EXPLAINING CREATIVITY

EXPLAINING CREATIVITY

The Science of Human Innovation

SECOND EDITION

R. Keith Sawyer

OXFORD

UNIVERSITY PRESS

UNIVERSITY PRESS

Oxford University Press, Inc., publishes works that further Oxford University's objective of excellence in research, scholarship, and education.

Oxford New York
Auckland   Cape Town   Dar es Salaam   Hong Kong   Karachi
Kuala Lumpur   Madrid   Melbourne   Mexico City   Nairobi
New Delhi   Shanghai   Taipei   Toronto

With offices in
Argentina   Austria   Brazil   Chile   Czech Republic   France   Greece
Guatemala   Hungary   Italy   Japan   Poland   Portugal   Singapore
South Korea   Switzerland   Thailand   Turkey   Ukraine   Vietnam

Copyright © 2012 by Oxford University Press, Inc.

Published by Oxford University Press, Inc.
198 Madison Avenue, New York, New York 10016
www.oup.com

Oxford is a registered trademark of Oxford University Press, Inc.

Library of Congress Cataloging-in-Publication Data

Sawyer, R. Keith (Robert Keith)
Explaining creativity: the science of human innovation/R. Keith Sawyer.—2nd ed.
    p. cm.
Includes bibliographical references and index.
ISBN 978-0-19-973757-4 (pbk) 1. Creative ability. I. Title.
BF408.S284 2012
153.3'5—dc22   2011014066

9 8 7 6 5 4

Printed in the United States of America on acid-free paper

PREFACE TO THE SECOND EDITION

A lot has happened since I finished writing the first edition of *Explaining Creativity* in 2003. There's been an explosion of new and exciting research on creativity and innovation—in neuroscience, cognitive science, assessment, education, and group creativity. This second edition has new chapters on all of these topics (seven new chapters in all), and every other chapter has been rewritten to incorporate new scientific studies.

Soon after the first edition was published in January 2006, three other overviews of creativity research were also published: Robert Weisberg's *Creativity* (April 2006), Mark Runco's *Creativity* (2007), and James Kaufman's *Creativity 101* (2009). Each of these books took an *individualist* approach, one that focuses on psychological studies of the creative person; in my first edition, I chose instead to focus on a *sociocultural* approach that emphasized social and cultural contexts (as noted by reviewers: Kaufman, 2007; Simonton, 2007). In addition to these textbooks, there are now four handbooks of creativity (Kaufman & Sternberg, 2006, 2010; Runco, 1997; Sternberg, 1999) and a two-volume encyclopedia (Runco & Pritzker, 1999).

As I studied these recent books, I became convinced that I should have included a more complete treatment of individualist approaches. The keyword for my first edition was *sociocultural*; the keyword for this edition is *interdisciplinary* because I bring together individualist approaches and sociocultural approaches. The new material on individualist approaches is found primarily in Chapters 3, 5, 6, 7, 9, and 10, which are completely new; I'm particularly excited about Chapter 10, where I describe the latest research in cognitive neuroscience—research that takes images of the brain while it's engaged in cognitive tasks related to creativity.

My goal is to present the most comprehensive overview of what scientists have learned about creativity. It's always a challenge to be comprehensive; as the old saying goes, the risk is that you focus on the trees and lose sight of the forest—if you pay too much attention to small details, you no longer see the big picture. Dean Keith Simonton (2007) grouped creativity overviews into two broad categories: those that focus on the "forest" and present a unified narrative approach (he mentions my first edition and Weisberg, 2006) and those that focus on the "trees" and describe every study that's ever been published (he mentions Piirto, 1992, 1998, 2004, and Runco, 2007). This second edition is much more detailed and comprehensive than my first; but still, I retain a narrative thread, and I make sure to bring all the research together to provide the field's consensus as a take-home message.

I've chosen to dedicate more attention to areas where the field has experienced controversy—for example, whether or not creativity is related to mental illness, or to what extent creativity tests are effective, or whether creativity is domain-general or domain-specific (or a bit of both). I've tried to be fair to all positions that have some basis in scientific studies. But at the end of each argument, I tell you what the consensus of the field is. After many years of research into these controversies, we have a pretty good idea of what the reality is.

Another reason I decided to unite individualist and sociocultural approaches in this second edition was my experience writing my 2007 book *Group Genius*. That book had three parts, and in the second part I reviewed research showing how often individual mental processes are influenced by collaborative conversations. Paul Silvia called this book an "integration of the sociocultural approach and the cognitive approach" and suggested that the book "could spark attempts to unify the sociocultural and cognitive traditions" (Silvia, 2007, p. 255). I liked that idea and realized no book had done that yet; here's my attempt.

In my first edition, I provided a broad historical and cultural context for creativity research. For these perspectives I went outside of the field of psychology; you can find excellent book-length treatments by Robert Paul Weiner (*Creativity & Beyond*, 2000) and Rob Pope (*Creativity: Theory, History, Practice*, 2005). In this second edition, I've further elaborated these reflective perspectives in an attempt to capture the collective creation that is "creativity research." I've combed through historical documents to assemble eight appendices that include key dates, publications, journals, conferences, and scholars that have advanced our understanding of creativity. This material is not gathered together in any other book, and I hope it will serve as a reference for everyone interested in the scientific study of creativity.

My ambition for this second edition is the same as it was for the first edition: to deliver on the ambitious title *Explaining Creativity: The Science of Human Innovation* by presenting everything that scientists have learned about creativity. I hope that this book will serve as a shared reference representing the state of the art and the consensus of the field. *Explaining Creativity* is for everyone who wants to learn what scholars today know about the science of human innovation.

ACKNOWLEDGMENTS

I have been studying and teaching creativity for over 20 years and have published several academic books on the topic. But when you write a book like this one, summarizing an entire field for the interested general reader, it's like learning the material all over again. It's been a wonderful experience! I begin by thanking Mike Csikszentmihalyi for introducing me to the field of creativity research. I thank all of my colleagues who work in the field of creativity research for sharing ideas and research in countless conversations. I owe a debt to my students, who have helped me discover how best to explain creativity. I'd like to thank all of the musicians, actors, and artists whom I've observed and interviewed through the years for sharing with me their perspectives on creativity. I am grateful to Abby Gross and Joanna Ng of Oxford University Press. And I'd like to thank my wife, Barb, who made this book possible.

CONTENTS

THE FIELD OF CREATIVITY RESEARCH

PART 1

CONCEPTIONS

CHAPTER 1

INTRODUCTION

Genius. Invention. Talent. And, of course, creativity. These words describe the highest levels of human performance. When we're engaged in the act of being creative, we feel we are performing at the peak of our abilities. Creative works give us insight and enrich our lives.

Creativity is part of what makes us human. Our nearest relatives, chimpanzees and other primates, are often quite intelligent but never reach these high levels of performance. And although advanced "artificially intelligent" computer programs hold the world title in chess, and can crunch through mounds of data and identify patterns invisible to the human eye, they still cannot master everyday creative skills.

Politicians, educators, and business leaders in the United States have realized that creativity and innovation are central to economic success (Business Roundtable, 2005; Council on Competitiveness, 2005; Sawyer, 2006e). Creativity is also needed to solve pressing social problems. The European Union dubbed 2009 "The European Year of Creativity and Innovation," pronouncing in its manifesto that "Europe's future depends on the imagination and creativity of its people" (2009, p. 1). Asian countries such as Singapore and China have announced major initiatives in creativity (Lau, Hui, & Ng, 2004; Singapore Ministry of Education, 2002). All of these countries have transformed from industrial economies to creative knowledge economies, where economic activity is focused on producing ideas rather than producing things.

Creativity will continue to increase in importance, due to several broad societal and economic trends:

1. Increasingly globalized markets result in greater competitiveness, even for industries that historically had been protected from significant challenge.
2. Increasingly sophisticated information and communication technologies result in shorter product development cycles.
3. Jobs that don't require creativity are increasingly being automated, or are moving to extremely low-wage countries.
4. Increasing wealth and leisure time in advanced countries (and beyond) have increased the demand for the products of the creative industries. As of 2007, the creative industries represented over 11% of U.S. GDP (Gantchev, 2007).

Despite its increasing importance, creativity hasn't received much attention from scientists. Until very recently, only a few researchers had studied creativity. Most psychologists instead study what they believe are more fundamental mental properties—such as memory, logical reasoning, and attention. But in recent years psychologists—along with increasing numbers of sociologists, anthropologists, biologists, and computer scientists—have increasingly turned their attention to creativity. Because creativity isn't a central topic in any of these fields, these scholars work without big research grants, and without a lot of attention from the leaders of their fields. Even so, their research findings have gradually accumulated, and our knowledge about creativity has now attained a critical mass. Perhaps for the first time, we hold in our grasp the potential to explain creativity.

Modern creativity research began in the 1950s and 1960s. This **first wave** of creativity research was focused on studying the *personalities* of exceptional creators (Chapters 3 and 4). In the 1970s and 1980s, researchers shifted their attention to the *cognitive approach*, a **second wave** based in cognitive psychology and focused on the internal mental processes that occur while people are engaged in creative behavior (Chapters 5, 6, and 7). In the 1980s and 1990s, the cognitive approach was complemented by the emergence of a **third wave**, the *sociocultural approach*, an interdisciplinary approach that focused on creative social systems: groups of people in social and cultural contexts (Chapters 11 through 15). This third wave includes research by sociologists, anthropologists, historians, and others.

After decades of research, we're closer than ever to an explanation of creativity. The problem is that each of the three waves has largely proceeded in "parochial isolation," in the words of leading creativity researchers Lucille Wehner, Mihaly Csikszentmihalyi, and István Magyari-Beck (1991, p. 270). Two other famous creativity researchers, Robert Sternberg and Todd Lubart (1999), also claimed that this lack of multidisciplinarity had blocked our understanding of creativity (p. 9).

My goal in this book is to address this problem by bringing together the three waves of creativity research—the personality approach, the cognitive approach, and the sociocultural approach—in what I call the *interdisciplinary approach*. In addition to the scientists who study the creative individual—psychologists, neuroscientists, and biologists—I also present research by scientists who study the contexts of creativity: sociologists of science and art, and anthropologists who study art, ritual performance, and verbal creativity in different cultures. For additional perspective, I occasionally draw on the work of scholars who study specific creative domains: musicologists, historians of art, scholars of theatrical performance, philosophers of science, legal scholars who study intellectual property—particularly in Part IV. By combining everything that scientists have learned about how people generate new things, the interdisciplinary approach provides us with a powerful explanation of creativity.

WHY EXPLAIN CREATIVITY?

The scientific study of creativity makes some people nervous. For example, practicing artists may worry, "Isn't the whole project just a mistaken attempt to impose the analytic worldview of science onto the arts? Isn't creativity a mysterious force that will forever resist scientific explanation?" Some artists worry that if they become too analytic, it could interfere with their muse. Other people are skeptical about corporations harnessing individual creativity for greater profit (Osborn, 2003). I believe that these worries are unfounded. Explaining creativity is important for many reasons.

Explaining creativity can help us identify and realize every person's unique creative talents. Without explaining creativity, it's easy to fail to recognize and nurture individuals with important creative abilities. If we hope to solve all of the pressing problems facing our society and our world, we must take advantage of the creative talents of everyone.

Explaining creativity can help our leaders to respond better to the challenges facing modern society. Researchers have discovered that creativity is an essential skill for effective leadership (Bennis & Biederman, 1997; Simonton, 1994). Creative leaders have much more impact because they can motivate their teams more effectively. Creative leaders are especially effective at handling novel challenges that force them to go outside the typical routines. At the beginning of this chapter, I pointed out changes in the modern economy that make creativity more important than ever (also see Florida, 2002). Before the 1980s, creativity was thought to be only occasionally important to a corporation; today, most business leaders believe that creativity is critical to the survival of their organization.

Explaining creativity can help us all to be better problem solvers. We each face problems in our everyday lives that require creative responses. Our society faces challenges like pollution, poverty, and terrorism. Some of these problems can be solved simply by a single individual having a good idea, but most of them will require groups of people working together.

Explaining creativity helps us realize the importance of positive, peak experiences to mental health. During peak experiences known as *flow,* people are at their most creative. Researchers studying *positive psychology* have discovered that flow and creativity contribute to a happy, fulfilling life (Csikszentmihalyi, 1990b). A better explanation of creativity can help people to achieve these positive, healthy experiences.

Explaining creativity can help educators teach more effectively. Educational psychologists are increasingly discovering the role that creativity plays in development and learning (Sawyer et al., 2003). In recent decades, psychologists have identified the step-by-step creative processes that underpin learning (Bransford, Brown, & Cocking, 2000; Sawyer, 2006b). Creativity is important not only to classroom learning but also to the critical informal learning that occurs in the preschool years—how to speak a first language, how to behave at the dinner table, how to make friends and engage in group play (Sawyer, 1997b).

Explaining creativity provides more than intellectual satisfaction; it will lead to a more creative society, and will enhance the creative potential of our families, our workplaces, and our institutions.

BEYOND HIGH ART

Almost all scientific books about creativity have been limited to those expressions of creativity that are highly valued in Western cultures.[1] By limiting their studies to "high" forms—to fine art painting rather than decorative painting, graphic arts, or animation; to basic science rather than

---

1. We find this bias in many books about creativity. Winner's 1982 book *Invented Worlds: The Psychology of the Arts* focuses on painting, music, and literature, and explicitly excludes what she calls "popular forms of art" such as television, jazz, and comic strips (p. 11). Wilson's 1985 book *The Psychology of the Performing Arts* focuses on "classical drama, music and opera" (p. i). Csikszentmihalyi's 1996 book *Creativity* is based

applied science, engineering, or technology; to symphonic compositions rather than the creativity of the violinist, the ensemble interaction of a chamber quartet, or the improvisation of a jazz group—these researchers have implicitly accepted a set of values that is culturally and historically specific. These biases must be discarded if we want to explain creativity in all societies, in all cultures, and in all historical time periods.

To explain creativity, we have to consider a broad range of creative behaviors, not only the high arts of Western, European cultures. In addition to fine art painting, symphonic performance of the European classical repertoire, and dramatic performance of scripted plays, a complete explanation of creativity must also explain comic strips, animated cartoons, movies, music videos, mathematical theory, experimental laboratory science, the improvised performances of jazz and rock music, and the broad range of performance genres found in the world's cultures. In this book, I examine creativity in non-Western cultures, and the creativity associated with the most influential contemporary developments in media and art—movies, television, computer software, music videos, multimedia, videogames, performance, and installation art.

The bias in creativity research toward the fine arts is a little out of keeping with the times; postwar America has been characterized by its valorization of spontaneity and improvisation, not only in performance but even in writing and painting: Black Mountain and beat poets, bebop musicians, abstract Expressionists, modern dance, and installation art (Belgrad, 1998; Sawyer, 2000). The visual arts have been heavily influenced by the creative potential of performance art, resulting in installation-specific pieces and multimedia works that integrate video images or taped sounds. That's why in Chapter 16, on visual creativity, I discuss not only fine art painting but also movies and installation art. And in Chapter 18, on musical creativity, I examine not only European symphonic composition but also the improvisational performances of jazz and of a broad range of non-Western cultures.

It's strange that psychologists in recent decades have been so focused on the fine arts; after all, within the arts themselves, such categories have increasingly been challenged and broken down since the 1960s (see Fry, 1970). In the 1960s, pop artists like Andy Warhol and Roy Lichtenstein broke the boundaries between high and low art, incorporating elements of advertising graphics and comic strips into their paintings. The Fluxus group began experimenting with performance and installation art, and in the following decades, installation art has become increasingly prominent within the mainstream art world. In the 1960s through the present, American popular music has experienced a flourishing of creativity that some believe is the historical equivalent to prior bursts of creativity in European symphonic music. In the 1970s, the New Hollywood era in film was a major creative break in movie production. In the 1980s, the advent of MTV and its music videos enabled a new burst of creativity among dance choreographers and film artists. And in the early years of this new century, the Internet has enabled participatory creativity; today, anyone can edit and post a video, a story, or a new song and share

on interviews with approximately 100 highly creative individuals; all of these individuals create in areas highly valued in dominant cultural groups in Western, European cultures: the sciences, the fine arts. Mumford (2003), in a review of two massive handbooks that surveyed the field of creativity research (Runco, 1997; Sternberg, 1999a), pointed out that they "talk about artists, scientists, and musicians at length, [but] I could find no mention of engineers, computer programmers, designers, marketing and advertising executives, consultants, or managers . . . there appears to be a tendency in the field toward a platonic, class-stereotypic view of the creative act" (p. 110).

it with the world. Although audiences have been declining for the so-called high arts, the audiences for these new creative forms are huge and continually expanding. Any serious study of creativity in the 21st century must explain the full range of human innovation.

TWO DEFINITIONS OF CREATIVITY

To explain creativity, we first need to agree on what it is, and this turns out to be surprisingly difficult. All of the social sciences face the task of defining concepts that seem everyday and familiar. Psychologists argue over the definitions of intelligence, emotion, and memory; sociologists argue over the definitions of group, social movement, and institution. But defining creativity may be one of the most difficult tasks facing the social sciences.

Creativity researchers can be grouped into two major traditions of research: an individualist approach and a sociocultural approach. Each of them has its own distinctive analytic focus, and each of them defines creativity slightly differently.

INDIVIDUALIST DEFINITION

The individualist approach studies a single person while that person is engaged in creative thought or behavior. This is the approach associated with first-wave personality psychology—which studies the traits of creative people—and second-wave experimental cognitive psychology—the branch of psychology that studies how people think, perceive, learn, and remember. Because individualists focus on single individuals, the individualist definition of creativity refers only to structures and processes that are associated with a single person.

Individualist definition: *Creativity is a new mental combination that is expressed in the world.*

- Creativity is *new*. The most basic requirement of a creative thought or action is that it must be novel or original. Repeating a previously mastered sequence of behaviors isn't creative; repeating a sentence verbatim isn't creative; speaking from memory isn't creative. Our minds spend large parts of every day engaged in non-creative activities—driving or walking the same route to work or school; preparing coffee and breakfast every morning; dialing a phone number; typing at a keyboard. These activities are non-creative because they repeat already mastered behavioral patterns.
- Creativity is a *combination*. All thoughts and concepts are combinations of existing thoughts and concepts. The mind is an immense web of symbolic material; most of it has been previously mastered, and simply recalling from memory isn't creative. Creativity involves a combination of two or more thoughts or concepts that have never been combined before by that individual.
- Creativity is *expressed in the world*. Creativity researchers can't study what they can't see. This is why the scientific definition of creativity has to exclude ideas that stay in a person's head and are never expressed, and ideas that no one else can see or understand. Under this definition, your nightly dreams aren't creative; ideas that you have but never write down or communicate to anyone else aren't creative.

The individualist definition is based on one of the oldest theories in psychology: *association-ism*. Well over 100 years ago, psychologist Alexander Bain (1818–1903) first argued that "new combinations grow out of elements already in the possession of the mind" (1855/1977, p. 572). Most of these combinations won't be completely new to the world, but as long as they're new in that person's mind, they satisfy the individualist definition. Creativity researchers refer to this as "little c" creativity. Little c creativity includes activities that people engage in every day: modifying a recipe when you don't have all of the ingredients called for; avoiding a traffic jam by finding a new way through side streets; figuring out how to apologize to a friend for an unintended insult; a child building a block tower (or even a baby stuffing peas into his nose for the first time). Thousands, or even millions, of people may have already solved those same problems, but as long as it's your first time, it meets the individualist definition.

How can we know if a combination is new for a particular person? Creativity researchers have developed a wide variety of clever experiments to do exactly this. For example, we can display three abstract geometric shapes and ask people to combine them to make an invention (see Chapter 6); we can present three randomly chosen words and ask people to write a story using them (see Chapter 3); or we can ask children to combine magazine photos to make a collage (see Chapter 3). Many other individualist measures of creativity are described in Chapter 3 on assessment.

SOCIOCULTURAL DEFINITION

The third-wave *sociocultural approach* studies creative people working together in social and cultural systems. Socioculturalists study how groups collectively generate innovation, and the structures and processes of social, cultural, and organizational systems that are creative. A jazz ensemble or a theater group is a fundamentally ensemble art form. A hit videogame or a computer-animated movie typically has 200 different creative people participating in its creation. A scientific paper that reports a new discovery often has 50 or 100 authors.

Even works that are generated mostly in solitude, like paintings, poems, or novels, are difficult to understand without incorporating the sociocultural level of analysis in addition to the individual level. That's because the only works that survive and that are disseminated to a broad public are those that successfully navigate a complex social and organizational system of gatekeepers, curators, and experts (see Chapter 11 on the sociology of creativity).

Sociocultural definition: *Creativity is the generation of a product that is judged to be novel and also to be appropriate, useful, or valuable by a suitably knowledgeable social group.*

The sociocultural definition of creativity requires that some socially valuable product be generated before the act or the person is called "creative." Only solutions to extremely difficult problems, or significant works of genius, are recognized as creative. This is sometimes called "big C" Creativity. All creations that satisfy this definition will by default also satisfy the individual or "little c" definition—because any product that is novel to a social group must also be novel to each individual within that social group.

The sociocultural definition is quite similar to definitions of *innovation* in organizations; Amabile (1988) defined innovation as "the successful implementation of creative ideas within an organization" (p. 126). Most business scholars distinguish between "creativity" as the ideas or products generated by individuals, and "innovation" as the successful execution of a new product or service by an entire organization (Sawyer & Bunderson, in press). The study of organizations is a central element of the sociocultural approach; we'll focus on organizations most directly in Chapter 12 on group creativity and Chapter 13 on organizations.

To satisfy the sociocultural definition, novelty to the creator isn't enough. Creators themselves can't know if their work is truly the first one in the history of the world; the identical creation might already exist, and the creator just doesn't know about it. Sociocultural novelty can be judged only by a social group, who can collectively determine whether an individual creation really is new. In addition, to satisfy the sociocultural definition, novelty isn't sufficient; the creation must also be *appropriate*, recognized as socially valuable in some way to some community. Appropriateness, like novelty, can be judged only by a social group.

The sociocultural definition of creativity has been widely adopted in creativity research—even by personality and cognitive psychologists.[2] That's because it's extremely difficult to scientifically define what is a "new combination" for an individual, under the individual definition. But there's a problem with including appropriateness as a criterion for creativity: because a work's appropriateness can be defined only by a society at a given historical moment, it becomes hard to distinguish creativity from worldly success and power. The influential creativity researcher Dean Keith Simonton accepted the appropriateness criterion and then argued that only eminent people can be said to be creative (1999b). You might prefer a conception of creativity that allows for unrecognized genius, people who are ahead of their time, or works that are simply so innovative that they are rejected as bizarre by the society, and thus aren't judged to be appropriate.

Although appropriateness may seem incompatible with creativity at first glance, it's not as bad as it may first seem. After all, creativity can't exist, even in principle, without appropriateness. For example, almost all musical compositions use the 12-tone Western scale—the notation system that all musicians learn in training—and are composed for instruments that are widely manufactured, distributed, and taught. Just because a work conforms to these conventions doesn't mean that we would say it's not creative. To be creative, you don't have to compose a work for a 42-tone scale, using instruments that don't exist and that no one knows how to play. If you did that, you'd be rejecting appropriateness but you'd certainly satisfy the "originality" criterion.

Composer Harry Partch (1949) became famous for doing exactly this. He spent his career writing such music, inventing and constructing his own unique instruments to perform his compositions (see Chapter 18). Certainly no one would disagree that his work is novel, nor that his work failed to satisfy criteria of appropriateness. And because it doesn't meet the appropriateness criterion, it's almost impossible to perform; it could be performed only if Partch himself guided a process that typically took about a year. First, Partch had a group of students build his instruments. After several months of construction, they would spend a few months learning Partch's idiosyncratic notation system and learning to play the instruments. After seven or eight months of work, the ensemble was ready to perform a few hours of music. Contrast this lengthy process with the eight hours or less of rehearsal that it takes a trained symphony orchestra to

2. The first wave of personality psychologists also emphasized that true creativity required not only novelty but also appropriateness (MacKinnon, 1962): "Novelty or originality of thought or action, while a necessary aspect of creativity, is not sufficient . . . It must to some extent be adaptive to, or of, reality" (p. 485). Stein (1961/1963, 1967, 1974) emphasized both novelty and usefulness at a point in time. The earliest published use of the little c/Big C terminology that I've found is in Stein (1987).

perform a new composition that follows the usual conventions, and we see the problems that face creators whose work is not appropriate—it's hard to display, disseminate, or perform.

Certain genres of music have an even more closely specified set of constraints; a sonata must have a certain form, or else it can't be categorized as a sonata at all. And just because all sonatas share many characteristics doesn't mean that all of them are the same, or that a new sonata is somehow only a copy of all of the other sonatas. Defining how different a work has to be to be considered a novel work is a complex issue facing critics and experts in many creative domains. For example, folklorists typically expect there to be some variation in the performance of traditional songs like Appalachian mountain tunes or Southern gospel songs, and even with performance variation, most of the audience would consider all of the variations to be instances of the same song, even though they aren't exactly the same.

Individual style provides another set of constraints that don't seem to be antithetical to creativity. Many listeners who aren't connoisseurs in a certain musical genre have had the experience of thinking "it all sounds the same." In recent years, I've heard this said of several rock bands, including the Grateful Dead and R.E.M., of all bluegrass music, and of anything played on the accordion. I'm sure that many people feel the same way about the harpsichord compositions of Bach, bebop jazz, or hip-hop. Just because a painter generates a painting that is recognizably in a certain style or genre doesn't lead us to say that it's "the same" painting as every other one in that style. Many painters' careers are characterized by first discovering a new style and then continuing to explore that style, for years or even decades (see my discussion of Cézanne on pp. 281–283). Many popular bands continue to play in the same familiar style for their entire careers. In both painting and music, one can point to the exceptional rare individual who develops a new style every few years—for example, Picasso and Madonna. These individuals are rare because art markets and galleries pressure artists to continue working in the same recognizable style, so that they'll generate a known product and thus develop a reputation and a market for that work. Record companies are infamous for insisting that popular bands under contract for multiple albums continue to produce albums that sound like their first big hit, because they know that fans become loyal to a band in part because they can count on consistency and reliability in style.

The scientific studies of creativity that I review in this book focus on both individual creativity and sociocultural creativity, both little c and big C Creativity. These two bodies of research are complementary; understanding the cognitive processes behind a single idea is important to understanding those earth-shattering innovations that change the world. And understanding the social dimensions of creative fields can also help us understand the cognitive processes that result in new ideas.

RELATED DEFINITIONS

The two-level definition of creativity is widely accepted by creativity researchers, with the two levels typically referred to as "Big C" and "little c" creativity. Some researchers have proposed three or more types of creativity, rather than only two. Taylor (1959) identified five types of creativity:

- *Expressive*: Independent expression, where the quality and originality of the product are not important, such as the drawings of children

- *Productive*: Artistic or scientific products that restrict and control free play and develop techniques for producing finished products
- *Inventive*: Inventors, explorers, discoverers; ingenuity is displayed with materials, methods, and techniques
- *Innovative*: Improvement through modification involving conceptualizing skills
- *Emergentive*: An entirely new principle or assumption around which new schools flourish

Kaufman and Beghetto (2009) argued for two levels of creativity in addition to Big-C and little-c:

- *mini-c*: The creativity inherent in the learning process, when children discover something for the first time
- *Pro-c*: Professional expertise in a creative domain that does not attain the level of transforming the domain

Feldman (2003) proposed a three-part definition, using the metaphor of a piano keyboard. High C is equivalent to Big C creativity; low C is equivalent to little c creativity; and middle C is roughly equivalent to Pro-c as proposed by Kaufman and Beghetto (see Morelock & Feldman, 1999).

This book is organized around two definitions of creativity, because they are widely accepted by scholars in the field and also because they correspond to the two primary levels of analysis that are found in the social world—individuals at a lower level of analysis and social entities at a higher, complex system level of analysis (Sawyer, 2005b). A complete explanation of creativity requires an explanation of both types—combining the sciences of the individual with the sciences of groups.

THE FOUR P FRAMEWORK

Many creativity researchers have been influenced by a four-part division of creativity research proposed by Mel Rhodes back in 1961, the *four P* framework:

- *Product*: Research that focuses on the products judged to be novel and appropriate by the relevant social group. Product creativity is almost always defined and evaluated using a sociocultural definition.
- *Person*: Research that studies the personality traits or personality types associated with creativity. Creative people are those identified with an individualist definition, or they are identified indirectly, as those people who have generated creative products. (See Chapter 3.)
- *Process*: Research that studies the processes involved during creative work or creative thought. (See Chapters 5, 6, and 7.)
- *Press*: Research that focuses on the external forces or "pressures" acting on the creative person or process, such as the social and cultural context. (See Part III.)

THE WESTERN CULTURAL MODEL OF CREATIVITY

Beliefs about creativity vary from country to country. Many readers of this book are likely to be living in the United States, and most people in the United States—and in the Western world more generally—share a set of implicit assumptions about creativity. Anthropologists refer to an integrated framework of assumptions as a *cultural model* (Holland & Quinn, 1987). Below, I identify ten features of the Western cultural model—I'll call them *creativity beliefs*. Chapter 14 contains a discussion of research on creativity beliefs in non-Western cultures; there's some overlap across cultures, but also many differences. As you read through these, ask yourself: How many of the ten beliefs do I believe? If you're from a non-Western culture, see how your own cultural model differs from these beliefs.

As you read through this book, I'd like you to keep these beliefs in mind and constantly evaluate them against the scientific evidence. As we journey through our survey of creativity research, we'll have many opportunities to consider whether or not each of these beliefs is supported by scientific research. Some of them are completely false; most of them are partially true, but a bit misleading. At the end of this book, in the final chapter, we'll return to these ten creativity beliefs and re-examine them from the new perspectives that we've gained from scientific research.

BELIEF 1. THE ESSENCE OF CREATIVITY IS THE MOMENT OF INSIGHT

Creative people get their great idea in a flash of insight. After that, all they have to do is execute it. They could even delegate its execution to someone else, because execution generally doesn't require creativity.

BELIEF 2. CREATIVE IDEAS EMERGE MYSTERIOUSLY FROM THE UNCONSCIOUS

Creative people have radical new ideas that come out of nowhere and that can't be explained by their prior experience.

BELIEF 3. CREATIVITY IS MORE LIKELY WHEN YOU REJECT CONVENTION

Creative people blindly ignore convention; convention is the enemy of creativity, because it blocks the pure inspiration welling up from the creative spirit. The best artists reject tradition and convention; they're not influenced by the prevailing ideas taught in art schools or advocated by rich collectors or influential museum curators. The best scientists reject the dominant theories that they learn in graduate school, and strike out on their own.

Variation: Children are more creative than adults.

BELIEF 4. CREATIVE CONTRIBUTIONS ARE MORE LIKELY TO COME FROM AN OUTSIDER THAN AN EXPERT

Sometimes the most creative people know the least about the domain. The leading people in any field are so bound up in the old way of doing things that they never have the great new ideas. It takes someone from the outside to see things in a new way; it's better if the outsider doesn't learn those old ways of doing things.

BELIEF 5. PEOPLE ARE MORE CREATIVE WHEN THEY'RE ALONE

Other people interfere with creativity; it's best to just go away by yourself. If you can, get yourself a cabin in the woods, like Thoreau at Walden Pond. Whatever you do, don't stay in the city center, where you're surrounded by people.

BELIEF 6. CREATIVE IDEAS ARE AHEAD OF THEIR TIME

Creative people are far ahead of their time, and their brilliance is not acknowledged during their lifetime. They're recognized only after death, when everyone else moves along to catch up with their vision.

BELIEF 7. CREATIVITY IS A PERSONALITY TRAIT

Creativity is a general personality trait, like IQ. If you're a more creative person, you'll be more creative at everything that you do. People who don't have much of this personality trait have very little hope of being creative.

Variation: Creativity is genetic, and some people are born with more of it.

BELIEF 8. CREATIVITY IS BASED IN THE RIGHT BRAIN

Creativity is in the right brain, and creative people display a "right-brained" pattern of behavior and thought.

General variation: Creative brains have identifiable biologic differences from uncreative brains.

BELIEF 9. CREATIVITY AND MENTAL ILLNESS ARE CONNECTED

Creative people are more likely to be mentally ill, and mental illness has a silver lining—it brings increased creativity. The inner turmoil associated with mental illness is the source of ideas and inspiration, so that when mental illness is treated, people become less creative.

BELIEF 10. CREATIVITY IS A HEALING, LIFE-AFFIRMING ACTIVITY

Creative activities are the fullest realization of human experience. They express the inner being of the person, and result in great personal fulfillment. Creative activities contribute to psychological health; this is why art therapy and music therapy are effective.

THE HOPE OF AN INTERDISCIPLINARY APPROACH

> *Creativity is precisely the kind of problem which eludes explanation within one discipline.*
>
> —Howard Gardner, in the first issue of the *Creativity Research Journal* (1988, p. 22)
>
> *Creativity arises through a system of interrelated forces operating at multiple levels, often requiring interdisciplinary investigation.*
>
> —Hennessey and Amabile, (2010, p. 571)

My goal in this book is to present all of the research on creativity—at both the individual level and the sociocultural level. My hope is to present a more comprehensive explanation of creativity than is possible with any one level of analysis—to take the interdisciplinary approach that Howard Gardner advised in the above epigraph from the inaugural issue of the *Creativity Research Journal* back in 1988. Many of my colleagues agree that it's time for an interdisciplinary synthesis; when Beth Hennessey and Teresa Amabile reviewed the research on creativity in 2010, they were struck by "a growing fragmentation of the field . . . investigators in one subfield often seem entirely unaware of advances in another" (p. 571). As long as the three waves of creativity research—cognitive, personality, and sociocultural—proceed on separate tracks, we will fail to explain creativity (e.g., Tardif & Sternberg, 1988, p. 429). My goal with this book is to help correct this situation, and bring together the full range of scientific perspectives.

Every bookstore contains books about creativity, but almost none of them are based on solid scientific research. Instead of reporting scientific findings, they often do no more than present the Western cultural model of creativity—but with catchy new terms and engaging anecdotes. My goal in this book is to take us beyond any one cultural model of creativity, and give us a scientific explanation of creativity. I've cast a broad net, and our journey will range far and wide—through psychology and sociology, through art history and literary criticism. So, keeping in mind that there is always more to learn—that science is, by definition, unfinished business— let's start our journey.

CHAPTER 2

CONCEPTIONS OF CREATIVITY

A s the applause swelled, Dr. Guilford took a deep breath, smoothed his tie and jacket, and began to walk to the podium. It was Sept. 5, 1950, and Dr. Guilford was at the peak of his long and illustrious career. He had dedicated his life to psychological research. He'd played a key leadership role during World War II, helping the U.S. military carry out the most massive testing program in history. And now, he had attained the highest honor that the discipline of psychology could give—he had been elected president of the American Psychological Association.

Every year, at the annual meeting of the Association, the president gives the keynote speech, and in 1950 at Pennsylvania State College, this was Dr. J. P. Guilford's moment (Fig. 2.1). Presidents traditionally use this opportunity to emphasize an important issue that they think deserves more psychological study. As Dr. Guilford began his talk, the hundreds of assembled psychologists in the room were shocked when they realized the topic he had chosen: the APA president had chosen to talk about creativity.

To understand why a professional psychologist in 1950 would be shocked to hear a speech about creativity from the APA president, you need to know a little about the field of psychology at the time. Since the 1920s, American psychology had been dominated by behaviorism—think of Pavlov's salivating dog and Skinner's experiments with pigeons. Behaviorists studied only behaviors they could see. Anything that happened inside the brain was off limits—they reasoned that because the mind couldn't be directly observed, it couldn't be studied scientifically. By the 1970s, this approach had been rejected by most psychologists, but 1950 was the heyday of behaviorism, and behaviorism didn't have much to say about creativity.[1]

A second prominent approach in 1950s American psychology was Freudian psychoanalysis. To a Freudian, creativity was a subliminal activity masking unexpressed or instinctual wishes; the people who chose to become artists were just redirecting repressed and unfulfilled sexual desires (Freud, 1917/1966, p. 467). The arts were based on illusion and the creation of a fantasy world, and were thought to be similar to a psychiatric disorder called neurosis (see Chapter 4, pp. 82–83).

---

1. Behaviorism's critics often pointed to the phenomenon of human creativity, and claimed that reinforcement methods couldn't teach creativity. Skinner realized the importance of this criticism, and repeatedly tried, although unsuccessfully, to respond (1968, 1972). Also see Epstein (1990, 1999) for a more recent behaviorist account of creativity.

FIGURE 2.1: J. P. Guilford. (Courtesy of the University of Southern California, on behalf of the USC Specialized Libraries and Archival Collections.)

A third reason that psychologists in 1950 didn't study creativity was that exceptional creativity was thought to be a byproduct of high intelligence. Soon after World War I, Lewis Terman of Stanford University adapted Frenchman Alfred Binet's new intelligence test for the United States, and for decades after that, the study of talent and human potential was dominated by the study of intelligence (see Chapter 3, pp. 52–58).

Modern creativity research began with Guilford's influential 1950 APA presidential address (Guilford, 1950). After Guilford's stamp of approval at the national psychology conference, studies of creativity blossomed. During the years that followed Guilford's address there were almost as many studies of creativity published in each year as there were for the entire 23 years prior to his address (Getzels, 1987; Sternberg & Dess, 2001).

Of course, one evening's talk can't change an entire scientific discipline overnight. But Guilford's APA address was the right message at the right time. In the years after World War II, the United States was an economic powerhouse, a machine exporting its products around the world, generating jobs for everyone. But the booming economy of the 1950s was very different from the 1990s information technology boom; there were no start-ups, no venture capital, no NASDAQ. Instead, almost everyone worked for a large, stable corporation, and the work environments were much more structured than in America today. IBM was legendary for requiring each employee to wear a white shirt and a navy blue suit, every day. Businesses were organized into strict hierarchies—almost like the military—and everyone knew their place in the pecking order.

Like the military, these companies were extremely efficient. But many thoughtful commentators were concerned. After all, the U.S. had just fought World War II to defend freedom, and its Cold War adversary—the Soviet Union—was criticized as a restricted and controlled society. So it was disturbing that U.S. society was beginning to seem increasingly constrained and regimented. By the late 1950s, Americans were increasingly worried about this "age of confor-mity," and a 1956 book called *The Organization Man* by William H. Whyte became a national bestseller. Its theme—that the regimented economy was resulting in an America full of uncre-ative, identical conformists—was echoed in similar books through the early 1960s. In 1961, management theorists Tom Burns and G. M. Stalker published an influential book arguing that these rigid hierarchical organizations were rarely innovative; instead, creativity came from com-panies with flat hierarchies, empowered workers, and authority distributed throughout the organization (Burns & Stalker, 1961). The research psychologists who studied creativity in the late 1950s and early 1960s were profoundly influenced by these nationwide concerns (as can be seen in transcripts of discussions at the five influential Utah conferences on creativity in 1955, 1957, 1959, 1961, and 1962: Taylor, 1959, 1964a, 1964b; Taylor & Barron, 1963).

Like Guilford, many of the early creativity scholars got their start during World War II, evaluating personality traits for the military. Donald MacKinnon and Morris Stein worked for the Office of Strategic Services, the predecessor to the CIA. They worked at the Assessment Center, a group that was charged with evaluating which people would best be suited for demand-ing roles overseas—irregular warfare, spies, counterespionage agents, and leaders of resistance groups (MacKinnon, 1978, p. xi). Guilford worked for the U.S. Air Force, developing tests to identify the intellectual abilities essential to flying a plane. After World War II, these military psychologists founded several research institutes to study creative individuals. MacKinnon founded the Institute of Personality Assessment and Research (IPAR) at the University of California at Berkeley in 1949. Guilford founded the Aptitudes Research Project at the University of Southern California in the early 1950s. Stein founded the Center for the Study of Creativity and Mental Health at the University of Chicago in 1952.

Creativity research was a high-stakes game during the nuclear arms race: in 1954, psycholo-gist Carl Rogers warned that "the lights will go out . . . international annihilation will be the price we pay for a lack of creativity" (p. 250). Around that time, the government began to give research grants to psychologists studying creativity—funding research to identify creative talent early in life, to educate for creativity, and to design more creative workplaces. The goal of this research was no less than to better understand freedom and its place in American society. As Morris Stein wrote at the time, "To be capable of [creative insights], the individual requires freedom—freedom to explore, freedom to be himself, freedom to entertain ideas no matter how wild and to express that which is within him without fear of censure or concern about evaluation" (1961/1963, p. 119).

In 1950, the government created the National Science Foundation, and one of its first pro-grams was the provision of fellowship funding to graduate students. To do this successfully, the NSF wanted to develop a test to identify the most promising future scientists. Personality psy-chologist Calvin W. Taylor led that research effort from 1952 to 1954; when he stepped down in 1954, he drew on his NSF connections to get funding for a series of conferences at the University of Utah on the identification of creative scientific talent, and the first one was held in 1955 (Taylor, 1964b; Taylor & Barron, 1963). The Utah Conferences brought together most of the first-wave personality psychologists studying creativity. The fifth conference in 1963 even attracted Harvard professor and legendary LSD guru Timothy Leary (Fig. 2.2).

Like Carl Rogers and Morris Stein, these creativity researchers believed they were defending freedom and helping to save the world from nuclear annihilation. Today, most people in America and in Europe agree with Stein that liberal democratic societies are those most conducive to creativity (Weiner, 2000). At the first Utah Conference in 1955, Frank Barron of the Berkeley

FIGURE 2.2: Participants in the 1963 Utah Conference on the identification and development of Creative Scientific Talent. (Frontispiece from Taylor, 1964a.) Front row, left to right: Taylor, Torrance, Drevdahl, Clark, Leary, MacKinnon, Guilford, Sprecher, Wight; second row: Westcott, Jablonski, Hyman, Datta, Fiedler, Parnes, Gamble; third row: Roberts, McRae, Mednick, Levine, Holland, Beittel; fourth row: Astin, McPherson, Mullins, Brust, Barron, Elliott, Ghiselin.

IPAR described the creative society; it had "freedom of expression and movement, lack of fear of dissent and contradiction, a willingness to break with custom, a spirit of play as well as of dedication to work" (1963b, p. 152). By 1960, creativity scholars began to sound as if they were writing the playbook for the hippie era that came only a few years later. In 1961, Morris Stein argued that "A society fosters creativity to the extent that it encourages openness to internal and external experiences . . . Societies that are full of 'don'ts,' 'shouldn'ts,' and 'mustn'ts' restrict freedom of inquiry and autonomy . . . [Society] discourages creativity to the extent that social pressures to conformity are so intense that deviations are punished directly or indirectly through social isolation and ostracism" (Stein, 1961/1963, p. 130). In 1962, Donald MacKinnon advised parents and teachers "to encourage in their children and in their students an openness to all ideas and especially to those which most challenge and threaten their own judgments" (1962, p. 493). Creativity researcher Frank Barron claimed to have first introduced Harvard's Timothy Leary to the psychoactive properties of the psilocybin mushroom (Barron, 1963a, p. 74). Leary would go on to become a famous champion of psychedelic drugs, widely known for his saying "Turn on, tune in, drop out." If you think parents were too permissive in the 1960s and after, you can't lay all the blame at Benjamin Spock's door (also see Hulbert, 2003).

People's ideas about creativity are always influenced by their society and their historical time. We shouldn't be surprised that postwar American psychologists emphasized a conception of creativity that fit exactly with a liberal democratic vision of society, one that contrasted the United States with the Soviet Union during the darkest years of the Cold War (see also Joncich, 1964).

Personality psychologists were largely unaware that their own conceptions of creativity were socially and historically unique (Raina, 1993; Stein, 1987). It turns out that what gets called creative has varied according to the historical and cultural period (Sass, 2000–2001, p. 57); these variations are the focus of this chapter.

HOW CONCEPTIONS OF CREATIVITY HAVE CHANGED OVER TIME

Many people who hold to the Western cultural model of creativity (see Chapter 1) believe that creative expression represents inner truth, the spirit of a unique individual. European Enlightenment humanism emphasized the divine nature of humanity; the human being became a sort of god. If creativity represents the purest expression of the spirit of the individual, it might capture the essence of this divinity (Becker, 2000–2001). Robert Weiner has argued that globalization is expanding this Enlightenment individualism beyond Europe, into a "global ideology of creativity" (2000, p. 113).

No past historical period would recognize today's concept of "creativity"; what we mean by that term has evolved through a complex historical and cultural process. The word "creativity" was invented in the late 19th century, when many people began to draw connections between the arts and the sciences. It appeared in an 1875 text *History of Dramatic English Literature*, by Adolfus William Ward (Weiner, 2000, p. 89), used in such a way as to suggest there is something similar across all disciplines (Weiner, 2000). The word doesn't appear in French or Italian until 50 years after that, and didn't appear in standard English dictionaries until after World War II (it's not in the second edition of the *New International Dictionary* in 1934, but it is in the *Third New International Dictionary* of 1961: Kristeller, 1983). The word comes from the English word "create," which derives from a hypothesized Indo-European root, *ker*, *kere* (to grow) via the Latin, *creatio* or *creatus* (to make or grow). But in the Roman era, this word was used for biological creation; *ars* and *artis* were more commonly used for human making (Weiner, 2000, p. 41).

Until the modern era, creativity was attributed to a superhuman force; all novel ideas originated with the gods. After all, how could a person create something that didn't exist before the divine act of creation? The Latin meaning of the verb "inspire" is "to breath into," reflecting the belief that creative inspiration was akin to the moment in creation when God first breathed life into man. Plato (427–327 BCE) argued that the poet was possessed by divine inspiration. Plato argued that the works of poets were entirely the invention of the Muses, who possess the poets and inspire them (Weiner, 2000, p. 35).

Plotin (204–270 CE) wrote that art could be beautiful only if it descended from God. The artist's job was not to imitate nature but rather to reveal the sacred and transcendent qualities of nature. Plato likewise held that all art was an imitation of nature; but for Plato, the nature that we see is an imitation of eternal ideas, so artworks are imitations of imitations (Weiner, 2000, p. 35). Art could be only a pale imitation of the perfection of the world of ideas (Honour & Fleming, 1999). Greek artists didn't blindly imitate what they saw in reality; instead, they tried to represent the pure, true forms underlying reality, resulting in a sort of compromise between abstraction and accuracy.

CONCEPTIONS OF THE ARTIST

Most people who live in the United States share a common set of beliefs about artists, one that derives from the Western cultural model of creativity. We think that most artists work alone. They're blessed with a special gift or genius. They have a uniquely valuable message to communicate, and generally have a relatively high social status. We believe that artworks should be signed by their creators; knowing who created a work is important to us. Art buyers seek out the best artists and buy their works. If you're one of the famous artists, your work will be collected by major museums. Imitations of your paintings aren't valuable, no matter how skillfully executed they are.

But these beliefs about artists are extremely recent. For example, the idea that an artist works alone is less than 200 years old. In the ancient system of apprenticeship in studios, artists worked in hierarchically structured teams. To learn art, a child—sometimes as young as the age of seven—was apprenticed to a master. All products of the studio were attributed to the master, even though a great portion of the work may have actually been completed by his assistants. The master acted as a sort of artistic director, composing the overall picture and executing only the most difficult portions.

The idea that the artist has high social status is also less than 200 years old. In the non-noble classes of Europe, status was based on economic success, and artists didn't make a lot of money. Artists were considered lower status than butchers and silversmiths, for example. This began to change during the Italian Renaissance, as artists began to be recognized for their knowledge and their genius. Nobility began to value art, and they competed with one another to take the best artists under their wing.

The idea that artists have a unique message to communicate is also only a few hundred years old. For most of European history, artists were considered primarily craftsmen. When a noble contracted for a work with a painter, the contract specified details like the quantities of gold and blue paint to appear in the work, the deadline, and penalties for delays (Baxandall, 1972). A contract in 1485 between the painter Domenico Ghirlandaio and a client specified that Ghirlandaio would "colour the panel at his own expense with good colours and with powdered gold on such ornaments as demand it . . . and the blue must be ultramarine of the value about four florins the ounce" (quoted in Baxandall, 1972, p. 6). In some contracts, artists were paid by the time worked rather than a fixed price for the completed work. These contract details show us that art was considered to be a trade—a very different conception of the artist than we hold today.

The idea that the artist creates a novel and original work that breaks with convention is only a few hundred years old. Before the Renaissance, creativity was associated with the ability to imitate established masters, and to accurately represent nature (Becker, 2000–2001, p. 46; Weiner, 2000). Although some people, including da Vinci and Vasari, argued that *genio* should not just be imitative, but should also incorporate originality, this argument did not become widely accepted until the late Renaissance (Lange-Eichbaum, 1930/1932).

During the Renaissance, Western conceptions of creativity began to change more dramatically. In the late 15th century in Florence, the idea became widespread that one could make a distinction between divine inspiration and human making. Art was still thought of as imitation, but as the direct imitation of divine ideas (rather than Plato's imitation of an imitation), and thus could surpass nature as we observe it (Weiner, 2000, p. 54). But the artist was not valorized; even Leonardo da Vinci didn't sign his works.

The first use of the word "create" in English was in 1589, by George Puttenham—in comparing poetic creation to divine creation (Weiner, 2000, p. 55). Artists began to differentiate themselves from craftsmen, and intellectuals began to think of what they did as something more than just craft or technique; the difference was that they could claim to "create"—unlike the mechanical arts. In the 18th century, poetry, music, and the visual arts were grouped together for the first time as "fine arts," and the word "creative" began to be applied to artists (Kristeller, 1983).

It was during Enlightenment humanism that the conception of man as an intentional creator began to flourish. In 1474, the Venetian city-state created the first regularized administrative system for granting patents, giving sole property to the originator for ten years (Merges, 1995). In 1624, Britain introduced patent protection for 14 years, granted to "the true and first inventor and inventors of such manufacturers" (Merges, 1995, p. 106; Weiner, 2000, p. 68).

These historical developments show that our current conception of the artist became widespread only about 200 years ago (Heinich, 1993). Many distinct developments converged in Europe to result in the modern Western conception of the artist. In the 15th century, the art of the portrait was born in Europe, a radical break with the prior tradition of painting only religious icons and scenes. Paintings and sculptures were increasingly signed by the artist in France, Germany, Flanders, and Italy. Consistent with Renaissance thought more generally, this was the beginning of the idea that the artist was a unique individual with his own perceptions and abilities, and that his paintings and his conceptions were unique. By the 16th century, the artist began to be seen as a member of a prestigious minority, working apart from any court or church. This was the beginning of an idea that has continued through the modern era: that artists are independent from society's normal standards of taste, that artists are inspired innovators, and that the function of art is to communicate the inner insights of the artist to the viewer.

The conception of the artist as internally driven by vision, inspiration, or imagination assumes that the creator doesn't know who will ultimately consume his creation, and furthermore assumes that it's not important for the creator to be aware of the ultimate audience. This historical situation was a result of the demise of patronage and the rise of mass audiences. Prior to that time, the artist was always working for a client—whether royalty, the church, or a rich merchant—with the goal of satisfying that client's demands (Clark, 1997, p. 11). Albrecht Dürer (1471–1528) produced the first works designed and published by the artist, not commissioned by a patron, and he was one of the first to sign his works (Weiner, 2000, p. 63).

From the 16th through the 18th centuries, the institutions of the art world were first established throughout Europe: museums, a tradition of art criticism and the study of the history of art, an art market with dealers and patrons. Schools for teaching art—run by the government and apart from apprenticeship in a studio—were founded in Florence in 1563 and in Rome in 1577. These state-run academies allowed aspiring artists to learn without apprenticeship to a master (Fig. 2.3).

And finally, in the Industrial Revolution, economic changes led to the end of the studio system. For centuries, apprentices had to learn how to make their own paints from scratch materials, and also to make their own paintbrushes; but after the 19th-century Industrial Revolution, an artist could purchase paints and brushes that were mass produced. The 19th-century French Impressionists are known for their radical new idea of painting outdoors, but this innovation would not have been possible without the invention of tubes of paint, which became available only in the 19th century. The modern concept of the artist—isolated, independent, inspired— could emerge only after all of these social and economic developments.

FIGURE 2.3: Woodcarving of a painting academy from the early 17th century. (Reprinted from Elkins, 2001, p. 17, Pierfrancesco Alberti Painter's Academy, early 17th century, Bartsch XVII.313.1. Used with permission of James Elkins.)

After several hundred years of broad social changes, during the 19th century Europeans began to see the artist as we conceive of him today: as a figure balancing the tension between the conventions of academic quality and the demand for originality (Heinich, 1993). For example, in the 19th century, anti-academism emerged in France—one of the first artistic movements to explicitly reject academic convention. Delacroix, Corot, and Courbet rejected the conventional hierarchy of subjects that placed historical and heroic scenes at the top, and instead painted realistic, everyday scenes—an important early influence on Impressionism.

Freudian psychoanalysis aligned readily with Romanticist thought. Freud argued that creativity emerged unpredictably from the unconscious mind, resulting from drives and conflicts that the creator is not consciously aware of. Freud's association between artistic creation and neurosis also aligned with a common strain of thought, in the late 19th century, that creative geniuses were somehow disturbed—similar to the mentally ill, physically sick, or criminals (see Chapter 4, pp. 82–83). Although Freud's psychodynamic theory has mostly been discarded today, these ideas about creativity remain a part of the Western cultural model.

Ironically, through the 20th century and increasingly after World War II in the United States, artists have been entering art schools in increasingly large numbers to be trained in the conventions of the art world. In the United States today, a greater proportion of working artists have the MFA degree than at any other time in history. Yet few of us are aware of the growing influence of formal schooling in fine art.

Today, at the beginning of the 21st century, most readers are likely to hold to the modern conception of the artist—a unique and inspired individual who expresses and communicates his or her unique vision through the art work. And of course, this conception is completely consistent with the Western cultural model of creativity. Yet this conception of the artist is no more than 200 years old.

RATIONALISM AND ROMANTICISM

Over the centuries, conceptions of creativity have veered between two broad ideas: rationalism and Romanticism. Rationalism is the belief that creativity is generated by the conscious, deliberating, intelligent, rational mind; Romanticism is the belief that creativity bubbles up from an irrational unconscious, and that rational deliberation interferes with the creative process.

Over 2,300 years ago, Aristotle's view of art emphasized rationality and deliberation, and stressed the conscious work required to bring a creative inspiration to completion. Aristotle gave credit not only to the Muses, but also to human skill and inspiration (Weiner, 2000, p. 36). The rationalist conception was dominant through the European Renaissance and Enlightenment, when reason was valued above all. Enlightenment conceptions of creativity emphasized rationality, proportion, and harmony. In 1650, Thomas Hobbes (1588–1679) called the invocation of the Muses the reasonless imitation of a foolish custom, "by which a man, enabled to speak wisely from the principles of Nature and his own meditation, loves rather to be thought to speak by inspiration, like a Bagpipe" (quoted in Smith, 1961, p. 24). Reason, knowledge, training, and education were considered necessary to create good art. When the term *originality* was coined, it meant newness and truth of observation, not a radical break with convention. The most original artists were those who best imitated nature (Smith, 1961).

During the 18th century, the term *genius* was first used to describe creative individuals (Becker, 2000–2001; Tonelli, 1973), and this new concept of genius was primarily associated with rational, conscious processes (Gerard, 1774/1966; Tonelli, 1973). Genius was associated with both scientists and artists, and was thought to be based in imagination, judgment, and memory (Becker, 2000–2001, p. 47).

The idea of the *imagination* emerged in England and Germany during the late Enlightenment in the 18th century (Engell, 1981; Taylor, 1989). The imagination "became the compelling force in artistic and intellectual life" from 1750 onward (Engell, 1981, p. 4). The imagination was the mental faculty responsible for generating novelty, and this conception would later form the core of the concept of "creativity" (Taylor, 1989). Theories of the imagination were a reaction against, and a rejection of, the abstract and mechanical formalism of the early 1700s, the empiricist idea that "Invention is nothing else but the habit acquired by practices of assembling ideas or truths" (Turnbull, 1740, I, p. 60; quoted in Engell, 1981, p. 70). Theories of the imagination made possible the conception of *genius*, which was due to an internal stimulus not explainable in terms of impressions received from the senses (Engell, 1981, pp. 79–80). Gerard's 1774 *An Essay on Genius* argued that "It is imagination that produces genius" (1774/1966, p. 26). Sir Joshua Reynolds' 13th discourse (delivered at the Royal Academy in 1786) was subtitled "Art Not Merely Imitation, But under the Direction of the Imagination" (Engell, 1981, p. 185).

In the late 1700s and early 1800s, writers in the English Romantic movement began to think that art might be created through nonrational processes (Abrams, 1984; Smith, 1961, p. 23). This line of thinking gradually evolved into the Romanticist belief that rational deliberation would kill the creative impulse (Abrams, 1953, p. 205). Instead of thinking rationally and deliberately, the artist should simply listen to the inner muse and create without conscious control.

The Romantics argued that creativity requires temporary escape from the conscious ego and a liberation of instinct and emotion, "the spontaneous overflow of powerful feelings," in Wordsworth's terms (1800/1957, p. 116). Shelley called it "unpremeditated art" (Shelley, 1901, p. 381, "To a skylark," line 5) and wrote: "Poetry is not like reasoning . . . this power arises from within, like the colour of a flower which fades and changes as it is developed" (Shelley, 1965, pp. 70–71).

The Romantics were revolutionary; they valued the artist's imagination more than mastery of the traditions of the past. Romanticism was the birth of contemporary notions of creativity—the idea that the poet or artist has a privileged status as the epitome of the human spirit (Engell, 1981). As these Romantic conceptions spread through Europe, artists began to be thought of as more than craftspeople.

The Romantics believed that creativity required a regression to a state of consciousness characterized by emotion and instinct, a fusion between self and world, and freedom from rationality and convention. These ideas weren't completely new; for thousands of years, scholars have connected creativity with altered or heightened states of consciousness. Plato used the term *enthousiasmos*, or "divine madness," to describe creativity. In ancient Greece, creativity was associated with demonic possession. A demon was a semi-deity and was viewed as a divine gift granted to selected individuals. Socrates, for example, attributed most of his knowledge to his demon (Becker, 2000–2001). Aristotle believed that creative individuals were *melancholic*; but this didn't mean he thought they were depressed; the word meant something different back then. In the Hippocratian humoral theory that held sway from ancient Greece through the Middle Ages, *melancholic* referred to one of four basic personality types, none of them associated with mental illness (Wittkower & Wittkower, 1963, p. 102). Qualities associated with the melancholic temperament included eccentricity, sensitivity, moodiness, and introversion. Emulating melancholia became a fad among young men in 16th-century Europe (Wittkower & Wittkower, 1963, pp. 98–105).

Although both Plato and Aristotle associated creativity with heightened states of consciousness, neither of them actually believed that mental illness contributed to creativity (see Chapter 9, pp. 163–176, for an extended discussion of the creativity–madness link). The belief that mental illness and creativity were related took its modern form during and after the Romantic era; the association of creativity with mental illness doesn't predate the 1830s (Becker, 2000–2001). The Romantics believed that clinical madness was an unfortunate side effect of extreme creativity. In the same way that melancholia became a trendy affectation in 16th-century Europe, mental illness became so in the 19th century; many of the Romantic poets began to embrace madness, and some claimed to experience mental anguish and madness simply because they thought they were supposed to. This self-fulfilling prophecy continues into our own time: because the Western cultural model suggests that creativity and madness are linked, writers and artists sometimes behave eccentrically, and even voluntarily exaggerate these aspects of their personalities in psychological tests (Becker, 2000–2001). After all, many creative individuals believe that being normal is the same thing as being typical, and they're eager to distinguish themselves from the average person.

Romanticism dominated the 19th century, but by the end of the century, "anti-Romanticism" was growing. The 20th century saw a rebirth of rationalism known as modernism. Modernism is characterized by isolation, coolness, and detachment (Abrams, 1984, pp. 109–144). The French modernist poets Baudelaire and Mallarmé both emphasized the importance of dispassionate deliberation and conscious craft (Abrams, 1984). In the early 20th century, poets like Ezra Pound formulated a modernist aesthetic that rejected the "mushy emotivism" of "romantic subjectiv-ism" (Sass, 2000–2001, p. 60). In the 1920s, Russian futurists and Czech formalists advocated a highly detached, analytic perspective on the world, one that stripped away the normal emotional and cultural associations of objects to instead focus on pure abstracted form (Sass, 1992).

Romanticism had one last burst in the predominantly rationalist 20th century, with 1950s postwar abstract Expressionism. The abstract Expressionists were said to create spontaneously from pure emotion and inspiration, unconstrained by planning, rational thought, or conscious filtering. However, even during the 1950s knowledgeable art experts were aware that this was a popular fiction. For example, Jackson Pollock's paintings—which in the popular conception simply involved flinging paint against canvas without forethought—were in fact carefully planned and composed. Pollack worked hard to master different techniques for dripping paint, experimenting with the results, and he composed his works in advance so that they'd give the appearance of maximum spontaneity.

Within only a few years, the avant-garde of art had moved on beyond these neo-Romantic conceptions. The contemporary arts of the 1960s onward—sometimes called "postmodern"—represented a return to rationalism. Postmodern art is critical of our culture's conceptions of creativity—deconstructing notions of spontaneity, originality, and individual genius (Sass, 2000–2001, p. 61). Minimalism and pop art explicitly rejected Romantic-era beliefs about art; they could not have been more obviously unemotional, carefully planned and executed, and in fact reveled in their own artifice by noting the parallels with advertising, product design, and comic strips. Andy Warhol famously said, "I want to be a machine" (quoted in Hughes, 1984, p. 48). Anti-Romanticism is prominent in postmodern art and theory, which rejects the ideals of authenticity, spontaneity, and personal engagement. This may be why the general public doesn't like modern art: because the average person still holds to Romanticist conceptions of creativity.

OTHER CONCEPTIONS

Contemporary Western cultural models of creativity often include the following elements, in addition to the ten core beliefs I identified in Chapter 1.

CHILDREN AND CREATIVITY

Most of us have heard it said that all children are naturally creative, and that all adults would be, too, if formal schooling hadn't interfered and smothered our natural creative impulse. In the lead article in a 1992 issue of the *Utne Reader*, Anne Cushman wrote, "For most of us, the extravagant creativity of childhood is soon crushed by the demands of parents, schools, and society" (p. 53).

This belief originated in the 19th-century Romantic-era belief that children are more pure, closer to nature, and that society gradually corrupts them as they grow to learn its customs and ways. These ideas about childhood didn't exist before the 19th century. In the early 20th century, modern artists like Kandinksy, Klee, Miro, and Dubuffet looked to children's art and often imitated a childlike style in their paintings (see Chapter 16, p. 310).

CREATIVITY AS SELF-DISCOVERY

Another common conception of creativity in the contemporary United States originated in the 1950s with the humanist psychologists, and is today often associated with the "New Age" movement: creativity is a form of self-discovery, therapy, and self-knowledge. It's quite common for famous creators to share the widespread cultural beliefs typical of their cultures. Composer Aaron Copland said that "each added work brings with it an element of self-discovery. I must create in order to know myself, and since self-knowledge is a never ending search, each new work is only a part-answer to the question 'Who am I?' and brings with it the need to go on to other and different part-answers" (Copland, 1952, p. 41). As one classically trained singer said, "If you choose a musical life, you have to recognize that you're not setting up something that you are going to do, but you're cultivating and fulfilling something that you are" (quoted in Berman, 2003, p. 20). Artists with this conception of creativity often speak of the courage required to pursue creative activity (an idea closely associated with existentialist Rollo May, 1959, 1969). In the New Age worldview, delving deep and discovering one's true self is one of the most highly valued endeavors, but it's also considered to be risky and difficult, a spiritual journey that results in personal transformation.

THE DEMOCRATIC VIEW OF CREATIVITY

"Creative", "Creation", "Creativity" are some of the most overused and ultimately debased words in the language. Stripped of any special significance by a generation of bureaucrats, civil servants, managers and politicians, lazily used as political margarine to spread approvingly and inclusively over any activity with a non-material element to it, the word "creative" has become almost unusable. Politics and the ideology of ordinariness, the wish not to put anyone down, the determination not to exalt the exceptional . . . have seen to that.

—Tusa, (2003, pp. 5–6)

The American ideology of democracy is the deep-rooted belief that everyone is equal (Menand, 1998; Rothstein, 1997; Stein, 1974). Many Americans today use "creative" as a complimentary term of praise. This ideology leads to a fear of making value-laden distinctions, a tendency to believe that everyone is creative, and that no one should judge what counts as good art, or even what counts as "art" (Wallach, 1997; Weiner, 2000). This ideology partly accounts for the resistance to introducing the sociocultural notion of "appropriateness" into creativity.

The humanist account of creativity as a form of universal self-actualization aligns naturally with American democratic ideals (Weiner, 2000, p. 106) and with the legendary American belief in the value of repeated self-reinvention, a belief that undergirds the self-help industry. As Weiner (2000) observed, many of the "how to" books about creativity today "move almost seamlessly between business innovation and personal self-help, between problem-solving and self-expression" (p. 106).

This ideology aligns well with individualist definitions of creativity, but not with sociocultural definitions. Science succeeds only because of the active involvement of a national network of critical review by journal editors, grant reviewers, and department chairs. The art world also requires that distinctions be made, that criteria be applied, and that selection and evaluation take place (Menand, 1998; Rothstein, 1997).

CREATIVITY AS ORIGINALITY

In 1917, Marcel Duchamp submitted a new work to be considered for an exhibition in New York: a simple urinal turned on its back, and signed with a fictitious name "R. Mutt." The exhibition's judges rejected the work and it wasn't displayed, yet soon after it was purchased by a wealthy collector, and today it remains one of the seminal works of 20th-century art, considered by some to be the origin of modern art. Duchamp's urinal challenged a core feature of our creativity definitions: a work should be original and unique. After Duchamp's shocking work, other artists began to experiment with the conventions of art itself, and art became reflexive, often commenting on itself and on the art world. The Dadaists experimented with many conventions of art: materials, techniques, durability, authenticity, even the importance of the "work" itself. They explicitly rejected any definition of art—as beautiful, tasteful, original, or spiritually inspired—and at times they tried to shock and disgust viewers.

In the United States, we tend to equate creativity with novelty and originality. But the high value that we place on novelty isn't shared universally in all cultures. In performance, for example, we find that in almost all cultures—including our own—improvisation is allowed only in informal performances; in formal settings, in contrast, improvisation is not allowed (Sawyer, 2003c). Formal performances must follow the movements of the dance, or the words of the script, verbatim. In most cultures, rituals forbid improvisation. This seems to be related to the power of ritual; a ritual can perform its supernatural function only if performed exactly, and a divergence from the appropriate dance or script would result in an ineffective ritual (see Chapter 19). In a traditional U. S. Christian wedding, the religious official is expected to say "I now pronounce you husband and wife"; an unexpected creative improvisation such as "I exclaim that you are now joined for life" or even "From henceforth you will be married" would be disturbing, generally not welcomed by the participants and audience (Sawyer, 2001a).

Traditional cultures tend to produce aesthetic objects that people in the United States associate with "craft" rather than "art," in part because they're typically functional objects—clothing, baskets, water vessels, hunting weapons. These artifacts have often been collected in the West, but not always by art museums—more typically they're found in "natural history" museums. We don't value these objects as highly because they seem to be mostly imitative, and our conception of creativity is focused almost exclusively on originality. But imitation is a long-established, deep-rooted form of cultural transmission, even in European fine arts (Delbanco, 2002; Gardner, 1973; Wicklund, 1989). For many centuries, and in many different societies, the ability to imitate and reproduce the acknowledged masters was highly valued, and developing this skill through practice was how one learned one's craft. Yet as Nicholas Delbanco, a director of an MFA program in writing, noted, "We've grown so committed as a culture to the ideal of originality that the artist who admits to working in the manner of another artist will likely stand accused of being second-rate" (2002, p. 59).

There are many creative domains that require individuals to insert as little of themselves as possible into the work. In translating a novel or poem into a different language, the translator is unavoidably creative; this is reflected by the fact that the translator receives attribution, and his or her name is published in the work next to that of the original author. But the ideal translator is one who most faithfully retains the creative spirit of the original, thereby keeping his or her own contribution to the translation as minimal as possible. Dubbing a foreign movie into one's own language requires that the translator develop a version of the original line that can most easily be spoken in the time that the foreign actor's mouth is moving, and it also requires the voice-over actors to match their delivery to the moving image. As with translation, the goal of the creator here is to keep his or her own contribution as minimal as possible. Although these are unquestionably creative activities, they're activities in which individual inspiration and originality would be detrimental to the work. Our culture tends to consider such activities to be less creative—exactly because the creator is more constrained.

All creativity includes elements of imitation and tradition; there's no such thing as a completely novel work. To explain creativity, we have to examine the balance of imitation and innovation, and the key role played by convention and tradition.

CREATIVITY AS FINE ART, NOT CRAFT

European cultures place a high value on the fine arts—those creative products that have no function other than pleasure. Craft objects are less worthy; because they serve an everyday function, they're not purely creative. But this division is culturally and historically relative. Most contemporary high art began as some sort of craft (Baxandall, 1972; Harris, 1966; Martindale, 1972). The composition and performance of what we now call "classical music" began as a form of craft music satisfying required functions in the Catholic mass, or the specific entertainment needs of royal patrons. For example, chamber music really was designed to be performed in chambers—small intimate rooms in wealthy homes—often as background music, the same way people today might turn on the stereo while they read or eat a meal. The "dances" composed by famous composers originally did indeed accompany dancing. But today, with the contexts and functions they were composed for long gone, we consume these works as fine art.

To take a famous example, photography is now considered an art; photographs are in the collections of all the major museums. But when the technique of photography was invented in 1839, it was considered a new technology and not a new art form. In 1844, the first major exhibition of daguerreotypes was not grouped with the artworks, but was in the Salon de l'Industrie Française. Between 1839 and 1890, photography was a mass market—focused on portraits—and there were very few aesthetic concerns (Denoyelle, 2002, p. 41). In 1852, the first exhibition of photographs with aesthetic intent was displayed at the Society of Arts in London, but these photographers remained marginalized—no market, no recognition—and photography, in the eyes of the art world, remained only a mechanical technique. Artists of the time were convinced that photography could never become an art, because the photograph wasn't created by human hands, like painting or sculpture.

How did photography became an art? An individualist would hypothesize that either those technicians working with the new tools gradually became more aesthetically skilled, or that established artists like painters and sculptors learned how to use the new technology and then applied their aesthetic abilities there. But what actually happened was that photographers themselves did not change at all; rather, the sociocultural system around them changed.

In 1890, Kodak introduced a cheap consumer camera that everyone could afford. This put the portrait studios out of business; the newly unemployed photographers needed a way to distinguish between what they did and this new popular photography. The movement of *pictorialism* was the response, with photographers attempting to imitate the artistic processes of painting;

rather than reproducible photos, they worked directly on the negatives and other materials of the process. They presented their works in art galleries, next to paintings. The elements of an art world began to form: collegial groups called "photo clubs," a journal called *Camera Work*, and shows and openings. However, art photography remained marginalized; their were no markets, buyers, or collectors, and museums were not interested in adding photos to their collections. Pictorialism eventually died out with the onset of the World War I. An art form can't survive without a market, venues for display, and collectors.

After World War I, when some painters began to make photographs that we now think of as art, those painters did not themselves consider their photography to be art. Man Ray, whom we remember today primarily for his photos, considered himself to be a painter. Brassaï, who wanted to become an artist, didn't believe that his photography realized that desire. Although demand for photographic skill grew with the expansion of daily newspapers and the demand for wartime news, documentary photographs in newspapers often did not even have a signature.

It wasn't until 1960 that a market for photographic art began to form in the United States. This development coincided with a rejection of many traditional notions of art: that it was the work of the hand, that each work was a unique creation. Prices remained modest, but collectors began to emerge, and finally, in the 1970s, a true art market was established, with control over the originality and rarity of the works (limited-edition prints), expositions, galleries, and museums. The most valuable prints are those where the negatives are lost; for this reason, some contemporary photographers destroy their negatives after making a predetermined number of prints. Where negatives remain available and unlimited prints could, in principle, be made, the market distinguishes between recent and "vintage" prints. Such a market requires experts who are able to look at a print and distinguish which year it was made from the negative.

In sum, it was not until the 1970s, well over 100 years after photography was invented, that photography took on the characteristics associated with art: the valuation of originality and uniqueness; the system of galleries, museums, and collectors; the supporting network of experts to evaluated value and confirm authenticity (Newhall, 1964).

Photography became an art only after the social system surrounding the activity became artlike, adopting the values and conventions of other established arts (Becker, 1982). Even today, the photos that conform more closely to the values of the art world are worth more—those made by the plasticians, who, like the pictorialists, produce unique prints by manipulating the developing process by hand (coloring a black-and-white photo, for example), and who create ephemeral scenes put together for the sole purpose of being photographed, only then to be disassembled.

The shift from craft to art happens over and over through history. It's always a social process, not a result of individual talent alone. As we learned earlier in this chapter, prior to the 15th century, painting was considered to be a craft and not an art, though this viewpoint shifted in the 15th century (Baxandall, 1972). To explain changing conceptions of creativity, the sociocultural approach is particularly valuable.

WHO CREATES?

The individualist definition associates creativity with the human mind, and associates the study of creativity with psychology. When we look for the creator of a created product, we instinctively look for a person (Kasof, 1995). The sociocultural definition emphasizes, in contrast, that creativity doesn't only emerge from human minds; many natural and social processes can generate appropriate novelty. These two definitions are complementary; our exploration of cognitive creativity can gain many insights from these other sources of creativity.

ANIMAL CREATIVITY

In 1917, Köhler (1925) described a chimpanzee who was able to solve a difficult problem. One by one, six chimpanzees were placed in a room with a banana suspended from the ceiling, out of reach. A wooden box was sitting on the floor in the corner. Five of the chimpanzees jumped repeatedly to try to get the banana, and gave up when they discovered it was too high. But the sixth kept looking at the box, then at the banana—and after five minutes, suddenly pushed the box under the banana, stepped up, and grabbed it. This action seems to meet our individualist definition of creativity: it was a new combination (box plus jumping).

Epstein (1990, 1999) demonstrated that pigeons can be taught in such a way that they solve the banana problem almost immediately. He trained pigeons until they'd mastered a repertory of different actions:

- First, he trained them to push a small box toward a green spot that was placed at random on the floor of the cage. (It takes weeks or months for a pigeon to learn this.)
- Second, he trained them to step up onto a box, starting with a short box and moving to progressively taller boxes. (After stepping up, they were rewarded with food.)
- Third, he trained them to step up onto a box, and peck a banana hanging from the top of the cage. (After pecking, they were rewarded with food.)

When three pigeons trained in this way were placed in a cage with a banana placed in a random location on the top of the cage, and with a box placed in a different location, they all took less than a minute to push the box to the spot directly under the banana, then to step onto the box and peck the banana (you can watch the video on YouTube). Doesn't this meet our individualist definition of a new combination, expressed in the world? After all, the pigeons had never before combined box pushing with box stepping and pecking.

Dissanayake (1988) noted that many animals—including birds and insects—engage in ritual behaviors that are reminiscent of dance or theater. Chimpanzees have been taught to paint using brush and canvas (Fig. 2.4). But in human art, specific information is communicated, and its content isn't predictable; it varies from one work to another. A second difference is that the human arts aren't instinctive; they're cultural activities that have to be learned.

A third difference is that the combinations discovered by Köhler's chimpanzee and Epstein's pigeons are combinations of observable behavioral sequences, whereas human creativity involves mental and conceptual combination. A fourth difference is that only very special animals can do this; five of Köhler's chimps gave up, and Epstein's three pigeons required months of training before they could solve the problem. But all normal people can combine concepts easily, without training (as we'll see in Chapter 6).

In any species, intelligent behavior involves some ability for adaptive, novel behavior. But the consensus among scientists is that creativity is a uniquely human trait.

FIGURE 2.4: A painting by Congo, a chimpanzee using a stiff-bristle paintbrush. (Reprinted from *The Biology of Art*, by D. Morris Knopf, 1962, plate 19. With permission of Desmond Morris.)

NATURAL CREATIVITY

The foundational insight of the Darwinian revolution is that all of the species in the world were created through natural processes of evolution—variation, selection, and retention. There was no intentional designer; rather, nature itself is the creator.

Prior to this foundational discovery of the 19th century, for centuries humankind believed that all species must have been created by a divine creator. The famous "watchmaker" argument for the existence of God originated in the mechanistic era of the 17th century. William Paley (1743–1805) began by noting that an object as complex as a watch must have an intelligent designer. Why, then, when faced with the even more extreme complexity of an animal, would one not also assume that there had been a creator? Yet Darwinian biology shows that natural species, although they were "created" in some sense, were not created by any intentional being; rather, they were created through unintentional natural processes. In this sense, nature itself is creative (see Chapter 9).

GROUP CREATIVITY

When we see a created product, we assume that a single person created it. In this, we aren't that different from those theologians of the 17th century who assumed that a complex object like a watch or an animal must have had a single intelligent creator (Skinner, 1968). But many created products are created by groups, organizations, and entire societies. In the modern era of mass production, the wristwatch isn't created by any single individual, but by a complex organization involving computer-aided design systems, microchips, factories in third-world countries, and international systems of distribution, manufacturing, and trade (see Chapters 12 and 13).

A jazz performance requires an entire jazz ensemble—for example, a drummer, a bass player, a pianist, and a horn player. The performance emerges from the interactions of four individuals working collaboratively; there's no way that such a performance could be created by a single, solitary individual. Of course, we can speak of the creativity of the drummer or of the saxophonist, but we can also speak of the creativity of the ensemble as a unit. And the group's creativity isn't a simple sum of the creative talents of the individual members; the group's performance is greater than the sum of its parts. Some combinations of musicians work well, and others don't; the same drummer might sound brilliant in one ensemble, yet only mediocre in another. To explain group creativity, we can't limit our focus to individual creativity; we must also consider group dynamics (Sawyer, 2003c).

Theater performances are ensemble performances, with an entire cast of characters. Although the cast is performing from a script written by a playwright, and has been guided by a director through countless rehearsals, the quality of each night's performance varies due to the group dynamics among the members of the cast. This group dynamic is carried to an extreme in improvisational theater, when the actors do not begin with a script or a plot, but rather create all of these dramatic elements on stage in front of a live audience. In this kind of group improvisation, no one can predict in advance what will happen. Even the best groups, filled with extremely talented actors, fall flat much of the time; a brilliant performance on Friday night might be followed by a dud on Saturday (Sawyer, 2003d).

Jazz and theater performances are created by groups, not by individuals. To explain group creativity, we have to focus on the processes of collaboration among group members. These are topics for Chapter 12 (group creativity), Chapter 18 (music), and Chapter 19 (acting).

SOCIETAL CREATIVITY

Who created the systems that underlie the U.S. economy—the trading mechanisms of the stock market, the legal system and the government oversight organizations that administer the market, the surplus capital that feeds the market? This is a trick question: no single person created these complex systems. Not even a single group or team created them; the systems emerged over decades and centuries, with contributions and modifications throughout by countless individuals and groups. The U.S. economy is a creation of the entire society, and it emerged over many life spans.

Cultural historians have attempted to explain why some societies, in some historical periods, seem to be more creative overall than others. In Renaissance Florence, an incredible creative explosion resulted in novel products that we still admire today, in architecture, sculpture, painting, and science (see p. 214). But no one creator was responsible for this burst of activity; the Florentine Renaissance was an emergent, collective, social phenomenon, and to explain creativity at the social level of analysis, we have to draw on social sciences like sociology, economics, and political science. We'll examine societal creativity in Chapters 11, 12, and 13.

CONCLUSION

Through the centuries, Europeans have held to different conceptions of creativity. Artists have been thought of as poorly paid tradespeople, and as divinely inspired geniuses. Creativity has swung between rational and Romantic conceptions. There hasn't been a single historically continuous definition of creativity. The message for us today is that the Western cultural model of creativity isn't universal. A science of creativity should be able to rise above these historical limitations, and take us beyond any one cultural model of creativity.

A second more subtle lesson to be drawn from this chapter is that these changing conceptions of creativity aren't random and unpredictable; they can be logically derived from broader properties of the society. The conceptions of art that a society holds follow logically from the styles and techniques of art, the social organization of the work, and the functions that art plays in that society. The deeply religious Europe of the Middle Ages associated creativity with the divine. Several broad shifts associated with the Renaissance led to a change in the conception of art. First, economic developments resulted in a demand for a new form of secular art—portraits and scenes of everyday life commissioned by the new business and trading classes. Second, during the Renaissance, the movement toward humanism led to an increasing emphasis on the uniqueness of the individual, and this resulted in a conception of the artist as uniquely inspired and talented, with a message and an insight to communicate that might not necessarily be divinely inspired. Third, the shift toward modern nonrepresentational art has often been interpreted as a response to broader social forces—the increasing mechanization of society or the maturing of photography as a more accurate representational medium in the late 19th century. Nonrepresentational art required yet another conception of creativity: creativity began to be conceived of as a break with conventions rather than as an imitation of nature, and art was reconceived as a way of experimenting with perception and representation.

MOVING AHEAD

We've now laid the groundwork to begin our explanation of creativity. We started by examining how conceptions of creativity have changed over the centuries. I identified the historical origins of many of the ten creativity beliefs of the Western cultural model (Chapter 1). A scientific explanation of creativity requires us to look critically at our own cultural model about how creativity works, and the scientific studies we'll examine throughout this book will allow us to determine which of our creativity beliefs are correct. But even if our cherished beliefs about creativity are challenged, we should welcome the science of creativity because it provides light by showing us how creativity really works. Only with true understanding can we improve the creativity of people, groups, organizations, and societies. The goal of creativity research is to explain all of these forms of creativity—to move beyond the cultural model of one culture at one historical point in time, and develop a science of human innovation.

KEY CONCEPTS

- Behaviorist and Freudian conceptions of creativity
- Conceptions of the artist: art as divine inspiration, imitation, imagination
- Rationalist conceptions of creativity—as generated by the conscious, deliberating, intelligent, rational mind
- Romanticist conceptions of creativity—as generated by the irrational unconscious, and repressed or blocked by the conscious mind

- Children and creativity
- Conceptions of creativity as self-discovery and as democratic
- Conceptions of creativity as original versus traditional and imitative
- Contrasts between fine art and craft

THOUGHT EXPERIMENTS

- Think of someone you know whom you think is particularly creative.
- Why do you think so?
- Is it because of some distinctive behavior, lifestyle, or way of talking or dressing?
- Is it because you've seen one of his or her created works and you thought that it was creative?
- Do you think this person would be considered creative by people from other countries and other cultures? Or is there something uniquely American about his or her creativity?
- If you have a pet—a dog or a cat—can you recall your pet doing anything that you would call creative?

SUGGESTED READINGS

Becker, H. (1982). *Art worlds*. Berkeley and Los Angeles: University of California Press.

Guilford, J. P. (1950). Creativity. *American Psychologist, 5*(9), 444–454.

Honour, H., & Fleming, J. (1999). *World history of art* (5th ed.). London: Lawrence King.

Negus, K., & Pickering, M. (2004). *Creativity, communication and cultural value*. London: Sage Publications.

Pope, R. (2005). *Creativity: Theory, history, practice*. London: Routledge.

Weiner, R. P. (2000). *Creativity and beyond: Cultures, values, and change*. Albany: State University of New York Press.

PART 2

INDIVIDUALIST APPROACHES

In Chapter 1, we encountered two definitions of creativity, each associated with a major approach to the study of creativity—the individualist approach and the sociocultural approach.

The individualist approach defines creativity as a new mental combination that is expressed in the world. *This "little c" creativity is novel for the person, but it doesn't have to be the first time it's even been done by a human being. That's why these mental combinations might not necessarily be something we would call "creative" in everyday language. It might be a child, learning how to add two numbers for the first time. It might be a new combination of two common words that are never associated, like "red water." It might be a commuter figuring out a new side road around a traffic jam, or a parent improvising on a family recipe.*

Part II focuses on individualist approaches—based on the study of exceptionally creative individuals, and also of ordinary people engaged in creative tasks. Chapters 3 through 7 provide a comprehensive overview of psychological research in the first two waves of creativity research—personality psychology and cognitive psychology. Chapter 8 summarizes attempts by cognitive scientists to develop computer programs that simulate various aspects of the creative process—research that's done by computer scientists working closely with psychologists. Chapters 9 and 10 summarize the science emerging from biological approaches to the study of the human brain.

Individualist approaches tend to be reductionist*—they analyze creativity by decomposing it into smaller units of thought and behavior. Each psychological experiment analyzes a distinct mental process; each brain imaging study focuses on specific brain regions. As you read through these studies, you may feel that you're lost in the trees and can't see the forest. At times, you may wonder what this or that experiment has to do with real-world creativity.*

I agree that individualist approaches sometimes can seem far removed from the real-world creativity we started out to explain. But these approaches provide a valuable part of the ultimate explanation of creativity— after all, creativity is based in mental structures and processes that are part of every normal human brain. Individualist approaches can provide us with answers about the basic building blocks of higher-level, observed human behavior. These studies don't explain "creativity" per se; instead, they explain basic mental processes that are components of creativity. The challenge, as we read through these studies, will be to not lose sight of the forest—and ultimately, to find a way to connect these scientific findings back to real-world creativity.

In contrast to the reductionism of the individualist approaches, the sociocultural approaches that we'll review in Part III tend to study real-world creativity; they analyze the whole phenomenon instead of reducing it to smaller individual and psychological components. Individualist approaches try to explain creativity from the bottom up, and sociocultural approaches try to explain creativity from the top down. Combining both approaches, we'll converge on a complete explanation of creativity.

C H A P T E R   3
_____

DEFINING CREATIVITY THROUGH ASSESSMENT

Guilford's 1950 presidential address focused on scientific and technological creativity, and he later seemed remarkably prescient when the Soviets beat the Americans into orbit with the launch of Sputnik in October 1957. The American response was a mobilization in the schools to attempt to identify and nurture scientific talent and creativity. An influential 1958 Rockefeller Brothers Fund report titled *The Pursuit of Excellence* identified creative talent as one of our great national resources (Rockefeller Brothers Fund, 1958). Parnes and Harding (1962) wrote, "We must develop a more creative trend in American education. We are in a brains race with Soviet Russia and the need is urgent" (p. vi).

For psychologists in the 1950s and 1960s, creativity was pretty much synonymous with scientific creativity; after all, most of this research was funded by the National Science Foundation. Researchers worked hard to develop a test that could identify children who were gifted and talented so that schools could nurture their talent and target them for high-creativity careers in science and technology (e.g., Parnes & Harding, 1962). The formal name of the Utah Conferences was "The Identification of Creative Scientific Talent." Standardized creativity measures began to be developed in the 1950s and 1960s, and this effort continues today. This chapter summarizes these creativity assessments.

Psychologists can't observe the mind directly; the mental structures and processes that psychologists study—whether motivation, personality traits, intelligence, memories, or emotions—are hypothesized unobservable entities called *constructs*. Although we can't see constructs directly, we can infer them from observable behavior. The first thing a psychologist does after proposing and defining a hypothesized construct is to *operationalize* the construct. Operationalization is a strict form of definition—it specifies a methodological procedure that can be used to measure the hypothesized construct in terms of observable behaviors.

Many people are nervous about providing strict definitions of creativity, such as the two main definitions I provided in Chapter 1—the individualist and the sociocultural definitions. But even if you agree that creativity can be defined, you might be skeptical that creativity can be operationalized and measured. Yet, as consumers of creative products, we assess creativity all the time:

- We choose which musicians, and which songs or albums, to buy.
- We make judgments about which movie directors are creative, and about which actors and actresses are creative.

- We discuss with our friends which videogames, YouTube videos, or mobile phone apps are creative.
- We have our favorite artists, poets, or novelists.
- We recognize certain jokes or cartoons as particularly creative.

Of course, these are all subjective judgments, rather than scientific measures—they're matters of personal taste. One person might rate the creativity of a musician or a YouTube video differently from another. But when the subjective judgments of many people are aggregated, what results are quantitative measures of creativity that can be used by creativity researchers:

- To assess the creativity of a Broadway musical, one has several measures to select from: length of run, dollars taken in at the box office, awards, reviews. Such measures have been used in a social network analysis of the creativity of the production teams that generated these musicals (Uzzi & Spiro, 2005; see Chapter 12 on group creativity).
- To assess the creativity of a fine art painter, one has several measures to select from: current auction prices of the paintings, how many major museums display the painter's works, how often the painter's work has been reproduced in an art history textbook, and others. Such measures have been used by economist David Galenson (2001) to identify intriguing patterns in French and American painters; see Chapter 15 on history and creativity.
- To assess the creativity of a scientist, one has several measures to select from: the number of journal articles published in academic journals; the frequency with which those journal articles are cited by other scientists as being important; and the number of awards, such as the Nobel prize, received by the scientist. Such measures have been used by many researchers, most notably by psychologist Dean Keith Simonton (1988b, 1997a; see Chapter 15).

Each of these measures represents a collective judgment by a large number of people with expertise in the creative domain. There are two issues with such measures that might occur to you immediately. First, do these numbers measure creativity, or something else? The value of a painting might be the result of trends in popularity that have a questionable relationship to actual creativity. This is a question about the *validity* of the above measures; a test is said to have *validity* when it measures what it claims to measure. For example, the box office of a Broadway musical might not truly measure creativity, if the theater audience prefers musicals that aren't the most creative ones. The first section of this chapter describes *test validity*, one of the most important issues in creativity assessment.

Second, these are all measures of exceptional levels of creativity—famous painters, scientists, or musicals. Thus these measures are designed for the sociocultural definition of creativity ("Big C" creativity). But research psychologists need a creativity test that works for everyone—to study creativity under the individualist, "little c" definition. This chapter describes many measures of creativity that can be used to study little c creativity, not just those exceptional creators who generate and sell their creative products. This chapter prepares you to understand the research in Chapters 4 through 10 by describing the tests that are used in that research.

THE REQUIREMENTS OF A GOOD TEST

Creativity assessment is one of the most controversial topics among creativity researchers, and what little consensus has developed still leaves a lot of room for multiple interpretations.

Before you can understand the state of creativity assessment, you need to know a little about how psychological assessments are developed.

Psychologists who develop and study tests are known as *psychometricians*. It's a well-established field of expertise, with over a century of science and math behind it; the first psychometrician was Francis Galton, who worked in the second half of the 19th century. Psychometricians have identified several characteristics that all psychological tests and measures should have; these fall into the two broad categories of *validity* and *reliability*.

VALIDITY

A test is said to be valid if it measures the psychological construct that you claim it measures. This is referred to as *construct validity*. The first basic test of construct validity is *face validity*—does it seem obvious that the test is measuring what it's supposed to? "On its face," in other words? If a proposed test has face validity, then the researcher moves on to more demanding procedures:

- *Convergent validity*—A measure has convergent validity if you can demonstrate statistically that other measures that are theoretically supposed to be related, are related. For example, different measures of creativity should be related.
- *Discriminant validity*—A measure has discriminant validity if you can demonstrate statistically that measures that shouldn't be related to your construct are not. For example, if your theory claims that creativity is distinct from intelligence, then the creativity score shouldn't be related to IQ.

After construct validity is demonstrated, a second important element of validity is *criterion validity*: does the test predict performance on some external criterion of creative performance? There are two subtypes of criterion validity:

- *Concurrent validity*—Does the test correlate well with a measure that has previously been validated?
- *Predictive validity*—Does the test predict creative performance in real life?

Researchers frequently use all of these forms of validity when discussing various measures of creativity.

RELIABILITY

A test is said to be *reliable* if it always gets the same result when applied to the same person. The word means the same thing it does when applied to any measuring tool; a voltmeter is reliable if it accurately reports the voltage between its two probes, and a bathroom scale is reliable if it reports your true weight. If you weigh yourself five times during the day, and the scale gives you a different weight each time, you should probably throw it out. That's why reliability is a necessary property of a good test; if a person gets a completely different creativity score each time he or she takes a test, that test would be an unreliable instrument.

There are roughly three important forms of reliability that are relevant to creativity research, although the first is the most important:

- Stability across time (test–retest reliability)
- Internal consistency—Multiple versions of the test should give the same results; different test items should give similar results (split-half reliability).
- Inter-rater reliability—With tests that require some human judgment to rate the performance, the ratings of multiple judges should be similar.

Without some evidence of reliability, it's extremely difficult to get a measure published and used. A test that isn't reliable is worthless.

THE CONSTRUCT OF CREATIVITY

Although validity and reliability are a bit technical (they require some complex statistics to formally demonstrate), it's important to understand these concepts because this is more than just a trivial mathematical exercise. Ultimately, it's about what creativity is and whether it exists at all—at least, in the form captured in the Western cultural model. If no test for creativity can be developed that's reliable, then it probably doesn't make sense to refer to creativity as a stable trait of a person.

And in fact, several scientists have argued that creativity is not a stable personality trait.

If no test can be developed that demonstrates that creativity has discriminant validity when contrasted with other personality measures—whether IQ or extraversion or tolerance for ambiguity—then our hypothesized construct of "creativity" probably doesn't really exist at all, and instead we should be studying those other constructs.

And in fact, several scientists have argued that creativity is not a distinct mental construct.

Now that we're armed with a basic understanding of good test design, and we understand the high stakes involved, we're ready to explore the field of creativity assessment.

CREATIVITY TESTS

Since creativity research began in the 1950s, well over a hundred creativity measures have been developed and studied (Hocevar & Bachelor, 1989). This section describes some of the most commonly used of these many assessments. The most widely used category of creativity test, the *divergent thinking test*, has its own extended section following this one.

RATINGS OF THE CREATIVE PERSON

One of the most common ways to measure creativity is to ask others who know the person well. School districts often rate students' creativity by asking their teachers to rate them. (However, teachers don't always accurately rate the creativity of their students; see Chapter 21 on education, pp. 389–390).

The researchers at the Berkeley IPAR identified exceptional creators by asking leading figures in each field to nominate their peers. Csikszentmihalyi (1996) likewise identified his 91 exceptional creators by asking senior people in the field to nominate "the most creative" in their field. The peer nomination method seems to work fairly well when applied to Big C sociocultural creativity.

RATINGS OF THE CREATIVE PRODUCT

At the beginning of this chapter, I listed several quantitative measures of a product's creativity. For an artwork, you can find its market value, or count how many times it appears in art history textbooks. For a research article that reports a scientific discovery, you can look up the *citation count*, the number of times the article is cited by later researchers. Then, when you average the ratings of all of a person's creative works, you can use that as an indirect measure of that person's creativity. If the average market value of an artist's paintings is high, you could reasonably conclude that the artist is creative. Note that these are sociocultural measures—they work only for Big C, exceptional creativity.

For little c, everyday creative products, several product ratings have been developed. Some of them ask a person to generate an artwork in the laboratory as part of the experiment. For example, the Barron Welsh Art Scale (Barron & Welsh, 1952; Welsh, 1969, 1975) asks a person to sketch an image, and the experimenter then scores the image based on Freudian concepts such as ego functioning, symbolization, and substitution. The Hall Mosaic Construction Test (Hall, 1972) gives a person 30 minutes to generate an 8 × 10-inch mosaic out of precut 1-inch squares that's then scored on six aesthetic dimensions by five expert raters.

Verbal creativity can be measured in a similar way; for example, people can be asked to generate a short story in the laboratory. In the IPAR Word Rearrangement test (Barron, 1963b), a person is given a list of 50 words—selected at random from common nouns, adjectives, and adverbs—and is told to make up a story that uses as many of the words as possible. The story is rated for originality on a 9-point scale.

The most widely used method of assessing little c product creativity is the *Consensual Assessment Technique (CAT)*. In the CAT, participants are asked to create a product—such as a poem, or a caption to a single-frame cartoon—and then the creativity of each product is rated by two or more experts in the field. The ratings of the judges are averaged, and the average rating is used as a measure of the creativity of the product. This technique was first used in Csikszentmihalyi's doctoral dissertation (1965) and first published in *The Creative Vision* (Getzels & Csikszentmihalyi, 1976). They asked MFA students to paint still lifes, and then asked a panel of five art school professors to rate the craftsmanship, originality, and overall aesthetic value of each painting. Perhaps the first use of the CAT with schoolchildren was Amabile (1982).

It sounds as if it would be too subjective, but multiple studies have shown that the ratings of experts generally correlate highly, for good inter-rater reliability, even with everyday creations like children's collages (Amabile, 1982; Baer, 1993; Kaufman et al., 2007; Kaufman, Baer, & Cole, 2009). For example, Runco and Vega (1990) had groups of three adults rate the creativity of children's ideas, and their levels of agreement were around 0.90 (on a scale from 0 to 1, this is fairly high); teachers, parents, and other adults gave the same ratings. In contrast, novice ratings aren't highly correlated, and novices shouldn't be used as raters with the CAT (Kaufman, Baer,

Cole, & Sexton, 2008). For example, Kaufman et al. (2009) found that expert ratings correlated with each other at 0.93 (a correlation of 1.0 means that every expert rated every work the same, so .93 means their ratings were extremely similar—almost identical), but novice ratings correlated with each other only at 0.53. So the CAT is one of the more expensive and time-consuming creativity tests to administer—you have to find and engage a panel of experts, and two or more have to rate each created product.

The CAT depends on the sociocultural criterion of *appropriateness as evaluated by a community*. But because it's used to assess little c creativity, and because rater judgments correlate highly, it's typically considered to be a measure of little c individual creativity rather than Big C sociocultural creativity.

SELF-REPORTS

Another common way to rate a person's creativity is to ask him or her directly. Torrance (1962) developed the first such test; his "Things Done on Your Own" scale presented students with a list of 100 creative activities, and asked them to "Include only the things you have done on your own, not the things you have been assigned or made to do" (p. 251). The 100 items included:

- Wrote a poem, story, or play
- Produced a puppet show
- Explored a cave
- Read a science magazine
- Grafted a plant or rooted one from a cutting
- Kept a daily record of weather
- Organized or helped to organize a club
- Made a poster for a club, school, or other event
- Drew up plans for (or constructed) an invention or apparatus
- Made up a recipe

Since Torrance's 1962 list, many self-report questionnaires have been developed; I describe four that are representative.

The Lifetime Creativity Scale

The Lifetime Creativity Scale (LCS; Richards et al. 1988a) asks people to list their occupations, responsibilities, accomplishments, and hobbies. An interviewer asks the questions and fills out the scoring sheet.

The Creative Achievement Questionnaire

The Creative Achievement Questionnaire (CAQ; Carson, Peterson, & Higgins, 2005) is given directly to the participant, who is asked to check off actual accomplishments in ten separate domains of creative accomplishment, such as "My work has won a prize at a juried art show."

The ten domains are visual arts, music, dance, creative writing, architectural design, humor, theater and film, culinary arts, inventions, and scientific inquiry. In each domain, seven different accomplishment items are provided, ranked by the level of achievement.

A factor analysis showed that the ten domains tended to group into three related areas: expressive creativity (visual arts, writing, humor) performance creativity (dance, drama, music), and scientific creativity (invention, science, culinary) (with architecture not related to any of these three).

Because many of the higher levels of achievement involve recognition by experts, both the LCS and the CAQ incorporate the sociocultural element of "appropriateness."

The Runco Ideational Behavior Scale

The Runco Ideational Behavior Scale (RIBS; Runco, Plucker, & Lim, 2000–2001) asks people to indicate how much they agree with 23 statements:

1. I have many wild ideas
2. I think about ideas more often than most people
3. I often get excited by my own new ideas
4. I come up with a lot of ideas or solutions to problems
5. I come up with an idea or solution other people have never thought of
6. I like to play around with ideas for the fun of it
7. It is important to be able to think of bizarre and wild possibilities
8. I would rate myself highly in being able to come up with ideas
9. I have always been an active thinker; I have lots of ideas
10. I enjoy having leeway in the things I do and room to make up my own mind
11. My ideas are often considered impractical or even wild
12. I would take a college course based on original ideas
13. I am able to think about things intensely for many hours
14. Sometimes I get so interested in a new idea that I forget about other things that I should be doing
15. I often have trouble sleeping at night, because so many ideas keep popping into my head
16. When writing papers or talking to people, I often have trouble staying with one topic because I think of so many things to write or say
17. I often find that one of my ideas has led me to other ideas which have led me to other ideas, and I end up with an idea and do not know where it came from
18. Some people might think me scatter brained or absent minded because I think about a variety of things at once
19. I try to exercise my mind by thinking things through
20. I am able to think up answers to problems that haven't already been figured out
21. I am good at combining ideas in ways that others have not tried
22. Friends ask me to help them think of ideas and solutions
23. I have ideas about new inventions or about how to improve things

RIBS has been demonstrated to have reliability and partial construct validity.

Gough's Adjective Check List

Gough's Adjective Check List (ACL) was originally a general personality instrument with 300 words, used at the Berkeley IPAR during the 1950s and 1960s; participants were asked to check those adjectives that best describe them (first published in Gough & Heilbrun, 1965). Out of the 300 words, Gough (1979) identified a subscale of 30 words that were predictive of creativity, which he called the Creative Personality Scale (CPS). The 18 adjectives positively associated with creativity are: capable, clever, confident, egotistical, humorous, individualistic, informal, insightful, intelligent, interests wide, inventive, original, reflective, resourceful, self-confident, sexy, snobbish, unconventional. The 12 adjectives negatively associated with creativity are: affected, cautious, commonplace, conservative, conventional, dissatisfied, honest, interests narrow, mannerly, sincere, submissive, suspicious. The total score is the number of positives checked minus the number of negatives checked. Gough (1979) found that scores on the CPS were correlated with ratings by knowledgeable experts over 12 samples totaling 1,701 subjects (a form of concurrent validity).

Domino (1970) developed a variant of the CPS: he started with Gough's 300 adjectives and found that 59 of them were associated with greater creativity (among freshman college students nominated and rated by their professors). The Domino Creativity Scale (Cr) is administered just like the CPS, but with Domino's 59 words instead of Gough's 30.

There's probably some gender and cultural bias in any adjective test; of the 1,121 college women and 760 college men whom Gough (1979) examined, the male average was 5.03 and the female average was 3.97. When you look closely at the list of adjectives, some of them seem to associate creativity with male-gendered stereotypes: egotistical and self-confident give you a plus, and sincere and submissive get you a minus.

REMOTE ASSOCIATES TEST

The Remote Associations Test (RAT; Mednick, 1962; Mednick & Mednick, 1967) begins with the assumption that creativity involves combining two concepts in a new way—the core of the individualist definition. Sarnoff Mednick, the developer of the RAT, extended this assumption with a second claim: he believed that combinations of two very different concepts—remote associations—would be more creative than combinations of very similar concepts. Mednick was inspired by historical research showing that breakthrough innovations often bring together material from different disciplines (see also Simonton, 1999b). For example, if 100 people are all asked to imagine the combination of a chair with a table, their imagined combinations would all probably involve a chair with a small, individual-sized table attached—something like a school desk. The combination is straightforward because both *chair* and *table* belong to the same category, *furniture*. But if 100 people were asked to combine a chair with a pony, many different answers would be suggested. A chair you sit on while grooming a pony? A chair that a pony sits in? A chair with its back carved in the shape of a pony's head? This is because *chair* and *pony* are from very different categories, so you have to form a "remote" association.

With education and learning, people tend to develop a few strong associations between related concepts. Mednick described this as a *steep associative hierarchy* (Fig. 3.1). Mednick argued that more creative people instead have a *flat associative hierarchy*, allowing them to make large numbers of remote associations between seemingly distinct ideas. To test a person's ability

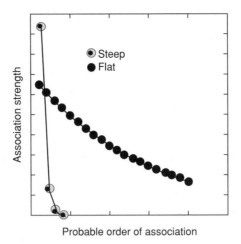

FIGURE 3.1: Steep and flat associative hierarchies according to Mednick's theory. (From *Origins of Genius: Darwinian Perspectives on Creativity* by Dean Keith Simonton, copyright 1999 by Oxford University Press. Inc. Used by permission of Oxford University Press, Inc.)

to form remote associations, Mednick created a special list of word triplets. In an RAT triplet, each of the three words is remotely associated with a fourth *target word*, and the task is to identify the target word. Try to find the target word for each of these five rows (answers are at the end of this chapter):

CREAM	SKATE	WATER
SHOW	LIFE	ROW
CRACKER	FLY	FIGHTER
DREAM	BREAK	LIGHT
HOUND	PRESSURE	SHOT

Because solving the RAT triplets forces a person to create a new combination, we know that a solution meets the individualist definition of creativity. And scoring the test doesn't involve any subjective judgment of appropriateness, as required by the sociocultural definition. Because of these strengths, the RAT has been used as a measure of creativity in several recent empirical studies (Ansburg & Hill, 2003; Isen, Labroo, & Durlach, 2004; White & Shah, 2006) and in a range of cognitive neuroscience studies (see Chapter 10).

Howard-Jones et al. (2005) developed a variant of the RAT: they asked people to write a short story using three words. There were two variables in the experiment: (1) People were either instructed to "be creative" or "be uncreative"; (2) People were given three unrelated words, such as the RAT triplets, or they were given three related words (magician, trick, rabbit). The stories based on unrelated words were rated (using the CAT) as more creative than the stories based on related words; and the stories where people were instructed to be creative were more creative than stories when they were instructed to be uncreative (see p. 49 below on experimenter effects).

With the unrelated words, even when they tried to be uncreative, they still wrote more creative stories than when they were trying to be creative with related words—additional evidence that combinations of distant concepts are more likely to be creative.

Although the RAT has several advantages, it has disadvantages as well. First, it's quite difficult for non-native speakers of English (Estrada, Isen, & Young, 1994). Second, it correlates highly with measures of verbal intelligence ($r = 0.49$), suggesting that it may not have discriminant validity with verbal intelligence tests (see pp. 55–57). Third, studies of creative breakthroughs have found that in most cases, insights result from associations with closely related material, rather than from extremely remote associations (Gough, 1976; MacKinnon, 1962; Perkins, 1983). We'll see in Chapter 20 that some of the most famous distant analogies in science are false reconstructions, such as Kekule's famous snake dream, which most likely never happened (pp. 373–374, note 2).

CREATIVE FUNCTIONING TEST

Smith and Carlsson's (1987, 1990) Creative Functioning Test (CFT) measures two hypothesized constructs: *ideational flexibility* and *creative strength*. The CFT presents a person with a series of still-life images generated by a professional artist, containing two primary objects. The images have a lot of shading and contours, so that it's fairly easy to see other things in the picture. Each picture is shown multiple times. At first, the picture is displayed for an extremely short period of time, just one fiftieth of one second, and the subjects are asked what they thought they saw. With such a short exposure, the answers at first have nothing to do with the actual image. Then the subjects see the same picture again, for a bit longer. The subjects don't know it's actually the same picture each time, and they typically report seeing different things each time they're shown the picture, until finally it's shown long enough that they can tell what the two objects are. The total number of different interpretations of the picture that a person gives before he or she reports seeing the two actual objects is the measure of *ideational flexibility*.

Then the same picture is displayed at shorter and shorter times. At first, the subjects recognize that it's the same picture over and over. Eventually, the time presentation is so short that they can't tell for sure. The *high creative strength* subjects start describing other, often idiosyncratic, images during this decreasing series. The *low creative strength* subjects keep saying that they see the same image, only that it gets darker or more fuzzy.

Carlsson, Wendt, and Rijsberg (2000) reported that the CFT has been validated by correlation with several other measures of creativity.

DIVERGENT THINKING TESTS

One of the most obvious differences between intelligence and creativity is that intelligence requires *convergent thinking*, coming up with a single right answer, while creativity requires *divergent thinking*, coming up with many potential answers. The first divergent thinking test was developed by Binet, the originator of the IQ test, in 1896 (Barron & Harrington, 1981, p. 446)—a test of open-ended, multiple-solution items. Similar measures of "imaginative abilities" proliferated through the early years of the 20th century.

During the 1950s and 1960s, many researchers developed tests of divergent thinking. Dr. Guilford himself led the charge, at the Aptitudes Research Project at the University of Southern California. His Structure-of-Intellect (SOI) model of the personality included *divergent production* (today referred to as "divergent thinking") as one of six *operations* (Guilford, 1959, 1967). The other operations were cognition, memory recording, memory retention, convergent production, and evaluation. Guilford proposed that divergent production involved four abilities: Fluency, Flexibility, Originality, and Elaboration.

Guilford and his team developed a large number of influential tests to measure the four components of divergent thinking; his tests have been adapted and used in two of the most widely used measures of divergent thinking (DT)—the Torrance Tests of Creative Thinking (TTCT; Torrance, 1974) and the Wallach-Kogan creativity tests (Wallach & Kogan, 1965). Both of these tests include the *unusual uses test* (Guilford, Merrifield, & Wilson, 1958). Subjects are asked to list as many uses as they can for a familiar object, like a brick or a coat hanger. The list is used to derive four component scores of DT: *Fluency* is measured by the number of responses; *Originality* is measured by the number of responses that are not provided by other participants; *Flexibility* is a measurement of the number of different categories that the responses group into; and *Elaboration* is a measurement of how descriptive each response is.

A second common way to measure the four abilities is Guilford's Consequences test (Christensen, Merrifield, & Guilford, 1953; also Guilford & Hoepfner, 1971). The Consequences test asks people to list the outcomes of unlikely events such as:

- "What would happen if gravity was cut in half?"
- "What would be the consequences if everyone suddenly lost the ability to read and write?"
- "What would be the consequences if none of us needed food any more to live?"
- "What would be the results if people no longer needed or wanted sleep?"
- "What would happen if the world was covered in water except for a few mountain tops?"

As with the Unusual Uses test, participants are scored on the total number of responses (fluency), the number of statistically rare responses (originality), the number of different categories the responses fall into (flexibility), and the degree of detail and description provided for each response (elaboration).

A third classic measure of DT is the *Plot Titles* test; two stories are presented without titles, and people are asked to list as many titles as possible for each plot. The titles are rated on a 5-point scale of cleverness (Barron, 1963b).

One problem with DT tests is that it's quite time-consuming for scorers to evaluate originality, flexibility, and elaboration for every response provided. Silvia, Martin, and Nusbaum (2009; also Silvia et al., 2008b) developed a quicker "snapshot scoring" method that allows each participant to be scored in just a few minutes. To do snapshot scoring, three raters look at the original handwritten response sheet for a participant, and then give a number from 1 to 5 as a rating of the overall creativity—basically, they just eyeball the list and go with their gut impression, rather than individually scoring every item listed. To evaluate the validity of this method, Silvia et al. (2009) gave people the Unusual Uses test with *brick* and *knife*. The snapshot method had reasonable validity, but lower validity than more time-consuming methods like *top-two scoring*, in which raters score all responses and then use the top two to assess the person's creativity.

TORRANCE TESTS OF CREATIVE THINKING

The most widely used paper-and-pencil test of creativity is a DT test called the Torrance Tests of Creative Thinking (TTCT; Torrance, 1974, 2008). The TTCT has been used in over 2,000 studies and has been translated into more than 32 languages (Frasier, 1990). E. Paul Torrance (1915–2003) based the TTCT on Guilford's concept of divergent production, and the TTCT contains many of the Guilford techniques. Torrance's tests were designed to satisfy one of the key goals of 1960s creativity research: to identify children with high creative potential so that they could be steered into careers requiring creativity, and to transform education to fully realize the creative potential of every student. Tests created by Guilford and by Torrance were widely used in the 1960s, particularly with young children. Today, the TTCT is the most widely used test of creativity for admission to gifted and talented programs (see Chapter 21).

The TTCT (Torrance, 1974, 2008) includes Verbal and Figural tests, and each includes a Form A and Form B that can be used alternately. The Figural forms have these subtests:

- Picture construction: Subject uses a basic shape and expands on it to create a picture.
- Picture completion: Subject is asked to sketch an interesting object, starting with an incomplete figure (Fig. 3.2).
- Lines/Circles: Subject is asked to sketch as many different objects as possible, each time starting with a pair of vertical lines (if Form A) or circles (if Form B).

The Verbal form has seven subtests. For the first three, the subject refers to a picture at the beginning of the test booklet. In Form A, the picture is of an elf staring at its reflection in a pool of water.

- *Asking*: Subject asks as many questions as possible about the picture.
- *Guessing causes*: Subject lists possible causes for the pictured action.
- *Guessing consequences*: Subject lists possible consequences for the pictured action.
- *Product improvement*: Subject is asked to make changes to improve a toy (like a stuffed animal).
- *Unusual uses*: Subject is asked to think of many different possible uses for a common object (like a paper clip).
- *Unusual questions*: Subject lists as many questions as possible about a common object (this item does not appear in later editions).
- *Just suppose*: Subject is asked to imagine that an improbable situation has happened, and then list possible ramifications.

FIGURE 3.2: Three examples of incomplete figures used in the TTCT (by author).

The Verbal and Figural tests correlate at 0.36, which isn't very high—suggesting these two tests are measuring two different constructs, not one single construct of "creativity" (Plucker, 1999).

Administration and scoring of the test is standardized; detailed norms have been created and are continually revised. The test is currently administered by the Scholastic Testing Service (www.ststesting.com, accessed Aug. 19, 2011). The original tests reported scores in the four DT components of fluency, originality, flexibility, and elaboration. In 1984, a revision resulted in different scores: two scores were added for the Figural tests—resistance to premature closure and abstractness of titles—and the flexibility score was removed because it was so highly correlated with fluency (Ball & Torrance, 1984; Hébert et al., 2002). Although STS continues to separately report fluency and originality, they correlate at 0.88 (Torrance, 2008), leading many researchers to use fluency as the single measure of creativity.

ARE DT TESTS RELIABLE AND VALID?

Although DT tests are widely used as measures of creativity—both in school settings and in research experiments—some scholars have raised serious questions about their reliability and validity. Other scholars defend DT tests and continue to use them in their research.

Reliability

In 2008, newspapers around the country reported the results of a fascinating experiment. People were shown either the Apple computer logo or the IBM logo, and then they were immediately given the Unusual Uses test of DT—they were asked to think of as many unusual uses as possible for a brick. People who were shown the Apple corporate logo got significantly higher scores on the brick test—both on fluency and on rated creativity of their uses. Among the subset of people who valued creativity highly, the half who saw the Apple logo came up with about eight unusual uses, and the others who saw the IBM logo came up with an average of just barely over five unusual uses (Fitzsimons, Chartrand, & Fitzsimons, 2008). If a person's test score can be modified so dramatically by such a simple manipulation, it raises serious questions about the reliability of the test. After all, a creativity test is supposed to measure a stable personality trait.

The Apple logo experiment is only one of many studies that challenge the reliability of DT tests. A survey of several hundred experiments evaluating DT tests showed that a person's score could be raised or lowered by changing the amount of time he or she was given to take the test, or the verbal instructions given to him or her in advance (Barron & Harrington, 1981, pp. 442–443). For example, many studies show that you can make DT scores go up if you change the instructions and tell people to "be creative" in their responses (e.g., Owen & Baum, 1985). If you know that generating more ideas gives you a higher creativity score, when you're given a test you'll just write down different ideas as fast as you can think. This suggests that DT is a strategy that can be selectively applied, rather than an unchanging trait of a person.

Some studies of the TTCT have argued for its reliability (see Kaufman, Plucker, & Baer, 2008, pp. 29–30; Plucker & Makel, 2010, p. 54). But these studies generally don't change the instructions or the test environment. The jury is still out on whether DT tests satisfy the criterion of reliability—and whether DT is an unchanging personality trait, or is instead a cognitive strategy that's selectively applied depending on the situation.

Validity

The first group of children given the TTCT were 200 elementary-school students in 1958. Torrance later added more children to the study. He continued to follow them into adult life, with a major follow-up in 1980, when they were on average 27 years old (Cramond, 1993; Torrance, 1981). Plucker (1999) got in touch with 220 of these students and had them fill out questionnaires reporting their publicly recognized creative achievements. He then had experts rate the quality of their three most creative achievements. The childhood Verbal TTCT score predicted adult achievement, but the Figural TTCT score did not. A predictive model that included both IQ and DT scores predicted just under half the variance in creative achievement, but the contribution of DT scores to this model was three times that of IQ. These longitudinal data seem to show that DT tests have predictive validity.

Other studies also provide some evidence for the predictive validity of DT tests (Milgram & Hong, 1993; Torrance & Safter, 1989). For example, Harrington, Block, and Block (1983) found that the number of high-quality responses on the Instances and Uses DT tests at the age of 4 or 5 predicted the children's creativity 6 and 7 years later, as rated by their sixth-grade teachers (at $r = 0.45$); the DT tests added predictive power beyond that of the IQ score alone. Runco (1984) also demonstrated that DT scores correlate with teachers' judgments of student creativity. (But there is research suggesting that teachers' evaluations of creativity aren't very accurate; see Chapter 21, pp. 389–390.)

These findings must be interpreted with caution, because the evidence for predictive validity becomes more positive under certain conditions, such as sampling only high-IQ children (Kaufman, Plucker, & Baer, 2008, p. 42). This could account for Torrance's findings, because those students had higher-than-average intelligence (Plucker, 1999, p. 109). Because the range of IQ scores represented in the Torrance sample was limited to a higher range than the general population, we can't draw any firm conclusions about the predictive validity of DT tests in the general population. In other words, what this study shows is that if you take a group of intelligent, above-average children, then DT scores differentiate their adult performance better than the (subtle) differences in IQ.

In a meta-analysis of many previous studies, Kim (2008) found that DT tests predicted adult creative achievement slightly better than IQ: DT scores were correlated with adult achievement at 0.216, while IQ scores were correlated at 0.167. This overall finding masks some differences: IQ predicted creative quantity better than DT; DT predicted creative quality better than IQ. Musical creative achievements were better predicted by IQ; art, writing, science, and social skills were better predicted by DT tests. Leadership was predicted equally by both. These aren't very large effects: the percentage of the variance explained is the square of the correlation, so a correlation of 0.20 means that only 4% of the variance is explained (.20 times .20 equals .04, or 4%).

In sum, the evidence for predictive validity of DT tests is mixed (Kaufman, Plucker, & Baer, 2008; Plucker & Makel, 2010, pp. 54–55; Silvia et al., 2008b). In general, high scores on these tests don't correlate highly with real-life creative output, as Guilford himself noted long ago (1970, 1971; also see Baer, 1993, 1993–1994; Cattell, 1971; Gardner, 1988, 1993; Kogan &

Pankove, 1974; Wallach, 1971; Weisberg, 1993). And although there remain some dissenters, most psychologists now agree that DT tests don't predict creative ability (see Kaufman, Plucker, & Baer, 2008, pp. 39–42).

There's one final problem with DT test design: there's little evidence for the construct validity of the four proposed ability subscores. One factor analytic study didn't find support for the four abilities as distinct constructs; instead, there was evidence for only one factor (Heausler & Thompson, 1988). For example, the subscores of uniqueness and fluency are highly related; Silvia (2008a) found a correlation of 0.89; the Torrance Test norms (Torrance, 2008) found 0.88.

CONCLUSION: BE CAREFUL WHEN YOU USE DT TESTS

Most models of the creative process propose that creativity begins with a DT stage—when lots of possibilities are generated—followed by a more critical evaluation stage (see Chapters 5, 6, and 7). And historical studies of many important creations—from Samuel Morse's telegraph to Charles Darwin's theory of evolution by natural selection—reveal that in early stages, a wide range of possibilities are examined (Sawyer, 2007). But DT is only one of the abilities required for successful creativity. Barron and Harrington (1981) reviewed hundreds of studies; in some, DT was correlated with other measures of creative achievement, but in others it wasn't—thus failing to demonstrate convergent validity (pp. 447–448). Creative achievement requires a complex combination of DT, convergent thinking, critical evaluation, and other abilities, and creative people are good at switching back and forth at different points in the creative process (see Chapters 5, 6, and 7).

A small number of creativity researchers argue that DT isn't important at all to real-world creativity. Weisberg (2006) reviewed several historical examples of exceptional creations—from Picasso's painting *Guernica* to the Wright brothers' invention of the airplane—and found no evidence that the creative processes behind these works began with a DT phase (pp. 474–475). Instead, from the beginning, the creative process was focused; there wasn't an early stage in which ideas were randomly produced. Perkins (1981), in a study of poets using talk-aloud protocols, found that there was no relationship between how fluently poets wrote and how good they were. Instead, he found that good poets wrote less, because they were focused on writing higher-quality products (pp. 167–168). Silvia et al. (2008a) concluded that DT isn't relevant to expert performance and that DT tests are relevant only for novices and beginners—the sort of people who usually take DT tests (p. 113).

After over 50 years of DT test study, the consensus among creativity researchers is that they aren't valid measures of real-world creativity. In an influential review of the research, Barron and Harrington (1981) concluded that we have no solid research proving that DT tests "measure abilities actually involved in creative thinking" (p. 447). Even Michael Wallach (1971, 1986), developer of one of the most famous DT tests in the 1960s, changed his views about DT tests by 1971, arguing that they didn't predict real-world creativity and didn't have criterion validity. The legendary trait theorist R. B. Cattell (1971) was a persistent critic of creativity tests, concluding that the test "is only a projection of the test constructor's personal view about what creativity is . . . oddity or bizarreness of response . . . comes close to mistaking the shadow for the substance" (pp. 408–409). (Other critical reviews include Brown, 1989, and Nicholls, 1972.)

The following statements about DT tests are representative of my colleagues in the field of creativity research:

- "Although divergent thinking is often considered to contribute to creativity, the constructs are not synonymous, and theorists over the past 20 years have moved toward more inclusive models of creativity in which divergent thinking plays an important but small role" (Plucker, Beghetto, & Dow, 2004; p. 85).
- "Such tests capture, at best, only the most trivial aspects of creativity" (Sternberg, 1985b, p. 618).
- "DT test scores have often failed to correlate significantly positively with plausible indices of creative achievement and behavior" (Barron & Harrington, 1981, p. 448).

A few researchers believe that DT tests can be used, with caution, as one way of estimating a person's creative potential (Runco, 1991a). Barron and Harrington cautiously concluded that "some divergent thinking tests, administered under some conditions and scored by some sets of criteria, do measure abilities related to creative achievement and behavior in some domains' (1981, p. 447). They concluded that because the demands for DT vary from field to field, general DT tests wouldn't necessarily correlate with creative achievement in any particular field.

IS CREATIVITY DISTINCT FROM INTELLIGENCE?

When psychologists began to study creativity in the 1950s, there was one dominant way of measuring human potential: the *intelligence quotient*, or IQ. The first modern IQ test was designed by Alfred Binet and Theodore Simon in France (Binet & Simon, 1916), and then adapted by Louis Terman of Stanford University (Terman, 1916). This test has changed dramatically but is still called the Stanford-Binet test. Lewis Terman was particularly interested in whether his IQ test, when administered to schoolchildren, could predict exceptional creative performance in adult life. After World War I, Terman used his new IQ test to identify a group of extremely high-intelligence youths, all with IQs of at least 140, and he kept in touch with them for decades. The nickname "Terman's termites" is often used to refer to this research pool of high-IQ individuals, the 1,528 highest-scoring children attending California's high schools. Terman stayed in touch with them through the ensuing 35 years (Terman & Oden, 1947, 1959). He discovered that high-IQ children achieve at a higher level than non-gifted children; IQ does indeed predict a degree of achievement in adult life. But within this group, additional IQ didn't result in higher accomplishment (Matarazzo, 1972). And none of the termites achieved the eminence of an Einstein or a Picasso (although two of them became eminent Stanford University professors of psychology: Lee Cronbach and Robert Sears). In one of his last papers, Terman concluded that not more than one third of these subjects were noticeably creative (Rhodes, 1961, p. 307). More famous than any of the 1,528 termites was a scientist who was rejected from the group when tested by Terman: William Shockley, the inventor of the transistor and a Nobel prize winner.

There were some critics who argued that Terman's subjects were all from California, and were rather homogenous socioeconomically. So Rena Subotnik and her colleagues replicated Terman's study with people who had graduated from Hunter College Elementary School in New York City between 1948 and 1960, with a mean IQ of 159 (Subotnik, Karp, & Morgan, 1989;

Subotnik, Kassan, Summers, & Wasser, 1993). Using the same survey that Terman had used in his 1951/1955 study, Subotnik essentially reproduced all of Terman's findings; her children grew up to be "productive professionals with stable interpersonal relationships and good mental and physical health" (Subotnik & Arnold, 1994, p. 5). Like Terman, she found no creative rebels, but many of them were successful doctors, lawyers, and executives.

A series of studies have shown that among a population of gifted children, variations in IQ don't predict adult eminence or distinction. There seems to be a minimum threshold of IQ that's required for great success; the best estimate from the research is that an IQ of 120 is necessary for adult eminence, but beyond that level a higher IQ doesn't increase the likelihood of success (Barron & Harrington, 1981).

Researchers have shown that creative adult artists, scientists, and writers get pretty high scores on tests of general intelligence (Barron & Harrington, 1981, p. 445). Up to the beginning of World War II, most psychologists agreed with Terman that creativity was simply a byproduct of intelligence, and that IQ was an accurate measure of creative potential. And there was a large body of research showing that IQ predicted school grades, job performance ratings, and many other adult variables. For example, IQ predicts about 10% of the variance in job performance. Although that might sound like a small percentage, it's still the best predictor we have; no other psychometric test has ever been shown to predict more than 10%. Because that leaves 90% of the variance, no researchers today believe that IQ is the only predictor of success in life (Sternberg, Conway, Ketron, & Bernstein, 1981).

During World War II, many American psychologists were employed by the military and tasked with developing tests to identify which men would be best suited to which roles in the military. In Chapter 2, we learned that many of these psychologists worked for the Office of Special Services; they quickly realized that IQ wasn't a very good predictor of who would be a good resistance leader, or who would be an effective spy behind enemy lines. This wartime experience predisposed them to look for other predictors of real-world performance, and creativity was one of the most obvious places to look.

If creativity were going to be a distinct topic for psychologists to study, then psychologists had to provide evidence that creativity was something above and beyond IQ, and that creativity could add predictive power above and beyond the variance already predicted by IQ scores. In psychometric terms, they had to demonstrate *discriminant validity* by developing a reliable measure of creativity, and then showing that it wasn't the same thing as existing measures of intelligence. The history of the attempt to distinguish creativity and intelligence is largely associated with the first wave of creativity research, from the 1950s through the 1970s.

WHAT IS INTELLIGENCE, ANYWAY?

In the late 19th century and the early 20th century, when psychometric tests of human ability were first being developed, psychologists began to notice that people who did well on one test tended to do well on others. For example, scores on tests of verbal fluency are correlated with scores on tests of math skills, visualization, and memory. Also in the late 19th century, public schooling was expanding rapidly, and educators noticed that students who got good grades in one subject tended to get good grades in the others. In an attempt to integrate these observations, Spearman (1923) proposed that all tests were actually measuring two factors—a general ability that he called *g*, and a task-specific ability, *s*. In the decades since, Spearman's statistical technique of *factor analysis* has been refined, and this has made it possible to measure how much of the performance on any specific test is probably due to *g*, general cognitive ability. Factor analysis is a statistical technique that allows you to group together many different variable measures, and then to examine whether they're distinct (i.e., have substantial unique variance) or whether some of the variables covary. Those that covary, above a certain statistical threshold, are identified as manifestations of a single underlying *factor*. Virtually all intelligence researchers today agree that cognitive ability is hierarchical, with the general factor *g* at the top of the hierarchy; below it are broad abilities like fluid thinking or working memory; and at the bottom are very specific, narrow abilities that are relevant to particular task domains (Carroll, 1993; A. S. Kaufman, 2009).

A complicating factor in the creativity–intelligence debate is that intelligence tests have changed substantially since the 1960s, when most of the initial studies were done that compared creativity and intelligence (see A. S. Kaufman, 2009, for a history). In the 1960s, most IQ tests weren't based in psychological research and theory, and weren't designed to measure *g* and the research-based ability factors, whereas today they all are (A. S. Kaufman, 2009). Even theory-based tests have changed in recent decades, because no single test can accurately measure *g*; every known test has components of both general and specific abilities. So the challenge is to bring together a wide range of specific tests and use all of those scores, combined with statistical techniques, to measure *g*. Since the 1960s, the focus has shifted from a small number of part scores, to a focus on as many as ten factors of intelligence, for example in the fifth edition of the Stanford-Binet (Roid, 2003), the Kaufman Assessment Battery for Children-Second Edition (KABC-II; Kaufman & Kaufman, 2004), and the Woodcock-Johnson-Third Edition (WJ-III; Woodcock, McGrew, & Mather, 2001). The ten-factor theory is known as the Cattell-Horn-Carroll (CHC) theory because it combines the Cattell-Horn theory of fluid and crystallized intelligence (Horn & Cattell, 1966; Horn & Noll, 1997) with Carroll's Three-Stratum Theory (1993; see McGrew, 2005, 2009, for an overview). Nearly all IQ tests today are based on CHC theory (Flanagan, Ortiz, & Alfonso, 2007, p. 18; A. S. Kaufman, 2009).

CHC includes ten factors of intelligence, each of which is in turn composed of two or more narrow abilities:

1. *Gf* (fluid intelligence; the ability to apply a variety of mental operations to solve novel problems, ones that don't benefit from past learning or experience)
2. *Gq* (quantitative knowledge)
3. *Gc* (crystallized intelligence; the breadth and depth of a person's accumulated knowledge of a culture and the ability to use that knowledge to solve problems)
4. *Grw* (reading and writing)
5. *Gsm* (short-term memory)
6. *Gv* (visual processing)
7. *Ga* (auditory processing)
8. *Glr* (long-term storage and retrieval)
9. *Gs* (processing speed)
10. *Gt* (decision speed/reaction time)

Today's intelligence tests measure no more than seven of these; *Gq* and *Grw* are domains of academic achievement, and *Gt* isn't measured by any major standardized test (Kaufman & Kaufman, unpublished). Today's various IQ tests generally measure between four and seven;

the popular Wechsler scales (WISC-IV and WAIS-IV) measure four abilities: verbal comprehension, perceptual reasoning, working memory, and processing speed (A. S. Kaufman, 2009).

In the earlier stages of the Cattell-Horn theory, fluid intelligence was hypothesized to be linked to creativity; *Gf* is related to coping with novel problems (Kaufman & Kaufman, unpublished). A recent study (Sligh, Connors, & Roskos-Ewoldson, 2005) found partial support for this link: they found a positive relationship between creativity and crystallized intelligence (*Gc*) for people with IQ below 120, and a positive relationship between creativity and fluid intelligence (*Gf*), among people with IQ above 120.

But most factor analytic studies suggest that creativity loads on the factor *Glr*, long-term storage and retrieval (see McGrew, 2009, p. 6). *Glr* subsumes the following narrow abilities (from Kaufman & Kaufman, unpublished, Table 1):

- Ideational fluency: Ability to rapidly produce a series of ideas, words, or phrases related to a specific condition or object. Quantity is emphasized instead of quality or originality.
- Associational fluency: Ability to produce a series of words or phrases associated in meaning to a word or concept with a limited range of meaning. Quality is emphasized instead of sheer quantity.
- Expressional fluency: Ability to rephrase an idea without losing its original meaning. Rephrasing is emphasized here instead of idea generation.
- Word fluency: Ability to produce words that have given characteristics.
- Figural fluency: Ability to draw as many things as possible when presented with a set of visual stimulus. Quantity is emphasized here instead of quality of originality. This is the nonverbal counterpart to ideational fluency.
- Sensitivity to problems: Ability to think of a number of different solutions to problems that are practical in nature, such as naming all the uses of a particular tool.
- Originality/creativity: Ability to produce original and unique responses to a given problem and to develop innovative methods for situations where there is no standard convergent way to solve a problem.

Most current IQ tests don't specifically measure *Glr* at all (including the Wechsler Intelligence Scale for Children IV and the Stanford Binet V), and those that do focus on other narrow ability components as well as ideational fluency and figural fluency (Kaufman & Kaufman, unpublished).

INTELLIGENCE AND CREATIVITY: DISCRIMINANT VALIDITY

Many people assume that creativity is distinct from intelligence, but the evidence for this is far from convincing. In the past 60 years, creativity researchers have repeatedly reported evidence that creativity is distinct from intelligence, only to have their evidence challenged by later studies. As early as 1962, Taylor (1962) reported that the psychologists assembled at the first three Utah Conferences on creativity all agreed that creativity scores and IQ scores measured distinct traits. Over 40 years later, Runco (2004) reported that "the separation [between creativity and intelligence] seems to have been widely accepted . . . the distinctiveness of creativity is rarely questioned" (p. 679).

But in the same year as Taylor's 1962 claim, the first book analyzing intelligence and creativity was published by Jacob Getzels and Philip Jackson (1962) at the University of Chicago. And they did *not* find clear evidence that creativity was distinct from intelligence. They used measures of both intelligence and of creativity, and they found that over a large number of students, on average the intelligence score and the creativity score were fairly similar. Different creativity tests correlated just as highly with intelligence as they did with each other. Getzels and Jackson (1962) didn't provide the correlation between combined creativity and intelligence scores; McNemar (1964) estimated this would have been at least 0.40. One year after the Getzels and Jackson book, Frank Barron's 1963 book *Creativity and Psychological Health* summarized the many IPAR studies, and reported that the correlation between creativity and intelligence was about 0.40. These studies showed that the creativity tests in use at the time didn't have discriminant validity or convergent validity.

In 1965, Wallach and Kogan published the results of another major study of schoolchildren, and these results were widely reported in the media: they found that a student's creativity score could *not* be predicted from his or her achievement score. They administered five measures of creativity and ten measures of achievement (however, these tests didn't measure g or IQ but rather school achievement: Cronbach, 1968). The creativity tests correlated with each other $r = 0.41$, the achievement tests correlated with each other $r = 0.51$, but the creativity and achievement tests didn't correlate ($r = 0.09$, not significant). This study seemed to demonstrate discriminant validity for the creativity tests.

Why did they get such big differences from the Getzels and Jackson (1962) study? According to Wallach and Kogan (1965), it was a result of how the tests were administered.[1] Getzels and Jackson (1962) gave the students paper-and-pencil tests for both creativity and intelligence, and in a similar classroom environment. Wallach and Kogan (1965) administered their creativity test in a very different way: they told the students it was a "game" rather than a "test," and they told the students to have fun. So it could be that the Getzels and Jackson study simply showed that children who do well on tests always do well on tests, whether it's an intelligence test or a creativity test (Runco, 2007).

Although the Wallach and Kogan study is still cited today as evidence that creativity and intelligence are distinct, the study had several methodological problems, and later analyses of the same data challenged their conclusion. Only three years later, the legendary psychologist Lee Cronbach (who had been one of Terman's termites) reanalyzed the Wallach and Kogan data and argued that their claims were not supported, due to various methodological errors (Cronbach, 1968). Silvia (2008a) reanalyzed the Wallach and Kogan (1965) data using latent variable analysis, a statistical technique that hadn't been invented in the 1960s. He found that latent originality and fluency variables correlated with intelligence at about $r = 0.20$, which is quite a bit higher than was reported back in 1965.

Wallach and Wing (1969; also see Wallach, 1971) found that creativity tests in combination with IQ tests, when given to college students, provided some additional predictive value of extracurricular activities and accomplishments than IQ tests alone. But the methodology they used made firm conclusions difficult. For example, the relation held only for accomplishments in art, writing, science, and leadership, but not in dramatics, music, or social service. Kogan and

---

1. Wallach later rejected this explanation (Wallach, 1971).

Pankove (1974) replicated the study to better tease out the different effects of creativity and intelligence tests, and found that creativity scores in fifth and tenth grade had no predictive relation with extracurricular activities or accomplishments assessed at graduation, whereas the fifth-grade IQ test was a powerful predictor. And when they examined the relation between creativity and each specific field, they didn't find any relation of creativity scores in fifth grade and nonacademic attainment in the seven fields surveyed—but they did find strong relations with IQ tests.

A review of all past studies by Batey and Furnham (2006) showed correlations between intelligence and DT tests to be between 0.20 and 0.40, which is a moderate to large effect; effects larger than 0.3 are in the top third of all effects published in psychology (Hemphill, 2003). Other recent studies have found similar correlations. Cho et al. (2010) found significant correlations between g (using WAIS) and TTCT Figural ($r = 0.32$) and TTCT Verbal ($r = 0.31$), and Kim (2005) conducted a meta-analysis of all previous studies that examined the relation between IQ and creativity test scores and found an average correlation of about 0.20.

These many decades of research show that creativity and intelligence are related. These studies are confirmed by biographical data on exceptional creators; all of the evidence suggests that the famous creators that we remember from history had intelligences far above average. However, intelligence predicts substantially less than half the variance in creativity measures, providing partial evidence for the discriminant validity of creativity tests.

Both creativity tests and intelligence tests have their uses. When is it most appropriate to use an intelligence test or a creativity test? Creativity tests are often useful:

- When traditional IQ tests don't measure all of a person's potential
- When there's a risk of stereotype threat in response to traditional tests
- When the subject has a learning disability that could affect scores on a traditional test
- When you need to assess creative abilities or potential in a specific area (writing, music, art)
- When you have a competition and you need to judge the winners, and you want creativity to be one of the criteria (such as with science fair projects)
- You're selecting students for a gifted and talented program

But the above research doesn't show that we can dispense with intelligence tests; in fact, it suggests just the opposite: creativity tests shouldn't be used alone, they should be used in combination with traditional intelligence tests. We'll return to this topic in Chapter 21 on education.

THRESHOLD THEORY

The *threshold theory* refers to the claim that IQ and creativity (as measured by DT tests) are correlated up to an IQ of 120, but above that, there's no relationship. The threshold theory was first suggested by Getzels and Jackson (1962) and later elaborated by Fuchs-Beauchamp, Karnes, and Johnson (1993). It fits a common-sense observation that creativity requires some minimal level of intelligence that's above average, but that once you have that level of intelligence, additional intelligence doesn't give you any additional increase in creative ability. Some scholars have even suggested that exceedingly high intelligence might interfere with creativity (Simonton, 1994; Sternberg, 1996).

But the majority of the evidence doesn't support the threshold theory (Runco & Albert, 1986; Sligh, Connors, & Roskos-Ewoldsen, 2005; Wakefield, 1991). Preckel, Holling, and Weise (2006) found relations between fluid intelligence and divergent thinking at all levels of intelligence. For various ranges of IQ, Kim (2005) combined 21 studies and found the following correlations between intelligence and divergent thinking: under 100, 0.260; 100 to 120, 0.140; 120 to 135, 0.259; above 135, –0.215. The differences between these ranges weren't statistically significant.

And even among those studies that claim to support the threshold theory, there's a methodological flaw: among the group with IQ over 120, the variance is smaller by definition—because the range of scores is smaller—making it statistically more difficult to find a significant correlation.

IS CREATIVITY DOMAIN-GENERAL OR DOMAIN-SPECIFIC?

The holy grail of creativity assessment research is a personality test to measure general creativity ability. A person's creativity score should tell us his or her creative potential in any field of endeavor, just like an IQ score isn't limited to physics, math, or literature. The first part of this chapter has revealed that efforts to develop such a test haven't been very successful.

But perhaps these efforts are misdirected; after all, creative people aren't creative in a general, universal way; they're creative in a specific sphere of activity, a particular domain (Csikszentmihalyi, 1988b; Feldman, 1974, 1980; John-Steiner, 1985). We don't expect a creative scientist to also be a gifted painter. A creative violinist may not be a creative conductor, and a creative conductor may not be very good at composing new works. There's substantial evidence that large portions of creative ability are *domain-specific* (Hirschfeld & Gelman, 1994; Kaufman & Baer, 2005). There may be some bit of real-world creativity that could be predicted by a hypothesized construct of general creativity, but that bit is much smaller than the domain-specific component. And that's probably the reason why creativity tests haven't been overwhelmingly successful: if there's no such thing as a domain-general creative ability, then no general creativity test could ever be successful (Baer, 1993–1994).

What's a domain? In Classic Greece, the domains roughly corresponded to the nine Muses of Greek mythology:

- Calliope: epic poetry
- Euterpe: lyric poetry/music
- Erato: love poetry
- Polymnia: sacred poetry
- Clio: history
- Melpomene: tragedy
- Thalia: comedy/pastoral poetry
- Terpsichore: choral song/dance
- Urania: astronomy/astrology

The most straightforward way to define a "domain" is to think of it as a recognized sphere of human accomplishment, such as ballet dancing, research in particle physics, political leadership, or business management. The different academic disciplines are each distinct domains—literature, music, psychology, biology. Psychologists tend to define a domain a bit more technically, in terms of the mental activities that underlie expertise in the domain. Here are four influential definitions:

- "A set of symbolic rules and procedures" (Csikszentmihalyi, 1996, p. 27)
- "A body of knowledge that identifies and interprets a class of phenomena assumed to share certain properties and to be of a distinct and general type" (Hirschfeld & Gelman, 1994, p. 21)
- "A given set of principles, the rules of their application, and the entities to which they apply" (Gelman & Brenneman, 1994, p. 371)
- "The set of representations sustaining a specific area of knowledge: language, number, physics, and so forth" (Karmiloff-Smith, 1992, p. 6)

What's shared by these definitions is the idea that a domain involves an internal, symbolic language; representations; and operations on those representations. The domain of music involves notes, melodies, harmonies, rhythms, and the like; the domain of physics involves formulas, empirically observed constants like the speed of light, and theories that have been supported by experimental evidence. Domains also involve a set of everyday practices; musicians know how to rehearse together, how to work with a conductor, and how to interpret a score; physicists know how to design an experiment, how to interpret results, and how to write an article for a scientific journal.

Most studies find that there are between three and seven distinct domains of human potential:

- Gardner (1983) proposed seven domains: spatial, linguistic, logical-mathematical, kinesthetic, musical, interpersonal, and intrapersonal. (Gardner [1999] added an eighth domain, naturalistic.)
- Holland (1997) proposed a model of vocational interests that contained six: realistic, investigative, artistic, social, enterprising, and conventional.
- Carson et al. (2005), using the CAQ, started with ten domains and through a factor analysis found they grouped into three factors: expressive creativity (visual arts, writing, humor); performance creativity (dance, drama, music); and scientific creativity (invention, science, culinary) (with architecture not related to any of these three).
- Kaufman and Baer (2004), in a study of 241 college students, found that nine rated areas of creativity actually grouped into three factors: empathy/communication (interpersonal relationships, communication, solving personal problems, writing); hands-on creativity (arts, crafts, bodily/physical); and math/science creativity (math, science).

Although these domains are quite broad, there's some evidence that expertise clusters into areas that are much more narrow and specialized than this. After all, being a concert pianist is a very different form of creativity than being a composer, a music theorist, a music teacher, or a conductor. Karmiloff-Smith (1992) called these *microdomains*, and suggested that they're found in school subjects as well: gravity within the domain of physics, pronoun acquisition within the domain of language, counting within the domain of math (p. 6). These more specific "microdomains" probably don't represent innate predispositions of a person; rather, they're likely to emerge after years of practice, education, and training.

A wide range of studies has shown that much of creative ability is domain-specific. Baer (1998) examined the creativity of products generated in four different domains—poems, short stories, collages, and math puzzles—by people of ordinary ability and no training. If the creativity of these products was due to a person's general creative ability, then the creativity of products in two different domains should correlate pretty highly. Instead, Baer found no correlations between creativity in the four domains. Conti, Coon, and Amabile (1996) analyzed 13 different cross-domain creativity correlations, and none of them were significant—on average, they predicted only 1% of the variance in each other. Runco (1989) found very small correlations (all under 0.20) between creativity on different kinds of artwork (crayon drawing of a limerick; collage of a dragon, cut out of paper with glitter and crayon details; a large picture decorated with crayons and colored pens and pencils), and he concluded that "visual creativity" is not a single domain, and that "composite scores should probably not be used as estimates of the creativity of children" (p. 187).

Sternberg (1999b, p. 304; Lubart & Sternberg, 1995; Sternberg & Lubart, 1991, 1995, 1996) found that divergent thinking was domain-specific; when he gave students DT tests in four areas—writing (write a short story with the title "The Octopus's Sneakers"), art (create a composition with the title "The Beginning of Time"), advertising (produce an advertisement for a new brand of doorknob), and science (how we might detect aliens among us who are trying to escape detection)—their scores of creative quality were correlated at about 0.4. These correlations indicate that there's a domain-general component of divergent thinking (also see Chen et al., 2006), but that most of the variance isn't due to domain-general abilities.

A HIERARCHICAL VIEW

The debate between domain-general creativity and domain-specific creativity has been active in recent creativity research (Kaufman & Baer, 2005; *Creative Research Journal* special issue, 1998, Volume 11, Issue 2). The consensus view in the field today is that creative performance depends on a domain-general component—which we might think of as general creative abilities and strategies—and a domain-specific component—expertise and knowledge in a specific domain (Amabile, 1983; Kaufman & Baer, 2005). And if this is true, then the ideal creativity assessment should be hierarchical—measuring both domain-general and domain-specific components. This would be analogous to contemporary intelligence tests, which also posit that human ability is hierarchically structured (see pp. 54–55).

Kaufman, Cole, and Baer (2009) asked several thousand subjects about 56 potential domains of creativity. Using factor analysis they found an overarching general factor and seven domain-specific factors: artistic-verbal, artistic-visual, entrepreneur, interpersonal, math/science, performance, and problem solving. The overarching general factor of creativity correlated quite highly with some domain scores: the highest was a 0.75 correlation with performance, and the lowest was a 0.05 correlation with math/science. This study showed that domain-general creativity may be more relevant to some domains than others.

SUMMARY

If one turns to the literature of creativity research and asks the simple questions: What is being measured? What is creativity? One soon realizes that the entire research enterprise moves on very thin ice.

—Mihaly Csikszentmihalyi, 1994, p. 143

Donald Treffinger (1986) called the early hopes placed in first-wave creativity research *the creativity quotient fallacy*: the belief that researchers would develop an equivalent to the IQ test for creative potential, one that could be just as easily administered and scored using a pencil-and-paper test booklet. Creativity researchers would be the first people to agree that school districts and state-mandated gifted education programs should evaluate creative potential so that they don't admit students based solely on IQ. But DT is only one component of creative potential, and other measures of creativity have their own problems. Different tests, each designed to measure creativity, often aren't correlated with one another, thus failing to demonstrate convergent validity (e.g., Alter, 1984; Baer, 1993). Another problem is that even though some of these tests correlate with creative achievement, the tests might in fact correlate with *all* achievement. Rather than measuring creativity, they might instead be measuring success and social achievement more generally—and IQ tests probably do a better job of that.

By the mid-1980s, many psychologists had given up on trying to measure creativity with a personality test (Cooper, 1991; Eysenck, 1990; Feist & Runco, 1993; Feldhusen & Goh, 1995; Nicholls, 1972; Rosner & Abt, 1974; Wakefield, 1991). Part of it was due to the perceived failings of previous efforts; but much of the turn away from assessment was due to a general shift in psychology away from the study of individual differences and toward the cognitive mechanisms that we all share. The research effort hasn't been abandoned entirely; many psychologists continue to work to develop better assessments. In recent years, schools have increasingly shifted toward outcome-based assessment as a way of evaluating the effectiveness of instruction. Advocates of creativity in schools need to have some way to demonstrate that one method of instruction is more effective at fostering creativity than another, and only an assessment that meets the psychometric standards of reliability and validity can do that (see Chapter 21 on education). This area warrants further research.

KEY CONCEPTS

- Test validity: construct validity, face validity, convergent validity, discriminant validity, criterion validity, concurrent validity, predictive validity
- Test reliability
- Consensual Assessment Technique (CAT)
- Remote Associates Test (RAT)
- Divergent thinking and its four components: fluency, flexibility, originality, and elaboration
- Unusual Uses test of divergent thinking

- Consequences test of divergent thinking
- Torrance Tests of Creative Thinking (TTCT)
- The threshold theory
- Domain-general and domain-specific creativity

THOUGHT EXPERIMENTS

- Think of the various creative products that you evaluate—by selecting them for purchase or consumption. How do you decide which music to buy, or which movies to see? On what criteria do you judge them? How did you develop those criteria?
- Do you know someone who is creative, but who isn't very smart? And vice versa, do you know someone who is extremely smart, but not at all creative?
- Think of a domain in which you've demonstrated some creative ability. Do you think that your creativity is specific to this one domain, or are you creative in general, and you've chosen this domain as your way to express that general creativity?

Answers to RATs: ICE, BOAT, FIRE, DAY, BLOOD

SUGGESTED READINGS

Brown, R. T. (1989). Creativity: What are we to measure? In J. A. Glover, R. R. Ronning, & C. R. Reynolds (Eds.), *Handbook of creativity* (pp. 3–32). New York: Plenum Press.

Kaufman, A. S. (2009). *IQ testing 101*. New York: Springer.

Kaufman, J. C., & Baer, J. (Eds.). (2005). *Creativity across domains: Faces of the muse*. Mahwah, NJ: Lawrence Erlbaum Associates.

Kaufman, J. C., & Kaufman, S. B. (unpublished). *Using intelligent testing to find creativity: Searching for divergent production in IQ tests with the cross battery approach.*

Kaufman, J. C., Plucker, J. A., & Baer, J. (2008). *Essentials of creativity assessment*. New York: Wiley.

Plucker, J. A. (1999). Is the proof in the pudding? Reanalyses of Torrance's (1958 to present) longitudinal studies data. *Creativity Research Journal, 12,* 103–114.

CHAPTER 4

THE CREATIVE PERSONALITY

I n 1949, at the University of California, Berkeley, Donald MacKinnon founded the Institute for Personality Assessment and Research (IPAR), with the goal of further developing and applying the various personality and ability tests that had been initially developed during World War II for the military. IPAR was founded with funding from the Rockefeller Foundation, and also received funding from the Carnegie Corporation (MacKinnon, 1978, pp. xi–xvii) and the Ford Foundation (Barron, 1968, p. 8). These are three of the most prestigious and competitive private foundations in the United States; their support of IPAR is evidence that its activities were considered nationally and culturally important.

Influenced by Guilford's 1950 APA lecture, one of IPAR's main goals was to scientifically determine the traits of the creative personality. Researchers at IPAR studied successful architects, inventors, engineers, writers, and mathematicians. At that time, creativity was often associated with being rebellious and unconventional (Griffin & McDermott, 1998; Sulloway, 1996), but from the beginning, the IPAR team was skeptical about the unproven stereotypes of the creative individual: "a genius with an I.Q. far above average; an eccentric not only in thinking but in appearance, dress, and behavior; a Bohemian, an egghead, a longhair . . . a true neurotic, withdrawn from society, inept in his relations with others" (MacKinnon, 1962/1978, p. 178). This was part of the cultural model of creativity in 1950s America.

There are two principal ways to study personality:

- One is to study personality *traits*—the smallest units of individual variation that are consistent, reliable, and valid. This was the approach taken at IPAR. In Chapter 3, we focused on various traits associated with creativity, such as divergent thinking (DT). This chapter reviews trait research at IPAR and beyond.
- The second way is to study *types*—to identify a finite set of personality types that can be used to categorize individuals. Personality type theories were not widely used by psychologists until the 1970s, after the heyday of IPAR. The best known of these is the *Myers-Briggs Type Indicator* (MBTI; Kiersey & Bates, 1978), but the one with the most research support is the *five-factor model* (Costa & McCrae, 1992). This chapter reviews a range of research that examines creativity and personality type.

Measures of ability (like IQ) and measures of personality have traditionally been viewed as separate domains, in part because measures of personality traits show very low correlations with IQ tests (Eysenck & Eysenck, 1975). Creativity resides in a middle ground between ability and personality; it's highly correlated with intelligence (see Chapter 3), and yet it's also associated with various personality traits.

This chapter begins with a review of the research on creativity and personality traits, and then reviews research on creativity and personality types. Then, I review the research on developmental changes in creativity, both in childhood and adulthood. Finally, I conclude by examining two opposed threads of research: one studying the link between creativity and mental illness, and the other studying the link between creativity and psychological health (Beliefs 9 and 10 of the Western cultural model).

CREATIVITY AND PERSONALITY TRAITS

IPAR developed a new method of personality assessment—much more expensive and labor-intensive than anything I described in Chapter 3. They began by asking experts to suggest names of particularly creative people in their field. These peer-nominated creators were then invited to travel to Berkeley, and live in a former fraternity house for a weekend with the researchers. The creators and researchers cooked and ate together, participated in informal discussions on selected topics like "great men of the twentieth century" and "planning the city of the future," and even shared midnight snacks in the kitchen. During the day, the visiting creators submitted to a battery of tests. This intensive method of evaluation was derived from a procedure that was first used during World War II by MacKinnon and others at the Office of Strategic Services (Barron, 1968, pp. 11–19). The Berkeley researchers found that their highly creative subjects had the following traits (MacKinnon, 1978):

- Above-average intelligence. Different professions scored differently on different submeasures of intelligence: writers scored highly on verbal intelligence, whereas architects scored highly on spatial intelligence.
- Discernment, observance, and alertness. They can quickly scan ideas and select those that are relevant to solving their problem; they have a wide range of information at their command.
- Openness to experience
- Balanced personalities. For example, creative men gave more expression to the feminine side of their nature than less-creative men: creative men scored relatively high on femininity, even though they didn't appear effeminate and they seemed not to be homosexual. (see Norlander, Erixon, & Archer, 2000)
- A relative absence of repression and suppression mechanisms that control impulse and imagery
- Pleasant and materially comfortable childhoods, although they recalled their childhoods as not having been particularly happy. MacKinnon called this the theme of remembered unhappiness (1978, p. 182). MacKinnon hypothesized that their home life was no different from anyone else's, but that the difference was in their perceptions and memories—they were more likely to remember unpleasant experiences because of their reduced repression.
- A preference for complexity. They enjoy discovering unifying principles that can bring order to complex, unfinished phenomena.

During the 1970s and 1980s, a wide range of other studies identified additional traits of creative people (Barron & Harrington, 1981; Feist, 1998; Tardif & Sternberg, 1988):

- Articulacy (verbal fluency)
- Metaphorical thinking
- Flexible decision making
- The ability to internally visualize problems
- Independence
- Tolerance of ambiguity
- Broad interests
- Attraction to complexity
- Willingness to surmount obstacles and persevere
- Willingness to take risks
- The courage of one's convictions
- High energy
- Independence of judgment
- Autonomy
- Self-control—a focus on a vision, and the ability to hold to routines and schedules (Dacey & Lennon, 1998, pp. 116, 120–121)
- Self-confidence, assertiveness, and belief in oneself as being "creative"
- Ability to resolve and accommodate apparently opposite or conflicting traits within oneself

Many of these studies found that the most important characteristic of creative people is an almost aesthetic ability to recognize a good problem in their domain; they know how to ask the right questions (see Chapter 5, pp. 90–93.) That's why highly creative people tend to be creative in one specific domain: it takes a lot of experience, knowledge, and training to be able to identify good problems. This aligns with research on domain specificity (Chapter 3, pp. 58–60), and research on how creative people master a domain (Chapter 5, pp. 93–95).

After two decades of research, MacKinnon and his team found that the "egghead . . . longhair . . . withdrawn" cultural model of the 1950s was almost completely false. The traits above are all habits of highly effective people, not of dysfunctional schizophrenics or alcoholics. Creative people are happy and successful and have well-balanced personalities.

Funding for IPAR efforts largely ended by the early 1970s, but by that time creativity research had spread to other universities, and studies of the creativity personality continued.

CREATIVITY AND PERSONALITY TYPES

During the 1970s, a debate raged between two prominent personality theorists, each proposing a different theory of personality traits and types. Hans Eysenck promoted his three-factor model of personality, measured with the Eysenck Personality Questionnaire (EPQ; Eysenck & Eysenck, 1975), with the three factors of Neuroticism, Extraversion, and Psychoticism (NEP). Raymond Cattell identified 16 personality factors (with 8 second-order factors), measured with the Sixteen Personality Factor Questionnaire (16PF; Cattell, Eber, & Tatsuoka, 1970). By the 1980s, a range of factor-analytic studies (see Chapter 3, pp. 54–55) convinced most personality researchers that neither of these models had it exactly right. Repeated statistical analyses revealed that there were five factor clusters—and that all of the other personality traits "loaded onto" one of these five factors. Factor analyses didn't support Cattell's 16 factors or Eysenck's NEP model. Also, there's not much factor-analytic support for the four/eight-factor Jungian model underlying the MBTI, and very few personality researchers use it, in spite of its popularity. Today, the five-factor model is the most widely used personality trait measure (Furnham, 2008). It's sometimes called the OCEAN model, for the acronym of the five factors:

- Openness to experience
- Conscientiousness
- Extraversion
- Agreeableness
- Neuroticism

These five factors have emerged in studies in a broad range of cultures around the world (McCrae & Costa, 1997). The most widely used test of the big five is discussed in Costa and McCrae (1992). Of the five, Openness to experience is most closely associated with creativity (Carson, Peterson, & Higgins, 2005; King, Walker, & Broyles, 1996; McCrae, 1987; Silvia et al., 2008b). Openness to Experience includes openness to fantasy (a good imagination); aesthetics (being artistic); feelings (experiencing and valuing feelings); actions (trying new things and having many interests); ideas (being curious and smart, and welcoming challenges); and values (unconventional and liberal).

Effect sizes vary depending on the creativity test used; in the studies I just cited, Openness predicts from 10% of the variance in creativity score (Furnham et al., 2009) to nearly 50% (Silvia et al., 2009), with most studies finding correlation coefficients in the range of 0.30. For example, McCrae (1987) examined the relations between six DT tests, Gough's CPS (see p. 44), and multiple measures of the five factors. Openness to Experience, measured as six facets (fantasy, aesthetics, feelings, actions, ideas, and values) was correlated with five of the six DT measures, and none of the other four factors was (the five rs ranged from 0.25 to 0.39). All six facets were correlated with these five measures. CPS scores were the most strongly related to Openness, although there was some evidence of a relation with Extraversion and Conscientiousness, and a negative relation with Neuroticism. Silvia et al. (2009) also found some evidence for a relation between Conscientiousness and creativity.

Although measures of creativity correlate with Openness to Experience, creativity isn't just the same thing as Openness; it seems to have some discriminant validity as a distinct construct. King et al. (1996) examined 75 college students, asking them to list their creative accomplishments in the past 2 years, as well as giving them the TTCT Verbal test and a five-factor model assessment. Controlling for SAT scores, the TTCT Verbal test was positively related to Openness to Experience and to Extraversion; creative accomplishments were negatively correlated with Agreeableness and positively correlated with Openness to Experience. The partial correlation of Openness and creative accomplishments, controlling for TTCT Verbal, was 0.38; the partial correlation of TTCT Verbal and accomplishments, controlling for Openness, was 0.25. These findings show that although creativity and Openness overlap, each explains some variance in creative accomplishments, independent of the other.

Using eight scales to measure the eight variables of the MBTI, Furnham et al. (2009) found that scores on the Consequences DT test were mildly correlated with Extraversion (rather than Intraversion), Intuition (rather than Sensing), and Perceiving (rather than Judging). The effect sizes were small; a regression equation with these effects accounted for a total of only 5% of the variance in the Consequences score.

These findings are all based on an assumption that creativity is a domain-general trait. But it's likely that the creative personality would vary across creative domains: an extravert would be less likely to choose a more solitary creative domain like writing poetry, whereas an introvert would be less likely to choose to become an actor or a politician.

KIRTON ADAPTIVE INVENTORY

Several researchers have adopted Kirton's measure of creative style, the *Kirton Adaptive Inventory* (KAI; Kirton, 1976). Kirton proposed that people fall into two creative styles, *innovator* and *adaptor*, and he proposed that creative style was distinct from the measured level of creativity—that both innovators and adaptors would get high and low creativity scores, in equal proportions, but that they would use different cognitive styles to do so. Innovators focus on doing things differently, and adaptors focus on doing things better. Scores on the KAI are normally distributed; a high score was called an "innovator" style and a low score was called an "adaptor" style. Kirton (1978) found no correlation between his three scales and DT tests, and argued that the KAI represented a personality type measure distinct from creativity.

There's some debate about whether the KAI actually measures distinct personality styles, or whether it's just another measure of a person's creative potential. Isaksen and Puccio (1988) found that TTCT correlates with KAI total score (0.23 fluency, 0.23 flexibility, 0.19 originality), suggesting that innovators are more creative than adaptors.

GENDER

There's no evidence of gender differences in creativity as measured using creativity tests. Kogan (1974) reviewed several 1960s-era studies of DT, ideational fluency, etc., and found no gender differences. Baer and Kaufman (2008) conducted a meta-analysis of the research, and likewise found no gender differences; they included studies in the United States, China, India, and Hong Kong. Earlier in this chapter, I cited the IPAR finding that the most highly creative individuals combine personality traits associated with both genders to a greater degree than others of their same gender. When firstborn children have an opposite-sex sibling, they score higher on creativity tests (Baer et al., 2005); being raised with a sibling of the opposite sex is associated with psychological androgyny, which is associated with greater creativity. The effects are increased as the number of opposite-sex siblings increases.

However, the differences in observed real-world creativity between men and women throughout history are significant (Simonton, 1994). These are certainly due to environmental and interactional factors, and require an explanation at the sociocultural rather than the individual level (Helson, 1990; Piirto, 1991; Simonton, 1994).

THE CREATIVE LIFE SPAN

Developmental psychologists have studied how creativity develops and evolves over the life span of the creative individual, looking at the influence of birth order, family, and community.

BIRTH ORDER

Are you more likely to be creative if you are firstborn, or later-born? Are only children more likely to be creative? Francis Galton, the founder of psychometrics, was perhaps the first to observe that firstborn and only sons were overrepresented in science (Galton, 1874, 1869/1962), and Havelock Ellis (1904) found the same pattern in other domains (see also Goertzel, Goertzel, & Goertzel, 1978; Torrance, 1962). Firstborns were overrepresented in Terman's group of gifted children (1925). In Roe's (1952a, 1952b) classic study, 39 of the 64 distinguished scientists were firstborn (15 of them were only children) and 13 were second-born, with only 12 remaining. Of the 25 who were not firstborn, 5 were the oldest male child, and 2 had an older sibling who died young. Firstborns typically represent more than half of the active scientists in any given discipline and have higher citation rates than later-borns. Csikszentmihalyi (1965) also found that the most original artists were more likely to be firstborns (p. 87); Feldman (1986) found that childhood prodigies were more likely to be firstborns.

But the birth order effect is controversial (see Schooler, 1972). Sulloway (1996) argued that firstborns are less likely to be innovative revolutionary scientists, because firstborns identify more with their parents and with authority, and are more invested in the status quo. There's some evidence that whereas firstborns are more likely to become famous scientific creators, later-borns are more likely to become artistic creators (Clark & Rice, 1982). Simonton (1994, 1999a) likewise argued that creative geniuses were generally not firstborns; he thought that firstborns and only children tend to make good leaders in times of crisis, but that middle-borns are better leaders in safe, peaceful times, because they are better listeners and compromisers.

What about family size? Are only children more creative, or are children from larger families more creative? Runco and Bahleda (1987) found higher DT in families with large numbers of children. In a recent study (Baer et al., 2005), firstborns with large numbers of siblings were more creative when those siblings were of a similar age. If you're the firstborn and your siblings are much younger, you're more likely to take on an adult-like role with them, and less likely to engage in peer pretend play with them—and it's the peer play that contributes to enhanced creativity (see pp. 71–73 below). They didn't find significant direct effects, but found evidence for the interaction effect with family size: firstborns with larger sibling groups are more creative when they have relatively more siblings close in age (less than three years of difference).

Evidence about family size and birth order is inconclusive. Based on current scientific knowledge, we can't say with any certainty whether firstborns or later-borns are more likely to be creative (as Baer et al., 2005, also concluded). It probably varies from one creative domain to another, and also with the type of problems facing the domain.

FAMILY INFLUENCES

Studies of hundreds of eminent people throughout history have found that between one third and one half of them had lost a parent before age 21 (Simonton, 1999b, p. 115). This is called *the orphanhood effect.* How could such trauma lead to creativity in adult life? One hypothesis is that the loss of a parent produces a bereavement syndrome, in which children become high achievers to emotionally compensate for the absence of the parent (Eisenstadt, 1978). A second hypothesis is that loss of the parent forces the child to develop a resilient personality simply to overcome the obstacles that face a life with only one parent. If a person grows up in a happy, financially stable family, he or she may just have it too good in childhood to be driven to greatness (Simonton, 1999b, p. 114). Goertzel and Goertzel (1962/2004) studied published biographies of 400 20th-century eminent creators and found that over 85% came from troubled homes. Many had parents who were eccentric, neurotic, or even incapacitated by psychological disorders. So a third hypothesis is that being an orphan leads the child into a life that is less conventional than that of peers with a happy, normal family life.

Of course, childhood trauma doesn't always result in a successful adulthood. Juvenile delinquents and suicidal depressives also display a higher-than-average incidence of parental loss, comparable to the higher rate among eminent individuals (Eisenstadt, 1978). And fortunately, with major advances in medicine during the 20th and 21st centuries, average life spans in developed countries are much longer than they've ever been in history, and the orphanhood effect, if it ever did exist, is largely a historical curiosity.

Being a first- or second-generation immigrant and being Jewish are highly correlated with creative achievement. Nearly 20% of Nobel prize winners have some Jewish background, far above their proportion in the world's population. These sociologic and demographic factors may correlate with creativity because they result in a sense of marginality in the individual, and realizing that you're marginal may play a role in creative eminence (this argument was first made by Thorstein Veblen in a famous 1919 paper). Howard Gardner's creativity research led him to propose that the "exemplary creator" comes from the provinces, from the margins of power rather than the capital city (1993; also see Simonton, 1988b, pp. 126–129; 1999a).

These studies have revealed that significant minorities of creative people grow up in marginal communities, or have some early life trauma (at least, in the first half of the 20th century). But still, more than half of the most creative people say they grew up in stable, happy families. When Csikszentmihalyi (1996) studied 91 eminent creators, he didn't find any evidence of early trauma in childhood. And when the creative architects studied at the IPAR recalled their childhoods, they described the classic upper-middle-class, educated, American lifestyle: fathers were effective in their demanding careers, mothers were autonomous and often had their own careers, religion was important but was not central or doctrinaire, families emphasized the development of a personal code of ethics, parents were not overly judgmental but encouraged the child's ideas and expressions, and the families moved frequently (MacKinnon, 1978). Ultimately, these findings can't be explained by personality psychology; these family characteristics demonstrate the ways that social class status reproduces itself across generations. Creative people are usually successful, and successful people generally have successful parents, as sociologists have known for decades.

FAMILY AND COMMUNITY VALUES

The Flauberts steered Gustave into law, but he rejected their wishes and went on to write the famous novel *Madame Bovary*. Claude Monet's parents wanted him to enter their successful grocery business, but instead he became a painter. Wassily Kandinsky—the man who some say invented abstract painting just before World War I—was a professional lawyer and didn't begin painting until the age of 30. French painter Paul Gauguin moved with his wife to her native city of Copenhagen, where she joined forces with her family in the attempt to get him to give up his art and choose an occupation that would allow him to support his family. Ultimately the conflict could only be resolved by divorce.

These were strong personalities who were willing to go against their families' wishes, but other creative people who face such conflicts choose not to make a commitment to a creative career. Many adolescents internalize the practical value system of their families—the belief that creative pursuits are impractical and not suitable for a respectable person, and won't allow you to make a living and support a family. Many parents steer their children away from creative careers because they believe that creative pursuits are low status, not financially rewarding, and, worst of all, selfish; after all, a responsible adult would choose to make money and support one's family. Other families don't want their children to become artists because they have conservative or religious value systems, and they reject the bohemianism of the art world.

To choose a creative career, a person has to believe that this life choice is morally worthy; the ambition to do great work is a driving force. Many creators first realize the necessity of this choice in adolescence. Every creator has to negotiate family and society: some lucky few have supportive, open-minded parents and relatives who provide all of the necessary support to nurture their creative talent; others are forced to rebel and to reject the practical value system of their families. The family dynamics involved in the career decision influence the creator for the rest of his or her career. These family issues are typically studied by psychoanalytic psychologists (e.g., Gedo, 1996; see pp. 82–83 later in this chapter).

Creative women face different societal forces than men. The pressure to be the breadwinner is still felt stronger in American men, for example, and this makes it harder for men to choose a creative career. Although women feel less pressure to be the breadwinner, until recently there was not much support in many segments of American society for women with independent, successful careers; they too are viewed as selfish when they pursue such paths. These cultural values probably contribute to the fact that large numbers of women enter art school, but professional artists are almost exclusively men (also see Guerrilla Girls, 1998).

CHANGES DURING CHILDHOOD

There are many parallels between the creative process of the artist or scientist and the developmental process that children undergo as they age and mature. For example, the core insight of constructivism—an influential developmental theory associated with many famous psychologists, including Jean Piaget (1896–1980) and Lev Vygotsky (1896–1934)—is that when children learn something new, they basically are creating or "constructing" that knowledge for themselves. The crucial assumption of Piaget's theory of intellectual development is that new psychological entities or "schemas" are constructed by the child. Learning is more than just the continuous accumulation of new knowledge; it's a creative reorganization of thought.

At the fifth Utah Conference in 1962, many creativity researchers agreed that developmental processes are the same as creative processes (including Westcott and Parnes: Taylor, 1964b, p. 113). In his seminal 1974 study of Darwin's creative process, Gruber (1974) explored the relation between Piagetian universal thought structures and Darwin's highly original ones, and he suggested that Darwin's thought structures were transformed through a Piagetian constructivist process (cf. Feldman, 1980). These parallels were elaborated in a 2003 book by leading creativity researchers including Mihaly Csikszentmihalyi, David Henry Feldman, Vera John-Steiner, and Robert Sternberg (Sawyer et al., 2003).

PLAY AND CREATIVITY

When children play together to enact dramatic roles in a pretend reality, it's called *sociodramatic pretend play*. Like all play, it's intrinsically motivated and self-directed; it's free from externally imposed rules; and it involves positive affect such as pleasure, joy, excitement, and fun. And like all play, it seems to have many similarities with adult creativity. In Freud's psychodynamic theory, both play and creativity involve a high degree of unconscious primary process thinking (see pp. 82–83 below). Russ (1996) developed a contemporary version of Freud's theory of play; like Freud, she argued that children and adults who have "controlled access to primary process thinking"—she called it *affect-laden cognition*—should be more creative thinkers (p. 35).

When children engage in sociodramatic pretend play, they constantly generate alternative possibilities to advance the play drama, and this is a form of DT. Some research has found that the amount or quality of pretend play is correlated with scores on DT (Dansky, 1980; Dansky & Silverman, 1973, 1975; Hutt & Bhavnani, 1976; Johnson, 1976; Li, 1978). Johnson (1976) reported strong correlations between social pretend play and both cognitive ability and DT; solitary pretend play wasn't correlated with these measures. Lieberman (1977) used a *playfulness scale* with kindergartners that measured physical spontaneity, manifest joy, sense of humor, social spontaneity, and cognitive spontaneity. In a study of 93 kindergarten children, she found significant correlations between playfulness scores and DT scores. However, these findings have been challenged on methodologic grounds. Pellegrini (1992, p. 25) pointed out that in many of these studies, both the experimenters and those testing for creativity knew the hypotheses and which conditions the children had been assigned to. When double-blind procedures were followed, Smith and Whitney (1987) couldn't replicate the relationship between play and creativity.

Sawyer (1997b) argued that it's the uniquely improvisational nature of social pretend play that contributes to its social and developmental benefits (see Chapter 12, Group Creativity, and Chapter 19, Theater, for more about improvisational creativity). The improvisational aspects of play include:

- *Contingency*: During the play dialog, each child's turn depends on the previous child's turn, and yet there's a broad range of possible creative acts. These actions are creative because they have to be both appropriate (the act has to make sense within the existing shared play world) and new (the act has to move the play drama forward).
- *Intersubjectivity*: Children work together to create a shared, jointly created play world, with pretend roles, personalities, and plot events. This collective action is quite similar to what goes on in creative adult collaborative groups (see Chapter 12).
- *Emergence*: The shared play world emerges incrementally, as each child contributes a small change to the plot, character, or scene by building on what has come before. Again, this process is quite similar to effective adult creative groups.

Sawyer (1997b) found that five-year-olds engaged in much more improvisational play than three-year-olds, and that they used *implicit* conversational strategies that were more similar to those used by adults in everyday creative conversations (Sawyer, 2001a). Sawyer concluded that improvisational pretend play was a valuable contributor to the development of the collaborative and conversational skills that are essential to group creativity in adults.

LONGITUDINAL STUDIES

The above studies examined children at a given point in time. In contrast, a *longitudinal study* tracks children across many years, and examines whether play in childhood can be used to predict creativity several years later. In the first longitudinal study, Russ et al. (1999) measured play in first grade, and then measured those children's creativity four years later in fifth grade. They used Russ's own Affect in Play Scale (APS) to measure the amount and type of affect in play (defined as how many of 11 different emotions are expressed by the children's characters), and the quality of fantasy and imagination in the play (defined as organization, elaboration of the plot, imagination, and repetition). To measure creativity, they used the Alternate Uses test (see Chapter 3), with six objects: newspaper, knife, automobile tire, button, shoe, and key.

There was partial evidence that the first-grade measures of play predicted creativity four years later; quality of fantasy in first grade predicted fluency scores on the Alternate Uses test in fifth grade (0.34), and degree of imagination in play predicted them too (0.42). But APS scores didn't predict creative activities and accomplishments, nor did they predict how creative their stories would be.

In a second longitudinal study, Mullineaux and Dilalla (2009) assessed realistic role play at age 5, and then assessed those same children, when they were 10 to 15 years old, with the Test for Creative Thinking-Drawing Production (TCT-DP; Urban & Jellen, 1993) and the Alternative Uses Measure (shoe, button, and key). The total amount of realistic role play at age 5 (during a 20-minute observation period) significantly predicted their scores years later on the Alternative Uses Measure ($r = 0.25$) and the TCT-DP ($r = 0.22$).

In sum, several studies have found intriguing relationships between the amount and quality of pretend play and a child's measured creativity years later. This correlation doesn't prove causation; we don't know whether the increased pretend play actually causes greater creativity, or whether the causal influence went the other way: more creative children might be the ones who play more. Or, a third factor might be responsible for both additional play and higher creativity scores—anything from verbal fluency to IQ to parental education levels. We need additional research on the potential connections between play and creativity.

PLAY INTERVENTIONS

Based on the above studies showing the developmental benefits of pretend play, some scholars have developed *play interventions* that aim to teach children how to play in a more developmentally advantageous way. Some of these interventions focus on enhancing creativity.

Li (1985) conducted a pretend play intervention—eight 20-minute sessions weekly over two months—that trained children in "open-ended fairy tale enactment." The intervention improved examiner and teacher ratings of creativity, and also improved originality scores on the Alternate Uses Test (paper towel, paper clip, screwdriver). The impact on creativity was surprisingly large;

the children who had the training had given only 2.13 original responses, on average, before the training, but shot up to 8.67 after the training. The scores of a control group of children who received no training actually declined slightly.

Garaigordobil (2006) created a dramatic play intervention for children aged 10 or 11. Half of the classes in two schools were given two hours a week in the play activities; the other half spent those two hours engaged in arts activities. The play intervention resulted in a substantial increase in performance on the TTCT Verbal ($r = 0.50$) and an even larger increase on the TTCT Figural ($r = 0.62$) scores.

These are fairly high effect sizes, and these studies should encourage more researchers and educators to explore the potential of play interventions. The evidence to date is pretty clear that play interventions increase creativity.

WORLDPLAY

Some children engage in an ongoing, elaborate form of fantasy play in which they create their own imaginary make-believe world. These imaginary worlds are called *paracosms* and this form of play is called *worldplay*. In worldplay, children repeatedly evoke their imaginary world, and over months or even years, they develop elaborate maps and populate it with imaginary people or beings. These occupants develop cultural practices, institutions, and stories. Some children sketch elaborate maps; some even invent alphabets and languages used by the occupants of the world. This is quite different from psychotic or disturbing fantasies; worldplay is a normal developmental activity.

Root-Bernstein and Root-Bernstein (2006) found that worldplay in childhood was higher among exceptional creators. Ninety MacArthur "genius" Fellows told about their worldplay in childhood, and the researchers compared these recollections with those of 262 college students at Michigan State University. Of the MacArthur Fellows, 26% created elaborate imaginary worlds in childhood; among the students, about 12% did. Another 20% of the Fellows reported some less elaborate form of paracosm in childhood. A second study confirmed this pattern: Goldstein and Winner (2009) found that professional actors recalled greater engagement in alternative worlds and inner worlds during childhood than a control group of lawyers.

Actors must inhabit alternative worlds every time they go on stage. And in the Root-Bernsteins' study, 57% of the MacArthur Fellows said that they actively invented and participated in imaginary worlds in their professional adult career—defined broadly to include films, plays, novels, and scientific visualizations. One Fellow working in the arts said "work involves creating a world with characters and a unique, specific logic"; one social scientist said his job involved the constant creation of "possible alternative worlds by reference to existing power arrangements, interest-forming patterns, etc."; one physicist said "to do theory is to explore imaginary worlds" (p. 416). This research suggests an intriguing link between childhood fantasy and professional creative work.

DEVELOPMENTAL CHANGES IN CREATIVITY

When Torrance (1968) examined the scores of children on his DT test, he noticed an intriguing trend: the scores declined in fourth grade. Torrance saw a decline in TTCT scores in 45% to 60%

of fourth-grade children, and an increase in only 11% to 38% of the students. Torrance called this pattern the *fourth-grade slump*, and hypothesized that the rigid and regimented nature of school was responsible for reducing children's natural creativity. Torrance's "fourth-grade slump" is widely cited, but there's very little empirical evidence for it (Runco, 2007, pp. 668, 679). Other researchers have tried to replicate Torrance's results, but without much success. Some studies saw a fourth-grade slump, but other studies found increases in creativity during the same age period. Charles and Runco (2000–2001) didn't find a slump in DT between third and fifth grade. Lau and Cheung (2010) assessed 2,476 Hong Kong Chinese students using their own electronic version of the Wallach-Kogan test, and found an increase from grade four to five; a decrease from grade five to six; a decrease from grade six to seven; and an increase from grade seven to nine. They concluded that overall, the developmental trend is that creativity increased; the largest drop, at grade seven, corresponded to a school transition in Hong Kong from primary to secondary school. A review of all of the studies by Mullineaux and Dilalla (2009) concluded that children's creativity continually increased, on average, although with occasional fits and starts.

Runco (2003, p. 76) concluded that the fourth-grade slump, if it occurs, isn't due to the highly structured school system, as Torrance thought; rather, if it occurs, it results from normal maturational processes, as children enter a "literal" or "conventional" stage in thinking and moral reasoning more generally, as part of a necessary developmental path towards the adult's "postconventional" stage (Gardner, 1973, 1982; Winner, 1982). So it's misleading to refer to these developmental changes as "slumps." The term persists because the belief that school squashes a child's natural creativity aligns with Romantic-era notions of the pure essence of childhood—of childhood as a pure state of nature, opposed to civilization and convention.

ADULT RECOLLECTIONS

There's a long tradition of starting with extremely gifted, expert adults, and then interviewing them to look backwards at how they become such high performers—a *retrospective interview* study. Some of these studies also examine the biographies of deceased eminent creators. The first such study was by Catharine Cox (1926), one of Louis Terman's doctoral students at Stanford. She identified 301 unquestionably talented, creative, and successful individuals—many of them deceased—and then looked into their biographies to identify what they had been like as children. How to determine the childhood IQ score of someone already deceased? Cox did it by examining biographical information, and determining at what age they acquired certain skills. They acquired those skills at younger ages than the average person, and this difference in age was used to calculate the IQ score (because IQ is the ratio of mental age to chronological age). Their childhood IQ scores averaged around 150. Within the group, Cox didn't find a correlation between IQ and the degree of eminence.

More recent studies have found several factors that are more important than IQ in adult success: social class, educational level attained, and personality traits, including ambition and motivation (Baird, 1982). Benjamin Bloom (1985) led a team of researchers who interviewed 120 of America's top concert pianists, Olympic swimmers, sculptors, tennis players, mathematicians, and scientists. They ranged in age from teenagers to the mid-30s. The researchers asked about childhood experiences, family support, teachers, mentors, and how their personal identity developed as they increasingly realized they were exceptionally gifted. The common developmental pattern across all six areas was that first, an initial intrinsic interest slowly gave way to an intensive technical study. Then, as they reached a top level of mastery, their initial enjoyment returned. They were supported in this journey by a network of parents, mentors, and teachers. Bloom, like Baird, found that drive and determination contributed more to success than natural talent (also see pp. 78–79).

But retrospective studies are limited—they can't tell us how the successful adults differ from other, equally promising children who didn't develop their potential as fully. For that we need longitudinal studies like Terman's (see Chapter 3, p. 50).

PRODIGIES AND SAVANTS

Some children with autism have amazing artistic skills; these individuals are known as *savants*. However, these artistic abilities are generally thought to be based on calculation and memory alone, rather than true creativity or originality (Selfe, 1977). For example, autistic artists are quite skilled at reproducing an image, sometimes even after only one quick glance, but they rarely create novel images that they haven't seen. Oliver Sacks (1970) described at length José, a severely autistic individual who'd always displayed a fascination with pictures in magazines, and frequently copied what he saw. José's concreteness of detail in representing nature, in particular, was always phenomenal, but as Sacks wrote, "His mind is not built for the abstract, the conceptual" (p. 228); rather, "the concrete, the particular, the singular, is all" (p. 229).

Prodigies and savants both are found in very specific domains—especially in music, chess, and math (Feldman, 1986). These are all domains with well-defined, well-articulated symbol systems. There may be a biological basis for performance in these rule-driven creative domains. When Howard Gardner developed his theory of multiple intelligences (1983)—the idea that intelligence isn't a general trait but is actually seven distinct mental abilities (see Chapter 21, p. 402)—he argued that the existence of prodigies in a domain was evidence that the domain had a basis in the biological brain. Savants provide additional evidence that you can't explain creativity without having a good theory of creative domains, and that creativity always has to be explained in the context of a specific domain (Chapter 3, pp. 58–60).

CHANGES DURING ADULTHOOD

During his voyage around the world on the *Beagle*, Darwin kept exceedingly detailed notebooks on his observations. After returning to his study in London, he continued to keep daily notes as he reexamined his data. In 1974, creativity researcher Howard Gruber published the first detailed study of these notebooks (Gruber, 1974). By looking carefully through Darwin's day-to-day entries, Gruber realized that the theory of evolution by natural selection didn't occur in a blinding moment of inspiration, an "aha" moment. Instead, the notebooks showed a more incremental process, a series of small mini-insights, each a key step in Darwin's theory. Darwin's creative inspiration didn't happen in a single moment; it was constructed day by day over a long period of extended activity. Gruber argued that the insight of evolution by natural selection wasn't what made Darwin great; Darwin was a genius because he was able to build a conceptual framework within which evolution by natural selection would make sense. Prior to Darwin, other theorists had proposed evolution by natural selection, but they're not considered the founders of modern evolution because they didn't successfully develop the conceptual framework within which that insight could be explained.

Gruber also discovered that creative people are successful because they tend to have multiple, overlapping, related projects under way at the same time (Gruber & Davis, 1988). During the many years that Darwin was developing his theory of evolution, he was also working on geology and on a nine-year study of barnacles. The overlapping projects tend to be at different stages in the creative process, and they all tend to be loosely related to each other (Root-Bernstein, Bernstein, & Garnier, 1993; Simon, 1974). Gruber called this a *network of enterprises*. Movement back and forth within this network allows cross-fertilization of ideas and material, increasing the likelihood of stumbling on a sudden solution. Gruber argued that what makes a person creative isn't a single insight or idea, but it's the bigger conceptual frameworks within which ideas emerge, are interpreted, and are given life and elaboration. The network of enterprises doesn't happen in a sudden insight; exceptional creativity is the work of a lifetime.

LIFETIME PEAKS

In his influential book *Age and Achievement*, Lehman (1953) presented evidence that individuals in different fields have their creative peaks at different ages. Lehman claimed that physicists peak in their 20s or 30s, biologists and social scientists peak in their 40s, and writers and philosophers peak throughout the life span. Writers and philosophers can breathe a sigh of relief, but these findings are disturbing to physicists, biologists, and social scientists—especially the ones already beyond their supposed "peak age." Should they just give up, retire, and let the young blood take over?

Many studies have explored creative peaks since Lehman's 1953 book. For example, McCrae, Arenberg, and Costa (1987) followed the same 825 men from 1959 to 1972 (with ages from 17 to 101). They gave them six different measures of DT and found that the measures increased for men under 40 and declined for men over 40. But although there's some evidence for these career peaks, it doesn't mean you're all washed up if you're already past the average age for your career. After all, these are only averages. Dennis (1958) noted that highly original work occurs in most arts and sciences up to age 70 and beyond. Simonton (1997a) found that the decline in annual productivity after the age of peak productivity is often quite small, and because exceptional creators are so much more productive than the average professional, even after a decline they remain far more productive than the average professional, even one who's at peak age (also see Chapter 15, History and Creativity, pp. 285–288). Csikszentmihalyi's "Creativity in Later Life" study (1996) found that most creators remain productive long after retirement. And since 2000, studies of scientific productivity have not found any decline, suggesting that scientists today stay productive right up to retirement (Stroebe, 2010; see Chapter 15, p. 288). There's still a lot we don't know about creative lives; this is a topic that warrants more scientific study.

CREATIVITY AND THE HEALTHY PERSONALITY: FLOW AND PEAK EXPERIENCE

In his childhood in the 1930s, young Mihaly loved to climb the hills of his native Hungary and the larger mountains just across the border in Czechoslovakia. Why does someone climb a mountain? The obvious answer to the question is "to get to the top," but Mihaly, like all mountain climbers, knew that he didn't climb mountains to get to the top. That's why mountain climbers answer the question with a half-joking reply, "Because it's there." Mihaly climbed for the sheer pleasure of climbing.

Mihaly's family left Europe to escape the terrors of World War II. As he grew into a young man, these painful childhood experiences led him to choose a career in psychology (interview in http://mmp.planetary.org/scien/csikm/csikm70.htm, accessed 8/19/2011). Mihaly Csikszentmihalyi found his way to the graduate school at the University of Chicago, the legendary but eccentric intellectual haven that's been called "a blend of monastery and Bell Labs" (DePalma, 1992, p. B11). Csikszentmihalyi studied with psychologist Jacob Getzels (1912–2001) and received his doctorate in 1965 for his studies of MFA students at the famed Chicago Art Institute.

In the 1950s, American scientific psychology was dominated by Harvard psychologist B. F. Skinner's behaviorist experiments with pigeons and rats. Everyone realized that creativity was difficult for behaviorists to explain. But among therapists, a new movement known as *humanistic psychology* was catching on. Abraham Maslow (1954) and Carl Rogers (1954, 1961) emphasized the importance of peak experience, inner motivation, self-actualization, and creativity. In grad school in the 1960s, Csikszentmihalyi was drawn to these theories because they had the potential to explain the pleasures he had always felt while climbing mountains (Fig. 4.1).

Abraham Maslow claimed that the most healthy people are the most creative (1959). Carl Rogers argued that the primary motivation for creativity is "man's tendency to actualize himself, to become his potentialities" (1954, p. 251). The existentialist psychologist Rollo May (1959) agreed with his humanist contemporaries in arguing that creativity is "the expression of the normal man in the act of actualizing himself . . . the representation of the highest degree of emotional health" (p. 58). Humanist psychology was a modern version of the 19th-century Romantic ideals about the source of human happiness being within the individual (see Chapter 2), and this is why most humanist psychologists largely viewed society as a constraint, an obstruction that interfered with self-actualization (cf. Maddi, 1975).

FIGURE 4.1: Mihaly Csikszentmihalyi mountain climbing in Colorado in 1992. (Courtesy of Mihaly Csikszentmihalyi.)

Behavioral psychologists spent decades studying how various external factors motivate individuals, but their study was limited to *external* rewards—those that came from the environment. The humanist psychologists were talking about something completely different: the rewards of self-actualization are *internal*. In 1950, Abraham Maslow's graduate advisor, Harry Harlow, had shown that monkeys would repeatedly solve mechanical puzzles despite the absence of food or any other reward (Harlow, Harlow, & Meyer, 1950). Harlow and his colleagues attributed the puzzle-solving behavior to a *manipulation drive*, and they called the behavior *intrinsically motivated behavior* because the monkeys did it for its own sake. This early study was followed by an increasing body of research on intrinsic motivation (see Deci, 1975, for an overview).

After seven years on the North Side of Chicago teaching at Lake Forest College, Dr. Csikszentmihalyi's successful research program led to a prestigious job at the University of Chicago in 1972, and he returned to the monastic intellectual community in the South Side neighborhood of Hyde Park. Along with Jacob Getzels, who was nearing retirement, he stayed in touch with those MFA students from the early 1960s as they pursued their careers as artists. These studies resulted in the 1976 book *The Creative Vision*, which reported the striking finding that the most creative and the most successful painters were those who had scored high on intrinsic motivation while in art school (Getzels & Csikszentmihalyi, 1976).

In the 1970s, Csikszentmihalyi (1975, 1990b) continued this research by studying everyday experience. He used a novel method that he invented: he gave people pagers and paged them randomly throughout the day. When the pager went off, they opened a special notebook and answered a few questions about what they were doing and how they felt. He called this the *experiential sampling method* (ESM). During the same period, he conducted interviews with top performers in a wide range of occupations. This research demonstrated that people in all walks of life feel at their peak when they're being their most creative (Csikszentmihalyi, 1990b).

Csikszentmihalyi called peak experience the *flow state*. Back in 1959, Rollo May was one of the first to describe this experience: *intensity of awareness, absorption, heightened consciousness, oblivious to the environment and to the passage of time* (p. 61). Csikszentmihalyi's research confirmed May's description; he found that people are more creative when they're in an experiential state that has the following characteristics:

- Clear goals
- High degree of concentration on the task
- A loss of self-consciousness
- Distorted sense of time
- Immediate feedback is continuous while engaged in the task
- Balance between level of ability and the challenges of the task
- A sense of personal control
- The activity is intrinsically rewarding
- A lack of awareness of bodily needs, such as hunger or fatigue
- The focus of awareness is narrowed to the activity itself, so that action and awareness are merged

When in flow, people are so motivated by the work that they often find themselves losing track of time. They focus in on what they're doing, they forget about everyday problems, and they're oblivious to distractions in the environment. These are extremely positive experiences; people tend to seek out tasks and environments in which flow is more likely to occur. Flow and creativity are closely linked.

DETRIMENTAL EFFECTS OF REWARD

For the individual to find himself in an atmosphere where he is not being evaluated . . . is enormously freeing. . . . If judgments based on external standards are not being made then I can be more open to my experience . . . Hence I am moving toward creativity.
—Carl R. Rogers, (1954, p. 257)

If ever there was a finding that has been worked and re-worked it is that evaluation has a negative effect on creativity.
—Stein, (1987, p. 419)

In the 1950s and 1960s, there was a debate among educators about whether to reward creative behavior. Most educators believed that grades would reduce student creativity. The positive reinforcement of grades seemed effective only at teaching the "stereotyped repetition of what works" (Schwartz, 1982, p. 57). Influential scholars such as Rogers (1954), Stein (1958), and Osborn (1953) argued that if we want to promote creativity, we have to remove all external evaluation. Torrance (1965) argued that instead of grades, schools should respond to creative activity with a "genuine respect for the child's creative needs and abilities—a recognition of their importance" (p. 42).

These longstanding beliefs about external rewards have solid backing in empirical studies. Decades of creativity studies have found that external rewards can easily short-circuit the benefits of the flow state. Even Harlow et al. (1950) found that when they later gave the monkeys food, it reduced their performance on the mechanical puzzles. It seems that when people know they'll be rewarded for the quality of their work, they can't stop thinking about that reward, and they find it impossible to get into the flow state where they're doing the task simply because they like doing it. The potential interference of extrinsic motivation was a key emphasis of Torrance's method for teaching creative behavior; he called his method *unevaluated practice* (Torrance, 1965).

In the 1980s, Teresa Amabile extended these early studies (Amabile, 1983, 1996). Her studies showed that when people are told they're going to be externally evaluated or rewarded for creative work, their level of creativity (and their intrinsic motivation) declines. It's because they focus on the expected reward, and that diverts attention from the task itself, and also from "nonobvious aspects of the environment that might be used in achieving a creative solution" (Amabile, 1983, p. 120).

But not all rewards are bad; many adults say that they work better and more creatively with the right external rewards—whether a raise, a bonus, or a promotion. Many students say they work better and more creatively because they're motivated to get good grades, or to get into a better university or graduate school. The discipline of microeconomics views people as rational actors who respond to incentives, and many of the predictions made by such models are supported empirically. Even Torrance (1965) found that competition among children resulted in greater fluency and originality on the assignment "improve a stuffed toy dog so that it will be more fun as a play toy" (pp. 143–144). And in a cross-cultural study of the effect, Hennessey (2003) found that in a more collectivist culture (Saudi Arabia), the expectation of a reward didn't undermine performance, suggesting that the effect might occur only in individualist cultures like the United States (see the discussion of individualist and collectivist cultures in Chapter 14).

The key is to design the external rewards carefully. Deci and Ryan (1985) found that if rewards are offered for taking part in an activity, or for completing an activity, they reduce intrinsic interest. However, if rewards are contingent on the quality of the work performed, they didn't reduce intrinsic motivation. A meta-analysis of 96 studies by Cameron and Pierce (1994) confirmed this finding, with the following overall results:

- Expected rewards *reduce* intrinsic interest, but unexpected rewards do not.
- Expected rewards that are granted regardless of the quality of performance *reduce* intrinsic interest.
- Expected rewards that are granted contingently on the quality of the performance *increase* intrinsic interest.

Eisenberger and Selbst (1994) found that certain kinds of rewards can increase creative performance on DT tests. First, the reward should be given only for a high degree of creativity; rewarding a small degree of creativity has a detrimental effect on creativity. If the reward is granted only for a high-quality performance, it increases intrinsic interest. Second, it has to be a small reward, or if it's a large reward, it has to be kept out of sight, so it doesn't absorb too much attention and thus reduce creativity (as Amabile's studies found). As Eisenberger and Cameron (1996) point out, the detrimental effects of rewards granted without concern for quality could simply be due to a "learned helplessness" response—if it doesn't matter how well you do, you'll feel helpless to influence the outcome, and that reduces your intrinsic interest.

Working adults often say that company incentives, if they signal the value of their contribution, are motivating and enhance creativity (Amabile & Gryskiewicz, 1987). Hennessey and Zbikowski (1993) found that when students perceive rewards to be informational, rather than controlling, they don't necessarily undermine creativity or intrinsic motivation. Amabile, Hennessey, and others have developed "immunization training" that teaches children about the potential negative effects of reward, and teaches them to view the rewards as informational. After such training, the expectation of a reward can often increase intrinsic motivation and performance.

If evaluation comes too early in the creative process, it can inhibit the generation of ideas. But during the selection and elaboration stages, it's essential. What Morris Stein wrote back in 1987 has been confirmed by research since then: "The effects of evaluation depend, in all likelihood on the context in which it occurs, the way in which it occurs, the evaluator, the creative person, etc. Evaluation cannot be avoided" (p. 419).

This research is particularly important for teachers who want to enhance children's creativity. First, the fears of the 1960s haven't panned out; it doesn't seem to be the case that rewards or grades always reduce creativity. But the research shows what to avoid: don't reward small effort, but only substantial effort; make sure that the reward is contingent on the quality of the work; make sure that the reward is not salient—in other words, don't spend a lot of time talking about it and if it's a tangible reward, don't put it right out in front of the students.

MOOD AND CREATIVITY

If the peak experience of the flow state is related to enhanced creativity, then that should be reflected in studies of mood and creativity. Sure enough, many experiments have shown that being in a good mood increases your performance on creativity tests.

Isen, Daubman, and Nowicki (1987) induced a good mood in one group of people by either giving them a small bag of candy, or having them watch five minutes of the comedy movie called *Gag Reel*, which had bloopers that were cut from three old television shows. Other groups of people engaged in physical exercise (two minutes of stepping up and down from a concrete block) or watched a movie about math facts (expected to have no impact on mood) or had a negative mood induced (watching five minutes of a film about Nazi concentration camps). In the first two experiments, they then gave everyone a classic insight problem that's fairly hard to solve: Duncker's candle task (see Chapter 6). Seventy-five percent of the people who watched the funny movie solved the problem, but only 20% of those who watched the movie about math facts did. Seeing the Nazi movie dropped the solution rate to 11%.

Also, on seven RAT items of moderate difficulty, a bag of ten pieces of candy, or five minutes of the comedy film, increased solution rates; those who watched the comedy film got an average of five of the seven right, while those who watched the math facts movie got only three right. Subramaniam et al. (2009) confirmed this study, finding that people who were in a good mood solved more RAT problems; furthermore, people in a good mood were more likely to report a sensation of insight when they got the answer.

These few studies of mood and creativity confirm the findings of the research on peak experience, flow, and intrinsic motivation: positive mood is associated with greater creativity.

CREATIVE SELF-EFFICACY

Self-efficacy refers to a person's beliefs in his or her abilities (Bandura, 1986). In contrast to self-esteem, which is a generalized sense of one's worth, self-efficacy refers more specifically to a person's beliefs in his or her ability to do well in a specific domain or on a specific task. *Creative self-efficacy* refers to a person's belief that he or she is or is not creative (Gist & Mitchell, 1992; Tierney & Farmer, 2002). It's assessed with questions like "I have confidence in my ability to solve problems creatively" (Tierney & Farmer, 2002, p. 1141). Creative self-efficacy is usually specific to a given domain; for example, a trained pianist may score highly on creative self-efficacy in music, but receive a low score on painting (Jaussi, Randel, & Dionne, 2007).

Most of this research has been in the workplace, and evaluates employee's beliefs that they can be creative in their work roles. Beghetto (2006a) used a simple three-item scale to assess creative self-efficacy:

- I am good at coming up with new ideas.
- I have a lot of good ideas.
- I have a good imagination.

Jaussi et al. (2007) used the following questions:

- In general, my creativity is an important part of my self-image.
- My creativity is an important part of who I am.

- Overall, my creativity has little to do with who I am (reverse coded).
- My ability to be creative is an important reflection of who I am.

Tierney and Farmer (2004) studied 191 workers at a Midwest chemical company and found that creative self-efficacy explained 35% of employee creativity. Choi (2004) studied 430 students at a business school and found that creative self-efficacy explained 34% of the variance in creative performance. If your job is less complex, then newcomers have higher creative self-efficacy than old-timers, but if the job is more complex, then newcomers have lower self-efficacy (Tierney & Farmer, 2002, p. 1144). There's some evidence that the predictive validity of self-efficacy on complex tasks is weaker than for performance on simple tasks (Gist & Mitchell, 1992, p. 206).

It makes sense that differences in self-efficacy are associated with differences in skill level. If you're effective at something, then you'll probably notice that and become more confident. But research suggests that the causality goes the other way too: people who think they can perform well on a task do better than people who think they'll fail (Tierney & Farmer, 2002). Some studies show that self-efficacy can be enhanced through training, and afterwards, performance increases (Gist & Mitchell, 1992). These findings are intriguing, and they suggest the potential role of creative self-efficacy in creative performance. One potential problem is that it's not clear to what extent creative self-efficacy is different from other creativity constructs; we need more studies to demonstrate the construct validity of measures of creative self-efficacy.

CREATIVITY AND THE DISTURBED PERSONALITY: THE PSYCHOANALYTIC APPROACH

> An artist is once more in rudiments an introvert, not far removed from neurosis. He is oppressed by excessively powerful instinctual needs. He desires to win honour, power, wealth, fame and the love of women; but he lacks the means for achieving these satisfactions. Consequently, like any other unsatisfied man, he turns away from reality and transfers all his interest, and his libido too, to the wishful constructions of his life of phantasy, whence the path might lead to neurosis.
>
> —Sigmund Freud, (1917/1966, p. 467)

Psychoanalysis has long associated creativity with access to more primitive, unconscious modes of thought—sometimes called *primary process thought*. Many schools of 20th-century art were influenced by Freud's psychoanalytic theories. Expressionism, dadaism, and surrealism were based in part on the idea that art involves the revelation of unconscious material. According to Freud, the creative insight emerges into consciousness from primary process thought. Freud argued that creativity involved the same mental processes as daydreams, fantasies, and full-fledged neuroses (1907/1989). Psychoanalytic theory explains the frequently noted connections between art, dreams, and children's play; they all involve regression to a more primitive developmental state, the intrusion of primary process thought and unconscious repressed drives into consciousness.

Regression involves a return to behavior patterns characteristic of an earlier stage of personality development. When repressed unconscious material is released, it usually causes psychological problems. That's why psychoanalytic theorists generally expect to see a connection between creativity and mental illness. For example, Freud's collaborator, Alfred Adler—the man who first proposed the concept of the "inferiority complex"—argued that the arts were *compensatory phenomena*—they're produced to cover up some inadequacy or inferiority (May, 1959, p. 56).

But by the 1950s and 1960s, creativity researchers convincingly demonstrated that most creative people didn't manifest any symptoms of neurosis. As a result, psychoanalytic theorists modified their theories; they started to believe that creativity involved both primary processes and secondary processes. Creative people are able to partially control regression and can use it in service of a conscious goal; this "regression in service of the ego" is constructive rather than destructive (Kris, 1952). Kubie (1958) argued that unconscious conflicts actually have a negative effect on creativity—because for the most part they're fixed and repetitive. Kubie instead attributed creativity to the *preconscious*, which rests between the conscious and unconscious portions of the mind. Rothenberg (1979) claimed that the creative process is "not only *not* primitive but [is] consistently more advanced and adaptive than ordinary waking thought" (p. 43).

From the 1950s onward, the consensus among psychoanalytic psychologists has been that the creative person manages a sophisticated balance between primary and secondary process thinking, and that this balance would be hard to maintain in the presence of mental illness. The relationship between the unconscious and the conscious mind is still central to several influential contemporary theories, even those that aren't psychoanalytic (as we'll see in Chapter 5). But psychoanalytic theorists no longer believe that creative people are more likely to be mentally ill. We'll examine the relationship between creativity and mental illness at more length in Chapter 9 (pp. 163–176).

CONCLUSION

After decades of creativity research, we've identified a large number of personality characteristics associated with high levels of creativity. Real-world creativity doesn't seem to be the result of any one personality trait; exceptional creators seem to combine many different traits and abilities, in a complex mix. Amabile (1983, 1988) emphasized three broad personality factors: task motivation, domain-relevant skills, and creativity-relevant processes. The first, task motivation, is based on her research on intrinsic motivation (described in this chapter). The second captures the domain-specific elements of creativity, and the third represents the domain-general elements (Chapter 3, pp. 58–60). Sternberg and Lubart's (1996) *investment model* identified six broad personality factors: intelligence, knowledge, cognitive style, motivation, personality, and environmental context. Creative people are happy and productive, and tend to be quite successful—nothing like our myth of the tortured lone genius.

Guilford's 1950 APA address jumpstarted the modern era of creativity research. But during the 1960s, creativity researchers in the United States increasingly turned away from the Cold War focus on military and technological goals, towards a focus on individual expression and radical school reform—consistent with the broader societal movements active in the United States at that time. As a result, by 1970, government and military support for creativity research virtually disappeared (Feldman, Gardner, & Csikszentmihalyi, 1994, pp. 1–9) and studies of the creative personality slowly came to an end (Feist & Runco, 1993, p. 280). By 1980, many creativity researchers concluded that the first wave of creativity research—the 30 years of study into personality traits and creative potential in childhood—had failed to achieve its goals (cf. Feldman, Csikszentmihalyi, & Gardner, 1994; also see Glover, Ronning, & Reynolds, 1989).

A special personality is required to make the choice for creativity, to knowingly choose the kind of lifestyle associated with the career, to be able to sustain the dedication and commitment to the work. Studies of the creative personality continue to be done by contemporary psychologists, using updated instruments and theories such as the big five personality model. Some of the most promising research is focused on the underlying cognitive processes that creative people use. In the next three chapters, we'll learn about the mental processes associated with creativity.

KEY CONCEPTS

- Personality traits versus personality types
- Five-factor (OCEAN) model of the personality
- Orphanhood effect
- Constructivism and creative learning
- Sociodramatic pretend play
- Longitudinal study
- Play intervention
- Worldplay and paracosm
- The fourth-grade slump
- Network of enterprises
- Peak experience and flow
- Intrinsic motivation and detrimental effects of reward
- Creative self-efficacy
- Primary process thought
- Compensatory phenomena

THOUGHT EXPERIMENTS

- Did you engage in worldplay—the creation of an elaborate imaginary world—in childhood?
- Think of a time that you were in "flow"—the state of peak experience. What were you doing, and what contributed to the flow state?
- Think of one of your teachers or mentors—someone older than you for whom you have a lot of respect. What words first come to mind when you try to describe what this person is like?
- Would you say that this person is effective and successful in life?
- Did this person work hard? Was he or she highly motivated?
- Would you say that this person is creative?

SUGGESTED READING

Barron, F., & Harrington, D. M. (1981). Creativity, intelligence, and personality. *Annual Review of Psychology, 32*, 439–476.

Feldhusen, J. F., & Goh, B. E. (1995). Assessing and accessing creativity: An integrative review of theory, research, and development. *Creativity Research Journal, 8*(3), 231–247.

Gruber, H. E. (1988). The evolving systems approach to creative work. *Creativity Research Journal, 1*, 27–51.

MacKinnon, D. W. (1962/1978). What makes a person creative? In D. W. MacKinnon (Ed.), *In search of human effectiveness* (pp. 178–86). New York: Universe Books. (Originally published in *Saturday Review*, Feb. 10, 1962, pp. 15–17, 69).

Piirto, J. (1999). A survey of psychological studies in creativity. In A. S. Fishkin, B. Cramond, & P. Olszewski-Kubilius (Eds.), *Investigating creativity in youth: Research and methods* (pp. 27–48). Cresskill, NJ: Hampton.

Stein, M. I. (1987). Creativity research at the crossroads: A 1985 perspective. In S. G. Isaksen (Ed.), *Frontiers of creativity research: Beyond the basics* (pp. 417–427). Buffalo, NY: Beary Limited.

THE CREATIVE PROCESS, PART 1

I n the 1970s, shortly after funding for IPAR and other personality studies had declined dramatically, a second wave of psychologists began to study creativity in a new way (Feldman, Gardner, & Csikszentmihalyi, 1994). Research psychology was changing dramatically during the 1960s and 1970s. *Cognitive psychology* began to replace both the behaviorism and the personality psychology that had been dominant in American psychology after World War II. Instead of studying traits and personality differences, cognitive psychologists analyze mental processes that are shared by all individuals. Cognitive psychologists examine the representational structures of the mind, their interconnections, and the mental processes that transform them. They explain creativity by showing how it emerges from the cognitive abilities that everyone shares.

Although cognitive psychologists focus on the mental abilities that everyone shares, they acknowledge that some people are more creative than others. But rather than explaining these differences in terms of personality traits, cognitive psychologists believe that they can best be understood in terms of variations in the use of specific, identifiable processes—such as the flexibility of stored cognitive structures, the capacity of memory and attention systems, and other basic cognitive principles. Second-wave cognitive psychology isn't opposed to first-wave personality research; they're complementary, and we need them both to explain creativity.

THE EIGHT STAGES OF THE CREATIVE PROCESS

Over the centuries, philosophers have developed two competing theories about the creative process. *Idealist theorists* argue that once you have the creative idea, your creative process is done. It doesn't matter whether or not you ever execute your idea, or whether anyone else ever sees it; your creative work is done once your idea is fully formed in your head. This idea is often called the "Croce-Collingwood" theory, after two philosophers who promoted it in the 20th century (see Sawyer, 2000). It shows up in the Western cultural model as Belief 1, "the essence of creativity is the moment of insight."

Action theorists, in contrast, argue that the execution of the creative work is essential to the creative process. Action theorists point out that in real life, creative ideas often happen while you're working with your materials. Once you start executing an idea, you often realize that it isn't working out like you expected, and you have to change what you had in mind. Sometimes a final product emerges that's nothing like your beginning idea. Perhaps the purest example of action creativity is jazz improvisation. Because it's improvised, musicians don't know what they'll play in advance; the notes emerge in the moment, from the complex give-and-take among the members of the ensemble. In improvisation, performers start playing without knowing what will emerge.

Many of the creativity beliefs associated with the Western cultural model are more consistent with the idealist theory than the action theory. We tend to think that ideas emerge spontaneously, fully formed, from the unconscious mind of the creator (Belief 2). In this chapter, and the next two, we'll see that the idealist theory is false; only an action theory can explain creativity. Creativity takes place over time, and most of the creativity occurs while doing the work. The medium is an essential part of the creative process, and creators often get ideas while working with their materials. If the idealists were right, it would be almost impossible to study creativity scientifically—if all of the action is in the head, a scientist can't observe it. We're lucky that the idealist theory is wrong, because action theories have a big advantage: they make it easier for scientists to observe and explain the creative process.

Psychologists have been studying the creative process for decades, and they've observed that creativity tends to occur in a sequence of stages. The simplest model of the creative process is a two-stage model sometimes called *the balloon*—an expanding stage of *divergent thinking* where many possibilities are generated, followed by *convergent thinking* as you converge on the one best idea. The balloon is a useful shorthand, but most theories of the creative process have expanded upon the simple balloon model to propose four or more stages, giving us a deeper understanding of the mental activities that people engage in when they're creating. This chapter, and the next two, are organized around an integrated framework that captures the key stages of all of the various models that psychologists have proposed (Table 5.1).

This integrated framework describes eight stages of the creative process:

1. *Find and formulate the problem.* The first step is to identify a good problem and to formulate the problem in such a way that it will be more likely to lead to a creative solution.
2. *Acquire knowledge relevant to the problem.* Creativity is always based on mastery, practice, and expertise.
3. *Gather a broad range of potentially related information.* Creativity often results from alert awareness to unexpected and apparently unrelated information in the environment.
4. *Take time off for incubation.* Once you've acquired the relevant knowledge, and some amount of apparently unrelated information, the unconscious mind will process and associate that information in unpredictable and surprising ways.
5. *Generate a large variety of ideas.* Unconscious incubation supports the generation of potential solutions to the problem, but conscious attention to the problem can also result in potential solutions.
6. *Combine ideas in unexpected ways.* Many creative ideas result from a combination of existing mental concepts or ideas.
7. *Select the best ideas, applying relevant criteria.* The creative process typically results in a large number of potential solutions. Most of them will turn out not to be effective solutions; successful creators must be good at selecting which ideas to pursue further.

Table 5.1: Sawyer's Eight Stages of the Creative Process, and How They Correspond to Other Process Models

	Wallas (1926)	Creative Problem Solving (Isaksen, Dorval, & Treffinger, 2000)	IDEAL cycle (Bransford & Stein, 1984)	Robert Sternberg (2006)	Possibility thinking (Burnard, Craft, & Grainger, 2006)	UK QCA (QCA, 2005)	Synectics (Gordon, 1961)	Mumford's group (Scott et al, 2004)	IDEO (Kelley, 2001)
Find the problem		Framing problems	Identify problems, define goals	Redefine problems	Posing questions	Questioning and challenging		Problem finding	
Acquire the knowledge	Preparation	Exploring data	Learn	Know the domain			Groundwork	Information gathering	
Gather related information			Look		Immersion	Envisaging what might be	Immersion		Observation
Incubation	Incubation	Constructing opportunities	Explore possible strategies	Take time off	Play	Keeping options open		Concept search	
Generate ideas	Insight	Generating ideas		Generate ideas	Being imaginative	Exploring ideas	Divergent exploration	Idea generation	Brainstorming
Combine ideas		Developing solutions		Cross-fertilize ideas		Making connections and seeing relationships		Conceptual combination	
Select the best ideas	Verification			Judging ideas		Reflecting critically on ideas	Selection	Idea evaluation	
Externalize ideas	Elaboration	Building acceptance	Act and anticipate outcomes	Sell the idea, persevere	Self-determination		Articulation of solution, development and transformation, implementation	Implementation planning and action monitoring	Rapid prototyping, refining, implementation

8. *Externalize the idea using materials and representations.* Creativity isn't just having an idea; creative ideas emerge, develop, and transform as they are expressed in the world.

The consensus resulting from cognitive psychology is that creativity isn't a single, unitary mental process. Instead, creativity results from many different mental processes, each associated with one of the eight stages.

STEP 1: FIND THE PROBLEM

> *We say that a question well put is half resolved. True invention thus consists in posing questions. There is something mechanical, as it were, in the art of finding solutions. The truly original mind is that which finds problems.*
>
> —Paul Souriau, 1881, p. 17; translation in Wakefield, (1991, p. 185)
>
> *The formulation of a problem is often more essential than its solution . . . . To raise new questions, new possibilities, to regard old questions from a new angle, requires creative imagination and marks real advance in science.*
>
> —Albert Einstein & Leopold Infeld, (1938, p. 92)

Many cognitive psychologists argue that creativity is essentially just a form of problem solving, and they compare the stages of the creative process to the stages involved in problem solving (Flavell & Draguns, 1957, p. 201; Guilford, 1967; Kaufmann, 1988; Klahr, 2000; Klahr & Simon, 1999). In a seminal 1962 article, Newell, Shaw, and Simon first stated a view that remained influential for decades: "creative activity appears simply to be a special class of problem-solving activity" (p. 66). Even J. P. Guilford argued that creativity was quite similar to problem solving (1967, pp. 312–331). When psychologists study problem solving, they present people with fairly well-defined problems: the starting state is clearly specified, the goal state is well understood, and it's fairly obvious which actions will get you from the start to the goal. Newell et al.'s *general problem solver* (GPS; 1962) proposed that problem solving occurred in an imaginary "problem solving space," sort of like a topographic map. You begin at the starting state, and your challenge is to find a "solution path" through the space toward the goal. As Bransford and Stein (1984/1993) put it in their book about problem solving: "A problem exists when there is a discrepancy between an initial state and a goal state, and there is no ready-made solution for the problem solver" (p. 7). Because you can't see the entire map, you have to use various strategies that are likely to move you closer to the goal, even though you're not quite sure which direction the goal state is.

But in the real world—whether in the arts, science, or business—problems are rarely neatly presented. The only place you're likely to be asked to solve well-defined problems is on a test. Instead, most creativity occurs when people are working on *ill-defined problems*: (1) they can't be solved through rote application of past experience; (2) the problem situation isn't clearly specified; (3) the goal state isn't clearly specified; (4) there may be many different end states; (5) there are multiple potentially viable paths to the end state (cf. Mumford, Baughman, & Sager, 2003). Solving well-defined problems involves primarily convergent thinking; solving ill-defined problems involves a higher degree of divergent thinking.[1] For ill-defined problems, the first "problem" to be solved is identifying and formulating the problem (for a review, see Jay & Perkins, 1997). With truly transformative creativity, you might even create an entirely new "search space" with a radically new topography and geography.

Creativity researchers have discovered that exceptional creativity more often results when people work in areas where problems are not specified in advance, where a big part of success is being able to formulate a good question (Beittel & Burkhart, 1963; Csikszentmihalyi, 1965; Getzels, 1964; Mackworth, 1965). As a result, many creativity researchers now believe that creativity involves *problem finding* as well as problem solving.[2]

PROBLEM FINDING IN ART

Although we don't usually associate the word "problem" with painting, one of the first studies of problem finding was a study of the creative process of fine art painters. In 1962, a research team from the University of Chicago spent a year at the School of the Art Institute of Chicago, one of the top art schools in the United States. The lead researcher was Mihaly Csikszentmihalyi, and his driving question was: How do creative works come into being? First, he designed an "experimental studio" to capture the usual process of painting. The studio contained two tables; one table was empty, and the other table held 27 different objects—things like a bunch of grapes, a steel gearshift, a velvet hat, a brass horn, an antique book, and a glass prism. The aspiring artists were instructed: "Choose some of these objects, rearrange them as you please on the other table, and draw them. You may spend as much time as you want selecting the objects and drawing them."

Csikszentmihalyi discovered that there were two very different approaches that artists used in this experimental studio. The first type of artist took only a few minutes to choose a few objects from among the 27 presented. They sketched an overall composition in a couple of minutes, and then they spent the rest of their time completing the composition. In other words, they quickly chose a visual "problem," and then they invested most of their effort in solving that problem.

The second type of artist couldn't have been more different. It seemed like they had trouble making up their minds: they spent five or ten minutes looking at the 27 objects, turning them around to see them from all angles. After they'd picked some objects and started sketching, they'd change their mind again and put one object back and get a different one. After drawing for 20 or 30 minutes, they'd get a new idea, and their sketch would completely change. Finally, after up to an hour like this, they would settle on an idea and then finish the sketch in five or ten minutes.

Csikszentmihalyi enlisted a team of five professors at the Art Institute to help him determine which artworks were more creative (this was the first use of the Consensual Assessment

---

1. However, complicating the picture, psychologists haven't found any relationships between divergent thinking and problem-finding ability (Starko, 1999, p. 90).

2. These terms were first used by Mackworth (1965). There are some parallels with Kirton's (1988) ideas about creative styles; his *adaptors* are the problem-solving people and his *innovators* are the problem-finding people.

Technique; see Chapter 3, pp. 41–42). He created an art show where all of the sketches were hung on the walls (without the artist's names), and he asked the five professors to rate the creativity of each sketch. When he averaged the total creativity score for each painting, he discovered that the artists who spent all of their time formulating their visual problem had generated far more creative paintings.

Five years after graduation, Csikszentmihalyi tracked down all 31 of these students to find out who had the most successful careers as artists, and who was most respected by art critics. About half of them had stopped doing art altogether. The other half, the successful artists, were the ones who had used a problem-finding style five years before while in art school.

Moore (1985) replicated these findings with middle-school student writers; he found that the problem-finding style predicted more original compositions. Moore (1990, 1993) also compared expert teachers to student teachers, and found that the expert teachers did much more problem finding; for example, the experienced teachers asked higher-level questions than student teachers, and they explored the environment more fully before acting.

Arlin (1974, 1975) found that the quality of questions asked during an experimental problem-finding task was predicted by four other individual measures: (1) a Piagetian measure of formal operational thinking; (2) elaboration as measured on DT tests; (3) adaptive flexibility as measured on Guilford's matchsticks problems; and (4) expressional fluency, as measured on DT tasks.

Runco and Okuda (1988), in a study with talented and gifted science and math high-school students, used a problem-finding methodology first used by Wakefield (1985): students were presented with three "Instances" DT tasks ("Name all of the things you can think of that move on wheels"), and then were asked to create their own problem ("Here we would like *you* to choose a category, and *then* list instances of it"). They were instructed to choose a category that had a lot of instances, because a longer list was better. They found that students generated more ideas on the problems they came up with than on the presented items. They also found that performance on the invented problems added significantly to the prediction of creative accomplishment, beyond scores on the presented tasks.

Okuda, Runco, and Berger (1991) gave 77 elementary-school children this standard problem-finding task, and then asked them to generate real-world problems related to home or school life, as follows:

> Now I would like you to think of different problems in school [or home] that are important to you. You may write down problems about school, teachers, rules, or classmates [or parents, brothers, sisters, chores, or rules]. Take time, and think of as many problems as you can. (p. 47)

The real-world problem-finding measures were the best predictors of scores on the Creative Activities Check List—better than the standard problem-finding tasks, and better than DT measures. The correlation was quite high ($r = 0.58$).

Mumford et al. (1996b) also found that scores on a problem-construction task were better predictors of creative problem solving than standard DT tests. In a later study, Mumford et al. (2003) gave subjects 6 ill-defined problems, and then showed 16 different restatements of the situation that might be used to define the problem. Subjects were told to select four that they thought would be most useful in helping them understand the problem situation. The more creative students tended to select restatements that emphasized high-quality approaches and high-quality restrictions. The researchers concluded, "People who frame an ill-defined problem in terms of viable solution strategies and restrictions on feasible approaches are more likely to perform well on creative tasks" (p. 35).

PROBLEM FINDING AND CONTEMPORARY CULTURE

At the beginning of a painting class in 1992, instructor Michell Cassou began by asking his students, "How many of you came here with your first painting already done in your head?" Half of the students raised their hands. Cassou continued, "If you paint that painting, you'll just be copying what you've already done." These students came to the class holding to the idealist theory, that creativity is when you have the idea. Instead, Cassou told his students to "open themselves to the moment," without predetermined plans (Cushman, 1992, pp. 54–55). The problem-finding creative style can be explained only with an action theory.

American society in the 20th century valorized spontaneity. But this emphasis on problem-finding creativity is relatively recent (Belgrad, 1998; see Chapter 2). Prior to the 19th-century Impressionists, who were influenced by the naturalism and spiritualism of the earlier Romantic writers, painters were definitely *not* supposed to paint without prior planning. The great academies of Europe, such as the École des Beaux-Arts in France, taught the importance of choosing an appropriate subject (ideally, a historical or mythological theme), of carefully composing its placement on the canvas, of experimenting with color mixes for each portion of the painting, and of sketching and painting preliminary drafts or "studies" before beginning the actual work. This was how painting had been done in Europe for centuries. But today, problem finding is more important to creativity than it's ever been.

STAGE 2: ACQUIRE KNOWLEDGE

After you've defined and formulated the problem, the second stage is to learn everything relevant to your problem. Most domains of creative activity have been around for many lifetimes—the centuries of European fine art painting, or the decades of empirical research in particle physics. Without first learning what's already been done, a person doesn't have the raw material to create with. That's why an important part of the creative process is to first become very familiar with prior works, and internalize the symbols and conventions of the domain. Creativity results when a person somehow combines these existing elements and generates a new combination.

Based on extensive studies of the biographies of exceptional creators throughout history, creativity researchers have discovered that it takes approximately ten years of study in a domain before a person makes his or her first major creative contribution (Gardner, 1993). This *ten-year rule* was first discovered in 1899, when *Psychological Review* published a study showing it takes ten years to become an expert telegrapher (Bryan & Harter, 1899). In 1973, cognitive psychologists Herbert Simon and William Chase estimated that international-level chess players required at least ten years of study (p. 402). Gardner (1993) demonstrated that creative individuals, in a wide variety of domains, tend to come up with major breakthroughs after ten years of deep involvement in the domain. The ten-year delay is evidence of the importance of learning the domain—the language and conventions of a creative discipline.

People who reach the top of their profession also spend that ten years in an especially valuable way. They engage in a special kind of learning that Anders Ericsson called *deliberate practice* (Ericsson, Krampe, & Tesch-Römer, 1993; Ericsson et al., 2006). In one of his many studies of expertise, Ericsson et al. (1993) asked all of the violinists at the Berlin music academy to keep a weekly record of how much they practiced, and exactly how they did it. After their first two years in the academy, the top violinists had practiced twice as many hours as the average student! Deliberate practice isn't just playing the same song over and over; it requires working on tasks that are a little bit beyond what you're capable of doing, but that can be mastered with concentration and feedback.

Studies of expertise by Ericsson and others have found that performance at the top world-class level is only possible after a person has invested 10,000 hours of deliberate practice in the domain. This number has been demonstrated to hold in domains as varied as chess, medicine, programming, physics, dance, and music. At five days a week, with four hours a day of deliberate practice, you'd reach the 10,000-hour mark in exactly ten years—the same number that other researchers derived from their biographical studies of exceptional creators.

Some domain knowledge is internalized in a passive and direct way; the student of physics has to learn Maxwell's equations and Einstein's theories exactly. But in deliberate practice, domain knowledge can be creatively transformed even while it's being learned. When artists walk through a gallery, they view paintings very selectively, looking for ideas or inspirations that can solve creative problems that they are currently working with. This can lead them to see something in a painting that its creator may not have intended. When scientists read a historical work by a long-dead theorist, they read into the work whatever perspectives or issues they are currently working with.

The deep learning associated with deliberate practice results in a deeper knowledge than simple memorization of facts and procedures (also see Chapter 21). Mumford et al. (1996a) demonstrated that how you encode the information that you learn influences your later ability to be creative with that knowledge. The researchers asked people to read through cards providing different sorts of information. People who spent more time on factual information, who discounted irrelevant information, and who attended to inconsistent information tended to produce higher-quality and more original problem solutions.

No one can be creative without first internalizing the domain, and this is why scientists now believe that formal schooling is essential to creativity. In modern science, for example, you can't even begin to work in a domain without first getting a PhD. However, the role played by schooling in creativity is complex (see Chapter 21). Even in science, where schooling is perhaps more important than in art, high grades aren't strongly correlated with adult achievement (see Simonton, 1988b, pp. 118–126).

Some studies have found that creativity is an inverted-U function of educational level; after a certain point, additional formal education begins to interfere with creativity. Figure 5.1 presents a curve derived from 192 creators from the Cox (1926) sample. In 1926, the education level corresponding to peak creativity was somewhere between the junior and senior years of college. Of course, these data are from an earlier era, and as the sciences have become progressively more complicated, this peak has shifted to the middle of graduate study (Simonton, 1984c, pp. 70–73).

Up to at least graduate school, then, formal schooling doesn't interfere with creativity; it's just the opposite. To participate successfully in a field, the young individual must internalize the domain. But the inverted-U pattern shows that there's some truth to the idea that schooling can

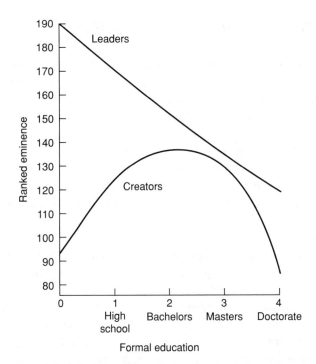

FIGURE 5.1: Curves of the relationship between formal education and ranked eminence for leaders and creators. (Redrawn from *Journal of Creative Behavior*, volume 17, 1983. "Formal Education, Eminence, and Dogmatism," pp. 149–162, by D. K. Simonton. Reprinted with permission of Creative Education Foundation. Copyright 1983.)

get in the way. After getting just enough education to internalize the domain, further training may oversocialize a person, resulting in a rigid, conventionalized way of thinking.

The intense learning associated with exceptional creativity continues outside of school and early in one's career. Zuckerman's (1974) study of Nobel laureates found that highly creative individuals actively seek out mentors, and they're selected by other highly creative individuals for training. Torrance (1983) found a correlation between having a mentor and the number of recognized creative contributions (also see Nakamura, Shernoff, & Hooker, 2009). Mentoring is particularly helpful in developing the ability to identify good, promising problems.

Exceptional creators tend to start learning their domain very early in life. When the psychologist Vera John-Steiner (1985) interviewed over 100 exceptional creators in the 1970s, she learned that all of them became immersed in their area of interest at a fairly young age. Pablo Neruda, in his autobiography, wrote that he "gobbled up everything, indiscriminately, like an ostrich." Painter Brent Wilson, who grew up in a very small town, remembers spending hours with every new issue of *Life* magazine (p. 90). Twenty years later, Professor Mihaly Csikszentmihalyi interviewed 91 exceptional creators, and he also found that in childhood, they displayed a "keen curiosity" and "intense interest" (1996, p. 156). Exceptional creativity is based in a long history, a lifetime of deep absorption into learning the domain. Creativity Belief 4 of the Western cultural model, that outsiders are more creative, is completely false.

STAGE 3: GATHER RELATED INFORMATION

After defining the problem and mastering the domain, the third stage of the creative process is to remain constantly aware of your environment, and to absorb information from a wide variety of sources. Creative thought is associated with a particular sort of perception: one that's active and alert to opportunities relevant to your problem.

Our intuition about how sight works is that our brain simply stores a copy of what the eye sees, like a camera. But that can't be right, because then you'd still need another part of your mind to examine the mental picture and make sense of it. At some point your mind has to get out of this infinite regress and actually interpret what's being seen—your mind has to break it up and process it into units that have meaning. And these units of meaning are probably not stored in anything like two-dimensional, photographic form (Ramachandran, 2004). This mental process involves creativity and transformation.

Rodolfo Llinas, a professor of physiology and neuroscience at NYU medical school, argued that our view of the world is a projection created by the brain. Scientists used to believe that visual data from our eyes were processed upwards, through the visual cortex, into the higher brain regions that are responsible for thinking and creativity. But the past decade of evidence from brain studies has discovered something very different: there are thousands of neurons that send information from the higher brain regions back into the visual cortex. Less than half of the connections entering the visual cortex actually come from the eyes; the other neurons come from the brain. Neuroscientists don't yet fully understand exactly how these higher- and lower-level pathways combine to form our visual perceptions of the world, but Dr. Llinas made a surprising claim: there's no essential difference between waking and sleeping, because in both states, our brain actively constructs our view of the world. Dr. Llinas has estimated that our perception is based only 20% on information coming from outside of us; the other 80%, your mind fills in.

Creativity involves being aware of a wide variety of information in your environment, and being able to spot opportunities to link new information with existing problems and tasks. Psychologists have identified a variety of perceptual techniques associated with creative thought. People are more creative when they structure their information search, retaining only the information necessary to understand the problem situation (Mobley, Doares, & Mumford, 1992). People are more creative when they absorb relevant categories and information, and that requires you to be critical and evaluative as you decide which information to look for (Mumford et al., 2003).

Exceptional creators use special techniques to see more effectively and more efficiently. For example, using the right categories can make it easier to see gaps and difficulties, as David Perkins (1981) demonstrated with a visual search task (pp. 79–81). First, he asked people to search a list of random letters and, as fast as possible, tell him whether the letter "x" was in the list. Try it yourself with this list: r, x, v, s, w; you can do it reasonably fast. But then Perkins asked people to tell him if there was an "x" in this list: a, e, i, o, u. Everyone is faster at the second decision than the first, because the category of "vowels" allows you to see very quickly that there is no "x". The good news is that people create new categories every day, and that means you can learn to scan for unusual and potentially relevant information by creating a new category or set. Creative people are better at seeing gaps, at spotting difficulties, at noticing opportunities and flaws (Perkins, 1981, p. 285).

STAGE 4: INCUBATION

Instead of thoughts of concrete things patiently following one another . . . we have the most abrupt cross-cuts and transitions from one idea to another . . . the most unheard-of combinations of elements, the subtlest associations of analogy; in a word, we seem suddenly introduced into a seething cauldron of ideas, where everything is fizzling and bobbing about in a state of bewildering activity.

—William James, (1880, p. 456)

After defining a good problem, after learning everything there is to know about it, and after absorbing new information from the environment, the fourth stage is to give your mind time to process all of that information—to search for new and appropriate combinations, creative solutions to the problem. Exceptional creators throughout history have said that their best ideas emerge from an unguided, unconscious process that creativity researchers call *incubation*. To provide time for incubation, many creative people force themselves to stop working periodically. They take time off from the hard, focused work to engage in an unrelated activity—gardening, walking—or to work on another problem for a while. Former CEO of Citicorp John Reed, responsible for introducing the first street-level ATMs back in the 1970s, said, "I do my best work when I have some alone time. It often happens when I'm sitting around a hotel room, I'm on a trip and nothing's going on, I sit and think, or I'm sitting on a beach . . . and I find myself writing myself notes." Physicist Freeman Dyson said that his daily insights come while he's shaving or taking a walk. Economist Kenneth Boulding takes a 40-minute bath every morning, and reported that ideas often come to him then (all quoted in Csikszentmihalyi & Sawyer, 1995).

In Chapter 4, we learned that creative people multitask in networks of enterprise; they make sure that they're working on more than one project at the same time. While they're consciously attending to one project, the others are incubating. The unconscious mind seems to be able to incubate on many projects at once "in parallel," unlike the conscious mind, which can focus on only one thing at a time (also see Csikszentmihalyi & Sawyer, 1995).

Perhaps the most famous example of incubation followed by insight comes from the famous Greek mathematician, Archimedes. His cousin, King Hiero of Syracuse, asked him to solve this problem: he'd ordered a crown made of gold, but he was suspicious that some cheaper silver had been used inside, and then just coated with gold. Archimedes wasn't allowed to cut inside or damage the crown. But he knew that silver weighed more than gold. Taking a bath one day, he noticed that as he slowly got into the tub, the water level rose. He suddenly had the insight that a heavier object would displace more water, and was so excited that he ran outdoors, into the street, naked, shouting, "Eureka!" which in Greek, meant "I have found it!"[3]

3. Like so many stories about creative insight, this almost certainly never happened. For one thing, the first written version of the story was almost 200 years afterward. Second, the scale had already been invented, and Archimedes could have just used that to measure the weight of the crown. Third, it's actually quite difficult to measure the amount of water displaced; the surface tension of the water makes the measurement difficult.

Many creators use cooking metaphors to describe incubation: they talk about "keeping things on the back burner," or "providing fuel for the fire," and they say that creativity takes time to "stew" or "bubble up." During incubation, ideas and thoughts combine rapidly in an almost undirected way. Einstein wrote in a letter to Hadamard that "the psychical entities which seem to serve as elements in thought are certain signs and more or less clear images which can be combined . . . This combinatory play seems to be the essential feature in productive thought" (in Hadamard, 1945, p. 142). With luck, incubation leads to the fifth stage: an idea emerges in a sudden flash of insight. Research on incubation is closely related to research on insight, the fifth stage that we'll read about in Chapter 6.

Freudian psychoanalysis presented the first theory of what's happening during incubation: powerful unconscious instinctual drives, often erotic in nature, are directing the mind in an inner unconscious conflict between id and superego. This *primary process thought* then enters preconscious thought, which is dominated by *secondary process thought*. The conscious mind is largely passive in reacting to these underlying forces. Kris (1952) modified Freud's original theory and argued for a more active role for the conscious mind of the artist, which he called "regression in the service of the ego"—the successful creator is someone who intentionally recruits the primary process of the unconscious.

Creativity researchers have largely abandoned these psychoanalytic theories of incubation, but today's most prominent theories are attempts to answer the same question: what's the role of the unconscious mind in creativity? Today's cognitive psychologists refer to a *dual-process theory* that includes two systems: one automatic, nonconscious, and implicit; the other using controlled processes and marked by subjective awareness and attentional focus (e.g., Bargh & Morsella, 2008; Chaiken & Trope, 1999; Strack & Deutsch, 2004). The conscious system has a limited capacity and processes information sequentially; the unconscious system has far greater capacity (Dijksterhuis & Nordgren, 2006) and operates in parallel (Lieberman et al., 2002).

Creativity researchers are unlikely to be there right at the moment when an exceptional creator has that great idea that leads to a Nobel prize. But a wide variety of fascinating experiments have studied small, everyday moments of incubation. The remainder of this chapter describes these findings.

EXPERIMENTAL EVIDENCE FOR INCUBATION

The first question that researchers have to address is whether anything at all is happening during incubation. It could be that the unconscious mind isn't working on the problem at all, that creativity progresses only during conscious attention. The "no incubation" hypothesis became attractive as psychologists began to reject the Freudian psychoanalytic framework; after all, for many decades unconscious incubation had been closely tied to Freud's theories of repression, regression, and primary process thought.

But even though Freud's explanation has been rejected, there's substantial experimental evidence that something unconscious is going on during incubation. To demonstrate an *incubation effect*, the researcher has to create an experimental condition where two different groups of people begin working on a task that is difficult and requires a creative insight to solve. One group of people is interrupted while they're working on the task but before they've solved it; then, they're given a task that forces them to consciously focus on something different; and finally, they're allowed to return to the original problem. The other group works continuously on the problem. If the unconscious mind works actively towards a solution, the first group—the one interrupted in the middle—should be more likely to have the insight that solves the problem. If the unconscious mind isn't doing anything, then both groups should solve the problem at similar rates.

Patrick (1986) used an experimental design that would be likely to reveal if an incubation effect exists. He gave subjects RAT triplets (see Chapter 3, pp. 44–46) and compared continuous work to three types of interruption. He also examined whether high-ability RAT solvers benefited more from interruptions than low-ability RAT solvers. The three types of interruption were designed to take a person's conscious mind progressively farther away from the problem. The four conditions were:

- Continuous work: eight minutes on each triplet
- Two minutes on each triplet, then an interruption that switched to a different triplet (not very far removed); the interruptions continued at two-minute intervals until each triplet had been worked on a total of eight minutes
- Identical to condition 2, except that in between each two-minute period the experimenter engaged the subject in five minutes of small talk (medium removed)
- Identical to condition 3, except that instead of conversation, subjects spent five minutes on a mental rotation task (far removed)

He used only triplets that subjects hadn't been able to solve during an ability-testing phase; they'd spent three minutes looking at the triplet and failed to solve it, thus ensuring they were at an impasse. The results showed an interaction effect by ability: high-ability subjects solved the most problems when interrupted by the rotation task, and low-ability subjects solved the most in the interruption with another triplet condition. The only significant main effect was the contrast for high-ability subjects between mental rotation and continuous work, showing an incubation effect for getting far away from the problem, but only for high-ability subjects. So the incubation effect was quite limited—only to one condition and only for high-ability subjects.

Beeftink, van Eerde, and Rutte (2008) gave people three relatively cryptic crossword puzzle clues to solve. They compared three conditions:

- Continuous work on one problem at a time for six minutes
- An interruption condition where people had to switch between the three puzzles after three minutes, thus working on each puzzle twice
- A condition where people could switch between the three puzzles whenever they wanted, for a total work time of 18 minutes (6 minutes on each of the three puzzles)

The results provided evidence of an incubation effect; they found that the third condition, where people could switch tasks at will, led to solving more insight problems and to fewer impasses than either other condition.

Wells (1996) interviewed 213 college professors and found that creative productivity (as measured by total number of publications) was correlated ($r = 0.21$) with a work practice of *forced incubation*, defined as intentionally ignoring or putting aside a manuscript. The professors reported that they often have new ideas during that time. Forced incubation is different from the sort of unintended and unexpected incubation that subjects get in incubation effect experiments, because it's under the conscious control of the creator, but it's more similar to the everyday experience of creative work.

Ellwood et al. (2009) reviewed 50 studies of the incubation effect and found that more than 75% found an incubation effect. But because the studies used such different methodologies, it's hard to know exactly what's going on during incubation. They pointed out that most studies of incubation have focused on the RAT, which involves convergent thinking, so they created a divergent thinking experiment—they gave participants an Unusual Uses test (list as many possible different uses for a piece of paper), and then created three conditions:

1. Work continuously four minutes
2. Work for two minutes, are told they are done, switched to do the Myers-Briggs for five minutes, and then to their surprise, they are given another two minutes to continue to generate different uses
3. Work for two minutes, given a related task for the break (produce as many synonyms as you can for this word), and then given another two minutes

In condition 2, with the unrelated break (Myers-Briggs), people generated 9.8 ideas after the break; in condition 3, people generated 7.6 ideas after the break; among those who worked continuously, 6.9 ideas were generated in the final two minutes. These numbers show a statistically significant incubation effect for divergent thinking.

The bulk of experimental evidence supports an incubation effect—being interrupted and forced to work on an unrelated task increases solution rates for creativity-related problems.

THEORIES OF INCUBATION

There are several influential hypotheses of what happens in the mind during incubation, and experiments have tested each of these:

1. You continue consciously working on the problem. Even if you're doing something else, your conscious mind might be multitasking and still partially attending to the problem you've put aside. Nothing is going on in your unconscious mind. In an experimental setting, a researcher can make sure this isn't happening by giving people *distractor tasks* that are designed to occupy the conscious mind during the interruption.
2. Rest. You got mentally exhausted working on the problem, and your mind gets a chance to relax and recover. Experiments can evaluate this hypothesis by using distractor tasks that are more or less related to the creative task; during a less-related distractor task, the portions of the mind related to the original creative task could recover from mental fatigue, but during a highly related task, those parts of the brain would remain active.
3. Selective forgetting. If your mind is fixated on a wrong solution path, incubation might allow your mind to become less attached to that incorrect solution, thus freeing you to discover a more fruitful path forward (also called the *forgetting fixation hypothesis*: Smith & Blankenship, 1989). Insight problems are typically designed so that people are misdirected down the wrong solution path, often by presenting irrelevant or misleading information in the wording of the problem. It could be that when this incorrect path fades, after the solver realizes it can't be correct, the correct solution—which had been

overshadowed by the fixation—reaches conscious awareness, thus accounting for the sudden sensation of insight.

4. Random subconscious recombination. Various bits of relevant information, stored in long-term memory, are recombined through a random process. The creative person "just happened to be standing where lightning struck" (Campbell, 1960, p. 390). Simonton called these associations "chance permutations" (1988b, pp. 6–8; 1997b). When these random processes generate something relevant to the problem, it moves into conscious awareness. This hypothesis has largely been rejected by psychologists, however, because it conflicts with everything we know about how the mind works (Boden, 1994a, p. 7; Johnson-Laird, 1987; Kaufman, 2003; Perkins, 1994).

5. Spreading activation. Related concepts in memory are gradually activated through the mind's semantic network. Researchers can study this hypothesis by examining how quickly people respond to related "primes" that are presented during the incubation period; these studies are described in Chapter 6.

6. Directed subconscious recombination. The subconscious mind actively works toward solution of the problem, below the level of awareness. This is the original psychoanalytic hypothesis of Freud, Kris, and others; the combinations are "active, directed forms of cognition in which the creator intentionally and in distinct ways brings particular types of elements together" (Rothenberg, 1979, p. 11). There's no easy way to evaluate this hypothesis using experimental designs, and it's largely been rejected by creativity researchers (e.g., Perkins, 1981, p. 57).

Many empirical studies have evaluated these various theories. Kohn and Smith (2009) conducted an incubation experiment with RAT triplets. Half of the participants were given a misleading cue, designed to induce fixation on this incorrect answer. The other half didn't get a misleading cue, so they weren't fixated on an incorrect answer. Then, the researchers tested two conditions that might lead to an incubation effect:

- Complete interruption (the triplet was removed, and subjects did a digit-monitoring task that occupied their attention)
- Partial distraction (the triplet remained on the screen while they did the task)

An incubation effect was observed with complete interruption (0.05 solution rate for no incubation and 0.10 solution rate with incubation) but not partial distraction. There was no incubation effect for problems that were unsolved but were not given a misleading cue. This is evidence for hypothesis 3, selective forgetting, and evidence against hypothesis 1, the conscious work hypothesis that during incubation your conscious mind is continuing to think about the problem.

Seifert et al. (1995) concluded that most studies favor hypotheses 2 and 3, *rest* and *selective forgetting* (p. 83). They called their theory *opportunistic assimilation*; here's how it works. When you get to an impasse and stop working, you still have "failure indices" in long-term memory. This allows all of the information you gathered, and the steps and dead ends that you took, to be easily recalled—"like a nearly completed jigsaw puzzle" (p. 87). Simon (1977) and Schank (1988) similarly argued that preparation serves to index useful items in memory—which they called *scenarios* or *schemas*—that are indexed in such a way that they can be retrieved when similar problems are encountered in the future. Langley and Jones (1988) argued that people have insight experiences during incubation when "retrieval is cued by some external event" (p. 190).

In this theory, during incubation, no active processing is taking place. But as you go about your day, you may eventually encounter an external object or situation that's relevant to the unsolved problem; this environmental stimulus then cues the recall of the failure indices, and you assimilate the new stimulus into the stored representation of the problem. Additional evidence for the opportunistic assimilation theory was provided by a study by Lockhart, Lamon, and Gick (1988). They presented people with 15 different insight problems, including the following:

> A man who lived in a small town married 20 different women of the same town. All are still living and he never divorced a single one of them. Yet, he broke no law. Can you explain?

The solution is that the man is a clergyman. The researchers came up with two types of hints, corresponding to the two hypothesized possibilities. In the first one, the *declarative form*, they first gave subjects the sentence "It made the clergyman happy to marry several people each week." In the second one—the *puzzle form*—they gave the sentence "The man married several people each week because it made him happy"; then, a few seconds later, they presented the word *clergyman*. The puzzle form at first causes you to form the inappropriate conception—that the man is marrying each woman himself—and then you get the clue that allows you to reconceptualize. In the first case, you never form the inappropriate conception, and never have to reconceptualize.

The people who read the declarative form ahead of time didn't do any better than people who didn't get any clue at all; they weren't able to transfer the clue to the new problem. But the people who got the puzzle version did far better. This is evidence that they had stored "failure indices" that allowed them to connect that information to the new problem more quickly. This study suggests that you're more creative later if you actually solve a similar problem yourself, instead of someone just telling you the answer. There are obvious implications for education and creativity (see Chapter 21).

Hypothesis 5, the *spreading activation hypothesis*, also has some empirical support (Eysenck, 1993; Langley & Jones, 1988; Yaniv & Meyer, 1987). The spreading activation mechanism was first proposed by Yaniv and Meyer (1987), who gave people a rare-word definition task—they presented a definition for an obscure, rare word, and then asked the person if they knew what the word was. In most cases, they had no idea what the word was. Then, still without telling them what the word was, the researchers gave them a *lexical decision task*: a technique that presents research participants with either a word or a pseudo-word (letter strings that are pronounceable but aren't real words, like "tuke" or "plone") and then asks them to classify it as a word or not, as quickly as possible. Reaction times were faster to the rare word that had been defined than to unrelated control words and to non-words, especially when a person reported having a "feeling of knowing" after seeing the definition, even though he or she couldn't think of the word.

Sio and Rudowicz (2007), in a study with Chinese GO players, also found support for the spreading activation hypothesis. They gave people RAT triplets, and for those triplets a person couldn't solve, Sio and Rudowicz gave the person a variant of the lexical decision task, in which half of the people were presented with words that were conceptually related to the unsolved RAT and the other half saw words that were completely unrelated. Some of the RAT triplets were designed to result in a fixation on an incorrect answer, but only for people who knew a lot about the game of GO. They found an incubation effect only for these GO-misleading RATs, and only among GO experts. This study demonstrated that the exact process of spreading activation depends heavily on a person's domain expertise.

In sum, there's experimental evidence to support hypotheses 2, 3, and 5: incubation works because it gives people's minds a rest; because it provides an opportunity to become less fixated on incorrect solutions; and because it provides time for spreading activation in the unconscious mind. In the real world, it's likely that taking time off also provides opportunities for "opportunistic assimilation"—as you go about your daily activities, you may randomly encounter a stimulus that is related to your problem, one that connects to the "failure indices" that remained when you stopped working. This is another reason why Stage 3—actively being aware of potentially relevant information—contributes to creativity.

THE ROLE OF THE CONSCIOUS MIND

Does the conscious mind interfere with creativity, or is it essential to creativity?

Evidence that the conscious mind interferes with creativity includes Schooler's findings on verbal overshadowing. Schooler, Ohlsson, and Brooks (1993) gave two groups of people the same problems, half of them insight problems and half of them non-insight problems. Half of each group was asked to talk out loud while working on the problems—a "think aloud" task that kept their conscious mind active. The other half of each group worked silently on the problems. Compared to the silent group, the people who verbalized were substantially less likely to solve the insight problems, but performed the same on non-insight problems.

Verbalizing solution attempts could interfere with solving insight problems because it leads people to focus on their initial, incorrect representation longer; or because it leads them to focus on the more reportable incremental reasoning processes associated with non-insight problem solving; or because it disrupts spreading activation (Schooler et al., 1993). They concluded that the conscious talking disrupts the nonreportable unconscious processes involved in insight problems, whereas non-insight problems didn't rely on nonreportable processes (Schooler & Melcher, 1995).

However, most studies suggest that the conscious mind plays an essential role in creativity. In the real world, most of the daily work of creativity is conscious and directed (Sternberg, 2003). And there's experimental support for the important role of the conscious mind. For example, many studies show that when people are instructed to "be creative," they generate more creative ideas (e.g., Howard-Jones et al., 2005). Baumeister et al. (2007) presented people with the following "popcorn story" written by Seyba (1984) and adapted by Eisenberger and Rhoades (2001), and asked people to generate either "titles" or "creative titles":

> You are a tiny golden kernel of popcorn lying in the bottom of a frying pan. Look around you and see the other popcorn kernels that are snuggled up close to each other. Feel it heating, getting warmer, hotter, now burning underneath you. Close to you a popcorn kernel explodes. One by one other popcorn kernels pop to life. White clouds appear to be bursting out all around you. The sound of popping drums in your ears. You are cramped, uncomfortable, steaming hot, sweating, dizzy. Your whole body feels too tight. You are trapped within a too tight suit. Suddenly, you, the popcorn kernel, feel yourself exploding, bursting. All at once you are light and fluffy. Bubbling up

and down with other popcorn. At last the popping sound begins to quiet. Just an occasional pop, pop, and at last silence. (Baumeister et al., 2007, p. 140)

Creative titles included PANdemonium, Popcorn Puberty, and A-pop-calypse. Less creative titles included Popcorn, Pop Pop, and Popcorn Kernels. People who were instructed to generate "creative titles" did, in fact, generate more creative titles—suggesting that the conscious intention to be creative results in increased creativity.

In two related experiments, Baumeister et al. (2007) demonstrated that when they interfered with conscious processing during creative tasks, it *reduced* creativity. The first study was with 12 jazz guitarists. They asked the 12 jazz guitarists to play solos in three different conditions: first, they played a normal solo; second, they played a solo while counting backwards from 917 by sixes (a high cognitive load); third, they played a solo while counting forward from 15 by ones (a low cognitive load). The low-cognitive-load solos were rated to be as creative as the normal solos, but the high-cognitive-load solos were significantly less creative (even though the solo was technically correct, holding to the right rhythm and scale). The second study asked people to draw pictures while listening to a song. Half of the people were asked to listen closely to the song and count the number of times the vocalist sang the word "time" in the lyrics. The people who had the active listening task generated less-creative drawings.

In sum, when they occupied the conscious mind with an unrelated task, people were less creative. If the conscious mind were interfering with the creativity of the unconscious, then occupying it should enable greater creativity by the unconscious—but just the opposite happened, suggesting that the conscious mind and the unconscious mind work together to generate the highest levels of creativity.

SUMMARY

The research presented in this chapter shows that the conscious mind plays an important role in the creative process. Stages 1, 2, and 3 are predominantly conscious and directed. Even Stage 4, incubation, occurs only in the context of ongoing conscious work—you benefit from incubation only if you work hard on a problem beforehand, and then continue to work hard on it afterwards.

It's impossible to study authentic, real-world creativity under controlled experimental conditions. After all, exceptional creativity is rare, and it takes a long time—months or years (see Perkins, 1981, pp. 49–57). Even if we didn't see an incubation effect in the laboratory, that wouldn't mean it didn't occur in the real world, with a motivated person working for days or months on a problem (Olton & Johnson, 1976). Psychologists have demonstrated incubation effects in laboratory tasks, but the effect might be even larger, or slightly different, in the real world.

Now we continue our exploration of the eight-stage creative process by moving on to Stage 5, generating ideas, and Stage 6, combining ideas.

KEY CONCEPTS

- Idealist theory versus action theory
- Divergent thinking versus convergent thinking

- Problem finding versus problem solving; ill-defined problems
- The ten-year rule
- Deliberate practice
- Think aloud task
- Incubation effect
- Distractor task
- Selective forgetting hypothesis
- Spreading activation hypothesis
- Opportunistic assimilation

THOUGHT EXPERIMENTS

- Think of a time when you made something that you think was particularly creative— a school project, a written report, a mechanical device, a block tower, a painting, or a musical performance.
- What mental process led to its creation?
- Did you have a lot of training and expertise in the domain? If not, what prepared you to make this creative product?
- Did you have the idea all at once, fully formed, and then all you had to do was make it? If so, what preceded the insight—what preparation did you do, and was there an incubation period?
- Or did you begin with only the germ of an idea, having mini-insights throughout the process, so that the final product was not exactly what you started out to make?
- Would you call this a problem-finding or a problem-solving type of creativity?

SUGGESTED READINGS

Csikszentmihalyi, M., & Getzels, J. W. (1988). Creativity and problem finding in art. In F. H. Farley & R. W. Neperud (Eds.), *The foundations of aesthetics, art & art education* (pp. 91–116). New York: Praeger.

Ellwood, S., Pallier, G., Snyder, A., & Gallate, J. (2009). The incubation effect: Hatching a solution? *Creativity Research Journal, 21*(1), 6–14.

Ericsson, K. A., Krampe, R. T., & Tesch-Römer, C. (1993). The role of deliberate practice in the acquisition of expert performance. *Psychological Review, 100*(3), 273–305.

Feldman, D. H. (1974). Universal to unique. In S. Rosner & L. E. Abt (Eds.), *Essays in creativity* (pp. 45–85). Croton-on-Hudson, NY: North River Press.

Feldman, D. H., Csikszentmihalyi, M., & Gardner, H. (1994). *Changing the world: A framework for the study of creativity*. Westport, CT: Praeger.

Gardner, H. (1993). *Creating minds*. New York: Basic Books.

Scott, G., Leritz, L. E., & Mumford, M. D. (2004). The effectiveness of creativity training: A quantitative review. *Creativity Research Journal, 16*(4), 361–388.

THE CREATIVE PROCESS, PART 2

M any exceptional creators report that their best ideas emerge unexpectedly during incubation, in an "aha" or "eureka" moment that creativity researchers call *the moment of insight* (Sternberg & Davidson, 1995). In the Western cultural model, creativity is associated with this moment of insight (Belief 1), and insights are thought to emerge mysteriously from the unconscious mind (Belief 2). In Chapter 5, we examined studies of unconscious incubation (Stage 4), and studies of the three conscious stages that precede incubation. These studies show that although the unconscious mind plays an important role in creativity, its process is not mysterious; creativity involves standard cognitive processes and structures.

So what happens when the moment of insight occurs? What's the source of new ideas? In this chapter, we continue our exploration of the creative process by examining psychological studies of the mental processes involved in Stage 5, generating ideas, and Stage 6, combining ideas.

STAGE 5: GENERATE IDEAS

> *The mind being prepared beforehand with the principles most likely for the purpose . . . incubates in patient thought over the problem, trying and rejecting, until at last the proper elements come together in the view, and fall into their places in a fitting combination.*
>
> —Alexander Bain, *The Senses and the Intellect* (1855/1977, p. 594)

In this epigraph, Alexander Bain concisely stated the very first psychological theory of insight: the *associationist theory* that new ideas are combinations of existing ideas (also see Chapter 1, p. 8). Associationist theories were at the core of behaviorism, a psychological paradigm that was dominant in American psychology for the first half of the 20th century. But one group of psychologists rejected associationism: the *Gestaltists.* "Gestaltism" takes its name from the German word that means "form," and Gestaltists argued for the holistic, irreducible nature of thought (Duncker, 1926; Wertheimer, 1945). In 1926, the German Gestaltist Karl Duncker published the first study of creative insight. He began by criticizing the associationist views of the famous American psychologist William James, that sudden insights are the result of having a lot of information and being able to make connections between facts. Instead, Duncker pointed out that some problems are solved suddenly, so fast that no chain of connections could explain the discovery.

To prove his argument Duncker created a series of 20 ingenious puzzles that he claimed couldn't be solved by incremental associations. If he could demonstrate that the problems were solved suddenly, rather than slowly and incrementally, that would be support for the Gestaltist theory and against associationism. One of Duncker's most famous problems is the x-ray problem:

> Suppose you are a doctor faced with a patient who has a malignant tumor in his stomach. It is impossible to operate on the patient, but unless the tumor is destroyed the patient will die. There is a kind of ray that can be used to destroy the tumor. If the rays reach the tumor all at once at a sufficiently high intensity, the tumor will be destroyed. Unfortunately, at this intensity the healthy tissue that the rays pass through on the way to the tumor will also be destroyed. At lower intensities the rays are harmless to healthy tissue, but they will not affect the tumor either. What type of procedure might be used to destroy the tumor with the rays, and at the same time avoid destroying the healthy tissue?

Duncker showed this problem to 42 people, and only 2 got the solution, and even then only with hints from Duncker (see the answer at the end of the chapter). By asking people to talk aloud as they tried to solve each problem, Duncker was able to identify a series of typical stages. First, they were drawn to an obvious solution, but they quickly realized that it couldn't work. Gestaltists called this an *impasse*; your mind is *fixated* on that solution, and you're blocked from seeing the problem any other way.

One of the most famous insight problems is the nine-dot problem (Fig. 6.1). If you're having trouble solving the nine-dot problem, put it aside, and now try to solve this problem quickly:

Add one line to IX to make six.

Most people find this quite difficult. It's because you've made two *unwarranted assumptions*: first, that the added line must be straight, and second, that you're trying to make "VI," which would be six in Roman numerals. The solution is to add a curved line, an S, to IX to make SIX.

The nine-dot problem is hard because people make the unwarranted assumption that the four lines have to stay within the box itself; the solution requires that your pencil lines extend outside of this box—thus the famous saying "Think outside the box" (the solution is at the end of this chapter). When you solve an insight problem, Gestaltists argued that it's not due to incremental chains of association; it's because you overcome the fixation, resulting in a sudden *restructuring* of the problem that allows you to realize the solution. In Chapter 5, we learned that

FIGURE 6.1: The nine-dot problem. Connect the nine dots with four connected straight lines without lifting your pencil from the paper.

many cognitive psychologists theorize that problem solving is a search through a multidimensional problem space (pp. 90–91). Insight problems are designed to make that impossible. The solver has to transform the problem space, or move to a completely different problem space (Kaplan & Simon, 1990).

Many of Duncker's classic insight problems are still used today by creativity researchers, such as the candle problem (Fig. 6.2). You're given a box of thumbtacks, some matches, and a candle; your challenge is to light the candle and mount it against the wall.

The candle problem demonstrates another frequent cause of an impasse: *functional fixedness* (Glucksberg, 1962). The solution is to empty the box of thumbtacks and tack it to the wall to create a tiny shelf for the candle, but you're fixated on the function of the box as a container, and that prevents you from seeing that the box could also function as a shelf.

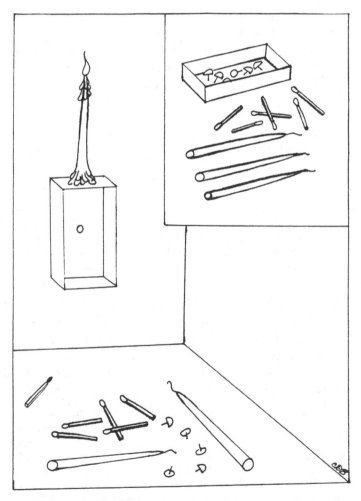

FIGURE 6.2: The candle problem. Using only the items in the picture, mount the candle on the wall and light it. (From page 49 of Dominowksi, R. L., & Dallob, P. (1995). Insight and problem solving. In R. J. Sternberg & J. E. Davidson (Eds.), *The nature of insight* (pp. 33–62). Cambridge: MIT Press.) © 1995 Massachusetts Institute of Technology, by permission of The MIT Press.

In sum, the classic insight experience has three stages. First, a person gets stuck. This is called a *fixation* or *impasse*, and it often results from being misled by ambiguous or irrelevant information in the problem (Dominowski & Dallob, 1995; Smith, 1995). Second, the person reinterprets the problem and applies a new conceptual framework (Schooler, Fallshore, & Fiore, 1995) or restructures the problem (Dominowski & Dallob, 1995). Third, solvers experience their solution as sudden and surprising (Bowden, 1997; Davidson, 1995; Metcalfe, 1986a, 1986b; Metcalfe & Wiebe, 1987; Schooler, Ohlsson, & Brooks, 1993). They're not consciously aware of how they overcame the problem (Gick & Lockhart, 1995; Ohlsson, 1992; Schooler & Melcher, 1995).

Insight problems are very different from *non-insight problems* like simple math equations or trivia questions. Non-insight problems are also called standard, analytic, or incremental problems. Many psychological experiments compare the mental processing involved in insight and non-insight problems to gain understanding into the mental processes involved in creativity. Solving insight problems seems to involve several creativity-related cognitive abilities. DeYoung, Flanders, and Peterson (2008) found that three different cognitive abilities are useful in solving insight problems: divergent thinking, convergent thinking, and breaking frame. Measures of these three abilities each independently predicted insight problem-solving performance.

Rebus problems can also be used to study insight. See if you have a minor sensation of insight when you solve the following three rebus problems.

GSGE	ECNALG	BAN ANA
GESG		
SGEG		

To show you how it's done, here's the answer to the first one, on the left: SCRAMBLED EGGS. (The other answers are at the end of this chapter.)

Boden's (1999) theory of transformational creativity is a modern variant of Gestaltist theory. Boden argued that although some forms of creativity are associations of existing elements, the most important creativity involves a transformation of a conceptual space. Using a linguistic analogy, Boden observed that generating a new sentence from the rules of grammar—a sentence that no one had ever said before—would be creative but it wouldn't be surprising. But transforming a conceptual space is like someone who develops a modification to the rules of grammar themselves, so that completely new kinds of sentences can now be uttered, sentences that wouldn't have been possible, or would have sounded nonsensical before. This kind of creativity couldn't be the result of associations between existing elements, because it would change the way associations themselves could be made.

FIXATION

Gestaltists argue that insight problems are hard because they lead you to "fixate" on an incorrect solution, and this results in an impasse that can be resolved only by a complete restructuring of the problem, never by an incremental series of associations (Weisberg & Alba, 1981). One everyday example of fixation is the tip-of-the-tongue (TOT) phenomenon, when you're trying to remember a person's name, and you've almost got it, but it's just out of your mental reach (Roediger & Neely, 1982; Smith & Dodds, 1999). One study found that 53% of reported TOTs were the result of the incorrect word or name coming to mind first, thus blocking retrieval of the correct word or name (Reason & Lucas, 1984). It's easy to exaggerate TOT fixation simply by displaying false competitors. Once you read the names of these three navigational devices—compass, astrolabe, and protractor—it becomes more difficult to remember the word for the instrument that measures the angle from the horizon to a star in the sky. (It's at the end of this chapter.)

Using similar techniques, researchers have exaggerated the effects of fixation in the laboratory. Smith and Blankenship (1989) found that people did more poorly on rebus problems when they were prompted with a misleading hint. Smith (1995) found that people did worse on partial word completion problems (like L _ D _ E R—the correct answer is LADDER) if they were first presented with a similar but incorrect word (like LEADER).

Finke et al. (1992, pp. 153–158) reported several examples of design studies in which design students and design professionals were presented with either an example design first, or no example. Even when they were told "create something as different from the example design as possible," they were still fixated on the example. Ward (1994) asked people to imagine, draw, and describe animals that might exist on another planet "very similar to earth." He discovered that people assume certain core properties of animals: they all have at least one major sense organ—eyes, ears, legs (98%); their bodies are symmetrical (98%); and they have at least one major functioning appendage like an arm or leg (92%). In a second experiment, Ward asked a different group of people to imagine animals on a planet "very different from earth." On another planet, all of these things might, of course, be different—but the percentages for the second experiment were almost identical to the first.

Experiments like these reveal that imagination is often highly structured; people tend to generate new things that are similar to what they already know. And these experiments demonstrate that fixation and structured imagination interfere with the ability to generate more unusual, original solutions.

IS INSIGHT INCREMENTAL OR SUDDEN?

Gestaltists argue that with creative insight, the mind doesn't incrementally get closer to the solution; the insight happens all at once, as a total restructuring of thought. This claim is related to the research on incubation in Chapter 5. If the Gestaltists are right, then nothing is happening during incubation up until the moment of insight itself. But if unconscious processing is occurring during incubation, and that processing brings you incrementally closer to the solution, that would be evidence against the Gestaltist theory, and (potentially) evidence for associationism.

Several researchers have addressed this question by designing clever experiments that can evaluate whether people get gradually closer to the solution during incubation. Metcalfe (1986, 1987) seemed to confirm the suddenness of insight solutions. She compared non-insight problems with insight problems like the following:

- Imagine that you're a landscape gardener, and your client tells you to plant four trees. But the client wants each tree to be exactly the same distance from each of the other three. How will you do it?

- Find 10 coins. Arrange the 10 coins so that you have five rows, with four coins in each row. How will you do it?

People were asked to solve five insight problems and five non-insight problems. While they worked, every 15 seconds the experimenter pressed a mechanical clicker and asked the subjects to make a mark on a special sheet of paper that indicated how close they thought they were to the solution. A mark at the far left meant they were very cold, and a mark at the far right meant they were very hot. While solving non-insight problems (algebra and trivia problems), the subjects felt warmer and warmer right up to the solution; but for the insight problems, they kept feeling cold until, suddenly, they got the solution. These studies seemed to side with the Gestaltists.

But maybe people are getting closer to the solution during incubation, and they just aren't consciously aware of it. Weisberg and Alba (1981) argued that insight problems are not hard because of fixation, but because you don't have enough of the right kind of prior experience. Most people have a lot of experience with connect-the-dot games, and so when they see the nine-dot problem, they start by going from dot to dot. They soon realize that this strategy doesn't work, but they don't have any experience with other strategies.

Weisberg and Alba wondered what would happen if people were given a hint—if they were told to go outside the boundaries of the square. But when people were stumped, and the researchers gave them the hint, almost everyone stayed stuck. Then they got another hint: the researchers drew the first line of the solution. A few more people were able to get it. When the researchers showed the remaining people the second line of the solution, everyone solved the problem. Showing people simple hints didn't help that much—they had to be shown almost half the solution before they could finish the task.

In their next experiment, Weisberg and Alba trained people to connect the dots in triangles by going outside the triangles (Fig. 6.3). People who received this training did much better on the nine-dot problem. Extending this work, Lung and Dominowski (1985) found that more people solved the nine-dot problem after they'd had practice on other dot-connecting problems that required lines to be extended beyond the dots—9% of the control group solved the problem, but 22% of those who had previous practice solved it. And if in addition to practice they were advised to consider a line-extending strategy, their success rate shot up to 59%.

Perkins (1981) used talk-aloud protocols as people solved insight problems, like the 544 BC coin that an antique dealer realized was a forgery ("How does he know?"). The talk-aloud protocol forces people to make conscious what might normally be unconscious. Perkins found that you can always see the series of mental steps people take toward getting the solution, and rejected the Gestaltist argument (Perkins, 1981, p. 71).

Kotovsky and Fahey (in Kotovsky, 2003) videotaped 32 people solving insight problems, and like Metcalfe, took feeling-of-warmth ratings every 30 seconds. Watching the videotapes, they noticed that many people generated the correct solution early on but didn't realize it was a solution (their warmth ratings didn't increase) and recognized that it was the solution only

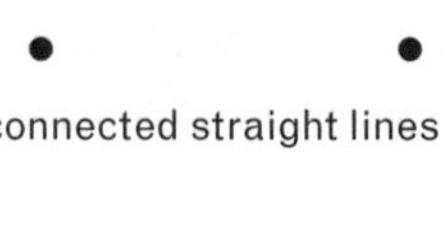

•   •

•   •

FIGURE 6.3: Connect the dots with two connected straight lines without lifting your pencil from the paper.

several minutes later. In other words, people generate the solution without realizing they've done so.

There's other evidence that the mind is getting closer to the solution, based on experiments using a priming paradigm: when people work on an RAT triplet but don't get the answer, they're then faster at reading the actual target word than they are at reading an unrelated word (Beeman & Bowden, 2000; Bowden & Beeman, 1998). Interestingly, this effect is stronger for the left visual field (right hemisphere) than for the left hemisphere (Bowden & Jung-Beeman, 2003a; Fiore & Schooler, 1998).

Bowers et al. (1990) developed two new tasks to examine unconscious processes: the dyads of triads (DOT) task and the accumulated clues task (ACT). The DOT task presents subjects with two RAT triplets; the three words of the coherent triad had a fourth target word, but the three words of the incoherent triad did not:

A	B
PLAYING	STILL
CREDIT	PAGES
REPORT	MUSIC

Answer: Triplet A, CARD

Subjects were asked to solve the coherent triad, and if they couldn't, to select which one they thought was the coherent triad. When subjects who couldn't identify the answer word were forced to choose A or B, a greater number of them chose the real triplet—58% (better than guessing, which would have put them at 50%).

In the accumulated clues task, Bowers first chose a target word, and then created a list of 15 words that were all remote associates of that word. For example, for the word SQUARE the 15 words were: times, inch, deal, corner, peg, head, foot, dance, person, town, math, four, block, table, box. Bowers found that the average person had a first hunch after 10 words and were pretty sure after 12 words. A lot of the time, they reported getting a sudden "Aha!" sensation, as if the idea had suddenly popped into their head in a discontinuous fashion. But even before people knew they were getting closer, their guesses got closer and closer to SQUARE, in a strikingly linear pattern (Fig. 6.4). But these same people often said the answer had come to them in a sudden flash of insight—even though the researchers had just gathered data showing it didn't happen that way (Bowers, Farvolden, & Mermigis, 1995).

SUMMARY

These experiments contradict several Gestaltist beliefs about creativity:

1. *We're blocked from creativity by our past experiences and our unwarranted assumptions.* To the contrary, Weisberg and Alba (1981) found that eliminating the false assumption makes the problem only slightly easier.
2. *When you break out of your fixation, the solution should come quickly and easily in a spark of insight.* Instead, the "outside" hint opens up a new problem-solving domain, but that domain also requires expertise and prior experience.

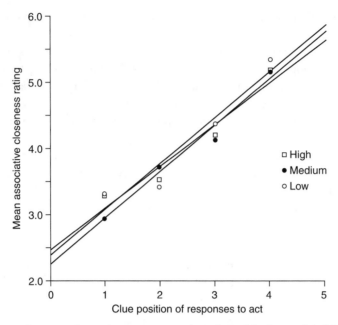

FIGURE 6.4: **Average closeness of guess to answer as people performed the Accumulated Clues Task (ACT), grouped into high/medium/low by how quickly they got the answer.** (From page 91 of Bowers, K. S., Regehr, G., Balthazard, C., & Parker, K. (1990). Intuition in the context of discovery. *Cognitive Psychology, 22*, 72–110.)

3.   *Insight solutions are independent of prior knowledge.* In reality, training in similar problems helps immensely.

Creativity isn't about rejecting convention and forgetting what you know. Instead, it's based on past experience and on existing concepts. These findings are consistent with studies of incubation in Chapter 5 in that they provide evidence for the spreading activation theory of incubation.

In the Western cultural model, great creative insights represent a complete break with the past, and they're more likely to occur when you reject convention. But research on the moment of insight hasn't supported this belief. There's now a consensus among scholars that the moment of insight can be explained in terms of previous experience and acquired knowledge. Becoming more expert, and acquiring more knowledge, prepares you for more and better insights rather than interfering with them.

STAGE 6: COMBINE IDEAS

Psychological studies of insight suggest that the Gestaltist theory is largely false. Rather than a sudden restructuring, the mind seems to gradually get closer to the correct solution. And that's pretty consistent with the associationist theory that creativity occurs when existing ideas combine together. The existing ideas that form the new mental structure aren't new; they're familiar ideas and conventions that are already in the domain and that have been internalized by the creator.

But the 19th-century associationists never explained the mechanisms whereby associations are formed in the mind. Fortunately, the past several decades of research in cognitive psychology have revealed a great deal about how the mind combines ideas.

CROSS-FERTILIZATION

All decisive advances in the history of scientific thought can be described in terms of mental cross-fertilization between different disciplines.

—Arthur Koestler, (1964, p. 230)

Throughout history, many creative advances have resulted from combinations. That's one reason that successful creativity is more likely when you work on multiple projects at the same time; while you're hard at work on one project, the other projects are incubating beneath the surface. And incubation often brings together ideas from more than one project, resulting in a combination that the creator hadn't been consciously aware of.

Other combinations result when people switch fields, introducing techniques or modes of thought that are already standard in another domain. This is particularly common in science (Koestler, 1964; Simonton, 1988b, p. 127). Landsteiner's previous background in chemistry facilitated his isolation of blood groups; Kekulé's early desire to become an architect may have influenced the way he thought about the structural basis of organic chemistry; and Helmholtz said that his invention of the ophthalmoscope resulted from an interest in optics that predated his training as a physician.

Some researchers hypothesize that field-switchers have more novel insights because of their marginality. This is Belief 4 of the Western cultural model: that outsiders are more likely to have breakthrough ideas. Because they're at the margins of the discipline, the thinking goes, they'll be more likely to have innovative ideas because they're less constrained by the domain (Black, 2000). But scientists haven't found any evidence that marginality contributes to creative output. Other researchers explain these multidisciplinary insights by appeal to *analogical thinking*—the idea that analogies between distinct domains allow the individual to perceive patterns in a way that wouldn't be apparent to someone working in only one domain (see below).

The best explanation seems to be that if you have multiple projects and multiple domains internalized, you'll have a larger pool of basic ideas. As a result, your chance of having an interesting new combination during incubation goes up significantly (Simonton, 1988b, p. 128).

CONCEPTUAL COMBINATION

Our understanding of creativity cannot be complete without a detailed and rigorous treatment of the cognitive processes from which novel ideas emerge.

—Thomas B. Ward (2001, p. 350)

Of all of the mental processes studied by cognitive psychologists, the ones thought to be most relevant to creativity are conceptual combination, metaphor, and analogy (Mumford & Gustafson, 1988, p. 27; Ward, Smith, & Vaid, 1997a, 1997b). It's creative to combine two concepts to make a single new one; for example, a "boomerang flu" is a flu that goes away and then returns. In analogies, some properties from one mental model are transferred to another; famously, de Mestral had the idea for Velcro when he began to wonder how burrs clung to his clothing (Hill, 1978).

Combining concepts is a basic human cognitive ability; you can easily imagine concepts like PANCAKE BOAT and RUBBER ARMY. Maybe a pancake boat is a very flat boat, with a low profile that allows it to go under low-lying bridges. Or, it could be a new kind of restaurant that serves breakfast while touring the harbor. These creative combinations probably have properties that aren't held by the component concepts. A RUBBER ARMY might have the property "makes a good toy for a boy" but most people don't think of "good toy" when they hear the words army or rubber. Properties that aren't true of either base concept are called *emergent attributes*, and people are incredibly creative in coming up with emergent attributes for noun combinations. Hampton (1987) asked people to imagine nine different new concept pairs, like "a piece of furniture that is also a fruit" and "a bird that is also a kind of kitchen utensil." People came up with 170 properties—an average of 19 properties for each pair. For "a piece of furniture that is also a fruit," emergent attributes included "Regenerates itself" and "Grows slowly." For "a bird that is also a kitchen utensil," attributes included "Serrated beak" and "Strong jaw."

Hampton found that people rarely come up with emergent attributes when they combined familiar conjunctions, such as "birds that are also pets," because they simply recall instances of that category—like a parrot—and list properties of the parrot, such as "talking." Emergent attributes are much more likely for combinations that result in imaginary objects, because these often require complex problem solving and they have to develop stories about how it might work.

Before we can explain how the mind combines or reorganizes concepts or ideas, we need a theory of what a mental concept looks like. Since the 1970s, cognitive psychologists have proposed *schema* or *frame* models that represent a concept as a data structure, with variables or "slots" that can be set to different values. For example, the schema for "vehicle" would include slots for:

- *Number of wheels* (two for a motorcycle, four or more for a truck, but with a default value of four for a car)
- *Number of seats* (again, a default value of four). Slots can themselves be filled with representationally complex concepts; the "seat" in the vehicle schema can be a motorcycle seat or a car seat, which have very little in common.

Each concept is stored in the mind as a set of *properties* and the *values* of each property. For example, the concept "spoon" has properties and values "shape: long and thin," "function: holds liquid," "size: (large or small)" and "material: (wooden, metal, or plastic)." For many concepts, the properties interact with each other; most of us think that wooden spoons are large spoons and that metal spoons are smaller. Noun concepts are complex and include many properties and values. In contrast, adjectives are simple, often having only one property and one value (the adjective "red" has the property "color" and the value "red").

In a simple model of conceptual combination, the *selective modification model* (Smith & Osherson, 1984), the adjective's property and value modify that property of the noun, but everything else stays the same.

Hampton (1987) proposed a second model of conceptual combination, the *attribute inheritance model*: the combination inherits all of the properties of the component concepts—with the constraints that no features that are impossible for one of the components will be inherited, and necessary features of each component must be inherited. For example, a "car boat" is the union of the properties of both car and boat: has four wheels, has four seats, has a propeller coming out of the bottom, and floats. In this model, no novel properties emerge, and conceptual combination is essentially not creative. But his model works only for combinations where the members of the compound set are also members of the component sets (all "car boats" are both "cars" and "boats"). When the combination requires one of these constraints to be violated, as with "fruit furniture" (furniture is durable, but fruit is perishable), people have to generate emergent attributes. Properties that are true of one concept but incompatible with the other are discarded; a pet shark can't be "warm and cuddly" as most pets are. If two properties are incompatible, you have to choose one; a pet "lives in a domestic environment" but a shark "lives in the ocean" and a pet shark can live in only one place. When combining, you'll pick the one that's most compatible with all of the other properties of the new concept.

Some combinations can't be explained by this simple additive model of combination. For the combination "small spoons," the "material" property is more likely to be "metal," but for the combination "large spoons," the "material" property is more likely to be "wooden," implying that the size and material properties are not independent (Medin & Shoben, 1988). When Wisniewski (1997) examined cases when speakers combined nouns to make novel concepts, such as "car boat" and "boomerang flu," he discovered that in many cases, the two component concepts themselves change when they're combined. For example, you're likely to envision a car boat to be a convertible, because boats typically don't have roofs covering the passengers; and its wheels are likely to be recessed in the bottom, rather than visible at the sides like a normal car. Thus conceptual combination isn't simply additive, but involves *emergence*—the combination is "greater than the sum of the parts," and the component concepts are changed as they merge into the higher-level concept.

In a third form of combination, *property mapping*, you take just one value from one concept and merge it with the second concept. Wisniewski and Gentner (1991) gave the example of "pony chair" as a combination that can't be explained by selective modification or attribute inheritance. If you combine "pony chair" and imagine a brown-and-white chair, this is what you're doing: taking the "color: brown and white" value of pony, and setting the color property of chair to the same value.

In a fourth, more complex form of combination, you look for a relation that can bring the two concepts together. When imagining a "book box," you might think of the relationship of "containing"; "box" is the container and "book" is what is contained.

A fifth model, the *concept specialization model* (Cohen & Murphy, 1984), proposes that general knowledge drives the combination of categories. The properties of the combination "apartment dog" can't be determined without knowing a lot about apartments and dogs and how they interact (dogs are not lived in by people, for example!). This model seems closest to what we mean by *creative* combination, because the way to construct the combination isn't obvious and algorithmic; it requires creativity, and the combination manifests emergent properties.

The most creative combinations result from a sixth process known as *structure mapping,* in which you take the complex structure of one concept and use it to restructure the second concept. There are two different kinds of structure mapping, *internal structure* and *external structure.* If you combine "pony chair" and envision a chair shaped like a pony, that's internal structure mapping—you took the internal structure of a pony and applied it to the chair. If you instead envisioned a small chair, that's external structure mapping. What you're thinking of isn't a chair that's smaller than a pony, but a chair that's smaller than other chairs—in the same way that a pony is smaller than other horses.

ENHANCING THE CREATIVITY OF COMBINATIONS

The more similar two concepts are, the easier it is to use the simpler strategies of combining properties and values. When concepts are very different, you have to use the more complex strategies of property mapping or structure mapping, and these strategies result in the most novel and innovative combinations. Wisniewski (1997) compared how people combined similar entities ("skunk squirrel") and very different entities ("hatchet squirrel") and found that only the distant combinations had emergent features. Wilkenfeld (1995, unpublished) and Poze (1983) also found evidence that combinations that are more remote are more creative. Wilkenfeld (1995) compared similar combinations (guitar harp) and distant combinations (motorcycle carpet), and found that the distant combinations resulted in more emergence (see summary in Ward, Smith, & Finke, 1999, p. 203). Mumford, Baughman, and Sager (2003) found that people's tendency to create high-quality and original new features for the new category that they've combined is related to their performance on creative problem-solving tasks (p. 59; cf. Finke et al., 1992). These findings confirm Mednick's proposal that creativity involves remote associations— the claim underlying the remote associates test (RAT; see pp. 44–46).

Wisniewski and Gentner (1991) came up with some words that were relatively similar, and other words that were very different. They did this by identifying important dimensions that apply to all nouns, such as "artifact" versus "natural," and "count noun" (nouns that can be preceded with numbers, like "five chairs") versus "mass noun" (nouns that can't be numbered, like "sand" or "paper"). Then they gave subjects pairs of concepts that varied on these dimensions, and pairs that did not. For example, a "pony chair" combines a natural concept and an artifact concept, both count nouns; "snake paper" combines two concepts that are different in two ways: one is natural and one is an artifact, and one is a count noun and the other a mass noun (Table 6.1). They discovered that the further apart two concepts are, the more likely it is that a creative idea will result.

There's intriguing evidence that with very simple instructions, people can be encouraged to generate more original and higher-quality combinations. Baughman and Mumford (1995) found if they asked subjects to identify the shared and unshared features of different categories, they generated more original, high-quality new categories. Mumford et al. (1997) found that when people combined related categories, feature-mapping instructions contributed to quality and originality; when they combined unrelated categories, metaphor instructions contributed. And when subjects were asked to think about category features, and also to think metaphorically about what those features might represent (bird flight symbolically represents "freedom"), they generated more original, higher-quality category combinations than in a simple feature-search-and-mapping procedure. These findings lead us to the next section, about the importance of metaphor and analogy in creative thinking.

Table 6.1: Concepts Combined in the Experiments in Wisniewski and
Gentner (1991)

Group 1: Count nouns		Group 2: Mass nouns		Group 3: Count nouns	
Natural	*Artifact*	*Natural*	*Artifact*	*Natural*	*Artifact*
Frog	Box	Clay	Candy	Elephant	Book
Moose	Chair	Copper	Chocolate	Fish	Car
Robin	Pan	Sand	Glass	Pony	Clock
Skunk	Rake	Stone	Paper	Snake	Ladder
Tiger	Vase	Sugar	Plastic	Squirrel	Pencil

METAPHOR AND ANALOGY

There's historical and anecdotal evidence that new ideas often result from *conceptual transfer*, also known as metaphorical or analogical thinking. Some of the most significant advances in science originated in analogies (from Holyoak & Thagard, 1995, pp. 186–188):

- Sound/water waves
- Earth/small magnet
- Earth/moon
- Light/sound
- Planet/projectile (Newton's apple)
- Lightning/electricity
- Respiration/combustion
- Heat/water

Metaphors are conceptual combinations that involve mapping a *vehicle* concept onto a *topic* concept. Similarly, analogy involves mapping knowledge from a *base* domain to a *target* (Gentner, 1989). In the metaphor "Children are sponges," *children* is the topic and *sponges* is the vehicle. In the analogy "Sound is like water waves," *sound* is the topic and *water waves* is the vehicle. The underlying cognitive processes are the same as with conceptual combination; understanding metaphors and analogies involves mapping features or information from one concept to another—from the vehicle to the topic. *Sponges* have the property of *soaking things up*; when this property is mapped to *children*, it suggests that children "soak up knowledge." Figurative combinations are even more creative: a "dirty dog" refers to a person who's just done something bad, and a "dirty mind" is said of someone who thinks vulgar thoughts.

In the 1960s, the famous consulting firm Synectics, Inc. used four forms of analogy to help businesses generate creative insights (Gordon, 1961, pp. 36–53):

- *Personal analogy*: Personal identification with the elements of the problem. If you're designing a new banking system, imagine yourself as the bill, being mailed to the customer and eventually returned with payment.
- *Direct analogy*: Compare parallel concepts or technologies (sound to water waves). Synectics later renamed this technique *Example* (Prince, 1970).
- *Symbolic analogy*: Use poetic phrases, objective and impersonal images to describe the problem—aesthetic, holistic, immediate. Synectics later renamed this technique

Book Title—the task is to develop a two-word, poetic title for your book about X (Prince, 1970).

- *Fantasy analogy*: "How do we in our wildest fantasies hope this will work?"

"Metaphor" tends to be a literary term, typically referring to verbal comparisons or properties. The metaphor "My love is like a rose" transfers the property "beautiful" from a rose to a person, but no other features of the rose transfer. In contrast, "analogy" refers to a transfer of whole structures and relations; it's often three-dimensional and spatial, referring to process or mechanism. The analogy that resulted in Velcro—the mechanism that gets a burr stuck in a dog's fur might be transformed into a clothing fastener—transfers the entire spatial mechanism; no verbal processing is involved.

Ortony's (1979) *salience imbalance model* is inspired by a subtle difference between a metaphor and a conceptual combination: with metaphor, properties that are salient in the vehicle aren't central to the topic. Salient properties of sponges include that they're used for cleaning, they can be held in your hand, and they don't weigh much, and none of these properties are applied to "children" in the metaphor "children are sponges." In a conceptual combination like "bathroom sponge," the salient features of sponge are central to the combination and they remain part of the combination. Analogies often involve salient properties—for example, with the analogy between water and sound, some conceptions of water have the property of "waves"—but not always.

Gentner (1989) explained analogical reasoning with a *structure mapping theory* that distinguishes between attributes (simple features like size, weight, color) and relations (higher-order relations between components or features). Most conceptual combinations are combinations of attributes, but don't combine relations. Research has shown that people tend to choose analogies based on attributes, but that these analogies tend to be superficial; better success results from focusing on relations. For example, Gick and Holyoak (1980) studied Duncker's original x-ray problem (p. 108 above), by first giving subjects an analogous story to see if they would be able to "transfer" the solution to the x-ray problem:

> A fortress was located in the center of the country. Many roads radiated out from the fortress. A general wanted to capture the fortress with his army. The general wanted to prevent mines on the roads from destroying his army and neighboring villages. As a result the entire army could not attack the fortress along one road. However, the entire army was needed to capture the fortress. So an attack by one small group would not succeed. The general therefore divided his army into several small groups. He positioned the small groups at the heads of different roads. The small groups simultaneously converged on the fortress. In this way the army captured the fortress.

If you've already looked up the answer to the x-ray problem at the end of the chapter, you can spot the parallels. (If not, take a look now at the "dispersion" solution at the end of this chapter.) The researchers gave ten people this story, and then gave them the x-ray problem and told them to use the fortress solution to help them solve it. In a first experiment, seven of them got the answer right away; for the other three, the researchers told them again to think back to the fortress story, and after the hint, those three got it too. Ten other people heard the x-ray problem but not the fortress story, and none of them came up with the dispersion solution. Gick and Holyoak told everyone to talk out loud into a microphone while they thought about the problem; when they later studied the tapes, they found a process of gradual, incremental work toward the solution—once again, no evidence for sudden insight.

In another experiment, people were given the fortress problem first, and then given the tumor problem, either with a "hint" to think about the previous problem, or no hint. With a hint, 11 of 12 (92%) got the solution; only 3 of 15 in the no-hint condition solved it (20%). In a final experiment, after the fortress story but with no hint to use it, 41% solved the tumor problem; then with a hint to think about the fortress problem while solving the tumor problem, another 35% got the solution.

These experiments show that people often don't notice the relevant analogies, and don't always use what they know to solve problems. The key is to notice or remember a source problem, and then to transfer over to the target the relevant aspects of the source. But noticing a good source problem is difficult; it helps to focus on deeper underlying relations, rather than surface properties. Sometimes, creative people make their own analogies by constructing a source that doesn't actually exist, or by modifying the source to make it fit the target better. Additional research is needed on these creative processes.

IMAGERY

The research I've reviewed so far focuses on a type of thinking known as *propositional* or *linguistic*. Since the 1970s, psychologists have known that our minds have another deep-rooted mode of thinking: the spatial or visual mode. Researchers have discovered that invented images are more likely to be novel if they bring together unusual parts or are combined in unique ways—consistent with the above studies of remote combinations (Finke & Slayton, 1988). Finke (1990) asked people to combine three-dimensional shapes (Fig. 6.5) to create an invention in a product category (Table 6.2). The parts can be combined in any way, they can be any size, and they can be made of any material. Two of the shapes can be distorted: shape 6 is a wire or string that can be any shape and length, and shape 7 is a tube that can be any shape and length.

Finke (1990) hired independent judges to rate the creativity of every student's invention. Amazingly, over one third of the students came up with new inventions that a team

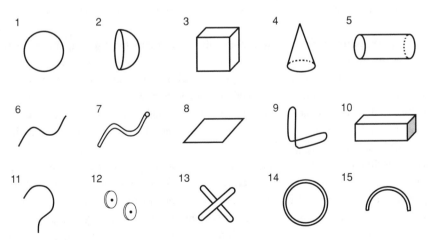

FIGURE 6.5: Give yourself one minute to use any three shapes to make an interesting, potentially useful object. (Based on shapes in Finke, 1990, p. 41)

Table 6.2: Invention Categories

1. FURNITURE
2. PERSONAL ITEMS
3. TRANSPORTATION
4. SCIENTIFIC INSTRUMENTS
5. APPLIANCES
6. TOOLS AND UTENSILS
7. WEAPONS
8. TOYS AND GAMES

of independent judges rated as both practical and original. What's most interesting is how the students came up with these new ideas. When they started, they had no idea of what they were going to create. But as they began to experiment, putting the parts together in various ways, what unfolded was unpredictable and surprising, even to the creators and even to Finke, who designed the experiment. Forty-nine of the 175 inventions were judged to be creative.

Finke (1990) conducted a second experiment with a different group of students. He assigned them three shapes at random, and told them to combine the shapes to make "an interesting and potentially useful object." They weren't told anything about an invention category. Then, after their invention was finished, Finke gave them a randomly assigned invention category, and told them to reinterpret their invented shape—but without changing how it looked—so that it functioned as an invention within that category. When the category was assigned *after* the combination was made, 65 of 120 were creative—a much higher proportion of creative inventions than the first experiment.

The lowest rate of creative inventions was generated in a third experiment, when the category was randomly assigned but people were allowed to select any three parts. Only 17 of 193 inventions were creative. To summarize:

- Assigned category, choose any three parts: 17 of 193 are creative
- Assigned category and three parts: 49 of 175 are creative
- Assigned three parts and then category after combination: 65 of 120 are creative

You might think that reducing the constraints would make the students more creative, but just the opposite happened. With so many choices, it was too easy to start with a fixed idea of what they wanted to create, and then just pick and choose the objects and category that best realized their pre-existing concept. The original task, with more constraints, forced them to start creating before they knew what they were doing, thus allowing unexpected insights to emerge. And in particular, when people were forced to re-interpret their own combination, their creativity shot up dramatically.

These experiments confirm the importance of problem finding, because when people don't know the category, and have to re-interpret their existing combination, they have no choice but to do problem finding. When people create using a problem-finding style, the creations often seem to have been intended from the beginning, even though they emerged unpredictably from a combinatorial process. Finke (1990) called this *the illusion of intentionality*, and it's one of the factors that contribute to our false belief in the idealist theory of creativity.

TYPES OF INSIGHTS

In this chapter I've reviewed psychological research on the two stages of idea generation: generating ideas (Stage 5) and combining ideas (Stage 6). These studies can help us understand the various kinds of creative ideas that people have.

Ohlsson (1992) followed Gestaltist theory and proposed three forms of restructuring:

- Elaboration—A representational change resulting from the addition of new information. This is necessary if the original representation is incomplete.
- Re-encoding—Rejecting some of the original interpretation and developing a new representation.
- Constraint relaxation—Changing an inappropriate representation of the goal state. For example, with the nine-dot problem, the inappropriate representation is the unwarranted assumption that the four lines have to be inside of the nine-dot box.

Cunningham et al. (2009) proposed six mechanisms that people might use to solve an insight problem, and they argued that most so-called insight problems include three or more of these six:

1. The need to redefine spatial assumptions (moving an object, changing perspective)
2. The need to change defined structures or forms (dismantle, change, or restructure an existing form or figure and then develop something new)
3. The degree of misdirection involved (insight problems that contain misleading information)
4. The difficulty in verifying what the solution would look like: with the ten-coin triangle problem, solvers know exactly what the solution will look like. With the nine-dot problem, the goal state isn't directly visible.
5. The sequential character of the problem: Some problems can be solved with a number of steps, getting you incrementally closer to the problem; others can't.
6. Figure–ground reversals

Weisberg (1995) presented the following dimensions that can be used to classify insight problems:

1. Does the problem involve a discontinuity in thinking? If yes, proceed to question 2.
2. Does the discontinuity come about through restructuring? If the solution is similar to the initial incorrect solution, then there has been no restructuring. If it requires a change in analysis, then there is restructuring. Proceed to question 3.
3. Is restructuring the only way the solution can come about? If there are other ways of producing the solution, then this is a "hybrid insight problem"; if not, it is a "pure insight problem."
4. If a hybrid insight problem, then we have to ask, in every case and for every subject, was restructuring actually used in this case?
5. If a pure insight problem, then we can ask the key question: How did restructuring happen?

Under this strict definition, many so-called insight problems aren't really insight problems at all.

Sternberg's *propulsion model* (Sternberg, 2003) metaphorically envisioned creative contributions as trajectories in space—similar to the early cognitive "search space" theories of creativity (Chapter 5, pp. 90–91):

- Replication: Keep the field where it is
- Redefinition: Redefine the field from a different viewpoint
- Forward incrementation: Move the field forward, in the direction it is already going
- Advance forward incrementation: A more rapid forward movement than the expected rate
- Redirection: Redirect the field to a different direction
- Reconstruction: Move the field back to an imagined past state, but with the goal of redirecting
- Reinitiation: Start the field from scratch
- Integration: Bring together two formerly distinct ways of thinking

Also working in the cognitive search space tradition, Boden (2004b) distinguished between three types of creativity:

- Combinatorial—Bring together familiar concepts in unfamiliar and surprising ways. Does not involve a conceptual space.
- Exploratory—Within an existing conceptual space, existing styles or rules are used to generate novel structures/ideas (identify a new point within the conceptual space).
- Transformational—Some defining dimension of the conceptual space is altered.

These distinctions have a complex relationship with the little c/Big C distinction I presented in Chapter 1. All solutions of insight problems represent little c creativity, because they're novel for the person, but they (mostly) aren't Big C creative. In general, it seems that many of the most significant historical creations have emerged from the more transformative forms of insight; Sternberg's *reinitiation* or *integration*, or Boden's *transformation*. But in some cases, exceptional creativity has resulted from more straightforward processes such as *redefinition* and *combination*. A creation's ultimate social importance can't be predicted from the mental processes involved; it results from a social process, as described in Chapters 11 through 15.

CONCLUSION

> *The range of viewpoints [on insight] . . . spans the entire spectrum from those who imply that creativity is little more than building on an initial insight to those who deny that moments of insight have any importance whatsoever for creative processes. The majority view, however, falls in between, with flashes of insight discussed as small but necessary components of creativity*
>
> —Tardif and Sternberg, (1988, p. 430)

This epigraph is from the conclusion to Sternberg's 1988 book *The Nature of Insight*. Now we have over 20 more years of research and a much clearer understanding of what happens during incubation and insight. The consensus view emerging from the research has confirmed Tardif and Sternberg's "majority view" in 1988: although creativity rarely comes fully formed in a magical moment of insight, the daily work of a creator is filled with small moments of insight-like ideas.

Every so often a creator will have a subjective experience of a moment of insight. But even though it may seem sudden to the creator at that moment, in retrospect it can always be traced to the prior work that the creator was engaged in. By analyzing the sketches and notebooks leading up to the insight, we see that each innovation resulted from a connected, directed, rational process (Weisberg, 1986, 1993). For example, Jackson Pollock's paintings are now known to have emerged from a long process of careful deliberation, and not from a sudden insight in the middle of the night followed by a binge of paint pouring. Charles Darwin's groundbreaking innovation—the theory of natural selection—is now known to have emerged from a multitude of smaller, incremental insights (Gruber, 1974). This history is lost unless there are detailed notebooks (like those left by Darwin) or video recordings (made by creativity researchers who happen to be present during the process). But in every case where researchers have access to this kind of detailed record, they can trace the final product from a complex series of small mini-insights that are closely tied to the work of the moment.

We're very far from Creativity Belief 4, that major contributions are more likely to come from people far outside an area. This is most clear from studies of Stages 1 and 2 of the creative process; only experts in a domain have the knowledge to identify good problems. In this chapter, we've learned that creative ideas are more likely to emerge when your mind is filled with relevant and closely related material. However, there's a partial truth to this creativity belief: major contributions come from people who can bring in a different conceptual framework and integrate it with their deep expertise. For greater creativity, it's better if you aren't so narrowly specialized that you have blinders on, unaware of everything else in the world. Cross-fertilization and distant combinations are often the source of surprising creative insights.

KEY CONCEPTS

- Associationist theory
- Gestaltism
- Insight and non-insight problems
- Impasse, fixation, and functional fixation
- Unwarranted assumptions
- Restructuring
- Cross-fertilization
- Conceptual combination
- Metaphor, analogy, and conceptual transfer
- Creative imagery
- Types of insight

THOUGHT EXPERIMENTS

- Can you think of a sudden moment of insight that happened to you recently? What were you doing when it happened? What occurred in the days leading up to it?

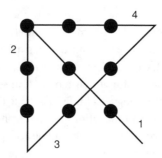

FIGURE 6.6: Solution to nine-dot problem.

- Have you ever combined two things that weren't supposed to go together? (Children do this all the time, for example when they mix root beer and Sprite.) What gave you the idea? Did it work well?
- Do you spend all of your time focused on one particular area? Or are you more of the kind of person who dabbles in a lot of different things? In either case, what are the lessons for you from this chapter and the one before?

ANSWERS TO PROBLEMS

Tumor problem dispersion solution: Use many separate rays, originating at different devices located around the body, and each at a low intensity. If they are oriented so that all of the rays converge on the tumor, the intensity at that point will be sufficient to destroy it, without damaging any surrounding tissue.

Rebus problems: backwards glance; banana split

Navigational device: sextant

SUGGESTED READINGS

Boden, M. (2004). *The creative mind: Myths and mechanisms* (revised and expanded second edition). London: Routledge.

Bowers, K. S., Farvolden, P., & Mermigis, L. (1995). Intuitive antecedents of insight. In S. M. Smith, T. B. Ward & R. A. Finke (Eds.), *The creative cognition approach* (pp. 27–51). Cambridge: MIT Press.

Csikszentmihalyi, M., & Sawyer, R. K. (1995). Creative insight: The social dimension of a solitary moment. In R. J. Sternberg & J. E. Davidson (Eds.), *The nature of insight* (pp. 329–363). Cambridge: MIT Press.

Finke, R. (1990). *Creative imagery: Discoveries and inventions in visualization*. Hillsdale, NJ: Erlbaum.

Finke, R. A., Ward, T. B., & Smith, S. M. (1992). *Creative cognition: Theory, research, and applications*. Cambridge: MIT Press.

Holyoak, K. J., & Thagard, P. (1995). *Mental leaps: Analogy in creative thought*. Cambridge, MA: MIT Press.

Ward, T. B., Smith, S. M., & Vaid, J. (1997a). Conceptual structures and processes in creative thought. In T. B. Ward, S. M. Smith, & J. Vaid (Eds.), *Creative thought: An investigation of conceptual structures and processes* (pp. 1–27). Washington, DC: American Psychological Association.

C H A P T E R 7

THE CREATIVE PROCESS, PART 3

I n the Western cultural model, creativity is associated with Stages 5 and 6, generating ideas and combining ideas (Beliefs 1 and 2). But extensive studies of the creative process have revealed that much of creativity occurs in Stage 7, selecting ideas, and Stage 8, externalizing ideas. These aren't just simple "implementation" activities; they actively contribute to creativity. After discussing these two stages, I conclude this chapter by summarizing all eight stages, what the eight-stage model leaves out, and how the later chapters will build on this material to complete our explanation of creativity.

STAGE 7: SELECT THE BEST IDEAS

> *It is not merely a question of applying rules, of making the most combinations possible according to certain fixed laws. The combinations so obtained would be exceedingly numerous, useless and cumbersome. The true work of the inventor consists in choosing among these combinations so as to eliminate the useless ones.*
>
> —Poincaré, (1913, p. 28)

After a new insight or combination emerges into consciousness, the creator has to evaluate the insight to determine if it's really a good idea. After all, many creative insights turn out to be bad ideas, even though they were appealing enough to jump from incubation to consciousness. Scientific insights may turn out to be wrong; business innovations may not work for some technical reason; new artistic ideas that sound good in theory might look banal, derivative, or uninteresting once executed. This critical thinking stage is sometimes referred to as *convergent thinking*. In the two-stage "balloon" model, convergent thinking follows the idea generation or "divergent thinking" phase of the creative process.

The evaluation stage is fully conscious; to be effective, the creator has to draw on an immense amount of knowledge about the domain. Is the insight an idea that someone already had in the past? Is the insight kind of interesting, but trivial? How can this insight be integrated with the creator's existing body of work? Or does it require a complete rethinking of a career, perhaps something the creator isn't prepared to do at this time? How can this insight best be connected to other work that's going on in the domain? Evaluation and revision contribute directly to creativity by leading to greater originality and impact (Lonergan, Scott, & Mumford, 2004).

Blair and Mumford (2007) reviewed the literature on idea evaluation and identified 12 attributes that people use when evaluating ideas:

1. Risky (high probability of incurring a loss)
2. Easy to understand
3. Original
4. Complete description (provides detailed steps needed to make the idea work)
5. Complicated
6. Consistent with existing social norms
7. High probability of success
8. Easy to implement
9. Benefits many people
10. Produces desired societal rewards
11. Time and effort required to implement
12. Complexity of implementation

Then they conducted an experiment to see which of these attributes were most often used. They gave participants the task of reviewing grant proposals to a fictional nonprofit organization. They found that people preferred ideas that fit social norms, were likely to produce the desired outcomes quickly, were complex to implement, were easy to understand, and benefited many people. They were likely to reject risky and original ideas. But when they were placed under time pressure, people selected riskier and more original ideas—suggesting that what people are doing with their extra time is screening out risky and original ideas.

A second study (Dailey & Mumford, 2006) found that when people evaluate new ideas, they consider two main issues: the resources needed to implement the idea, and the consequences of implementing the idea. In this study, students were given three new ideas from either the education or public policy domains; the six real-world ideas related to private vouchers; transforming a large urban high school; turning around low-performing schools; reducing subway graffiti; community crime prevention; and neighborhood redevelopment. The students were asked to evaluate each idea on ten resource considerations and on ten outcome consequences (similar to the above list). The students were overly optimistic in their evaluations compared to what actually happened when the idea was implemented in the real world. But surprisingly, Dailey and Mumford (2006) found that students who had more familiarity with the domain of education or public policy were even *more* optimistic—more likely to underestimate resource requirements and overestimate positive consequences. This is probably a case of having just enough knowledge to be dangerous, as the saying goes—a bit of familiarity, but not full domain expertise (p. 379).

Evaluation decisions are based on the creator's internalized model of the domain and field; these allow a quick evaluation of novelty and appropriateness (Bink & Marsh, 2000; Csikszentmihalyi & Sawyer, 1995). So evaluation processes should be domain-specific. Horng and Lin (2009) found that the evaluation of new culinary dishes is based on a combination of professional technique, aroma, taste, and texture, color, modeling and arrangement, garnish, dishware, handling of ingredients, and overall assessment. Eisenberg and Thompson (2003) found that evaluations of improvised music are based on perceived complexity, creativity, and technical goodness.

With most creative works, many different evaluative criteria are relevant, and it's not always obvious which of the various criteria are the most important, or how they relate to each other.

For example, there's often a tension between evaluating an idea for its correctness or appropriateness, and evaluating an idea for its originality. The balance changes over the course of a career, and the field and domain continue to change as well, requiring a change in evaluative criteria to stay current: a scientific discovery that's novel in 1960 isn't likely to seem novel in 2010.

THE PRODUCTIVITY THEORY

Many creators say that the best way to have a good idea is to have a lot of ideas, and then just get rid of the bad ones. I call this the *productivity theory*. Poet W. H. Auden said that "the chances are that, in the course of his lifetime, the major poet will write more bad poems than the minor" because they "write a lot" (quoted in Bennett, 1980, p. 15). Geniuses are wrong in a similar proportion to everyone else; they generate more wrong ideas than average folks simply because they generate more ideas overall (Weisberg, 1986). Galileo insisted that planets traveled in a circular orbit, even with the increasing evidence for comets' elliptical paths; Darwin undermined his evolutionary theory with the doctrine of pangenesis, now known to be false; and Einstein persisted in arguing for a unified theory, and rejected quantum mechanics.

In addition to such anecdotal evidence, quantitative research supports the productivity theory. Simonton (1988a, 1988b) measured the raw productivity of historical creators, and also identified the creations that had stood the test of time as truly significant works. He found a strong relationship between productivity and significant creations: when comparing individuals, the creators who had the highest overall lifetime output were the people most likely to have generated a significant work. Even when he measured year-to-year productivity within a single person's lifetime, he found that the most productive periods were the times when a creator was most likely to have generated a really significant work (1988b, pp. 88–91). A 1998 study of patented inventions (Huber, 1998) found that in a group of 408 full-time inventors, those with the most patents were those whose patents were judged the most significant.

At first glance, the productivity theory seems to defy common sense. It seems that the person who's really productive must be a little sloppy, cutting corners and generating second-rate work. It seems like the most important works would require a lot of time and energy to generate; the person who generates a really important work should be the one who dedicates all of his or her energies to that one project. We can all conjure up an image of a solitary creator, working alone for years in isolation, growing increasingly eccentric, until he finally comes out of the lab or studio to reveal the masterpiece that will change the world. But this doesn't happen very often; it's more of a myth than a reality.

THE RELATION BETWEEN GENERATING IDEAS
AND EVALUATING IDEAS

Aren't convergent thinking and critical thinking the complete opposite of creative thinking? If so, then these should turn out to be distinct constructs, and people who are good at generating ideas might not be good at critically evaluating them. For example, Sternberg and Lubart's (1995) triarchic model suggests that analytic ability and creative ability are distinct and don't covary. However, most creativity studies have revealed that creative people are good at critically evaluating their many ideas and selecting the best one, and that creativity is enhanced by a close relationship between divergent and convergent thinking.

Runco (2003) argued that real-world creativity requires both idea generation and critical evaluation abilities; in several studies, he showed a relationship between DT scores and accuracy of judging the originality of their own ideas. Runco and Dow (2004) asked people to complete three DT tasks (uses, pattern meanings, and consequences) and asked those people to go back and grade the creativity of their ideas. A high grade was considered accurate if the idea was unique or uncommon. They found that DT scores correlated with accuracy scores: people with lots of unique ideas also were better at grading their ideas. Runco and Chand (1994) found that evaluative accuracy for one's own ideas was correlated with the production of original ideas on two different tasks ($Rs = 0.48, 0.61$). Evaluative accuracy is related to DT among adults (Runco & Vega, 1990) and children (Runco, 1991b).

Silvia (2008b) had people complete four DT tasks (two Unusual Uses tasks: brick and knife, and two instances tasks: things that are round and things that make a noise) and then asked them to pick their top-two most creative ideas for each task. Three raters then rated all of their responses on a scale of 1 to 5. It turns out that people's choices of their top two responses covaried strongly with judges' ratings. People high in Openness had more creative responses on the DT tasks, and their evaluations were more accurate (their top-two choices were more likely to match the judges' ratings); people high in Conscientiousness had the opposite pattern. Idea generation was highly related to evaluation ability; people who generated more ideas were also more likely to choose two ideas that matched the judges' ratings.

These studies are all in the laboratory and don't require any domain expertise, so it's hard to say what their implications are for real-world creative domains. But the findings are consistent with what we know about Big C creative work; we know that creativity requires a substantial amount of domain knowledge (see Chapter 5), and domain expertise contributes both to the ability to generate original ideas, and also to the ability to judge the most original ideas.

EVALUATING YOUR OWN IDEAS VERSUS EVALUATING OTHERS

> *Because contributors themselves remember their hardships and frustrations, they will have very different favorites among their conceptions in comparison with those of their contemporaries. Creators are thus not the best judges of their own work.*
>
> —Simonton, (1988b, p. 90)

In general, people mostly agree when they rate the creativity of others—as we learned from studies of the consensual assessment technique (Chapter 3, pp. 41–42). Runco and Vega (1990) had groups of three adults—teachers, parents, and other adults—rate the creativity of children's ideas. Their inter-rater agreement was around 0.90. The originality of each idea was then measured by calculating how common the idea was—they counted up the number of individuals who gave each idea, and ideas listed by fewer individuals were rated as more original. The accuracy of each adult rater was then determined by how closely their ratings matched this originality measure. When the adults were told to rate the *popularity* of each idea rather than the creativity of each idea, their ratings more closely corresponded to the originality measure.

But social psychology has often found that people judge their own and others' actions differently. Judgments of others tend to focus on the person, and judgments of self focus on the context. This is known as *the divergent perspectives hypothesis*. There haven't been many studies of whether this applies to creativity judgments. Perkins (1981, pp. 122–125) reported a series of experiments that show that people's judgments of how confident they are that they have made the right decision are completely unrelated to how accurate they actually are. Many effective creators seem to realize this, because they often put a work or idea aside and evaluate it again later, or solicit feedback from a trusted colleague. In general, people are more accurate in rating their own ideas for uniqueness, and more accurate in rating others' ideas for popularity (Runco & Chand, 1994; Runco & Smith, 1992).

SUMMARY

The man who first proposed the concept of divergent thinking, J. P. Guilford (1967), argued that all five of his proposed operations—cognition, memory, divergent production, convergent thinking, and evaluation—proceed in parallel during the creative process, with "evaluation all along the way" (p. 329; also see Runco, 2003, and Sawyer, 2003b). Stage 1, finding a good problem, requires evaluation: it's important to be able to select which question or problem is the best one to focus on. Stages 2 and 3 require evaluation too: you have to decide what to learn, and what to look at. Mumford, Supinski, et al. (1996a, 1996b, 1996c) found evidence that when people were asked to select concepts that would help them solve problems—an activity associated with Stages 2 and 3—those who selected concepts that were loosely organized around long-term goals generated higher-quality and more original solutions. In Stage 4, your subconscious mind is constantly deciding what to focus on in the external environment that might be potentially related to your ongoing work. Mumford et al. (2003) provided evidence that some evaluation precedes the divergent thinking of Stage 5.

The ability to accurately judge the creative potential of an idea is essential to being an effective creator. The above studies demonstrate significant relationships between evaluation ability and other measures of creativity, such as DT tests. Although we generally think that the critical thinking of evaluative thought follows a more creative stage, evaluation is likely to be a constant presence in the creator's work.

STAGE 8: EXTERNALIZE THE IDEA

Making things is a physical business, expressed in effort and sweat . . . It is not a period of quiet reflection but a real intellectual and physical engagement with the material.
—John Tusa, (2003, p. 11)

Creativity research has tended to focus on the early stages of the eight-stage creative process—particularly on the idea-generating stage. But a lot has to happen to make any idea a reality. Successful creators are skilled at executing their ideas, predicting how others might react to them and being prepared to respond, identifying the necessary resources to make them successful, forming plans for implementing the ideas, and improvising to adjust their plans as new information arrives. These activities are important in all creativity, but are likely to be even more important in practical domains such as technological invention and entrepreneurship (Mumford, 2003; Policastro & Gardner, 1999).

This final stage is mostly conscious and directed; it's where the creator takes the raw insight and molds it into a complete product. Most creative insights aren't fully formed; the creator has to use his or her immense domain knowledge—in particular, how to work using the materials and techniques of the domain—to convert the idea into a finished work. Monet had the idea to paint a haystack in a field at different times of the day and the year; but his idea wouldn't have gone anywhere unless he also had the painting skills to mix the right colors, to hold and to move the brush to make the right strokes, and to compose the overall image to get the desired effect. A person might have a new idea about how to design a computer word processor, but that idea would be lost to history if the person didn't know how to write computer programs.

Many people hold to the idealist theory and think that this final stage isn't really "creative" *per se*; it's no more than a straightforward execution of the idea. Having the idea is the creative part of the process; making the idea a reality might involve skill, craftsmanship, and dedication—but not creativity. However, researchers have discovered a lot of creativity during this final stage. Externalizing an idea often results in other ideas and follow-on ideas. And the most creative people don't wait until their idea is fully formed before they start externalizing it; in the early stages of the process, when the idea may be just an intuition or a bare outline, they start putting it out in the world. Externalizing is essential to the problem-finding process that's used by the most successful creators (Chapter 5, pp. 90–93).

It's not that hard to demonstrate that externalization can contribute to creative thinking. First, try to solve this problem in your head:

> A man had four chains, each three links long. He wanted to join the four chains into a single, closed chain. Having a link opened cost two cents and having a link closed cost three cents. The man had his chains joined into a closed chain for fifteen cents. How did he do it?

Most people find this problem almost impossible to solve mentally. If you can't get the answer, then sketch the four chains on a piece of paper and try it again, using your pencil to move the chains around. Once it's sketched out, most people find it much easier to solve.

In Bransford and Stein's (1984) IDEAL problem-solving framework, "Externalizing" is one of five core elements of effective problem solving (it's the "E" in "IDEAL"). Try this problem, from their book:

> There are three separate, equal-sized boxes. Inside each box are two separate, small boxes, and inside each of the small boxes are four even smaller boxes. How many boxes are there altogether? (p. 29)

People who try to solve this problem in their heads find it to be difficult. Performance always improves when people draw pictures of the problem; try it yourself. It's because the problem is a bit too complex to represent and solve mentally, and this is true of most real-world creative domains. If you've solved it in your head, there's a good chance you'll overlook one aspect of the problem (see the answer at the end of this chapter).

John-Steiner (1985) interviewed over 70 exceptional creators—from composer Aaron Copland to author Anaïs Nin—and studied their diaries and notebooks. She also studied the notebooks of another 50 historical creators such as Diego Riviera, Leo Tolstoy, and Marie Curie. She found that the one characteristic that all these creative people shared—across such varied fields as painting, theater, and science—was how often they put their early thoughts and inklings out into the world, in sketches, short writings in notebooks, and quick prototypes. Instead of one big leap, their ideas emerged over time as they engaged with these external images. Many of these exceptional creators use an "inner shorthand" to make their creative ideas visible, which John-Steiner called "languages of the mind." Exceptional creators often report using visual images, or visual analogies, to come up with creative solutions (Shepard, 1978). Albert Einstein, for example, always said that he thought in pictures: "words do not play any role in my thought; instead, I think in signs and images which I can copy and combine" (Hadamard, 1945, p. 142). Like Einstein, many engineers and physicists say that visual analogies are central to their creativity (John-Steiner, 1985, p. 212).

Perkins (1981) described how Rudolph Arnheim analyzed the process that Picasso used to generate his famous painting *Guernica*. Arnheim was able to do this because Picasso made 61 sketches and took 7 photographs of his work as it unfolded. Perkins pointed to the similar examples of Darwin's notebooks and Beethoven's musical drafts, and concluded, like John-Steiner, that exceptional creators always work with concrete representations (p. 218).

Larkin and Simon (1987) found that when they gave experts a verbal description of a problem, the first thing they did was to make a visual diagram—which helped them search for relevant information, recognize important patterns and relations, and manage the complexity of the problem challenge. Verstijnen (1997) found that people who used sketches during a task discovered more problems, and solved more problems, than people who didn't sketch. Meyer (1989) found that when people used visual diagrams, they were better at coming up with improvements to inventions.

Finke and Slayton (1988) asked people to combine three randomly chosen shapes (Fig. 7.1) and "make a recognizable figure." Independent judges determined that 15% of the 872 resulting combinations were creative. When they asked people what strategies they used, they said they started combining parts in a trial-and-error fashion and waited to see what emerged—a bottom-up strategy requiring externalization, rather than a more top-down strategy of mentally deciding on an overall final design and then trying to fit parts into it.

Markman, Yamauchi, and Makin (1997) assembled pairs of people in their lab and had them build LEGO spaceship models together, using the required 52 pieces, along with the picture of the finished product on the box. The twist was that one of the two people was forbidden to touch

FIGURE 7.1: Imagine combining three of the shapes to make a recognizable shape or pattern. (Figure 1 on page 253 of Finke, R. A., & Slayton, K. (1988). Explorations of creative visual synthesis in mental imagery. *Memory & Cognition, 16*(3), 252–257. Copyright 1988 Psychonomic Society, Inc. With kind permission from Springer Science+Business Media B. V.)

the pieces, and the other wasn't allowed to see the picture. So they had to talk constantly to finish the spaceship. After finishing, each person was asked to sort the pieces into groups and to name each group. They came up with categories like *bar* (for a thin brick), *tile* (for a flat brick), or *prism* (an odd-shaped piece that was triangular). They also grouped the bricks according to their function in the model, like *rocket* for a piece that went at the back of the spaceship.

The researchers then asked a separate group of people to build the model all alone, with no need for communication. When the people in this second group were later asked to sort the pieces, they just piled them according to color. Talking about building the spaceship had caused the first group to create richer, more complex categories.

The key is to identify the right way to represent the problem (Day, 1988); with most creative problems, there are many different possible ways to externalize it, and the most effective way to represent a problem changes with the nature of the problem. Some problems are easier to solve with a verbal representation; others are easier visually or mathematically (Halpern, 1989; Hayes, 1989). In many cases, when people have trouble making progress, it's because they're using external representations that aren't the most appropriate ones (Day, 1988).

Although I've placed *externalizing* as the final and eighth stage, in creative lives it happens throughout the process. I've already pointed out that the problem-finding style of work is unavoidably dependent on externalization, and I showed you that you're more likely to have insights about the four-chain problem when you externalize it. Furthermore, externalizing is often critical to Stage 7, selection, because it can be hard to tell if an insight is a good one without building or sketching the idea, at least part way. Exceptional creators almost always end up modifying the initial insight during externalization. The raw insights that emerge from Stages 5 and 6 are nothing but rough outlines; the creator usually experiences a continued cycle of mini-insights and revisions while elaborating the insight into a finished product.

Finke, Ward, and Smith (1992) provided a potential explanation of the value of externalizing. In their two-stage Geneplore model, first *generative processes* generate cognitive structures. Generative processes include memory retrieval, association, mental synthesis, transformation, analogical transfer, and category reduction. Then, *exploratory processes* are used to examine the implications of these cognitive structures; exploratory processes include attribute finding, conceptual interpretation, functional inference, contextual shifting, hypothesis testing, and searching for limitations (1992, p. 2). They argued that exceptional creators often generate and externalize *preinventive structures* during the first stage—ambiguous, preliminary, or prototype version of an idea that can be interpreted in many potential ways during the exploratory stage. Certain preinventive structures lend themselves to creative interpretation during the exploration stage; they have the properties in Column 3 of Table 7.1.

McNeill (1992) studied gesturing in a wide range of storytelling and problem-solving situations and found that gesturing often contributes to thinking. He discovered that when people aren't allowed to gesture, they find it harder to solve problems. Schwartz (1995) found that when people gestured with their hands, they solved gear problems like this faster:

> Five meshing gears are arranged in a horizontal line much like a row of quarters on a table. If you turn the gear on the furthest left clockwise, what will the gear on the furthest right do?

Individuals and groups can solve these problems pretty easily, but they have to twist their hands in the air to simulate the gears turning. But Schwartz discovered that when two people worked together on these problems, they used more gestures, and as a result they discovered the

Table 7.1: The Geneplore Model

Generative Processes	Preinventive Structures	Preinventive Properties	Exploratory Processes
Retrieval	Visual patterns	Novelty	Attribute finding
Association	Object forms	Ambiguity	Conceptual interpretation
Synthesis	Mental blends	Meaningfulness	Functional inference
Transformation	Category exemplars	Emergence	Contextual shifting
Analogical transfer	Mental models	Incongruity	Hypothesis testing
Categorical reduction	Verbal combinations	Divergence	Searching for limitations

(Based on p. 20 of Finke, R. A., Ward, T. B., & Smith, S. M. (1992). *Creative cognition: Theory, research, and applications.* Cambridge: MIT Press.)

underlying *abstract parity rule*: If the number of gears is an odd number, the first and last gear turn in the same direction. Only 14% of people working alone discovered the rule, but 58% of the pairs did. It's because the pairs had to communicate to solve the problem, so they externalized their thoughts more frequently and in a greater variety of ways.

Do you really have to externalize it in the world? Maybe there's a cheaper and easier shortcut: you just visualize it in your mind's eye. Finke et al. (1992, p. 59–60) tested this hypothesis and found that mental imagery was just as creative as physical manipulation of the shapes. When Helstrup and Anderson (1991) replicated this experiment, they found that in the physical condition people were able to generate more patterns than with mental imagery (but not more creative patterns). Verstijnen et al. (1998) redid the experiment with experienced sketchers and found that when they externalized their visual process, they were much more creative. But with non-experienced sketchers, there was no difference—as with the previous studies.

Mental visualization can be a useful technique, but it works for only relatively simple problems. As the number of parts increases, externalization becomes increasingly important, because with complex mechanical combinations, your mind doesn't have the conscious capacity and working memory to represent it internally (Finke et al., 1992, p. 60).

These studies of externalization show that it's much more than a simple "implementation" or "execution" of an idea that's already fully formed in the mind. Just the opposite: externalizing early ideas, and then manipulating and working with them, contributes directly to the still-emerging and uncertain creative process. This is why the famous product design firm IDEO instructs their groups to "be visual," "get physical," and "the space remembers" (Boynton & Fischer, 2005; Kelley, 2001). As John Tusa says in the epigraph above, creativity takes "effort and sweat," not just "quiet reflection." This research supports the action theory and rejects the idealist theory (Chapter 5) and challenges two of the beliefs of the Western cultural model: Belief 1, that the essence of creativity is the moment of insight, and Belief 2, that creative ideas emerge mysteriously from the unconscious.

GOING BEYOND STAGE THEORIES

> *You have these ideas, and then you work on them. As you work on them, you get new ideas . . . one makes the other one come out.*
>
> —Sculptor Nina Holton, quoted in Csikszentmihalyi & Sawyer, (1995, p. 353)

In the daily stream of thought these . . . different stages constantly overlap each other as we explore different problems.

—Graham Wallas, (1926, p. 81)

The eight-stage model is a useful way of capturing all of the cognitive processes involved in the creative act. The eight stages are domain-general; the creative process in all domains, from science to technological invention to fine art painting, involves these stages. But creativity rarely unfolds in a linear fashion. The mental processes associated with the eight stages can overlap, or cycle repeatedly, or sometimes appear in reverse order. This is why some creativity researchers prefer to describe them as eight "disciplines" or "habits of mind" that are associated with highly creative individuals; some of the models I cited in Table 5.1 (p. 89) are presented this way, including Burnard et al., 2006, and Scott et al., 2004.

When we do intensive biographical studies of the origins of transformative discoveries and inventions, we see that creativity emerges over time in a complex, nonlinear fashion. Many creative products evolve over months and years, so these biographical studies involve a lot of work—poring over journals, notes, preliminary drafts, and letters. One of the most influential biographical studies was Howard Gruber's close reading of Darwin's journals. Gruber's analysis of how Darwin's theory emerged over 13 years filled a rather large book (Gruber, 1974). Most such studies require a book to tell the whole story—other examples include Seth Shulman's story of the Wright brothers, Glenn Curtis, and the airplane (2002), and Tom Standage's story of how the telegraph emerged from Samuel Morse's 12-year effort (1998). Creativity researchers are still fleshing out theories about these long-term processes: how long creative periods are sustained, and how one multiyear period is succeeded by a shift to another research question or another style of visual representation (cf. Gruber, 1988; Feinstein, 2006; Nakamura & Csikszentmihalyi, 2003). These questions can't be answered using the experimental methodologies that predominate in psychological research; they require more qualitative, biographical methods. These *ontogenetic studies* have found that creators work on many problems at the same time, and that in most creative careers, an insight often generates more questions than it answers. A creative insight that generates good questions is more valuable than one that conclusively answers every known question but doesn't suggest any further research. The task of solving a good question leads to the reformulation of difficult problems and the generation of completely new questions.

Rather than coming in a single moment of insight, creativity involves a lot of hard work over an extended period of time. While doing the work, the creator experiences frequent but small mini-insights. Unlike the mysterious insight of our Western cultural model, these mini-insights are usually easy to explain in terms of the hard conscious work that immediately preceded them. We still don't know exactly what goes on in the mind, but we do know that insights are based in previous experiences, they build on acquired knowledge and memory, and they result from combinations of existing mental material.

Psychoanalytic theorists were some of the first to explore the cyclical nature of mini-insights. Arieti (1976) noted that "complex works that can be divided into parts" involve a series of insights, with incubation occurring throughout the creative process, and he concluded that the stages of creativity aren't separated through time (p. 18). Rothenberg (1979) argued that creation isn't found in a single moment of insight but is "a long series of circumstances . . . often interrupted, reconstructed, and repeated" (p. 131). He criticized stage theories, arguing that "the temporal distinction made between inspiration and elaboration in the creative process is an incorrect one; these phases or functions alternate—sometimes extremely rapidly—from start to finish" (p. 346). And Vinacke (1952) argued that in many creative fields, especially fine art, the final work results from a series of insights beginning with the first draft or sketch and continuing until the work is completed. Incubation doesn't occur in a particular stage but operates to varying degrees throughout the creative process. For example, poems and plays don't emerge suddenly or completely but are gradually developed through a process of many incubations and insights (see Chapter 17).

At the end of our exploration of the eight-stage creative process, it seems clear that the moment of insight is overrated. It's only one small component of a complex creative process, and it's not all that mysterious. The typical creator experiences many small mini-insights every day, and these mini-insights can be traced back to the material he or she was consciously working on. We only think we see dramatic leaps of insight because we didn't observe the many small, incremental steps that preceded it. Instead of the light bulb, a better metaphor for an insight would be the tip of an iceberg, or the final brick in a wall. Creative activities require problem solving and decision making throughout the process, and each one of these decision points involves a small amount of creative inspiration; when these mini-insights are viewed in the context of the ongoing creative work, they no longer seem so mysterious. Creativity researchers today agree that "creativity takes time . . . the creative process is not generally considered to be something that occurs in an instant with a single flash of insight, even though insights may occur" (Tardif & Sternberg, 1988, p. 430).

The mythical view of a moment of insight overly simplifies the complexity and hard work of most creativity. Instead of a single glorious moment, creators experience small insights throughout a day's work, with each small insight followed by a period of evaluation and externalization; these mini-insights only gradually accumulate to result in a finished work, as a result of a process of hard work and intellectual labor of the creator.

SUMMARY

> Artists of all kinds . . . work regularly, daily—some work every day of their lives, long hours, too—systematically and intensively . . . Most reach their end by repeated addressing of the problem, whether on the canvas, the poet's notebook, or the composer's score. . . Some continue to revise work even after it appears to be completed. . . In almost every case the acts of creation represent a huge accrual of effort, of second and third thoughts, doubts, hesitations, uncertainties and inner debate.
>
> —John Tusa, (2003, p. 10)

Our three chapters about the creative process have given us a fairly detailed understanding of creativity:

- Creativity is not a special mental process, but involves everyday cognitive processes.
- Creativity results from a complex combination of basic mental capabilities.

- Creativity does not occur in a magical moment of insight; rather, creative products result from long periods of hard work that involve many small mini-insights, and these mini-insights are organized and combined by the conscious mind of the creator.
- Creativity is always specific to a domain. No one can be creative until he or she internalizes the symbols, conventions, and languages of a creative domain.

Decades of research show that innate creative talent is overrated. The research confirms the wisdom of Thomas Edison's famous aphorism: "genius is one percent inspiration and ninety-nine percent perspiration" (Bartlett, 1955, p. 735). Researchers have discovered that creativity is largely the result of hard work. There's no magic, no secret.

Although these are all important scientific findings, we haven't yet explained creativity. Psychology provides only one piece of the complex explanation of creativity that modern science has developed. In the next three chapters, we'll explore exciting new individualist approaches to the study of creativity: computation, biology, and neuroscience. And after that, in Part III, we'll broaden our scope to examine sociocultural approaches to creativity.

A problem with studying the cognitive mechanisms that underlie each of the eight stages is that complex human activities like creativity are built out of many mental mechanisms. It's a long way from conceptual combinations like "car boat" to the development of creative products that transform a domain (as noted by Simonton, 1997b; Ward, Smith, & Vaid, 1997a, p. 4), and one might reasonably wonder whether exceptional creativity really occurs in the same way. For the most part, cognitive psychologists haven't examined real-world creativity directly; instead, they focus on everyday cognitive processes (Ward, Smith, & Vaid, 1997a, p. 1)—little c creativity rather than big C creativity.

Most big C creative innovations are complex combinations of many concepts, not a single concept. The leap from a single conceptual combination to a world-changing creative innovation is a pretty big one. For example, Dunbar (1997) found that creative ideas in science emerge over the course of a collaborative meeting, from a series of small changes, each produced by a different cognitive mechanism—one by analogy, another by induction, yet another by causal reasoning (see Chapter 20). Cognitive psychology can help us understand each of these component mechanisms, but it may not help us much with understanding the complex processes that ultimately result in the emergence of Big C creativity, because these influential works probably contain hundreds of concepts in complex combinatorial relations (cf. Ward, Smith, & Vaid, 1997a, p. 18). Although creative insights emerge from simple underlying cognitive processes, the emergence of a full-fledged creative product, over time, is often so complex that it can't be traced to any one mental event or process (Finke, Ward, & Smith, 1992, p. 8). For these reasons, many prominent creativity researchers believe that the experimental psychology I've reviewed in these three chapters cannot, alone, provide a full explanation of exceptional creativity (Csikszentmihalyi, 1988a; Simonton, 1997a).

IMPLICATIONS FOR ASSESSMENT

The cognitive approach suggests that the more creative individuals are those who develop and use alternate understandings; identify facts that are inconsistent with these understandings; apply multiple understandings while they are solving a problem; and reorganize elements within an understanding (Mumford & Gustafson, 1988, p. 32). This sounds an awful lot like everyday, ordinary problem solving—like those early cognitive psychologists who argued that creativity was just problem solving, back in the 1960s and 1970s (see pp. 90–91). Creativity is based on the same common cognitive capabilities as is problem solving. But it's the unique combination of cognitive capabilities that results in the emergence of that special behavior that we call creative.

Much creativity research still uses the DT tests that emerged in the 1950s and 1960s (see Chapter 3). But we now have a much better understanding of the cognitive processes underlying creative behavior, and that gives us a potential framework for developing new forms of assessment—tests that could measure, among other things, conceptual combination skills, problemfinding skills, and reinterpretation skills (cf. Mumford, 2003). This is a promising area for future research.

AFTER THE EIGHT STAGES

The eight stages lead up to the generation of a creative work: a product that can be shared, discussed, and communicated. What typically happens next is that trusted colleagues or mentors provide editorial suggestions, and the creator takes those to heart and returns back to the work. Revising and improving isn't always a straightforward task; it often involves creativity as well, so the creator has to revisit the eight stages. Very little creativity research has focused on this process of revision, the dialog that occurs with the work itself after a first draft has been generated. This is a promising area for future research.

The eight stages of creativity focus exclusively on what goes on in the creator's mind. But there's substantial evidence that real-world creativity is deeply collaborative and embedded in social organizations, and creativity researchers have neglected the more collaborative elements of creativity (Mumford, 2003; Sawyer, 2007). For example, the product design firm IDEO has formalized an approach to creativity that's based in real-world creative work processes (Kelley, 2001). It has five stages—understand the market, observe real people, visualize new concepts, evaluate and refine prototypes, and implement the new concept—and none of the five is purely individual. Social and organizational approaches to creativity will be the topics of Chapter 12 on group creativity, and Chapter 13 on organizational creativity.

KEY CONCEPTS

- Convergent thinking
- The productivity theory
- The divergent perspectives hypothesis
- Externalization
- The nonlinearity of the creative process
- Assessments based on cognitive psychology research

THOUGHT EXPERIMENTS

- Think of a time you had an idea that, upon closer examination, turned out to be not such a good idea. What evaluative process made that clear? Why didn't you see it right away?

- Are you a scribbler? For example, during a lecture or while on a phone call? Does scribbling help you think?
- Do you tend to draw concrete pictures of abstract ideas and concepts? If not, give it a try the next time you're working with abstract, conceptual material.
- Select one of the eight stages, and propose a way to assess a person's ability to successfully engage in that stage.

ANSWER TO PROBLEM

There are 33 boxes (3 large, 6 medium, and 24 small).

SUGGESTED READINGS

Bransford, J. D., & Stein, B. S. (1984/1993). *The IDEAL problem solver* (2nd edition). New York: W. H. Freeman and Company.

Dailey, L., & Mumford, M. D. (2006). Evaluative aspects of creative thought: Errors in appraising the implications of new ideas. *Creativity Research Journal, 18*(3), 367–384.

John-Steiner, V. (1985). *Notebooks of the mind: Explorations of thinking.* Albuquerque, NM: University of New Mexico Press.

Perkins, D. N. (1981). *The mind's best work.* Cambridge, MA: Harvard University Press.

Runco, M. A. (Ed.) (2003). *Critical creative processes.* Cresskill, NJ: Hampton Press.

Silvia, P. J. (2008). Discernment and creativity: How well can people identify their most creative ideas? *Psychology of Aesthetics, Creativity, and the Arts, 2*(3), 139–146.

COMPUTER SIMULATIONS OF THE CREATIVE PROCESS

In October 1997, an audience filed into the theater at the University of Oregon and sat down to hear a very unusual concert. A professional concert pianist, Winifred Kerner, was performing several pieces composed by Bach. Well, actually, not all of the pieces had been composed by Bach, although they all sounded like they were. This was a competition to determine who could best compose pieces in Bach's style, and the audience's task was to listen to three compositions, one by Bach and the others by two different composers, and then vote on which was the real thing. Yet this information-age competition had a novel twist: the audience had been told that one of the composers was a computer program known as EMI (Experiments in Musical Intelligence) developed by David Cope, a composer and a professor of music at the University of California, Santa Cruz. The audience knew that of the three compositions, one would be an original Bach, one would be a composition by Steve Larson—a professor of music theory at the University of Oregon—and one would be by EMI. For each of the performances, the audience had to choose which of the three composers had generated it.

The audience first voted on Professor Larson's composition. He was a little upset when the audience vote was announced: they thought that the computer had composed his piece. But Professor Larson was shocked when the audience's vote on EMI's piece was announced: they thought it was an original Bach! After the concert, Professor Larson said, "My admiration for [Bach's] music is deep and cosmic. That people could be duped by a computer program was very disconcerting" (quoted in Johnson, 1997, p. B9). (Compositions by EMI in the styles of composers from Bach and Beethoven to Stravinsky and Webern can be heard at: http://artsites.ucsc.edu/faculty/cope/, accessed Aug. 22, 2011.)

Back in 1962, the famous cognitive scientists Allen Newell, J. C. Shaw, and Herbert Simon predicted that "within ten years a computer will . . . compose music that is regarded as aesthetically significant" (1962, p. 116). They weren't just bluffing; already by 1958, they'd written a computer program for the ILLIAC computer that composed music using Palestrina's rules of counterpoint, and the composition was performed and recorded by a string quartet (p. 67). Thirty-five years later, at the University of Oregon, their prediction finally seemed to come to pass.

The first computer was conceived by Charles Babbage in the 19th century; he called it the Analytical Engine. His complicated contraption of gears, pulleys, and levers was never built, but it caused a lot of Victorian-age speculation. Babbage's friend Ada Augusta, the Countess of Lovelace, famously wrote that "the engine might compose elaborate and scientific pieces of music of any degree of complexity or extent . . . [but] the Analytical Engine has no pretensions whatever to *originate* anything. It can do whatever we *know how to order it to perform*" (Augusta, 1842, notes A and G).

Like Lady Lovelace long ago, most of us don't believe that computers can be creative. If EMI seems creative, then many of us would attribute that creativity to programmer David Cope; after all, the computer is only following the instructions that Cope provided in his line-by-line program. There is no place for the computer in the Western cultural model of creativity. Computers are incompatible with the Romantic and New Age idea that creativity is the purest expression of a uniquely human spirit, an almost spiritual and mystical force that connects us to the universe. Very few books about creativity research contain anything about these programs, which I call *artificial creators*.[1] This omission is surprising; although I have many criticisms of artificial creators, they're without doubt some of the most intriguing and exciting developments among the individualist approaches to creativity. In this chapter, we'll examine some of the most successful artificial creators.

Artificial creators are developed by researchers in the field of *artificial intelligence (AI)*. Since the 1950s and 1960s, these computer scientists have been developing computer programs to simulate human cognitive processes; one of the first was the *general problem solver* I described in Chapter 5, and one of the most famous of these programs is Deep Blue, IBM's chess-playing program that defeated the world champion, Garry Kasparov, in 1997. The field of AI is deeply interconnected with cognitive psychology, and many artificial creators are simulations of the cognitive processes we learned about in Chapters 5, 6, and 7.

AI researchers generally conceive of creativity as a set of mental operations on a store of mental structures. For example, Dasgupta's (1994) *computational theory of scientific creativity* describes creativity

> solely in terms of (1) symbolic structures that represent goals, solutions, and knowledge and (2) actions or operations that transform one symbolic structure to another such that (3) each transformation that occurs is solely a function of facts, rules, and laws contained in the agent's knowledge body and the goal(s) to be achieved at that particular time (Dasgupta, 1994, p. 39).

The claim that creativity is rule-governed is directly opposed to the Western cultural model of creativity. It's also incompatible with some models of the creative process that we reviewed in Chapters 5, 6, and 7. But even among researchers who believe human creativity is very different from these computer programs, there are many who nonetheless agree that these simulations have intriguing implications for our theories of the creative process.

THE ARTIFICIAL PAINTER: AARON

Harold Cohen was an English painter with an established reputation when he moved to the University of California, San Diego in 1968 for a one-year visiting professorship. He worked

---

1. A notable exception is Boden's 1991 book *The Creative Mind*, republished in 2003 in a second edition by Routledge.

FIGURE 8.1: A painting by Harold Cohen's computer program AARON. (Reprinted with permission of Harold Cohen)

with his first computers there, and after the experience he chose to stay in the United States and explore the potential of the new technology. In 1973, while Cohen was a visiting scholar at Stanford University's Artificial Intelligence Laboratory, he developed a program that could draw simple sketches. He called it AARON (Fig. 8.1). In the decades since, Cohen has continually revised and improved AARON. AARON and Cohen have exhibited at London's Tate Gallery, the Brooklyn Museum, the San Francisco Museum of Modern Art, and many other international galleries and museums, and also at science centers like the Computer Museum in Boston (McCorduck, 1991).

Each night, he programs AARON to generate 150 pieces; he selects the best 30, and then decides to print about 5 or 6 (Cohen, 2007). Cohen thinks of AARON as "an apprentice, an assistant, rather than as a fully autonomous artist. It's a remarkably able and talented assistant, to be sure, but if it can't decide for itself what it wants to print . . . then, clearly, it hasn't yet achieved anything like full autonomy" (Cohen, 2004).

Harold Cohen's system is the best-known and most successful example of a computer program that generates visual art. An ever-growing number of artists are making electronic art; recent years have witnessed exhibits and criticism (see Candy & Edmonds, 2002). Cohen trained AARON to create drawings by using an iterative design process; at each stage, Cohen evaluated the output of the program, and then modified the program to reflect his own aesthetic judgment about the results. We can see the history of this process in his museum exhibits: AARON's earlier drawings are primarily abstract, its later drawings become more representational.

Starting in 1986, Cohen worked at getting AARON to draw in color. He developed a "rule base" for how it would develop a complete internal model of which colors would go where. AARON's design benefits from Cohen's years of expertise: "nothing of what has happened could have happened unless I had drawn upon a lifetime of experience as a colorist. I've evidently managed to pack all that experience into a few lines of code, yet nothing in the code looks remotely like what I would have been doing as a painter" (Cohen, 2007).

Some would say that AARON isn't creative, for the same reason that Lady Lovelace gave: because the programmer provides the rules. Cohen agrees that AARON doesn't demonstrate human creativity because it's not autonomous: an autonomous program could consider its own past, and rewrite its own rules (Cohen, 1999). AARON doesn't choose its own criteria for what counts as a good painting; Cohen decides which ones to print and display. In one night, AARON might generate over 50 images, but many of them are quite similar to one another; Cohen chooses to print the ones that are the most different from one another (personal communication, Jan. 14, 2004). To be considered truly creative, the program would have to develop its own selection criteria; Cohen (1999) was skeptical that this could ever happen. Cohen's process of creating AARON fits in well with what psychologists have learned about the creative process (Chapters 5, 6, and 7): his creativity was a continuous, iterative process, rather than a sudden moment of insight or the creation of a single brilliant work.

You might say that the drawings aren't by AARON, that they're really by Cohen—Cohen, along with a very efficient assistant. Cohen (2007) agreed that the paintings are his: "I'll be the first artist in history to have a posthumous exhibition of new work," and he's called AARON his "surrogate self" (2007). But attributing ownership and authorship to Cohen is a little too simplistic; it doesn't help us to explain the creative process that generated these drawings. As Cohen pointed out, "it makes images I couldn't have made myself by any other means" (2004). To explain how these drawings and paintings were created, we have to know a lot about the program, and about how AARON and Cohen interacted over the years. Explaining artificial creativity requires new approaches, and raises new questions.

THE ARTIFICIAL MATHEMATICIAN

The Artificial Mathematician (AM) program was developed by computer scientist Doug Lenat (1977, 1983). Lenat taught AM 100 simple mathematical concepts, and then gave it about 300 general rules for transforming these concepts. These transforming rules include generalizing, specializing, inverting, exemplifying, and combining concepts. As AM runs, it plays around with the 100 starting concepts, using the transforming rules to add new concepts to the pool. Each new concept is evaluated to determine if it's "interesting," and if it is, it's further transformed. To determine which new concepts are interesting, Lenat gave AM another set of rules. These rules include the conservation rule, which states that "if the union of two sets possesses a property that was possessed by each original set, that is interesting," and the emergence rule, which states that "if the union of two sets possesses a property that was lacking in each original set, that is interesting."

Starting from the 100 basic concepts, AM has generated many valuable arithmetic ideas, including addition, multiplication, prime numbers, and Goldbach's conjecture. As a result, Lenat claimed it's creative. Lenat later developed a more advanced version of AM called EURISKO. It adds to AM the ability to transform its own rules, and it does this with a second set of rules describing how the main rules can be transformed. For example, one of these "meta-rules" lowers the probability that a given rule will be used, if it has been used already a few times without resulting in anything interesting. Other meta-rules generalize the basic rules, or create new ones by analogy with old ones. EURISKO has had some surprising successes. It came up with an idea for a three-dimensional unit for a computer chip that could carry out two logical functions simultaneously, and this idea was awarded a U.S. patent for its innovation. It also was able to defeat human players in a national competition of a battleship war game (Boden, 1999, p. 366).

Like EMI and AARON, AM raises interesting questions about creativity. These programs seem to satisfy the individualist definition of creativity—they come up with new combinations that are expressed in the world. When AM started it didn't know about addition or multiplication, so its discovery of both of these is novel under our individualist definition. In addition, the works generated by EMI and AARON seem to meet the sociocultural definition—they're new to the world, and are judged creative by expert musicians and artists.

However, experts disagree about whether or not AM is creative (Rowe & Partridge, 1993). The first and biggest problem is that AM generates a huge number of ideas, and most of them are boring or worthless; Lenat has to sift through all of the new ideas and select the ones that are good. But as we saw in Chapter 7, evaluation is one of the most important stages of creativity. A second problem is that during development, Lenat was able to keep adding new rules if he noticed that AM wasn't coming up with anything interesting. We'll never know how much of this sort of massaging and revising took place during the development of the program. After all, AARON makes good art today because Cohen spent 40 years revising the program to suit his taste. A third factor reducing its creativity is that Lenat continually guides AM's processing, pointing out a concept that he thinks AM should explore more fully.

Yet like EMI and AARON, even AM's weaknesses can help us to explain creativity. We can learn a lot about human creativity as we examine how these programs differ from it. Artificial creators can help us to clarify our own definitions and conceptions of creativity.

ARTIFICIAL WRITERS

Several computer scientists have attempted to write programs that can write literature or poetry. Although these writings won't win any prizes, they can help us to explain creativity.

For example, how would you explain the fact that programs that write poetry have been more successful than programs that write prose? It isn't because poetry is easier to write; it's because human readers are used to reading meaning into ambiguous poems. In other words, when we read a poem, we expect to be doing a lot of interpretive work, providing much of the meaning ourselves. As a result, the program doesn't have to be so good at writing meaning into the poem (Boden, 1999, p. 360).

Story-writing programs can't yet write prose that's artfully constructed or that's pleasurable to read. Instead, they focus on creating interesting plots, with characters that have motivations, and actions that make sense in the context of those motivations. These programs—like the pioneering TALE-SPIN program (Meehan, 1976, 1981)—start with scripts that represent stereotypical behavior, and character motivations and their likely resulting actions, including help, friendship, competition, revenge, and betrayal.

TALE-SPIN represents character motivations, but it has no concept of an overall narrative structure, or how those goals can best fit together to make an interesting story. It generates stories, but it has no ability to evaluate the resulting stories, or to modify them to satisfy some aesthetic criteria. Thus, like AM, it's missing the evaluation stage. A more recent program known as MINSTREL (Turner, 1994) makes a distinction between the overall goal of a good story and the goals of the characters; a character's goals may be rejected if they don't fit into the overall structure of the narrative. MINSTREL relies on 25 transformative rules called TRAMS, for Transform, Recall, Adapt Methods. Some of the most common TRAMS are "ignore motivations" and "generalize actor"; one of the less common TRAMS is "thwart via death." MINSTREL's stories aren't great, but they're not horrible, either; when people are asked to judge the quality of the stories—without knowing that they're computer-generated—they usually guess that the author is a junior-high-school student.

MINSTREL has an extra stage of evaluation that's not present in TALE-SPIN. TALE-SPIN uses the characters' different motivations to construct plots, but those motivations often don't fit together to make a coherent narrative. But MINSTREL fixes this problem with an extra stage of evaluation; motivations are created for each character, but then MINSTREL evaluates them all to see which ones will work best to make a coherent narrative. MINSTREL still doesn't contain the ultimate evaluation stage—it doesn't have the ability to examine the stories that it generates to determine which ones are the best.

THE ARTIFICIAL ORCHESTRA

AI programmers have begun to realize that intelligence isn't always a property of solitary individuals; collaborating groups are sometimes more intelligent working together than individuals working alone. This is reflected in the field of distributed artificial intelligence, "DAI" for short, in which developers program many independent computational entities—called agents—and then let them loose in artificial societies to interact with one another. What emerges is a form of group intelligence called *distributed cognition*.

This field has only existed since the mid-1990s, and in the past couple of years, these techniques have been used to simulate the group dynamics of distributed creativity (Sawyer & DeZutter, 2009). At MIT's Artificial Intelligence Lab, James McLurkin (2002) developed a robotic orchestra with 40 robots, each with a sound synthesizer chip (Fig. 8.2). The robots worked together to make collective decisions about how to split a song into parts, so that each robot would know which part to play on its sound chip. This simulated orchestra didn't need a conductor or an arranger to play together; that would have been centralized cognition, and McLurkin's orchestra was a classic example of distributed cognition.

In 2003 at Sony's Computer Science Lab in Paris, a second virtual orchestra performed. Eduardo Miranda had developed a virtual orchestra with 10 computerized performers. But rather than perform an existing score, Miranda used the theories of distributed cognition to have them collectively create their own original score. Each player was programmed to be able to generate a simple sequence of musical notes. But more important, each player was programmed to listen to the other players, to evaluate their novel sequences, and to imitate some of them with variations. Miranda then left his virtual orchestra to "rehearse" for a few days; when he came back, the orchestra had produced haunting melodic streams. This was distributed creativity; the melodies were created by a group of 10 virtual players, independent agents that worked together to create (Huang, 2003).

FIGURE 8.2: James McLurkin's Robotic Orchestra. (Photo courtesy of iRobot. Reprinted with permission.)

Creativity researchers have discovered that creative work often occurs in collaborative social settings (Chapter 12). These collaborative orchestras are based on these new research findings; distributed creativity simulates creative collaboration. With these exciting new developments, the computational approach is shifting away from a purely individualist approach.

THE LESSONS OF ARTIFICIAL CREATIVITY

These programs seem to meet the individualist definition of creativity: they generate new combinations that are expressed in the world. But although these programs generate new combinations, they don't seem to do it like people do. These artificial creators do not simulate very many of the cognitive processes and structures that psychologists have associated with creativity (as pointed out by Finke et al., 1992, p. 14). But future efforts along these lines, if they were guided by interdisciplinary teams of psychologists and computer scientists, could help us explain creativity. First, programs could be developed to simulate and test different theories of the incubation stage. Does incubation occur by guided analogy or by random combination? We could try simulating both in an artificial creator, and observe the differences in behavior. Second, programs could be developed to explore in detail how concepts are structured, stored, and combined—again, by simulating each theory in a computer program and then comparing the results.

Artificial creators also teach us by virtue of what they leave out. None of these programs models emotion, expression and communication, motivation, or the separate generation and evaluation stages distinctive of human creativity.

CRITICISM 1. COGNITION AND EMOTION

AI is based on the claim that the mind is a computational device. AI limits its study of the human mind to cognition—rational, analytic, linear, propositional thought. These programs are especially helpful in understanding the cognitive components of creativity: analogy, metaphor, concepts and conceptual spaces, sequential stages, and transformative rules. But artificial creators don't model emotion, motivation, or irrationality. As a result, the best artificial creators can hope to do is to simulate those elements of human creativity that rely on cognition.

CRITICISM 2. PROBLEM FINDING

Computers are useless. They can only give you answers.
—*Pablo Picasso (Byrne, 1996, 2:623)*

We saw in Chapter 5 that the first stage in the creative process is asking a good question; creativity researchers call this problem finding. But artificial creators never have to come up with their own questions; their human creators decide what problems are important, and how to represent the problem in computer language. Artificial creators simulate problem solving rather than problem finding (Csikszentmihalyi, 1988a).

This doesn't bother some AI researchers, those who believe that creativity isn't much different from everyday problem solving (see pp. 90–91). They argue that most creativity really is problem solving; after all, most of us don't experience problem-finding insights on a regular basis, and even genius-level creators don't find problems every day. But most creativity researchers believe that problem finding can't be explained as a type of problem solving; coming up with good questions requires its own explanation.

CRITICISM 3. CREATIVITY CAN'T BE ALGORITHMIC

Teresa Amabile (1983, 1996) argued that to be creative, a task can't be algorithmic (p. 35). An algorithmic task is one where "the solution is clear and straightforward," and a creative task is one "not having a clear and readily identifiable path to solution" so that a new algorithm must be developed before the task can be accomplished. As an example, Amabile said that if a chemist applied a series of well-known synthesis chains for producing a new hydrocarbon complex, the synthesis would not be creative even if it led to a product that was novel and appropriate; only if the chemist had to develop an entirely new algorithm for synthesis could the result be called creative (p. 36). Amabile's (1983) definition of creativity, although it predates most of the work on computational creativity, excludes the possibility of computer creativity, because computer programs are algorithmic by definition.

AI researchers would respond that this definition is unfairly limited; after all, it seems that many creative products result from algorithmic processes. Why shouldn't we agree that the chemist's new hydrocarbon complex is creative? And it raises a critical definitional problem: How can we know which mental processes are algorithmic, and which ones are truly creative? After Picasso and Braque painted their first Cubist paintings, were all of the Cubist paintings they did afterward just algorithmic? After Bach composed his first minuet, were all of his later minuets just algorithmic? Most of us wouldn't be satisfied with such a restrictive definition of creativity. Still, it seems that Amabile is on to something. If an algorithm tells you what to do—if you follow a set of existing rules to create—most of us would agree that's less creative than if you come up with something without using existing rules, or if you invent a whole new algorithm.

CRITICISM 4. NO SELECTION ABILITY

Although these programs generate many novel outputs, the evaluation and selection is usually done by a person. But in Chapter 7, we learned that the evaluation stage is just as important as the incubation and insight stages. For example, many creative people claim that they have a lot of ideas, and simply throw away the bad ones. And researchers have discovered that creators with high productivity are the ones who generate the most creative products (see Chapter 15).

Lenat's AM math theorem program generates a lot of ideas that mathematicians think are boring and worthless (Boden, 1999, p. 365). But AM doesn't have to select among its creations; Lenat himself painstakingly sifts through hundreds of program runs to identify those few ideas that turn out to be good ones.

David Cope, EMI's developer, carefully listens to all of the compositions generated by EMI and selects the ones that he thinks sound most like the composer being imitated. EMI itself has no ability to judge which of its compositions are the best. When EMI is trying to imitate Bach, Cope said that one in four of the program runs generates a pretty good composition. However, Bach is easier for EMI to imitate well than some other composers; the ratio for Beethoven is one good composition out of every 60 or 70 (Johnson, 1997).

The Western cultural model of creativity emphasizes the unconscious incubation stage and the moment of insight; we tend to neglect the hard conscious work of evaluation and elaboration. Artificial creators show us how important evaluation and elaboration really are. Evaluation often goes hand in hand with Stage 8, the execution and elaboration of an insight; yet artificial creators never "execute" in the embodied way that a human creator does—hands-on work with paints and brushes, or trying out a melody on a piano to see how it works. Evaluation can't be done effectively without a deep understanding of the domain—the conventions and the language of a creative domain, and the history that resulted in the body of existing works that's known and shared among creators in the area. In the Western cultural model, the domain isn't that important; we tend to think that conventions are constraints that limit the individual's creativity.

Because artificial creators don't evaluate and execute their own creations, they implicitly assume an idealist theory of creativity instead of an action theory (Chapter 5). Yet scientists believe that the idealist theory is wrong; evaluation and elaboration play central roles in human creativity. Artificial creators can simulate divergent thinking, insight, and novelty, but these are only half of human creativity; evaluation, selection, and execution are equally important.

CRITICISM 5. WHAT ABOUT THE DEVELOPMENT PROCESS?

The programmers who develop artificial creators rarely analyze their own debugging and development process. But typically, early versions of a program produce many unacceptable or uncreative outputs, and the programmer has to revise the program so that these don't happen in later versions of the software. Only by becoming familiar with the development cycle of the program—with how the programmers sculpt and massage its behavior through successive and iterative revisions—could we really understand the role played by the human meta-creator.

All of these artificial creators were developed by programmers who were also creatively talented in that particular domain. Donald Cope was a professional composer before he started EMI; Harold Cohen was a successful painter before beginning work on AARON. Only a talented musician would be able to "debug" the Bach-like compositions of EMI; a non-musician wouldn't have the ability to judge which versions of the program were better. Only a talented visual artist like Harold Cohen could tell which paintings by AARON were better paintings; a non-artist wouldn't be able to select between different versions of the program and choose a promising future path for development.

Because we never hear about the development process, we don't know how the programmer's creative choices are reflected in the program; it's easy to come to the incorrect conclusion that the programmer simply wrote a program one day, and out popped novel and interesting results. Programming an artificial creator is just like any other creative process—mostly hard work, with small mini-insights throughout, and with most of the creativity occurring during the evaluation and execution stages.

ARTIST—TECHNOLOGY COLLABORATIONS

> Imagine a scene: in a darkened room a moving image is projected onto a large screen. In front of it, several people are moving rapidly in different directions, waving their arms and simultaneously watching the screen. They might be laughing or chatting to one another or quietly observing the shapes, colours and sounds that are continually changing as if in reaction to the movements of those present. As a matter of fact that is exactly what is happening. In today's world of art and technology this is an interactive or "participatory" art experience. Together, artists and technologists have created spaces in which infra-red sensors detect people's movements and by detecting the movements in the space, a computer generates visual images and sounds which are displayed so that everyone can see the artwork as it evolves.
>
> —Linda Candy and Ernest Edmonds (2002, p. xi)

For over 20 years, visual artist Jack Ox has been using technology to translate music into visual images (Ox, 2002). Ox's GridJam system is Internet-based and supports collaborative musical improvisation among players at different geographic locations. Computer sound files and three-dimensional visualizations come together in a virtual performance space. Musicians can improvise together no matter where they are in the world; they can hear and see each other in the GridJam interactive environment. Building on such a virtual environment, it's a small additional step to add nonhuman musicians to the mix, or to write programs that transform each musician's riffs before they reach the other musicians. As with many of these new artistic uses of technology, the product that results is a hybrid creation, part human and part computer.

Computer technology is increasingly being used in creative ways by artists to create multimedia interactive works of art. Sometimes these creations are called *art systems* rather than art works, because "system" emphasizes that the viewer participates in the creativity (Cornock & Edmonds, 1973). In art systems, the role of the artist is no longer to create a product; it's instead to create a set of rules that structure the relationship between the audience and the artwork (Candy, 2002, p. 263). This new form of visual art emphasizes interaction, participation, and collaboration.

The history of artists using computers in their work extends back at least to 1963, when the magazine *Computers and Animation* began its annual competition of computer art (Candy & Edmonds, 2002, p. 5). Many of these first computer artists were inspired by the writings of the Russian constructivists; in the 1920s, long before the invention of the digital computer, Russian artists like Malevich proposed that mathematical or geometric algorithms could be used to aid in the generation of visual art (Malevich, 1919/1968). In January 1965, perhaps the world's first gallery exhibit of computer art was displayed by Georg Nees at the Studio Galerie at the University of Stuttgart. These works were produced with a graph plotter, and generated by programs written by Nees. Later that year, A. Michael Noll and Bela Julesz showed computer graphics at the Howard Wise gallery in New York. In 1968 in London, many of these works appeared in the Cybernetic Serendipity exhibition held at the Institute for Contemporary Art, curated by Jasia Reichardt, who later produced *The Computer in Art* (1971). The interdisciplinary science, art, and technology journal *Leonardo* was founded in 1968.

This was really cutting-edge work; in the 1960s, computers were big and expensive. There were no personal computers, and most computers were owned by big businesses and by the military. Almost no one predicted how much more sophisticated and inexpensive computers would become. By the 1990s, as powerful personal computers became widely available, artists' uses of technology increased dramatically. One of the main venues for this exciting new work has been the "Creativity and Cognition" conference series. The first was held in 1993 at the University of Loughborough, England, and they're now held biannually in odd-numbered years.

This type of creativity doesn't fit well with our creativity myths. Contrary to the classic image of the painter working alone in a studio, 62% of the artists who work with technology collaborate with others (Candy, 1999). Scientific studies of these artist–technology collaborations have found that they have a lot in common with the design processes of engineering teams. These collaborative teams use group creative processes; the creative process is a hierarchically organized, planned activity, an opportunistically driven mix of top-down and bottom-up strategies (see Chapter 12).

To explain art systems like these, we have to analyze not only the mental processes and personality of the creator, but also the group dynamics and collaborations of systems of people. We need to combine individualist and sociocultural approaches to explain artist–technology collaborations.

CONCLUSION

People seem to like computer art. Audiences at EMI concerts and gallery viewers at shows of AARON's paintings react the same way that they do to human creations. When Dr. Cope sits at the piano and plays computer-composed Chopin for people, audiences respond just as they would to a human composer; they act as if a creative being is reaching out to them through the music. When people look at an AARON painting, they instinctively try to interpret what it means—what is the artist trying to say?

Computer art raises an interesting possibility: the viewer may contribute as much to a work as the artist does. After all, people also see images of Elvis in dirty windows and think their cars have quirky personality traits. Artistic meaning isn't only put into a work by the artist, but is often a creative interpretation by the viewer. Many influential theories of art emphasize audience reaction rather than the creator's intention.[2]

These programs meet the individualist definition of creativity, and some of them seem to meet the sociocultural definition, too. But artificial creators are missing several important dimensions of the human creative process.

EVALUATION

Artificial creators are never responsible for the evaluation stage of the creative process. The programmers decide when the program has discovered something interesting; many times when such a program runs, nothing interesting results. These computer runs are discarded and never reported. In contrast, human creators have lots of ideas, and an important part of the creative process is picking the most promising ones for further elaboration.

EXECUTION

Artificial creators come up with an idea, and that's the end of their creative process. Their creative process matches the idealist theory—the theory that the creative process is complete once the creative idea has been conceived in the head (Chapter 5). But scientific studies of creativity have revealed that's not the way humans do it. People have most of their insights during the execution and elaboration of the work; to explain human creativity, we need an action theory. Computer artists don't need to act in the world to create; they don't work the same way that human artists do.

COMMUNICATION

Artificial creators don't have to communicate and disseminate their novel work to a creative community. Yet as we'll see in our examination of sociocultural approaches in Part 3, the communication stage is complex and involves immense creativity. Attempting to communicate a creative work often feeds back to fundamentally transform the creative process itself.

---

2. For example, German literary theorist Wolfgang Iser (1978) argued that a literary text provides only a rough guideline to the reader; the reader's job is to create an aesthetic experience by interacting with the text. Reader-response theorists also include even more radical literary theorists; most famously, Stanley Fish (1980) has argued that there is *nothing* in the text that's not put there by the reader (see Chapter 17, pp. 333–334).

Artificial creators are interesting both for their successes and also because they show us the limitations of the individualist approach to creativity. Artificial creators are weakest when it comes to the social dimensions of creativity. Because they don't have to evaluate, execute, or communicate, they don't contain the important conventions and languages that allow communication between a creator and an audience. Because they create according to an idealist theory, there's no creativity during the execution stage. In human creativity, the execution stage is often deeply collaborative, as we'll see when we turn to sociocultural approaches in Part 3.

KEY CONCEPTS

- Artificial intelligence and artificial creators
- Distributed artificial intelligence and distributed creativity
- Creativity as opposed to algorithmic, rule-governed behavior
- Art systems and artist–technology collaborations

THOUGHT EXPERIMENTS

- When you use a word processor to write, does that influence the type of writing that you do? In other words, do you write differently than when you write with pencil and paper?
- Have you ever used a computer program to draw, paint, design a website, or compose or produce electronic music? Does the design of the program influence your creative process, or affect the final created product?
- Would you say that the computer is a collaborator in your creativity? Or is it just a very complicated tool, like a pencil on steroids?
- Has your personal computer ever done anything that you didn't expect? Would you say that this unexpected behavior was creative?

SUGGESTED READINGS

You can read more about AARON at Harold Cohen's website: http://crca.ucsd.edu/~hcohen/ (accessed Aug. 22, 2011).

You can listen to songs composed by EMI at David Cope's website: http://artsites.ucsc.edu/faculty/cope/ (accessed Aug. 22, 2011).

Boden, M. A. (1999). Computer models of creativity. In R. J. Sternberg (Ed.), *The handbook of creativity* (pp. 351–72). New York: Cambridge.

Candy, L., & Edmonds, E. (Eds.). (2002). *Explorations in art and technology*. Berlin: Springer.

Cope, D. (2001). *Virtual music: Computer synthesis of musical style*. Cambridge, MA: MIT Press.

Csikszentmihalyi, M. (1988a). Motivation and creativity: Toward a synthesis of structural and energistic approaches to cognition. *New Ideas in Psychology, 6*(2), 159–176.

McCorduck, P. (1991). *Aaron's code: Meta-art, artificial intelligence, and the work of Harold Cohen*. New York: W. H. Freeman.

C H A P T E R   9

BIOLOGY AND CREATIVITY

On April 18, 1955, the famous physicist Albert Einstein died in Princeton, New Jersey. He had requested that his body be cremated. However, he was such an exceptional genius that the Princeton pathologist Dr. Thomas S. Harvey removed his brain and quickly placed it in formaldehyde to preserve the nerve cells. Medical doctors and psychologists hoped that by close examination of Einstein's brain, they might gain insight into what made him so smart. But none of the studies of Einstein's brain were able to identify any significant biologic differences between his brain and the average brain.[1] Except one: his brain weighed only 1,230 grams, much less than the adult male average of 1,400 grams.

Einstein's brain became an almost religious icon in our secular age. Even during his lifetime, Einstein's brain was examined by the primitive brain science of the time: electrodes were attached to his head to record his brain waves while he thought about his theory of relativity. This would happen only in a culture that believed that differences between people are biologically based.[2] We believe that exceptional genius must be hardwired in the brain, and that the explanation for extreme creativity must be biological (Belief 8 of the Western cultural model). We look at Einstein's brain rather than his education, or family environment, or work habits.

Since Einstein's death in 1955, contemporary U.S. culture has increasingly "biologized" human behavior—whether it is a search for "the gene" for musical ability, obesity, creativity, or homosexuality. Americans are increasingly likely to attribute behavior to innate biologic causes, often on the basis of flimsy research evidence (Peele & DeGrandpre, 1995). We tend to think that we can explain every aspect of the human personality by looking into the genetic code deep inside the individual's cells. This broad cultural attitude has many concrete manifestations:

1. The best-known studies were conducted by Harry Zimmerman, Einstein's personal physician; the UCLA neuroscientist Marian Diamond; and the Canadian brain researcher Sandra Witelson. Zimmerman found nothing unusual (Burrell, 2004, p. 279). Diamond and Witelson, however, thought they had found the secret of Einstein's brain; Diamond published her findings in 1985 in *Experimental Neurology*, and Witelson published hers in 1999 in the prestigious medical journal *The Lancet*. However, each of these studies was quickly shown to be flawed, and the special features of Einstein's brain that they wrote about ended up amounting to nothing (see the extended discussion in Burrell, 2004, pp. 282–290). However, the fascination never ends; the *Wall Street Journal* published a story that did little more than recycle the discredited Diamond and Witelson studies on May 22, 2009 (Hotz, 2009a).

2. This is not only an American fixation; Lenin's brain was removed by Soviet scientists after his death in 1924 for examination.

newspaper and television science reporting focuses on every new genetic discovery, and government agencies fund cognitive neuroscience and behavioral genetics at much higher dollar amounts than most other social and behavioral sciences. Because of this general cultural attitude, many readers of this book are likely to be receptive to the idea that there might be a creativity gene that makes the human species the most innovative one on the planet, or that genetic differences between people might make one person more creative than another.

But most scientists believe that there is no creativity gene.[3] The psychological findings of Chapters 5, 6, and 7 show us that there can't be such a gene; the research shows that creativity is based in everyday cognitive processes—the same mental abilities that are used in non-creative activities. And we'll see in Chapter 10, on cognitive neuroscience, that when people are engaged in creative tasks, they use brain regions that are commonly used in a wide range of everyday activities. Although there might be genes related to these general cognitive abilities, these large bodies of research show that there can't be genes that are specific to creativity.

This chapter has three main themes. First, I discuss the famous left brain/right brain studies. Second, I discuss studies of mental illness and creativity, from Hans Prinzhorn in the 1920s through contemporary studies of schizophrenia and manic-depressive disorder (including studies of drugs, alcohol, and creativity). Third, I discuss theories of how creativity evolved along with the human species. The chapter immediately following this one reviews contemporary cognitive neuroscience: studies that use the relatively new methodology of brain imaging.

RIGHT BRAIN OR LEFT BRAIN?

Since the dawn of the new science of psychology in the early 19th century, scientists hoped to identify the specific functions of each region of the brain. The first 19th-century psychologists to map the brain were called *phrenologists*. Figure 9.1 is a reproduction of an image of the brain from 1826, showing where phrenologists believed that different personality traits were located. The first impression you get from looking at the list of "brain organs" is that many of these traits sound really old-fashioned—few psychologists today believe that "benevolence" and "secretiveness" are reliable and valid personality traits (see Chapter 4). Studying the history of personality psychology is humbling for a psychologist because the traits always change as the times change.

If you look a little closer at Figure 9.1, you'll notice that there's no organ for creativity. The absence of a creativity organ suggests that phrenologists didn't believe creativity was a brain-based personality trait. This absence in 1826 is consistent with historical research showing that the Western cultural model of creativity originated only in the mid-19th century, as Romantic conceptions spread through society (see Chapter 2).

SPLIT-BRAIN PATIENTS

By the 1960s, brain science had advanced significantly, with new tools that allowed more accurate mappings of brain functions onto brain regions. Beginning in the 1960s, neurobiologist

---

3. A notable exception is Stanford anthropologist Richard Klein; see note 6.

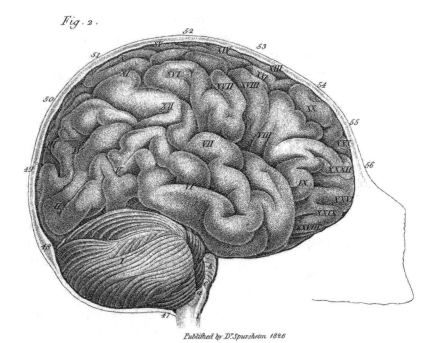

Fig. 2.

Published by D.ʳ Spurzheim 1826

FIGURE 9.1: A phrenologist's view of brain organization and function. (Reprinted from Johan Kaspar Spurzheim, 1826.) Guide to the Principal Zones: I. Organ of amativeness; II. Organ of philoprogenitiveness; III. Organ of inhabitiveness; IV. Organ of adhesiveness; V. Organ of combativeness; VI. Organ of destructiveness; VII. Organ of secretiveness; VIII. Organ of acquisitiveness; IX. Organ of constructiveness; X. Organ of self-esteem; XI. Organ of love of approbation; XII. Organ of cautiousness; XIII. Organ of benevolence; XIV. Organ of veneration; XV. Organ of firmness; XVI. Organ of conscientiousness; XVII. Organ of hope; XVIII. Organ of marvellousness; XIX. Organ of ideality; XX. Organ of mirthfulness; XXI. Organ of imitation; XXII. Organ of individuality; XXIII. Organ of configuration; XXIV. Organ of size; XXV. Organ of weight and resistance; XXVI. Organ of coloring; XXVII. Organ of locality; XXVIII. Organ of calculation; XXIX. Organ of order; XXX. Organ of eventuality; XXXI. Organ of time; XXXII. Organ of melody; XXXIII. Organ of language; XXXIV. Organ of comparison; XXXV. Organ of causality

Roger Sperry began to study split-brain patients—six Californian patients whose two brain hemispheres had been surgically separated in an attempt to control their severe epileptic seizures (Gazzaniga, 1970; Sperry, Gazzaniga, & Bogen, 1969). (Later, a different series of split-brain patients were studied at Dartmouth Medical School.) In 1972, Robert Ornstein's best-selling book *The Psychology of Consciousness* popularized the idea that the two hemispheres play different roles in our mental lives (1972; also see Ornstein, 1997). During the 1970s, this work began to receive media coverage, and one of the ideas that emerged was that creativity was based in the right brain. For example, Betty Edwards's 1979 book *Drawing on the Right Side of the Brain* told artists how to be more creative by releasing the power of their right brains. And today, decades later, many people think that creativity is a right-brain function.

The left hemisphere (LH) and the right hemisphere (RH) of the brain are highly connected—a bundle of between 100 and 200 million axons connects the two. That's a huge number; it's more neuronal connections than connect the cerebral hemispheres to the lower brain areas for sensation, vision, hearing, and taste (Bogen & Bogen, 1988, p. 295). This bundle of nerve fibers is called the *corpus callosum*; there are at least seven other such bundles, called *commissures*, connecting the two hemispheres, but the corpus callosum is the biggest one.

Split-brain patients have had their corpus callosum surgically severed, a procedure reserved for very extreme cases of epilepsy. Because the two sides of the brain can no longer communicate with each other, Sperry was able to create experimental tasks that could be presented to only one hemisphere. For example, using a specially constructed laboratory, an image could be presented only to the right visual field, and then the subject was asked to respond in some way using his or her right hand. Because both the right visual field and right hand are connected only to the left brain, the behavior observed would be strictly a product of the left brain. The same task could then be presented to the left visual field and left hand (which connect only to the right brain), and the results compared. Such studies revealed that although the two hemispheres are anatomically identical, the two sides of the brain have subtle differences in function. The best example of functional specialization is language; over 95% of right-handers have language specialization in the LH. Being left-handed doesn't mean that you're right-brain dominant for language; about 70% of left-handers process language in the LH, 15% process it in the RH, and 15% process language bilaterally (Springer & Deutsch, 1981/1993, p. 22).

After only a handful of patients had undergone this procedure, the surgeons realized how dramatically it affected brain function, and they developed a modified version of the procedure that severs only three fourths of the corpus callosum nerve fibers, leaving intact the posterior one fourth. This modified procedure cures the epilepsy, and no visible behavioral or experimental symptoms can be observed (Bogen & Bogen, 1988, p. 295). Consequently, there were never more than a small handful of such patients.

In the 1970s, the popular media took hold of these research findings, and soon it became widely believed that the left brain was the rational mind, while the right brain was the creative mind. This is the origin of the popular conception that "left brain" and "right brain" represent personality traits and that some people are dominant in one or the other hemisphere.

These studies from the 1960s and 1970s, combined with evidence from brain lesion studies, have found that, roughly speaking, the RH is associated with more "holistic" processes (rapid, complex, whole-pattern, spatial, and perceptual processes) and the LH is associated with more "analytic" processes (verbal, analytic, and linear processes) (Springer & Deutsch, 1981/1993). The RH is dominant for recognizing and identifying natural and nonverbal sounds, whereas the LH is dominant for recognizing and identifying language. The RH is better at depth perception, at maintaining a sense of body image, at producing dreams during REM sleep, at appreciating and expressing emotion aroused by music and the visual arts, and at perceiving emotional expression in others (Restak, 1993). In general, studies have found that the LH is the dominant hemisphere, and the RH plays a supporting role by handling perceptual functions such as facial recognition and attentional monitoring (Gazzaniga, 1995, 2000). For example, in split-brain patients verbal IQ measures don't drop for the LH, and problem-solving ability remains intact, but the RH isn't capable of higher-order cognition (Gazzaniga, 1995, p. 226).

So where's creativity? In perhaps the earliest application of the split-brain studies to creativity, Bogen and Bogen (1969) suggested that the LH inhibited RH function, thus blocking creativity. But today most neuroscientists reject this "inhibition" model, and instead believe the hemispheres work together in creativity, each contributing a different strength (also see Kaufman et al., 2010). Even Bogen and Bogen (1988) eventually rejected their earlier "inhibition" claims, instead proposing that ideas are generated during incubation in the RH, the other creativity stages happen in the LH, and "a greater than usual hemispheric interaction" happens during the most creative moments (Bogen & Bogen, 1988, p. 295). Carlsson, Wendt, and Risberg (2000) and Hoppe and Kyle (1990) proposed that the RH contributes a different modality of information, which is subsequently used by the LH. For example, symbolization and imagery might start in the RH and then get verbalized in the LH. Hoppe (Hoppe, 1988; Hoppe & Kyle, 1990) examined the split-brain patients and concluded that creativity depends on information passing across the corpus callosum. Springer and Deutsch (1981/1993) proposed that convergent thinking is a left-brain strength, with divergent thinking in the right brain. Goldberg, Podell, and Lovell (1994) proposed that the LH is responsible for routine cognitive strategies, and the RH for novel cognitive strategies.

These findings about hemispheric localization are only very general; the story is actually much more complicated. For example, when people both with and without musical training are asked to recognize fragments of music, there are interesting differences in hemispheric specialization. Those who had no formal training carried out the task in the RH, whereas those with formal training used both hemispheres equally (Bever & Chiarello, 1974). In non-musicians, the LH specializes in the perception of timing and rhythm, and the RH in pitch and timbre perception. In musicians, the pattern shifts: the LH becomes much more involved (Zaidel, 2009). In general, researchers have discovered that it's too simplistic to associate any particular domain of creative activity with either hemisphere; rather, the various components of skill required for performance in any creative domain are located throughout the entire brain—components like motivation, inspiration, performance, perception, and evaluation—and they move around as domain expertise increases. Because of these well-documented expertise-related shifts, hemispheric localization can't be completely genetic or innate.

These theories might remind you of the psychoanalytic theories we encountered in Chapter 4, such as the "regression in the service of the ego" theory of Kris (1952). Modern versions of such theories include the *Janusian thinking hypothesis* of Rothenberg (1979), or the *primary process/secondary process model* of Martindale (1990). Or, they might remind you of the creative process models in Chapter 5 that suggest creativity involves two related but complementary mental abilities—divergent thinking followed by convergent thinking. The consensus of creativity researchers is that creativity involves a cycling between two qualitatively distinct modes of thought, but it doesn't seem to be the case that these distinct modes are localized in different brain hemispheres.

LESION STUDIES

In addition to split-brain patients, studies of brain localization have been done on patients with brain lesions resulting from strokes, and with head injuries sustained during wartime. Most of these studies are, of necessity, done on people without artistic training and without exceptional creativity in any given domain; after all, brain damage is rare, only a small percentage of people are highly talented in any creative domain, and the odds of finding a brain-damaged creative person are consequently very small.

For example, scientists have compared the drawings of people with LH and RH damage (Gardner, 1975; Warrington, James, & Kinsbourne, 1966). In one study, subjects were asked to copy a picture of a house. Those with LH damage drew simpler images with fewer details. Those with RH damage drew confusing pictures in which the overall form is incorrect, but within this

(a)   (b)

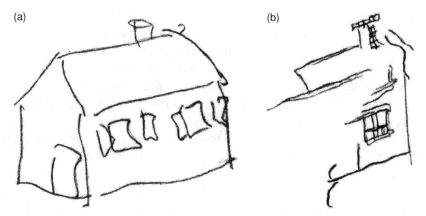

FIGURE 9.2: **(a) Sketch of a house by a right-handed patient with LH damage (drawn with the nonparalyzed hand). (b) Sketch of a house by a right-handed patient with RH damage.** (Reprinted from Gardner, H. (1975). *The Shattered Mind*, pp. 306, 307. With permission of Howard Gardner.)

hodgepodge, specific segments of the house might be quite detailed—a chimney with each of the bricks carefully drawn, for example (Fig. 9.2).

These studies show that both hemispheres play a role in drawing, with each hemisphere making a different but essential contribution. The LH seems to function to capture details and the RH captures the overall image. In general in such studies, the RH seems to be dominant for holistic perception, with the LH dominant for analytic skills—the same results found in split-brain studies.

The story gets yet more complicated when we consider the very small population of artistically trained individuals with brain damage. Zaidel (2005) studied 15 artists with unilateral brain damage (painters and composers). They were able to continue working and their style remained recognizable. Also, published cases of artists with slowly advancing brain degeneration show that they retain their skills, style, and creativity long into their illnesses—including Parkinson's, Alzheimer's, and other dementia. This strongly suggests that neither hemisphere specializes in art, and no specific localized region controls artistic production.

In trained painters, there's some evidence that the LH plays a less important role (Alajouanine, 1948). Other studies show that loss of linguistic skills, an LH function, doesn't severely affect the ability to paint (Zaimov, Kitov, & Kolev, 1969). And RH damage doesn't cause trained painters to lose the ability to capture the overall form of an image, as it does in untrained painters. One possible explanation is that training distributes skills more evenly throughout the brain. But this is only a hypothesis; it's impossible to explain these differences given the current state of scientific knowledge. We can't draw firm conclusions because among these subjects, the sites of their brain lesions weren't identical.

Many art critics have observed that there seems to be a heightened emotionality and expressivity in the works of established artists after RH strokes. In a famous example, painter Lovis Corinth suffered RH damage and began to draw in a bolder, more intense, and more emotionally expressive style than before his stroke (Kuhn, 1925, p. 107). LH damage doesn't have the same effect, suggesting some as-yet-unknown connection between the RH and emotionality in art.

The results of localized brain damage change depending on the creative domain. Because language, of all brain functions, is perhaps the most localized—usually in the LH—writers who suffer LH lesions often never write again, whereas writers with RH damage can write, but nonetheless suffer subtle difficulties—such as an impaired ability to understand metaphorical uses of language (Winner, 1982, p. 345). Music is the most complex case of all, made more complex because there are so many distinct musical abilities—composition, performance, perception, and technical skill with an instrument. Studies show that the many components of these skills are distributed throughout the brain, and that brain damage has different effects on trained and untrained musicians.

WHERE IS CREATIVITY?

There's no scientific evidence for the widely held notion that creativity takes place in the right hemisphere. No one has ever found a specific brain location for creativity (also see Chapter 10). And there's no scientific basis for the popular belief that there are two broad personality types, corresponding to a dominant "right brain" or a dominant "left brain" (as we learned in Chapter 4).

Brain research has found that brain damage usually reduces or completely terminates creative expression (Restak, 1993, p. 170). Split-brain patients show low creativity on tests of language and thinking. Researchers now believe that creative people have heightened communication between their hemispheres (Hoppe, 1988). A recent study (Whitman, Holcomb, & Zanes, 2010) found that subjects with higher TTCT scores showed more cross-hemispheric collaboration in a cross-visual field semantic priming task. This and other studies suggest that the hemispheres work more closely together in creative thought than they do in uncreative thought (Lezak, 1995, p. 69).

The idea that creativity is in the right brain is false, a myth that's lasted long past its time. Scientific research shows that creativity is not a specific, identifiable trait that can be localized to one region of the brain. Creativity is located in different parts of the brain depending on the domain; different subcomponents of ability in a single domain are located throughout the brain; and the location of these different subcomponents seems to differ in trained and untrained individuals. Creativity involves the whole brain.

MENTAL ILLNESS AND CREATIVITY

In Chapter 4, we learned about two very distinct theories of human creativity that have been influential in the history of psychology. On the one hand, Freudian theory held that creativity is driven by repressed desires and is a kind of neurosis. On the other hand, the humanist psychologists argued that creativity represents the peak of a healthy human personality. These two theories are both represented in the Western cultural model of creativity (Beliefs 9 and 10). Humanist psychology is an important element of "new age" approaches to art and music (see Chapter 22), and it supports the use of art and music in therapy. These perspectives assume that engaging in creative practice is a healthy, healing activity—in direct contrast with the belief that creativity and mental illness are somehow linked. So which is correct? Is there a link between creativity and madness?

Madness is devastating and limits one's ability to function in everyday life, but we often think that the madness brings along with it a special wisdom, a ready access to the deep, unconscious sources of creative imagination. It's easy to think of famous examples of writers, artists, and scientists with mental diseases. Virginia Woolf was sexually abused as a girl, suffered severe mood swings as an adult, and committed suicide. Sylvia Plath experienced episodes of psychotic depression, and committed suicide. Ernest Hemingway was a notoriously heavy drinker, suffered bouts of depression, and committed suicide.

Dr. Janos Maron, founder of the Living Museum—a gallery founded in 1983 at the Creedmoor Psychiatric Center in Queens Village—said that "the creative juices of the mentally ill flow more freely . . . if you're not mentally ill, you have to work much harder to get up to that level of creativity" (quoted in Budick, 2002). The idea that mental illness and creativity are linked has taken on the status of a cultural myth; most Hollywood movies that feature a mentally ill character will portray that character as unusually creative. *A Beautiful Mind* (2001) implies that the Nobel prize–winning economist John Nash derived his brilliance in part from his schizophrenia; other such films include *Rain Man* (1988) and *Shine* (1996).

The idea that madness and creativity are linked originated in the early 1800s and became more sophisticated with Freud's psychoanalytic theories of primary process thought. Perhaps the first scientist to link creative genius and madness was the psychiatrist and criminologist Cesare Lombroso (1891/1984), better known for his theory of the "born criminal"—that you could predict who would become a criminal by examining facial features such as large jaws, high cheekbones, and big chins. Lombroso famously argued that geniuses suffered from a wide array of "degenerations"; he provided a long list of historical geniuses who were short, lame, hunchbacked, club-footed, unusually lean and emaciated, more likely to stammer, and more likely to be sterile. They love to wander, which he called "vagabondage" (p. 18), and they sleepwalk. According to Lombroso, you could visually identify geniuses because they have asymmetric skulls; Lombroso's book includes sketches of the skulls of Kant, Volta, and others. Lombroso analyzed many biographies for evidence: he found that Horace, Aristotle, and Plato were unusually short; Cicero, Erasmus, and Napoleon were "emaciated" or extremely thin; other geniuses stammered, were sickly as children, were left-handed, or were sterile.

Although influential at the time, this theory had little empirical support and was long ago abandoned. We know today that none of this is true. So how did Lombroso, who claimed to be presenting "scientific" results, get it so wrong? It's because he violated several tenets of good scientific practice:

1. *Define your experimental condition*: The "experimental condition" is the subset of the population within which your hypothesis should hold true. For Lombroso, there are actually two: all "degenerate" people, and all geniuses. **Lombroso didn't clearly and explicitly define his criteria for genius, and he didn't examine the population of all degenerate people.**

2. *Identify a control group*: The "control group" is a group of people who are identical to the experimental condition in every way except for the independent variable of interest. Without an appropriate control group, the risk is that some *confounding variable* could be responsible for any observed difference, so you can't know for sure if your hypothesis is true even if you observe a difference. **Lombroso didn't examine a control group.**

3. *Randomly sample from the conditions*: In most cases, the researcher can't study every person from the population in every condition. There are far too many geniuses, under Lombroso's definition, for him to include all of them in his study. Likewise, there are far too many degenerate people. If you don't randomly sample, the risk is that you'll

"cherry-pick" individuals who are more likely to support your hypothesis. **Lombroso didn't randomly sample among geniuses; he didn't sample the population of degenerate people at all.**

4. *The researcher should be blind to the condition*: When diagnosing each person in the study, the researcher shouldn't know which condition that person falls into. Otherwise, it's a natural human instinct to have your hypothesis confirmed, and researchers run the risk of seeing what they want to see in the data. **Lombroso wasn't blind to the condition; he interpreted the data himself and was biased to see what he was looking for.**

These huge methodological errors show why Lombroso's conclusions aren't warranted. He went through history and cherry-picked famous people who had some suggestion of mental illness, and he broadly interpreted the evidence so that it would favor his hypothesis. He didn't examine all degenerate people to see if they had a higher degree of genius than the general population (which his theory predicted).

Let's take another example. Many people have observed that popular musicians are often drug users, and have hypothesized that using drugs somehow makes you a better musician. So how would you design an experiment to test this hypothesis?

1. *Define your experimental condition*: In this case, all musicians. Keep in mind that this means not just men; not just young musicians (to avoid a potential confound of youth); not only popular musicians, but also striving bands who aren't yet popular (to avoid a potential confound of fame); and all musical styles, from rock, pop, and hip-hop to polka, bluegrass, gospel, and classical (to avoid a potential confound of self-fulfilling stereotypes associated with certain styles). Ideally, it means not just musicians in one culture (like the United States), but in practice most researchers have to limit their subjects to their own culture.

2. *Identify a control group*: People who aren't musicians

3. *Randomly sample from the conditions*: Your experimental sample should include not only the stereotypical young male pop or rock band, but also the 60-year-old bassoonist in the local symphony orchestra; church organists and choir members; piano and guitar teachers in local communities; music teachers and band leaders from public high schools.

4. *The researcher should be blind to the condition*: Although this is often difficult, ideally you would have access to a file on each person's lifestyle and history of drug use without knowing whether they are in the experimental condition or the control condition.

Doing this thought experiment, you'll quickly realize that the hypothesized link between music and drug use had many unstated assumptions hidden in it—assumptions about youth, musical genre, gender, lifestyle, and popularity. After all, very few people think that middle-aged church choir members have drug abuse problems. If you don't design your experiment carefully, you won't be able to prove that any link you observe isn't due to one of these confounding variables. Several researchers have examined whether there's a link between drugs, alcohol, and creativity in various domains, and they've found no evidence for such a link (see pp. 176–177).

Two mental disorders have been most closely associated with creativity: schizophrenia and manic-depressive disorder. As we review these studies, keep in mind the potential methodological errors made by Cesare Lombroso; they remain surprisingly common in modern studies of the creativity–madness link.

CLASSIC STUDIES

Soon after Cesare Lombroso's book, Havelock Ellis (1904) selected 1,030 names from the *Dictionary of National Biography* and found that only 4.2% had suffered from mental illness, 8% from melancholia, and 5% from personality disorder. These numbers weren't much higher than the general population, so he concluded that there was no relationship between genius and mental illness (1904, p. 191). Bowerman (1947) replicated Ellis's 1904 study and found only a 2% incidence of mental illness.

Juda (1949) spent 16 years analyzing German artists and scientists who worked between 1650 and 1900. She investigated 19,000 in total, and interviewed 5,000 of them. Of this large number, 294 were highly gifted: 113 artists and 181 scientists. 63.7% of the artists were normal; another 27.4% were placed in an odd category called "psychopaths" that included "schizoid eccentric," "emotionally unstable," "weak characters," and "excitable and high strung." 11.5% had outright psychosis; 2 committed suicide. Among the 181 scientists, 75.5% were normal. 14.4% were "psychopaths," 12.7% had psychosis, and 3 committed suicide. These numbers are only slightly higher than in the general population, and Juda concluded, "There is no definite relationship between highest mental capacity and psychic health or illness . . . Psychoses, especially schizophrenia, proved to be detrimental to creative ability" (p. 306).

Goertzel and Goertzel (1962/2004) identified 400 eminent people by selecting those who had at least two biographies written about them. They found less than a 2% rate of mental illness among a group of 400 eminent individuals they studied; only five had psychiatric illness requiring hospitalization. This is lower than the general population. They also found that there was a lower-than-average incidence of mental illness among the parents, brothers, and sisters of the 400 (1962/2004, pp. 237–238).

Post (1994) studied 291 biographies of famous men. Post made his diagnoses on the basis of information printed in the biographies. None of the 291 subjects met the criteria for any DSM-III diagnosis, so he coded if they had one or more of the criteria for a disorder; only visual artists and writers had an elevated number of criteria.

These four classic studies with large databases—Ellis, Juda, Goertzel and Goertzel, and Post—suggest that eminent geniuses aren't any more likely to suffer from mental illness than the rest of us. Yet there are more recent studies that more closely explore the link between creativity and two specific mental disorders: schizophrenia and bipolar disorder.

SCHIZOPHRENIA

At the beginning of the 20th century, the German psychiatrist and art historian Hans Prinzhorn managed a clinic for the mentally ill in Heidelberg, Germany. He believed in art therapy, and he gave many of his patients paints, brushes, and canvases and encouraged them to paint, even though most of them had never painted before. In the 1920s, he published a collection of fascinating paintings created by hospitalized schizophrenics (Prinzhorn, 1922/1972); these paintings

FIGURE 9.3: *Medical Faculty*, by schizophrenic artist Adolf Wolfli, 1982. (Reprinted with permission of Adolf Wolfli-Stiftung Kunstmuseum, Bern. Photograph from Adolf Wolfli Foundation, Museum of Fine Arts, Bern. Copyright 1982.)

made a big impact on the art world, and modern painters like Jean Dubuffet began to collect the paintings and to imitate aspects of them in their own works (see Chapter 16, pp. 308–309). Schizophrenic paintings have several distinctive features: a compulsive working style and a focus on detailed ornamentation, so that every single square inch of the canvas is filled with intricate material; a focus on local detail, with little attention to composition or integration; and repetition of patterns (Fig. 9.3).

The publicity surrounding Prinzhorn's clinic led many scientists to believe that creativity and schizophrenia are linked. Schizophrenics have lost contact with reality; many artists live within their own inner world. Schizophrenics have hallucinations; artists see things in unusual and unconventional ways. Freudian psychoanalysis associates creativity with primary process cognition entering the conscious mind, and schizophrenics have all sorts of seemingly irrelevant ideas pop into their heads without conscious control, and at least on the surface, this seems similar to the moment of creative insight (Eysenck, 1995).

But rigorous scientific studies haven't found associations between schizophrenia and creativity (see the papers collected in a special issue of the *Creativity Research Journal*, 2001, Volume 13, Issue 1). Although some of the patients at Prinzhorn's clinic in Heidelberg generated some fascinating art, quantitative surveys suggest that less than 2% of mental hospital inmates began to engage in any form of creative activity (Kris, 1952; Winner, 1982, p. 362). The older focus on a link between schizophrenia and creativity is now thought to be due to the overly broad conceptions of schizophrenia that prevailed prior to the third edition of the official *Diagnostic and Statistical Manual* (DSM) in 1980. American diagnostic criteria have narrowed considerably (Sass & Schuldberg, 2000–2001).

Barron and Harrington (1981) concluded in their review of the literature, "the core charac-teristics of the creative person . . . are certainly not those of someone in the throes of a bout with schizophrenia, nor even of the schizotypic personality" (p. 462). Why did so many people, including psychologists, believe so long in a connection between schizophrenia and creativity, when there was so little evidence for it? It was because they were misled by Western cultural myths. Schizophrenia, particularly among psychoanalysts, was thought to involve a regression to a primitive Dionysian state, to infantile forms of irrationality (Sass, 1992). This conception of schizophrenia is almost identical to Romantic ideas that creativity involves spontaneous, emo-tional expression, not constrained by rational judgment, and that the artist is similar to a child (see Chapter 2).

BIPOLAR DISORDER

Two studies have found that almost half of all writers suffer from major depression (Andreasen, 1987; Jamison, 1993, 1995), and a third study found that as many as 10% of writers and poets have committed suicide (Ludwig, 1992). But if a writer were severely depressed all the time, he or she would never get any writing done. That's why some psychologists have proposed that writing creativity is related to bipolar disorder, also known as *manic-depressive illness* (Jamison, 1993). Bipolar disorder is characterized by extremely active or "manic" periods, alternating with low-energy depressive periods. Jamison (1993, 1995) argued that the manic phase exaggerates the incubation processes that lead to an original creative insight, and the normal and depressive phases allow the reflection necessary for evaluation and elaboration.

Kinney and Richards (2007) argued that there's evidence of an elevated prevalence of mood disorders (depression and manic-depressive illness) in exceptional creators in the fine arts. Gartner (2005) argued that successful entrepreneurs throughout history have been hypomanic. Kaufman (2005) studied poets in Eastern European countries and found that they were more likely to suffer from a mental illness than other types of writers.

There's a big problem with these studies: many of the creators who are tagged as manic-depressive are already dead, and researchers can't actually interview them. Instead, they have to make the diagnosis from the historical record, and it's almost impossible to diagnose individuals who are long deceased; recall the methodological errors made by Cesare Lombroso. Louis Sass (2000–2001) has argued that Jamison's studies of manic-depression in writers resulted in a self-fulfilling prediction, because she adopted an exceedingly broad definition of affective psychoses (p. 66).[4] And in a further complication, many of Jamison's subjects are literary figures from the Romantic tradition, and not many are creative people from other spheres of human activity (sci-ence, engineering, musical performance) and pre- or post-Romantic periods. One of her studies

---

4. Arnold (1992, 2002) hypothesized that some of these creators suffer from porphyria. Arnold (2002) said, "There is no cause and effect relationship between insanity and creativity" (Arnold, 2002). He argued that Vincent van Gogh suffered from an inherited disease, porphyria, which is exacerbated by malnutri-tion, infection (from gonorrhea), smoking, and absinthe drinking; because these traits were quite common among artists, those with an inherited tendency toward porphyria would have manifested its symptoms (Arnold, 1992).

analyzed major British and Irish poets born between 1705 and 1805, a cohort whose creative productivity overlapped considerably with the Romantic period (1780–1830). Sass (2000–2001) argued that the link with affective disorders advocated by Jamison (1993) and others is heavily based in Romantic notions of creativity—and also in a certain pre-modern style of art that was more prominent in the 19th century.

In Chapter 2, we learned that writers in the Romantic period held to a cultural belief that creativity and madness were related (Becker, 2000–2001). When creative people believe that creativity and madness are linked, they often invite madness and purposely volunteer evidence of madness in lifestyle and in diagnostic examinations. Nicolson (1947) found evidence that writers exaggerated their symptoms, consistent with the Romantic cultural conceptions that we find in Coleridge (see Chapters 2 and 17). This can make it almost impossible to accurately determine the presence or absence of mental illness, when you're reading a biography over 100 years later.

Critique of Bipolar Studies

Earlier in this chapter, I itemized the methodological errors that led Cesar Lombroso to erroneously claim that geniuses were physically degenerate. How do the above studies compare? Did they manage to avoid these common methodologic mistakes? It turns out the answer is no, and psychologists have uniformly rejected these studies due to their methodological flaws.

Andreasen was the only interviewer for her subjects, with no independent corroboration. She selected the writers herself, from a highly constrained group—professors at the Iowa Writer's Workshop (and she selected the controls, too). And she knew who was a writer and who was a control. We don't know whether the writing professors were actually creative or productive at the time of the interviews; maybe they stopped writing and returned to teaching because their mental illness made writing impossible. And she used an interview she developed herself, and applied a very broad diagnostic criterion: any "vague hypomanic experience" (1987, p. 1289).

Jamison used only the subjects' own reports of treatment, with no independent diagnostic criteria. She used a hand-picked sample; a controlled selection procedure wasn't used. Like Andreasen, she used her own diagnostic criteria, which considered "more energy than usual," "elevated mood," and "increased productivity" to be evidence of hypomania. The total percentage of mental illness is accounted for completely by the poets and playwrights in her sample; there was no elevated degree of mental illness among the other fields. And Jamison herself famously suffered from manic-depressive illness, resulting in an obvious bias in favor of finding positive correlates of the condition (Jamison, 1995).

Arnold Ludwig's Study

A third study that's often cited as evidence of a link between creativity and mental illness is more comprehensive, and thus requires more attention. Ludwig (1995) selected everyone whose biography was reviewed in the *New York Review of Books* between 1960 and 1990. This resulted in 1,004 eminent people; three fourths were men. He then read up to four biographies on each subject, for a total of 2,200 sources. He classified them by profession, and then he used a Creative Achievement Scale to rate their relative eminence.

Table 9.1: Lifetime Prevalence of DSM-III-R Disorders in
U.S. Residents Aged 15 to 54

Disorder	Lifetime Prevalence (%)
Affective disorders	
Major depressive episode	17.1
Manic episode	1.6
Dysthymia	6.4
Any affective disorder	19.3
Anxiety disorders	
Panic disorder	3.5
Agoraphobia without panic disorder	5.3
Social phobia	13.3
Simple phobia	11.3
Generalized anxiety disorder	5.1
Any anxiety disorder	24.9
Substance abuse disorders	
Alcohol abuse without dependence	9.4
Alcohol dependence	14.1
Drug abuse without dependence	4.4
Drug dependence	7.5
Any substance abuse/dependence	26.6
Other disorders	
Antisocial personality	3.5
Nonaffective psychosis (includes schizophrenia and related)	0.7

(Kessler et al., 1994, p. 12)

For comparison rates of mental illness, he used the Epidemiological Catchment Area (ECA) survey, involving interviews with 20,000 Americans (Robins & Regier, 1991). ECA found substantially lower rates than another mental health survey of 8,098 Americans aged 15 to 54, which found the following lifetime prevalences (Table 9.1).

In Ludwig's analysis, lifetime rates of depression in his eminent sample were quite elevated: 77% for poets, 59% for fiction writers, 47% for nonfiction writers, 46% for music composition, 50% for artists (p. 138). The lifetime rate of mania was as high as 17% for theater, 11% for nonfiction, 13% for poetry, and 13% for architecture (p. 140). Lifetime rates of psychosis were 17% for poets, 11% for sports, and 10% for music composition (p. 142).

These are pretty big numbers. And compared to Jamison and Andreasen, Ludwig invested a huge amount of effort and had an immense sample. But there's a serious problem with Ludwig's analysis: he didn't publish his diagnostic criteria, so we don't know exactly how specific or broad they may have been. He probably used overly broad diagnostic criteria: while reading the biographies, he coded potential evidence of mental illness both for "definite/strict" and for "probable/permissive," and all of his analyses use the more permissive criteria (p. 131). But with the control group, diagnosis was likely to be more similar to the strict criteria used by professional psychiatrists, so the comparisons with the control group probably aren't valid.

CONCLUSION: CREATIVE PEOPLE ARE NOT MENTALLY ILL

The connections between creativity, schizophrenia, and manic-depressive illness are intriguing, but when you review all of the scientific research, the bottom line is that there isn't convincing evidence of a connection between mental illness and creativity. Despite almost a century of work attempting to connect creativity and mental illness, evidence in support of a connection has been remarkably difficult to find. The few studies that found evidence for a link are barely more scientific than Lombroso's 19th-century work. Rothenberg (1990) concluded, "The need to believe in a connection between creativity and madness appears to be so strong that affirmations are welcomed and quoted rather uncritically" (p. 150). The consensus of all major creativity researchers today is that there's no link between mental illness and creativity.[5]

The four classic studies I reviewed above found no evidence of a link. In another classic study of creativity and physical health, Nicolson (1947) found that writers were no less physically healthy than non-writers—for example, 32 eminent British writers between the 14th and 19th century had remarkable longevity, with 10 of them living beyond the age of 70 (also see Runco, 2004, p. 666). He also noted that only two of them had any signs of mental illness, and these were during brief periods in an otherwise long and healthy life.

In Chapter 4, we learned about humanistic psychologists, and the work of Mihaly Csikszentmihalyi, who showed that creativity is a state of "peak experience" or "flow," residing at the very top of Maslow's hierarchy along with self-actualization. Most research shows that creativity is associated with high mental health and stability (e.g., MacKinnon, 1962; Runco, 2004, p. 659; Runco & Richards, 1997). Barron (1963a, 1969, 1972) always emphasized that his studies of exceptional creators found no evidence of pathology; he found that artists, scientists, and others demonstrated exceptional psychological health. Terman's 35-year longitudinal study, with its five volumes, found that the high-IQ "termites" were in good health and had normal personalities (Terman, 1925).

But if there's no link, then why are there so many famous historical creators with symptoms? Ludwig (1995) pointed out several aspects of artistic professions that might result in a spurious link: artistic occupations don't police their borders to keep people out, like other professions that require licensure—so if you have some "issues" that would keep you out of most respectable professions, the arts can't keep you out. And because our society has so many stereotypes about artistic professions being unconventional, it becomes a self-fulfilling prophecy: no one gets upset (and no one can fire you) if a painter is eccentric or unconventional, but they might get upset if it's their medical doctor or their accountant (also see Nicolson, 1947). As the novelist Jeanette Winterson pointed out, "Creative people get away with bad behavior. We aren't expected to conform" (2009, p. W3). In other words, any apparent correlation between mental illness and

---

5. All overviews of creativity research reject any link: Weisberg (2006) says it's a myth. Kaufman (2009) says the studies are flawed, and it's not proven. He also says that even though his own work is cited as evidence of a link, he never said that, "nor would I say that today" (p. 128). Runco (2007) concluded that "there are indications that creativity has benefits for health" and that there are many flaws with the research claiming a link with madness, and concluded "this area receives so much study because it is newsworthy" (p. 152). I agree with Kaufman's final word: "Psychologists who are interested in these areas should make sure they are not glorifying illness, stigmatizing creative people, or generally causing havoc" (J. C. Kaufman, 2009, p. 130). Also see Glazer, 2009; Rothenberg, 2001; Schlesinger, 2009; Waddell, 1998; Silvia & Kaufman, 2010.

the arts could simply be due to public expectations associated with the Western cultural model; if you're a military officer or a minister, you'll hide any eccentric behaviors, whereas if you're a writer or a painter, you'll exaggerate them.

If anything, mental illness interferes with creativity. In real life, John Nash, the schizophrenic mathematician who was the subject of the 2001 movie *A Beautiful Mind*, accomplished his greatest mathematics before his illness took hold. Most creative people afflicted with mental illness believe that their disease interferes with their creativity. With Sylvia Plath, for example, there was no question that her severe depression negatively affected her work. As she put it, "When you are insane, you are busy being insane—all the time . . . When I was crazy, that was all I was" (quoted in Ludwig, 1995, p. 4). Most creative people who suffer from mental illness are relieved to get rid of their symptoms after treatment with therapy or prescription drugs (Friedman, 2002).

A MORE NUANCED CLAIM

By the 1990s, it was pretty clear to everyone that creativity and mental illness were not linked, and that in general people with diagnosed mental illness were less creative than the average person, while exceptional creators tended to have high mental health. But then another hypothesis emerged: perhaps it's not full-fledged mental illness that's related to creativity; rather, perhaps it's an elevated tendency towards mental illness, but one that never becomes clinical. Today, those few scholars who still believe there's some link between creativity and mental illness have pulled back to this more nuanced claim (e.g., Eysenck, 1995; Glazer, 2009; Kinney & Richards, 2007).

THE SCHIZOTYPAL PERSONALITY

Full-fledged schizophrenia is detrimental to creativity, but perhaps creativity is enhanced by an elevated tendency toward schizophrenia, one that never crosses the line to diagnosed mental illness. This influential hypothesis was first proposed by psychologist Hans Eysenck (1916-1997). In a 1947 book, Eysenck proposed a two-dimensional model of personality, Extraversion and Neuroticism (Eysenck, 1947/1961); beginning in the 1970s, he proposed a third major personality trait, Psychoticism, and he argued that it's correlated with creativity in normal populations. *Latent inhibition* refers to the varying ability of the brain to screen from current attention stimuli previously experienced as irrelevant, and people who score high on measures of Psychoticism have an *over-inclusive cognitive style*, resulting from a reduction in latent inhibition (Eysenck, 1994, 1995). Eysenck developed the *Eysenck Personality Questionnaire (EPQ)* to assess his three proposed personality traits (Eysenck & Eysenck, 1975, 1976). Psychoticism is characterized by traits including aggressive, cold, egocentric, impersonal, impulsive, antisocial, unempathetic, and tough-minded (Eysenck, 1993, p. 155). But these people aren't clinically ill; when Eysenck studied a large number of exceptional creators, he discovered that psychoses (including schizophrenia and manic-depressive disorder) were rarely found in creative people in any field (1995)—consistent with the studies I reviewed above. According to Eysenck, Psychoticism is normally distributed in the population, and only extreme outliers manifest clinical levels of psychosis.

A few studies have found some evidence for Eysenck's hypothesized relationship between creativity and Psychoticism. Woody and Claridge (1977) gave 100 Oxford students five tasks from the Wallach-Kogan measure of divergent thinking and found that Psychoticism (measured with the EPQ) correlated 0.32 to 0.45 with the total number of responses produced, and 0.61 to 0.68 on the number of unique responses. Rushton (1990) compared 52 university professors and found that publication and citation counts correlated 0.26 ($p < 0.05$) with Psychoticism. Among 69 professors across Canada, enjoyment of research correlated 0.43 ($p < 0.01$) with Psychoticism, assessed using self-ratings.

However, most creativity researchers have rejected Eysenck's claims. The above studies are the exception; most studies have failed to find a relationship between Psychoticism and DT scores (reviewed in Reuter et al., 2005). Other scholars have challenged the above studies that report that eminent artists and scientists score higher on Psychoticism (Claridge, 1993). Reuter et al. (2005) used six different creativity measures (two each figural, verbal, and numeric) and found no correlation between Psychoticism and any of the tests (see also Dudek, 1993; Schuldberg, 2000-2001). Claridge (1993) noted that the Psychoticism scale hasn't met criterion validity and noted that diagnosed psychotics don't have high scores on the Psychoticism scale, as Eysenck's theory predicts. Csikszentmihalyi (1993) pointed out that less than 3% of the variance in DT scores is predicted by Psychoticism scores.

Although Eysenck's three-trait model of the personality was once highly influential, it's not widely accepted today among personality theorists. Personality theorists generally converge on the five-factor model (see Chapter 4), and from that research we know that Openness to Experience is correlated with creativity. Reduced latent inhibition (LI) has been associated with susceptibility to schizophrenia, and reduced LI is also associated with the big five personality trait Openness to Experience (McCrae, 1987) and with creative achievement (King, Walker, & Broyles, 1996). Carson, Peterson, and Higgins (2003) found decreased LI in high lifetime creative achievers compared to low creative achievers (as measured with the CAQ, see Chapter 3). So perhaps Eysenck's findings regarding Psychoticism and creativity are a replication of this five-factor finding, which has nothing to do with psychosis or any other mental illness.

CYCLOTHYMIA

A second variant of the nuanced claim is that creativity is related to *cyclothymia*, a mild form of bipolar disorder in which a person has mood swings from mild depression to euphoria but stays connected to reality. The mood swings are far less severe than bipolar disorder, the hypomania doesn't became actual mania, and most such people don't need long-term treatment. One variant of cyclothymia is Eckblad and Chapman's (1986) proposed personality construct, *hypomania*. Hypomanic personalities are cheerful, optimistic, extraverted, self-confident, and energetic, and sometimes irritable, rude, reckless, and irresponsible. Meyer's (2002) *hypomanic personality scale* was designed to identify "upbeat, gregarious and energetic people who sometimes become too euphoric and overactive" (p. 653). Scores on a hypomanic scale predicted later bipolar disorder; about 25% of hypomanics are diagnosed bipolar within 13 years (Meyer, 2002). Meyer found that higher levels of Openness to Experience are associated with higher levels of hypomanic symptoms (at $r = 0.25$), although Openness is not related to bipolar illness itself (Meyer, 2002).

There's some evidence that mood disorders have a partial genetic basis. And if so, relatives of bipolar or cyclothymic patients might have an undiagnosed but elevated tendency toward mood disorder, and this might cause them to be more creative than people without relatives with mood disorder. Richards et al. (1988a, 1988b) examined this possibility by studying a sample of 77 subjects. They compared an "index group" of 17 manic-depressives, 16 cyclothymes, and 11 normal first-degree relatives, with 33 controls. Of the 33 controls, 15 were normal and 18 had a diagnosis other than mood disorder. They found two significant contrasts: the "index group" had higher creativity than the controls—but this finding was completely due to elevated creativity in the 11 normal relatives. Contrasts weren't statistically significant between the three index groups of manic-depressives, cyclothymes, and the 11 normal first-degree relatives, although the 11 normal relatives were slightly higher in creativity (with a score of 2.6) than the bipolar subjects themselves (cyclothymes, 2.5; manic-depressives, 2.2). The 33 normal control subjects averaged a creativity score of 2.3; the differences with cyclothymes (2.5) and manic-depressives (2.2) were not statistically significant . But because the first-degree relatives had higher creativity than the controls, the authors concluded that elevated creativity might be associated with "risk for mood disorders" (Kinney & Richards, 2007, p. 229).

These studies have numerous methodological errors—most commonly, defining the supposed "tendency" so broadly that it includes creativity practically by definition. But even if you're swayed by those who argue there's evidence for a potential correlation between creative achievement and some undiagnosed tendency toward mental illness, there are three very different explanations for such a relationship:

1. The elevated tendency makes you more likely to be creative.
2. Participating in creative activities elevates your tendency.
3. There is some third personality factor that increases both creativity and the elevated tendency (sensation seeking, high energy, Openness to Experience, etc.).

The myth of the mentally ill creator generally aligns with number 1: there's something about mental illness that makes you more likely to be creative. Some advocates of the link have used the evolutionary term "compensatory advantage" to argue that mental illness survives through evolution because it confers the advantage of occasionally great creativity—in the same way that sickle-cell anemia is an illness that results from a genetic adaptation that confers immunity to malaria (Richards et al., 1988b).

But any potential relationship is just as likely to be explained by number 2: there may be something about participating in creative activities that elevates your scores on these various criteria. This second explanation is more likely, because many people who participate in fine art painting or writing novels spend years with little money and remain relatively obscure during that time. It could make even the strongest person a bit depressed to be unable to afford the basics of life while receiving no accolades or recognition from society. And the high productivity associated with creative accomplishment is associated with many of the rather mild behaviors that qualify you for the hypomanic phase of cyclothymia. If a researcher is combing through a biography and looking for evidence of struggle or tension in the early career of just about anyone who's poor and ignored, it won't be hard to find. Creators in many domains don't display elevated levels of mood disorder; these are the domains that society tends to reward financially, such as scientific creativity, entrepreneurship, and technological invention.

THE MYTH PERSISTS . . .

The few studies that claim to find a link between creativity and mental illness are deeply flawed—inadequate sampling methods, reliance on written materials to conduct diagnoses, variability in diagnostic criteria, and absence of control groups (see Richards, 1981, p. 296). When relatives of eminent creators are included, the problems are compounded; as Nicolson (1947) pointed out, "If the grandfather or grandmother of an author can be shown to have possessed a weak chest or a tendency to rheumatism, their unhappy grandchild is accused . . . of being congenitally neurotic" (p. 710). These are many of the same methodological errors that were made by Lombroso in the 19th century, and that led Albert and Runco (1999, p. 23) to call him a "charlatan" and his methods "fraudulent" (p. 27).

Given what we've learned about creativity in Chapters 5, 6, and 7, it's not so hard to explain why mental illness and creativity aren't connected. First, much of creativity involves working with existing conventions and languages; you can't just make up your own separate universe. (Well, you *can*—like the composer Harry Partch, Chapter 18—but you face immense obstacles.) Second, creative success requires networking and interacting with support networks, and this requires social skill and political savvy (see Chapters 11, 12, and 13). Third, creativity is mostly conscious hard work, not a sudden moment of insight (see Chapters 5 and 7), and getting the work done takes a highly effective person.

The mental illness myth is based in cultural conceptions of creativity that date from the Romantic era, as a pure expression of inner inspiration, an isolated genius, unconstrained by reason and convention. As we saw in Chapter 2, rationalist conceptions of creativity emphasize conscious deliberation and reasoning; only during Romantic cultural periods do people think that emotionality and madness somehow contribute to creativity. The modernism and postmodernism of 20th-century art is more rationalist than Romantic (Becker, 2000–2001; Sass, 2000–2001).

Given this preponderance of evidence, the only claim that remains at all plausible is that some creators, in a limited number of creative domains, in certain European cultures, and in certain historical time periods, may be slightly more towards the mentally ill end of the spectrum even though they're not clinical. But convincing evidence even for this highly restricted claim has not yet been found. If such evidence were one day to be provided, we still would not know whether this tendency precedes and then enhances creativity, or whether the career and financial difficulties inherent in a few select creative domains exaggerate those tendencies in otherwise normal individuals. But the research of almost a century is pretty clear: clinical levels of mental illness *reduce* creativity. And in most cases—most creative domains, most cultures—there's no evidence even for the subclinical hypothesis.

So why are we still talking about mental illness and creativity?

The first possible reason is because of our Western cultural model. The myth persists among science journalists because it makes a good story. In September 2009, *ScienceDaily* (Keri, 2009) reported a Hungarian study focusing on a variant of neuregulin 1, a gene that normally plays a role in a variety of brain processes, but that's also associated with a greater risk of mental disorders, including schizophrenia and bipolar disorder. The researchers asked for volunteers "who considered themselves to be very creative" and gave them the Just Suppose test and the lifetime Creative Achievement Questionnaire. Those who had the gene variant were more likely to have higher scores on these tests. But there are so many potential confounding factors—from IQ to personality variables—that no clear conclusions can be drawn.

Again, in May 2010, *ScienceDaily* reported a study seeming to show that the dopamine system in healthy people with high DT scores "is similar in some respects to that seen in people with schizophrenia" (de Manzano et al., 2010). These studies may or may not mean anything significant (noting the problems with DT scores identified in Chapter 3), but what's more telling is that these articles are introduced as if science had convincingly connected creativity and mental illness: "In order to examine the link between psychosis and creativity" (2009); "Creativity is also linked to a slightly higher risk of schizophrenia and bipolar disorder" (2010). These claims are false and aren't supported by any scientific evidence.

But there's another reason that I think is motivating some of the scientists who continue to claim there is a link. Keep in mind that these are almost always psychiatrists, rather than research psychologists. Gordon Claridge, in a preamble to a 2009 special issue on madness and creativity, put it this way: "The purpose of researching the madness/creativity connection is not to rubbish the original but troubled mind; it is rather to give optimism to the mentally ill and their kin" (p. 754). Kinney and Richards (2007) observed that when mood disorder patients are told there's a link between their disorder and heightened creativity, it increases their morale and self-esteem. And they're more likely to take their medication when they're told "if you can control your disorder you have great creative potential" (p. 233). Psychotherapists, in an understandable desire to help their suffering patients, could quite naturally be led to over-interpret what is rather weak evidence.

DRUGS AND CREATIVITY

In the early 1990s, when Sweden was cracking down on a perceived high level of alcoholism in that country, there were major debates in two Swedish newspapers: many Swedish authors claimed that drinking was necessary to aid their creative writing (Norlander, 1999). Perhaps alcohol inhibits the "conscious" stages of creativity (preparation, portions of illumination, and verification) and disinhibits incubation and insight (Norlander, 1999). Biographical and interview studies of writers suggest that they're more likely to use alcohol to help them generate ideas. It's a widely held belief that writers drink more than the general population. So is it true?

Ludwig (1995), in his review of the biographies of historical creators, found higher rates of alcohol dependence than the general population in theater (60%), music performance (40%), sports (32%), visual arts (29%), fiction (41%), nonfiction (27%), and poetry writing (34%) (p. 133). He found an elevated occurrence of drug-related problems in music performance (36%), actors (24%), and fiction writers (19%) (p. 135). But as I already pointed out when discussing Ludwig's study, he used a broad, over-inclusive measure of such behaviors, so it's hard to know how reliable these numbers are.

Most studies haven't found any creative benefit to alcohol or drug use. Norlander and Gustafson (1996, 1997, 1998) administered alcohol to subjects at various stages of the creative process and found either no effect or a diminished creativity, with some exceptions. In (Norlander & Gustafson, 1996) they gave two bottles to each of sixty subjects to take home, and created three groups of twenty subjects. For the control group, the two bottles contained tonic water; for the alcohol group, the two bottles contained 1 ml of 100% alcohol per kilogram of body weight, mixed with an equal volume of tonic water; for a placebo group, the two bottles contained tonic water with vodka essence. The three groups received instructions to "drink all of one bottle before going to bed tonight and the other bottle before bed tomorrow night," and they gave them a notebook to continue jotting down ideas on a problem that they had been presented with in the lab. The subjects with alcohol in their bottles generated more ideas and more original ideas in the notebooks, but the quality of the ideas was the same as the placebo and control groups (Also see Norlander & Gustafson, 1997). When writers either had alcohol or not, on the Purdue DT test, the alcohol group scored lower on flexibility and higher on originality (Norlander & Gustafson, 1998). Apart from these mixed findings, their other studies found either no effect or a reduction in creativity.

There's no evidence that alcohol, marijuana, LSD, or other drugs enhance creativity (Rothenberg, 1990). Plucker and Dana (1998) found that having a history of alcohol, marijuana, or tobacco usage wasn't correlated with creative achievements. Bourassa and Vaugeois (2001) found that if you smoke marijuana before a DT task, there's no positive effect for new users, but there's a negative effect for experienced users. Jos Ten Berge (1999) reviewed French- and German-language studies from the 1960s with psychedelic drugs and painters. No studies found that drugs enhanced creativity; in fact, just the opposite—they concluded that painting under the influence resulted in the "greatest artistic banalities" and that the work was "unreal, inane, or baroque kitsch" (p. 269).

When Jenny Boyd (1992) interviewed 75 popular musicians, she found that almost all of them had stopped using drugs and alcohol altogether because of the negative effect on their creativity. Guitarist and singer David Crosby perhaps said it best: "The problem with the drugs is that . . . they become so debilitating that the creative process stops entirely . . . for the last three years of my life, I didn't write anything . . . So much for the drugs and hash creativity theory" (Boyd, 1992, p. 200). As Kaufman (2009) concluded, "any connection between drug use and creativity is largely one manufactured in the drug user's mind" (p. 124).

ATTENTION-DEFICIT/HYPERACTIVITY DISORDER

There have been anecdotal reports that ADHD individuals display higher creativity, but empirical studies have yielded mixed results (White & Shah, 2006). ADHD individuals have a deficit in executive inhibition, and some theories of creativity (e.g., Eysenck on Psychoticism) posit a relationship between decreased inhibition and creativity. A higher level of executive inhibition would be expected to enhance performance on a convergent thinking task such as the RAT, because it helps you to suppress partial solutions that are matches for just two of the words, and because it helps you to stay on task long enough to find the solution. In contrast, a lower level of executive inhibition might enhance your ability to generate original responses on DT test.

White and Shah (2006) gave ADHD and non-ADHD college students the Unusual Uses test for *brick* and *bucket*. They also gave them 18 RAT word triplets to solve in five minutes. The ADHD group performed better on the Unusual Uses task but worse on the RAT. The relationship between ADHD and creativity is complex; further research is necessary.

THE EVOLUTION OF CREATIVITY

Most of the aesthetic objects found by archaeologists are designed to be worn—strings of beads and shells, brightly colored, and etched with repetitive patterns. Such objects probably communicated information about kinship or status. These decorative objects would be necessary only in a society so large that it would be impossible to personally know every other member. These larger societies also probably were characterized by increasing social competition, as distinct groups came into contact as they moved into new lands, and aesthetic objects could have served a function here as well (Henderson, 2003). Creativity seems to have evolved in tandem with increasingly complex social organization.

Most scientists agree that people who look like us had evolved by at least 130,000 years ago (Wilford, 2002)—but it took much longer before these early ancestors first acted like us. Scientists disagree about when, where, and how these anatomically modern humans began to display creative and symbolic thinking. Some scientists believe that the anatomic brain was fully evolved as of 130,000 years ago, but the ability for creativity remained hidden until society became more complex; others believe that some as-yet-undetected genetic advance resulted in a later change in brain wiring. This latter group argues for a *creativity explosion*, a sudden emergence of creative ability that occurred about 20,000 years ago (Pfeiffer, 1982) or perhaps 50,000 years ago (Klein & Edgar, 2002). These dates were originally proposed as a time of creative "explosion" because many of the cave paintings found in Europe date from then. These archaeologists hypothesized that some change suddenly occurred that led to the onset and rapid dissemination of painting—perhaps a biological change in the brain, perhaps a cultural innovation, disseminating through Europe like any other fashion.[6]

But most archaeologists reject the explosion theory altogether and believe that art evolved along with the human species, in a gradual and progressive fashion. These scientists point to recent discoveries in Africa and the Middle East, arguing that they support an older, more gradual evolution of creative behavior, one that isn't centered in Europe. For example, Dr. Christopher Henshilwood (Henshilwood et al., 2002) found objects that were 77,000 years old in South Africa that were decorated with symbolic patterns, suggesting that their creators had the capability for symbolic thought and creativity. Lorblanchet (2002) examined hand-carved stones found in Africa dating back 2 million years and noticed that many of these carvings were made using stones with pleasing colors and textures. He concluded that these primitive people must have used aesthetic taste to pick out these stones rather than other, more ordinary ones.

In *The Descent of Man*, Charles Darwin speculated on the evolution of art, suggesting that our sense of beauty is shared with other animals, including birds and apes, and that music was the origin of human language. Miller (2000, 2001) followed Darwin in proposing that aesthetic preferences derive from sexual selection through mate choice. Darwin observed that in most species, females tend to select mates, and in most human societies the males adorn themselves more than females. Animals choose partners based on visual indicators of fitness, and evolution shows many examples of ornamentation that advertise fitness—the tail of a peacock being the most famous example. The tail is an effective signal of fitness because only healthy peacocks can grow and support such tails. Miller argued that art works in the same way; it's a "signaling system" focused on sexual selection for courtship. In support of Miller's theory,

6. Richard Klein has recently argued that the discovery of the FOXP2 gene—apparently linked to linguistic ability—demonstrates that creativity may have also suddenly evolved with the mutation or emergence of a new gene (Henderson, 2003). FOXP2 seems to have mutated less than 200,000 years ago, the right time frame to potentially be a cause of the creativity explosion that Klein argues happened about 50,000 years ago.

Kenrick et al. (2010) noted that "talented artists, musicians, or writers frequently show off their creative outputs to others and may receive very high levels of . . . romantic interest as a result . . . and reproductive opportunities" (p. 298; see also Griskevicius et al., 2006). If art is a signaling system, then styles of art should evolve that could be produced only by a high-fitness artist— someone with high intelligence, creativity, hand–eye coordination, and lots of free time to learn difficult skills. Miller argued that although aesthetic tastes vary across cultures, all art requires virtuosity.

An alternate theory is associated with Ellen Dissanayake, who rooted the arts in two universal human activities: play and ritual. Many nonhuman animals also engage in play and ritual behaviors, providing additional evidence of their biologic basis. She claimed that in primitive societies, the arts "are in most instances intimately connected to ceremonies or ritual practices" (1988, p. 74) and that even in modern European societies, an autonomous sphere of art for art's sake is a relatively recent innovation. The development of Western music was inseparable from the Christian liturgy; through the 16th century, visual art was connected with Christian practices as well; and drama had its origins in Greek rituals. Art, play, and ritual share many features; they're social, they involve make-believe and the use of metaphor, they're each fundamentally communicative, with their own special language in which otherwise incommunicable things can be said, and they each involve exaggeration and repetition.

These theories remain controversial. Other evolutionary psychologists argue that art has no adaptive value and didn't evolve due to natural selection. Instead, they believe that art is a byproduct of other adaptations; art products satisfy us because they push "pleasure buttons" that evolved for other purposes—the ability to perceive symmetry and color, for example. Evolutionary psychologist Steven Pinker argued that the arts take more time than other activities that could accomplish the same evolutionary functions; because they're inefficient, they couldn't have evolved solely for that function (Crain, 2001, p. 35).

Evolutionary perspectives have filtered into professional criticism in the arts. The field of *biopoetics* uses Darwinian ideas to analyze literary works, for example, by analyzing the evolved cognitive structure of the brain to determine what makes us prefer one work over another (Carroll, 1995). For example, our preference for plot structures and narrative forms might be a result of natural selection.

You might expect artists to resist the idea that one of the deepest spiritual and personal elements of our being had its origin in our genes. After all, the evolutionary-psychological idea that human behaviors might be genetically based has been resisted by a broad range of both social scientists and humanists, because it seems to imply a deterministic view of human nature, the impossibility of development and change, and the undemocratic idea that individual differences may not result from the opportunities provided by one's environment, but might be hardwired in the genes. Herrnstein and Murray's 1994 book *The Bell Curve* was almost universally criticized for its claim that intelligence was genetically based and was passed on from parents to children.

But instead, Dissanayake's 1988 book *What Is Art For?* was welcomed by art educators, art therapists, and working artists because of her conclusion that the arts are a fundamental element of human nature and that the arts serve a basic human need. School districts with tight budgets frequently view the arts as an unnecessary frill, the first part of the school instructional budget to be cut, and Dissanayake's book seemed to provide an argument that the arts had value on par with the sciences. In 1991, the National Art Education Association invited her to give the keynote speech at its annual conference, and she received a standing ovation.

IS CREATIVITY A HERITABLE TRAIT?

If creativity is selected by evolutionarily pressures, then it should be *heritable*—passed from generation to generation through the genes. One of the best ways to evaluate heritability is through twin studies. Francis Galton conducted the first twin study in 1875 (Galton, 1875), as a way of comparing the relative importance of nature and nurture, and there have been hundreds of twin studies published since then. To conduct a twin study, you have to find equal numbers of both monozygotic and dizygotic twins. Monozygotic twins, also called "identical twins"—about one third of all twins—are genetically identical, while dizygotic twins, also called "fraternal twins"—about two thirds of all twins—are no more alike genetically than brothers and sisters born at different times. Both types of twins are presumably subject to the same environmental influences during their developmental years, because both pairs of twins are born at the same time and raised in the same family. On many traits, we'd expect both types of twins to be more similar than two random people, because of the environmental influences of being raised in the same family. But the critical factor in determining heritability is that traits that are genetic should show higher inter-twin correlations for monozygotic than for dizygotic twins. If both types of twins are equally similar on a trait, it's generally thought not to be heritable and thus not genetic.

Barron (1972) administered a range of tests associated with creativity to just over 100 pairs of twins. Two groups of adolescent twins were used: one group of Italian twins from Rome and Florence, and the other a group of American twins studied at the Institute of Personality Assessment and Research (IPAR) at the University of California, Berkeley. Of the five traits measured that were hypothesized to be connected to creativity, only two of them showed evidence of heritability: adaptive flexibility and aesthetic judgment of visual displays (pp. 176–177). However, on the two traits thought to be most closely connected to creativity—ideational fluency (divergent thinking) and originality—there was no evidence of heritability.

Other twin studies have also found no evidence that creativity is heritable. Vandenberg (1968) found no evidence of heritability in divergent thinking scores. Nichols (1978) conducted a meta-analysis of the twin literature, and averaged all of the correlations; he found that the divergent thinking scores of monozygotic twins were correlated at 0.11 more than those of dizygotic twins, which wasn't statistically significant—and this was the smallest difference of all measures studied, smaller than general intelligence, memory, verbal fluency, and many other measures. In perhaps the most comprehensive study, Reznikoff, Domino, Bridges, and Honeyman (1973) studied 117 pairs of monozygotic and dizygotic twins found through the Connecticut Twin Registry, which maintains a list of all multiple births in Connecticut since 1897. They administered a battery of 11 tests of creativity, including the RAT and five of Guilford's trait measures. They couldn't find any convincing evidence of a genetic component to creativity; of all 11 tests, only on the RAT were monozygotic twins more similar than the dizygotic twins. However, they found that twins overall had more similar scores on all of the measures than random pairs from the general population. Because there was no significant difference between the two types of twins, the best explanation is that twin similarity results from their similar environment.

Only one study found strong evidence that creativity is heritable, using the Creative Personality Scale (CPS; see Chapter 3, p. 44). Waller et al. (2003) examined CPS scores of 78 twins from the Minnesota Study of Twins Reared Apart. When twins are reared apart, they don't share the same family environment, so any similarities are most likely due to genetics.

CPS scores of the monozygotic twins correlated at 0.54; CPS scores for the dizygotic twins was close to zero. But given the lack of evidence for heritability in every other twin study, these findings should be interpreted with caution. One problem with using the CPS in a twin study is that we know that scores on the CPS are correlated with gender (see Chapter 3, p. 44), and all monozygotic twins are the same gender, but not all dizygotic twins are.

The argument that creativity emerged suddenly due to a genetic change has been batted around in anthropologic circles for several decades. But creativity is not heritable, and most scientists don't believe that creativity has a unique genetic basis. Of course, the general cognitive functions of the brain are inherited, but proper operation of the complex brain involves a vast array of different processes and regions (as we'll see in the next chapter), and these emerge during a person's development through a complex and long-term process of genetic expression that's heavily influenced by the environment (Pfenninger & Shubik, 2001; see also Elman et al., 1996).

CREATIVITY AS EVOLUTION

Prior to Darwin, people thought that the amazing complexity and beauty of the natural world could be explained only by the presence of an intelligent creator. The complexity of the human eye or hand was taken as evidence of prior design. But Darwin's theory was, above all, a theory of the creative force of impersonal evolution—Darwin explained the origin of new species without appealing to any intelligent organizing force, by showing how random changes were selected by their consequences—the faceless, distributed, and random process of evolution. The three-stage evolutionary process of blind variation, selection, and retention could explain all life on Planet Earth.

Darwin's theory of natural selection isn't such a bad theory of the creative process. The creative ideas that emerge from incubation are the "variation"; the evaluation stage provides the "selection"; and the execution of the work into physical form is "retention." This evolutionary theory of creativity was first argued in an influential 1960 article by Donald Campbell; he called his theory *evolutionary epistemology*. Inspired by evolutionary metaphors, a group of creativity scholars known as the Epistemology Group met several times in England between 1994 and 1997 to explore how technological innovation is like biological evolution (Ziman, 2000). Evolutionary concepts have been applied to cultural development in an interdisciplinary field of study known as *memetics* (e.g., Dennett, 1995). To some degree, this is common sense. After all, the business press routinely talks about new technologies in biological terms, referring to "market niche," and using terms such as "fitness," "survival," and "symbiotic."

The behaviorist B. F. Skinner also proposed an evolutionary theory of creativity, and he used that theory to draw a pretty radical behaviorist conclusion: "It is not some prior purpose, intention, or act of will which accounts for novel behavior; it is the 'contingencies of reinforcement'" (1972, p. 353). After all, Skinner reasoned, new species are created even though there is no intentional, willful creator behind their origin. So why should we assume that new ideas require purpose and intention? Referring to this theory of creativity, Skinner wrote, "For the second time in a little more than a century a theory of selection by consequences is threatening a traditional belief in a creative mind" (1972, p. 354). (For Skinner to compare himself to the great Darwin is typical of the chutzpah that helped make him a media figure in his day.) Behaviorism was often criticized for being unable to explain creativity; Skinner's ingenious response was to claim that creativity was only a myth anyway.

The main problem with the evolutionary metaphor is that it implies that the variation stage is random and unguided by the conscious mind. But in Chapter 5, we learned that most creativity researchers think that the incubation stage is guided in some way—by conceptual structures, by association networks, or by unconscious processes of evaluation. And if incubation is guided, the evolutionary metaphor of blind variation and selective retention doesn't really apply. (There are many other problems with applying biological evolution to cultural evolution; see Orr, 1996.)

CONCLUSION

Biology is the smallest level at which we could explain creativity. Biology's units of analysis are genes, DNA, and cells and regions of the human brain. In general, scientists agree that explanations at such lower levels of analysis are more general, more universal, and more powerful and have fewer exceptions than explanations at higher levels of analysis—like the explanations of psychology or sociology. It always makes scientific sense to start your study by attempting to explain something at the lowest possible level.

The biological research I've reviewed in this chapter provides very little help in explaining creativity; mostly the research serves to dispel some widespread myths. Creativity is not coded in our genes. Creativity isn't heritable. Creativity isn't in the right brain; it's a whole-brain function, drawing on many diverse areas of the brain in a complex systemic fashion. And there's no evidence of a link between mental illness and creativity.

In recent years, an exciting new biologic approach has emerged that has even greater potential to help us explain creativity—the brain imaging technologies that are used in *cognitive neuroscience*. These technologies, much more than the older methods reviewed in this chapter, have the potential to help us understand which parts of the brain are involved in creative thought, and what are the underlying mental mechanisms of creativity. For this, we turn to the next chapter.

KEY CONCEPTS

- Split-brain studies: corpus callosum, commissure
- The tenets of good scientific practice
- Schizophrenia, schizotypy, and creativity
- Bipolar disorder, cyclothymia, and creativity
- Drugs and creativity
- ADHD and creativity
- The evolution of creativity
- Heritability and creativity

THOUGHT EXPERIMENTS

- Is your level of creativity about the same as your parents?
- According to your parents, did you show a special creative talent very early in childhood? Do you think you were born with that talent?

- Did your parents do anything while you were growing up to encourage your creative abilities? If your parents hadn't done those things, would you still be just as creative now? Or, if they had done more, would you be more creative now?
- Think of one of the most creative people you personally know. Does he or she have any signs of mental illness?

SUGGESTED READINGS

Becker, G. (2000–2001). The association of creativity and psychopathology: Its cultural-historical origins. *Creativity Research Journal, 13*(1), 45–53.

Campbell, D. T. (1960). Blind variation and selective retention in scientific discovery. *Psychological Review, 67,* 380–400.

Ludwig, A. M. (1995). *The price of greatness: Resolving the creativity and madness controversy.* New York: The Guilford Press.

Prinzhorn, H. (1972). *Artistry of the mentally ill.* New York: Springer.

Reznikoff, M., Domino, G., Bridges, C., & Honeyman, M. (1973). Creative abilities in identical and fraternal twins. *Behavior Genetics, 3*(4), 365–377.

Sass, L. A. (2000–2001). Schizophrenia, modernism, and the "creative imagination": On creativity and psychopathology. *Creativity Research Journal, 13*(1), 55–74.

C H A P T E R   1 0

COGNITIVE NEUROSCIENCE AND CREATIVITY[1]

When cognitive psychology emerged in the 1970s, there was no way to directly observe what was happening in the mind, so psychologists developed a series of experimental techniques that allowed them to infer what must be happening in the mind, based on how people act in highly controlled settings in the laboratory. This *experimental cognitive psychology* provided the research summarized in Chapters 5, 6, and 7.

Beginning in the 1990s, an exciting new technology became available to cognitive psychologists: *brain imaging*. Brain imaging allows psychologists to see what's happening in the brain while people are thinking. The technology uses powerful machines—originally developed for medical diagnoses—to develop three-dimensional images that show how brain activity changes while the mind is engaged in cognitive tasks. Brain imaging is at the core of the new field of *cognitive neuroscience*. In a cognitive neuroscience experiment, the researcher designs a simple task for the research participant. The participant engages in the task while his or her head is positioned inside the brain scanner. By examining brain activity while a person is engaged in a particular task, researchers can make inferences about which areas of the brain are associated with that task. Cognitive neuroscience has made great strides in a very short period of time, and funding agencies have been generous, so we can expect new developments to continue.

The fundamental assumption guiding all cognitive neuroscience is that all of our sensations, thoughts, and mental processing are based in the biological brain, and that when we have a subjective experience of a mental event, the neuronal activity of the brain that occurs at the same time is responsible for that experience. All scientists today accept this assumption and reject various 19th-century dualist theories that the mind is somehow different from the biological brain.

Cognitive neuroscience builds on two older methods. The first is *lesion studies*, studies of how cognitive abilities change after a debilitating brain injury that affects only one local part of the brain. Injuries that selectively damage the brain result from strokes; during World War II,

1. I would like to thank Aaron Berkowitz, Edward Bowden, Mark Jung-Beeman, Charles Limb, and Todd Braver for comments and advice on this chapter. Portions of this chapter were previously published as: Sawyer, R. K. (2011). The cognitive neuroscience of creativity: A critical review. *Creativity Research Journal*, *23*(2), 137-154. Copyright © 2011 Taylor and Francis.

many such injuries resulted from battle. The problem with lesion studies is that lesions indiscriminately affect a variety of brain regions, and it can be difficult to determine the exact location of the lesion. A second, older method is to insert electrodes through the skull and into the brain of an experimental animal; electrodes can detect exactly which neurons are active. The problem with this method is that it can't be used with humans. The brain imaging methods available today to cognitive neuroscientists are much more valuable than either lesion studies or electrodes because they allow us to examine normal, healthy brains, engaged in tasks designed by researchers.

I begin the chapter with a whirlwind introduction to three influential brain imaging technologies: EEG, PET, and fMRI. These technologies are rather complicated, and I can provide only a relatively short summary. But don't skip over the technical introduction; if you don't understand how these methods work, you won't be able to understand exactly what the specific studies mean. Science reporters love brain imaging studies, and just about every month you'll see a news story about "the location" of one or another human ability or personality trait, or you'll read that a certain region "lights up" or "turns on" when we're engaged in a particular task. These stories are almost always misleading. Not long ago, a friend who had read one of these news stories asked me, "Isn't creativity in the right anterior cingulate cortex?" The answer is no, and creativity isn't located in any other specific brain region, either. After reading this chapter, you'll realize why that's the case, and you'll be prepared to understand what these experiments really mean.

BRAIN ANATOMY

The brain is made up of between 100 and 150 billion neurons. Each neuron connects with between 1,000 and 10,000 other neurons, at connections called *synapses*. A neuron receives signals through short tentacles called *dendrites*; it sums up those signals to determine the strength of the signal it sends down its one single *axon*. Each axon has as many as a thousand or more *axon terminals*, each of which transfers signals to the dendrites of other neurons. Most axons connect to nearby neighbors, but a small percentage of neurons have extremely long axons that can send signals across the brain. All neurons are constantly *firing*, sending neurotransmitters from the axon across the synapses to the dendrites. The strength of the signal is how many times per second it fires. A relatively calm neuron fires less than 10 times per second; a highly active neuron fires between 50 and 100 times per second.

Cognitive neuroscientists focus on the *neocortex*, the thin layer of "gray matter" on the outside of the brain, because it's responsible for all higher-level mental functions. The neocortex is about 5 mm thick (Huettel et al. 2009, p. 185). Inside the brain, below this outer layer, is the "white matter"; this large area is filled with the longer axons that connect distant parts of the brain. It appears to be white because the axons are covered with *myelin*, a fatty substance that increases the efficiency and speed of the axon's electrical transmission. The neocortex appears to be gray in contrast, because it contains the neuronal cell bodies and the blood vessels that supply blood to the brain.

If you've ever seen a picture of a brain, you'll remember that it's wrinkled (Fig. 10.1). Neuroscientists say that it's *folded*, and this is because the folds allow more of the outer cortical layer to fit into the skull. The tops of the folds—the part that's pressed right up to the skull—are

(a)

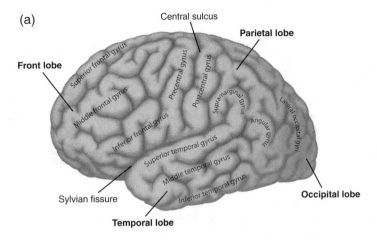

Central sulcus

Parietal lobe

Front lobe

Superior frontal gyrus

Middle frontal gyrus

Inferior frontal gyrus

Precentral gyrus

Postcentral gyrus

Supramarginal gyrus

Angular gyrus

Lateral occipital gyri

Superior temporal gyrus

Middle temporal gyrus

Inferior temporal gyrus

Sylvian fissure

Temporal lobe

Occipital lobe

(b)

Right hemisphere

Central sulcus

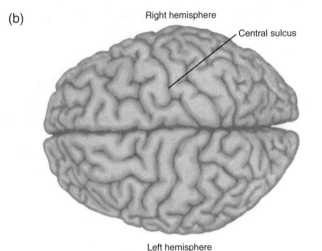

Left hemisphere

FIGURE 10.1: Gross brain anatomy. (a) Lateral view of the left hemisphere. (b) Dorsal view of the cerebral cortex. The major features of the cortex include the four cortical lobes and various key gyri. Gyri (singular is "gyrus") are separated by sulci (singular is "sulcus") and result from the folding of the cortex. (From p. 71 of Gazzaniga, M., Ivry, R. B., & Mangun, G. R. (2002). *Cognitive neuroscience: The biology of the mind* (2nd ed.). New York: Norton. Copyright (c) 2002 by W. W. Norton & Company, Inc. Used by permission of W. W. Norton & Company, Inc.

called the *gyri*; the crevices are called *sulci*. The total surface area of the cortex is about 2,300 cm squared—about the size of a 12-inch pizza—but two thirds of that is within the depths of the sulci.

HOW IT'S DONE

Cognitive neuroscientists primarily use three different brain imaging methods: EEG, PET, and fMRI. Each has its own strengths and weaknesses; two of the methods are sometimes used in combination to take advantage of their complementary strengths.

EEG

Neurons transmit signals down the axon and the dendrites via an electrical impulse. *Electroencephalography (EEG)* uses sensors placed on the scalp that measure electromagnetic fields generated by this neural activity. EEG detects the electrical activity at the dendrites—the receiving end of the synapse. If many neurons and their dendrites are lined up in parallel, and if many of them are receiving signals at the same time, then a tiny magnetic field is created. In the cerebral cortex, neurons and dendrites are aligned in parallel, so a detectable electromagnetic field is generated. Neurons aren't necessarily aligned in the basal regions of the brain, and that electrical signal is weaker at the scalp; thus, in general only cortical activity is studied using EEG.

In the most common arrangement, 20 sensors are placed on the head in standard locations. (More specialized studies use as many as 256 electrodes.) In an EEG study, a person is presented with a stimulus. In many studies, the person is asked to evaluate the stimulus, and then told to press a button if a particular condition holds. The EEG that's recorded right after the stimulus is presented, or right at the time that the decision is made and the button pressed, is called an *event-related potential (ERP)*.

The neurons in the brain are constantly firing, and the brain always generates electric waves of amplitudes between 50 and 200 microvolts. The ERPs that psychologists are interested in are much smaller—usually just a few microvolts. As a result, in an EEG experiment, the participant is given the same activity 50 or even 100 times; then, mathematical algorithms are used to average over all of the trials (Fig. 10.2). The normal brain waves of 50 to 200 microvolts cancel each other out, and what remains is the change in brain activity that's directly related to the stimulus event—the ERP. EEG signals of interest to cognitive scientists occur in the frequency range of 1 to 50 Hz, and ERP signals typically occur in 0.5 to 20 Hz.

Different frequency bands of the brain's electromagnetic field indicate different sorts of brain activity:

- Delta waves (0.5–4 Hz)—during deep sleep
- Theta waves (4–8 Hz)—greater in childhood; implicated in encoding and retrieval of information
- Alpha waves (8–13 Hz)—occur while awake, while relaxed with the eyes closed
- Beta waves (13–30 Hz)—increased alertness and focused attention
- Gamma waves (>30 Hz)—still not well understood, but have been implicated in creating the unity of conscious perception

Cognitive neuroscientists typically study alpha, beta, and gamma waves.

The advantage of EEG is that it can detect the brain's response to the external stimulus event essentially immediately—to the microsecond. This is referred to as a high *temporal resolution*. The disadvantage is that EEG can't tell us much about where the neurons are that are causing the change in the electromagnetic field; this weakness is referred to as a low *spatial resolution*. Even though there are 20 electrodes positioned around the skull, an ERP at any particular electrode doesn't necessarily mean that the ERP was caused by neurons immediately underneath that electrode, because electromagnetic fields extend across the brain. To identify the brain regions associated with neuronal activity, we need technologies capable of a higher spatial resolution—PET and fMRI.

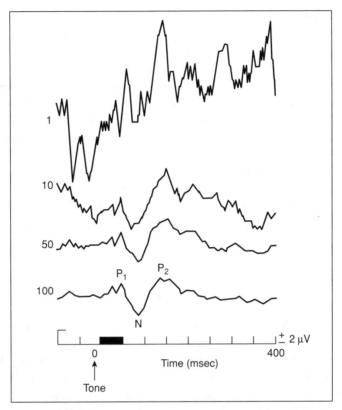

FIGURE 10.2: In EEG experiments, participants are presented with the same stimulus or task up to 100 times, and the EEG waves are averaged across all of the tasks to reduce the signal-to-noise ratio and reveal the ERP associated with the task. These are waves of the EEG in response to presentation of an audio tone at time 0. The topmost wave represents a typical EEG from a single trial; the other waves represent averaging across 10, 50, and 100 trials. This is done for each electrode, and each will have a slightly different ERP profile. (From *Fundamentals of Human Neuropsychology*, 5e by Bryan Kolb and Ian Q. Whishaw. © 2003 by Worth Publishers.)

PET

When neurons in a particular region of the neocortex are firing more rapidly, that region is said to have *elevated neuronal activation*. As a result of elevated activity, the neurons require more oxygen, and blood flow is greater to that region. *Positron emission tomography (PET)* indirectly measures neuronal activity by detecting local changes in regional cerebral blood flow (rCBF). PET works by introducing a radioactive tracer into the bloodstream; where there's more blood flow, there's more radiation. A radioactive isotope of oxygen is often used that decays rapidly—a fast decay is important to reduce the amount of radiation exposure. O-15 is the most commonly used oxygen isotope; it has a half-life of 122 seconds.

During a PET experiment, a person is given a cognitive task that can be done in approximately the time it takes for the oxygen isotope to decay. After approximately 40 seconds, most of the O-15 isotope has decayed and the signal has peaked. While he or she is engaged in this task, the associated brain regions will increase in neuronal activation; rCBF will increase to those regions; and the increased radioactivity is detected by the PET scanner—a large doughnut-shaped device with the head placed at the center. The result is a three-dimensional representation of the brain activity associated with the cognitive task.

PET has a fairly high spatial resolution; the technology is able to measure the neuronal activity associated with a neocortical region of about 5 mm³. This 5-mm³ space is called a *voxel* for *volume element*—the word has an "x" in it because it's derived from "pixel," the term for the two-dimensional "picture element" that's used in televisions and computer screens. The size of the voxel is referred to as the *spatial resolution* of the image; smaller voxels equals higher spatial resolution. On average, neural density in the neocortex is 20,000 to 30,000 neurons per 1 mm³, and the number of synapses in a cortical space of 1 mm³ is close to 1 billion. This means that in the typical study we'll read about in this chapter, each voxel effectively contains 5.5 million neurons and about 50 billion synapses (Logothetis, 2008, p. 875).

Compared to EEG, PET has a very low temporal resolution; whereas EEG detects the ERP essentially immediately, PET requires a full 40 seconds (the time associated with the isotope decay) to measure elevated brain activity.

fMRI

Functional magnetic resonance imaging (fMRI) emerged a few years after PET but has rapidly become the most widely used brain imaging technique. It's been called "the most important imaging advance since the introduction of X-rays" in 1895 (Logothetis, 2008, p. 869). The fMRI machine detects the ratio of oxygenated to deoxygenated blood, because each affects the magnetic field differently. The ratio is referred to as the *blood oxygen level-dependent (BOLD)* signal. When neuronal activation increases in a region of the neocortex, blood flow increases faster than the neurons can use the oxygen, causing the BOLD signal to increase.

fMRI is used much more than PET because the machines are more readily available, the spatial resolution is higher, and you don't have to inject radioactive tracers with each trial, allowing hundreds of trials, which can then be averaged. (With a PET experiment you can do at most about 30 trials, because you have to inject the radioactive isotope just before each trial; 12 to 16 trials is more typical.) Also the temporal resolution is higher; with PET, you average over 40 seconds engaged in an activity (because even the fastest isotopes decay over 40 seconds), but you can get an fMRI image every two seconds, allowing for an event-related fMRI, similar to the ERP you get from EEG. As with EEG, changes to any single event are impossible to detect because of the complexity of brain response; when you average the responses to 50 trials, you average out the unrelated brain activity fluctuations and you see the signal related to the event being studied.

There are three challenging problems with fMRI that result from its dependence on BOLD signal changes. First, BOLD increases above the resting state only between 1% and 3% at maximum neuronal activation. When cognitive neuroscientists report increased activation in a particular brain region, they're reporting an increase that's never greater than 3% above the comparison baseline state of the normal neuronal firing rate. Second, when neurons increase in activation, the BOLD signal doesn't increase immediately; the initial rise doesn't occur for several seconds after the increase in neuronal activity, the peak is 4 to 6 seconds later, and it doesn't decline back to baseline for 15 or 20 seconds (Fink et al., 2007; Huettel et al., 2009). The delay varies between individuals, so experiments have to correct for that variation. And, the delay varies across different brain regions even in the same person; there's no known way to normalize these variations, but they're not large. Third, the spatial location of BOLD doesn't always correspond exactly to the neurons that are increasing in activation, because BOLD detects the anatomic locations of the blood vessels that supply the neurons, not the location of the neurons themselves (Huettel et al., 2009). For accurate localization, fMRI has to detect blood flow in the tiniest capillaries, the ones immediately next to the neuronal bodies, but there are much larger blood vessels that feed those capillaries. fMRI technology is largely able to focus only on the smallest capillaries, but this ability varies subtly with different cortical regions. Researchers who use fMRI have developed techniques to account for these problems, but it will always be an inexact methodology because of one final challenge: when neurons become more active, blood flow increases not only right next to those neurons, but also over a bigger area that extends to a few millimeters distant, where there may be no increase in neuronal activity (Huettel et al., 2009, p. 179).

COMBINING METHODS

Because these technologies have complementary strengths, they can be used together to develop fairly elaborate understandings of how activity in the biological brain corresponds to human mental functioning. One of the most common approaches used today is to use EEG for its high temporal resolution; then to use fMRI with the same task for its high spatial resolution; then to combine the two findings for a full picture of the brain's activity.

STATISTICAL IMAGE AVERAGING

With EEG and fMRI, it's not possible to study just one response to a single event, because there are large changes in the EEG signal or BOLD signal that are always occurring as part of the brain's normal activity. So in an EEG or fMRI experiment, each participant has to do the same task tens or even hundreds of times, and the ERP is averaged across all of these trials; the normal background variation of the brain's EEG wave or BOLD signal is then averaged out, and what remains is the ERP of interest. So when a specific voxel shows "elevated neuronal activation" in a particular task, the brain isn't necessarily engaging these regions every time it engages in the task; what we're seeing is an average over lots of repetitions of the task.

Standard Brains

To account for the ordinary variability in human brains, cognitive neuroscientists don't study a single person. Instead, they perform the same experiment on many people, they do statistical image averaging across all of the brains, and then they use statistical algorithms to identify the average location of the brain activation in an experiment, across all of the subjects' brain images, averaged together to generate a single "average" brain image.

Every one of us has slightly different fingerprints, even though they all look like fingerprints. And every one of us has a recognizable face, even though all faces have the same two eyes, one mouth, and one nose. In a similar way, each human brain is slightly different, even though the overall organization of all brains is quite similar. Heads come in different sizes and shapes: some more narrow, some shorter front to back. This means that to compare two brains, you have to mathematically adjust the size of all of the brains so that they're basically the same. Most researchers adjust the brains to align with a *standard brain* as published in standard neuroscience atlases. Otherwise, normal anatomic variation would make averaging impossible.

Even after doing this, brains differ in the size of the different gyri and the location of folds in the brain; the location of sulci can vary by as much as a centimeter. There's at present no method for manipulating each brain's detailed structure to conform to a standard. To accommodate this natural variation in brain structure, most studies use a mathematical technique known as *smoothing*—which spreads out the observed activation, thus increasing the chance of overlap among different individuals when statistical image averaging is done.

Movement

Whenever you move your hands, or bend your knee, or turn your head, large regions of the brain are active, including vast areas of the neocortex, where higher-level thought takes place. Even blinking an eye, or twisting your head a tiny bit, or moving your eyes to the side even while your head is stationary, or twitching a leg muscle, causes neuronal activation that can interfere with the image. With the EEG, eye and eyelid movements create electric frequencies in the same range as the EEG signal. For these artifacts, there's a standard "correction" that subtracts out the artifact. When there are a lot of artifacts, it's often possible to interpolate the signal from the neighboring electrodes. But sometimes the artifacts are severe and the trial has to be rejected completely.

As a result, it's important for participants to remain completely still during these experiments. Typically the head is physically restrained, and participants are asked not to move, but even so, heads often still move enough to affect the results. There are algorithms that are used to correct for head movement with the fMRI. And with fMRI, the vocal tract causes electromagnetic activity in the same range as the BOLD signal, making it difficult to design experiments during which participants talk. In most experiments, participants are given a small handheld device with a single button and are instructed to push the button depending on what they perceive. This requires only one finger to move a short distance.

PAIRED IMAGE SUBTRACTION

Three facts about the brain make cognitive neuroscience challenging:

- First, every neuron is always firing, so researchers always refer to relative activation levels, rather than neurons being "on" or "off."
- Second, it's not the case that when we stare off into space, all of our brain's neurons are firing only at a low activation level. Large parts of the brain are always fairly active.
- Third, there are parts of the cortex that always increase in neuronal activation whenever we engage in any cognitive task.

Cognitive neuroscientists are interested in all of these aspects of the brain; however, most of the time they try to identify specific cortical regions that increase in activation in one kind of task but not in others.

The methodology that allows researchers to identify specific brain regions associated with specific tasks, despite these three challenging facts, is called *paired image subtraction*. In every experiment, the first thing that's done is that a brain image is taken during a carefully selected "control state" or "baseline state." The participant lies still and does nothing, or performs some simple comparison activity. This baseline is sometimes called the *rest state*. Then, this baseline image is subtracted from the image that results during the task condition. The key to designing an effective experiment is to design two tasks that are identical in every way except for one small change that's the cognitive function of interest. The subtraction cancels out the normal activation levels of all of the neurons that don't undergo any change in activation level (facts 1 and 2) and it cancels out all of the neurons that change in activation level the same way in both conditions (fact 3). The image that results shows the differences in activity between a task condition and the baseline of brain activity (Fig. 10.3). A specific brain region might be increasingly active in both the experimental and control conditions, but if the increase is greater in the experimental condition, the visual display will show heightened activation for the experimental condition.

Paired image subtraction makes a key assumption: *pure insertion*, meaning that the additional cognitive process can be inserted into the baseline process without indirectly changing

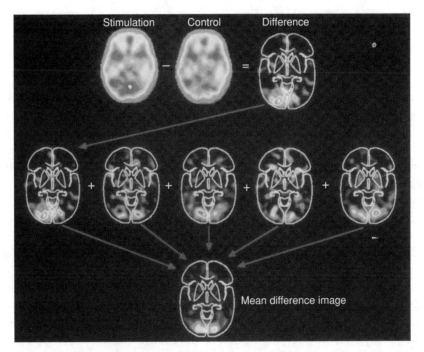

FIGURE 10.3: In the upper row of these PET scans, the control condition (resting while looking at a static fixation point) is subtracted from the experimental condition of looking at a flickering checkerboard 5.5 degrees from the fixation point. The subtraction produces a slightly different image for each of five subjects, as shown in the middle row. Statistical image averaging across these five subjects results in the image at the bottom. This procedure is always used to generate the images you see in research reports and in media coverage of these studies. Brain PET scan taken from the book *Images of Mind* by Michael I. Posner and Marcus E. Raichle. Copyright © 1994, 1997 by Scientific American Library. Reprinted by permission of Henry Holt and Company, LLC.

any of the activity associated with the baseline process. But this assumption is probably rarely the case, because the brain is complex and nonlinear (Logothetis, 2008, p. 871). There's no way to detect these indirect changes.

COGNITIVE CONJUNCTION

Some studies make use of the technique of *cognitive conjunction*. They have people do two slightly different tasks, such that each of the tasks shares one common cognitive component. Then, they do a paired image subtraction for each of the conditions against the resting state. Finally, they identify which regions of heightened activation are shared across the two tasks; these regions are presumably associated with the common cognitive component.

MIND WANDERING AND INCUBATION

> *Watching older kids study, or try to study, I saw after a while that they were not sufficiently self-aware to know when their minds had wandered off the subject . . . Most of us have very imperfect control over our attention. Our minds slip away from duty before we realize that they are gone.*
> —Legendary teacher John Holt, in *How Children Fail,* (1964, pp. 7–8)

We learned in Chapter 5 that incubation often results in the sudden emergence of a good idea. And all of us have experienced the phenomenon of *mind wandering,* when our thoughts drift away from the task at hand to something completely unrelated. We shift away from a primary task to process some other, personal goals, but in a way that's not obviously goal-directed or intentional. There's some evidence that people prone to mind wandering score higher on tests of creativity (Hotz, 2009b; Tierney, 2010). What happens in the brain when the mind is wandering? Recent studies of the brain's idle states can potentially help us answer this question.

The brain is always active, even when the research participant is just lying in the scanner, staring at the ceiling, wondering what's for dinner that night, whether he got his parking ticket validated, or whatever. That's why the first step of any brain imaging study is to take a *baseline* or *resting* image of the brain, so that it can be subtracted from the brain while it's actively engaged in the task of interest. The most common resting state is to have the participant focus on a simple "X" target that's displayed in the same location where the stimuli will be presented. Some experiments simply average out a few brain images taken in the seconds before the experiment starts (while the participant is probably wondering when it's going to start).

The brain accounts for about 2% of body weight but uses about 20% of all the energy the body consumes, even in a resting state with the eyes closed. When your mind starts thinking hard about a difficult problem, the brain's energy consumption rarely increases by more than 5% (Raichle, 2009). And I've already noted that from minimal to maximal neuronal activity, the blood demand almost never increases more than 3%. So it's not surprising that fMRI studies have shown that the brain's resting state is quite similar to the problem-solving state, to conceptual processing, and to memory retrieval (see citations in Smallwood & Schooler, 2006, p. 955).

During waking hours, people's minds wander between 15% and 50% of the time, depending on the task. For example, people's minds are wandering 20% of the time they're reading, and half of those times they're not even aware that their minds are wandering (Smallwood & Schooler, 2006, p. 956). Mind wandering, which is closely related to daydreaming, is dominated by typical life events and is rarely focused on fantasy (Andrews-Hanna et al., 2010; Singer & Antrobus, 1963). Mind wandering varies with fatigue, with alcohol, and with the difficulty of the task. Kane et al. (2007) found that it averaged 30% in an experiential sampling of everyday life, and that it varied depending on working memory capacity. In people with high working memory capacity, their minds wandered less when the task required focused concentration, but their minds wandered more when task demands were low.

Klinger (2009) found that on average, people have about 4,000 thoughts of all kinds during a typical day, each averaging 14 seconds in length, and that half of these qualify as "daydreaming," defined as undirected mind wandering or thought that is at least partially fanciful (p. 228). He hypothesized that even in cognitively demanding tasks, there would be a minimum rate of daydreaming of about 10% of the time.

Raichle (2009) identified a *default network*—parts of the brain that are active in the resting state but that, intriguingly, become less active when engaged in various cognitive tasks. Brain imaging has found that the default network continues to be active in tasks that involve passive sensory processing, but it tends to reduce its activity with tasks with high central executive demand—which is exactly what you'd expect with mind wandering. Mason et al. (2007) found that when people were engaged in a task they had practiced on, allowing them to daydream, the default network was more active than when they were engaged in a novel task. These same regions reduce in activity when you become unconscious (Andrews-Hanna et al., 2010). Christoff et al. (2009) found that the default network was most active when people's minds were wandering and they weren't aware of it. There's evidence that task performance is more severely disrupted by mind wandering when you're not aware it's happening.

Studies of mind wandering reveal that we spend more of our daily lives engaged in an incubation-like state than we probably realize. People typically are consciously aware of only half of their mind-wandering episodes. I propose an intriguing hypothesis: mind wandering serves to provide us with moments of "mini-incubation" that contribute to creative thought by temporarily taking our minds away from the problem at hand and providing a brief opportunity for insight to occur.

CREATIVE INSIGHT

The very front of the brain is associated with all of the highest, most deeply human abilities— what are sometimes called "controlling" and "executive" functions of the brain (Srinivasan, 2007). From brain lesion patients, we've long known that patients who have lesions in this area "lack initiative, foresight, activity and ability to handle new tasks . . . impaired in voluntary shifting and choice" (Goldstein, 1944, p. 192). Representational systems, such as symbols and verbal meanings, are processed in the frontal lobes.

Dietrich (2004) hypothesized that conscious and deliberate creativity is driven by the front of the brain, but that spontaneous insight emerges from three cortices behind and under the frontal cortex—the temporal, occipital, and parietal (TOP). The TOP areas are devoted primarily to perception and to long-term memory; they receive many neuronal axon signals from the lower, sensory brain systems. The frontal lobe doesn't receive direct sensory input; it integrates already highly processed information from the TOP to enable even higher-level cognitive behaviors like abstract thinking, planning, willed action, working memory, and attention. Chapter 6 surveyed the research on the moment of insight, studies that typically use "insight problems" and make the assumption that the problem can be solved only with a moment of insight. Brain imaging technologies are ideally suited to identifying the brain regions associated with creative insight.

One problem with using insight problems in brain imaging studies is that many people say they solve them without actually having an experience of insight. Instead, they say that they worked systematically and incrementally toward the solution. For example, the three-word RAT puzzles summarized in Chapter 3 are sometimes solved without an accompanying sensation of insight. Perhaps the sensation of insight is purely a subjective feeling of emotional intensity or excitement at having found the problem, but it doesn't actually contribute to solving the problem. Weisberg (1986) has argued that insight and non-insight problems are solved through exactly the same cognitive processes, and that insight is largely a myth.

The methodology of cognitive neuroscience is perfectly suited to determining whether insightful solutions result from different brain activity than solutions with no insight. Mark Jung-Beeman and colleagues at Northwestern and Drexel Universities (Jung-Beeman et al., 2004) conducted a series of experiments to determine what happens in the brain when people are solving insight problems. Their study was designed to address three questions:

1. Is there any unconscious processing that immediately precedes the sudden conscious awareness of the insight? Several studies in Chapter 6, using the "priming" experimental methodology, suggest an affirmative answer.
2. Are there different cognitive and neural mechanisms involved in having an insight solution versus ordinary problem-solving processes?
3. Does the sudden "Aha!" experience reflect a sudden change in the brain?

Solving problems with insight and without insight are likely to both involve many of the same cognitive processes and neural mechanisms. But insight solutions seem to require distant or remote associations; the brain area associated with associative relations is the anterior superior temporal gyrus (aSTG) of the right hemisphere. Language comprehension studies show that sentences and complex discourse increase aSTG activation in both hemispheres, and that when distant semantic relations are used, the right hemisphere (RH) aSTG is more active.

Their first experiment used fMRI with 13 subjects. They used 124 RAT triplets (see Bowden & Jung-Beeman, 2003b), and gave the participants 30 seconds to identify each target word. As soon as they identified the word, they pressed the button in their hand. The researchers asked them to say the word out loud, simply to confirm that they had the correct word. Then, they were asked to press the button again if they had a feeling of insight.

Fifty-nine percent of the problems were solved, and people reported feeling insight for 56% of these solutions. They examined six seconds of brain activity around the time of the first button press. The subjects who reported having a sensation of insight showed a heightened brain activation in the RH aSTG compared to those who didn't have the insight sensation.

The temporal resolution of fMRI isn't high; in this experiment, one brain image was taken per second. Thus, the findings from this experiment might reflect simply a subjective experience of insight, and it's that subjective experience that corresponds to the RH aSTG—but that region might not have anything to do with the insight itself, just with the sensation of insight. The real question is, was the problem actually solved differently when subjects felt they were having an insight? To answer that question we need a higher temporal resolution—so the researchers did exactly the same experiment and compared the time–frequency analyses of the EEGs of insight solutions and non-insight solutions.

They found that there was a burst of gamma-wave activity in the front RH (but not left hemisphere [LH]) associated with insight solutions about 0.3 seconds before the solution button-press, but not with non-insight solutions. In other words, when people reported a feeling of insight, they had a burst of frontal RH brain activity just before they pressed the button, but not when they solved without insight. The researchers interpret this as the sudden conscious availability of the solution word: the moment of insight.

However, the activity continued to increase for a full second after the button was pushed, suggesting an alternative explanation: they might reflect the excitement of getting the solution—an effect of the solution rather than a cause (see Sheth et al., 2008). But the burst of gamma activity in the EEG began before the button press, rather than after it. In another study (Jung-Beeman, Bowden, & Haberman, 2002), when insight was reported, there was greater neuronal activity in the RH superior temporal sulcus for the final two seconds before participants solved the problems than when no insight was reported. Two seconds is long enough that it most likely precedes the subjective conscious awareness of knowing the solution.

In another study (Kounios et al., 2006), different alpha wave patterns *preceded* the *presentation* of the problem when insight solutions were reported. There was no difference in the EEG between getting the answer versus not getting the answer, suggesting that subjects were doing the same basic sort of mental work whether or not they got the answer. In Experiment 2, the researchers obtained an fMRI to identify the brain regions before the problem was presented. Preparation preceding the presentation of problems that were then solved with insight involved greater activity of the anterior cingulate cortex (ACC). In other words, you could predict whether insight would be used even *before* the person saw the problem! They conclude that ACC activity is responsible for the alpha-wave mid-frontal activity detected with the EEG.

Sheth et al. (2008), using EEG, found brain differences up to eight seconds before the solution when the problem was solved with insight. They observed a reduction in beta power (15–25 Hz) over the parieto-occipital and centro-temporal regions with: (a) correct versus incorrect solutions (compared ten second pre-response); (b) solutions without a hint versus with a hint (compared ten second pre-response); (c) success after the hint is provided versus no success (they examined ten seconds before the hint and ten seconds after); and (d) self-reported high insight versus low insight. Gamma-band (30–70 Hz) power was increased in the right fronto-central and frontal regions for (a) and (c). Lower alpha was increased for insight versus non-insight solutions in the central-parietal region. The most intriguing result was that for those who were stumped and then got a hint, the brain activation pattern was different, even before the hint was presented, for those who eventually got the answer versus those who didn't.

Luo and Knoblich (2007) presented insight problems (Example: "the thing that can move heavy logs, but cannot move a small nail"; answer: "river") followed by either hints that lead to restructuring, or hints that reinforced the incorrect structuring. When they provided a restructuring hint, they observed activation in the bilateral superior frontal gyrus, the medial frontal gyrus extending to the cingulate cortex, and the bilateral posterior middle temporal gyrus. They also found ACC activation with insight problems versus non-insight problems. Interestingly, ACC activation declined with time, suggesting that subjects were developing general strategies to deal with this sort of word problem.

Fink et al. (2009) found an increase in alpha synchronization in frontal brain regions and a diffuse and widespread pattern over parietal cortical regions. Alpha synchronization was higher in response to more free associative tasks (like the Alternative Uses test, a Name Invention task), and more original ideas were associated with stronger increases in alpha activity than conventional ideas. Their fMRI found strong activation of LH frontal regions, particularly the left inferior frontal gyrus (also found by Jung-Beeman, 2005).

Sandkuhler and Bhattacharya (2008) gave people RAT triplets; they could press a button if they were stumped, and right away they'd be shown a hint: the first letter of the target word, or half of the letters of the target word. The first two seconds while they were reading the problem was used as a baseline. They found strong gamma-band responses in parieto-occipital regions for sudden versus nonsudden solutions (38–44 Hz). They also found increased upper alpha-band response (8–12 Hz) in the right temporal regions, suggesting active suppression of weakly activated solution-relevant information, for initially unsuccessful trials that after a hint led to the correct solution.

One of the interesting benefits of cognitive neuroscience is that it can tell us the full range of tasks that a particular brain region is implicated in. From a large number of experiments, we know, for example, that the RH prefrontal cortex also experiences elevated activation with problems requiring a set-shift transformation, and on tasks involving sequential thinking when a belief–logic conflict causes a change in the reasoning process; and it helps make available a set of alternative and less probable word meanings in a lexical task.

Vartanian and Goel (2007) summarized several studies focused on *hypothesis generation* and *set shift*: a movement from one state in a problem space to a very different state, with no obvious incremental step-by-step transition (also see Goel & Vartanian, 2005). These included studies on Guilford's match problems (requiring rearranging matches to generate a specified number of squares), which compared a divergent condition (generate all of the possible ways this problem could be solved) to a convergent condition (subjects were presented with a hypothetical solution and asked to say whether it was correct). Hypothesis generation activated left dorsal lateral prefrontal cortex (PFC) and right ventral lateral PFC (vs. baseline). When subjects got a correct solution—which was evidence of a set shift—only the left dorsal lateral PFC was still increased in activation versus baseline.

With anagram problems, right ventral lateral PFC was activated when problems were solved without any hint ("Can you make a word with CENFAR?") versus given a specific semantic category as a hint ("Can you make a country with CENFAR?"). They concluded that hypothesis generation in open-ended settings activates a network that includes right ventral lateral PFC, for both spatial and linguistic stimuli. These are different areas than the ones implicated in insight studies—there, it's the right temporal lobe. In another study, they found that activation in right dorsal lateral PFC covaried with the total number of solutions generated in response to match problems—which could be the result of working memory, cognitive monitoring, or conflict resolution.

Kounios et al. (2008) also studied anagram problems, and focused on the resting state. They split everyone into two groups based on how they said they solved anagram problems: one group with people who were more likely to report solving a problem with insight (the "high insight" group [HI]) and another group who were less likely to report using insight (the "low insight" group [LI]). HI people had different resting-state EEGs (the resting state is the period just before the anagram was shown to them) compared to LI people. LI people had more high alpha—which indicates less activity in the visual cortex—than the HI group. This suppression of activity was greater in the LH. The LI group had greater beta-1 EEG as well, suggesting more focused visual attention. The HI group had more RH activity, in low alpha, beta-2, beta-3, and gamma frequency ranges. Kounios et al. explained these findings by suggesting that a person's likelihood of using insight to solve a problem is influenced by the characteristics of the prior resting state; they could predict the likelihood that you'd use insight to solve an anagram by analyzing your EEG during the resting state just before they showed you the anagram. The tendency to use insight or not remained stable through the course of the experiment; people used the same amount of insight in the second half of the experiment as in the first half, for example, and many other studies have shown that resting-state EEG is relatively stable over time.

In the above experiments, the brain regions that display elevated neuronal activity aren't some mysterious nether regions of the brain; other brain imaging studies show that they're involved in a wide range of cognitive tasks, many of which we don't associate with creativity *per se*. The RH aSTG is implicated in integration across sentences to extract themes; to form coherent memories for stories; to generate the best ending for a sentence; and to repair grammatically incorrect sentences. The ACC is implicated in monitoring for competition among potential responses or processes; in voluntary selection; in conflict monitoring; in decision making; and in unrehearsed movements (see Berkowitz & Ansari, 2008, p. 541). Some studies suggest that the ACC is involved in suppressing irrelevant thoughts. Neuronal activity in the ACC was elevated with insight solutions, suggesting that shifting the mind away from an answer that you've discovered is incorrect involves cognitive control mechanisms similar to those involved in suppressing irrelevant thoughts.

STUDIES OF DIVERGENT THINKING

There's a variety of evidence that the RH is more effective at semantic processing of distant associates (Bowden & Jung-Beeman, 2003a; Howard-Jones et al., 2005). And there's some evidence that the prefrontal part of the RH supports processing of distant associations (Seger et al., 2000).

Howard-Jones et al. (2005) used the three-word short story task described in Chapter 3 (pp. 45–46). Recall that they created four conditions using two variables: (1) instructing subjects to "be creative" or "be uncreative"; (2) providing subjects with three unrelated words (flea, sing, sword), or three related words (magician, trick, rabbit). While in an fMRI scanner, the participants were given 22 seconds to generate a story. After they left the scanner, they were asked to recall a random sample of 20 of the stories they had generated (five stories from each condition). Using paired image subtraction to subtract the "uncreative" condition image from the "creative" condition image, they observed an increase in prefrontal activity, including bilateral medial frontal gyri and left ACC. When participants were combining unrelated words as opposed to related words, additional activity was also found in bilateral ACC and right medial frontal gyrus.

As with the insight studies, these brain areas aren't unique to creative tasks; they're involved in a wide range of cognitive tasks. Left prefrontal activation occurs in word-association tasks and sentence-completion tasks. Increased ACC activity has been linked to a wide range of tasks with increased information-processing demands, including selecting items from episodic memory. Making divergent associations requires increased conflict monitoring; the ACC and the PFC are associated with additional conflict monitoring (Howard-Jones et al., 2005, p. 248) and with insight solutions (see above).

CREATIVE BRAINS VERSUS NON-CREATIVE BRAINS

The methods of cognitive neuroscience aren't able to reliably analyze the activity within a single person's brain, but they can be used to identify differences between groups of people, so long as there are enough people in each group to do statistical image averaging in each group. A few studies have examined differences in neuronal activity between people who get high scores on creativity tests and people who get low scores. In one of the earliest studies, using EEG, Martindale and Hines (1975) found that creative people show higher levels of alpha-wave activity when engaged in creative tasks like the Alternate Uses Test and the RAT, whereas medium- and low-creative groups had low alpha-wave activity.

Carlsson et al. (2000) used the Creative Functioning Test (CFT; see p. 46) to select a high-creativity and a low-creativity group (each with 12 male right-handed students). They then presented three tasks that were expected to activate the frontal lobes increasingly: the lowest expected activation was for an automatic speech task (count aloud, starting with 1); the next higher activation was a word fluency task (say all the words you can think of that start with the letter "f" or "a" or "s"); and the final activation was a divergent thinking task (say as many uses as you can think of for a brick). Only the divergent thinking task was expected to activate RH areas associated with creativity. Low creatives had more elevated LH during the word fluency task; high creatives had more elevated RH during the brick test. (Strangely, the automatic counting task resulted in higher blood flow than either of the other two tasks; the researchers don't know why.) The biggest differences, when comparing brain activity on the f-a-s task and on the brick task, were elevated anterior PFC in creatives (both hemispheres) and decreased fronto-temporal and anterior PFC activity for low creatives (particularly in the RH).

They concluded that high creatives use bilateral prefrontal regions on the brick task, while low creatives used mostly LH. High creatives had more increased activity in these regions, compared to the f-a-s task, than low creatives—whose brains looked about the same in the f-a-s and the brick tasks.

Chávez-Eakle and her team (Chávez-Eakle, 2007) compared six individuals with TTCT scores in the 99th percentile with six individuals at the 50th percentile by giving them the Unusual Uses test. The high scorers on the Verbal TTCT had greater cerebral blood flow in the right precentral gyrus; the high scorers on the Figural TTCT had greater cerebral blood flow in the right postcentral gyrus, left middle frontal gyrus, right rectal gyrus, right inferior parietal lobe, and right parahippocampal gyrus—indicating that "a bilaterally distributed brain system is involved in creative performance" (p. 217), although most of the elevated activity is in the RH.

These studies provide some evidence that in less creative people, the RH is slightly less active. But ultimately, these studies found that high creatives show patterns of bilateral hemispheric activation, consistent with the studies described in Chapter 9. As we've seen from other studies in this chapter and in Chapter 9, it's misleading to say that creativity is "in" the RH (also see Feist, 2010, p. 118; Kaufman et al., 2010, p. 221); keep in mind that with all brain imaging studies, the differences in neuronal activation reported are never more than 3% above baseline state.

STUDIES OF MUSICAL IMPROVISATION

A series of intriguing experiments have recently been conducted with trained musicians engaged in a variety of musical tasks. In the first such study, 11 professional pianists improvised while their heads were in the scanner, using a special keyboard with one octave of 12 keys (white and black). The musicians could hear what they were playing through scanner-safe headphones. They were instructed to improvise a simple melody based on an eight-note melody that was displayed to them, and then asked to reproduced the improvised melody (Bengtsson, Csikszentmihalyi, & Ullen, 2007). This resulted in "improvise minus reproduce" subtraction images. Then, the pianists freely improvised but without memorizing and reproducing the improvisation, and this resulting in "freeimp minus rest" subtraction images.

When the image of a brain reproducing an improvised melody was subtracted from an image of the brain improvising that melody for the first time (the "improvise minus reproduce" condition), there were significant brain differences in many regions including the right dorsolateral prefrontal cortex (DLPFC) and right presupplementary motor area; bilaterally in the rostral portion of the dorsal premotor cortex; temporal lobe activations in the left posterior superior temporal gyrus (STG), and the fusiform gyrus; and bilateral occipital activity in the middle occipital gyrus. Essentially, all of these areas were also activated in the conjunction between improv-reproduce and freeimp-rest. The right DLPFC is activated in many other free choice tasks, including word generation, number generation, word-stem completion, and sentence completion. A range of studies show that the DLPFC is centrally involved in planning and performing novel and complex behavioral sequences, including language and thought. Several of the other active areas are also activated in movement sequence production.

Berkowitz and Ansari (2008) studied 12 classically trained pianists engaged in four different tasks. The researchers designed a special five-note keyboard that the subjects could play with the fingers of one hand, moving only the fingers and not the hand. The keyboard had middle C through G, the white keys only. The subjects listened through scanner-safe headphones.

As with all cognitive neuroscience studies, the most important thing was the subtle differences between the different tasks that would be revealed by paired image subtraction; each task required a slightly different degree of improvisation. Before the experiment, the subjects were taught seven different five-note patterns that were extremely simple: either five presses of the same key (CCCCC, DDDDD, EEEEE, FFFFF, GGGGG), an ascending scale (CDEFG), or a descending scale (GFEDC). In their first task, the pianists played any of the five-note patterns, in any order they chose. Thus they had to make a decision every five notes, resulting in a rather small degree of melodic improvisation. In the second melodic improvisation task, the pianists continuously invented five-note melodies—thus making a decision every note.

Both of these tasks were performed with or without a metronome that clicked two beats each second. With the metronome, subjects were told to play only one note per click. With no metronome, subjects were told to improvise rhythmically as well as melodically. This design allowed the researchers to isolate the brain regions associated with three different activities: rhythmic improvisation alone, melodic improvisation alone, and both types of improvisation combined.

Using the cognitive conjunction technique, the conjunction of the brain images during the two melodic improvisation tasks was associated with increased neural activity in the dorsal premotor cortex, ACC, and inferior frontal gyrus/ventral premotor cortex, all in the LH (which was expected, since the task was performed with the right hand).

As with the insight and the divergent thinking tasks, these brain regions are the same ones that are used in a wide variety of everyday cognitive tasks. The dorsal premotor cortex is involved in a wide variety of motor tasks, including selection and performance of movements. ACC, which is implicated in insight and in divergent thinking, is involved in many cognitive tasks, including unrehearsed movements, decision making, voluntary selection, and willed action. The third region is part of Broca's area, typically associated with language production and understanding, or more generally with producing and processing sequential auditory information.

In sum, improvisation involves brain regions that are involved in generating and comprehending sequences, making decisions among competing alternatives, and creating a plan for the motor execution of that sequence. These are domain-general brain regions, suggesting a role for domain-general mental processes in creativity.

Limb and Braun (2008) used a more realistic improvisational musical task. They compared two conditions, using six trained jazz musicians: (1) subjects played a previously memorized jazz composition, while accompanied by a jazz quartet they could hear through headphones; and (2) subjects improvised over the same chord sequence, while hearing the same accompaniment through their headphones. Their keyboard had 35 full-sized keys.

The researchers also saw activation in the same three brain regions. But because the tasks were so much more complex, they found changes in activity in over 40 brain regions. Many of these are likely to be not specific to music or to improvisation, but related to general cognitive activity such as attention, working memory, and task complexity. One particularly interesting result was a decrease in activity in almost all of the lateral PFCs, particularly in the lateral orbital PFC and the DLPFC, suggesting inhibition of regions involved in monitoring and correction. They observed increased activation in superior and middle temporal gyri (STG and MTG) and ACC, as well as many other areas. They observed increased activity in the medial PFC, which has been associated with autobiographical narrative. The decreased activity was in the regions associated with consciously monitoring goal-directed behaviors.

As Berkowitz pointed out, "the brain imaging results from these two studies correlate quite well with artists' experiences of improvisation" (2010, p. 144). Improvisation involves brain regions associated with the skills that underlie improvisational thought: selection and performance of movement, decision making, language processing and sequential auditory information, and inhibition of monitoring. And as with all of the studies we've reviewed so far, no brain areas are uniquely associated with improvisation; all of these brain areas are involved in a wide variety of cognitive tasks, many of them not considered to be creative.

DIFFERENCES WITH TRAINING

We now know that the adult brain can generate new neurons, contrary to a previous belief that all neurons are present at birth. And neuroscientists have discovered that the brain is a lot more *plastic* than we previously realized—in other words, patterns of neuronal activation can change over time with experience. Of course, our brains must change any time we learn something—even the name of a person we met yesterday—but brain plasticity is much more extensive than simple fact learning; the structure of the brain itself can change. These changes can take years; for example, more fluent speakers of a second language process that language differently than less fluent speakers (Reiterer, Pereda, & Bhattacharya, 2009). But the brain is plastic enough to rewire itself in as little as a few weeks. One study showed that when the ACC is damaged, people can't talk for a few weeks, but then speech comes back to them as their brain is rewired to work around the damage (Posner & Raichle, 1994).

Brain imaging studies have found that people with musical training actually think about music differently, people with artistic training think about art differently, and people with dance training think about dance differently.

MUSIC TRAINING

When listening to music and when generating music, the brains of trained musicians show different patterns of activation. Berkowitz and Ansari (2010) compared trained musicians with non-musicians in a simple five-note improvisational task. The key difference was that the musicians deactivated the right temporoparietal junction while the non-musicians did not. This region is engaged in bottom-up stimulus-driven processing; deactivation of this region occurs to inhibit attentional shifts toward task-irrelevant stimuli during top-down, goal-driven behavior. Thus, musical training seems to result in a shift toward inhibition of stimulus-driven attention, allowing for a more goal-directed performance state. Schlaug (2006) demonstrated that trained musicians process a pitch memory task using different brain regions than non-musicians.

ART TRAINING

Bhattacharya and Petsche (2005) used EEG to compare artists (MFA graduates from the Academy of Fine Arts in Vienna) and non-artists mentally composing a drawing (while staring at a white wall) and found significantly different patterns of functional cooperation between cortical regions. Comparing the tasks to rest, artists showed stronger short- and long-range delta-band synchronization and non-artists showed enhanced short-range beta- and gamma-band synchronization, primarily in frontal regions; comparing the two groups during the task, artists showed stronger delta-band synchronization and alpha-band desynchronization, and strong

RH dominance in synchronization. Well-mastered tasks typically show greater coherence or synchronization across cortical regions. For example, expert chess players show stronger delta-band coherence than novices when anticipating chess movements. They interpret these differences as due to more advanced long-term visual memory, and extensive top-down processing.

DANCE TRAINING

Fink et al. (2009) compared expert professional dancers with beginning dancers who had just completed a first class in basic dance. They asked them to wear EEG electrodes while they mentally performed either an improvised dance or a classic waltz. They also did an Alternative Uses test (tin, brick, sock, ballpoint pen), and during these tests, the dancers showed stronger alpha synchronization in post-parietal brain regions. During improvisation imagery, dancers showed more RH alpha synchronization than the novices, while there were no differences with the waltz. They interpret increased alpha synchronization as inhibition (of processes not directly relevant), or top-down control.

These studies show that brain activation patterns are not genetic and are not prewired at birth. Neuronal activation can change fairly dramatically in response to environmental influences, experience, and learning.

CONCLUSION

> *[Creativity] cannot be reduced simply to the neural circuitry of an adult brain and even less to the genes behind our brains.*
> —Neuroscientist Antonio R. Damasio, (2001, p. 59)
>
> *If there was something truly distinctive in the brains of great men, great women, depraved hoodlums, or murderers, it would have been discovered by now. But nothing has turned up . . . all human brains look essentially alike.*
> —Burrell, (2004, p. 306)

Although this research methodology is still in its infancy, it has already contributed greatly to our understanding of creativity. We now know that many regions of the brain are active when people are engaged in creative tasks. And cognitive neuroscience has shown that when people are engaged in creative tasks, the same brain areas are active that are active in many everyday tasks—even in ordinary tasks that we don't think of as requiring any creativity at all. In sum, these studies show:

- Creativity is based in ordinary, everyday brain processes, not in a distinct part of the brain. Every normal, healthy human being is capable of engaging in these brain processes; they're required for everyday functioning.
- There's no evidence for the popular belief that creativity is located in the RH of the brain. Many regions of the brain, in both hemispheres and pretty much equally, are active during creative tasks.

The bottom line is that creativity is not localized to a specific brain region. That's consistent with the cognitive research we examined in Chapters 5, 6, and 7, which showed that creativity involves a wide variety of cognitive abilities. Each of these cognitive abilities is itself a complex and emergent property of the biological brain; each involves many brain regions at a moment in time, and each requires many successive moments in time. Creativity can't be reduced to a single brain region at a single moment in time—the mythical flash of insight.

There are several issues to keep in mind when considering this sort of experiment:

1. Neuroscientists agree that pretty much all cognitive function involves many parts of the brain all at once; regions that show elevated neuronal activation are scattered all over the brain. The colorful images that we occasionally see in a magazine, with a small bright red dot showing "the location" for whatever, result from *averaging* and *subtraction*; what we're not seeing in that image are the many brain regions that are active in both conditions, before the subtraction. If we focus too much on localization, we lose sight of the reality that what goes on in the brain is diffuse and distributed.

2. It's hard to use brain imaging studies to make claims about causation; an area may be activated during a task but not play a critical role in performing the task; rather, it might be "listening" to other brain areas that provide the critical computations.

3. These findings result from averaging across many trials, typically about 50 per experimental condition. The brain area reported in the research paper isn't necessarily active in every single trial; it's just statistically more likely that it's active in one condition versus another. So it's incorrect to say that "creativity is located in the ACC" or even "the right hemisphere," although a quick read through the above studies might misleadingly give that impression. This is why I've put so much information about the methodology at the beginning of this chapter: to dispel simplistic notions that these methodologies are telling us "where" certain functions are located in the brain.

4. For the most part, what cognitive neuroscience has discovered are facts that are largely already known from the classic experimental methods of cognitive psychology (Carey, 2006, p. 4). In the 1970s, these experiments had discovered that verbal information and visual information were represented differently in the brain—so when brain imaging shows that these two types of information result in different patterns of neuronal activation, no one is surprised. Researchers also had discovered that implicit memory and explicit memory were distinct long before cognitive neuroscience demonstrated that each corresponded to a different pattern of neuronal activation.

5. The scanners are large and expensive. People have to lie down and remain completely still while they listen to the loud whirring of the scanner's motor. Bodily movements, even quite small ones, activate large regions of the brain and overwhelm the signal associated with the mental processing of interest, so there's no hope of being able to study people engaged in normal activities in their everyday contexts.

Future technology can be expected to give us better and better images. However, there are limitations of these methods that cannot be overcome.

First, the temporal resolution of PET and fMRI can never be increased dramatically because the response of the blood system is so sluggish. After neuronal activation increases, blood flow doesn't become elevated in the associated region for about 4 seconds, and it takes 15 seconds for the blood system to settle back to its resting state, so we will never be able to do trials more often than every 20 seconds or so. Spatial resolution, however, will get much higher with increasing magnetic field strength; Logothetis (2008) predicts that slice thicknesses will decline to 0.5 mm, with voxel sizes two or three orders of magnitude smaller than at present (p. 871). But an increase in spatial resolution probably won't advance cognitive neuroscience very much, due to the normal variations among brains that require averaging and smoothing, and also due to the fact that BOLD is itself not localized to one narrow location.

Second, the spatial resolution of EEG will never get much higher due to the diffuse nature of the electric fields in the skull.

In addition to these technical issues, there's one final problem: the mental processes studied are quite small compared to the mental complexity and long-term cognitive processes that are associated with real-world creativity. The reductionist approach of cognitive neuroscience works fine with some brain functions—for example, perceptual systems like vision, because vision is processed in a fairly regular way through a specific set of neurons. But with higher cognitive functions such as creativity, problem solving, language, decision making, memory, etc., our thoughts and behaviors are *emergent complex phenomena*: they involve many distinct neural groups, scattered throughout the brain. Any meaningful creative product is likely to have behind it tens or even hundreds of these brief mental events. Imagine a writer composing a poem; each selection of a single word is likely to result from multiple events of association and insight. And after a first draft is completed, the process of editing and revising will involve hundreds more such mental events. Each of the eight stages of the creative process is likely to be realized in a distinct set of brain states. And in a creator's life, these mental moments occur over long period of time, where the mind's processing is interspersed with solitary interactions with external representations, and social interactions with others working in the area. These two latter processes can't be localized in the brain—the role of external representations requires attention to externalization processes (Chapter 7), and the role of social interaction requires study of the interactional dynamics of those groups (Chapter 12).

Cognitive neuroscience is an exciting and important component of the explanation of creativity. These studies all show us that creativity is not localized in one brain region; rather, creativity emerges from a complex network of neurons firing throughout the brain. These findings paint a complex picture of the relationship between brain science and creativity.

KEY CONCEPTS

- Lesion studies and electrode studies
- Neurons: synapses, axons, dendrites, axon terminals
- Brain anatomy: gray matter, white matter, sulci, gyri
- Electroencephalography (EEG)
- Event-related potential (ERP)
- Temporal and spatial resolution
- Positron emission tomography (PET)
- Voxel
- Functional magnetic resonance imaging (fMRI)
- Blood oxygen level-dependent (BOLD) signal
- Statistical image averaging

- Paired image subtraction (with baseline or rest state)
- Cognitive conjunction
- Mind wandering

SUGGESTED READINGS

Berkowitz, A. L. (2010). *The improvising mind: Cognition and creativity in the musical moment.* Oxford, UK: Oxford University Press.

Gazzaniga, M., Ivry, R. B., & Mangun, G. R. (2002). *Cognitive neuroscience: The biology of the mind* (2nd edition). New York: Norton.

Posner, M. I., & Raichle, M. E. (1994). *Images of mind.* New York: Scientific American Library.

Ward, J. (2006). *The student's guide to cognitive neuroscience.* Hove, UK: Psychology Press.

PART 3

SOCIOCULTURAL APPROACHES

In Part II, we learned about research in the individualist approaches—the first wave of personality psychology (1950s through 1960s) and the second wave of cognitive psychology (1970s to the present). We also had over-views of exciting new research in biology and in the computer simulation of creativity. Individualist approaches to creativity have given us a fairly good understanding of what goes on in the mind when people are engaged in creative activity. These approaches are most helpful in explaining little c, individualist creativity—defined as a new mental combination that's expressed in the world. But to explain Big C, sociocultural creativity—something that's new to the world, and is appropriate to an ongoing domain of activity—we need to go beyond studies of the individual, because only social groups can collectively evaluate originality and appropriateness. Individual-level explanations are the most important component of the explanation of creativity, and that's why I started the book with them. But individuals always create in contexts, and a better understanding of those contexts is essential to a complete explanation of creativity.

Part III focuses on sociocultural approaches, which define creativity as something that's new to the world—the first time it's ever been done by anyone. And novelty alone isn't enough; it also has to be appropriate *to some ongoing domain of creative activity. If you generate something genuinely new and appropriate, you'll be known to others in your chosen domain, and your work could influence others for decades to come. Because domains evolve and change, "Big C" creativity is culturally and historically specific; socioculturally defined creativity could change from one country to another, and from one century to another. Sociocultural definitions accept this context-dependent element of creativity and attempt to develop ways to rigorously define creativity within a particular historical and cultural location.*

In contrast to the reductionism of the individualist approaches, sociocultural approaches are holist—they attempt to explain the messy complexity of real-world creativity without breaking it apart into constituent components like conceptual combination, divergent thinking, or analogical reasoning. Holist approaches are necessary to explain the complex relationships between individuals and groups, cultures, and organizations.

Each individual is a member of many overlapping social groups. Each social group has its own network, with links among different members of the group. Each social group has its own structure, an overall organization that determines where each person fits in, and what role each person will play in the group. Sociologists are scientists who study these networks and organizations, and how human groups can accomplish tasks and perform at levels beyond the capability of the individual, and we'll explore the findings of their research in Chapters 11, 12, and 13.

Each individual is a member of a culture, with its own implicit, unspoken, and unwritten rules about how the world works, about what's important, about what categories are used to break up and understand the world. Creativity itself is culturally defined; some cultures don't even have a concept of creativity, and in many others the concept doesn't look anything like our own. Anthropologists are scientists who are trained to delve inside a culture and capture its hidden, unspoken rules. Anthropologists have learned a lot about creativity in the past few decades, and we'll explore this research in Chapter 14.

Finally, each individual creates as a representative of a certain historical period. This is harder to recognize with our own creativity, but it becomes obvious when we look back 100 or 200 years at the creative products that were generated in another era. You don't have to go back 100 years to see that creativity is always a product of its time; probably half of all U.S. college students, when presented with a pop song they've never heard before, can identify the year it was recorded simply based on its stylistic and formal features. We can't explain why all songs recorded in 1973 sound similar by studying musicians' motivations, cognitive processes, or personalities. We need another sort of explanation for the similarities in creative products within a given time period, a level of analysis above the individual, a way to explain the historical context of human creativity, and we'll explore the findings of historians in Chapter 15.

We've prepared for this exploration by starting with individualist approaches. Although the chapters to come emphasize the contexts of human creativity, creativity doesn't exist without the individual. Each approach represents only one piece of the explanation of creativity; we need an interdisciplinary approach to explain creativity. Once we finish exploring the sociocultural approaches, we'll move on to Parts IV and V of the book, where we'll use the full power of the interdisciplinary approach, combining both individual and sociocultural perspectives, to explain a wide range of creative activities.

CHAPTER 11

THE SOCIOLOGY OF CREATIVITY

No partial intelligence can so separate itself from the general mass as not to be essentially carried on with it . . . The most profound thinker will therefore never forget that all men must be regarded as coadjutors in discovering truth.

—Auguste Comte, *Positivism,* 1842/1854, vol. 2, p. 522

The great problems are handed on from generation to generation, the individual acting not primarily as an individual but as a member of the human group.

—Max Wertheimer, 1945, pp. 123–126

Another late night in another smoke-filled Chicago jazz club. It was 2 a.m. and pianist Howie Becker was having trouble staying awake during the chord changes. Part of the problem was that it was a Monday night, and as all jazz musicians know, Monday is the night for an open jam session—when musicians from many bands come together in a single club and take turns on the bandstand. An open jam starts with a house band—piano, bass, and drums—that provides the musical backdrop for a rotating series of visiting saxophone and trumpet players. And on this Monday night, Becker's band was the house band, and the club was filled with horn players—some of them professionals from other local bands, but others aspiring beginners who frankly didn't deserve to be sharing the same stage. Yet the egalitarian ethos of an open jazz jam required that they be given the same opportunity as everyone else.

Becker was getting tired of Monday nights. Each horn player takes his turn on the stage and then sits down with a drink to socialize. But the pianist has to play all night long, playing accompanying chords, or "comping," behind all of the solos. This can get pretty boring for a pianist, because there are only so many different ways you can arrange the chords while comping on a song. A typical soloist might play through the song eight times, followed by five or six other players. Add that up, and Becker was comping through the same song almost 50 times. In fact, by 2 a.m. he had already dozed off a couple of times *while playing*; when Becker briefly fell asleep, none of the other musicians noticed—he kept playing just fine.

Pianist Howard Becker is now a famous sociologist.[1] He played piano in Chicago in the 1950s to support himself while in the legendary sociology doctoral program at the University of Chicago. One of his earliest scientific studies was about the Chicago community of jazz musicians. And years later, in 1982, he published *Art Worlds*, an influential book on the sociology of art. In *Art Worlds*, Becker chose to focus not on the internal mental process of the artist; rather, he expanded the focus out to the contexts surrounding the artist. He examined the networks of support that are necessary for creative work to take place—the gallery owners, patrons, and educated viewers, the manufacturers of paints and canvasses, the educators at art schools. And perhaps most intriguing, he examined our society's conceptions of art and the artist, and why we call some activities "art" while calling other activities "crafts" or "hobbies."

As a sociologist, Becker was also interested in the standards and conventions shared by an art world. Becker knew that the reason complete strangers could play together on a Monday night was because they all knew the same rules about how the music was supposed to work. For example, the first horn player to solo on a song might solo for five times through the song, or as long as eight or nine times through the song, depending how his inspiration moved him. But the musicians knew that the second musician, and every one after that, had to solo the same number of times as the first. Why? No one ever talked about it; this was an unwritten rule. Becker's insider interpretation was that if the second musician played fewer times, it would imply that he was a less creative musician, without as much inspiration as the first guy. On the other hand, if he took up more time, it might look like he was trying to show up the first guy, trying to prove that he had more ideas. This unwritten rule emerged from the deeply egalitarian ethos of the jazz community (Becker, 2000). Becker also realized that if he could keep playing even while he was starting to nod off, the conventions of comping on piano had to be pretty structured. If jazz piano required true innovation and creativity every single moment, then certainly a person couldn't be just barely awake and keep doing it.

The Western cultural model of creativity is inspired by 19th-century Romantic images: the starving poet who can't afford to leave his barely furnished apartment; the genius composer with the stub of a chewed pencil, working out a symphony in his head while he lies in bed, sick and alone; or the visionary painter, out of step with convention and his peers, whose work never leaves his studio until long after his miserable death. But today more than ever, the most important forms of creativity in our culture—movies, television shows, big science experiments, music videos, popular songs, computer software, video games—are joint cooperative activities of complex networks of skilled individuals. The Internet has enabled new forms of distributed creativity like Wikipedia, YouTube, flickr, and the open-source Linux operating system. A jazz group is a perfect metaphor for these forms of collaborative creativity (Sawyer, 2003c, 2007). With collaboratively created products, it's extremely difficult to apply our individualist conceptions of creativity (Fig. 11.1).

It's ironic that the United States today has one of the most individualist cultural models of creativity in history, because perhaps more than in any other society, creativity in the United States is a collective, institutional activity (Garber, 2002). The creative products that U.S. society is best known for today—including movies, music videos, the Internet, and video games—are all

---

1. He tells the story of falling asleep at the piano in Becker, 2000.

FIGURE 11.1: A team of glass-blowers completing one of the "Venetian" series of sculptures in the Dale Chihuly Studio. Chihuly stands at the back, overseeing the work. (Reprinted from *The Origins of Creativity* by Pfenninger and Shubik, 2001. "Form From Fire," D. Chihuly, photograph by Russell Johnson. With permission of Oxford University Press Inc.)

made by organized groups of highly specialized individuals. To explain the creativity of complex collaborating groups, we need a scientific perspective that allows us to understand how groups of people work together, and how the collective actions of many people result in a final created product. The scientific discipline that studies complex cooperative networks of activity is sociology, and this chapter contributes to our explanation of creativity by drawing on sociological research and findings.

THE SOCIOCULTURAL DEFINITION OF CREATIVITY

Originality as such does not assure the excellence of a work of art . . . In the field of the arts, there are many works that are quite original but not especially good, and there are works of limited originality that attain a high degree of aesthetic quality. . . In the fields of the sciences, scholarship, and philosophy no original idea is of any worth that does not also claim to be true.

—Kristeller, (1983, p. 110)

In Chapter 1, we learned that sociocultural definitions of creativity include two important features: the product or process must be *novel*, and it must be *appropriate* to some domain of human activity. The sociocultural approach started with the 1983 appearance of Teresa M. Amabile's book *Creativity in Context* (also see Amabile, 1982; Hill & Amabile, 1993). Amabile examined the first-wave personality tests that measured an individual's originality, and she discovered that there was often an implicit subjective assessment built into these tests. In these psychometric tests, originality was often scored by a team of raters, and these raters were applying their own criteria of novelty and appropriateness to make these judgments. Amabile concluded that social appropriateness could never be avoided in creativity research, not even by personality researchers who claimed to be focusing on individual traits and processes. She proposed a *consensual definition* of creativity: a product is creative when experts in the domain agree it's creative (Amabile, 1982, p. 1001; 1983, 1996, p. 33). If experts from a domain come to a consensus, it means the product is appropriate in that domain. If creativity can't be defined without appropriateness, and appropriateness can be defined only by the people working in a domain, then the definition of creativity is fundamentally and unavoidably social. Appropriateness is defined by social groups, and it's culturally and historically determined (Amabile, 1982, p. 1010).

The legendary creativity researcher Mihaly Csikszentmihalyi had always been interested in the great fine artists of the European tradition; he had a particularly strong interest in the Italian Renaissance of the 1400s. When he was a young child, he lived for a while in Venice, a few steps from St. Mark's Square. Later his family moved to Florence, where every morning he walked past Brunelleschi's elegant Foundling Hospital with its sculpted ceramic façade. As a teenager, he lived on the Gianicolo Hill in Rome, overlooking Michelangelo's great dome. Why did the city of Florence experience such a dramatic and sustained burst of creativity during the Renaissance? Csikszentmihalyi knew that the answer couldn't be strictly psychological; it would be highly unlikely that simply through genetic luck, a lot of creative people just happened to be born in Florence at the same time. He knew that explaining the Florentine Renaissance required a knowledge of historical, social, and economic factors. For example, the Italian nobles had a virtual monopoly on the lucrative trade with the Orient. They had a political structure—a multiplicity of sovereign states, principalities, and republics—that encouraged competition for the best artists and artworks. They had a high level of education among the middle classes, and this resulted in widespread support for the arts. They had the good fortune to be the second home of choice for expatriate intellectuals fleeing the crumbling Byzantine Empire to the east. Csikszentmihalyi's knowledge of this period kept him from reducing creativity to a purely psychological explanation. Like Amabile, Csikszentmihalyi realized that creativity isn't just a property of individuals, but is also a property of societies, cultures, and historical periods (Csikszentmihalyi, 1988b, 1990a, 1996, 1999).

During the 1980s and 1990s, creativity researchers refined the insights of Amabile and Csikszentmihalyi to develop the *systems model* of creativity (Fig. 11.2; see Feldman, Csikszentmihalyi, & Gardner, 1994). The systems model contains three components: the person, domain, and field. The person is the source of innovation; a person begins the process by developing a created product. But that alone can't be called creative, because the product might not be novel, and it might not be appropriate. Novelty and appropriateness are judged by people who are experts in that creative domain: the field. If the field decides that the product meets these criteria, the product enters the domain, where it's preserved and disseminated to other members of the field. Works that are rejected by the field don't enter the domain, and are often forgotten and destroyed.

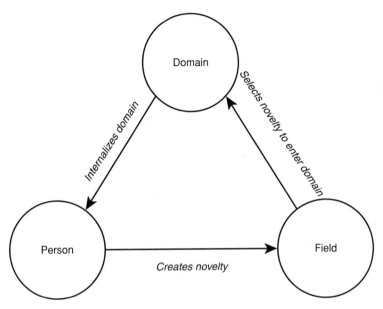

FIGURE 11.2: The sociocultural model of creativity.

The systems model is, at its root, the evolutionary process applied to ideas (see Chapter 8). The individual generates *variation*, corresponding to genetic variation and mutation. The field serves the *selection* function, corresponding to natural selection in biologic evolution. And the domain accomplishes *retention* of desirable variations.

THE FIELD

Morris Stein was one of the most important first-wave creativity researchers. Stein had worked in business and was deeply familiar with marketing research on how new products are disseminated and adopted by consumers. In an early version of the sociocultural approach, he analyzed the *intermediaries* of the field that legitimize certain works as creative and deny that status to others—sometimes they're called *gatekeepers* (Stein, 1961/1963, 1967, 1974). Intermediaries include the patrons who provide emotional and financial support; experts like authorities and critics; and transmission agents who disseminate the work to the public, such as gallery owners, salesmen, advertising agencies, publishers, bookstores, and opinion leaders. Stein also studied how innovations are adopted by the public; he distinguished different categories within the audience—early adopters, early majority, late majority, and laggards—drawing on influential marketing research (Rogers, 1962).[2]

2. Even prior to Stein, sociocultural theories of creativity had appeared in literary theory and aesthetics; for example, in the 1930s Walter Benjamin had argued that every historical situation alters and "translates" a work so that it can never again be what it originally was for the artist and his initial audience (as described by Marcuse, 1970).

Csikszentmihalyi used the term *field* to refer to the group of intermediaries who determine what's accepted and disseminated. As Stein first pointed out, the field is a complex network of experts, with varying expertise, status, and power. After a person creates a product, it's submitted to the field for consideration, and the field judges whether or not it's novel, and whether or not it's appropriate. In science, the field would include the journal editors and peer reviewers of submitted articles, the heads of top departments at major universities, and the senior scientists who review grant proposals at government agencies. In painting, the field would include gallery owners, museum curators, editors of national art journals, reviewers at Washington funding agencies, and faculty at leading MFA programs. These influential gatekeepers determine not only which created products are published but also what types of creative work will receive funding. French sociologist Pierre Bourdieu's (1993) influential theory of cultural production emphasizes that the field is constituted by economic and power relations among subgroups, and analyzes creativity as a sort of market transaction between producers and consumers. Sociologists of science have argued that the field determines which creative events history will later judge to be significant discoveries, in a complex social and historical process of retrospective attribution (Brannigan, 1981; Schaffer, 1994; see Chapter 20).

Members of a field tend to agree with one another in judgments of who and what is creative. In the IPAR study of architects (Chapter 4), 40 top architects were selected and then rated by 11 editors of major architectural journals, and each of the 40 rated all of the others. The two groups' judgments correlated at 0.88, a remarkably high rate of agreement. As in architecture, in almost all creative domains the experts agree. Researchers have studied the effect of training on aesthetic judgment in many domains, and they've found that the more expert the pool of raters, the more in agreement their ratings will be. Naïve, untrained evaluators of paintings provide ratings of quality that are all over the map. But when the same painting is evaluated by a group of art experts, it receives remarkably consistent ratings (Child, 1968). Trained experts agree because they've internalized the conventions of their domain, and these conventions include criteria for judgment.

The eight stages of the creative process presented in Chapters 5, 6, and 7 are all stages that occur within a single individual. But after Stage 8, "Externalize," is complete, and a product is generated, successful creative individuals still have a lot of work to do—and that later work mostly involves social interaction with the field. They have to choose the best style and location to present their idea to the field. They have to choose the right time, using their knowledge of personalities and institutions. They have to develop a narrative about how their creation fits into the ongoing historical development of the domain, drawing on their knowledge of what will resonate with other members of the field. They have to be savvy about the politics of the field, to convince the members of the field to select their creation.

THE DOMAIN

The domain consists of all of the created products that have been accepted by the field in the past, and all of the conventions that are shared by members of the field—the languages, symbols, and notations (also see Ward, Smith, & Vaid, 1997a; see Chapter 3, p. 59, for alternate definitions). The domain of jazz is what allowed Becker's jam session to work. The domain of classical music consists of the best-known works composed by Bach, Beethoven, Wagner, Schoenberg, and perhaps a hundred others. The domain of Western music also includes the standard system of musical notation, the set of instruments that are manufactured and that musicians know how to play, and the conventions of performance practice for each genre and composer.

To become a member of the field, a person has to first learn everything about the domain. That's why every successful creative career starts with a long period of training and preparation (see Chapter 5, pp. 93–95). A composer won't create a brilliant symphony without first absorbing a huge amount of information about prior styles and genres—standard song forms like sonatas and fugues; the different capabilities and weaknesses of different instruments; how to represent all of this on the page using musical notation. An aspiring jazz musician can't even sit in with a band without years of practice (Berliner, 1994): if you aren't prepared to play jazz, you'll be laughed off the stage and you won't be invited back.

COULDN'T THE FIELD BE WRONG?

The systems model often bothers people who hold to the Western cultural model of creativity. In this cultural model, society and culture are thought to be constraining and uncreative; truly exceptional creators are thought to be light-years ahead of their colleagues in the field. What about those individuals whose brilliance isn't recognized in their lifetimes, but who are later identified as creative? Don't those examples show that the field is often wrong? The creativity of plant breeder Gregor Mendel and that of painter Vincent van Gogh were not recognized until after their deaths, right?

Well, not really. Commonly cited cases like Mendel and van Gogh include large portions of Romantic myth. I describe the real story behind the Mendel myth in Chapter 20 (pp. 378–379), and van Gogh's paintings were selling quite well soon after his untimely death. Quantitative measures across large numbers of artists and scientists reveal that it's rare for unrecognized creators to be reevaluated as brilliant after their deaths. Scientific and artistic reputation remains remarkably stable over time, even across centuries (Over, 1982; Simonton, 1984c). For scientists, the number of citations to their publications stays the same from year to year (with correlations in the upper 0.90s); this consistency of reputation is found across generations as well. In psychology, no one who was out of favor in 1903 was in favor in 1970, and no one in favor in 1903 had been rejected by 1970 (Over, 1982, p. 60). Reputation in the arts and humanities is also very consistent over time (Farnsworth, 1969; Rosengren, 1985; Simonton, 1984c).

In all creative domains, a person's reputation is more stable over time than the reputation of any of the individual creative works that reputation is based on (Simonton, 1976). Creators with enduring reputations are those who've created a large body of diverse contributions, and their status doesn't rise or fall with the fate of any single creative work. If one work becomes dated or falls out of favor, another has high odds of being rediscovered. Often, the contributions for which historical scientists are best known today aren't those that earned them fame in their own lifetimes; for example, Einstein is now most famous as the father of relativity theory, but his 1921 Nobel prize was granted for work he did in 1905 on the photoelectric effect.

THE AUDIENCE

All works of art or stylistic cycles are definable by their built-in idea of the spectator.
—Leo Steinberg, (1972, p. 81)

The work of artistic creation is not a work performed in any exclusive or complete fashion in the mind of the person whom we call the artist. That idea is a delusion bred of individualistic psychology . . . This activity is a corporate activity belonging not to any one human being but to a community.
—R. G. Collingwood, (1938, p. 324)

Every year, investors spend millions of dollars creating movies and Broadway plays that fail to connect with an audience, even though the gatekeepers in the field had selected them over hundreds of other ideas. Every year, scientific journals publish articles that will never be cited by other scientists and will have almost no impact on future research, even though those articles were selected by expert editors and reviewers. The intermediaries in the field play a critical role in evaluating creative works, but after they've made their choices, the ultimate test for a creative work is whether or not it's accepted by a broad audience.

Sociologists have discovered that audience members aren't all the same. They can be grouped depending on their level of expertise and how connected they are to the creators who work in the field (Fig. 11.3). We've already learned about the intermediaries at the center of the field. Works selected by these intermediaries then pass outward, to connoisseurs, amateurs, and the broad public.

CONNOISSEURS

The audience's inner circle is filled with the connoisseurs, those people who know the most about the domain. Connoisseurs have been socialized into the domain almost as thoroughly as

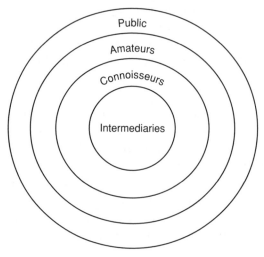

FIGURE 11.3: Nested audiences.

the intermediaries of the field. They play a disproportionately important role in the audience; they know more, they're more active, they're more opinionated, and less experienced people trust their opinions.

A large percentage of the audience at any dance performance have themselves had some training in dance, and as many as 15% of all theater tickets sold in New York are sold to students in drama programs (Becker, 1982, p. 53). Hans Haacke's surveys of art gallery visitors revealed that between 40% and 60% were either artists or art students (Haacke, 1975, pp. 17, 42).

Many successful artists and musicians have fans who closely follow their careers; these connoisseurs may remember more about the artist's past work than the artist himself. Fans expect similar work in the future, and they get angry when their favorite artist shifts styles. Popular bands know that the audiences at their next tours will want to hear the hits from their past albums; if they dare to play new music, the fans will want those new songs to sound pretty much like the old ones. Bands ignore the fans at their peril; they know that their core fans are those most likely to buy their new CDs.

Stravinsky's comic opera *Mavra* was quite different from the ballets that made him famous, *Petrushka* and *Rite of Spring*; it was much simpler and based in folk music genres. The audience at the premiere of the work was disappointed not to hear the familiar Stravinsky sound (White, 1966, pp. 59–60). When American photographer Edward Weston, who was famous for still lifes and landscapes, started producing bitter and political images during World War II (like "Civilian Defense," a nude woman lying on a couch wearing nothing but a gas mask), his best fans became his most bitter critics (Becker, 1982, p. 291).

All artists are deeply aware of who their fans are and what they like. Most of them try to satisfy their fans; the fans have an influence on the creative process, even if the creator is alone in a room in the woods. Of course, an artist can choose to ignore the fans and do whatever he or she wants. But when artists choose to create works that their existing fans won't like, they know they'll have to struggle to connect with a new audience, and that's often a tough decision to make. In one way or another, fans play an indirect role in the creative process.

FANS OF UNPOPULAR GENRES

If you like an art form that isn't widely popular—modern dance, polka, early silent films—you may very rarely get to see that art. A person who's interested in these marginal art forms has to be a little more active than a person who prefers mainstream fare (Becker, 1982, p. 67). If you like network sitcoms and Top 40 songs, you can be confident that you'll never lack for entertainment, because there are massive industries and large audiences that ensure such genres will always be easily available to you. But if your taste runs to obscure black-and-white sitcoms from the early 1950s era of television, or new compositions in the European art music tradition, you may need to band together with like-minded people and actively organize to create opportunities to view these forms.

Fans of marginal art forms often form informal associations, because they realize that without their active support, the genre might die out altogether. For example, the typical American city is lucky to have even one modern dance or contemporary classical music ensemble; in my home of St. Louis, we have one of each. But even in a midsized city like St. Louis, these groups get very small audiences and never make enough money from ticket sales to be self-supporting. If serious fans want to be able to see a marginal art form, some of them have to donate significant money and become patrons, or else the group will fold. To take a different example, polka music is another marginally popular genre in St. Louis. Performances aren't even advertised in the local weekly newspaper. Instead, all of the local fans subscribe to a newsletter and pay membership dues every year to ensure that they'll continue to have opportunities to hear polka. Christian music groups tend to be advertised through churches rather than in the newspapers. Other genres outside the mainstream include hypertext fiction, with groups organizing primarily over the Internet (see Chapter 17, pp. 329–330), or obscure black-and-white movies, with film societies typically based at local universities.

Marginal art forms like polka and contemporary dance can survive only because fans of the genre have decided to provide financial support, free services, and their own social network. Such groups often engage in outreach efforts, trying to increase their membership by broadening their audience. You can't explain creativity in these marginal creative genres without understanding the important role played by the audience.

AMATEURS

In the fine arts, amateurism is diffused through society. In France, 47% of all people over 15 years of age have practiced one of the fine arts—fiction writing or poetry, painting, musical performance, or dance—and 22% have done so within the past year (Donnat, 2002, p. 70). Amateur participation at museums, concerts, and theaters is highly correlated with educational level, much more so than with income. Amateur participation in the fine arts is also related to gender; among amateur dancers and writers, there are twice as many women as men, and even in music and painting, there are more women. Only with guitar and drums are there more men.

Most amateurs are exposed to their art while still in school; it's rare for an adult to take up a new creative activity. Some hard-core amateurs continue to paint or to play an instrument throughout life. Some of these amateurs are almost semiprofessional and may even continue to hope for some professional success with their hobby. A much larger group engages in the activity for relaxation; they don't stay in touch with what's going on in the field and they know it will always remain a hobby for them. And the biggest group of amateurs is exposed to the art while in school but give it up after college. Even though they don't actively engage in the art, because of their knowledge of the domain they're much more likely to attend performances or art events, and they're much more likely to enjoy and understand them.

A large pool of amateurs doesn't guarantee an audience for cutting-edge new works. Most amateurs are pretty conservative in their tastes. Among amateur painters in France, only 12% of them do any contemporary art; 76% of them do figurative art; 75% of them do landscapes and still lifes; and 16% of amateur painters say outright that they don't like contemporary art (Donnat, 2002, p. 73). The same numbers would probably result from an interview with amateur musicians about contemporary composers. Cutting-edge works tend to draw their support from the inner-audience circles: the connoisseurs.

THE GENERAL PUBLIC

At the outermost circle of the audience is the general public. The public has very little power over what art gets recognized, distributed, and valued. Their only choice is whether they attend museums or concerts. Their interest can be measured only collectively, in mass numbers.

But for many creative domains—like movies, TV shows, or music recordings—the size of the audience is a key measure of success. The intermediaries of the field often keep track of audience size and demographics, and this way the collective choices of the general public can have an indirect influence on future creative works.

SOCIAL CLASS AND THE AUDIENCE

> *From information about an individual's age, sex, race, social background, and primary group membership, one could make a reasonable attempt at predicting his musical preferences.*
>
> —W. Ray Crozier and Antony Chapman, (1981, p. 268)

The kind of art you like tells people a lot about you. Since at least the 1960s, high-school students have identified themselves by their musical preference. When I was in high school in the 1970s, part of an adolescent's self-identity was whether he or she was "into" rock, disco, or reggae. The genres change every few years; adolescent self-identity in the 1990s was attached to rap, metal, or jam bands. These preferences become even more closely tied with identity in certain musical subcultures, such as the 1990s subcultures associated with goth, deadheads, ska, and rockabilly (Epstein, 1994). These choices aren't only a reflection of aesthetic preference; white suburban boys are drawn to rap because of its associations of tough, authentic, inner-city street culture as much as for its formal musical properties.

There are huge class differences in consumption of art (Dimaggio & Useem, 1978). Cross-cultural studies have found that variability within societies is greater than variability across societies (Anderson, 1976; Berlyne, 1971; Ross, 1976). In other words, your social class is a better predictor of what you'll like than what country you grew up in. Working-class people often feel that certain forms of art are "not for us" and are directed at a higher stratum of society. For example, a 1978 study found that blue-collar workers were underrepresented in art audiences; in a 12-month period, only 10% of a large sample had attended the theater, and only 4% a symphony concert. In general, the high arts—fine art, ballet, classical music—tend to draw interest from the upper middle class. Educational level is the best predictor of audience composition, occupation is the second-best predictor, and income is the least effective predictor (Crozier & Chapman, 1981). People don't consume art simply because they can afford to; they consume art because they've been trained to do so, either by their families or by their schooling. French sociologist Pierre Bourdieu (1979/1984) argued that by consuming culturally valued creative products, individuals increase their store of cultural capital. Bourdieu's analyses of French society discovered correlations between a person's consumption patterns and the educational level of his or her parents, demonstrating that cultural capital is transmitted from parent to child through socialization practices.

Several studies found that higher socioeconomic status correlates with appreciation of classical music, the preference for complex paintings, and the preference for abstract paintings. There are three possible explanations for these differences. First, social-class differences might be related to personality differences, and it's actually the personality differences that account for the different preference. Second, exposure to art and training in art increase the preference for it, and socioeconomic status increases the likelihood of exposure to high art. Third, art prefer-ence is a social-class identifier, and during socialization, children learn what types of art "people like them" are supposed to like.

Some postwar researchers argued for the first explanation: these differences in attendance are due to differences in personality. Because different social classes raise their children differ-ently, the children might grow up with different personality traits characteristic of their social class. For example, middle- and upper-class families were once thought to raise children with a higher "preference for complexity," and several studies identified correlations between social class and the degree of complexity of the artworks preferred (Crozier & Chapman, 1981, pp. 259–262). Other researchers hypothesized that higher-income families raised children who would prefer abstract art, while working-class families would raise children who preferred simplicity and photographic realism (Kavolis, 1968).

The second explanation for social-class differences in aesthetic preference is that different social classes provide their children with different opportunities to engage in art. Higher-income families are more likely to provide their children with painting or music lessons, and are more likely to take them to museums or concerts, and it's this familiarity that leads to social-class dif-ferences in adult preferences for art. The problem with this second explanation should be obvi-ous to anyone who hated going to the museum as a child: in many cases, the activities that parents force on their children result in a *decrease* in preference for that activity. American chil-dren who grow up in regions that were heavily settled by German immigrants, like Milwaukee and St. Louis, are likely to hear a lot more polka music than children in other regions, but if anything this is likely to increase their dislike of polka. And staff workers at modern art muse-ums, like gallery attendants, janitors, and security staff, don't gradually come to enjoy modern art any more than their working-class peers who don't have such exposure to art.

Both the first and the second explanations implicitly accept that high art really is better, and try to explain why it is that lower-class people don't "get it." The personality-based explanations suggest that lower-class people score low in some important personality trait and this lack pre-vents them from appreciating high art; the exposure explanations assume that if you're exposed to high art, you'll realize its superior value and begin to appreciate it. Most of these studies were conducted in an earlier era, in a time when the reign of high art had not yet been challenged by the pop art of the 1960s, and by the increasing influence of popular culture and the media from the 1970s on. And most of these studies were conducted by researchers who themselves implic-itly believed in the objective superiority of the high arts of the European canon. These explana-tions don't work if you don't think high art has any objective superiority, and they don't work to explain aesthetic preferences outside of high art, which are the preferences that most of us have most of the time—a high-school student's preference for jam bands, metal, or rap.

The third explanation is the one that most scientists now accept: children are socialized to learn that certain forms of art are associated with certain group identities, and expressing a pref-erence for those forms is a way of expressing their identity as a member of that group. Since at least the 1950s, scientists have known that music plays a role in the identity construction of youth. Research connecting music preference and group identity in young people extends back to the 1970s and has confirmed the importance of group identity in musical preference (Chapman & Williams, 1976; Frith, 1978).

This third explanation actually has little to do with aesthetic preference *per se*, but rather with the desire to be seen to be consuming and enjoying a certain style of work. For example, think of the middle-aged executive who attends the symphony because all of his company's vice presidents also attend, or of the couple who attends the museum opening because "all of our friends" will be there. This third explanation also explains preferences for non-high art in a way that doesn't implicitly privilege high art. For example, think of the college student who attends the concert because everyone in her dormitory will be going, and who likewise would never consider attending the symphony because there will not be any other college students there.

PRESTIGE EFFECTS

When we like a work of art, we usually say it's because of something about the work itself. But it turns out that our judgments of artistic quality are often influenced by the prestige of the context—whether the painting is by a famous painter, or whether we see it hanging in the art museum. Scientists have tested the role of prestige effects by showing people relatively unknown paintings of similar quality, and then telling half of them that the painter is a great master and telling the other half that it's by a beginning art student. Or they might tell half of them that the painting is a masterpiece and the other half that it's a minor work. Or they might tell them different prices that the work sold for at auction.

Studies of prestige effects have a long history; in 1929, Farnsworth and Beaumont selected 10 paintings by unknown painters and asked college students to rate them. For each painting, two alternative descriptions were prepared, one that reported that the painting was an important work by a great master that had fetched a high price at auction, and another that said that the painting was a relatively minor work by a student. The ratings of the pictures varied as predicted, according to the description. Similar effects have been experimentally reproduced in judgments of literature and music (see Crozier & Chapman, 1981).

There are individual differences in susceptibility to prestige effects; some people are more easily swayed by the consensus of expert opinion. Susceptibility seems to be inversely related to background knowledge; subjects without much knowledge of art are more sensitive to prestige cues (Michael, Rosenthal, & DeCamp, 1949; Mittler, 1976). Knowledgeable subjects are more likely to trust their own judgment and are more willing to be critical of the experts' consensus.

Prestige effects, however, have small effect sizes in these experiments, and they seem to emerge only when there aren't any other criteria that can be used to make aesthetic judgments (Mumford, 1995). For example, in these experiments the works to be compared are, by design, essentially of identical quality; people would be less likely to be swayed by prestige effects if the works were more obviously of different quality (Crozier & Chapman, 1981, p. 255).

The findings emerging from prestige effect studies can best be explained using a sociological approach. Sociology explains most of the difference in aesthetic preference by looking at factors like socialization practices and group identity. We don't need to know much about a person's individual psychology or personality traits to make predictions about what kind of art he or she will like; we can make pretty good predictions just by knowing the person's social situation.

ASSESSMENTS OF SOCIOCULTURAL CREATIVITY

Neither "novelty" nor "appropriateness" can be measured at the individual level. "Novelty" means new to the domain, and the domain exists outside of any single individual; "appropriateness" can be judged only by a social evaluative process. As a result, sociocultural assessments can never be purely objective; a group must perform the assessment, and different groups at different times might come to different conclusions. The telegraph was novel and appropriate in 1844, when Morse first sent a message between Baltimore and Washington (Standage, 1998), but it would not be new or useful today.

Patent law uses a variant of the sociocultural definition to determine what's a patentable invention. To be patentable, an invention must meet three criteria: it must be new, useful, and *non-obvious*—you can't get a patent for something that anyone could have figured out. Well, not exactly "anyone"—it has to be non-obvious to a member of the field, someone who's an expert in the domain. Patent law refers to such an individual as "a Person Having Ordinary Skill In The Art," or the oddly catchy acronym, PHOSITA. The legal process that determines whether something is creative (i.e., patentable) is a deeply sociocultural process—involving courts, precedents, oral arguments, friend of the court briefs, etc.

As with patent law, sociocultural tests are almost always applied to a creative product rather than directly to a person. The creativity of the products generated is sometimes then used to assess the creativity of the person. One of the most widely used sociocultural measure of creativity is the Consensual Assessment Technique (CAT; Amabile, 1982, 1996; see Chapter 3, pp. 41–42). Another common form of sociocultural test is to measure the impact of a created product. With a scientific article, this can be done by counting the number of times that later articles reference it (see Chapter 15, History, pp. 292–293). With artworks such as paintings, impact can be measured using the market value of the painting, or the number of times the painting appears in an art history textbook (see Chapter 15, pp. 281–283).

Most of our culture's important creative products are too large and complex to be generated by a single individual; they require a team or an entire company, with a division of labor and a careful integration of many specialized creative workers. Group creativity involves *distributed cognition*—when each member of the team contributes an essential piece of the solution, and these individual components are all integrated to form the collective product (Sawyer & DeZutter, 2009). The following three sections describe assessments of creativity designed for organizational innovation, for organizational climate, and for entire regions and countries.

ASSESSING ORGANIZATIONAL INNOVATION

Many measures have been proposed to compare the creativity of different companies. Typically, several variables are incorporated into a formula (referred to as a "composite" measure); the most commonly used variables are the number of patents granted; the total expenditures on research and development; and the percentage of revenues originating from products introduced in the previous five years. For example, each year the Boston Consulting Group (BCG) conducts a survey and publishes a ranking of the most innovative global companies, in its own report and in *Business Week* magazine. In 2010, 1,600 senior executives worldwide responded to the survey. The composite ranking formula was:

- Survey respondents' list of most innovative companies: 80%
- Shareholder returns: 10%
- Revenue growth: 5%
- Margin growth: 5%

In the 2010 survey, the top ten most innovative companies were:

1. Apple
2. Google
3. Microsoft
4. IBM
5. Toyota
6. Amazon.com
7. LG Electronics
8. BYD Company
9. General Electric
10. Sony

BCG also surveyed companies to ask what metrics they use internally to measure their success at innovation. The responses, ranked from top to bottom, were (Andrew et al., 2010, p. 10):

- Customer satisfaction: 45%
- Overall revenue growth: 40%
- Percentage of sales from new products or services: 35%
- Higher margins: 29%
- New-product success ratios: 27%
- Return on innovation spending: 26%
- Projected versus actual performance: 26%
- Number of new products or services: 25%
- Time to market: 20%
- Patents: 15%

It's not clear whether these variables are measuring creativity or some other organizational characteristic. For example, the top two items on the BCG list have no obvious relationship to creativity and innovation, because they could result from many other factors unrelated to creativity (such as greater efficiency or productivity). Likewise, 20% of the BCG ranking comes from general success measures such as shareholder return.

In an attempt to address some of these problems, the U.S. National Science Foundation in 2009 launched its first-ever *Business R&D and Innovation Survey (BRDIS)*, developed jointly with the Census Bureau—replacing the previous survey, which had been conducted every year since 1953. The composite instrument for 2009 included:

- Total worldwide R&D expenditures
- Patents applied for and issued
- Patents licensing revenue
- Intellectual property transfer
- Number of new products and services introduced in the previous three years
- Percentage of total sales due to those new products and services
- Percentage of R&D devoted to new business areas or product lines
- Relationships with academia
- Percentage of R&D employees to total staff

Companies were required to break out these figures by business area and to report the numbers separately for their domestic and their overseas operations. The first release of data was announced in May 2010.

ASSESSING ORGANIZATIONAL CLIMATE

Several organizational scholars have developed measures of an organization's innovation potential by measuring its *organizational climate*. I review three: CCQ, KEYS, and TCI (see Mathisen & Einarsen, 2004).

1. The Creative Climate Questionnaire (CCQ; Ekvall, 1996) is designed to measure organizational conditions that may stimulate or block creativity and innovation. It's a questionnaire administered to employees that asks 50 questions related to four areas:
   - Mutual trust and confidence; support for ideas; open relationships
   - Challenge and motivation; commitment to the organization's goals
   - Freedom to seek information and show initiative
   - Pluralism in views, knowledge, and experience; exchange of opinions and ideas
2. KEYS (Amabile et al., 1996) uses a questionnaire to measure eight organizational characteristics that are related to creativity, and two criterion measures of the organization's actual performance:
   - Organizational encouragement of creativity
   - Supervisory encouragement of creativity
   - Work group supports for creativity
   - Sufficient resources
   - Challenging work
   - Freedom and a sense of control over one's work
   - Organizational impediments to creativity
   - Workload pressure that leads to distraction from creative work
   - Criterion 1: Actual creativity of the organization
   - Criterion 2: Actual productivity of the organization
3. The Team Climate Inventory (TCI; Anderson & West, 1998) focuses on the immediate work group rather than the entire organization. This instrument is used as a team development tool, so that team managers can use the results to improve team innovation. TCI questions focus on four factors:
   - The team's objectives and visions are clearly defined, shared, and attainable.
   - The team welcomes equal participation in decision making, and it is safe to present new ideas.
   - The team has a shared concern with excellent performance toward the objectives.
   - Attempts to introduce new ideas and procedures are expected, approved of, and supported.

Mathisen and Einarsen (2004) examined data on the reliability and validity of these measures, and they concluded that KEYS and TCI have acceptable scientific quality, but CCQ doesn't yet have enough studies to demonstrate reliability and validity.

ASSESSING NATIONS AND REGIONS

Many national governments and organizations have developed overall measures of a nation's creative capacity. Versions of the *European Innovation Scoreboard (EIS)* have been published annually from 2001 (published by the Enterprise and Industry Directorate-General of the EU). The number of countries participating was 37 in 2007. This is a composite index; the 2008 version incorporates 29 indicators in seven categories (Hollanders, 2009):

- Human resources: Secondary-school and university graduates per 1,000 population aged 20 to 29; participation in lifelong learning per 100 population aged 25 to 64
- Finance and support: Public R&D expenditures as a percentage of GDP; venture capital as a percentage of GDP
- Firm investments: Business R&D expenditures as a percentage of GDP; IT expenditures as a percentage of GDP
- Linkages and entrepreneurship: Small and medium-sized enterprises (SMEs) innovating in-house as a percentage of all SMEs
- Throughputs: Patents per million population; trademarks per million population
- Innovators: SMEs introducing product or process innovations as a percentage of SMEs
- Economic effects: Employment in knowledge-intensive services; medium and high-tech manufacturing exports as a percentage of total exports

Based on the composite EIS, in 2008 the top innovators were Denmark, Germany, Finland, Sweden, and the United Kingdom. Japan and the United States weren't included, but a subset of 17 indicators were available for those countries, and these showed that the innovation performance of Japan was 38% above and the United States was 28% above the EU-27 average.

Richard Florida's *Creativity Index* (Florida, 2002) is a composite used to measure the creative potential of 268 geographic regions (Metropolitan Statistical Areas [MSAs]) in the United States. It includes:

- Patents per capita
- High-tech regional industrial output as a percentage of total U.S. high-tech industrial output
- Percentage of a region's total economic output that comes from high-tech industries, compared to national percentage
- Fraction of all U.S. gay people in the area divided by fraction of the total U.S. population who live in the area
- Fraction of all artistically creative people who live in a metropolitan area divided by the fraction of the total U.S. population who live in that area
- Racial integration index: Census track ethnicity composition in relation to composition of the whole MSA
- Percentage of creative occupations of total employed

The index isn't as rigorous and robust as some others (Saltelli & Villaba, 2009), but it's been influential in economic development discussions in the United States and internationally (Peck, 2005).

CONCLUSION

In this first chapter of Part III, we've explored how sociologists and social psychologists explain creativity. It's very different from the individualist approaches of Part II. Instead of assuming that all of the interesting things to explain are inside a person's head, sociologists assume that the most important things to explain are *outside* of people's heads—the social groups that we belong to; the networks of affiliations; the complex structures of modern creative work in large institutions; the complex and varied types of audiences who view, attend, purchase, and consume creative products; the nature of the market that governs the transactions between creators and consumers.

If our primary interest is in the creativity of teams, organizations, regions, and countries, individualist approaches are of limited value. Of course, creative companies must contain individuals who have creative ideas, but the overall creativity of the company isn't a simple additive summation of the creativity of all of the individuals in the company, due to *social emergence* (Sawyer, 2005b). Patterns of interaction, social network links, and the subtleties of organizational climate all play an important role. These will be our focus in the next two chapters.

For a sociologist, creativity is always identified and judged within a social system. The social system includes complex systems of social networks (the field) and complex languages and systems of conventions (the domain). Many of the psychologists who study creative individuals have also adopted the sociocultural definition of creativity; they define creativity as novel and appropriate by reference to a field and a domain, and they use sociocultural assessments such as the CAT.

Only a sociocultural approach can explain those creative products that are generated by large, complex groups of people—movies, video games, computer applications—or by small, intimate ensembles like jazz groups or brainstorming work teams. There's no single creator for many of these modern creative products. Throughout the chapters of Part IV, we'll see examples of creative products that are fundamentally collaborative, group creations. This is why a purely individualist approach to creativity can't provide a complete explanation of human innovation.

KEY CONCEPTS

- The systems model of creativity: person, domain, field
- Intermediaries
- Consumption of creative products and personal identity
- Prestige effects
- Patent law definition: new, useful, non-obvious
- Composite rankings: of businesses, regions, and countries

THOUGHT EXPERIMENTS

- Have you ever been creative in a domain where you had no training or experience whatsoever? If so, how do you know you were creative—did someone in that domain's field tell you so?

- Think of the most creative thing you've ever done. How much training and experience had you had in that creative domain? How do you know it was creative? Were there any members of the field who examined your product and evaluated it?
- Have you ever had a supportive, collaborative relationship with a senior member of a field—an editor, a reviewer, a producer or director, a curator, a college professor? Or if not, do you think of those sorts of people as obstacles, and never as helpers?

SUGGESTED READINGS

Amabile, T. M. (1982). Social psychology of creativity: A consensual assessment technique. *Journal of Personality and Social Psychology, 43*(5), 997–1013.

Becker, H. (1982). *Art worlds*. Berkeley and Los Angeles: University of California Press.

Crozier, W. R., & Chapman, A. (1981). Aesthetic preferences: Prestige and social class. In D. O'Hare (Ed.), *Psychology and the arts* (pp. 242–78). Brighton, Sussex, England: Harvester Press.

Csikszentmihalyi, M. (1988b). Society, culture, and person: A systems view of creativity. In R. J. Sternberg (Ed.), *The nature of creativity* (pp. 325–39). New York: Cambridge University Press.

Sawyer, R. K. (2003). *Group creativity: Music, theater, collaboration*. Mahwah, NJ: Erlbaum.

C H A P T E R   1 2

GROUP CREATIVITY

[Thomas] Edison is in reality a collective noun and means the work of many men.
—Francis Jehl, Edison's longtime assistant, referring to the fact that Edison's
400 patents were generated by a 14-man team (Kelley, 2001, p. 70)

In group creativity, a product is created by a group, a work team, or an ensemble (John-Steiner, 2000; Paulus & Nijstad, 2003; Sawyer, 2003c, 2007). For example, the improvisations of a jazz ensemble are group creations. To explain jazz creativity, scientists focus on the musical interaction among members of the ensemble (Sawyer, 2003c). Of course, each musician is individually creative during the performance, but the creativity of the group as a unit can be explained only by examining social and interactional processes among the musicians (see Chapter 18, Music). No one can generate a performance alone; the performers have to rely on the group and on the audience to collectively generate the emergent performance. In improv theater, the actors always ask the audience members to shout out suggestions before they begin to improvise a scene, and many groups stop in the middle of a scene to ask the audience to tell them what should happen next (see Chapter 19, Theater). As with all humor, the actors assume that the audience shares a large body of cultural knowledge and references, and in this way the audience indirectly guides their improvisation; it wouldn't work for the audience unless both actors and audience were from the same social group.[1]

The past 30 years have seen a huge growth in research on organizational innovation (Grønhaug & Kaufmann, 1988; King & Anderson, 1995; West & Farr, 1990), but only in the 1990s did this research focus closely on groups. This recent shift is critical, because most business innovations originate in groups (Evans & Sims, 1997). And many business leaders today believe that when people work in groups, they'll be more creative than individuals working alone.

---

1. Portions of this chapter are based on a literature review I did with Stuart Bunderson: Innovation research in organizational behavior, by Keith Sawyer and Stuart Bunderson, in *Innovation: What do we know?*, edited by Anjan Thakor. To be published by World Scientific Publishing.

There's some scientific support for the belief that groups are more creative than individuals (Larey & Paulus, 1999; Taylor, Berry, & Block, 1958). But many people have had the opposite experience—of finding themselves in a dysfunctional group, one that made everyone less creative and less productive than they might have been otherwise (Lencioni, 2002). Too many groups fall into *groupthink*, a state of lazy, shared consensus where no one wants to rock the boat (Janis, 1972). This chapter reviews evidence that groups are more creative, and contrasting evidence that groups are sometimes less creative. At the end of the chapter, we'll have a good idea of how to organize groups so that they'll be maximally creative.

Getting groups right is critical because collaboration is rapidly becoming the norm in science and in invention. It's important to funding agencies to know how important groups and teamwork are to scientific innovation. Most of the basic research in the United States is funded by the National Science Foundation (NSF) and the National Institutes of Health (NIH). They could choose to award many small grants to individuals, or long-term, larger awards to large teams. What does the research show about how they should spend their money?

Wuchty, Jones, and Uzzi (2007) analyzed huge databases—of 19.9 million scientific papers over 50 years, and 2.1 million patents—and found that the amount and degree of collaboration have increased dramatically over the decades. First, the databases allowed them to determine which papers, and which patents, had one author, two authors, or more. Two or more authors means that the creation was collaboratively generated. In science, the average team size (number of co-authors) doubled over 45 years—from 1.9 to 3.5 authors per paper. Science has become a lot more complex, and requires a lot more funding, and that might account for the larger team size. But the databases also had data about the social sciences and the arts and humanities; social science research hasn't increased in scale and cost the same way particle physics and medicine have. Even in the social sciences, collaboration has become a lot more important. In 1955, only 17.5% of social science papers had two or more authors; in 2000, 51.5% of those papers did. And although papers in the arts and humanities still are mostly sole authored (over 90%), the trend over the past 50 years has also been toward more collaboration.

The historical data show that collaboration is becoming more widespread. But has all of this collaboration increased creativity? Wuchty et al. (2007) used the same databases to examine whether the collaborative products were better. The databases allowed them to determine the impact and influence of each paper and patent, because those databases keep track of how many times the paper or patent was cited by a later publication. Having more citations means a more influential paper, and having more citations has been shown to correlate with research quality. Over the 50-year period they studied, teams generated more highly cited work in every research area, and in every time period.

Nemeth and Goncalo (2005) confirmed this finding: as the number of authors increases, the number of citations increases, too. And they showed an additional fascinating pattern: when the authors were from different universities, the number of citations increases even more. Distant collaboration enhanced creativity more than local collaboration, and that's probably because it brings together multiple perspectives; researchers in the same university department will be more similar to each other and will share more implicit understandings.

Multiple studies show that teams generate better scientific research, and more important inventions, than solitary individuals. And Wuchty et al. (2007) discovered that the creative advantage for teams has increased over the past 50 years. Although teams generated more highly cited work back in 1955, by 2000 the advantage of teams over sole individuals had become even greater. In 1955, team-authored papers received 1.7 times as many citations as sole-authored papers; in 2000, they received 2.1 times as many.

Table 12.1: Contrasts Between the Input–Output (IO) and Process Approaches

Input–Output	Process
Analyzes variables	Analyzes processes
Variables are what happens before and after group interaction	Process is what happens during group interaction
Typically done in controlled laboratory conditions	Typically done with real-world teams
Typically quantitative and statistical	Typically qualitative
Provides evidence about how to structure inputs for maximum effectiveness, but is limited in detailed advice and understanding	Can provide detailed advice and understanding, but with limited generalizability and lower standard of scientific proof

There are two broad approaches to the study of groups. The *input-output (IO)* approach analyzes how different group inputs result in different group outputs. The inputs could be task instructions, incentives, group composition, and resources provided. The output is some measure of group effectiveness. This approach almost always compares groups in different experimental conditions; the groups are carefully assembled in the laboratory by randomly assigning people to join groups of other people they most likely don't know. However, the IO approach has also been done using "virtual experiments" by examining real-world organizations that have many teams engaged in similar tasks—for example, hundreds of copier repair teams (Wageman, 1995) working nationally for the same leading copier company. The IO approach typically uses quantitative measures, and often can provide statistical measures of the significance of observed relationships.

The IO approach provides valuable practical information about how to create groups that perform most effectively. But its weakness is that it can't tell us *why* a group performs well or not; the team's creative process is treated as a "black box." The second approach, known as the *process* approach or the *mechanism* approach, looks inside the black box to examine the group processes that explain the observed relations between inputs and outputs. Process studies are typically *qualitative*—extensively analyzing only a handful of groups, possibly even just one, by transcribing their dialog and analyzing how work unfolds over time (Table 12.1).

This chapter is divided into two major sections, each corresponding to one of these influential approaches to the study of group creativity.

INPUT–OUTPUT APPROACHES

There are two primary variables that have been extensively studied using the IO approach: the effect of group composition on group performance, and the effect of different process instructions on group performance.

GROUP COMPOSITION

Research shows that more diverse groups are more creative. Bantel and Jackson (1989) found that diversity in the functional backgrounds of members of top management teams in the banking industry was associated with more organizational innovation and, particularly, innovations in administrative processes. Similarly, Hambrick, Cho, and Chen (1996) found that the diversity of top management teams in the airline industry (measured as the differences in functional background and education) was associated with competitive moves that were seen as bolder and more innovative by industry observers. Keck (1997) studied firms in the cement and computer industries and found that when top management teams were more diverse in their functional affiliations, a company adapted more successfully to changes in the business environment. Management teams are more likely to pursue novel strategic directions when they're diverse in functional affiliation or educational background (Lant, Milliken, & Batra, 1992; Wiersema & Bantel, 1992). The literature on minority influence (e.g., Nemeth, 1986) suggests that the presence of even one group member who disagrees with the majority can deepen cognitive processing and lead to more reflective and integrative outcomes.

But there's also evidence that diversity can reduce group effectiveness. Some studies have found no relationship between diversity and creativity, or even a negative relationship (Ancona & Caldwell, 1992). Diversity can make interpersonal relations more complex; it can heighten group conflict; and these downsides could potentially offset the advantages. In a study of 76 top management teams, Knight et al. (1999) found that teams with greater diversity of functional backgrounds experienced higher interpersonal conflict and had more difficulty achieving consensus. Higher group diversity has been shown to lead to higher levels of intra-group conflict (Jehn, Northcraft, & Neale, 1999; Pelled, Eisenhardt, & Xin, 1999).

We can reconcile these conflicting findings by designing groups that manage diversity carefully:

1. Cognitive diversity (different educational, regional, or functional backgrounds) contributes to group creativity, rather than ethnic, national, or gender diversity *per se*.
2. There is an optimal degree of diversity: too much or too little reduces creativity.
3. Diversity works only if the group develops a shared sense of purpose and a shared commitment to the group's goals (Van der Vegt & Bunderson, 2005).
4. With complex tasks, diverse groups perform better; heterogeneous teams produce more ideas than homogenous teams (Kurtzberg, 2005).

SUPERSTARS

How important is it for a team to have one "superstar," a brilliant leader who can bring everyone together? In science, for example, a superstar is a brilliant scientist who teams up with others to collaboratively conduct research and who co-authors with other scientists. Azoulay, Zivin, and Wang (2010) developed a clever way to address this question using a natural experiment: they examined what happened to research productivity when an academic superstar suddenly dies while he or she is still actively engaged in scientific research.

The researchers analyzed the co-authors of 112 eminent life scientists. On average, each superstar had published with 47 co-authors in his or her career. That number alone is astonishing and shows how collaborative modern science is. Following the death of the superstar, his or her coauthors suffer a lasting quality-adjusted decline in productivity of 5% to 8%. For one person to have that impact across 47 co-authors is astonishing, and the authors found that this decline was lasting. Because there were so many co-authors, the researchers were able to compare different potential explanations for the decline. For example, they were able to show that the decline wasn't because they had shared personal connections (like working together at the same funding agencies or on editorial boards). The best explanation was that the decline results from the loss of "an irreplaceable source of ideas" (p. 552). For example, co-authors whose work was more closely related experienced a sharper decline in output than co-authors who worked on less related topics. These findings suggest that the superstar increases collaborative success by sharing and disseminating ideas among members of his or her network of co-authors.

TASK DESIGN

Teams generate innovation through interaction among members of the team. If the interactions are predictable and scripted, or if they're too strongly controlled by the team leader or by the strict norms and procedures of the organization, then no unexpected innovations will emerge. Teams are more likely to generate innovation when the group task design allows for a group process that is emergent, unpredictable, and improvisational (Sawyer, 2007). Yet research also shows that completely unstructured team interactions aren't ideal; the introduction of an appropriate task design to guide the team's creative process can enhance the innovation potential of the team.

One of the most common creativity task designs is *brainstorming*. Osborn (1948, 1953) coined the term "brainstorming" to describe his method of creative problem solving, and Gordon's *synectics* (1961) was also based on the belief that group thinking is always superior to individual thinking. Brainstorming continued to be a widely used technique through the dot-com era of the late 1990s and up to the present; Tom Kelley, founder of the famous Silicon Valley design firm IDEO, proclaimed that "brainstorming is the idea engine of IDEO's culture" (Kelley, 2001, p. 56; also see Chapter 22, pp. 411–412). Each designer at IDEO spends 5% to 10% of his or her time engaged in brainstorming sessions.

Brainstorming is based on two principles that Osborn called "deferment of judgment" and "quantity breeds quality." *Deferment of judgment* means that idea generation should be strictly separated from idea evaluation. From these two principles, Osborn proposed the following four guidelines for a brainstorming session (Osborn, 1948, p. 269). First, no criticism; don't evaluate any of the ideas; brainstorming is for idea generation and evaluation is to come later. Second, "freewheeling" is encouraged; the wilder the idea, the better. Third, quantity is the goal; the more ideas presented, the more likely that more creative ideas will be among them. Fourth, everyone should look for combinations of previous ideas and improvements on previous ideas. Osborn claimed that following these rules would more than double the ideas generated by group members.

Despite the continued popularity of group brainstorming as a technique, there's a substantial body of research showing that groups are less effective at generating ideas than the same number of people, working alone, who later pool their ideas—what has become known as a *nominal group* (because the individuals are working alone, they are a group in name only). In addition to the quantity of ideas, several studies have measured the quality of the ideas generated, using measures of originality or feasibility.

The first study that found that group brainstorming inhibits creativity was published in 1958 (Taylor, Berry, & Block, 1958). Taylor et al. asked subjects to brainstorm for 12 minutes, either individually or in four-person groups. Nominal groups were formed from the subjects who had brainstormed individually; for each nominal group, the ideas generated by four individuals were combined, eliminating redundant ideas. Taylor et al. found that the nominal groups generated twice as many different ideas as the real groups. In recent years, multiple studies have confirmed this 1958 finding that brainstorming groups, on average, generate half as many ideas as a similar number of solitary individuals. Diehl and Stroebe (1987) reviewed 22 experiments; in 18 of them, the nominal groups outperformed the real groups. In only four—all involving two-person groups—there was no difference. Other studies have found that real groups generate lower-quality ideas than nominal groups (as reviewed in Diehl & Stroebe, 1987; Paulus, Larey, & Dzindolet, 2001; Stroebe & Diehl, 1994). In a meta-analytic review of these studies, Mullen, Johnson, and Salas (1991) concluded that both quantity and quality of ideas are lower in real groups than in the comparison nominal groups. Quantity of ideas and number of good ideas are typically highly correlated; Diehl and Stroebe (1987, 1991) found a correlation of 0.80 between quantity of ideas and number of good ideas—quite similar to the finding that fluency and originality correlate at 0.88 on the TTCT (Chapter 3, p. 51).

These findings are surprising to most people because brainstorming is often a lot of fun. Especially in a homogenous group, there's high team cohesion and positive affect, and positive affect leads groups to perceive higher levels of creativity (Kurtzberg, 2005). But Kurtzberg (2005) found no correlation between a team's self-ratings of creativity and their actual measured ratings. And brainstorming groups always say that they were more creative than they would have been if they had worked alone, even though the research shows just the opposite. This has been called *the illusion of group effectiveness* (Homma, Tajima, & Hayashi, 1995; Paulus, Larey, & Ortega, 1995; Rowatt et al., 1997).

FACTORS THAT MAKE BRAINSTORMING MORE OR LESS EFFECTIVE

By the mid-1980s, there was a strong consensus among creativity researchers that face-to-face groups were less creative than nominal groups, a phenomenon that became known as *productivity loss*—referring to the lost productivity of groups compared to solo individuals. This resulted in a second phase of brainstorming research: the attempt to discover the factors that caused this productivity loss in the hopes of understanding how to design groups to be more creative. In an influential early study of productivity loss in groups, Steiner (1972) distinguished two forms of productivity loss: *motivation losses* and *coordination losses*. Motivation losses might occur if something about the group situation lowers the motivation of group members below that of subjects who work alone; Steiner identified two motivation losses, *free riding* and *production matching*. Coordination losses result from the difficulties in coordinating individual contributions to the group product; Steiner identified two coordination losses, *evaluation apprehension* and *production blocking*.

Motivation Losses

Free riding refers to a classic phenomenon studied by social psychologists: individuals in a group might "free ride" on the efforts of others. For example, in a group of six individuals, one of the individuals might reason that if he were to stay quiet and relax a bit, the other five members would generate plenty of ideas and no one would ever notice his silence. Several brainstorming researchers have attributed productivity loss to free riding (e.g., Stroebe & Frey, 1982). All the group members know that their ideas will be summed at the end of the session, so they might feel that their individual contribution is less identifiable. And group members might reason that their contribution is less important, and thus more dispensable (Kerr & Bruun, 1983).

The free-rider interpretation accounts for several findings from brainstorming research. Bouchard (1972) introduced a rule that participants had to give their ideas in a predetermined sequence, and if they couldn't think of a new idea, they had to say "pass." Bouchard found that this rule increased group productivity, suggesting that making contributions identifiable reduces free riding. Bouchard and Hare (1970) examined groups of size five, seven, and nine and found that the larger the group, the bigger the productivity loss for the interactive group. The free-riding hypothesis predicts that increases in group size would increase dispensability and decrease identifiability, and that explains the increase in productivity loss with larger groups (Bouchard & Hare, 1970).

If the group is told that quantity is the only measure of their performance, then the task becomes additive, and every single contribution is important. If the group is told that quality or originality is the goal, then group members who think they're less creative might think their ideas are more dispensable.

Production matching refers to a phenomenon where individuals compare their own performance to that of the other group members, and they try to match their level of production to that of the others. It's well known that setting ambitious goals can increase performance, including with idea generation (e.g., Hyams & Graham, 1984). Paulus and Dzindolet (1993) reasoned that because brainstorming is a new situation for most people, they're not sure about what would be the appropriate level of productivity. Consequently, they reduce their uncertainty by comparing their performance to that of others in the group. If this hypothesis is correct, then there should be a convergence of individual productivity towards the mean. In an experimental comparison of interactive and nominal brainstorming groups, Paulus and Dzindolet (1993) found that the number of ideas generated by individuals were more highly correlated in the interactive groups than the nominal groups, providing support to the production-matching hypothesis. Paulus and Dzindolet examined two additional assumptions: first, in the early phases of the brainstorming session, individual productivity is inhibited due to coordination losses (see below); due to production matching, the low performance becomes a group norm and keeps productivity down. However, the evidence for this was inconclusive. They found that there was less decrease in productivity, over the 25-minute session, for interacting groups than for nominal groups; however, even in the interacting groups, there was a decrease in productivity—on average, in the first five minutes, the interacting groups generated 12.9 ideas, and in the final five minutes, they generated only 5.5 ideas. This seems inconsistent with the hypothesis that the group establishes a low norm at the beginning, which then remains constant through the entire session.

Coordination Losses

Evaluation apprehension or *social inhibition* suggests that group members are monitoring the quality of their own ideas and resist voicing all of the ideas that occur to them—contrary to the brainstorming instructions to "freewheel" and not worry about criticism. This might occur in a group setting because people are afraid of negative evaluations from other group members;

however, in the solitary nominal condition, those who will be reviewing the ideas generated are not physically present, reducing the potential risk of negative evaluation. Early support for social inhibition came from a study by Collaros and Anderson (1969), who manipulated the perceived expertise of group members in the brainstorming group. The logic behind the experiment was that each individual would be more inhibited if he or she thought the other members were experts. The experiment had three conditions: *all experts*, when each member of the group was told that all other members had previous experience with such groups; *one expert*, when each member of the group was told that only one unidentified member of the group had previously worked in such a group; and *no experts*, when no such instructions were provided. The results were consistent with the predictions: productivity was highest in the *no expert* condition and lowest in the *all expert* condition. In a post-experiment questionnaire, the subjects reported more feelings of inhibition in the *all expert* condition.

Another study, by Maginn and Harris (1980), generated inconsistent findings. Their study examined only subjects working alone to generate ideas. Half of the subjects were told that there were three judges on the other side of a one-way mirror who were listening to their ideas and rating them for originality. These subjects generated just as many ideas as the subjects who didn't think there were observers, thus finding no evidence for social inhibition.

Diehl and Stroebe (1987) further examined this hypothesis by comparing individual (solo) brainstorming on controversial topics and uncontroversial topics. For their controversial topic with German subjects, an example question was "How can the number of guest workers be reduced?" This is quite controversial politically in Germany, where the study was conducted. Positions on the issue are highly polarized; policies designed to encourage guest workers to return to their home countries are associated with right-wing attitudes, for example. They further manipulated evaluation apprehension by telling some subjects that their ideas would be evaluated by others. They found that subjects generated fewer ideas with controversial topics, and fewer ideas when they were told their ideas would be evaluated.

Production blocking refers to any aspect of a group's dynamic that results in a reduction in the number of ideas generated. There are several factors that could result in production blocking. First, in a group setting only one person can talk at a time, whereas the nominal group members, working alone, can all generate ideas in parallel. Second, if people can't voice an idea right when it occurs to them, they might forget the idea before they get a chance to speak, or they might suppress the idea if they think of a criticism or a reason why it might not work. If, on the other hand, a person manages to keep that idea in mind until the others have finished speaking, the mental rehearsal of that one idea prevents him or her from thinking of additional ideas during that time. Third, group members have to listen closely to other people's ideas, and that leaves them with less mental energy to generate their own ideas. Research shows that productivity loss increases as the size of the group increases (Bouchard & Hare, 1970).

Diehl and Stroebe (1987) conducted an experiment that demonstrated that production blocking was a major cause of productivity loss in brainstorming groups. They built special communication devices to introduce blocking into the nominal group condition. All four subjects were instructed to speak their ideas into a microphone. Each subject worked alone in a separate room, but all four microphones were connected through a sort of switchboard that acted like a traffic light—allowing only one person to talk at a time. Underneath each microphone was a display of four lights, one corresponding to each group member. Whenever one person was talking, the subject's own light turned green, and the other three turned red. When a person stopped talking for 1.5 seconds, his or her light was switched off, and another person could talk. To further compare the potential role played by social inhibition, Diehl and Stroebe created one condition in which the subjects wore headphones, allowing them to hear the contributions of the others, and a second condition where the subjects didn't wear headphones and couldn't hear each others' ideas.

The results suggested that production blocking explained almost all of the productivity loss. Nominal groups generated about 100 ideas and face-to-face brainstorming generated about 55 ideas, consistent with prior studies. In the nominal group condition where subjects could hear each other, the groups generated about 35 ideas; in the condition where they could not, they generated about 40 ideas. Although the hearing condition, which might be expected to introduce social inhibition, resulted in somewhat fewer ideas, the difference wasn't statistically significant, suggesting that social inhibition doesn't result in a statistically significant increase in productivity loss beyond what's explained by production blocking. Furthermore, it suggests that the need to listen to others, thus splitting cognitive capacity between listening and idea generation, isn't the cause of production blocking. The cause of productivity loss seems to be the reduction in speaking time available to individuals when brainstorming, compared to solitary individuals in a nominal group.

To further evaluate this hypothesis, Stroebe and Diehl (1994) compared four-person nominal groups given 5 minutes to generate ideas with four-person interacting groups given 20 minutes. This condition would allow each individual in the interacting condition to have the same amount of speaking time available as the solo individuals in the nominal group. They found that the interacting groups generated significantly more ideas than the nominal groups—on average, 60.75 ideas versus 47.50 ideas. This might suggest that interacting groups can be more productive—however, these groups not only have four times as much time to talk, they also have four times as much time to think.

To determine whether productivity loss is caused by limited speaking time or by limited thinking time, Diehl and Stroebe (1991) conducted a variation on the above experiment. They again gave the brainstorming group 20 minutes, but also gave the solo individuals in the nominal condition 20 minutes. However, the solo individuals were allowed to speak their ideas only for a total of 5 minutes; this was measured with a voice-controlled clock, and the individuals weren't allowed to speak any more ideas after their 5 minutes was up. The results were quite interesting: nominal groups whose individuals could speak only 5 of 20 minutes were almost as productive as nominal groups whose individuals were allowed to talk for the entire 20 minutes, and their productivity was significantly higher than the interacting group that had 20 minutes.

In this experiment, the solo individuals in the nominal group, and the interacting individuals in the brainstorming group, each had 5 minutes to talk. The only difference was that the solo individuals could talk whenever they wanted, whereas those in the interacting group had to wait until someone else was finished talking. This study suggests that the waiting time is responsible for productivity loss in brainstorming groups.

A fourth cause of production blocking is *topic fixation*. On any typical brainstorming problem, the ideas generated tend to fall into categories. For example, a common question used on brainstorming experiments with college students—"think of ways to improve your university"—results in ideas that cluster in categories such as improving parking, improving the dining options, improving instruction or classrooms, etc. Ideally, a brainstorming session should generate ideas from as many distinct categories as possible; however, social tendencies in face-to-face groups might limit the range of idea categories considered. First of all, a range of studies has shown that groups tend to talk about information that everyone shares, and tend not to talk about information held only by one individual, known as a *hidden profile* (see below, pp. 242–243). Second, groups seem to display a tendency toward early consensus, leading to a convergent group style rather than a divergent group style (Aldag & Fuller, 1993).

Larey and Paulus (1999) evaluated the topic fixation hypothesis by developing a measure of *flexibility*, the total number of categories generated by a group. They had four-person nominal and interactive groups spend 15 minutes generating ideas for "How to improve the campus"; each idea generated was assigned to a category by the researchers. As with prior studies, nominal groups generated almost twice as many ideas (56 vs. 31). Nominal groups generated ideas in significantly more categories (17.2 vs. 12.1). In a further measure of the topic fixation hypothesis, the researchers analyzed all the ideas stated and calculated the probability that an idea would come from the same category as the idea that was stated just before. A ratio was calculated: the probability of staying in a category over the probability of moving to a new category. Interactive groups were much more likely to stay in the same category (ratio = 0.321 vs. 0.196 for solo individuals).

FIXING BRAINSTORMING

Fortunately, there is additional research that suggests that brainstorming groups can be made more effective by (1) clearly specifying the goals, (2) using a trained facilitator, (3) using "brainwriting" or electronic brainstorming, and (4) using groups to select ideas.

Clearly Specified Goals

Clear goals increase the effectiveness of brainstorming (Litchfield, 2008). Osborn pointed out back in 1948 that "Meetings drift aimlessly when a clear statement of the problem is lacking" (p. 269); IDEO says its brainstorms require "a well-articulated description of the problem at just the right level of specificity" (Kelley, 2001, p. 57). A group is less likely to generate new and useful ideas if the goals specified are vague, unclear, or too broad in scope.

Trained Facilitator

Several studies have found that groups with a trained facilitator are more effective (Isaksen & Gaulin, 2005; Offner, Kramer, & Winter, 1996; Oxley, Dzindolet, and Paulus, 1998). Offner, Kramer, and Winter (1996) began by training 12 graduate students in effective facilitation techniques, in two sessions of about two hours each. They then compared 20 four-person groups with a facilitator, 20 four-person groups with no facilitator, and 5 nominal groups. The found that the groups with a facilitator generated significantly more ideas than those with no facilitator. Further, they found that groups with a facilitator generated about as many ideas as the nominal groups.

Oxley, Dzindolet, and Paulus (1996) compared the performance of solo individual brainstorming with groups without a facilitator and with groups with highly trained facilitators (three hours of training), trained facilitators (one hour of training), and untrained facilitators (selected at random from the subjects assigned to the group). As with Offner et al., they found that the groups with highly trained facilitators generated as many ideas as nominal group members. They also found that groups with highly trained facilitators outperformed groups with trained and untrained facilitators. In addition, they found one area where the groups with highly trained facilitators outperformed even the nominal group—in the final 5 minutes of the 20-minute session, these groups generated almost twice as many ideas as the nominal groups. These findings suggest that if the session were even longer, the groups that had a highly trained facilitator might have significantly outperformed the nominal groups.

Brainwriting and Electronic Brainstorming

Brainwriting is an extension of brainstorming that involves writing ideas down on paper, both to keep a better record of all the ideas and also to reduce potentially negative group effects. *Method 635* is a brainwriting method in which six people each generate three ideas and write them on a sheet of paper. They then pass each sheet five times, with each person adding new ideas to each sheet each of the five times. A typical Method 635 session takes about five minutes. Method 635 is particularly good at generating names or slogans (Geschka, 1993).

Perhaps the first study of electronic brainstorming, where participants interacted via a computer network, was conducted by Nunamaker, Applegate, and Konsynski (1987). In the following years, this and other research resulted in a series of software products designed to support group creativity, a software category generally known as *group decision support systems (GDSS)*. A GDSS is generally used with a face-to-face group; each member of the group sits in front of a computer, and all of the computers are networked. Rather than speak ideas out loud, participants type their ideas into their computer; each idea is then immediately displayed on the other participants' screens.

Gallupe, Bastianutti, and Cooper (1991) experimentally tested the system developed by Nunamaker et al. (1987) and found that when four-person groups brainstormed using the GDSS, productivity loss did not occur: they generated as many ideas as nominal groups (50 vs. 53.20). And electronic brainstorming generated more ideas than face-to-face brainstorming (50 vs. 39.80). Gallupe and Cooper (1990) compared the speed of typing an idea to the speed required to say the idea and found that typing an idea took longer—which should have resulted in reduced productivity for electronic brainstorming, instead of the increased productivity actually observed.

Dennis and Valacich (1993) compared nominal and electronic brainstorming groups of sizes 6 and 12. Consistent with Gallupe et al. (1991), they found a nonsignificant difference in productivity with groups of size 6 (electronic brainstorming 55.42 ideas; nominal 65.81 ideas). However, 12-person electronic brainstorming groups were significantly more productive than 12-person nominal groups, generating 136.44 ideas versus 107.06 ideas. Their interpretation, based on observation of these groups in action, was that the electronic brainstorming groups benefited from the synergy that resulted from reading each others' ideas. Also, they observed that nominal group members appeared to run out of ideas, generating fewer towards the end of the session, whereas this didn't occur in the electronic brainstorming condition.

The increased productivity of electronic brainstorming is consistent with the above research on production blocking and evaluation apprehension (participants won't be nervous about their ideas being evaluated, because no one knows who generated each idea).

Use Groups to Select Ideas

Several studies demonstrate that groups are better at selecting good ideas than are solitary individuals. After conducting a brainstorming experiment where the task was "identify uses for a paper clip," Larey (1994) had a different set of subjects evaluate each idea generated and rate its creativity. Judgments were made by interactive groups and by nominal groups. Accuracy of judgments was determined by comparing the creativity ratings of the group or individual with a creativity rating generated by averaging the ratings of ten independent judges. Interactive groups were more accurate than individuals at rating the creativity of the ideas.

In another study, groups who were instructed to come up with one best idea generated a better idea than individuals instructed to generate a single best idea (Williams & Sternberg, 1988)—additional evidence that the group is better at selecting good ideas.

Brainstorming is more effective when groups have clear criteria for what counts as a good idea. Osborn's instruction to "avoid criticism" is of questionable value. For example, Postmes, Spears, and Cihangir (2001) found that priming a group with a "critical thinking norm" rather than a "consensus norm" resulted in a dramatic increase in performance: only 22% of the consensus norm groups selected the best option, but 67% of the critical thinking norm groups did. Galinsky and Kray (2004) found similarly dramatic effects in a study of groups tasked with solving a mystery. They primed some groups with a "counterfactual mindset," a critical way of thinking that promoted consideration of alternative possibilities; only 23% of the groups without this prime solved the mystery, but 67% of groups with the counterfactual prime solved the mystery.

HIDDEN PROFILES

One of the hypothesized benefits of groups versus solitary individuals is that groups bring more relevant information to bear on a problem. Each member of the group is likely to have somewhat different information and skills, particularly if the group is composed of members from diverse backgrounds. So if each member contributes his or her own unique knowledge to the group discussion, the group collectively would have more information than any one individual working alone. Wegner's (1986) theory of *transactive memory* suggests that social groups often seek ways to coordinate how they collectively store and use information, and that groups implicitly assign responsibility for sub-domains of information to specific members. The implication of this theory is that many groups succeed by relying on each member having unique information.

However, Stasser and Titus (1985, 2003) found that this hypothesized benefit of groups is rarely realized. They asked four-person teams of college students to evaluate three imaginary candidates for the president of their student body. The candidates were each given attributes and political positions that had previously been identified as desirable, neutral, or undesirable through an earlier survey of students. Candidate A possessed more desirable traits than the other two (B and C were identical in their desirability). When a group member received complete profiles of all three candidates, 67% of them chose Candidate A (the remaining third split their votes between B and C). When four students, all of whom had received complete profiles, came together in a group and talked about the candidates, 83% of the groups chose Candidate A.

But what happens when no single individual sees the complete profiles? Stasser and Titus (1985) tested two other conditions, where each individual participant had only a subset of the profile information. In a second experiment they called "hidden profile/consensus," each member received a different subset of Candidate A's desirable traits, and a different subset of Candidate B's undesirable traits. As a result, from the perspective of any one member, Candidate B now appeared to have more positive and fewer negative traits than Candidate A—even though collectively the four team members had the complete information that had enabled them to select Candidate A in the first experiment. A third experiment with a condition they called "hidden profile/conflict" was similar to "hidden profile/consensus" in how it selectively distributed information to shift support away from Candidate A, except that two of the four members received a subset of information that favored Candidate B and the other two received a subset of information that favored Candidate C.

In these hidden profile conditions, pre-discussion votes by each individual member selected Candidate A only 25% of the time. But when the four came together to discuss the candidates, did they exchange their information so that they collectively learned that Candidate A is the best? Just the opposite occurred: in the second experiment (where Candidate B seemed the best initially), after discussion, support for Candidate B *increased* from 61% to 71%. In the third experiment, votes for Candidate A *dropped* after discussion, from 21% to 12%.

These findings show that groups often fail to share unique information. The practical lesson is that groups should be encouraged to share unique information. However, simply mentioning the unique information is not enough; Stasser, Taylor, and Hanna (1989), and later Larson et al. (1996), found that even if a unique piece of information was shared, it was less likely to be remembered and repeated by other members than was shared information. Stasser and Titus (2003) hypothesized that introducing unique information, and repeating unique information, incurs a social cost. Lower-status group members were less likely to repeat unique information than high-status members (Larson et al., 1996).

COMPETITION

Contests, prizes, awards, and competitions have been widely used to foster creativity among teams (Birkinshaw & Lingblad, 2001; McKinsey & Company, 2009). The motivation behind intergroup competition is that it increases a positive sense of challenge for each competing group and enhances group flow by increasing coherence and a sense of shared mission (Baer et al., 2010). Baer et al. (2010) manipulated the degree of competition and found that increasing competition also increased the creativity of the group, using a consensual assessment measure by a three-judge panel who rated novelty and usefulness.

PROCESS APPROACH STUDIES

It's difficult to study group processes by using an experimental methodology, because when a group is allowed to work together on a task, it becomes almost impossible to control for all of the many variables that are relevant to the interaction, even if the group is brought into a laboratory and given a carefully specified and limited task to talk about. And in any case, most interaction researchers believe that it's important to study interaction as it occurs in real-world settings; this is referred to as *naturally occurring conversation*. A group of people in a laboratory, working on an artificial creative task, may talk very differently than they would in the real world.

It's difficult to fully explain group creativity by focusing on individual thought and action in isolation from the entire discursive context (Sawyer, 2003c). That's why experimental methods are rarely used to study group processes; instead, researchers often use a qualitative method known as *interaction analysis* (Sawyer, 2006a). Group process researchers focus on discourse and communication as a sort of externally visible distributed emergent knowledge (cf. Greeno, 2006; Kelly, Crawford, & Green, 2001, p. 268; Middleton & Edwards, 1990, p. 23; Sfard, 2002). Interaction analytic methods correspond to the sociocultural observation that knowledge and learning are often properties of groups, not only individuals (Hutchins, 1995; Rogoff, 1998).

GROUP DEVELOPMENT

Research shows that most groups go through a similar developmental process, from the moment they form to the time they break up. There are many theories about how groups develop through time; one survey of 20 different models found that they all proposed a *starting stage* in which group members get to know each other, set group goals, define member roles, and develop somewhat stable patterns of behavior; *crisis stages* in the middle; and an *ending stage* when the group has reached maturity and completes the group's business and prepares its final product (Chidambaram & Bostrom, 1996). The most famous model of group development is that of Tuckman (1965; Tuckman & Jensen, 1977), which proposes five stages:

- *Forming*: High anxiety, uncertainty, and politeness. Group members are concerned with psychological safety, reducing uncertainty, and defining boundaries.
- *Storming*: Conflict, power struggles, definition of roles. The internal structure of the group is developing; different members or coalitions may have different ideas about how to proceed.
- *Norming*: The group settles on a consensus goal, structure, roles, and a division of labor. Communication shifts from internal negotiation to the shared task.
- *Performing*: A high-performing group in which members are comfortable and share information openly. Each person knows the strengths and expertise of the others, and tasks are distributed optimally.
- *Adjourning*: Tasks are completed and the group breaks up.

Tuckman's group development model has been empirically validated (Decuyper, Dochy, & Van den Bossche, 2010), although not all groups advance through all of the stages; some groups never attain the optimal "performing" stage.

GROUP FLOW

When groups are performing at their peak, many scholars compare them to improvising jazz groups (Eisenberg, 1990; Kao, 1996; Miner, Bassoff, & Moorman, 2001; Weick, 2001). In both a jazz group and a successful work team, the members play off of one another, with each person's contributions inspiring the others to raise the bar and think of new ideas. Together, the improvising team creates a novel, emergent product, both unpredictable and yet more suitable to the problem than what any one team member could have developed alone.

When groups are challenged to undertake novel tasks, or when the task itself isn't well understood or hasn't been clearly specified, the group's collaboration can't be scripted or planned out in advance; this sort of planning works well to enhance efficiency but blocks innovation precisely because it's designed to reduce the variance of what occurs between the group members. When innovation is required, the group's challenge is to generate a solution that is unexpected, unpredictable, and unplanned.

In my book applying improvisational models to group creativity, I (Sawyer, 2007) extended Csikszentmihalyi's concept of *flow*—the state of peak experience (see Chapter 4, pp. 76–79) from the individual to the group. When a group is performing at its maximum effectiveness, I refer to it as being in a state of *group flow*. Group flow is characterized by the following ten characteristics:

1. Match between group and goal. If the group's goal is well defined, then a high degree of structure, cohesion, and shared knowledge are necessary to attain peak performance. But if the group's goal is ill defined, as is the case with most creative tasks, then peak performance requires a lower degree of structure and more diversity of backgrounds.
2. Close listening. Rather than plan ahead what is to be said, everyone's statements are genuinely unplanned responses to what has just been said.
3. Complete concentration. The group is fully focused on its task, without external distractions.
4. Being in control. The group has autonomy and authority to execute.
5. Blending egos. Each person's ideas build on everyone else's, so that at the end, no one can remember who contributed what.
6. Equal participation. Everyone participates equally. This generally requires that everyone have a similar level of expertise and authority.
7. Familiarity. Some degree of familiarity is necessary, because it results in *tacit knowledge* that enables better communication. But too much familiarity means that there is no possibility of unexpected connections that result in new ideas.
8. Communication. The group members are always in communication, always talking.
9. Keep it moving forward. Each person builds on and elaborates the ideas generated by the others.
10. The potential for failure. The real potential for failure motivates peak performance, but only if the group is working in an environment that welcomes failure as a necessary and frequent correlate of innovation, rather than punishing failure.

When groups are improvising, in a state of group flow, creativity occurs through the following process:

1. Innovation emerges over time. There's no blinding flash of insight that solves the group's problems. Rather, there's a constant series of small insights, which accumulate over time to result in the creative outcome.

2. Innovation emerges from the bottom up, not the top down. Effective creative groups aren't dominated by a single strong person, and they're not guided by agendas, plans, or policies. They are *self-managing groups*; groups that collectively manage themselves are more adaptive, agile, and innovative.

3. The meaning of each contribution becomes clear only afterwards. Ideas are proposed, and only with later discussion does it become clear exactly how an earlier idea fits into the emerging total picture.

4. There are many dead ends. Even the most effective teams can't avoid them, but they are effective at identifying when they're at a dead end, and backing up to start down a new path.

Groups tasked with innovation may not follow a linear developmental sequence such as the one proposed by Tuckman. In his five-stage model, groups define their goals and their task structure in the "norming" stage before they get down to serious work. But for innovative groups, much of the work involves identifying goals—problem finding—and group structures and norms need to remain fluid, varying as new ideas and understandings emerge.

SUMMARY: MAKING GROUPS MORE CREATIVE

Groups are more creative than individuals when they've worked together for a while; when they share a common set of conventions and knowledge and yet also have complementary sets of expertise; and when the organization rewards group collaboration. Groups are more creative than individuals when the amount of shared knowledge corresponds to how well the problem is understood. If the group has to find a new problem, it's better if they don't share the same background and expertise; if the group has to solve a known problem, it's better if they share more similar expertise (Sawyer, 2003c, 2007).

Taggar (2002) studied both the individual and the group level simultaneously. He found evidence for a multi-level mediating factor that he called *team creativity relevant processes (TCRP)*, capturing such emergent factors as peer inspiration and motivation, organization and coordination, and "individualized consideration" (eliciting different ideas and viewpoints). He found that groups perform best when they contain creative members (using an aggregated measure of total group creativity) *and* when they have effective TCRP. Low TCRP can neutralize the effect of having all high-creativity group members. Team processes are emergent properties of the group in interaction; the group's creativity is more than a simple sum of the individual members' creativity.

Although real groups underperform nominal groups on ideational fluency tasks such as brainstorming, many studies have identified other tasks on which real groups outperform nominal groups:

- Spatial problems: Groups outperform a comparable number of individuals when the problems involve three-dimensional spatial information and transformation (Schwartz, 1995).
- Complex problems: Groups outperform a comparable number of individuals on problems of moderate difficulty that require understanding of verbal, numeric, or logical conceptual systems (Laughlin et al., 2006).

- Problem finding: Cognitively diverse groups outperform individuals when the nature of the problem isn't well understood, and the problem must be formulated.

In most real-world settings, groups are tasked with problems that tend to have these characteristics. Rarely do real-world groups engage in the ideational fluency tasks that are used in laboratory brainstorming experiments.

CONCLUSION

People love to be in group flow (Eisenberg, 1990). As a result, the companies that create an improvisational work environment will be better able to attract and retain the most creative professionals. The best manager is one who can create an environment in which free collaborative improvisation can flourish, and this requires an almost Zen-like ability to control without controlling. As is written in the *Tao Te Ching*:

> The existence of the leader who is wise is barely known to those he leads. He acts without unnecessary speech, so that the people say, "It happened of its own accord." (Rosenthal, 2003, Section 17)

Many business leaders believe that collaboration, openness, and a lack of hierarchy and rigidity are the keys to business creativity. In business, the bottom line is what the whole organization creates collectively. There might be a lot of creative employees, but if they work in a stifling organizational structure they won't innovate. We can't explain group creativity only by looking inside the heads of the smartest employees. We need an approach that explains group dynamics and creative collaboration, organizational structures and corporate cultures, and market penetration and dissemination.

KEY CONCEPTS

- Groupthink
- Input–output approach (IO) and process approach
- Cognitive diversity
- Brainstorming
- Nominal group
- Productivity loss
- Hidden profiles
- Interaction analysis
- Group flow
- Self-managing groups

THOUGHT EXPERIMENTS

- A jazz performance, by definition, could not be created by a single solo performer. Think of some other creative activities that require a group.

- Think of the various formal groups that you've been a part of—whether a sports team, a music ensemble, a work group, or a volunteer or nonprofit. Which groups were successful? Which groups were not? How would you explain these differences?
- Think of an informal, emergent group that you've been a part of—a group of friends, a secret club in elementary school, roommates in college. How did the group form? What kept it going? How did it end?
- Did this group have any private jokes, or special slang words that no one else understands? Can you remember who created those inside jokes and terms, or how they were selected by the group for continued use?
- Of all the groups you've been a part of, which one was the most fun? Was that also the most effective and successful group?

SUGGESTED READINGS

John-Steiner, V. (2000). *Creative collaboration.* New York: Oxford.

Kao, J. (1996). *Jamming: The art and discipline of business creativity.* New York: HarperCollins.

Kelley, T. (2001). *The art of innovation: Lessons in creativity from IDEO, America's leading design firm.* New York: Doubleday.

Paulus, P. B., & Nijstad, B. A. (2003). *Group creativity: Innovation through collaboration.* New York: Oxford.

Sawyer, R. K. (2007). *Group genius: The creative power of collaboration.* New York: BasicBooks.

CHAPTER 13

ORGANIZATIONAL CREATIVITY

This process of Creative Destruction is the essential fact about capitalism. It is what capitalism consists in and what every capitalist concern has got to live in.

—Economist Joseph Schumpeter, 1942/1975, p. 83

According to the famous economist Joseph Schumpeter, creativity is the core of capitalism. New innovations displace the old, often leading to radical transformations and creative destruction. Creative destruction, with rapid advances in technology, was a fact of life in the United States in the late 20th century. At the beginning of the 21st century, creativity had become the key factor driving the U.S. economy (Florida, 2002) and many other leading world economies.

Creativity researchers have discovered that you can't explain organizational creativity using a strictly individualist approach. To explain any case of important innovation, we need to examine teamwork and collaboration, overall organizational structures and culture, and contextual factors such as the market and the regulatory climate. Creativity researchers have demonstrated what executives intuitively know: that organizational creativity occurs in complex social systems.

One of the best-known recent examples of technological innovation is the Windows operating system.[1] Who created it? Many people will answer by saying that the Microsoft corporation created Windows. Microsoft released its Windows 3.1 operating system in 1990.

But the minority of computer users who are devoted to the Apple Macintosh tell a different story. They know that the most distinctive features of Windows—its graphical user interface (GUI)—appeared years earlier in the Macintosh. The Apple Macintosh was the first successful

---

1. The following narrative is taken from a variety of sources, including messages posted by Oliver Steele in March 1988: http://www.stanford.edu/~siegman/interface_history.html; by Bruce Horn, who worked in the LRG of Xerox PARC from 1973 to 1981, and then worked at Apple from 1981 to 1984: http://www.mackido.com/Interface/ui_history.html and http://mxmora.best.vwh.net/brucehorn.html; by Jeff Raskin, who began working at Apple in 1978 but had frequently visited Xerox PARC in the mid-1970s: http://mxmora.best.vwh.net/JefRaskin.html (all sites accessed 8/23/11).

consumer computer to have a GUI with windows, menus, and a mouse pointing device, and it was released years before Microsoft Windows, in 1984.

However, Apple didn't create Windows either. The critical creative ideas that we associate today with Windows were created in the 1960s and 1970s. An early version of a GUI was thought up all the way back in 1945 by Vannevar Bush, who called his invention the *memex*. In the 1950s, Douglas C. Engelbart explored Bush's idea while working for the Advanced Research Project Agency (ARPA) of the Department of Defense. When this funding ran out, Engelbart and his team of engineers moved to a cutting-edge research facility that Xerox founded in 1970 known as the Palo Alto Research Center, or PARC for short.

Up to the 1970s, the key ideas for a windows-and-mouse user interface had remained in the research laboratory. But in 1973, Xerox PARC put these ideas together and released the world's first personal computer, the Alto (Fig. 13.1). The Alto had windows and a mouse-controlled cursor. It used a laser printer—a radical new technology also developed at PARC—and you could connect several Altos using a network known as Ethernet, also developed at PARC. This was a highly influential computer, far ahead of its time; today, every computer has windows and a mouse, and almost every office uses laser printers and Ethernet. But Xerox chose not to market the Alto because it would have cost the customer $40,000. In 1981, Xerox released a less expensive version, the Star, for $16,000, but the market had already settled on much cheaper personal computers like the Apple II, and the Star failed to sell.

Steven Jobs, Apple's founder and CEO, was given a couple of tours of Xerox PARC in 1979, and he was inspired by the innovative user interface. He instructed his developers to get to work

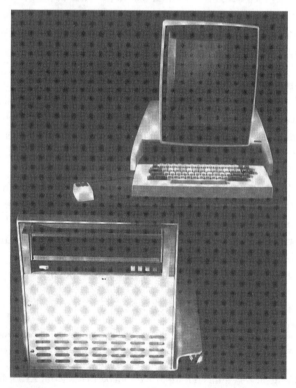

FIGURE 13.1: The Alto Computer, created by the Xerox Palo Alto Research Center in the 1970s, was the first windows-and-mouse computer. (With permission of Smithsonian Institution, image no. 90–2234.)

on a similar type of computer, and by 1981, Apple had hired about 15 of the Xerox developers to work on two GUIs: the Lisa and the Macintosh.[2]

The Lisa and Macintosh teams worked pretty much independently, and they sometimes duplicated each other's innovations, resulting in multiple discoveries. The engineers sometimes chose different solutions for the same problem. For example, where the Mac had a mouse for cursor control, the Lisa used a touch-sensitive pad next to the keyboard. The Lisa was released first, in January 1983, but at $10,000 it was too expensive for average consumers and was doomed like the Alto and the Star. The Macintosh (commonly referred to thereafter as a "Mac") was released at an affordable price in 1984, and the rest is history.

Apple invited Microsoft developers in-house between 1981 and 1984, during the development of the Mac, because Microsoft developers were writing application software for it. Microsoft liked the Mac operating system and offered to pay a licensing fee to use it. When Apple refused, Microsoft announced the creation of Windows in 1983 (although the first version would not be released until August 1987).

Knowing that Xerox PARC developed the first windows computer still doesn't explain how Windows was created. What we know today as the Microsoft Windows GUI is a conglomeration of many mini-insights that originated in university research labs. The first interface that used direct manipulation of graphic objects was the influential Sketchpad system, which was the topic of Ivan Sutherland's 1963 MIT Ph.D. thesis. Sketchpad contained many features that later became central to windows operating systems: icons, a way to select icons by pointing, and the ability to move them by clicking, moving, and clicking again in the new location. David Canfield Smith first used the term "icon" for screen objects in his 1975 Stanford Ph.D. thesis on Pygmalion. Smith later became one of the team members who designed the Xerox Star. Each of the mini-insights that together make up the GUI emerged from a collaborative team of individuals, and tracing sole authorship is nearly impossible (Table 13.1).

Table 13.1 is only an approximation. No one knows exactly which research group first came up with each of these ideas, and the origins of many of them are contested. It seems likely that many of the ideas were cases of multiple discovery. After all, it's not that big of a leap of insight to look at radio buttons and think of extending the idea to check boxes. But even if these attributions are correct, it doesn't provide much support to the individualist view of creativity, because most of these creative innovations emerged from an entire research team: the Lisa project at Apple, for example, or the Learning Research Group (LRG) at Xerox PARC. And even the innovations that are attributed to specific people—like the idea of turning a trackball upside down to create a mouse—occurred in collaborative contexts, and it's probably unfair to give all of the credit to any one individual.

Many of these creative innovations build on each other. For example, the first screen pointer was a light pen; it had to touch the screen to work. Because the pointer was physically touching the screen, there was no need for a pointer icon to be displayed on the screen. In the 1970s, researchers at Xerox PARC took this idea and elaborated it. They realized that a trackball could

---

2. This history may overstate the linearity of influence; Jeff Raskin began to work at Apple in 1978 and became a founding member of the Macintosh team, and although he was aware of the developments at Xerox PARC, he also noted that many of their ideas predated Xerox, as well; for example, he cited his own 1967 thesis on graphic user interfaces. And a lot of the Macintosh and Lisa operating systems had been developed even before Jobs visited PARC in 1979 (see sources in note 1).

Table 13.1: Source of Invention of Various Components of the Windows GUI

Invention	Year	Source
Screen pointer (lightpen touching screen)	1963	Ivan Sutherland's Sketchpad project
Pointing device, now with on-screen pointer	mid-1970s	Doug Englebart and SRI
Mouse (an upside-down trackball)	1963 (?)	Doug Englebart and SRI
Cursor changes that show system status (arrow to egg timer)	mid-1970s	William Newman and Xerox PARC
Menus	mid-1970s	Learning Research Group (LRG) at Xerox PARC
Pop-up menus	mid-1970s	Dan Ingalls (LRG)
Pull-down menus	1983	Lisa team at Apple
Disabling (graying) of inactive menu items	Uncertain	Lisa team at Apple (1983) or Ed Anson (1980) or Xerox PARC (1982)
Menu bar	1983	Lisa team at Apple
Scroll bars	mid-1970s	LRG
Radio buttons	mid-1970s	Ted Kaehler (LRG)
Check boxes	mid-1970s	LRG (?)
Drag-and-drop movement of icons	1984 (?)	Jeff Raskin and the Macintosh team

be used instead of a light pen, but because the ball didn't actually touch the screen, a pointer had to be placed on the screen to indicate the current position. The insight for the mouse was that the trackball could be placed on the bottom of a small box, and that the box's movement would cause the trackball to move because of friction with a rubber mouse pad. Each of these creative insights was a small, incremental elaboration on a preceding series of insights. The idea for a mouse that would control an on-screen cursor didn't appear suddenly, full grown, in a burst of insight in 1975. It was a rather small extension of a long series of mini-insights extending back at least to 1963.

The history of the windows-and-mouse GUI provides us with several insights into organizational creativity.

Each innovation builds incrementally on a long history of prior innovations. The creative products that the consumer sees, that are successful in the market, rarely spring to life full grown. The consumer rarely sees the long historical path of small, incremental mini-insights that accumulate to result in the emergence of the final product. The explanation of this process requires an action theory rather than an idealist theory (see pp. 87–88).

Innovations emerge from collaborative teams. Although a single person may become associated with a specific idea, it's hard to imagine that person having that idea apart from the hard work, in close intimate quarters, of a dedicated team of like-minded individuals. And most innovative products require many insights, each of them coming from a different team member (Evans & Sims, 1997; Sawyer, 2007; Wicklund, 1989).

Multiple discovery is common. In the words of MIT Media Lab cofounder Nicholas Negroponte, "innovation is inefficient" (2003, p. 34). There were several organizations each developing GUIs—two separate teams within Apple, a Microsoft team started in 1983, and even more teams within Xerox PARC—and many critical ideas emerged in multiple teams independently, or by drawing on ideas that predated all of those groups.

There is frequent interaction among the teams. Members of a team occasionally visit and view what is being done by another team. And key employees frequently transfer allegiances, taking their expertise from one team to another (Tuomi, 2002).

A product's success depends on broad contextual factors. How much does it cost? Who and what sort of person can afford it? Is it compatible with other products and practices that are already embedded? How well is it marketed?

Innovation emerges from a complex social and organizational system. We can't explain business creativity without a sociocultural explanation of the complex organization from which innovation emerges. We have to understand not only the individual team members' creative processes but also the nature of teamwork and collaboration, and the roles played by organizational structure and market forces (Grønhaug & Kaufmann, 1988; King & Anderson, 1995).

INNOVATION VERSUS CREATIVITY

> *History proves that great inventions are never, and great discoveries seldom, the work of any one mind. Every great invention is either an aggregate of minor inventions or the final step of the progression.*
>
> —Mel Rhodes, (1961, p. 309)

In a sphere of activity far removed from the mainstream of creativity research, a huge group of highly paid professionals has spent decades poring over the arcane details of creativity and innovation. Who could these neglected creativity scholars be? They're the lawyers connected with the field of intellectual property rights. Many of these scholars believe that a strong patent office, and a legal system with the power to protect intellectual property so that creators are rewarded for their work, has been a major factor contributing to creativity in the United States.

In Washington, D.C., on Oct. 16, 2002, the U.S. Patent and Trademark Office celebrated its 200th anniversary by bringing together 37 members of the National Inventors Hall of Fame. They hold hundreds of patents. The White House Office of Science and Technology Policy has estimated that 52% of the nation's growth since World War II has come through invention (Leary, 2002). The U.S. Patent and Trademark Office awards 3,500 new patents each week; every year, it receives 326,000 patent applications; and in over two centuries, it has granted more than 6.3 million U.S. patents. These large numbers qualify the office as one of the world's greatest experts on creative innovation.

The U.S. Patent and Trademark Office website tells us what it takes for an innovation to be patentable:

Any new and useful process, machine, manufacture, or composition of matter, or any new and useful improvement thereof (from http://www.uspto.gov/web/offices/pac/doc/general/what.htm [accessed 10/15/10])

This definition emphasizes the two components of the sociocultural definition of creativity: a product that is both "new and useful," both novel and appropriate to some domain of activity. The patent office website even provides a helpful elaboration of what "useful" means:

> The term "useful" in this connection refers to the condition that the subject matter has a useful purpose and also includes operativeness, that is, a machine which will not operate to perform the intended purpose would not be called useful, and therefore would not be granted a patent.

The statutory definition of what can be patented has been elaborated and refined through decades of case law, common law, and patent office regulations and practices. As a result, the definition of invention may be the most rigorous definition in the entire field of creativity (Huber, 1998).

The Patent Act, 35 U. S. C. §103, forbids issuance of a patent when "the differences between the subject matter sought to be patented and the prior art are such that the subject matter as a whole would have been obvious at the time the invention was made to a person having ordinary skill in the art to which said subject matter pertains." This clause led to the *nonobviousness* standard: a patent can be issued only to ideas that would not have been obvious to another person working in the same area—what is known as a PHOSITA, an acronym for "Person Having Ordinary Skill In The Art." In *KSR v. Teleflex*, the Supreme Court ruled that it had become too easy to receive a patent, because the nonobviousness standard had not been applied rigorously. This court decision excluded "ordinary innovation" from intellectual property protection because any PHOSITA could have generated it (Sawyer, 2008). Not all combinations are patentable—only those combinations that are not obvious, and that have unpredictable results.

Innovation isn't simply the creation of something new. In the development of the windows GUI, many people created new technologies in the 1960s and 1970s that didn't become viable products until they all came together in the Apple Macintosh in 1984. Innovation involves both the creation of a new idea, and the implementation, dissemination, and adoption of that idea by an organization (West, 2002, 2003). Often the original insight changes significantly as it's executed, so much that it's essentially reinvented (Grønhaug & Kaufmann, 1988). Explaining these processes requires an interdisciplinary approach that focuses not only on the individual who originates the idea but also on the entire organizational system, and the complex social and interactional processes that result in implementation, dissemination, and adoption.

THE ENTREPRENEURIAL PERSONALITY

One of the classic definitions of entrepreneurship is "the relentless pursuit of opportunity without regard to resources currently controlled" (Stevenson & Sahlman, 1989, p. 104). A second definition is more useful for psychologists: "entrepreneurship is the process of recognizing and pursuing opportunities . . . with a view to value creation" (Chell, 2007, p. 18). Under these definitions, entrepreneurs are people who can recognize opportunities—what creativity researchers typically call "problem finding"—and have the motivation to pursue them, while remaining focused on value creation—what creativity researchers would call "appropriateness."

The personality traits associated with the entrepreneur include (Chell, 2008):

- *Need for achievement*: The drive to excel, to attain a goal
- *Internal locus of control*: People believe themselves to be in control of their destiny.

- *Risk-taking propensity*: Pursuing an idea when the probability of success is low. However, this is calculated risk; the outcome is perceived as achievable.
- *Opportunity recognition*: People who effectively recognize opportunities have substantial domain knowledge; they engage in trial and error and counterfactual thinking (mental simulations of various possible outcomes of an action or event); they remain extremely alert to the business environment, and they perceive that environment accurately.
- *Proactive orientation*: They are active agents who take initiative to bring about change.
- *High self-efficacy*: In the relevant areas of marketing, innovation, management, risk-taking, and financial control
- *Social competence*: Ability to network and socially adapt
- *Intuition*: Ability to envision future possibilities
- On the big five personality traits (see Chapter 4, p. 66), only Conscientiousness was found to be related to long-term venture survival (Amit, Glosten, & Muller, 1993; Ciavarella et al., 2004). Yet when managers are compared to entrepreneurs, managers score higher on Conscientiousness, and also on Agreeableness (Envick & Langford, 2000).

Arenius and Minniti (2005) studied 51,721 *nascent entrepreneurs*—people who founded a new enterprise for the first time (as opposed to *serial entrepreneurs* and *portfolio entrepreneurs*)—and found that:

- The likelihood of becoming a nascent entrepreneur decreases with age.
- Males are more likely than females to become nascent entrepreneurs.
- Employed people are more likely than the unemployed or retired to become nascent entrepreneurs.
- Positively related personality traits include opportunity perception, confidence in one's skills, and knowing other entrepreneurs.
- Fear of failure is negatively correlated with being a nascent entrepreneur.

Miner (1997) studied 100 entrepreneurs and identified four different entrepreneurial personality types:

- *The personal achiever*: Scores high on Need to achieve, Desire for feedback, Strong personal initiative, Commitment to organization, Belief that one person can make a difference, Belief that work should be guided by personal goals
- *The empathetic supersalesperson*: Scores high on Capacity to empathize, Desire to help others, Belief that social processes are very important, Belief that sales force is crucial to carrying out company strategy
- *The real manager*: Scores high on Desire to play a corporate leader role, Decisiveness, Positive attitudes toward authority, Desire to compete, Desire to stand out from the crowd
- *The expert idea generator*: Scores high on Desire to innovate, Love of ideas, Belief that new product development is crucial to carrying out company strategy, Desire to avoid taking risks

The difficulty in identifying an "entrepreneurial personality" is that founding and running a successful venture involves many procedural stages over months and years. In a study of which

Stanford MBA alumni become entrepreneurs, Lazear (2005) found that those with more balanced skill sets—the jack-of-all-trades—were more likely to become entrepreneurs, and highly specialized people were less likely. Many distinct competencies are required, from recognizing an opportunity and formulating the problem (perhaps the most creative stage of the process) to exploiting the opportunity, identifying markets, securing financial backing, recruiting staff with relevant expertise, protecting intellectual property, defending against competitors who enter the same market, and managing the revenues and costs so that the business is profitable. Other than the first stage, the later stages are not likely to involve any higher degree of creativity than any other managerial activity, although they almost certainly involve different managerial talents.

THE COLLABORATIVE WEB

New products aren't created by individual minds; they emerge unpredictably from a complex network of organizations and markets. Evolution explains how biological complexity emerges with no designer; the *systems model* applies the evolutionary metaphor to explain sociocultural creativity (see Chapter 11). Once an individual has an idea, that idea enters a marketplace, an ecosystem of competing ideas. Corporate executives have many new ideas to choose from, but no single executive is in complete control, because business organizations are themselves sociocultural systems that behave in unpredictable ways, and some ideas might fit better with the organization's ecology than others. And once an idea is turned into a product and marketed, it enters the sociocultural system of the marketplace, where it has to compete with other products. The outcome of market competition is not designed; technological developments emerge unpredictably.

New technologies often have unintended effects. When the Defense Department funded the ARPANET in the 1960s and 1970s—the network that we all now know as the Internet—their purpose in networking the large mainframe computers at Defense Department research sites was to allow resources to be shared. These mainframe computers were expensive, and the Defense Department thought they could buy fewer computers if users at each location could run programs on less-busy computers at other locations.

By the early 1970s, ARPANET had developed a single standard for transferring files between computers. Ray Tomlinson, a developer at Bolt, Beranek and Newman, an ARPANET contractor, realized that users at different computers could send messages to one another, with each message being transferred as a small file. However, he had to add one tiny feature: senders needed a way to indicate which person was supposed to receive the file. On the spur of the moment, Tomlinson decided to separate the person's name and the computer's name with the @ sign. He wrote the program off-duty and unofficially shared it with a few colleagues in late 1971. In 1972, it was added to the operating system, so that every ARPANET computer had a version installed. Tomlinson's mail program caught on like wildfire. Soon after that, Tomlinson's program was replaced by an e-mail program that used a different technology, with dedicated e-mail features. By 1973, 75% of all network traffic was e-mail, and this was a complete surprise to the experts who had planned and funded the ARPANET. They hadn't even included e-mail in their original design for the network, and Tomlinson's program wasn't an officially authorized project. Through most of the 1970s the Defense Department viewed e-mail as an illegitimate use of expensive computer resources, but they tolerated it because they hoped it would lead more research sites to join the network.

So who created e-mail? Although it wouldn't have been possible without the ARPANET, the network's creators didn't create e-mail. And although Tomlinson created the program that supported e-mail, that wouldn't have been possible without the network. And the idea might have been lost to history if researchers across the country hadn't started using it, each person making his or her own decision. The dissemination and success of the innovation was a distributed, emergent, social phenomenon, not planned, organized, or even predicted by anyone. And in this, innovation is like evolution: design without a designer, creativity without a creator.

New products are created by complex social organizations—what I call *collaborative webs* (Sawyer, 2007). The selection of products is accomplished by an even more complex organization: the market. The interdisciplinary approach allows us to study collaborative webs at multiple levels of analysis, combining individualist and sociocultural approaches.

THE INDIVIDUAL IN THE ORGANIZATION

In the Western cultural model of creativity, we generally think that the social and cultural context can only be a constraint to creativity. One interview study of corporate engineers found that they almost always associated the context with interference and inhibition (Talbot, 1993). When these engineers think about context at all, they think about how their boss doesn't like novelty or overrides their decisions, about how information doesn't flow freely, or how other departments aren't willing to cooperate. They also complain about short-term managerial thinking, rigid hierarchical structures, or overly tight financial controls. It's not surprising that these engineers associate context with constraint, because in the Western cultural model of creativity, that's the only role that context is allowed to play. It's much more difficult for us to realize the supporting, enabling, and enhancing role that contexts play in creativity, because those functions don't have a place in the Western cultural model.

In the 1950s and 1960s—the first wave of creativity research—it was thought that the most creative organization would be the one that least interfered with individual autonomy (Rockefeller Brothers Fund, 1958). This was consistent both with a fear of a society filled with "organization men," and with the individualist personality focus of creativity research (see Chapters 2 and 4). However, contemporary research has demonstrated that companies that focus on individual talent—a trendy approach in the 1990s—tend to fail. No company was more sold on freeing individualist talent than the Enron Corporation, for example, which famously went bankrupt in 2001 after the discovery of systematic accounting fraud. Enron's failings have been directly tied to its focus on "the talent myth" (Gladwell, 2002). The problem is that such a focus leads one to believe that an organization's creativity is a simple additive function of the creativity of its employees. But in real corporations, the organization's creativity is a complex and emergent property, depending not only on the employees but also on the structures that organize them, and the joint practices that they engage in together (King & Anderson, 1995). Organizational creativity isn't additive, and that's why it's not possible to make a company more creative simply by hiring more creative people. Several successful U.S. organizations, such as Southwest Airlines, Wal-Mart, and Procter & Gamble, hire ordinary people from midlevel universities rather than the top students from Harvard's business school. Their organizational systems explain their creativity and success. The sociocultural approach is required to explain how such companies innovate.

SOCIAL NETWORKS

Teams never operate in a vacuum; each team is part of a broader organizational context. As long ago as 1961, Burns and Stalker made the seminal argument that *organic* organizational structures (decentralized, with flexible policies and procedures) are more likely to promote innovation than *mechanistic* organizational structures (centralized control and formalized procedures). Aiken and Hage (1971) empirically demonstrated that this was the case in a study of 16 organizations in a Midwestern U.S. city. In the classic book *The Social Psychology of Organizing*, management guru Karl Weick (1969) similarly argued that smaller, "loosely coupled" organizations are more adaptive than carefully planned organizations. In an influential 1983 book, Henry Mintzberg used the term "adhocracy" to refer to one of five organizational forms, the one with the flattest organizational structures and smaller teams. Management theorists have consistently argued that these looser, more improvisational organizational forms are more innovative (e.g., Mintzberg, 1983; Quinn, 1985; Sawyer, 2007).

Organizational context shapes, directs, and constrains organizational innovation in a variety of ways. But one of the most important means by which organizational context influences innovative activity within an organization is by shaping the way in which organizational members interact, share information, compare knowledge, and combine ideas. In other words, organizational structure and context—the "formal" organization—affects innovation largely by shaping and constraining the "informal" organization (i.e., the network of interactions between and among organization members). For creative problem solving, the informal organization has been shown to matter more than the formal organization (Hargadon & Bechky, 2006). In many highly innovative organizations, innovation emerges from informal teams that emerge outside of the formal organization (Sawyer, 2007). Breakthrough innovations often result when information flows through the informal organization in ways that foster unexpected connections among disparate ideas (Hargardon, 2003).

In recent decades, researchers have made significant strides in assessing and evaluating the informal organization through the use of *social network analysis (SNA)*. A social network consists of a set of nodes, each representing an individual, and links between nodes, representing a relationship. These relationships have been conceived in different ways. First, a network link or "tie" could be defined in terms of its strength (Granovetter, 1973). Stronger ties are characterized by more emotional closeness, more frequent and longer interactions, and mutual and reciprocated judgments of the importance of the relationship (Hansen, 1999; Wegener, 1991). (Some researchers have suggested that these may be distinct dimensions of tie strength, and may have different outcomes: Marsden & Campbell, 1984; Perry-Smith, 2006.) Second, a network tie could be defined in terms of the content of communication. Are people exchanging advice? Political support? Information needed to complete a task?

One of the most solid findings of SNA is that strong friendships aren't good for creativity. This may seem counterintuitive; but it's because (1) we tend to have close relationships to people who are like us, and (2) our good friends typically know each other. As a result, social networks strong in friendship tend to be groups where everyone knows each other, and where individual knowledge and attitudes tend to converge over time (Burt, 1992). Thus it's less likely that a person will encounter a surprising new view from a friend—and hearing the same views and the same information that one already holds doesn't contribute to creativity (Perry-Smith, 2006; see pp. 233–234 on team diversity).

In contrast, so-called *weak ties*—where two people are linked, but not very strongly—are more strongly associated with creativity (Perry-Smith & Shalley, 2003, 2006). In contrast to strong ties, weak ties are people who interact only infrequently, and for shorter durations each time. A person is more likely to acquire new information from a weak tie than a strong tie, because strongly connected nodes tend to have the same sources and share the same information. Furthermore, a weak tie does not require a strong emotional bond, and as a result individuals may be more tolerant of differences (Coser, 1975; Granovetter, 1982). Strong ties are more typical between similar people (Ibarra, 1992; Lincoln & Miller, 1979; McPherson, Smith-Lovin, & Cook, 2001). In a study of an applied research institute, Perry-Smith (2006) found that individuals with more ties with other researchers were more creative.

Weak ties facilitate creativity by (1) providing a greater amount and diversity of new information that is related to an ongoing problem, and (2) providing exposure to cognitive diversity—different approaches and perspectives. Several studies support these claims:

- In a study of 772 artists, Simonton (1984a) found that more distant relationships were associated with greater artistic eminence. The most creative artists were those with connections to highly distinguished artists, which Simonton called *paragons*. And in general, artists were more creative if they lived during a period with more living paragons—suggesting that simple exposure to exceptional creators enhances creativity. There's some evidence that this finding extends to organizational contexts. Zhou (2003) found that individuals were more creative when they had more creative coworkers. This relationship was stronger for individuals who started out being less creative. Working with other creative people helps you to learn creative behaviors and ways of thinking by watching them (Shalley & Perry-Smith, 2001).
- Perry-Smith (2006), in a study of an applied research institute, found that individuals with many acquaintances, rather than a few close colleagues, were more creative.
- In a study of a Scandinavian telecommunications company, Rodan and Galunic (2004) found that managers who were connected to other managers with different knowledge bases were more innovative.

The opposite of a loosely connected organizational network would be a network where all ties are strong ties, and where the same people are all connected to each other. This sort of network is referred to as *densely connected*. Managers with dense networks have been found to be less adaptable, and less likely to modify their networks when the task environment changes (Gargiulo & Benassi, 2000).

Uzzi and Spiro (2005) analyzed a network of 2,092 people who worked on 474 musicals between 1945 and 1989. They analyzed the creative success of each musical using measures like critics' reviews and financial success. For each musical, a unique team of six freelance individuals is brought together: a composer, a lyricist, a librettist (who writes the plot and dialog), a choreographer, a director, and a producer. The strength of a tie between two of these professionals was measured by how many musicals overall they had worked on together. They found an inverse U relationship between the connectedness of a team and musical success; up to a point, increased connectedness resulted in increased success, and beyond that point, an increase in connectedness had a negative impact on creative success.

Connections expose a team to new sources of creative material. But if the network is totally connected, you get less diversity of ideas, and the group risks falling into a rut of conventional styles. Recall the research in Chapter 12 showing that brainstorming groups without a sufficient amount of diversity fall into groupthink and end up being less innovative that solitary workers (pp. 235–242). The most creative organization is the one with good connections between teams, but where teams still have independence and autonomy.

In sum, social network analyses have converged on the finding that both too-dense and too-unconnected networks are bad for creativity; the ideal network is one that has both dense connections and loose connections, and is often referred to as a *small world network*.

TEAMS AND CREATIVITY

The above findings seem to be in tension with findings in team research that highly cohesive teams are more effective—because a highly cohesive team is, by definition, densely connected. Highly cohesive teams have more satisfied group members and greater consensus (Beal, Cohen, Burke, & McLendon, 2003; Sethi, Smith, & Park, 2001). A meta-analysis by Balkundi and Harrison (2006) found that teams with dense interpersonal networks were better at attaining their goals, and that when team leaders were more central in the group's network, the team performed better.

Given the above research, however, we might expect that more cohesive teams are less creative. There's one study that suggests this is the case (Perry-Smith & Shalley, 2006)—that instead, groups with weak ties with one another are more creative. And a host of studies have found that teams with high degrees of consensus are more prone to make bad decisions, because of the risk of groupthink (Janis, 1972). A second tradition of research has found that there's no relationship between a group's member satisfaction and the team's effectiveness; this is called *the illusion of group effectiveness* (see Chapter 12, p. 236).

When team members have weak external ties, the team is more likely to be creative. Ancona and Caldwell (1992) found that socially isolated teams weren't very innovative, compared to teams with informal relationships outside the team. Weak external ties can help a team gain political support and acquire resources, but they can also work as conduits for the flow of diverse information (Ancona & Bresman, 2007; Cummings, 2004; Hansen, 1999; Tushman, 1977). Balkundi and Harrison (2006) found that when a team's manager was more central to the organization's inter-team network, the team performed better. These weak ties increase the likelihood that a team can think in more flexible ways and come up with a broader range of unique solutions to problems. Individuals with outside connections are more likely to receive new information and new perspectives (Fleming & Marx, 2006). Sutton and Hargadon (1996) argued that certain types of firms, such as design consultancies, prosper by acting as *knowledge brokers*—their entire business model is premised on many weak ties to a wide range of organizations.

CENTRALITY

In addition to an individual's pattern of network links, there's a large body of research that an individual's location within the overall organizational network is important to promotion, advancement, and power (Blau & Alba, 1982; Brass, 1984, 1992; Cross & Cummings, 2004;

Sparrowe et al., 2001). Imagine a large social network, with several hundred nodes, and all of the links between the nodes mapped out. Although two different individuals may both have the same number of links, one individual's links may be more strategically placed—they may be more *central*. "Centrality" refers to the degree to which a person is in the middle of the network, loosely speaking. There are least three ways to define the centrality of a node: (1) the number of contacts; (2) *betweenness*, or the extent to which a node falls between pairs of other points on the shortest path between them; and (3) *closeness centrality*, a measure of the average of the shortest distances to all other nodes in the network, so that the person who can reach the largest number of others with the fewest links is more central. This third measure of closeness is the one most frequently used; a more "closeness central" node can reach other nodes through a minimum number of intermediary nodes and is therefore dependent on fewer intermediary positions, and thus it measures the degree of independent access to others. Brass (1984) found that higher-centrality individuals, measured using closeness, were more likely to be promoted and were rated as more influential.

Burt (1992) introduced the seminal concept of the *structural hole* in order to capture the benefits that individuals derive from these weak ties. Imagine an organization with two distinct work groups. If there's no contact between the two groups, this creates a *structural hole*: an opportunity for an individual to connect to both groups, and thus act as an *information broker* between the two groups. Burt (1992) argued that individuals who occupy these structural holes gain power and hold unique information. His research found that they're promoted faster, and they receive larger bonuses. Ideas from individuals who occupy structural holes are judged to be more innovative (Burt, 2004). And, when structural holes are filled, an organization is more able to accept new ideas (Burt, 2004).

Research is inconclusive on the link between centrality and creativity. On the one hand, it might seem that centrality would lead to less creativity; after all, research suggests that more densely connected individuals are less creative and less adaptive, and being more central seems related to dense links. On the other hand, greater centrality might result in a broader range of perspectives, and access to a wider variety of organizational subcultures, which would enhance creativity. Some research suggests that centrality is related to the ability to successfully "sell" a novel idea (Fleming & Marx, 2006; Mehra, Kilduff, & Brass, 2001; Obstfeld, 2005). As long ago as Rogers (1962), network centrality has been associated with the successful diffusion of a new idea. Although Burt (2004), in widely cited research, found that structural holes lead to good ideas, there was no evidence that these good ideas were actually implemented in successful products or processes. Individuals who occupy structural holes get their unique ideas by combining distinct bodies of knowledge, but then they have the difficult task of bringing together very different groups of individuals to turn that idea into a reality. Obstfeld (2005), in a study of an engineering division of a car company, found that engineers who worked to bring together disconnected people were more likely to be involved with successful innovation.

CULTURAL DIFFERENCES IN INNOVATION

Through the 1970s and the 1980s, Americans often looked to the Japanese economy with envy. Japanese companies were achieving market penetration in a wide range of industries traditionally dominated by American companies: automobiles, consumer electronics, steel. Although Japan had an older image as the land of conformity and imitation, it was Japan that gave the world the Sony Walkman and the VCR.

But all things go in cycles. Following the extended slump in the Japanese economy that began in the early 1990s, the "lost decade," Japan engaged in a serious bout of self-examination, and many Japanese themselves began to believe that their culture was too focused on consensus and conformity, and that this prevented the innovation necessary to bring the Japanese economy out of its slump. With the U.S. economy thriving during Japan's lost decade, many Japanese focused on the innovative power of the United States.

Anthropologists have described the United States as individualist and the Japanese as collectivist (see Chapter 14). Many other Asian countries are also said to be collectivist, and leaders in other Asian countries have similar concerns about innovation and creativity. After Japan's lost decade, business leaders there began to think that a more individualist cultural style might lead to increased innovation. The thinking was that a culture that values connections, consensus, conformity, and rule making might be too risk-averse. For example, a famous Japanese saying goes: "The nail that sticks up gets hammered down." The Japanese have even named the problem "Big Company Disease," with its symptoms being a bloated bureaucracy, endless meetings, and complex and seemingly unnecessary management practices.

But how can one executive change something as longstanding and entrenched as a cultural value system that prizes consensus and connection? It may seem impossible, but some corporations are trying by developing programs, hiring consultants, or sending their professionals to Silicon Valley. Yet results have been mixed; culture is extremely resistant to change. For example, the Toshiba corporation introduced flexible working hours in 1994, focusing on its most creative employees. The employees didn't even have to come into the office as long as they got their work done. But three years later, in 1997, most of these people continued to come into the office during regular working hours, and very little had changed.

Individualist and collectivist attitudes affect each person's creative style. Japanese managers prefer a bustling environment when thinking about ideas, whereas Europeans prefer to be alone (Geschka, 1993). Europeans expect stimulation from lectures, seminars, and conferences, whereas Japanese go to the city center and visit bookshops, supermarkets, and theaters. In the preliminary phases of idea generation, European managers talk with internal and external experts and colleagues in the same area; Japanese managers talk with private acquaintances of the same age, regardless of their area. These findings are preliminary but intriguing. Certainly, more cross-cultural research along these lines will be necessary for a complete explanation of creativity. The next chapter explores cultural differences in creativity.

KEY CONCEPTS

- Patent definition: new, useful, and nonobvious
- The entrepreneurial personality
- The collaborative web
- Social network analysis: weak ties, centrality, structural holes, knowledge brokers
- Organic and mechanistic organizational structures

THOUGHT EXPERIMENTS

- Have you worked in a large organization, whether corporate or nonprofit? What procedures and practices were you taught? Do you know where those procedures and practices came from? Of the things you had to know to do your work in this organization, were there some that no one taught you, that you had to learn on your own? Of the things that you were taught, how many of them were written down in an official book of corporate procedures?
- Tomorrow, make a note of the creative technological products that you use throughout the day—the washing machine, the computer, the telephone, the automobile. Try to imagine a time before they existed, and see if you can imagine what insights could lead to that product's invention.

SUGGESTED READINGS

Chell, E. (2008). *The entrepreneurial personality: A social construction* (2nd edition). London: Routledge.

Florida, R. (2002). *The rise of the creative class and how it's transforming work, life, community and everyday life*. New York: Basic Books.

Sawyer, R. K. (2007). *Group genius: The creative power of collaboration*. New York: BasicBooks.

Sawyer, R. K. (2008). Creativity, innovation, and obviousness. *Lewis & Clark Law Review, 2*(12), 461–487.

CHAPTER 14

CULTURE AND CREATIVITY

The light dove cleaving in free flight the thin air, whose resistance it feels, might imagine that her movements would be far more free and rapid in empty space.

—Immanuel Kant, *Critique of Pure Reason*, 1781/1900, p. 6

T he sociocultural approach emphasizes the important roles played by the domain and the field. In the Western cultural model of creativity, the domain—the set of conventions, past works, and standard ways of working—just gets in the way of creativity; the true creator ignores the domain and breaks all of the conventions (Belief 3). But creativity researchers think of the domain as a kind of creativity language. Of course, you have to learn a language before you can talk; it's impossible to communicate without sharing a language. In the same way, it's impossible to create anything without the shared conventions of a domain. Even though you use the same words and grammatical rules as everyone else, you still manage to create a novel utterance almost every time you speak. And just because the creator accepts the conventions of a domain doesn't mean he or she isn't creative.[1]

Kant's dove can fly only because of the invisible support of tiny air molecules. There could be no flight without air. The dove might feel the air only as resistance, and wish for the air to go away; but of course, in a vacuum the dove would fall to the ground. The air is a metaphor for the creative domain; many creators are frustrated by the constraints of the domain, but without the domain they wouldn't be able to create at all. If you have trouble expressing yourself to a friend, do you blame the constraints of your native language? Of course not; without that language, you couldn't even begin to express yourself.

Kant's air is a metaphor for culture, the subject of anthropology. When you think of "anthropology" your first image is likely to be of the archaeologist, digging for ancient bones or pottery in a remote desert environment. But archaeology is only one branch of the discipline

---

1. Theories that compare creativity to language and communication have a long history, beginning with R. G. Collingwood (1938) and John Dewey (1934); see Sawyer, 2000, for a comparison. For an influential sociocultural elaboration of these ideas, see John-Steiner, 1985.

of anthropology. In this chapter, we'll be concerned with another branch known as *cultural anthropology*: the study of living, active cultures. Cultural anthropologists often say that their job is to "make the familiar strange, and the strange familiar." Most anthropologists choose to study a culture that's as different from their own home culture as possible. They then use a research method called *ethnography* or *participant observation*, living as a member of the culture for at least one or two years. The goal of this experience isn't just to learn about the other culture; unavoidably, while learning about a radically different culture, they learn a lot about their own implicit cultural beliefs, thus "making the familiar strange."

Anthropologists use the word *culture* in a way that's related to common contemporary phrases like "popular culture," "mass culture," and "subculture." But it's a little more complex than that, and anthropologists have debated the definition of culture ever since Edward Tylor (1871/1889) proposed one of the first definitions in the late 19th century:

> Culture . . . is that complex whole which includes knowledge, belief, art, law, morals, custom, and any other capabilities and habits acquired by man as a member of society. (p. 1)

In the 1960s, a school of American anthropology known as *symbolic anthropology* developed a slightly modified definition of culture. Clifford Geertz (1966/1973) defined culture as:

> An historically transmitted pattern of meanings embodied in symbols, a system of inherited conceptions expressed in symbolic forms by means of which men communicate, perpetuate, and develop their knowledge about and attitudes toward life. (p. 89)

When you define culture in terms of symbols, culture becomes something like a language—and that's where anthropology connects to the sociocultural approach. A creative domain is like a small cultural sphere. And a domain is like language, in that you can't create anything without a domain, even though most of the time you're unaware of its importance. Cultures are systems of interrelated domains, and culture influences creativity primarily through influences on domains (Csikszentmihalyi, 1999, p. 317).

Beginning in the early 1980s, anthropologists began to examine how cultures transform and reinvent themselves. Cultural change always involves creativity. But this kind of creativity is very different from fine art painting or musical performance because it's a creativity of everyday life. In cultural creativity, novelty is a transformation of cultural practices and appropriateness is the value to a community. This approach is different from individualist conceptions of creativity because it emphasizes the creation of *practices*, not the creation of *products* (Rosaldo, Lavie, & Narayan, 1993).

Imagine an unschooled folk musician in a time long before the invention of sound recording. She gives repeated performances of the same song, a song that's never been written down. In each performance, she embellishes the melody a little differently; she might add a few words or modify a phrase to signify the context of the performance—the holiday, the audience members, or the time of year. And every other performer who sings the song adds his or her personal style to the performance. After a hundred years pass, the song will be different, even though no one person is responsible.

An older generation of anthropologists and folklorists argued that these performance variations weren't significant. They argued that they were more like personal quirks than really different performances—like differences in handwriting or in a person's accent. But today anthropologists believe that the creation of novelty through these subtle variations is an essential part of many creative domains, particularly in performance (see Chapters 18 and 19). After all, the difference between creating a completely new work and simply varying an existing one is a matter of degree.

Members of a younger generation select from the traditions they inherit, but then they elaborate and transform those traditions. In the normal, everyday process of cultural transmission, there's always both invention and imitation. Even when members of a culture believe they're not changing the traditions, they can't help changing, due to universal cultural processes that have been well documented by anthropologists. Once anthropologists realized that cultural transmission was not a mechanical replication of the past, they realized that creativity is always a part of culture (Bruner, 1993). Everybody in a culture participates in its reproduction and its evolution—not only special figures like musicians or storytellers. Cultural creativity is found in the practices of everyday life—eating, sleeping, everyday conversation—not only in ritual or shamanic performance. Creativity is a common part of everyday life; culture can't survive without continued improvisation and embellishment.

INDIVIDUALISM AND COLLECTIVISM

Anthropologists have documented an amazing variety of cultural practices and beliefs around the world. Of all of the ways to compare cultures, perhaps the most widespread is the individualism–collectivism contrast (Markus & Kitayama, 1991; Triandis, 1995).[2] Collectivist cultures are those in which people are integrated into strong, loyal groups. These cultures value group goals and outcomes over the individual. The self is defined by reference to the group, and to one's position in it; there's not a firm separation between individual and group. In individualist cultures, in contrast, the ties between individuals are looser. Individualist cultures value individual needs and interests over those of the group, and they value personal outcomes and goals more than social relationships. The self is defined as an inner property of the individual, without any necessary reference to the group. These are differences in degree; even individualist cultures may have some collectivist elements, and vice versa.

Cross-cultural research has found that the U.S. culture is extremely individualist. For example, studies of family sleeping arrangements have found that over 90% of the world's cultures practice *co-sleeping*, in which the newborn child sleeps in bed with the parents until at least the age of two (Morelli, Rogoff, Oppenheim, & Goldsmith, 1992). When members of such cultures are told about the U.S. practice of providing newborn infants with their own cribs—and even their own rooms—they're horrified, and consider it to be tantamount to child abuse. When Americans are asked to justify the practice, they provide medical explanations, to be sure, but they also provide explanations that are telling in their implicit valuing of individualism: "He was old enough to be by himself" or "She was ready" (Morelli et al., 1992, p. 609). Many parents explicitly say that separate sleeping arrangements will foster independence in the child; in one interview study, 69% of parents emphasized that sleeping alone would foster independence and

2. These cultural differences may even affect the neural structure of the brain during development; see Park & Huang (2010).

self-reliance (Morelli et al., 1992). A contrasting example is Japanese culture, which practices co-sleeping, and which is usually considered to be a highly collectivist culture. Japanese parents believe that their infants are born as separate beings; they must be encouraged to develop inter-dependent relationships with community members to survive, and co-sleeping is thought to be essential to that process.

In experimental studies of cultural differences, many scholars have used the Individualism-Collectivism Test (I-CT) developed by Triandis (1994, 1995). The I-CT is a questionnaire administered to individuals, and it results in a single score on a linear scale; a lower number indicates a more collectivist individual. Zha et al. (2006) used the I-CT to compare American and Chinese doctoral students, and found that Americans scored higher on individualism (25.92) and Chinese scored higher on collectivism (18.73).

In individualist cultures—like the United States—individuals emphasize how they are unique, different, and better than others. They tend to see themselves as separate from others. In such cultures, people believe that artists embody these traits to an extreme—artists are unique, more different, and more separate than the average person. In collectivist cultures, in contrast, people emphasize that they are ordinary, similar to, and no different from others, and rather than separateness, they emphasize their connectedness (Fiske, Kitayama, Markus, & Nisbett, 1998; Markus & Kitayama, 1991). And as we'll see below, in collectivist cultures, artists are perceived—and perceive themselves—very differently.

Works of art serve different cultural functions in individualist and collectivist cultures. In individualist societies like the United States, some functions of art include:

- *Expression*: Allowing the individual to express his or her inner experience
- *Therapy*: Providing an outlet; it's therapeutic to express through art
- *Communication*: Allowing the creator to communicate his or her unique vision or message to an audience
- *Entertainment*: Entertaining an audience during leisure time
- *Enlightenment*: Educating an audience, or raising spiritual awareness

All of these functions derive from the individualism of U.S. culture. The functions of art are largely to support the individual, and to reward and acknowledge individuality. The individualism of Western cultures is directly related to Belief 10 of the Western cultural model—the belief that creativity contributes to self-actualization and expresses the inner being of a person.

In many small-scale cultures, art serves a more collectivist function: ritual effectiveness. If a shaman's carved mask doesn't fit in with the conventions of the domain, it's not perceived to be bad art, but rather it's perceived to be ineffective at accomplishing its function of controlling spirits. The Hawaiian ritual poetry known as *kaona* can be composed only by specialists because it uses veiled and hidden meanings that can be obtained only through special linguistic constructions. If the words are changed by a non-expert, it could make the poem ineffective and perhaps even harmful (Kaeppler, 1987). The same is true of Hawaiian ritual dance; the dance has to be performed in exactly the right way, or else it won't accomplish its ritual function. If the desired outcome doesn't come to pass, members of such a culture typically attribute the failure to errors in performance.

The Lega are an African people who live in a dense tropical rainforest in Zaire (Biebuyck, 1973). At the center of their culture is the *Bwami* association, a cult that controls sorcery and initiation rites. During *Bwami* ceremonies, carved wooden animals are used by performers to communicate critical educational messages, but they aren't valued for their aesthetic form. What's most important is that the carving is exactly like the previous carving that served the same function, a "true equivalent or substitute of what existed before" (Biebuyck, 1973, p. 178). The owner of a particular carving will trace its history by referring not only to the current object, but also to all prior objects that it was designed to replace. Again, because ritual effectiveness is the key criterion, imitation and replication are emphasized more than the unique qualities of any given object, even though there's variation even among objects that are claimed to be exact replicas.

EXPERIMENTAL CULTURAL DIFFERENCES

Many studies have examined cross-cultural differences in performance on creativity tests. There's a widespread concern within Asian countries that they're not as creative as the United States and Europe, and experiments with a variety of creativity tests seem to confirm this. For example, most studies with the TTCT show higher scores in America than in Asian countries. Jellen and Urban (1989) gave their Test for Creative Thinking-Drawing Production (TCT-DP) to children in 11 countries and found that America, England, and Germany outperformed China, India, and Indonesia. Zha et al. (2006) compared American and Chinese performance on a measure of creative potential, the Creativity Assessment Packet (CAP, a form of DT test: Williams, 1991). The average score of the Americans was 175.54, and the average of the Chinese was 149.83. Niu and Sternberg (2002) reviewed several studies showing that Americans scored higher on DT tests than Indian children, Arabic youth, and adults in Japan, Hong Kong, Taiwan, and Singapore. However, they also found several studies showing superior Asian performance on DT tests, particularly on the figural form of the TTCT (for example, Zha et al., 2006, p. 357).

It's hard to draw solid conclusions from these studies. For one thing, these DT tests were all originally developed in America, and thus may be biased toward Western conceptions of creativity and may underestimate the creativity of Asians (Leung, Au, & Leung, 2004; Niu & Sternberg, 2002; Rudowicz, 2004). These tests may reward an individualist type of creativity, and Asians may be stronger on a collectivist type of creativity that's not measured by the tests—for example, collectivist individuals might be more effective in creative groups or in complex organizations (see Chapters 12 and 13). These possibilities have not been studied and represent opportunities for future research.

In China, Taiwan, Hong Kong, and Singapore, creativity was traditionally undervalued, but this has been changing rapidly (Niu, 2006). In Taiwan, creativity is constantly discussed in the media and is a national priority frequently discussed by politicians. In Singapore, the national ministry of education has made creativity central to its national curriculum (see Ministry of Education Singapore, 2002). Choe (2006) reports a strong emphasis on creativity in South Korea. *The International Journal of Creativity and Problem Solving* was founded in Korea in 1990 and is published in English. Its original name was "The Korean Journal of Thinking and Problem Solving"; the name was changed in 2009 to reach a more international audience.

These efforts, combined with reforms under way in primary and secondary schools (see Chapter 21), are likely to affect these national comparisons in the coming years.

DIFFERENT ARTISTS

Up to the middle of the 20th century, many anthropologists held to theories of creativity that were derived from the Western cultural conception of the artist as a marginal outsider, a uniquely creative visionary. Anthropologist Victor Turner believed that artists were marginal people who attempt to avoid the stereotypical roles provided by their culture; he compared the artist to the prophet (1969). The cultural psychologist George Devereux likewise associated art with the outsider, arguing that art was a way for a society to stay healthy by channeling the least socializable impulses productively (1961). Economist Thorstein Veblen, in a famous 1919 paper, attributed the intellectual prominence of Jews in Europe to their marginal outsider status.

These scholars gave voice to the Western cultural model's beliefs that the artist is a misunderstood outsider, ahead of his or her time (Belief 4), breaking the conventions that bind the rest of us (Belief 3), and remaining unconcerned about the social sanction that might follow. But new anthropological research has found that such beliefs, while common in individualist cultures, are not found in collectivist cultures. In individualist societies, the creator is considered to be the apotheosis of the individual, but in collectivist societies, the creator is considered to be the apotheosis of the group. In collectivist cultures, the artist is rarely marginal.

Between 1969 and 1971, anthropologist Marjorie Shostak lived with the !Kung San, a group living on the northern fringe of the Kalahari Desert in Botswana and Namibia (Shostak, 1993). While studying creativity in this culture, she discovered that art was central to !Kung San life; there were many musicians, healers, bead-weavers, and storytellers. To explore creativity in this culture, she began by asking members of the culture to direct her to their most creative members. But she found that this didn't work; when she asked them who the best bead-weavers or musicians were, her question was greeted by an embarrassed silence. When pressed, a person would simply list the names of every bead-weaver or every musician, claiming they were all equally "the best" (p. 56). She later found that the reason for their reticence was their egalitarian and collectivist culture: no one was supposed to be of higher status or superior to anyone else.

On her second trip to the !Kung in 1975, Shostak asked people to judge photographs of bead-weavings that she had collected during her first field trip from 1969 to 1971. These weavings had already been judged and ranked by curators at the Museum of Primitive Art (now part of the Metropolitan Museum of Art) in New York City. Again, she found that people weren't willing to rank the weavings, even when they'd been done in another village and they didn't know the artist. Eventually she found one artist who was willing to evaluate the weavings in private with her, but that artist would not do this in public if members of her own culture were present.

!Kung San artists have to manage a difficult balancing act: expressing a unique individual voice while avoiding any aura of superiority. Talented artists, just like talented hunters, are expected not to brag about it, and generally don't receive any reward or status for their skill. Shostak found that this created problems for powerful, idiosyncratic artists, because their persona didn't fit with the !Kung conception of the creative individual. She wrote about Jimmy, a !Kung musician whom she believed generated the most creative compositions. Many other musicians played his compositions, so they had clearly been judged as creative by other musicians in the culture. Surprisingly—given their egalitarian ways—everyone was willing to say that Jimmy was unusually gifted. Shostak explained that they were able to acknowledge this status difference only because he was so clearly an outsider. He had trouble finding a wife, he lived miles apart from any village, and by his own admission no one liked him; the name "Jimmy" itself testified to his outsider status, because almost no !Kung have Western names. But although he was recognized as a gifted musician, no one respected him, valued him, or considered him a real member of their group.

Jimmy had no acknowledged role in the !Kung culture because artists aren't expected to be the isolated, inspired, unique, convention-breaking individuals that we imagine them to be in the United States. Jimmy conforms well to Western cultural conceptions of the artist. But among the !Kung San, there's no way to remain a member of the group while playing a role as the unique, idiosyncratic, gifted artist.

SHAMANS: THE ORIGINAL PERFORMANCE ARTISTS

Modern theater is often thought to have originated in shamanic ritual performance (see Chapter 19). In all cultures, shamans face the tension between the uniqueness of their individual experience and the need to publicly express their experience to the community. A shamanic vision of the otherworld is extremely personal, by definition; otherwise, any member of the culture could have had the same experience. However, the shaman must then communicate that experience through the conventional role of the shaman in that culture.

In many cultures, shamans wear masks during their performances, and it takes a lot of skill to carve an effective mask. The masks are designed to represent the spirits that the shaman encountered during his or her possession state, and help to translate his or her experience into something that the community can share. Although the vision is personal to the shaman, he or she must dramatize the experience and give it public expression (Layton, 1991, p. 195). Each culture recognizes a certain set of conventions for depicting spirits on masks, and a different set of conventions is often followed for ritual performance and for more popular, everyday celebrations.

These carved masks are obvious candidates for works of art, and they're collected and displayed by most major museums in the West. But taken out of their cultural context and displayed on the wall, it's easy to mistake them for the same kind of aesthetic object as the sculptures and paintings that artists in Western cultures generate. However, the motivations and processes whereby they are generated are different; the creative process is different; the conception of creativity is different; and the conception of the role of the creator is different.

Sometimes shamans carve their own masks, but more often they hire an expert carver to do it for them. The shaman describes his or her personal vision to the carver and integrates established traditional conventions for depicting certain types of spirit. Sometimes the shaman carves the face of the spirit and then lets another carver do the rest of the mask; sometimes the shaman sketches a quick outline on the surface of the wood, and the carver executes the design. But each carver then provides his own creative touch. The fact that certain carvers are commissioned is evidence that members of the culture think that some carvers are better than others. But the masks aren't chosen simply because they're beautiful; they're chosen because they're thought to be more effective at accomplishing their ritual function of controlling spiritual powers (Ray & Blaker, 1967).

CHANGING CONCEPTIONS OF PRIMITIVE ART

So-called "primitive" or "ethnographic" art first came to prominence in Europe at the very beginning of the 20th century, and contributed a great deal to the foundation of modern art

FIGURE 14.1: **(a) Pablo Picasso, *Nude*, 1907.** (With permission of Estate of Pablo Picasso/Artists Rights Society (ARS), New York. Copyright © 2004.) **(b) A Senufo figure of the Ivory Coast, Africa.** (New York University, Institute of Fine Arts, Visual Resources Collection. Copyright © Walker Evans Archive, The Metropolitan Musuem of Art.)

(Goldwater, 1938/1967; Fig. 14.1). Painter Paul Gauguin personified the primitivism of modern art, writing that "you will always find nourishing milk in the primitive arts" and that "barbarianism has been a rejuvenation for me" (quoted in Goldwater, 1938/1967, pp. 66–67). These conceptions of primitive art were based on false ideas about primitive cultures that were widely held by Europeans at that time. They falsely thought that primitive societies were static and unchanging, and that they displayed no creativity because they emphasized tradition and convention. Their art was thought to be limited in its forms and unchanging in its patterns. Many European anthropologists and artists alike thought of this art as the collective expression of a culture, and thought that individual creativity played almost no role in such art (see Goldwater, 1938/1967; Layton, 1991).

When Picasso and Gauguin discovered the art of non-Western societies, they called it primitive art because they thought this art came from an ancient time in the past, because they thought these cultures hadn't changed in thousands of years. The term *primitive* implies a historical trajectory in which the origins and early development of our own Western art can be seen in these modern yet non-industrialized small-scale societies. However, anthropologists have since learned that these contemporary societies have also undergone centuries of artistic evolution and are likely to be far removed from their own origins (Layton, 1991, pp. 1–3). Because culture is fundamentally creative, culture is always changing, even primitive culture. The term *primitive* is based on a false idea of the static, unchanging nature of these societies (Kuper, 1988). Based on decades of research, anthropologists of art now realize that the world is filled with diverse and independent artistic traditions, each of which has undergone the same centuries of independent evolution as our own. The paintings of the aboriginal Australians or the carvings of the Amazonian highland Indians don't come from some distant forgotten past time of the human species.

Scholars no longer use the term *primitive art* for two reasons. First, it's difficult to know what constitutes a significant innovation in the art form of another society. Even in Western cultures, creativity isn't opposed to convention and shared themes, but rather is always embedded in complex symbolic domains of creative conventions. A person who knows very little about Baroque music may have difficulty distinguishing compositions by Bach, Vivaldi, and Mozart, and most Americans think that all polka sounds alike. Second—as we'll learn later in this chapter—it's common to exaggerate the degree of innovation of our own art forms, simply because we're intimately familiar with the domain and can detect even minor variations.

Innovation and tradition are not opposed, as in the Western cultural model; they're always intimately and dialectically related. Some domains are more receptive to innovation, while others encourage consistency with conventions, and we can begin to look for broader cultural factors that might help us to explain these differences. We can then take these insights and use them to better understand these differences among domains in our own societies.

CONCEPTIONS OF CREATIVITY

> *The definition and testing of creativity may be as much based on the same kind of culture-bound presuppositions and biases as are the definition and testing of intelligence.*
>
> Donald MacKinnon, (1978, p. 202)

The Western cultural model emphasizes invention, novelty, rejection of tradition, self-actualization, and a celebration of individual accomplishment. According to Rudowicz (2004), these are foreign to Chinese ideals of respect for the past and maintaining harmony with nature (p. 59). In the Chinese language, there's no word that easily translates as "creativity." Throughout Chinese philosophy, creativity was viewed as an inspired imitation of nature (Rudowicz, 2004, p. 60)—quite similar to Renaissance European conceptions of genius as imitating nature (see Chapter 2). Individuals are not responsible for invention, because they are simply following nature and discovering truth. As with European art prior to the Renaissance, most Chinese classics aren't signed, and many works were collaboratively generated (Rudowicz, 2004, p. 61). Even when a single creator could be identified, this was generally avoided because that would lead to humiliation and pity.

In collectivist cultures, tradition isn't considered to be opposed to creativity; creativity is thought to take place within a network of customs, beliefs, and societal structures. Chinese researchers and educators link creativity to ethical and moral standards (Rudowicz, 2004, pp. 61–62) in a way that has no parallel in Western conceptions of creativity. When Chinese students and educators were interviewed about creativity, Rudowicz (2004, pp. 64–65) found that Hong Kong Chinese students' conceptions overlap with Western conceptions, but there are some differences: Chinese conceptions include "contributes to society's progress," "inspires people," and "is appreciated by others" (p. 65). When Hong Kong Chinese are asked to nominate the most creative people, their list is dominated by business people and politicians; artists, writers, and composers rarely appear on the lists (Rudowicz, 2004, p. 69). When Americans are asked the same question, they typically nominate people in the arts or media.

Korean conceptions of creativity have some overlap with Western conceptions (Lim & Plucker, 2001): when asked about creativity, people in both cultures emphasize perseverance, independence and deviance, and cognition and motivation. However, Koreans see the creator as a loner, and this is considered undesirable because of the high value placed on social responsibility in Korean culture.

Niu and Sternberg (2002) reviewed a range of studies of the cultural models of creativity in Asian countries (including China, Korea, Japan, and India) and the United States. Indian scientists describe the creative personality as curious, self-motivated, risk-taking, and open-minded. They believe they're less creative than Western scientists due to the Indian cultural values of obedience and social etiquette (Kapur, Subramanyam, & Shah, 1997; Niu & Sternberg, 2002).

Western societies place more value on intrinsic motivation, and Asian societies place more value on extrinsic motivation—particularly the desire to please their parents (Ng, 2001, p. 113). Asian societies also place a high value on "face" and managing one's social image; Western research on motivation would generally place these concerns in the "extrinsic motivation" category, and in the Western cultural model, these concerns are thought to interfere with the individual's pure expression and thus to block creativity.

The Western cultural model of creativity is deeply connected to the individualism of most Western cultures. And it finds its purest expression in the United States, perhaps the most individualist of the world's cultures. In the United States, people tend to believe that creativity is the expression of a unique individual; that there are individual differences in talent that are probably innate; that a created work is invested with the unique emotional and personal experience of the creator. And above all, this cultural model values innovation and breaking conventions. As a result, creators in Western cultures are likely to emphasize these aspects of their works— exaggerating the novel features of their work and talking about how they struggled with the limitations of the conventions of their domain. In part because they're expected to, creators talk about what they're trying to communicate with their work, and what personal experience led them to create this particular work. The now-required "artist statement" encodes this cultural belief; an artist can't get a gallery show without composing a statement specifying what inner state led to this work, and how he or she intended to communicate and express that state in this work (see Chapter 16). And the legal system of copyright requires that a new work be original, or else the artist is said to be plagiarizing or is required to pay royalties. Our system of copyright is another societal and cultural force causing artists to exaggerate the novelty of their work.

In collectivist cultures, conceptions of creativity are radically different. In these cultures, it's important for the work *not* to be different. In large part, that's because individuals in collectivist cultures emphasize that they are ordinary, similar to, and no different from others. And in small-scale cultures, artworks are supposed to be the same so that they'll be ritually effective. As a result, creators tend to emphasize exactly the opposite qualities of their work; they deny that the work contains any innovation, and they claim that it accurately represents tradition, even when Western outsiders perceive a uniquely creative talent.

The anthropologist Anthony Forge (1967) described the Abelam, a New Guinea culture in the southern foothills of the Prince Alexander Mountains, to the north of the Sepik River. They have an elaborate wood-carving tradition associated with the cult of the clan spirits, and Forge noted that the artist must work "within fairly narrow stylistic limits" (1967, p. 81). The carvings were designed to represent the clan spirits, and the artists insisted that their works were in the ancestral style. Yet Forge also found carvings being used that he was able to determine were almost 100 years old, and these were visibly different from the new ones. When Forge confronted members of the culture with these apparent differences, they ignored the differences or claimed that they weren't significant.

A similar pattern was found by folklorist Albert B. Lord (1960) in his study of South-Slavic epic poetry. Performers had always insisted that each story was performed identically on each occasion, and that the stories were told the same way that they'd been told by their ancestors. However, by using tape recorders, Lord discovered that these Serbo-Croatian epics were performed differently each time. The same song, sung by the same singer on multiple occasions, could vary in length by as much as several thousand lines. Even when the storytellers swore they were repeating verbatim the same story they had told a week ago, a close analysis of the audio-tapes showed that the words used were actually very different, although the structure of the story—the meter and the rhyme—remained the same. When performers were confronted with these differences, they refused to acknowledge that they represented significant differences, and they insisted that the song was indeed the same on each occasion.

In individualist cultures, creators emphasize the innovation in their work, and in collectivist cultures, creators emphasize that their work is *not* innovative. But close scientific study has found that both of these views are partially wrong. Creators in individualist cultures draw heavily on conventions and tradition; creators in collectivist cultures display individual style and novelty in their works. There's more creativity in following tradition than Westerners generally believe, as documented repeatedly by anthropologists—including Hughes-Freeland (2007) with Javanese dance, Nakamura (2007) with Japanese calligraphy, and Mall (2007) with south Indian *kolam* women's folk art, patterns rendered in rice flour on the thresholds or the floors of houses and temples, to ritually clean the areas. Whether you live in an individualist or a collectivist culture, your culture's conceptions of creativity influence how you see creative works.

CONTINUITY AND CHANGE

> *Originality is the art of concealing your sources.*
> —Unknown, quoted in Byrne, (1996, 3:489)

Some creators are more likely to use the conventions of a traditional domain, to make works that are recognizably similar to what has come before. Other creators are more likely to innovate, to emphasize novelty, to make works that contain elements not found in any prior works. In the United States, we value the innovator and disparage the traditionalist as derivative or imitative. Our individualist conception of creativity leads us to believe that whether a person's creations emphasize continuity or change, it must be because of some inner personality trait or mental processes unique to the creator.

But because collectivist cultures don't define creativity in terms of the novelty of the work, it's not possible to explain why an artist emphasizes continuity or change by analyzing his or her psychological makeup; to explain such differences, we have to examine the culture of the artist. In the following sections, I'll discuss several different cultures and show how they provide incentives to continuity or incentives to change. We'll see that sometimes we can't explain creativity without appealing to culture.

CULTURAL INCENTIVES TO CONTINUITY

In the traditional Asmat culture of New Guinea, men achieved status through headhunting (Gerbrands, 1967). Wood-carving provides a vehicle to express the symbolism important to the culture in which men are thought to be spiritually related to trees, in part due to their creation myth that people emerged from carvings done by an ancient culture hero. Aesthetic carvings are of two types: ritual objects that are used once and then left to rot in the forest, and everyday goods that are frequently used, like the handles of spears and paddles, or musical horns used to warn of an impending attack.

Most men in this culture occasionally carve everyday objects, but certain men are recognized for the better quality of their objects. There's no formal training; some men are just drawn to it or have a talent for it, and teach themselves by observation and practice. Those recognized as better carvers are occasionally approached and asked to produce a carving for use on a ritual occasion—a drum, shield, or ancestor pole. These talented carvers don't occupy a distinct social role; they engage in the same daily activities as any other man. However, while they're creating a carving for a client, the client takes over the daily tasks that the artist would otherwise have performed, and also provides meals for the carver.

Although members of this culture have opinions about which artists are better, their decision of which artists are the best is not based solely on aesthetic criteria. Older artists are considered to be better, because older men are thought to be closer to the spiritual world portrayed in the carvings. Prestige at headhunting contributes to the status of an artist, because the rituals use the carvings as a way of increasing the effectiveness and power of the headhunters (Layton, 1991, p. 16).

The importance of ritual effectiveness is an incentive to continuity. Continuity is encouraged by several other factors: carvers don't occupy a distinct social role; everyone does some carving; and the carvers' reputations depend partly on non-aesthetic qualities such as age and prowess at headhunting.

The Asmat are perhaps closest to the older stereotype of primitive art as traditional, an expression of the spirit of the community, and unchanging. However, even in this culture there are individual differences in style and talent, and these differences are recognized and acknowledged by the Asmat.

CULTURAL INCENTIVES TO INNOVATION

Now let's examine a creative domain in a non-Western culture that provides incentives to innovation rather than incentives to continuity. During the 1960s, Marion Wenzel studied house decorations in a part of Africa known as Nubia, along the Nile River straddling the border between Egypt and the Sudan (Wenzel, 1972). The area was about to be flooded by the construction of the Aswan Dam, and the houses would be submerged forever. These decorative facades had existed only since the 1920s, and they'd first been designed by Ahmad Batoul, in the area north of Wadi Halfa. Other men had copied him; they competed with him by developing their own recognizable personal styles, and soon some of them were even better known than Batoul, even though he'd created the domain. In 1972, Wenzel was able to study cultural change by examining a range of villages along the Nile, because she knew that the genre had originated in the north, where Batoul had worked, and then slowly disseminated south along the river. Therefore, she assumed that the situation 75 miles to the south was similar to what the north must have been like 40 years earlier.

In the south, if a builder decorated a house after completion, he expected nothing more than a tip. It was rare to find an individual who was a full-time decorator; builders could make more money by building a house, and the women of the house could do the plaster decoration themselves. But by 1925 in the north, the occupation of plasterer had already become prestigious, a distinct profession. By 1940, the best-known decorators were successful enough to hire subcontractors to apply the plaster, so that they could focus on the decoration. These artists had no pressure to conform to any traditional role conception, because the status was completely new, and market competition drove both an increasing division of labor and an increasing differentiation of style.

Market competition was an incentive to innovation. When the originator, Batoul, began to face competition from imitators, he developed several distinctive new motifs that set his work apart. This, in turn, inspired his competitors to introduce distinct motifs of their own (Wenzel, 1972, pp. 109–111). The competition for business encouraged artists to innovate and to explore the potential of traditional designs for creative variation. At the same time, the decorators had to conform to local expectations of how a house should look. For example, customers often wanted shining plates on the facade because they would "divert the evil eye" (Wenzel, 1972, p. 123).

In contrast to the Asmat culture—where cultural forces required continuity—in Nubia, cultural forces provided incentives to novelty and innovation. We can't explain creativity in these cultures by analyzing the personality traits of the Asmat and Nubian artists. To explain these forms of creativity, we have to look to the unique nature of the two cultures, using an anthropological approach.

ECONOMIC STATUS AND INNOVATION

In many cultures, the degree of novelty in an artwork is related to the artist's position in a complex web of social and economic relationships. Forge (1967) described a painting of a ceremonial Abelam house that introduced a design variation: a narrow band of stylized leaves that were similar to the traditional pattern, but had some obvious differences. He wrote that "some of the older men were against it; [but] the two artists and their helpers were adamant—they were both of high reputation and no alternative artists were available . . . [and] this innovation was much admired in the surrounding villages" (p. 81). Because the artists were highly respected and well established in the community, the elders eventually accepted the innovation. But if the artists had been beginners of lower status, they would have been forced to paint the house again and do it the way the elders wanted.

Silver (1981) studied modern Asante wood carvers and found that the innovativeness of a person's style was almost completely explained by his status in the community. The village that Silver studied was established during the 19th century by the king as residence for a craft guild that supplied royal regalia, and to whom the king granted a monopoly on wood carving. But after conquest and colonialism, an open market emerged, and several different statuses of carver emerged. The highest-status carvers were prosperous and well known. These established carvers often produced innovative work; although it reproduced traditional Asante proverbs, it used a nontraditional "naturalistic" style. The success of an innovation was unpredictable; because there was a greater market for conventional carvings, innovation was economically risky. Because of the risk, middle-ranking carvers didn't innovate; they had to create dozens of carvings every week simply to support themselves. However, the middle-ranking carvers adopted the successful innovations of the higher-ranking carvers, and their works kept evolving. The lowest rank of carvers were desperate to earn income, and had no prestige to fear losing. They typically created carvings for export to Europe, and this work imitated carving styles that were well known in Europe as "African" styles but were not authentic Asante styles; these carvers were never taken seriously locally.

Like the Asante wood carvings, many traditional crafts are no longer purchased by members of the culture—either because Western collectors have priced them out of the market, or because the traditional cultural practices that used those objects have been lost to modernity and colonialization (Graburn, 1976). Artists in many third-world cultures no longer produce art for local consumption, but instead for affluent Western collectors. These artists are under extreme pressure to create works that conform to Western expectations of primitive art: handcrafted objects that communicate to the Westerner's friends that the owner has traveled to an exotic place. In many cases, these objects aren't really traditional; for example, with Native American art, many tribes' indigenous styles have been replaced by the Santa Fe and Oklahoma Schools of the early 20th century—because art buyers think that these styles "look like" Native American art (Weiner, 2000, p. 157). Innovation isn't rewarded by the international tourist market.

In all three of the cultures I just described—the Asmat, the Nubian, and the Asante—individual artists have different talents and styles, and an individualist approach could help us understand these differences. But in each of these cases, the cultural approach is also necessary to fully explain creativity. We need to understand a lot about the culture to explain the degree and the nature of the innovation that is generated by each artist.

IS CREATIVITY VALUED?

Societies can't survive without reproducing themselves from generation to generation. Otherwise, the society loses coherence and fades away, lost to history. For the most part, when sociologists study societies around the world, they see a great deal of stability in the social structures, norms, and functions over time. Perhaps the main function of social systems is to maintain the status quo (Merton, 1949/1968). Because creativity often disrupts the status quo, it's often not welcomed; as Machiavelli famously wrote in *The Prince*,

> And it ought to be remembered that there is nothing more difficult to take in hand, more perilous to conduct, or more uncertain in its success, than to take the lead in the introduction of a new order of things. Because the innovator has for enemies all those who have done well under the old conditions, and lukewarm defenders in those who may do well under the new. (1982, Chapter VI)

The existentialist Salvatore Maddi (1975) claimed that this was still the case in today's modern societies, despite the high social value we say we place on creativity: "the social structures and publics involved are not prepared to accept changes or disruptions affecting their own lives. Actually, in traditional, primitive, preindustrial societies there is little pretense that creativity is a virtue. What leads toward change is rather frankly regarded as dangerous in such contexts" (p. 181). We see this today in many communities that are centered on fundamentalist religious belief, for example in many parts of the Muslim world, and in smaller religious communities in the United States.

The United States, as a relatively young country founded in a revolutionary break with the past, tends to place a high value on innovation and change. Many international observers believe that this attitude has contributed to the high degree of technological invention associated with the United States. There's some evidence that individualism contributes to innovation: Shane (1992, 1993) compared the per-capita number of patents across the world and found a higher patent rate in more individualistic countries (also see Lubart, 2010).

CONCLUSION

Individualist approaches explain creativity by looking inside the person. In contrast, anthropology explains creativity by looking to the culture within which the creativity occurs. In this chapter, we've seen that anthropologists can explain a lot about creativity without knowing anything about the personalities or the mental processes of the creators. They can explain the degree of innovation or imitation in a given artwork—both how that varies between cultures, and how that varies among artists in the same culture. They can explain why a given culture has a distinctive conception of what an artist is, and how an artist works—by exploring whether that culture is individualist or collectivist. For example, the United States is extremely individualist, and anthropologists explain the Western cultural model of creativity by showing how it emerged from the individualism of Western cultures.

Without anthropological research, we would never know how many different conceptions of art and styles of creative activity exist in the world. We might never know that Western cultural conceptions of creativity are unique. We might never learn that the Western cultural model of creativity isn't globally universal.

Even in collectivist traditional cultures, there are individual differences, and the individualist approach can help us to explain those differences. But individualist explanations become more powerful when they are contextualized within an explanation of society and culture. In many cultures, an artist's creative style is determined by his or her status or family connections. And in many cases, artworks can be explained by the economic system. These explanations limit the scope of individualist explanation, because we know that individuals can vary only within these broader constraints. To explain creativity, we must not only *include* sociocultural approaches; in many cases, we must *begin* with them.

KEY CONCEPTS

- Culture
- Performance product versus performance practice

- Individualism and collectivism
- The dialectic of innovation and tradition
- Non-Western cultural models of creativity
- Incentives to continuity and to change

THOUGHT EXPERIMENTS

- Have you ever traveled or lived overseas? If so, you probably realized for the first time how much living in the United States influenced your attitudes and approaches to life. Can you think of any of these differences that might relate to creativity?
- Think of a domain that you are particularly creative in. When you meet other people who create in that domain, would you say that your backgrounds are similar? Or does your background stand out somehow?
- Most people who read this book start out with the typical creativity myths of the isolated lone genius, ignoring convention, perhaps on the verge of mental illness. Did you? Where do you think you learned this conception of creativity? Do you still believe that it's basically correct? After all, deep-seated cultural conceptions are very resistant to change.
- If you still think your view is right, how do you explain the different conceptions of creativity held by other cultures? Are they simply wrong?

SUGGESTED READINGS

Bruner, E. M. (1993). Epilogue: Creative persona and the problem of authenticity. In S. Lavie, K. Narayan, & R. Rosaldo (Eds.), *Creativity/anthropology* (pp. 321–334). Ithaca, NY: Cornell University Press.

Layton, R. (1991). *The anthropology of art* (2nd ed.). New York: Cambridge. [Especially recommended: Chapter 5.]

Raina, M. K. (1999). Cross-cultural differences. In M. A. Runco & S. R. Pritzker (Eds.), *Encyclopedia of creativity, Volume 1* (pp. 453–464). San Diego, CA: Academic Press.

Rosaldo, R., Lavie, S., & Narayan, K. (1993). Introduction: Creativity in anthropology. In S. Lavie, K. Narayan, & R. Rosaldo (eds.), *Creativity/anthropology* (pp. 1–8). Ithaca, NY: Cornell University Press.

Shostak, M. (1993). The creative individual in the world of the !Kung San. In S. Lavie, K. Narayan, & R. Rosaldo (Eds.), *Creativity/anthropology* (pp. 54–69). Ithaca, NY: Cornell University Press.

CHAPTER 15

HISTORY AND CREATIVITY

Time is the greatest innovator.

—Francis Bacon (1561–1626) (1868, *Essays*,
in *Works*, Volume 12, p. 160)

Paul Cézanne was one of the most important painters of the 19th century. Born in 1838, Cézanne had a long and productive career. Cézanne's paintings became more and more valuable throughout his life; his most valuable works were painted just before his death in 1906. The later paintings sell for more, and art professionals judge them to be more important (Galenson, 2001). This makes sense; after all, painters should become increasingly skilled with age, and their works should become increasingly more influential in the art world, and more valuable on the art market.

However, Cézanne's career pattern is not universal among artists. Pablo Picasso, born in Spain in 1881, also worked primarily in Paris. Picasso also had a long productive career, working right up to his death in 1973. However, while Cézanne painted his most important works late in life, Picasso painted his most valuable and most important works early in his career—while he was still in his 20s—and his output became increasingly less important over the rest of his life (Fig. 15.1).

Explaining such differences is the job of the art historian. Art historians are trained to consider individual works and individual artists, often paying close attention to their financial and personal circumstances, the social and political context of their time, and the inner psychology of the artist that resulted in the unique message and style of his or her works. Art historians generally focus closely on one artist or one period, and they explore how overall styles and genres develop over time.

When trying to explain the very different careers of Cézanne and Picasso, an art historian would typically proceed by closely studying the changes in style and technique across the two painters' careers, attempting to identify what led Cézanne's work to improve in quality while Picasso's declined. Art historians are also centrally concerned with the influence of one painter on another; paintings that have more impact on other artists tend to be considered more valuable, so the art historian might want to explore why Picasso's early works were more influential,

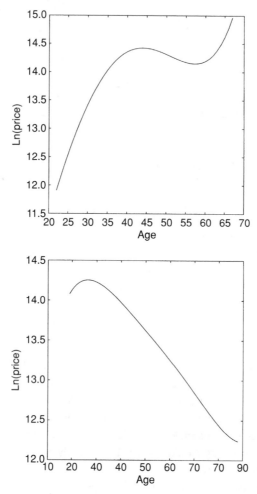

FIGURE 15.1: (a, top) Estimated age–price profile for Paul Cézanne (1839–1906). (b, bottom) Estimated age–price profile for Pablo Picasso (1881–1973). (Reprinted by permission of the publisher from *Painting Outside the Lines: Patterns of Creativity in Modern Art* by David W. Galenson, p. 15, Cambridge, MA: Harvard University Press. Copyright © 2001, by the president and Fellows of Harvard College.)

whereas Cézanne's later works seemed to be. This explanation would typically be in terms of the formal properties of those works and how they could be shown to have influenced the formal properties of later works.

This is an *idiographic* approach, meaning that it focuses on the close analysis of single cases—individual artists and individual works. An idiographic explanation of the differences between Cézanne and Picasso can teach us much about the two artists and their careers. However, it turns out that the career-long patterns that distinguish Cézanne and Picasso are not unique to those two men; there's a deeper pattern at work that we can see only when we look at many artists at once.

Figure 15.2 contains data for 42 French painters, indicating their birth date and the age at which they painted their most important painting—again, as valued by the market and by the experts. Figure 15.3 contains similar data for 57 American painters (both figures are based on

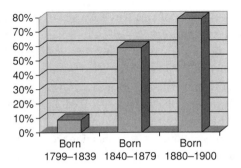

FIGURE 15.2: French painters, grouped by birth year, and the percentage of each whose peak career age was under 40 years, using data from Galenson (2001).

data in Galenson [2001]). These tables show that the age at which artists paint their most important works varies depending on when they were born; for those born early in the 19th century, the most important works were painted late in life, but for those born nearer to 1890, the most important works were painted early in life. Cézanne, born 40 years before Picasso, is typical of his generation's painters, as Picasso is of his. The idiographic approach of the art historian is not equipped to explain these broader patterns. Although it's good for the in-depth analysis of individual painters and individual works, it's not well suited to the explanation of broader patterns that apply across many artists or across many historical periods.[1]

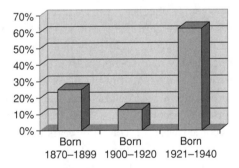

FIGURE 15.3: American painters, grouped by birth year, and the percentage of each whose peak career age was under 40 years, using data from Galenson (2001).

1. Galenson explained these patterns by hypothesizing that the art world changed to increasingly value problem-finding creativity (which he called "experimental painting"); the 19th century, in contrast, valued "conceptual execution," the increasingly skillful implementation of a well-studied and well-worked idea, and these market forces encouraged problem-solving creativity. See Chapters 5 and 16, where Getzels and Csikszentmihalyi (1976) found that problem-finding artists were more successful; their conclusion is that problem-finding artists are better artists. But Galenson's work suggests another interpretation: although our contemporary art market values problem-finding artists, this has not always been the case. Consequently, it may be too simplistic to claim that problem-finding artists are more creative, as Getzels and Csikszentmihalyi do; rather, the picture seems more complicated, and it seems that problem-finding artists are more valued only in certain historical periods (and in certain cultures and societies, as Chapters 14 and 16 suggest).

In recent decades, a few scholars of creativity have begun to use *historiometric* methods to analyze these broad patterns. Historiometry—also known as cliometry, after Clio, the ancient Greek Muse of history—is the numeric study of historical patterns. When you attach numbers to historical events, you can spot lawful numeric relationships across historical periods; historiometricians hope to identify universal historical laws, laws with explanatory, predictive, and perhaps even deterministic power (Martindale, 1990). All human inquiry, from art history to particle physics, is divided between this sort of nomothetic study of lawful, generalizable patterns, and the idiographic study of unique events that don't repeat (Nagel, 1961, p. 547). Because creativity research is a borderline, interdisciplinary study, it combines the approaches of both the sciences and the humanities, the nomothetic and the idiographic (Gardner, in Sawyer et al., 2003, p. 233).

In this chapter, we'll learn about historiometric explanations of creativity. Idiographic explanations of creativity are relevant, by definition, to single cases only; nomothetic explanations, because they apply across multiple cases, can explain broader patterns. If I used the idiographic approach in this chapter, I'd have to choose a few specific artists or scientists and delve deeply into their creative process and their productive output. But we'd have trouble generalizing from these few artists to develop a scientific explanation of all creativity.

Most art historians deny that there are universal laws of art history. They argue that historical events are not repetitive, but are individual and unique. Yet even those historians who prefer to pursue an idiographic approach agree that each individual creates as a representative of a certain historical period. This is harder to recognize with our own creativity, but it becomes obvious when we look back 100 or 200 years at the creative products that were generated in another era. After taking a couple of college courses in English literature, most people can identify, within 50 years or so, when a given paragraph was written, even without knowing its author. All of the music that was composed in the early 1800s can be recognized as being from that period, almost to the decade, by many people with expertise in classical music. A basic course in art appreciation equips one to identify the historical period and perhaps even the painter of paintings that one has never seen before. And over half of all U.S. college students, when presented with a pop song recorded since 1970 that they have never heard before, can identify when it was recorded within a couple of years (I've confirmed this in my own classes). Most of the creators of these products weren't intentionally trying to sound like their historical period. Just the opposite; bands in the 1970s and 1980s were trying to sound unique and different, and at the time no doubt believed that they were doing something distinct from everyone else.

If you've ever attended an MFA show—which every art school requires its students to participate in before graduation—you're likely to get the impression of an incredibly diverse range of styles. But the creations of our own time always seem more diverse than they are. James Elkins, an art school professor, wrote about his reaction after he looked at graduation exhibition catalogs from decades ago:

> Art school catalogs from the turn of the century are filled with reproductions of student paintings that look like slavish copies of John Singer Sargent or Henri de Toulouse-Lautrec, and exhibition catalogs from the 1950s show hundreds of students' works that emulate abstract expressionism. The lesson I draw . . . is that fifty years from now even the most diverse-looking work will begin to seem quite homogeneous. Works that seemed new or promising will fade into what they really are: average works, mediocre attempts to imitate the styles of the day. . . . In the oldest catalogs the students' work

seems to be all done by one person, and in the newest, each student seems to be a lone innovator. (2001, p. 68)

How can we explain the similarities in creative products within a given time period? The explanation can't be found in the motivations of the creators, in their cognitive processes, or in their personalities. The individualist approach is the wrong level of explanation. We need to look above the individual, to the historical context of human creativity.

CREATIVITY OVER THE LIFE SPAN

The historiometric method has grown in use since the 1970s, largely under the influence of Professor Dean Keith Simonton of the University of California, Davis. Historiometry was, actually, the first method applied to the study of creativity; the first historiometric analysis of creativity was published by the French mathematician and sociologist Adolphe Quetelet (1835/1969; also see Simonton, 1999a). Quetelet was one of the first scientists to use statistical methods in the social sciences. For example, he counted the number of plays produced by English and French playwrights over the course of their careers. When he plotted their year-by-year productivity on a graph, he saw an inverted-U shape. Their output increased up to a peak age, and then declined gradually. Quetelet also found that the quality of the plays that a playwright wrote in any given year was related to the total amount of creative output generated in that year.

The recent rebirth of the historiometric method championed by Simonton has confirmed that these 19th-century patterns still hold for today's creators. Creative output tends to be an inverted-U function of *career age*, the length of time the individual has been working in the domain. Productivity in any given year increases as the individual continues to work in a creative domain, until it reaches a peak level; then, after some number of years, the productivity level begins to decline, and declines gradually through the remainder of the life span. Simonton (1988b) explained this with a formula based on the cognitive theories of Chapters 5, 6, and 7: he hypothesized an *ideation rate* that indicates the rate at which the incubation process will generate new configurations of mental elements, and an *elaboration rate* that indicates the rate at which these new ideas are elaborated into communicable form. The ideation rate is higher at the beginning of a career, when there are more free, unorganized mental elements. The elaboration rate is proportional to the backlog of new configurations that await elaboration. Simonton used these two rates to generate an equation for creative productivity at any given point in the life span:

$$p(t) = c(e^{-at} - e^{-bt})$$

Figure 15.4 shows a typical productivity curve generated by Simonton's equation, assuming that $a = 0.04$, $b = 0.05$, and $c = 61$, with t starting at the chronological age of 20. The equation generates the widely observed inverted U for career productivity, in this case with a peak in the early 40s. Figure 15.5 shows the actual productivity curves taken from the lives of creative individuals in different domains; they match the equation pretty well (data from Dennis, 1966).

These patterns are fascinating. After all, it's not obvious that there would be a late-career decline; individuals tend to become increasingly famous and to earn increasingly larger salaries

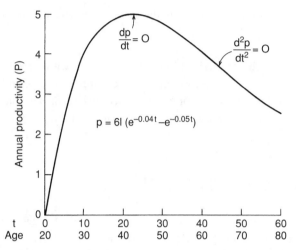

FIGURE 15.4: The relation between career age, time, and annual production of creative ideas, *p(t)*, according to Simonton's (1984) model. In this figure, *e* is the exponential constant, the ideation rate *a* = 0.04, the elaboration rate *b* = 0.05, and the initial creative potential *m* = 305. (Reprinted from *Developmental Review*, 4(1), p. 86; Simonton, 1984, "Creative Productivity." With permission of Elsevier. Copyright © 1984.)

throughout their careers. It might have been the case that individuals would experience multiple creative peaks, perhaps every 5 or 10 years.[2] Without the historiometric method, it might be hard to convince someone that career productivity was an inverted U.

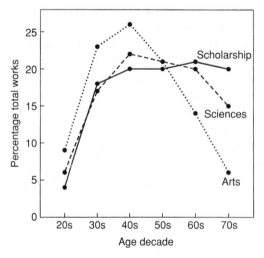

FIGURE 15.5: Typical age curves for three general domains of creativity, based on data from Dennis (1966). (Reprinted from *Psychology, Science, and History*, Simonton, 1990. With permission of Yale University Press. Copyright © 1990.)

2. Using more idiographic methods, Gardner has proposed a 10-year rule, which states that creators' significant innovations tend to be separated by 10-year gaps (also see Chapter 5, pp. 93–94).

It's also not obvious that quality of output would be related to quantity, nor that an individual's best work would come in the year when he or she generates the most overall output; we usually think that quantity and quality are opposed, and that if a person is generating a lot of work then it must be slipshod or not fully thought through. An individual who works long and hard for years on a single project, investing a lot of energy and making sure everything is exactly right, might be expected to generate a more important work than a colleague who is churning out works every month. Yet historiometric data tell us that in the years when an individual is generating the most products, he or she is most likely to generate his or her most important work—the *productivity theory* of Chapter 7 (p. 131). The single best predictor of scientific fame is the number of times other scientists refer to the author's publications, and the primary predictor of this citation count is the scientist's total output. The correlation between overall career productivity and citation count ranges from 0.47 to 0.76, depending on the individual (Simonton, 1988b, p. 84).

In all of these studies, there are exceptions that prove the rule. For example, we can find perfectionists who devote all of their efforts to a small number of publications that are of high quality, and also scientists who publish a lot of relatively low quality items (Cole & Cole, 1972). That's why we could never discover the underlying pattern without the use of a historiometric method that averages across many creators.

Every creative domain has its own characteristic inverted-U shape that tends to apply to all individuals working in that domain. Each domain has a typical peak age of productivity, the age at which the most significant innovation of a career is typically generated; and each domain has a distinctive shape to its U curve, with different slopes to the rise and decline. Physicists often joke to one another that if they haven't done Nobel prize–winning work by the age of 30, they should hang up their hats—and historiometric analysis has confirmed that the inverted U for physics has a peak around the age of 30. Most other disciplines peak later in life; social scientists tend to reach peak productivity in their 40s or 50s, and humanities scholars in their 50s and 60s.[3]

These typical career trajectories can be explained with the sociocultural model of Chapter 11. Remember that sociocultural theory argues that before becoming creative, individuals must become socialized into the field and internalize the domain. In this approach, individuals wouldn't be expected to be productive or to generate important works until they'd fully internalized the domain. This explanation can account for the early rising part of the typical inverted-U career trajectory; output and importance increase as the domain is increasingly mastered.

Sociocultural theory can also explain why different domains have different peak ages. Csikszentmihalyi (1996, p. 39) observed that those domains that have a young peak age tend to be those with an intricate, highly articulated body of domain knowledge that is clear and logically consistent; in contrast, domains with an older peak age tend to be those in which the domain is more loosely defined, with greater ambiguity in its basic terms and concepts. This corresponds to the findings that mathematics, physics, and chess have many young masters, whereas history and philosophy have many older creators generating important works.

Simonton used his equation to explain these variations in the productivity curve across creative domains. The information-processing requirements for each domain are unique; each

---

3. Note that the actual curves are in terms of career age rather than biological age, so these numbers in terms of biological age are only approximations, because not everyone starts a career at the same age.

domain has a characteristic ideation rate, the rate at which new configurations are generated by the incubation stage, and each domain has a characteristic elaboration rate, the rate at which those new ideas can be elaborated into communicable form. For example, in theoretical physics and pure mathematics, both the ideation rate and the elaboration rate may be high, resulting in a career peak at a relatively young age followed by a quick drop (Simonton, 1988b, p. 72). Simonton (1988b) took the data generated by Dennis (1966) for productivity rates across the life spans of hundreds of creators, and using different values of a and b in his equation was able to replicate the documented career peaks in different disciplines: poets peak at a career age of 19 years, mathematicians at 26, and historians at 40 (note that because most careers don't start until around the age of 20, you can expect to add about 20 to these numbers to get the person's actual age at career peak). In some creative domains, productivity doesn't decline as much later in the career; those domains are characterized by a low elaboration rate, such that the new ideas "back up" and can never all be communicated (Simonton, 1988b, pp. 72–73).

Historians have observed that the peak age for scientific productivity was about 25 years of age in the year 1500, but by 1960 it was 37 (Zhao & Jiang, 1986). The increasing complexity of scientific domains seems to have caused this increase; this complexity would make the ideation and elaboration rates decline, and this results in a later career peak. Jones (2010) studied 700 Nobel prize winners and technological inventors in the 20th century and found that over the course of the century, the greatest achievements occurred at later and later ages; the mean age at great achievement rose by about six years over the century, and in 2000, the peak age was 36 to 40. His data showed that the peak age increased because early age innovation is declining, and that's a result of the increased educational demands required to acquire the knowledge necessary to contribute an innovation. At the beginning of the 20th century, great minds began their work at age 23; at the end, at age 31. There's been no increase in the productivity of innovators beyond middle age to make up for this shortened career, and as a result, there's been a decline in innovative output per researcher over the century. Jones estimated as much as a 30% decline in life-cycle innovation, on average, over the 20th century, due to the shorter careers of researchers today.

Since 2000, studies of scientific careers (Feist, 2006a; Gingras et al., 2008; Joy, 2006; Kyvik & Olsen, 2008; see Stroebe, 2010) have not found any productivity decline with age. In an attempt to explain the discrepancy with the earlier studies, Stroebe (2010) pointed out that the earlier studies had made several methodologic errors. For example, some earlier studies found a productivity decline simply due to the *base rate fallacy*: because science has grown at a rapid rate through the 20th century, there have always been more young scientists than older scientists, and thus younger scientists would be overrepresented in journals and research grants simply because there are more of them. A second possible explanation for the earlier findings is that young scientists today are receiving better training in graduate school, and might be more productive than today's elder scientists were at the beginning of their careers—in other words, the older scientists haven't experienced a decline in productivity, they were simply always less productive.

So even if scientific productivity used to decline with age, it doesn't seem to be the case today. One additional possible explanation is that when U.S. scientists were forced to retire at 65 by mandatory retirement laws, they naturally started winding down their research laboratories a few years prior to retirement, and stopped applying for multi-year grants (Stroebe, 2010). But in the United States, mandatory retirement for professors was made illegal in 1994, allowing scientists to continue doing research later in life.

CREATIVITY ACROSS TIME PERIODS

Historiometry reveals hidden patterns in creative output that are difficult to explain with an individualist approach. Of course, individualist approaches are an important part of the explanation of creativity, and they've been an important element in historiometry. But at the same time, the patterns that Simonton found make it clear that the individualist approaches can't explain all of the data.

Perhaps even more intriguing than life-span studies are historiometric analyses across many time periods; these analyses often reveal broad, long-term trends in creativity that hold true across individuals, across creative periods and domains, and even across many societies. Galenson's comparison of Cézanne and Picasso is a good example of the potential of such an approach.

Martindale began his historiometric study (1990) by outlining a sociological theory of creativity, a set of fundamental social laws.[4] He began by noting that society can tolerate only a small amount of novelty on a regular basis. However, creativity requires novelty. So what allows society to tolerate or even to encourage novelty, despite its general preference for rules and routines? Martindale proposed that it's societal habituation, a social version of a long-established psychological phenomenon—the gradual loss of interest in repeated stimuli. Habituation results in a pressure for novelty, and this demand is generally met by people who can supply the demand: artists. Novelty increases the arousal potential of an artwork, thus countering the society's habituation.

Just after a new style of art is created, the works in that style are relatively simple because the style itself is so novel that habituation is not a problem. Yet the longer the style stays around, the more the society will habituate to works in that style, and novelty and arousal potential will continue to increase. Eventually, the potential for that style to incorporate novelty is used up, and the only way to keep avoiding habituation is for the society to jettison that style, and to generate a new style.

Martindale associated arousal potential with the *primordial content* of a work. He measured "primordial content" by counting the words or concepts in the text that he believed emerged from the primary process thought of the creator—based on the psychoanalytic concept of regression in the service of the conscious mind (Chapter 4). Primary process thought is free-associative and undirected, and thus increases the probability of novel combinations of mental elements (1990, p. 57). Martindale associated primary process thought with the incubation and insight stages of creativity, and contrasted it with the more conscious, analytic style of thought associated with the other stages (p. 58). Increased regression and primary process thought should increase the arousal potential of a work. The works that are selected and valued at any given moment in history will be those that balance habituation and arousal potential in exactly the way that society requires at that historical moment.

Martindale tested his theory's predictions by coding the primordial content and arousal potential of works that were not only created in but also selected by society at each historical

---

4. His sociological concepts were named after psychological concepts but they are not psychological as he used them; rather, he applied concepts from the psychological domain to social groups (see Sawyer, 1993).

moment.[5] His theory predicted that (1) arousal potential will increase over time, (2) styles will change periodically, (3) primordial content will increase within each style, and (4) primordial content will decline when a new style is introduced. He tested the four predictions by examining French, British, and American poetry, European and American painting, Japanese prints, and other genres.

In his most ambitious analysis, Martindale evaluated these predictions by coding and analyzing over six centuries of British poetry, from 1290 to 1949. He began by dividing the 650 years into 33 successive 20-year periods, and selecting the top seven poets in each period by ranking their quality and influence on the basis of the number of pages devoted to them in the *Oxford Anthology of English Verse* (Martindale, 1990, p. 118). Martindale then randomly sampled poetry segments from poems written by each poet. To evaluate his first prediction, Martindale coded the arousal potential of each segment by using a formula based on the uniqueness and difficulty of the words found in the texts. Although this measure doesn't represent syntax, overall composition, or the meanings of the words—all of which could reasonably be expected to have an impact on a poem's arousal potential—Martindale's data nonetheless showed the predicted increase over the 650-year period (Fig. 15.6).

Martindale's second, third, and fourth predictions were tested by using quantified measures of the primordial content of each poem. As with arousal potential, he defined primordial content by first developing a list of 3,000 words that were associated with primordial content in psychoanalytic theory (p. 92), and then he counted the number of those words that appeared in the writing of each poet. As with arousal potential, primordial content rose over time, but this time with periodic oscillations superimposed (Fig. 15.7). By eyeballing the graph, Martindale discovered that the drops in primordial content corresponded to commonly agreed-upon stylistic changes in poetry.

These are ambitious and fascinating studies: any time all four predictions of a theory are supported across six centuries of data, you have to pay attention. The historiometric approach will never replace traditional idiographic art history, but it can obviously be a useful partner in historical explanations of creativity.

Like Martindale, many historiometric researchers have examined the fluctuations in creativity across nations, cultures, and civilizations. They've found that historically creative individuals don't appear randomly in every year or decade; rather, they're clustered into periods of high creativity that are separated by much longer periods of creative stagnation. For example, Yuasa (1974) used archival data to determine the relative scientific "prosperity" of each nation from 1500 to the present. He defined a country as the world's creative center if the proportion of scientific output from a country was at least 25% of the entire world (p. 81), and he documented the following shifts in the center of scientific creativity:

- 1540–1610 Italy (Florence, Venice, Padua)
- 1660–1730 England (London)
- 1770–1830 France (Paris)
- 1810–1920 Germany (Berlin)
- 1920–present United States

---

5. The necessarily sociocultural dimension of this selection process is implicit in Martindale's account; he didn't examine the sociological and historical processes that would explain why the works from a given historical period were selected and preserved for so many centuries.

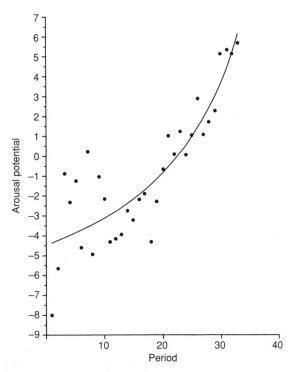

FIGURE 15.6: Martindale's measure of the arousal potential of a poem increases through 650 years of British poetry, from 1290 through 1949. (Reprinted from *The Clockwork Muse* by Colin Martindale. Copyright © 1990 by Colin Martindale. Reprinted with permission of Basic Books, a member of Perseus Books, L.L.C.)

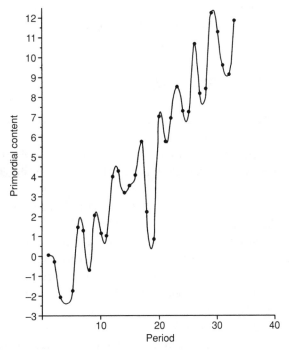

FIGURE 15.7: Martindale's measure of primordial content of a poem increases while oscillating, through 650 years of British poetry, from 1290 through 1949. (Reprinted from *The Clockwork Muse* by Colin Martindale. Copyright © 1990 by Colin Martindale. Reprinted with permission of Basic Books, a member of Perseus Books, L.L.C.)

The data within each of these "golden ages" form a productivity curve similar to that for the individual lifespan: an inverted-U shape with a single peak of maximum creativity. Political upheaval has often been suggested to result in a collapse of central control that then later leads to increased creativity, with a one-generation lag (Barnett, 1953). Yuasa likewise hypothesized that political revolution played an important role. For example, the French Revolution in 1789 and the preceding ferment led to France's period of dominance. But once a nation becomes a hub of scientific activity, a decline begins. Eventually, the potential of the scientific revolution loses its ability to generate new ideas. Just as with individual productivity, eventually the number of potential new configurations that can be derived from this initial set of cultural elements will decline.

For this pattern to be realized in individual productivity curves, the age of scientists should increase as the golden age progresses—because on average, older scientists are less productive. And in fact, several historiometric researchers have provided evidence that a country's science declines as the average age of its scientists passes 50 (Simonton, 1988b, pp. 100–101). As a result of these suggestive studies, some scholars have hypothesized that older scientists are less receptive to innovative ideas. This has been called *Planck's principle*, after the theoretical physicist who believed that the 20th-century developments in relativity theory and in quantum mechanics would take hold only after the older scientists, trained in Newtonian physics, died off: "a new scientific truth does not triumph by convincing its opponents and making them see the light, but rather because its opponents eventually die, and a new generation grows up that is familiar with it" (1949, pp. 33–34). But there's no empirical evidence for Planck's principle. Simonton reported that 94% of the variance in receptivity to a novel idea is due to factors other than a person's age (1988b, p. 103). There are many examples of very old scientists who immediately grasp the genius and truth of the latest innovations. Just because productivity drops doesn't mean that receptivity to the new ideas of others also drops.

THE HISTORY OF DOMAINS

Are creative domains driven by a few genius creators, or does everyone in the field make a small but important contribution? In science, two very different answers have been proposed: the Ortega hypothesis and the great-man hypothesis. The Ortega hypothesis (Cole & Cole, 1972) takes its name from a passage in *The Revolt of the Masses* by Spanish philosopher Ortega y Gasset: "Experimental science has progressed thanks in great part to the work of men astoundingly mediocre, and even less than mediocre" (1932, pp. 84-85). Practicing scientists sometimes say that science is like building a wall, with each member of the discipline contributing a brick; in Ortega's view, those who are acknowledged with fame and Nobel prizes just happened to be the ones who placed the last brick at the top of the wall. Newton famously said that he saw farther than other scientists because he stood on the shoulders of giants. This view has become newly popular among academics who reject great-man accounts of history in favor of more democratic and sociological accounts of scientific progress: "It is the aggregated contributions of thousands upon thousands of scientific foot-soldiers, junior officers, and men and women of middle rank that account for the great majority of scientific advances" (Waller, 2002, p. 158).

But there's some quantitative historical study that seems to support the great-man theory. For example, in physics, the most frequently cited papers don't cite lesser-known figures in the field; rather, often-cited papers tend to cite publications by often-cited predecessors, and similar results have been found for other scientific fields (Cole & Cole, 1972; Green, 1981; Oromaner, 1985). In any given year, around 35% of all existing papers are not cited at all; another 49% are cited just once, 9% twice, 3% three times, 2% four times, 1% five times, and the remaining 1% six times or more (Price, 1965). An extremely small percentage of all published papers has any impact on the field; based on citation counts, science seems more elitist than democratic.

However, this doesn't mean that only the top geniuses have any impact; many articles are written by mediocre scientists, simply because there are so many more of them, and by chance alone the odds favor that one out of this mass of articles will strike it big occasionally. Ultimately, citation studies can't definitively prove that the great-man hypothesis is right; they don't capture the role of scientists who informally interact with the author at conferences or in lab meetings, although their names never appear on an important publication (see Chapter 20).

STRENGTHS AND WEAKNESSES OF HISTORIOMETRY

Historiometry studies historical individuals whose work has passed the test of time (Simonton, 1999a, pp. 116–117). Because the work has passed the test of time, it's easier to resolve the basic question of who is creative; creative individuals and works are those that have made it into the history books, those that have been judged and selected by the field to have had a lasting influence after their creation. With contemporary works by living creators, it's harder to determine the creative value of the work. The downside of historiometric study of deceased creators is that we have limited information available; with living individuals, we can run experiments, or conduct extensive interviews, whereas with historical individuals we're limited by the historical record.

A problem facing all quantitative approaches in the social sciences is that the raw data of social life are not quantitative; social life is rich and complex. Nomothetic approaches have to somehow transform qualitative data into quantitative data, and this can sometimes be nearly impossible. Even in the best of circumstances, turning life into numbers means that some of the richness and complexity is lost, and we end up emphasizing certain aspects of the phenomenon and neglecting certain others. Critics can always argue that the researcher has chosen badly, transforming the wrong things into numbers and neglecting other important aspects of reality.

The benefit is that once the transformation has been accomplished, a wide array of statistical techniques are available that are fairly easy to apply. Inexpensive statistical software can be installed on any personal computer. These analyses don't require special expertise in art history or the history of science, and don't require the dedication of extensive and time-consuming research on specific creators. Once the numbers are in the computer, "one could study the history of any artistic tradition . . . without even knowing what the art form is, without knowing whether it is Chinese music or Greek vases" (Martindale, 1990, p. 14). Whether or not this is truly a benefit is debatable; idiographic art historians may wonder how valuable an explanatory approach is if you don't even have to know whether you're examining Chinese music or Greek vases.

The historical approach has the potential to identify broad, contextual findings that none of our other approaches would be able to explain. Whether or not you like the quantitative, number-crunching methodology, it changes the way you think about creativity. You can no longer think that Cézanne and Picasso are different just because they were born with genetically different styles of creativity, or because they had certain personality types. Now we know that Cézanne and Picasso are representative of entire generations; and to explain their differences, we have to explain why the generations are different, not only why two specific individuals are different. Knowing these patterns, you can't go back to a purely individualist approach.

KEY CONCEPTS

- Idiographic and historiometric methods
- Primordial content and arousal potential
- The Ortega hypothesis and the great-man hypothesis

THOUGHT EXPERIMENTS

- If I played for you a pop song recorded between 1970 and 2000, one that you had never heard before, do you think you could guess the year it was recorded? If so, why is that?
- When you hear a pop song from the 1920s, does it sound old-fashioned? Do you think it sounded old-fashioned back then?
- Think about something you've created—a song, a painting or drawing, a poem or short story. Think ahead to 30 years from now. In what ways will your creation seem dated?
- We generally think that we can be more creative when our lives are less pressured. But historiometric studies show that people tend to do their most creative, most important work in the years when they're busiest, when they're generating the most output. Has this happened to you? What does this finding tell you about the role of incubation and insight in creativity?

SUGGESTED READINGS

Galenson, D. W. (2001). *Painting outside the lines: Patterns of creativity in modern art*. Cambridge, MA: Harvard University Press. [Especially Chapters 1 and 2]

Martindale, C. (1990). *The clockwork muse: The predictability of artistic change*. New York: Basic Books. [Especially Chapter 4]

Simonton, D. K. (1997a). Creative productivity: A predictive and explanatory model of career trajectories and landmarks. *Psychological Review, 104*(1), 66–89.

Simonton, D. K. (1999a). Creativity from a historiometric perspective. In R. J. Sternberg (Ed.), *The handbook of creativity* (pp. 116–133). New York: Cambridge University Press.

PART 4

CREATIVITY IN THE DOMAINS

In Parts II and III, I've presented a wide range of approaches that scientists have used to explain different facets of creativity. These chapters have provided the scientific findings and the theoretical frameworks that we'll use as we move forward to explain creativity in specific domains. In Part IV, we'll explore creativity in different domains, ranging from painting to music to science, and in Part V, we'll explore everyday forms of creativity, including education and everyday life.

Throughout Parts IV and V, I'll be considering not only the psychological processes that lead individuals to be creative but also the social and cultural properties of groups that lead them to be collectively creative. Each chapter will be an interdisciplinary combination of individualist and sociocultural approaches. The modern science of creativity is interdisciplinary, because explaining creativity requires the combined insights of psychology, sociology, anthropology, history, and other disciplines.

CHAPTER 16

VISUAL ARTS

Art is the social within us, and even if its action is performed by a single individual, it does not mean that its essence is individual.

—Lev Vygotsky, *The Psychology of Art*, 1922/1971, p. 249

O f all the creative domains, painting seems to fit best into the Western cultural model of creativity. More than any other creative domain, we imagine the painter working in isolation, without influence from the external environment and without concern for convention. But it turns out that this image is mostly incorrect. Explaining painting requires both individualist approaches and sociocultural approaches. And because fine art painting is only one of the many visual arts, I'll also discuss installation art, comics, videos, and movies. The Western cultural model doesn't align very well with these genres of visual creativity.

By expanding the discussion beyond painting, I'm acknowledging a shift in the art world that's been under way since at least the 1960s, when Roy Lichtenstein began painting comic strip panels and Andy Warhol began silk-screening publicity photos of movie stars. By 1970, artists everywhere were talking about the crisis in painting, and even worrying about the end of painting (Fry, 1970). By 1990 the boundaries between fine art painting and other forms of visual creativity were so fuzzy that the Museum of Modern Art in New York City mounted a show titled "High & Low: Modern Art, Popular Culture" (Varnedoe & Gopnik, 1990). If we limited our focus to fine art painting, our explanation would leave out most of today's visual creativity.

WHO IS THE ARTIST?

The village of Nathdwara, in the southern part of the Rajasthan province of India, contains the Shri Nathji temple. It's an important temple, founded in 1671, and most of the town's economy is centered on services for visiting pilgrims. For example, many of the visitors buy religious paintings, known as *Mewari* paintings, painted by a local community of about 150 traditional painters (Maduro, 1976). To a Westerner, the paintings might all look similar, but the Mewari painters can identify at least 18 different genres of paintings, each with its own target market and contextual use. For example, miniatures based on scriptures are sold to visiting businessmen, often for resale to Western tourists; *pichwais* depict Shri Nathji and are used in ritual contexts. Each painter is known for being good at a few specific genres, and some specialize exclusively in just one of the 18 genres.

During his 18-month stay there from 1968 to 1970, anthropologist Renaldo Maduro discovered that the painters of Nathdwara are a distinct caste; there's very little interaction between them and the other people in the village. And like all castes in India, membership is determined by birth. Not just anyone can be a painter; you have to inherit the profession from your father. One painter said, "Painting is what I have to do for a living. My forefathers did it, and so we do it. It is our tradition, that's all" (quoted in Maduro, 1976, p. 4). Only a small percentage of the artists report experiencing a sense of individual psychological growth or personal struggle in their artistic work—almost the defining feature of a painter in the United States.

To examine whether the Western cultural model of creativity is universal, we have to consider conceptions of art found in other cultures, an anthropological approach that we first explored in Chapter 14. There are individuals in the big cities of India that a Westerner would recognize as modern, Westernized painters. But in the smaller cities like Nathdwara in the more rural areas, you can still find traditional communities of painters, working in uniquely Indian ways.

Mewari painting is a home-based industry; everybody in the family helps out. The women and younger children mix the paints in the morning, and cut the paper to its proper size. Paints are still made in the traditional way, from local stone and vegetable pigments, even though chemical powdered paint is now available. Older children and men make the brushes from squirrel hair or horse hair, and they do the painting and the marketing.

Maduro identified three different levels of ability. At the lowest ability level, the *laborers* paint stereotyped portraits that imitate traditional religious paintings. Because there are so many pilgrims, even these relatively untalented painters find a market for their works. The *master craftsmen* are technically competent and are respected, but they don't create anything original. At the highest level of ability are the *creative artists*. They don't always attempt to be original, but they occasionally create original works. Their best innovations are copied by the lesser painters in the village. And when they're copied, these creative artists don't get upset, as a Western painter might; copying is standard practice among these artists, and being copied is a sign of respect and prestige.[1] After all, Mewari painters are generally anonymous; they don't sign their works. When they were interviewed, the painters said that the most important qualities of a painter were humility, self-effacement, and lack of self-assertion.

In Hindu tradition, all the arts and crafts were handed down to certain individuals by Lord Vishvakarma, and artistic work is considered a sacred ritual. Most artists talk about the significance of Vishvakarma in their work (Maduro, 1976, p. 75). The painters think that their own creative energy comes from a range of sources that's quite different from what Western painters would say: *prana* life-force from the subtle body, one of the three bodies that Hindus believe we all have; a special hereditary birthright; and an internal store of creative power, or *maya rupa* (p. 129). These Hindu beliefs—too complex for me to fully explain here—profoundly affect the

---

1. Note the similarities with the three levels of Asante wood carvers, described in Chapter 14, p. 278.

way that painters think about their own creativity. The most creative painters often speak in spiritual terms; one painter said, "Creativity? Oh, it's all *maya rupa* . . . everything. This *maya* that I have inside me is thrown out into my art. This is a sacred truth . . . It is the dream of Brahman, and we painters contain a part of that force in us too because we are all part of Brahman" (quoted in Maduro, 1976, p. 141).

In Chapters 14 and 15, we learned to be careful not to assume that traditional painting has been the same since the beginning of time. And indeed, Mewari painting has changed over the centuries. As recently as 100 or 200 years ago, the best paintings were sold to royalty, and most of the remaining paintings were sold to rural Indian poor and middle classes. But with the introduction of printing presses and lithographs, the general population stopped buying paintings; they could buy the mass-produced versions for much less. Today, most Mewari paintings are sold to Indian and foreign tourists, and the market demands are completely different. There's less value placed on originality and on traditional standards of craftsmanship. The mass tourism market has encouraged standardization; paintings have become smaller so that they can fit into suitcases; and painters increasingly purchase brushes and paints to free up more time for painting, even though the colors of the manufactured paints don't look exactly like the homemade ones.

Painting in Europe was once not so different from Nathdwara. First of all, paintings by old masters were rarely painted entirely by them; the master was the leader of a workshop or studio, with a group of apprentices working with him. Like the Mewari painter's family, the master's studio worked as a team. Before the Industrial Revolution allowed the manufacture of tubes of premixed paint, European painters had to make their own paints. The master designed the composition, sketched in the rough outlines, and painted the parts of the painting requiring the most skill, like the faces of the central figures. Then the rest of the work was left to the apprentices, who painted the details of the clothing, the sky and the clouds, the buildings and furniture. We consider such a painting to be an authentic work of the master, but the creation of such a work is nothing like a contemporary painting. Today we expect a painting to be completely painted—every last brushstroke—by the artist whose name is signed at the bottom.

Because of the collaborative nature of the studio system, it's often difficult to attribute old-master paintings properly. Some apprentices started their own studios, and the hand of that apprentice is seen in the work of both his studio and his former master's studio. The concern with attribution reflects a contemporary conception of authenticity, the very modern idea that a painting has to be the work of a single isolated individual. We're more interested in attribution than the old masters were; back then, everyone knew that the master didn't paint every last brushstroke, and no one worried about it. Our fixation on attribution is an example of how a Western creativity belief—that paintings are the unique inspiration of a solitary individual—leads us to neglect the social networks and the systems of collaboration that result in many created works, including paintings.

In Chapter 2, we learned that our contemporary conceptions of creativity are culturally and historically formed. For example, Western conceptions of visual art have changed dramatically over the centuries. Renaissance-era contracts made it clear that painters were thought of as technicians, not artists; for example, the contract often specified the percentage of blue and gold in the painting (see p. 20). And the idea that a painter should work alone is a recent one; in most cultures and most time periods, paintings were made by collaborative teams. In both the studio system of Europe and in Mewari painting of India, artists worked collaboratively.

INDIVIDUALIST APPROACHES

Mewari paintings are very different from today's Western paintings. They're collaboratively created and aren't expected to break with convention. European painting was quite similar until the last century or two; our contemporary Western conception of the artist as an inspired, solitary genius originated only in the early 1800s. Still, many of my readers will want to know how contemporary Western painters work. Because the first wave of creativity research was heavily influenced by the individualism of the Western cultural model, psychologists in the 1960s spent a lot of time studying the personality traits of painters, and I'll begin by reviewing these studies. Then, I'll move beyond the stereotype of the lone genius, and I'll draw on contextual approaches to explain other genres of visual creativity.

THE PERSONALITY OF THE PAINTER

In general the arts establishment connives to keep alive the myth of the special, creative individual artist.

—Paul Willis, (1990, p. 1)

During the 1960s, Dr. Frank Barron was one of the top researchers studying creativity, and he worked with Donald MacKinnon at the Institute for Personality Assessment and Research (IPAR) at the University of California, Berkeley. These were heady times to be studying creativity in the countercultural environment of Berkeley, just across the bay from San Francisco. Dr. Barron was friends with famous figures like Dr. Timothy Leary and poet Allen Ginsberg. Dr. Barron chose to focus his studies on artists and art students (Barron, 1972), and his team gave classic personality tests to art students at the San Francisco Art Institute (SFAI) and at the Rhode Island School of Design (RISD). The RISD students were given the Minnesota Multiphasic Personality Inventory, known as the MMPI, and the SFAI students were given the California Psychological Inventory, or CPI.

RISD students scored higher than the general population on the traits of flexibility and psychological-mindedness; they were less well socialized, more impulsive, and less interested in making a good impression. They were poised, confident, and self-accepting. They reported a lower sense of well-being than average. Females and males had comparable personality profiles, except for the expected difference in measures of femininity.

SFAI students had higher-than-average scores on schizophrenia and hypomania. But these students weren't actually mentally ill; Barron interpreted these scores as indications of openness, unconventionality, and originality. (Also see the discussion of schizotypy and hypomania in Chapter 9, pp. 172–174.) Again, males and females were comparable. The overall personality profile wasn't so different from the RISD students: both groups were flexible, energetic, and open to experience.

One problem with personality trait research is that after a while, the personality traits measured by the tests seem historically dated. Remember the 1826 map of the brain in Chapter 9, with the traits of "amativeness" and "veneration"? Tests of creative people in the 1930s measured "sublimation and compensation," "coalescence of the instincts," and "constitutional delicacy"

(Raskin, 1936). These traits seem so foreign to us now, it's hard to even figure out what they might have looked like. The more recent narrative descriptions provided by Barron seem very much of our time: "The female student of design, like the male, is independent in thought, unconventional, flexible, creative, open. She approaches life with the same vigor, tempering spontaneity with an awareness of social necessities and a sensitivity to nuance. She also is complex, open to experience, and capable of dealing with the feelings of doubt such openness may bring" (1972, p. 45).

At many art schools, I've noticed that for some students, the idea of being an artist is just as important as actually doing art. Being thought of as creative is a central part of their identity. And particularly in the 1960s, art students probably wanted to be more unconventional and revolutionary than in any prior decade. That's why these tests, rather than measuring true creativity, may instead measure the traits of people who like to think of themselves as creative. Western cultural conceptions tell us that creative people should be unconventional, flexible, and open to experience; therefore people who want to be creative—or who want to be perceived as creative—often behave this way, or convince themselves they're this way (Kasof, 1995). This is basic human nature and it predates the 1960s. Romantic-era poets like Coleridge knew that they were supposed to conceive their poems in bursts of spontaneity, and that they were supposed to experience mental anguish and bouts of madness, and Coleridge made up stories about his creative process that fit this profile (see Chapter 17).

PROBLEM FINDING IN ART

I sometimes begin a drawing with no preconceived problem to solve . . . but as my mind takes in what is so produced a point arrives where some idea becomes conscious and crystallizes, and then a control and ordering begins to take place.

—Sculptor Henry Moore, (1952/1985, p. 72)

I do not seek, I find.

—Pablo Picasso (quoted in Byrne, 1996, 4:484)

The 20th-century painter Francis Bacon said that his work emerged from "the transforming effect of cultivated accidents of paint" (quoted in Ades, Forge, & Durham, 1985, p. 231). In this improvisational problem-finding painting style, Bacon said, "the creative and the critical become a single act" (p. 233). This modern style is very different from the carefully planned, composed, and executed works generated by European painters prior to the 20th century.

The 1950s New York action painters were perhaps the first to emphasize the process of painting rather than the end product. By the 1960s, the entire New York art scene—including filmmakers, performance artists, and musicians, as well as painters and sculptors (Tomkins, 2002b, p. 57)—was fascinated with process. In the 1960s, Robert Rauschenberg and other painters began to invite audiences into their studios as they painted, so that they could witness a "performance" of a work of art.

Creativity is often associated with the ability to solve problems. But as we learned in Chapter 5, many significant creative advances result from problem finding, when the problem is not known in advance but emerges from the process of the work itself. Some of the first studies of problem finding were done with artists during the 1960s (Beittel, 1972; Beittel & Burkhart,

1963; Csikszentmihalyi, 1965). In a classic study of problem finding in art, Getzels and Csikszentmihalyi (1976) identified 35 senior art students at the Art Institute of Chicago, and brought them each into a room with a table on which 27 objects had been placed. The artist was then asked to choose some of the objects and generate a pastel drawing based on them. The researchers found that the students tended to work in one of two styles (Figs. 16.1 and 16.2). Before beginning their drawing, the problem-solving artists examined and manipulated fewer objects, and the problem-finding artists examined more objects. Problem-finding artists chose more complex objects; chose objects that were more unusual, in that they were selected by fewer artists overall; and spent more time examining and manipulating the objects that they had selected. During the drawing itself, problem-solving artists composed the essential outlines of the final composition very quickly—in one extreme case, 6 minutes into a 55-minute session. Problem-finding artists took much longer—in an extreme case, the form of the final painting was not visible until 36 minutes into a 49-minute session, 73% of the total drawing time (Csikszentmihalyi, 1965, p. 32).[2]

The problem-finding artists generated drawings that were judged to be more original by five independent professional art experts (Csikszentmihalyi, 1965, p. 66). The problem-solving artists generated drawings that were judged to be more craftsmanlike.

Getzels and Csikszentmihalyi stayed in touch with these art students after they received their BFA degrees in 1963 and 1964. They measured their success in 1970 (Getzels & Csikszentmihalyi, 1976), and again in 1981 (Csikszentmihalyi & Getzels, 1988). They measured success by asking art critics, gallery owners, and peer artists to rate each former student's current reputation in the field. By 1970, 24% of the original group of 31 students had disappeared and none of the judges had heard of them; another 24% were known to have left the field of art. Twenty-three percent were doing art with some success, and 29% were well known with substantial reputations. By 1981, five of the 31 could not be found; an additional 13 were doing work completely unrelated to art—a combined total of 58%. The remaining 13 students (42%) were working in the field of art—a few as full-time fine artists, but most as teachers and graphic illustrators.

What personality traits back in their art school days best predicted artistic success later in life? The main one was problem finding: the art students who worked in a problem-finding style in art school were those most successful in both 1970 and in 1981.

Both individualist and sociocultural approaches are required to explain these results. We learned in Chapter 15 that the problem-finding style of art began to be valued only around the turn of the 20th century. Before this time, artists like Cezanne explored a single "problem" for their entire career, and they gradually got better at it; that's why Cezanne's later paintings are worth more. The Getzels and Csikszentmihalyi study wouldn't have gotten the same results 200 years ago—the problem-finding artists would not have been as likely to have had successful careers, and their work would have been less likely to have been judged creative. After all, even in the 1960s the problem-solving artists were judged to generate more craftsmanlike work, and 200 years ago, craftsmanship was more highly valued than originality.

---

2. These may not be fixed personality traits. Beittel (1972, Chapter 5) developed an instructional method to teach artists how to use the opposite style, and he found that it was fairly easy to teach artists to use both styles. In his theory, that's because both styles involve improvisational interactions with the act of painting, which he called "problem controlling" to contrast it with problem solving.

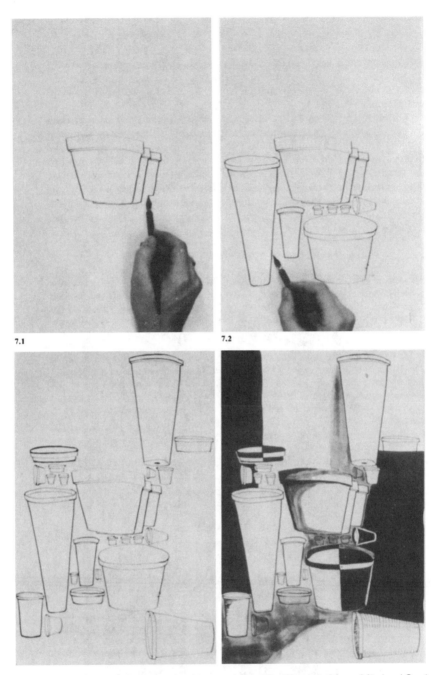

7.1

7.2

FIGURE 16.1: Photo sequence of problem-solving style of drawing. (Reprinted from *Mind and Context in the Art of Drawing,* 1972, K. Beittel. With permission of Joan Beittel, www.healingartssanctuary.com, accessed Aug. 25, 2011.)

FIGURE 16.2: Photo sequence of problem-finding style of drawing. (Reprinted from *Mind and Context in the Art of Drawing*, 1972, K. Beittel. With permission of Joan Beittel, www.healingartssanctuary.com, accessed Aug. 25, 2011.)

The 20th-century art world valorized process and spontaneity, and these values have affected our conceptions of creativity. The stereotype of Jackson Pollock, mindlessly pouring and dripping paint on a canvas while in a near-psychotic state, fits into our culture's conceptions of how the painter is supposed to work—in a burst of pure inspiration and without conscious restraint. But even Pollock painted with forethought and planning, realizing that art was impossible without norms and conventions: "Pollock learned to control flung and dribbled paint almost as well as he could a brush; if accidents played any part, they were happy accidents, selected accidents, as with any painter who sets store by the effects of rapid execution" (Greenberg, 1961/1996, p. 116). The painting process is conscious, intentional, planned hard work, sprinkled with frequent mini-insights, just like the creative process in any other domain (see Chapters 5, 6, and 7).

NEUROAESTHETICS

Neuroaesthetics is the study of the neural mechanisms underlying aesthetic experience (Skov & Vartanian, 2009, p. 3). Most of these studies focus on the aesthetic experience of the viewer of a work. Aesthetic experiences are quite common; we have many of them every day—faces, cars, and landscapes are beautiful, and we might experience an aesthetic response when embracing a loved one or listening to a historical narrative (p. 4). What makes an aesthetic experience different from an ordinary, non-aesthetic experience? Aesthetic theory has spent decades trying to answer this question. Arnheim (1974) applied the Gestalt laws of perception to art; Berlyne (1971, 1974) proposed an "experimental aesthetics" that was based in physiological arousal. These aestheticians and others have proposed a long list of features that define what is aesthetic, including:

- Symmetry
- Complexity or simplicity
- Novelty or familiarity
- Proportion or composition
- Semantic content versus formal structure

We don't have a good clear definition of what art is, and what makes it different from non-art. (We learned in Chapter 2 that to some extent, the distinction is one of cultural valuation rather than perception.) Neuroscience could help by identifying the brain regions involved in aesthetic experiences and then examining if and how those regions are similar to and different from neuronal responses to non-art objects.

Miller (2001; see Chapter 9) argued that aesthetic judgments emerged to communicate fitness, and that features like symmetry and repetition signaled virtuosity and thus the fitness of the artist. Jacobson et al. (2006) found similar patterns of neural activation when subjects were making aesthetic judgments and symmetry judgments: ten common areas were active. Symmetry was the most important factor in aesthetic judgments. But there were some differences when comparing the two: aesthetic judgments activated the right frontomedian cortex, bilaterally the superior frontal gyri, and the anterior cingulate cortex, and six other areas, and many of these regions have been previously implicated in social or moral evaluative judgments for persons or actions. Another study found that positive aesthetic response is related to activation in the orbitofrontal cortex in music, paintings, faces, odors, tastes, and touches (Brown & Dissanayake, 2009, p. 51).

Chatterjee (2003) argued that the brain's cognitive processing of non-aesthetic visual stimuli wasn't different from aesthetic stimuli responses; the difference was in the emotional responses. There are very few studies of the emotional mechanisms underlying the perception of art; in one of the few studies, Vartanian (2009) asked patients to rate paintings for how much they liked them; the brain areas involved in emotion and reward processing were active, and were more active when they liked the paintings more, including the visual cortex, the caudate nucleus, and the cingulate sulcus. This is evidence for the role of emotions in aesthetic judgment.

Neuroaesthetics is a new area, with much potential for future studies to increase our under-standing of the aesthetic experience.

CAN ART BE TAUGHT?

Out of a thousand art students, maybe five will make a living off their art, and perhaps one will be known outside her city. . . . It's the nature of fame, real quality, and genuine influence to be rare. In addition the mechanisms of fame are strongly random. Many interesting artists don't make their work at the right moment or show it to the right people. A bad critique, or bad weather on opening night, can be enough to topple a career. . . . Most artists do not make interesting art.

—James Elkins, (2001, p. 67)

In the early 1940s, there were 11 institutions offering the Master of Fine Arts (MFA) degree; today there are more than 180. In the 1940s, those attending the programs mostly had ambitions to become art teachers; today, many of them want to become professional artists. Today's art school is a historically and culturally unique institution, with its critiques and its MFA shows, and some professors have argued that art school doesn't teach how to make art at all (Elkins, 2001). And there are several types of art that are very difficult to make or even to learn about in art schools: art that takes more than one semester to complete (because students are graded each semester); art that requires the painter to work in a single style for a long period (because instruc-tors encourage variety); art that varies across many different styles (because art schools want students to develop a recognizable "voice"); art that requires naïveté—about perspective, com-position, color, or art history (because students are expected to know all of these things); art that requires years of mechanical preparation and practice (because art school is only two years long) (see Elkins, 2001, pp. 72–82). Art schools today focus on teaching the problem-finding style of creativity, and that's what the art world wants, as well. If you want to be a problem-solving type of artist, you were born 200 years too late.

Most art schools today don't focus on the technical skills of painting, drawing, and sculpting; rather, they emphasize the more intellectual and academic aspects of painting. Many art schools now use both grades and samples of paintings in their admissions decisions. Theresa Lynch Bedoya, vice-president and dean of admissions at the Maryland Institute College of Art, said that students with strong academic backgrounds produce more thoughtful art (Geraghty, 1997). In 1970, critic Harold Rosenberg suggested that the expansion of university MFA programs after

FIGURE 16.3: This cartoon makes fun of an art student talking artspeak. (Reprinted with permission of Eric Reynolds. Copyright © 1991, 2004 Daniel Clowes.)

World War II had resulted in the "cool, impersonal wave in the art of the sixties" (Tomkins, 2002a).

Higher academic ability generally results in more articulate students, students who can connect their work to art historical themes or to material they've learned in science or literature classes. Throughout the 20th century, it became increasingly important for artists to be able to tell a good story about their motivations for doing art, how the themes and images emerged from their personal life experience, and what message they hoped to communicate to the audience with their art: "as an artist, you have to be able to keep up a steady, intriguing patter while the potential customer wonders whether or not you're worth as much as you say you are" (Elkins, 2001, p. 53). Both MFA programs and galleries alike enforce this expectation; art school classes teach students to talk "artspeak" (Fig. 16.3), and they teach their artists how to write an effective "artist's statement." Artists have been making fun of artspeak and of the artist's statement since at least the irreverent 1960s. In a classic parody, Roger Lang explained his sculpture of a piece of pie on a plate:

> Pie was interesting to me first of all as food—then I found some triangular associations, geodesic, mathematical, sexual, using a pie wedge as a basis for plate decorations. Later, high in the sky, chicken pot pie, apple pie, cherry pie, and pie-eye thoughts pushed me into 3-dimensional usages. Fruit Pie is, after all, a very American food. Gradually, things accumulated and I came to think of pie as a vehicle for associations, things that come along for nothing, free. In addition, there are the visual changes which I impose, and I haven't even begun explorations of one-crust pies yet. Taking everything into account, pie is very rich. (quoted in Slivka, 1971, p. 43)

The jury is out on whether art can be taught. But even if art schools don't teach one how to make art, they can teach one how to talk like an artist, how to write like an artist, and how to participate in the art world. In their teaching practices, art schools implicitly accept a sociocultural approach.

BEYOND PAINTING: SOCIOCULTURAL EXPLANATIONS OF VISUAL CREATIVITY

In the second half of this chapter, we'll extend our explanation of visual creativity beyond painting. We'll see that outsider art—which is popular largely because it seems to confirm our individualist creativity beliefs—can be explained only using a sociocultural approach. Then we'll finish the chapter by examining some of the most widespread visual art forms of our contemporary culture—photographs, cartoons, and movies.

OUTSIDER ART

Everything changes but the avant garde.

—Paul Valéry (1871–1945) (quoted in Byrne, 1996, 3:528)

In January 1996 in New York City, artists, gallery owners, and wealthy patrons mingled in front of paintings, holding the always-present glasses of white wine. Thirty-five dealers displayed the works of hundreds of artists; 300 people attended the opening dinner. A very New York art scene, but with one difference: this show was the fourth annual New York Outsider Art Fair, and none of the hundreds of artists displayed was part of the New York art scene; many of them were visiting New York for the first time. Just a few months earlier, in November 1995, the American Visionary Art Museum had opened in Baltimore; it was designated in a Congressional resolution as "the official national museum, repository, and educational center for American visionary and outsider art," which was defined as "art produced by self-taught individuals who are driven by their own internal impulses to create" (quoted in Steiner, 1996). At the museum's opening exhibition, visitors could dine in the top-floor Joy America Café, directed by a self-taught chef whose outsider dishes included "Chinese dim sum with charred pineapple and coconut aioli." Two years later, in the spring of 1998, the first major retrospective show of outsider art was curated by the Museum of American Folk Art in New York City, and toured the country. In 2010, the Outsider Art Fair in New York City celebrated its 18th year.

The term "outsider art" dates back to an influential 1972 book by that title by British art historian Roger Cardinal. Cardinal's vision of alternative art was derived from French artist Jean Dubuffet's writings on the art of European mental patients (Peiry, 2001; also see Chapter 9, pp. 166–168). Dubuffet was interested in the paintings of children, primitives, and the mentally ill, grouping them all together because of his belief that these works were generated without the constraining influence of culture and convention. He was inspired by the legendary collection of paintings by mental patients of Hans Prinzhorn (1972). Dubuffet's term for this art was *art brut*, literally "raw art," and today Dubuffet is generally acknowledged as the grandfather of the outsider art movement. Like Dubuffet, Cardinal believed that such art was directly connected with the primordial source of all creativity because it was unconstrained by conscious attempts or subconscious influence to conform to art-world conventions. More recently, some dealers and critics call it *self-taught art* because they're offended by what they perceive to be the marginalizing or patronizing connotations of "outsider" (Fine, 2004, pp. 30–33).

Today's outsider art is mostly produced not by the mentally ill, but by rural, poor, uneducated people; if you saw one of these works you might call it folk art. In the 1970s, people began to drive the back roads of rural America, collecting craft objects and Americana, but they didn't think it was on the same level as fine art. It wasn't until 1981 that an exhibition, curated by Elsa Longhauser, presented folk art objects as fine art. Her exhibit followed the conventions of the art world, emphasizing individual authorship and objects that could be classified as paintings or sculpture, not only as utilitarian craft objects.

To explain what's unique about outsider art, we need the sociocultural approach. Outsider art isn't defined by any formal properties of the works themselves, but by their field and domain. Although the works may have been generated on the "outside," outsider art has its own field (curators, galleries that specialize in it, and patrons who collect it) and its own domain (the American Visionary Art Museum, the Museum of American Folk Art in New York City, the quarterly magazine *Raw Vision* with the masthead "Outsider Art—Art Brut—Contemporary Folk Art—Marginal Arts").

The history of outsider art, documented in books like Colin Rhodes' 2000 book *Outsider Art: Spontaneous Alternatives*, Lucienne Peiry's 2001 book *Art Brut: The Origins of Outsider Art*, and Gary Alan Fine's 2004 book *Everyday Genius*, is like a natural laboratory to test the predictions made by the sociocultural approach. Score one for the sociocultural approach: the outsider art world has developed just as predicted. Gary Alan Fine's (2004) five-year study of the outsider art community revealed that it had all of the same roles and relations as any other art world, and the field and the domain play the same roles. It *wasn't* "art" until this social system emerged to define it as such; "It becomes art only in the act of naming" (Rhodes, 2000, p. 22). Before these developments in the 1990s, more of us would have considered these works to be mere curiosities, or simple "folk art," an older term that's disliked by the outsider arts community because of its pejorative connotations. The contemporary interest in outsider art has brought it "inside"; paradoxically, just as it becomes recognized as "art," it loses its outsider status (Peiry, 2001).

THE ORIGINAL OUTSIDER ART

Some art historians date the beginning of modern art to the sunny afternoon when Picasso, taking a walk through the streets of Paris, happened to pass a shop specializing in African tribal sculptures and noticed a particularly interesting sculpted head in the window.[3] Soon after, Picasso's paintings were replicating these designs (Goldwater, 1938/1967; see Fig. 14.1, p. 272). Paul Gauguin decided that he couldn't paint true art while he was surrounded by the corrupting influence of Europe, and he left for the remote French island of Tahiti to find a natural, uncorrupted paradise. Gauguin's paintings while he lived in the South Pacific (between 1891 and 1893, and then from 1895 to his death in the Marquesas Islands of French Polynesia in 1903) are

3. This story is apocryphal; there are conflicting accounts of when and where Picasso first encountered African sculpture. Picasso said he happened on it on a chance visit in 1907 to the Paris anthropological museum. However, Matisse said that he had shown Picasso an African sculpture from his collection in 1906, in Gertrude Stein's apartment. Vlaminck said that Picasso first saw African sculpture in Derain's studio (Goldwater, 1938/1967, pp. 144–145).

(a)

(b)

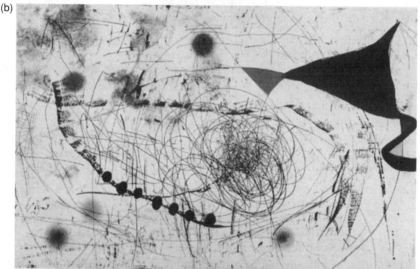

FIGURE 16.4: (a) Joan Miró, *Mediterranean Landscape*, **1930.** (b) Joan Miró, *La Manucure Évaporée*, **1975.** (Copyright © 2004. Artists Rights Society (ARS), New York/ADAGP, Paris.)

generally considered to be the source of modern painting's use of color; they influenced the movement known as Fauvism, which included influential painters like Matisse and Kandinsky.

Interest in primitive art spread quickly through Europe. African art was "discovered" almost simultaneously in both Germany (the *Die Brücke* Expressionist movement) and France (the Fauvists and Picasso, Matisse, and Derain) between 1904 and 1908. These European artists were attracted to the simplicity and intensity of expression in African art, which was thought to express pure emotion.

In addition to primitive art, many of the greatest modern artists—Kandinsky, Klee, Picasso, Miro, Dubuffet—collected children's art and used it as source material for some of the most significant breakthroughs of their careers (Fineberg, 1997, 1998; Goldwater, 1938/1967; Golomb, 2002).

These artists were influenced by the Romantic-era cult of childhood. They believed, as French poet Charles Baudelaire (1821–1867) famously wrote, that "genius is nothing more nor less than *childhood recovered* at will" (1863/1964, p. 8). They believed that children's art held the key to the internal world, spontaneous and free from conventions.

In 1902, Klee rediscovered his own childhood drawings in his parents' storage shed, and used material from them in many of his later paintings (Fig. 16.4). Kandinsky studied children's paintings in order to find a universal visual language, one before culture imposed its own images. He believed that "the talented child has the power to clothe the abiding truth in the form in which this inner truth appears as the most effective" (Kandinsky in 1912, quoted in Goldwater, 1938/1967, p. 128).

These so-called "outsiders"—children, primitives, and the mentally ill—have influenced art that's been at the core of the art establishment for over 100 years. Outsider art isn't new; what's new is that a domain and a field have emerged to redefine how we relate to the works.

INSTALLATION ART

The thesis of the end of Art has become a familiar slogan.
—Herbert Marcuse, (1970, p. 123)

Being an artist now means to question the nature of art.
—Joseph Kosuth (quoted in Rose, 1969, p. 23)

In the 1960s, painters got nervous. It was beginning to seem like all of the action was happening somewhere else. Art critics were talking about artworks like Robert Smithson's *Spiral Jetty*, 6,650 tons of black basalt and earth in the shape of a giant coil, 1,500 feet long, jutting out into the Great Salt Lake in Utah. Bruce Nauman made movies of himself anxiously pacing in circles. Donald Judd's work is so large and imposing that it's displayed in a private museum in Marfa, Texas, on 340 acres of a former Army base; one of the pieces displayed consists of 100 milled aluminum boxes installed in two converted artillery sheds. In 1977, Heiner Friedrich's SoHo gallery in New York became the permanent home of Walter De Maria's work *The New York Earth Room*, which is 280,000 pounds of dirt, spread 22 inches deep, across a 3,600-square-foot room. The room requires constant maintenance to maintain moisture levels and to clear away the mushrooms that keep popping up.

These works challenge the dominance of painting. They're known as *installation art*, a broad term for art that seeks to shape the environment for its reception, changing how people view and relate to the artwork. Installation artists don't just create art, they also create the contexts in which their work will be seen. It's as if they are creating a new kind of museum, a new kind of relationship with the audience.

Installation art reflexively comments on the experience of interacting with art. Like modern theater, which breaks the fourth wall and draws attention to its own conventions (see Chapter 19), installation art questions the boundary between artwork and audience, and questions the nature of art itself. But because such art breaks the most fundamental conventions of the art world, most people have never seen it. The art world's system of conventions—museums, galleries, traveling exhibitions, opening-night parties, mass mailings to museum donors—helps to disseminate a new work and makes it possible for the field to judge the work. Installation art can't be sold easily because it can't be displayed in any collector's home, and it can't be carried from one place to another. It's hard to have an opening-night party, because most of the dealers and collectors are in Manhattan, not in Utah or Texas. To view the art you have to make a pilgrimage to its remote unconventional location. It's hard to imagine a market in such art.

At first glance, installation art seems to reinforce the Western cultural model; these artists work in solitude and break all of the art world's conventions. But even installation artists have to pay rent and buy food. In the early years, many of the best-known installation artists were supported by independently wealthy private donors, resulting in a patronage system reminiscent of medieval Europe. How did these rich patrons know which artists to support? By seeking the advice of dealers and museum curators, creating a new mini-art world that operated much like the old traditional one.

By breaking the conventions of the art world, installation art calls attention to them. And at the same time, installation art teaches us why we have such conventions, and why they'll never disappear. Conventions, domains, and fields are required for art to exist as a social system, as a shared cultural activity that many people can jointly participate in. Installation art indeed breaks conventions. But the fact that most of my readers have never seen it reinforces the importance of those conventions.

PHOTOGRAPHY

Eugene Atget is today a famous French photographer known for his documentary-style photographs of everyday street life in Paris in the early 20th century. But he wasn't known as a photographer during his lifetime. Although he took thousands of photographs, few people knew his work. Just before his death in 1927, the young American photographer Berenice Abbott met him and thought his work was brilliant; when he died, she gained control of his negatives, examined thousands of them, and eventually chose to print the small set of photographs by which Atget is now known (Abbott, 1964). We usually expect the photographer himself to use his own creativity in this selection process. After all, Abbott selected only about 100 prints out of many thousands; how do we know Atget himself would have picked the same ones? So in this case, Atget and Abbott collaborated in the work that we today know as "Atget." After Abbott made Atget famous, other photographers went back to the same negatives and selected different photographs than she did.

The photographs in legendary Western photographer Ansel Adams's first book were selected from his negatives by Nancy Newhall; Adams was very much alive, but too busy to make the selections. Shouldn't we attribute Newhall as a collaborator in the creation of this first book? Both Atget and Adams became known from a body of work that reflected someone else's sensibilities and standards.

An art photograph, displayed on a gallery wall, is the result of a long sequence of small decisions. First, the photographer has to decide when to pick up the camera and point, and then when to press the shutter. Most photographers take far more photographs than they'll ever be able to print, knowing that they'll be able to review their contact sheets in the studio. Becker (1982) described taking 20,000 photos in preparation for an exhibit containing no more than 100 prints (p. 195). The most important decisions are made in the studio: which of the 20,000 photos is good enough to potentially result in a good print?

After the individual photographer has made his or her choices, the curators and gallery owners have to evaluate and select the photos of many different photographers. Only a minority of photographers ever receive a gallery show. And getting one gallery show doesn't result in fame or lasting reputation. For that to happen, many different galleries, curators, and patrons each have to individually decide to select that work. It's in this sense that "art worlds, rather than artists, make works of art" (Becker, 1982, p. 198).

Every artist becomes known from works that reflect the standards of the gatekeepers in the field. Especially with mass-produced works like books, movies, and music CDs, only works that are selected by the field for distribution ever reach a wide audience. The general public comes to know a creator "as selected by" multiple layers of intermediaries. Because evaluation and selection are critical parts of the creative process, these intermediaries become collaborators in the work.

MOVIES

Movies reach almost everywhere. No other art form mobilizes a national discussion in such a big way.

— Roger Ebert, (1997, p. A23), in an editorial arguing that
there should be a Pulitzer Prize for movies as an art form

It's a little strange that so much psychological research on visual creativity focuses on fine art painting when psychologists could be studying a much more widespread and more influential creative visual medium: Hollywood movies. When the Pulitzer Prizes were first created in 1917, movies weren't yet a respectable art form. And still today, there's no Pulitzer Prize for film, although there are prizes for fiction, drama, history, biography, poetry, and music. In the first half of the 20th century—when movies were new—people could still get away with arguing that movies really didn't deserve the same status as fine art; some scholars were viciously dismissive of American movies (German Marxist Theodor W. Adorno is perhaps the best known). But during the second half of the 20th century, almost everyone came to agree that film had attained a status as a creative art form, the equal of any other.

Movies don't fit in with the Western cultural model of creativity for several reasons. First, they're created by large teams of people, each with specialized skills, who have to work together collaboratively to generate the final product. Film scholars have occasionally attempted to impose the lone-genius myth onto movie creation, attributing the creativity to the director. But although the director has a unique creative position, unlike the painter, he or she can't create a movie without a large support staff (Simonton, 2011). The collaborative nature of movie production can't be explained with individualist approaches.

One of the most widely known examples of movie creativity is George Lucas's original *Star Wars* film of 1977. At first glance, the story of how *Star Wars* came to be made seems to fit into the lone-genius myth. In the mid-1970s, Lucas's original 13-page treatment of *The Star Wars* (as he originally called it) was rejected by Universal and by United Artists, even though Lucas had already had a big success with *American Graffiti*. Only Alan Ladd, then at Fox, considered it, and even then he had to work against the objections of the Fox board. But even this first script for

The Star Wars wasn't a burst of lone genius; Lucas spent over a year writing the 13-page plot summary and another year writing the first draft of the script. Even after all this work, his dialog still needed some help, and he got several other writers to help rewrite the script. After realizing the script was too long for one movie, he then broke it up into six separate movies (the first movie was called *Star Wars, Episode IV: A New Hope*). At a private screening of an early cut of the film for his friends and Fox executives, everyone hated it, thought it was a bad movie, was convinced it would tank, and was embarrassed for Lucas (Seabrook, 1997).

They were all wrong. The success is legendary. The first movie alone earned $323 million, more than any prior movie. It was the first movie to spawn a lucrative line of toys. And it funda-mentally changed how movies are made. Before *Star Wars*, cinematic elements were secondary to the narrative and the literary elements of the movie; now, the visual and cinematic elements are primary. Interestingly, few of the visual elements that Lucas used were themselves original. Film historians point out that many of Lucas's visuals were taken from past movies: the light sabers and Jedi Knights were inspired by Kurosawa's *Hidden Fortress*; the robot C-3PO was a character straight out of Fritz Lang's *Metropolis*; Harrison Ford's portrayal of Han Solo resembles *Butch Cassidy*. It's often said of Lucas that "he didn't actually invent anything" (Seabrook, 1997, p. 48).

So was Lucas truly creative, or did he just get lucky? In one sense *Star Wars* fits the tradi-tional genius myth narrative; he pushed through a creative vision in the face of opposition from the field, and he succeeded. But ultimately, the lone-genius myth doesn't fit unless we ignore big chunks of the story. The idea wasn't a burst of inspiration, but evolved over a five-year period. The script was collaboratively written by several people. Most of the visual elements were borrowed from prior movies, and the story, as is widely known, is based on common mythical elements analyzed by Joseph Campbell. Many movie experts thought that it was a bad movie—famously, Pauline Kael of *The New Yorker*.

From the sociocultural perspective, *Star Wars* has to be considered creative because it's been judged creative by the field. It made it through all of the usual filters by first getting funded and distributed by a major studio, and then by facing the test of the movie-going audience. Although some influential critics hated the movie, on balance the field has determined that it was creative. And since 1977, the ways that it changed the domain are increasingly clear.

Of all movies ever made, George Lucas's *Star Wars* is about as close as you can get to Western cultural beliefs about the creative artist, and even this story doesn't fit the beliefs all that well. But the great majority of movies aren't nearly as innovative or influential; most of them replicate what's come before, with only minor variations. According to Hollywood legend, there are only seven story lines underlying all movies and TV shows (Friend, 1998). Professional writers con-sciously stick with proven formulas, knowing that TV executives, advertisers, and viewers have grown to expect them. Many writers today use computer software that helps them to follow these rules (see Chapter 17). Explaining movie creativity requires a focus on collaboration, networks, divisions of labor, and markets.

CARTOONS

Like movies, cartoons are created by large organized teams of specialized individuals. They require a significant upfront investment of cash and expensive distribution through broadcast or cable television, and as a result, cartoons go through multiple layers of evaluation and modification long after the originating idea. Like sitcoms and movies, cartoons are usually created by collaborative teams of writers (see Chapter 17).

Here's a transcript of a story meeting of the artists working on the Cartoon Network's *Samurai Jack*, with the meeting led by creator Genndy Tartakovsky (the creator of *Dexter's Laboratory*). Andy (one of the artists) has come up with a new story idea. There are about ten people in the room. Other than Andy and Tartakovsky, whenever one of the others speaks up I've simply indicated "artist" (from Wilkinson, 2002):

Andy: We're looking to do the story we talked about, where Jack gets infected with a virus and it takes over his arm. Then it would slowly take over his whole body. Then half of him becomes evil, and he's going to fight himself.

Tartakovsky: How do we set it up?

Artist: Could he have battled Aku, and Aku has a cold, and he sneezes on him?

Tartakovsky: (nods) It's almost like we're at the end of another show with a great fight. Except this one starts with a battle. And he's fighting these robots, and Aku's commanding them. It's cold and drafty, and Aku starts sneezing, and says, "Oy, I've got to get some chicken soup."

Artist: Oy?

Artist: How do we get it out that he's infected?

Artist: We had talked about him showing a guy his face. And it's half in shadow.

Artist: He becomes Aku.

Artist: He becomes *Jaku.*

Artist: The more evil he becomes, the more erratic his body is.

Artist: Maybe somebody's getting robbed, he saves him, and the guy thanks him, and he's walking away, and in Jack's other hand is the guy's watch.

Artist: Do we need to find somebody to summon him? Is there a psychic battle with himself?

Artist: Or a fight in his head? I was thinking, he knows a place to cleanse himself—a monastery. And the monks help him.

Artist: The B story is no one's trusting Jack—they see him and they run.

Tartakovsky: It's always stronger if Jack can help himself. I like the image of Jack as Aku with one eye. I like it half and half. The more I think about it, the body of the show is him fighting himself.

Artist: He realizes he'd better get out of the city before he hurts someone, so he travels to a village.

Tartakovsky: I still want to keep it real simple, though.

Artist: At the monastery, they tie him up so he can't do any harm.

Tartakovsky: Does Aku know that Jack has what he has?

Artist: No, he's too sick.

It's clear from this brief excerpt of the brainstorming session that no single person is in charge. No one creates any more than anyone else. Even though the discussion started with Andy's story idea, Andy says nothing after getting it started. Tartakovsky doesn't dominate the group. The cartoon emerges from the discussion, and ends up being a collective creation of 10 people.

COULD WE MAKE THE ART WORLD MORE DEMOCRATIC?

What kind of art do Americans really want? If you took a poll of a random group of Americans, what art would they choose? Two conceptual artists from Russia decided to find out what kind of art Americans like by conducting a poll of their own. They asked 1,001 Americans about their favorite colors, forms, styles, and content; when they put Americans' top choices all together, they got a bluish landscape painting containing George Washington, a family of tourists, and a pair of deer, all in a painting about the size of a dishwasher (Fig. 16.5). Vitaly Komar and Alexander Melamid did similar polls in countries from China to Iceland (Kakutani, 1998; Wypijewski, 1997). They found a lot of overlap, and also some amusing national differences.[4] Based on the poll results, they painted each country's "most wanted" painting, and also its opposite, a painting that contained everything the culture most disliked (all paintings can be viewed on the Web, at http://www.diacenter.org/km/ [accessed Aug. 25, 2011]). These least-wanted paintings look a lot like abstract modern art. Later, they showed the paintings to focus groups, and they found that most Americans really did like the "painting by numbers."

This art—created by audience consensus—is clearly tongue in cheek, but it raises some interesting issues for creativity. Why shouldn't art reflect what the people want? Much of what we hear on our radio stations is directly influenced by polls of listeners conducted by the Arbitron

FIGURE 16.5: *America's Most Wanted Painting* (http://www.diacenter.org/km [accessed Aug. 25, 2011]), a painting generated by the artists Komar and Melamid, based on a survey of 1,001 adults that asked them what they most liked to see in a painting. (Reprinted with permission of Komar. Copyright © Komar & Melamid.)

4. Similar findings were reported by Kaplan and Kaplan (1989). Their work focused on aesthetic preferences for different images of nature, in a wide range of cultures and subgroups.

market-research corporation (see Chapter 18, p. 343). Best-selling novelist James Patterson distributed drafts of his books to "test readers" for feedback before releasing the books for publication. He changed the ending of his thriller *Cat & Mouse* in response to reader feedback; the novel reached number 2 on the *New York Times* bestseller list. The producers of the Broadway musical *Ragtime* hired a polling firm to help them revise the script in response to audience reactions; the show went through 20 drafts before opening night (Kakutani, 1997). And "super fans" who maintain popular websites have started to influence Hollywood decision making. While *The Hulk* (2003) was being produced, studio executives surfed the Web to see what aspects of the original comic strip were most important to the most serious fans. Internet fan sites have influenced the creation of many movies, including the *Lord of the Rings* trilogy (2001, 2002, 2003) and *Spider-Man* (2002) (Bowles, 2003).

Is this so wrong? Or would we rather side with the art world attitude that it doesn't matter what people think? When the art world of New York gathered at the Whitney Museum to discuss Komar and Melamid's project, many of them agreed that "talking about what *the people* want is absurd" (art historian Dore Ashton, quoted in Sante, 1998). It's only absurd given Western cultural conceptions of art—as the inspired outburst of the inner spirit of the artist, isolated, misunderstood, rejecting convention.

To explain today's most important forms of visual creativity, we need to move beyond painting. And when we move beyond painting, we need a sociocultural approach. Movies and cartoons are created collaboratively, and the intermediaries of the field play an increasingly important role. The example of photography shows us that evaluation and selection is often more important than incubation and insight, and this lesson extends far beyond photography. Even our contemporary conceptions of painting are historically unique and can be traced back to our Western cultural model and its origins in the 19th-century Romantic movement (Chapter 2, pp. 20–23).

KEY CONCEPTS

- Problem finding in art
- Neuroaesthetics
- Outsider art/art brut/self-taught art
- The cult of childhood

THOUGHT EXPERIMENTS

- Have you used a digital camera? Do you take pictures differently now that you know you can immediately delete a photo that doesn't look good?
- If you ever used a Polaroid camera, were you more careful about when you took pictures because you knew that each picture cost more than those taken with an ordinary camera?
- If you don't like abstract modern art, then how do you explain why it has dominated the art world for most of the 20th century? Have you ever said, "I may not know art, but I know what I like"?

- Would you agree with the following statement: "It doesn't matter what those gatekeepers in the field think, those snobby New York 'experts.' They don't get to say what counts as art." If so, then what alternative would you propose for how to select the best art works? Would it be a democratic system, like that of Komar and Melamid?
- Do you think we should do away with all criteria and selection? But if so, then we can no longer have galleries, art markets, and museums because those institutions all require that criteria be applied and choices be made. How do you think such institutions should function?
- Are movies art? Are they just as important as fine art painting? Or do you believe that there's something uniquely special about fine art painting?

SUGGESTED READINGS

Csikszentmihalyi, M., & Getzels, J. W. (1988). Creativity and problem finding in art. In F. H. Farley & R. W. Neperud (Eds.), *The foundations of aesthetics, art & art education* (pp. 91–116). New York: Praeger.

Elkins, J. (2001). *Why art cannot be taught: A handbook for art students.* Urbana, IL: University of Illinois Press. [Especially Chapters 2 and 3]

Fine, G. A. (2004). *Everyday genius: Self-taught art and the culture of authenticity.* Chicago, IL: University of Chicago Press.

Fineberg, J. D. (1997). *The innocent eye: Children's art and the modern artist.* Princeton, NJ: Princeton University Press.

Prinzhorn, H. (1972). *Artistry of the mentally ill.* New York: Springer.

C H A P T E R   1 7

WRITING

It is tremendously important that great poetry be written, it makes no jot of difference who writes it.

—Ezra Pound, 1954, p. 10

When the young American poet T. S. Eliot published *The Waste Land* in 1922—while only 24 years old—it won him an international reputation. *The Waste Land* has no plot, but is instead a loosely connected series of images that capture the disillusionment and disgust at the death and destruction caused by World War I. The disconnected organization of the poem reflects the fragmented and confused nature of modern urban life. Eliot later proved that he was no one-shot wonder; he had a long, productive, and influential career in the decades after this first great success, capped with a Nobel Prize in Literature in 1948.

Most of us assume that Eliot created *The Waste Land*. After all, his name is on the title page, and he was the one who cashed the check for the royalties. And after all, isn't poetry one of the most solitary, private forms of creativity?

Not in this case. *The Waste Land* was a collaborative creation; two other poets significantly modified Eliot's first typed manuscript: his friend and colleague Ezra Pound, and his wife, Vivien Eliot.

Pound was older and more experienced than Eliot, and his support was critical in Eliot's early career. Eliot had great respect for Pound and gave him the initial typewritten manuscript of his 800-line poem, asking for suggestions. Pound didn't hold back; he deleted entire pages from Eliot's first draft, moved stanzas around, and liberally reworded many lines. For example, the famous first line "April is the cruellest month" is line 55 of Eliot's first typewritten manuscript. Pound shortened Eliot's initial typed manuscript by half; the published poem came out at only 433 lines. Eliot's original manuscript had elements of parody and dry humor—its original title had been "He Do the Police in Different Voices"—and Pound removed all of it to focus on the bleak imagery. Eliot acknowledged his debt to Pound in his book's dedication: "For Ezra Pound, *il miglior fabbro*" (the greater craftsman).

Eliot's wife Vivien was a second important editor. After Eliot sought Vivien's advice, she also deleted lines from the original manuscript and suggested alternative wordings; she wrote one of the poem's memorable lines, near the end of part 2, "What you get married for if you don't want children?" (Eliot's original draft had "You want to keep him at home, I suppose.")

The original manuscript was lost for many decades, and no one realized that *The Waste Land* was collaboratively created until scholars rediscovered the manuscript in 1968 (Eliot, 1971). However, Eliot's reputation didn't suffer even though it now seemed that Pound had written more than half of the poem. Eliot is still considered to be the author of *The Waste Land*, even though the story of the poem's creation makes us question whether any one person should actually get all the credit.

At first glance, writing seems to be far removed from social and contextual influences. You don't need anyone's help to write poetry; you don't need to use complex tools; and you don't have to collaborate in a system of cooperative work. If you think of poetry as the private, personal expression of a person's inner vision, you might think that this story is abnormal. You might even feel that Eliot was cheating by drawing on the help of others, or that Pound interfered with Eliot's original vision. But these reactions stem from our Western cultural model of creativity. In reality, many successful writers seek out good editing, listen very closely to such comments, and are grateful for them. Eliot's story shows us that creative writing is often the result of collaboration. The story of *The Waste Land* has three important lessons to teach us about writing creativity.

LESSON 1: WRITING IS HARD WORK

The Western cultural model tells us that the inner voice of the creator is the unconscious, yearning to find expression. Many successful writers speak of the important role played by unconscious inspiration. Madeleine L'Engle, author of the classic *A Wrinkle in Time*, said that "a lot of ideas come subconsciously. You don't even realize where they're coming from" (quoted in Csikszentmihalyi, 1996, p. 256), and poet Mark Strand, chosen in 1991 to be poet laureate of the United States, said that "you don't know when you're going to be hit with an idea, you don't know where it comes from" (quoted in Csikszentmihalyi, 1996, p. 241; also see Clark, 1997).

In the Western cultural model, the words pour onto the page in a burst of inspiration. But that's Hollywood, not real life. English novelist Anthony Trollope described a very businesslike writing method:

> [A writer] should have so trained himself that he shall be able to work continuously during those three hours—so have tutored his mind that it shall not be necessary for him to sit nibbling his pen, and gazing at the wall before him, till he shall have found the words with which he wants to express his ideas. It had at this time become my custom . . . to write with my watch before me, and to require from myself 250 words every quarter of an hour. I have found that the 250 words have been forthcoming as regularly as my watch went. (Trollope, 1883/1989, p. 197)

Like Trollope, many famous writers are quite productive. John Updike has written well over 40 books; Joyce Carol Oates, 80 or more; other prolific writers include Stephen King, John Sayles, and James Michener. Can someone who works in such a businesslike way really be creative? Because the Western cultural model tells us that creativity emerges in a burst of inspiration from the unconscious, we naturally think that the inspired first draft is the best. If a work is really good, then it won't need much revision after this moment of insight. But this is a myth;

professional writers know that the first draft often needs heavy editing. Very few writers can attain their best without subjecting their spontaneous work to careful, tedious, time-consuming review and editing. In a famous 1846 essay, Edgar Allen Poe rejected the myth of inspiration:

> Most writers—poets in especial—prefer having it understood that they compose by a species of fine frenzy—an ecstatic intuition—and would positively shudder at letting the public take a peep behind the scenes, at the elaborate and vacillating crudities of thought . . . at the fully matured fancies discarded in despair as unmanageable—at the cautious selections and rejections—at the painful erasures and interpolations . . . which, in ninety-nine cases out of the hundred, constitute the properties of the literary *histrio*. (1846, p. 163)

This is a wonderful summary of the action theory of creativity, and a rejection of the idealist theory (Chapter 5). Contemporary writers work just as hard as Edgar Allen Poe. Lyric poet Anthony Hecht, winner of a Pulitzer Prize in 1968, said that "there's an awful lot of fussing and fiddling; I feel that the writing of a poem is a very conscious act" (quoted in Csikszentmihalyi, 1996, p. 251). After his initial inspiration, Strand critically examines everything, consciously drawing on all of his knowledge of past poets and conventions to rework the raw material. German poet Hilde Domin said that a very experienced poet will be able to apply the critical eye almost simultaneously along with the unconscious inspiration: "Like, for example, when you eliminate a word. In the beginning you eliminate it *after* you have written it. And when you are more skilled you eliminate it while you are writing" (quoted in Csikszentmihalyi, 1996, p. 248).

English writer Jessica Mitford engaged in a constant dialog with her unfolding drafts: "The first thing to do is read over what you have done the day before and rewrite it. And then that gives you a lead into the next thing to do" (John-Steiner, 1985, p. 8). Poet May Sarton wrote, "The poem teaches us something while we make it; there is nothing dull about revision" (1980, pp. 50–52). Creative writers almost all engage in a constant dialog with the page.

Many aspiring writers believe that their unconscious should do all of the good creative work for them; writing teachers have observed that this belief keeps these novices from getting started. Novelist Anne Lamott, in her writing advice book *Bird by Bird*, emphasized the importance of generating "shitty first drafts" (1994, p. 21), and Natalie Goldberg, in *Writing Down the Bones*, communicated much the same message, with rules like "keep your hand moving," "don't cross out," and "lose control" (Goldberg, 1986, p. 8). The first draft provides necessary raw material, but it's not anywhere near a finished product; it still requires the hard work of evaluation and elaboration.

LESSON 2: WRITING IS CONSCIOUS AND DIRECTED

Some editors are failed writers, but so are most writers.
—T. S. Eliot (in Charlton, 1980, p. 121)

The late Raymond Carver's story *Cathedral* is the last of 33 drafts of the work. Carver said he knew he was done with a story only when he got to the point that he went over it, adding only occasional commas, and then in the next revision, he began removing some of those same commas (Dutton, 2001, p. 189). Most people don't realize that professional writers sweat over every comma; such tedious work doesn't match the Western cultural model.

The belief that a poem springs to mind fully formed by the unconscious genius originated in the Romantic era. Romantic poets actively encouraged the public to believe in this myth, even when it wasn't true. You may have heard Coleridge's story about how he created the poem "Kubla Khan" all at once in an opium-inspired daze. But Coleridge's story is known to be false. For example, scholars have discovered an earlier version of the poem, and they know of many other examples where Coleridge lied about his work process (Schneider, 1953; also see Weisberg, 1988, pp. 170–171). Coleridge probably realized that the story about the opium would make the poem more interesting to a reading public suffused with Romantic myths about creativity. Coleridge's story tells us more about the Romantic-era conception of creativity than about his actual creative process, because we know that during his era, admitting to long periods of frequent revision would not have been consistent with Romantic-era conceptions of how true creativity worked.

When Rothenberg (1990) interviewed writers and poets, he didn't find a lot of evidence for spontaneous inspiration. Instead, he found evidence for Poe's view:

> Over and over again, my subjects have told me that they seldom knew what a poem was really "saying" until they were well into the writing, until they had actually finished it or, in some cases, until months or years later. (p. 41)

LESSON 3: WRITING IS A COLLABORATIVE AND SOCIALLY EMBEDDED ACTIVITY

Although both Pound and Vivien Eliot heavily edited Eliot's original manuscripts, we still credit the poems to Eliot alone. But editing can cross a line where we think it's too much, where we begin to wonder whether the "author" really should get the credit. Novelist Thomas Wolfe, author of *Look Homeward, Angel*, died in 1938, leaving about a million words behind, all unorganized and unfinished. Edward Aswell, an editor at Harper & Brothers, created two more books out of these scattered writings; he did it by creating composite characters drawn from separate bits of writing, and he sometimes added his own words. Aswell's efforts remained secret until the late 1970s, and when they became public, it diminished Wolfe's reputation.

When Raymond Carver died in 1988 at age 50 from lung cancer, he was considered by many critics to be America's most significant short-story author. His first collection of short stories, published in 1981 as *What We Talk About When We Talk About Love*, was critically acclaimed for its minimalist style. If there could be such a thing as an "outsider writer," Carver might qualify; he grew up in the rural northwestern part of the country and taught himself to write by taking a correspondence course. He lived in poverty and suffered from serious alcoholism. He seemed to represent a pure form of writing as the necessary expression of inner demons, and editorial collaboration doesn't fit well with such an image.

Gordon Lish was Carver's first editor, and he often claimed that he had so heavily edited Carver's early stories that they were as much his as they were Carver's. But his claim was never taken seriously; after all, stories authored by Lish himself had never been successful, and all authors rely on editorial advice to some extent. And yet critics had often noted that Carver's writing style seemed to change later in his career, after Lish was no longer his editor. The early stories, edited by Lish, are more minimalist and abstract in style, and the later ones are more sentimental and more elaborate in style. Literary critics had attributed this change to the fact that Carver seemed to become happier later in life, as he conquered his alcoholism and settled into a stable relationship with Tess Gallagher.

In 1991, Carver's manuscripts were made available to researchers, at the Lilly Library at Indiana University. When Carver's manuscripts were first examined—and they're covered with editorial marks in Lish's hand—Lish's claim didn't seem so ludicrous. The scratched-out text is often more than half of each page; Lish added entire paragraphs to some pages, and shortened many stories by deleting the last few paragraphs of Carver's original draft. In some stories, Lish cut 70% of the original words and replaced many of them with his own text; in others, stories ended up 40% shorter than Carver's initial draft (Max, 1998). A famous letter has come to light in which Carver begged Lish not to publish his book (Rich, 2007), but in another letter, just one week later, Carver praised what Lish had done, asking only for a couple of minor revisions (Campbell, 2009; Martin, 2009).

His widow, Tess Gallagher, spearheaded an effort to publish the original versions of those stories, even though his original publisher, Knopf, refused. In 2009, the original versions were published by Vintage as *Beginners*. A review of this new book concluded, "There is little doubt that [Lish] was substantially responsible for what we think of as the Carver style" (Martin, 2009). At least one reviewer of the original versions concluded that the Lish-edited versions were "cleaner, more vigorous, and more memorable" (Martin, 2009).

These stories challenge the Western cultural belief in the authenticity of a writer's output. We want to believe that we're reading the author's deeply personal and emotional experience, that the author finds catharsis by getting it out onto the page. But most writers receive help, and editors have always modified the writer's original text. Dr. Carol Polsgrove, a professor at Indiana University, said, "If you exalt the individual writer as the romantic figure who brings out these things from the depths of his soul, then yes, the awareness of Lish's role diminishes Carver's work somewhat. But if you look at writing and publishing as a social act, which I think it is, the stories are the stories that they are" (quoted in Max, 1998, p. 51). A new form of literary criticism known as *genetic criticism* has begun to focus on the evolution of manuscripts from drafts to published form, examining the collaborative process that involves editors, colleagues, and publishers (Deppman, Ferrer, & Groden, 2004). After all, why should we place such a high value on authenticity and purity with novels and short stories when we don't expect it of television sitcoms or Hollywood movies?

THE PSYCHOLOGY OF CREATIVE WRITING

A writer is somebody for whom writing is more difficult than it is for other people.
—Thomas Mann (quoted in Charlton, 1980, p. 57)

Writing is hard work. It takes dedication to craft and intense motivation. It's not pretty. Thomas Mann doesn't mean that nonwriters have an easier time with writing. What he really means is that writers are the only people who realize how hard writing actually is; people who think it's easy are naïve and are deluding themselves. They're amateurs who generate a first draft and then never go through the hard work of editing and revising it.

In the 1960s at the Berkeley IPAR, Barron (1972) conducted a series of intensive interviews and observations with 26 professional creative writers—including Truman Capote, Norman Mailer, Marianne Moore, and Saul Bellow. He found that the writers scored higher than the general public on several personality trait measures:

- Intellectual capacity
- Value placed on intellectual and cognitive matters
- Value placed on independence and autonomy
- Verbal fluency
- Conceptual thinking
- Flexibility

Piirto (2009) gave the Myers-Briggs Type Indicator to 15 successful female writers and to a comparison group of 15 female elementary-school teachers (also see Chapter 4, p. 67). Most writers preferred Intuition (N) over Sensing (S), and Perceiving (P) over Judging (J). This is consistent with Barron's (1968) findings; Barron also found a higher degree of introversion than extraversion.

Csikszentmihalyi's extended interviews of five creative writers (1996) identified several important common threads. First, the writers could be significantly creative only by first immersing themselves in the domain of literature. None of them were "outsider" writers; they all read a lot, they had strong opinions about other writers, and they memorized their favorite works. In other words, they internalized more of the domain than nonwriters. All five of them eventually became part of the field of literature—they became friends with other writers, contributed to insider journals, and gossiped about each other. They became intermediaries, teachers, and editors.

Second, the writers all emphasized the constant dialog between unconscious inspiration and conscious editing, between passionate inspiration and disciplined craft. They all agreed that it's important to listen to their unconscious. They kept notebooks nearby at all times so that sudden snippets of text or dialog could be quickly scribbled down for later evaluation. They worked in a problem-finding style, starting a work with only a phrase or an image rather than a fully composed plot, and the work emerged from the improvisational act of writing and revising. There was never a single big insight; instead, there were hundreds and thousands of small mini-insights. The real work started when many mini-insights were analyzed, reworked, and connected to each other; and as with every other type of creativity, many ideas that sounded good at first ended up in the trash.

Many creative writers talk about these mini-insights. Writers are constantly thinking, coming up with small bits of text that they write down in their notebooks. These are little snippets of a scene or a character, and the writer has no idea whether they'll ever be used in a finished published text. Poet Mark Strand starts writing this way: "I'll jot a few words down, and that's a beginning" (quoted in Csikszentmihalyi, 1996, p. 241). These pages are then stored in a folder or a notebook, frequently perused, and much later can be slipped into an ongoing story, one that was not even conceived when the original snippet was written. This is the hard work of writing, and it's why fiction is never only autobiographical reporting—characters in a novel are rarely exactly like any living individual, but are rather composites of observations of many people, strangers and intimates, built up over a long and hard day-to-day process of observation and writing.

Most creative writers use a problem-finding style; they don't know what they're doing until they've done it (Lamott, 1994, p. 22). Moore (1985) replicated the famous Getzels and Csikszentmihalyi study of artists (Chapter 16) with student writers. He found that student writers resembled art students in their problem-finding behavior; the writers whose stories were rated the most original by experts were the ones who used a problem-finding style.

POETRY AS AN ORAL ART

In the fall of 2002, rap recording mogul Russell Simmons produced the Tony Award–winning *Def Poetry Jam* on Broadway, bringing oral poetry into the heart of America's central entertainment district. Nine different poets reciting on stage in front of an audience—it might sound boring at first. However, this is poetry composed for the stage, not the page, and like other performance genres, the process is the product—it exists only in performance. Each poet was selected from the burgeoning small-club scene of poetry jams, a circuit that has resulted in a renaissance of what is often called "spoken word." The oral nature of the genre results in a return to certain core elements of poetry: the performative element, first of all, but also formal features like rhythm and rhyme that fell out of fashion in literary free verse. Literary values are secondary; these compositions often work better on stage than they do in private contemplation in the library. Only in performance would an audience see the hypnotic qualities of Staceyann Chin's description of lovemaking, or the posed militancy in the kung fu dandy poses of Beau Sia, the self-described "Chinese tornado."

Some people might argue that the theatrics of performance keep us from appreciating the underlying poetry. If it doesn't seem as creative when we study it in the library, then haven't we, in a sense, been fooled by the tricks of the performer? But this attitude is simply a manifestation of our culture's general distrust of performance creativity, and the higher value we tend to place on compositional creativity. This distrust of performance is pretty recent; historians agree that for thousands of years, poetry was primarily an oral, spoken genre.

Several scholars have studied how poetry is influenced by its oral roots. For example, because poetry was transmitted orally in cultures that were not literate, the structure of the poem had to be easy to remember. Cognitive psychologists have discovered that techniques associated with poetry, like alliteration, meter, and rhyme, increase the memorability of a text (Rubin, 1995). In other words, poetry doesn't have the distinctive features it does just because they look pretty on the page, or because they're fun to read; rather, they serve a very practical function of aiding in memory, a function that was, strictly speaking, no longer necessary after the introduction of literacy and written composition. Through most of human history, verbal creations had to be easy to remember; in oral cultures, all composed texts had features that we today associate with poetry, because otherwise they would not be remembered and would disappear from history.

In preliterate medieval Europe, a small cadre of trained scribes began to record traditional oral texts, fixing them on the page. This was time-consuming and expensive and could be done only for highly valued ritual texts. When the printing press was invented, it became economically possible to print a much wider range of texts. Until the growth of the novel as a prose genre in the 19th century, poetry continued to have the highest status of all written genres. The high value placed on poetry derived from its ancient pedigree, its historical association with religious texts, and the additional skill required to craft such texts.

ROMANCE NOVELS

We don't have to return to Trollope's day to find examples of prolific, hard-working writers with rigid schedules. Romance novel authors are quite prolific; many of the most popular writers publish several books every year. Authors in several other genres—westerns, detective stories, children's books—are equally prolific. Ian Fleming wrote the first James Bond novel, *Casino Royale*, in under 10 weeks (Storr, 1972, p. 40).

Romance novels are written by women for women. A sociological survey conducted in Britain in the 1960s found that over half of readers were full-time housewives, that they read the books to relax and to escape from everyday problems, and that many women read these books in secret, suggesting that there was something of a stigma attached to them (Mann, 1969). It's interesting that although these findings come from over 30 years ago from Britain, they're still true of the readers of today's romance novel in the United States; they are still read with a bit of guilt, and primarily by married mothers between the ages of 25 and 50, with about half not employed outside the home (Radway, 1991).

Are these novels "art"? Are they as creative as so-called "literary" novels? Even if the genres can be distinguished, is there a difference in the creative process whereby writers generate them? With this high level of productivity, you can't create everything from scratch each time. Higher productivity seems to require a higher amount of convention and structure, and a lower amount of originality. And indeed, the plots of romance novels are more formulaic than many other types of fiction. Many publishers of romance fiction have multiple series of novels, each designed to appeal to a different group of readers. These publishers have strict editorial guidelines for each series, "tip sheets" for writers that specify appropriate plot elements and character types, so that readers will get what they're expecting.

GROUP WRITING

> It is woefully difficult to write a play. A playwright is required by the very nature of drama to enter into the spirit of opposing characters. . . . The job of shifting oneself totally from one character to another . . . is a super-human task at any time.
>
> —Stage director Peter Brook, (1968, p. 33)

The 1970s TV show *M*A*S*H* is typical of how most sitcom episodes are written: not by a single solitary individual, but by a collaborative team of writers. Larry Gelbart was the head writer, but actor Alan Alda frequently collaborated with Gelbart on scripts, and in fact, he himself received writing credit for many of the episodes. The actors would go through the first finished draft of the script line by line and make comments, resulting in revisions before filming. In some cases, script ideas emerged from these discussions. In one episode, Alda's character, Dr. "Hawkeye" Pierce, decides to remove a man's appendix, even though the operation is unnecessary, so that the man won't have to return to the battlefront. One writer rejected this element of the plot, arguing that no good doctor would do such a thing. Mr. Alda argued in response that war sometimes overrode the normal ethics of everyday practice. As the argument continued, the cast collectively realized that the argument itself could be the core of a good script, so they rewrote the script to incorporate the debate into the story (Bennetts, 1986).

A situation comedy is a weekly television episode with approximately 22 minutes of performance time, with advertisements filling out a 30-minute schedule slot. The 22 minutes are broken into two acts, and usually the episode has a story that's resolved by the end of the episode. The scripts are developed by a staff of writers, with the executive producer or "show runner" the head of the team. Some teams have two or three executive producers. Other team members include writers with titles such as supervising producer, producer, executive story editor, and creative consultant. The conceptual outline of an episode is conceived by the entire group, in a meeting where stories are worked out scene by scene. Then each scene is assigned to one or two people who write the dialog. After these scenes are written, two or more rounds of comments and revisions by the team and writers follow. After multiple revisions, each resulting from a collaborative discussion among the writing team, the script is presented to the cast for a *table reading*. The table reading takes place on the stage, with network and studio personnel present, and it often results in suggestions for further revisions to the script. The last revision, called the final polish, is often done by the executive producer, perhaps with help from a few key staff members. Additional rewrites take place through the five days of rehearsal leading up to the final taping of the show, inspired by suggestions from actors or producers. Sometimes these suggestions are experimentally improvised by the cast, as they try out potential changes before sending the script back to the writing team.

In their interviews with comedy writers, Pritzker and Runco (1997) found that some teams were more collaborative than others, and in those teams "a sense of excitement and participation is experienced by everyone" (p. 123), and more creative scripts resulted. The writer Lynn commented on one such group: "It was more of a group thing—somebody having an idea and somebody else in the room adding to the idea and 'How about this?' 'How about that?'" (p. 124).

The collaborative writing style of *M*A*S*H* is typical of television. One reason that collaboration is essential is that each episode is only one in a whole season; the characters' personalities must be consistent, and their dialog has to make sense within the overall trajectory of the season and the series (Pritzker & Runco, 1997, p. 128). A second reason for collaboration is that different writers contribute different skills; some are better at constructing stories, others write good characters, and still others are the best joke writers. In many sitcoms a joke specialist joins the group on the last major rewrite to punch up the show's dialog.

With movie scripts, the process is often even more involved than with sitcoms, and extends over historical time as the script passes through the hands of multiple creative teams (Wolf, 1998). Hollywood types refer to this process as "script development." The script for the Dreamworks 1998 animated film *Small Soldiers* was originally written by Gavin Scott, purchased by Steven Spielberg in 1992, and revised four successive times by Anne Spielberg, Danny Rubin, Frank Deese, and Lewis Colick. Finally, yet another version by Danny Rifkin—this time incorporating Spielberg's suggestion that the soldiers be divided into two opposed factions—was approved for production in 1997. After this long creative process, the final product wasn't even that original. In 2000 Spielberg was sued by Gregory Grant, a short-film maker who alleged that Spielberg stole the plot from his 1991 short animation *Ode to G.I. Joe*; the short film contained similar plot elements of toy soldiers coming to life. Spielberg's production company defended itself by saying that neither of them had been creative; their defense was that the idea of "toy soldiers coming to life" was too generic to copyright.

When filming starts, the script isn't done—in fact, editing and rewriting accelerate. As Wolf (1998) reported, the first writers "merely stand at the head of a conveyor belt designed by producers and studios to precision-tool hits, sending their scripts along for subsequent handling by a small army of additional writers, each one specifically directed to beef up action scenes, to polish dialogue, to throw in some romance" (p. 32). The 1998 asteroid thriller *Armageddon* had eight different writers contributing to various portions of the script, all coming onto the project after the initial script had been developed by Jonathan Hensleigh and sold to producer Jerry Bruckheimer, and after the director and star had been hired. Tony Gilroy (*Devil's Advocate*) did a major rewrite on the first 15 pages of the script, with additional help from Paul Attanasio (*Quiz Show*, *Donnie Brasco*) and Jeffrey Abrams (*Regarding Henry*, *Forever Young*). Abrams then took the script and focused on the back stories of the individual driller-spacemen, and did additional scene work. Ann Biderman (*Smilla's Sense of Snow*) then rewrote the portions of the script relating to the romance between Ben Affleck and Liv Tyler, and also did work on the father–daughter conflict between Tyler and Bruce Willis. Shane Salerno edited and revised several of the action sequences, as Scott Rosenberg (*Beautiful Girls*, *Con Air*) wrote punchy humorous lines for Steve Buscemi and Ben Affleck. Robert Towne—perhaps Hollywood's most famous script doctor, with his fame originating in his credits as the writer of *Chinatown*, *Shampoo*, and others— then rewrote some of the more serious lines in the script that emphasized the world's potential elimination at the hands of the asteroid. During this process, Hensleigh, the original writer, served as a coordinator, collecting the pages of these many writers and cutting and pasting them together.

About 40 elite writers make their careers out of such script work. And there's nothing new to such a system; in the studio system of the 1930s and 1940s, writers were narrowly specialized, with some focusing on plot structure, and others filling in the dialog. Hollywood emphasizes collaboration because it believes that the group process will generate a more creative product than a single writer working alone.

COMPUTER-ASSISTED WRITING

Aspiring Hollywood screenwriters can purchase the software package *Final Draft* to help them write; the product's motto is "Just add words" (www.finaldraft.com [accessed Aug. 25, 2011]). As of July 2005, more than 200,000 copies had been sold. And it's not just for aspiring amateurs; it's been used to write many successful and well-known movies, including all of the *Lord of the Rings* (2001, 2002, 2003) and *Harry Potter* (2001–2011) movies. *Final Draft* has been endorsed by Hollywood insiders from director Oliver Stone to actor Tom Hanks.

What can writing software do for you, if you still have to "just add words"? Of course, it does the usual formatting and spell-checking associated with any word processor, but in addition, *Final Draft* actually supports and guides the creative process of the writer. For example, it contains an intelligent "expert problem solver" that suggests a three-act plot structure, and provides tools to enforce that structure; it supports writers by marking whether a problem is one of plot, character, or structure. Reports can be generated that collect all of a character's lines. It remembers character names, scene headings, and transitions. A "Scene Navigator" supports editing of scene descriptions and action shots. And *Final Draft* supports the collaborative script writing that's so common in movies and television, keeping track of who changed a line and when.

Other software packages also focus on supporting the creative core of the writing process. *Dramatica* provides "story development paths" and "structural templates for creating scenes or chapters" in novels, screenplays, and short stories (www.dramatica.com [accessed Aug. 25, 2011]). A "Story Guide" prompts the aspiring author with questions that lead the author from a basic concept all the way to a completed text. One question the software asks is: "At the end of your story, you want the audience to see your Main Character as having:" and then presents a multiple-choice list of items including "Changed," "Remained Steadfast," and "Skip this question for now." A "Story Engine" allows a small change in the dramatic structure to automatically update related plot elements elsewhere in the story. In their marketing literature, the company shows what the story engine for *The Great Gatsby* would look like: under "Plot Dynamics," the driver is "decision," the limit is "optionlock," the outcome is "failure." Other categories are "Character Dynamics" and "Thematic Choices." A "Character Builder" suggests archetypical characters and lists of personality traits, and can suggest what two characters' relationship should look once you've chosen their traits.

When authors wrote stories with quill pens, no one thought that the pen was a collaborator in the author's creativity; it was just a tool. When typewriters became widespread, they too were considered to be passive, transparent tools. But a software package like *Dramatica* somehow seems to be more than just a tool; it seems to cross a line into being a virtual collaborator. To explain this sort of computer-assisted creativity, we need to know a lot about the software, and we need to know a lot about the step-by-step creative process. We can't explain this creativity just by looking inside the writer's head.

HYPERTEXT AND THE AUDIENCE

The mantra of the so-called postmodern school of literary criticism is that readers create their own texts; the writer is not in control of the readers' response. Prior to postmodernism, the text was thought to be the printed letters on the physical pages of the book—in other words, a visible created product. The author was the creator, and the reader was a passive consumer. Today's postmodernists argue that the writer and reader collaborate to creatively generate the meaning of the work. The pages of the book aren't the created product; after all, they're static and lifeless. The act of reading is performative; the book provides a framework for the reading experience, but doesn't determine that experience. Readers bring books to life through the creative act of reading.

Postmodernism comes to life in a new genre of literature that's been made possible by the personal computer—the hypertext novel (Kakutani, 1997). The computer makes possible any organizational structure for a text; it no longer has to be linear, with one page following the other until the back cover is reached. In a hypertext, each virtual "page" is stored in its own computer file, and the pages are linked according to the author's sense of what story fragments might possibly be connected to what others. When a reader finishes a page, he or she is presented with on-screen buttons that branch in multiple narrative directions. Hypertext fiction has no beginning, middle, or end; the reader chooses where to enter and exit the story, and how to move through the story. After two decades of outsider cult status, hypertext gained a form of establishment legitimacy when several such novels were reviewed in *The New York Review of Books* in 2002 (Parks, 2002).

The hypertext author creates a world, a virtual environment something like a role-playing video game. Many hypertext novels take advantage of the multimedia capabilities of the computer screen, and include graphics and images alongside the text. The author's role is diminished because the reader participates actively in the construction of his or her reading experience.

For almost two decades, fans of hypertext fiction have predicted "a future in which traditional narratives would become obsolete, and discrete, self-contained books would also give way to vast interlinked electronic networks" (Kakutani, 1997, p. 41). There's no reason why each virtual page has to be written by the same author; in the late 1990s, "chain fiction" was invented, in which different segments of the hypertext are written by different authors (Kakutani, 1997, p. 41). These multivocal works make more clear than ever the collaborative nature of writing— collaborations including not only isolated creative geniuses we used to call "writers," but now directly including readers in the creative collaborative process. As Mark Taylor and Esa Saarinen (1994) wrote, "No hypertext is the product of a single author who is its creative origin or heroic architect. To the contrary, in the hypertextual network, all authorship is joint authorship and all production is co-production. Every writer is a reader and all reading is writing" (p. 6).

FAN FICTION

"Fan fiction" is the term for stories by amateur writers about characters from their favorite books, movies, and television shows. Long before the Internet, fan fiction circulated off the radar in obscure "zines," a now-obsolete term referring to small-print-run magazines usually generated with a mimeograph machine or a photocopier. Some of the earliest fan fiction was derived from the 1960s TV series *Star Trek*. The subgenres of fan fiction can get fairly elaborate; for example; "K/S fandom" refers to short stories that posit a sexual relationship between Captain Kirk and Spock; this genre originated in England in the late 1960s, and as of 2010 was circulated through the website beyonddreamspress.com (accessed Aug. 25, 2011). K/S is a subgenre of "Slash fiction," which refers to any fan fiction about same-sex relationships between fictional characters. (In contrast to K/S, the subgenre of "K&S" refers to fan fiction where Kirk and Spock are just friends.)

The website fanfiction.net carries fan fiction for just about any media property you can think of (accessed Aug. 25, 2011). A partial list as of September 2010 included *Lord of the Rings*, *Ghostbusters*, *M*A*S*H*, *Friday the 13th*, and *Calvin & Hobbes*. One of the most popular genres of fan fiction in the early 21st century was Harry Potter. Some of these authors are attracting mainstream success, with thousands of readers, and even getting book deals.

A librarian in Rathdrum, Ohio, spent ten years writing stories for the Internet about a character from Jane Austen's *Pride and Prejudice*. Simon & Schuster became aware of her work, and paid her a $150,000 advance to publish the stories in a series of three books. In Brooklyn, NY, a freelance copy editor became one of the most popular fan fiction writers of *Lord of the Rings* and Harry Potter stories; he received a three-book deal for a young adult fantasy series (Jurgensen, 2006).

Some typical patterns tend to recur in fan fiction. Many stories are prequels that explore the earlier history of important characters. Also common are *crossovers*, which combine characters from very different books—such as the Calvin character from the Calvin & Hobbes cartoon moving to England and becoming a wizarding student at Hogwarts ("The best seven years," at fanfiction.net). *Shippers* invent relationships between characters; the genre of "Slash" I described earlier is a subgenre of "Shipper."

In an earlier era, the publishing houses might have brought lawsuits against fan fiction writers for unauthorized use of their intellectual property. Now, the publishers mostly consider the activity to benefit their sales by increasing customer interest. The original authors usually feel flattered. However, publishers advise their authors not to read fan fiction that's based on their own works, because if they later write a sequel, one of these fans might claim that the real author stole one of his or her fake story plot lines.

Fan fiction is another example of the sociocultural process of creativity over time. Each work builds on prior works; nothing is completely original. With fan fiction, this is more obvious, but it's always the case. The proliferation of genres and subgenres is an emergent social process; once these subgenres are in place, the boundaries tend to be policed rather carefully. Readers choose what to read based on their favorite genres and subgenres. The Internet has accelerated these natural social processes of creativity and brought them into the mainstream.

WHAT LASTS: POSTHUMOUS PUBLICATION

After the death of a well-known and respected writer, what factors play a role in the posthumous development of a reputation? Most of us would say it's the body of work published by the writer during his or her lifetime; good work will eventually be recognized for its worth. In contrast, the sociocultural approach would argue that reputation is determined by the cooperative evaluation of the art world—social processes that continue even after the death of the author.

Posthumous publication is a tried-and-true way of keeping a deceased writer in the public eye. For example, there have been as many books published by writer Raymond Carver after his death as during his lifetime. Several of these posthumous short stories were found in unfinished form, by Tess Gallagher and Jay Woodruff, who transcribed them from typescripts and hand-written drafts (Campbell, 2009). Virginia Woolf's works have been published far more after her death, because her letters and diaries were released by her estate and eventually filled up over 30 volumes.

Some writers try to plan ahead for their career after death: Henry James rewrote his own books to be re-released after his death, and Norman Mailer left plans for an anthology of his greatest works that was released after his death. One way to influence history's opinion is to pick a good biographer. An official biographer is granted privileged access to original documents like letters and draft manuscripts, and other writers are forbidden to see such materials. These careful plans don't always work like the author might have hoped. Robert Frost selected his friend Lawrence Thompson as his biographer, but Thompson had begun to think less of Frost even before he'd passed on. Thomas Hardy chose a devious way to control his posthumous reputation: he secretly wrote his own biography and instructed his wife to release it under her name after his death.

Another common way to control your future reputation is by selectively destroying your files and papers so that only the most flattering stuff remains. Writers often establish exclusive arrangements for storage of their papers, negotiating the best deals with university libraries across the country. Saul Bellow has his papers at the University of Chicago; Toni Morrison's are at Princeton. Writers frequently spend years of their retirement selecting and ordering the materials. Their final creative act is the creation of their future reputation.

Some writers go to an extreme, burning every last paper in the attempt to prevent future generations from looking past the published work itself. After all, they reason, "During my lifetime I released exactly what I wanted published, and that's my gift to posterity; if I'd wanted my private papers released, I could have done so during my own lifetime and benefited from royalties on sales." Franz Kafka famously instructed his friend Max Brod to burn all his work "even to the last page"; in the end, Brod could not bring himself to carry out the instruction. Critics and readers are grateful the manuscripts exist, but that they do is Brod's choice and not Kafka's. Some executors make these selection decisions on their own. Ted Hughes, widower of Sylvia Plath, destroyed the last volume of her diary after her 1963 suicide, intending to protect their two children from further anguish. Lord Byron's friends burned his X-rated memoirs, fearing a scandal should they ever be printed.

Fans and relatives of deceased writers do all they can to build up a writer's reputation. Usually, the writer's spouse or another family member becomes the official executor of the estate and has complete control over the writer's letters, diaries, and manuscripts. The executor makes all of the above decisions—what will be published posthumously, who'll be the official biographer, where the archives will be stored. Without the executor's permission, the archival materials can't be quoted.

We can't explain historical reputation by looking only at the work, or only at the writer's personality. Reputation is collaboratively managed and it emerges from a sociocultural process.

THE DOMAIN OF WRITING

There are three rules for writing a novel. Unfortunately, no one knows what they are.
—W. Somerset Maugham (1874–1965) (quoted in Byrne, 1996, 3:490)

One of the most valuable insights of the sociocultural approach is that you can't create in a vacuum. In Chapter 14, we learned that the domain of culture is like the air that supports the wings of a flying bird; even though the bird might curse the wind because its friction slows her down, without the wind there could be no flight. In Chapter 11, we learned that creativity always takes place in a domain. The best metaphor for the domain is everyday language. You can't talk at all unless you've learned a language—the vocabulary, syntax, and idioms that you share with the other members of your culture. But just because you're all using the same language, it doesn't mean that you can never talk creatively. In the same way, the conventions of a creative domain enable the possibility of creativity.

The writers interviewed by Csikszentmihalyi (1996) all emphasize the importance of immersing themselves in the domain of the word. Writers, it seems, read more voraciously than anyone else. Many writing teachers say that their single most important piece of advice is to read constantly.

Can one be an "outsider writer"? It seems a contradiction in terms. After all, the definition of an outsider artist is someone who doesn't follow the conventions of a domain, but all writers follow the conventions of the language they use, the conventions of word meanings and grammar. The closest we could come to outsider writing would be a self-taught person who didn't actively participate in the field of creative writing. In 2002, Henry Louis Gates reported that he had purchased, at auction, the manuscript of a novel called *The Bondwoman's Narrative*, written by the slave Hannah Crafts in 1850 (Crafts, 2002; Gates, 2002). Prior to the Civil War there was an entire genre of slave narratives that were published and widely read; *Uncle Tom's Cabin* is the most famous. But this was the first original, pre-edited manuscript ever discovered. Crafts was an African-American slave when she wrote the novel, and it was lost, unread, in storage for over a century.

Slaves were forbidden to read and write, so Crafts certainly qualifies as being self-taught. And by being on the margins of society, Crafts seems to meet many of the other criteria now associated with outsiders. But even this apparently "outside" writer did not generate a completely novel, unconventional text. Gates's analysis of the novel revealed that it was, if anything, even more conventional than most novels of the time, and that it borrowed heavily from popular and widely available fiction of the era. For example, throughout Crafts' novel, there are entire passages lifted verbatim from several of Charles Dickens's novels (researchers have discovered that her master's library contained three of Dickens's novels). And the themes, characters, and events in the novel closely follow other popular fiction of the day.

This example suggests that there can never be an outsider writer. Paradoxically, the more outside you are, the more conventional your writing will be. Our individualist conceptions often lead us to believe that writers are more naïve, more self-taught, more inspired than they actually are. And many writers, editors, and publicists are only too happy to have us believe. But the truth is that writers always work in a sociocultural system, collaborating with members of the field, working with the conventions of the domain.

THE DEATH OF THE AUTHOR

A seminar essay by French literary theorist Roland Barthes, published in 1967, was titled "The Death of the Author." In it, he demolished the Western cultural view of the suffering, lone genius:

> The Author is thought to nourish the book, which is to say that he exists before it, thinks, suffers, lives for it . . . in complete contrast, the modern scriptor is born simultaneously with the text, is in no way equipped with a being preceding or exceeding the writing.

Barthes went on to present a view of literature as almost exclusively collaborative, imitative, and derivative: a text is "a multi-dimensional space in which a variety of writings, none of them original, blend and clash. The text is a tissue of quotations drawn from the innumerable centers of culture . . . the writer can only imitate a gesture . . . his only power is to mix writings, to counter the ones with the others." Barthes' view became gospel among post-structuralist, post-Marxist literary theorists through the 1970s, 1980s, and 1990s. Terry Eagleton called this the "dethronement" of the creative author (see discussion in Pope, 2005, pp. 7–10). Barthes' claim was that the author's identity or intended meaning was irrelevant to textual interpretation. This line of thought contributed to the influential *reader response theory* (Iser, 1978); Iser argued that a literary text provides only a rough guideline to the reader; the reader's job is to create an aesthetic experience by interacting with the text. The even more radical Stanley Fish (1980) argued that there is *nothing* in the text that is not put there by the reader.

These literary theorists may have seemed radical back in the 1970s, but the recent growth of hypertext fiction and fan fiction seems to fit beautifully with their claims. And they also align with the historical examples of writer collaboration I've summarized in this chapter, from T. S. Eliot to Raymond Carver. Even older examples of collaborative writing include the committee of about 50 men who composed the King James Bible (Nicolson, 2006); The Inklings, a writer's collaborative at Oxford University that included C. S. Lewis and J. R. R. Tolkien (Farrell, 2001); and even Shakespeare's plays, which were almost certainly collaboratively generated by the entire theater ensemble (Sawyer, 2009b).

But as a psychologist, it seems to me that these theorists go a bit too far in attributing all literary creativity to impersonal social and historical forces. They were a bit too influenced by Marxist and Hegelian social theories that attribute all creative force to history. (Many literary theorists have also began to retreat from such radical claims; see Eagleton, 2003; Pope, 2005.) I believe that individual psychological processes are a key component of writing creativity; the complete explanation will be interdisciplinary, bringing together individualist and sociocultural approaches.

KEY CONCEPTS

- The role of editing in the writing process
- The role of conscious thought and hard work
- The oral and theatrical origins of the written word
- Show runners, table readings, and Hollywood script writing
- Computer-assisted writing
- Hypertext
- Fan fiction
- The death of the author

THOUGHT EXPERIMENTS

- How often do you revise when you write?
- Do you write better at some times of the day than others?
- Do you prepare an outline before you start to write?
- Have you ever edited or been edited? What was it like? Did it improve the final product?
- Have you ever written poetry or fiction? Why? Did anyone read it?

SUGGESTED READINGS

Csikszentmihalyi, M. (1996). *Creativity: Flow and the psychology of discovery and invention.* New York: HarperCollins. [See especially Chapter 10]

Eliot, V. (1971). *T. S. Eliot The waste land: A facsimile and transcript of the original drafts including the annotations of Ezra Pound.* New York: Harcourt Brace Jovanovich.

Lamott, A. (1994). *Bird by bird: Some instructions on writing and life.* New York: Pantheon Books.

Max, D. T. (1998, Aug. 9). The Carver chronicles. *The New York Times Magazine,* 34–40, 51, 56–57.

Pritzker, S., & Runco, M. A. (1997). The creative decision-making process in group situation comedy writing. In R. K. Sawyer (Ed.), *Creativity in performance* (pp. 115–141). Norwood, NJ: Ablex.

CHAPTER 18

MUSIC

All art constantly aspires towards the condition of music.

—Walter Pater, 1873/1986, p. 86

Many people think that jazz musicians play whatever comes into their heads in a burst of unconstrained inspiration. But even the freest improviser plays within a musical tradition, and before you can improvise you have to learn that tradition (Alperson, 1984; Berliner, 1994). Young jazz musicians become aware of the structures and conventions of their domain through close listening. For example, they often listen to famous albums and copy the performances note for note. This helps them to develop a personal repertoire of phrases; sometimes, young improvisers sound just like the famous musician they've been copying. Trumpet players sound like Miles Davis or Wynton Marsalis, saxophonists like Coleman Hawkins or John Coltrane. No doubt, it takes a high level of skill to sound like a famous musician. But that's only the first step in a lifetime of learning how to play jazz.

Listening and practicing at home is an important part of learning jazz. But young musicians who have wonderful technique on their instruments, who can play extremely fast and flawlessly, often tend to be poor improvisers, because they haven't yet learned how to communicate musically with the ensemble. Musicians can't learn jazz by playing at home alone. To get really good, a musician has to attend uncountable jam sessions, and play in many different beginner bands (Berliner, 1994).

The late 20th century experienced an incredible flowering of musical creativity. In the 1950s popular music genres were limited pretty much to jazz and rock'n' roll. Even in the 1970s, record stores had perhaps three or four sections: classical, rock, jazz, or rhythm and blues. But by the 1990s, your run-of-the-mill mall music store had 20, 30, or more genres available, from reggae to world music to metal to trip hop. With the development of electronica, boundaries between genres began to fall; in electronica, computer-savvy producers use digital sampling to combine a century of American pop music in a single song.

Popular music has more in common with jazz than it does with high-status classical music. Like jazz, pop music is often improvised and performance-oriented, composers are not valorized as the sole creators of the tradition, and scores are rarely written down for later performance. Cultural critics from Theodor Adorno (2002) to Alan Bloom (1987) have attacked popular music from across the ideological spectrum—Marxism in Adorno's case, conservative American values in Bloom's case. But these criticisms often seem to be based in snobbish prejudice, derived from the ethnocentric assumption that European classical music is the standard of quality.

In this chapter, I'll explore musical creativity by comparing composition and performance. Explanations of musical creativity tend to emphasize one at the expense of the other. Our Western cultural model does a better job of explaining composition; we can easily imagine a composer alone in a room, working in a fever of half-crazed hard work, the lone genius of our romantic myth. The cultural model doesn't work as well with performance, because performance is deeply social, with an audience and co-performers. We've learned throughout this book that the Western cultural model has influenced creativity researchers as much as it has everyone else, and that may be why creativity researchers have focused on the creativity of composition rather than the creativity of performance (Sawyer, 1997a). To explain performance creativity, we need an interdisciplinary approach, one that combines both individualist and sociocultural perspectives. And once you realize how performance creativity works, you see that composition, too, requires an interdisciplinary explanation.

It's too simple to say that all pop music is improvised and all classical music is composed. For example, in a review of a performance by jazz pianist Ray Bryant, Hollenberg (1978) noted that his solos on two successive nights were note-for-note identical, and wrote: "Some of the freest sounding pieces of the evening were the most mechanical" (p. 42). Bryant isn't the only musician to use precomposed solos; many famous jazz improvisers have occasionally repeated solos note for note, including Jelly Roll Morton, several of Duke Ellington's soloists, and Oscar Peterson (Brown, 1981).

How could a composed piece sound more free and spontaneous than pieces that actually are improvised? Famous European composers including Bach and Beethoven were legendary improvisers, and many of them wrote compositions that were designed to sound like improvisations. These pieces are called "fantasias" or "impromptus," and Bach's fantasias are thought to be pretty close to written-out improvisations. Paradoxically, it takes a lot of compositional effort to create a work that sounds improvised.

Even more so than in jazz, many rock and pop performers compose their solos in advance. Unlike jazz, with a subculture that valorizes pure improvisation, rock lead guitarists don't mind admitting that they compose their solos. In interviews in *Guitar Magazine*, precomposed solos were often published, in detailed musical notation, alongside the interview. Like a Bach fantasia, even though the solos are composed, they sound improvised because they're composed according to the conventions of improvisation.

COMPOSITION

It's been said that different composers have different working styles. Some of them are said to compose in quick bursts, without any preparation or revision, so that the compositional process is essentially like an improvisation. Mozart and Schubert are often said to have composed in this manner. However, this common observation is a Romantic-era myth, without supporting historical evidence. In the last chapter we learned that Romantic poets like Coleridge made up stories about how they created their poems so that their creative process would seem consistent with the creativity beliefs of the day. In the 19th century, composers and their fans made up similar stories. For example, since the 1960s scholars have known that Mozart's creative process was controlled by a consistently practical approach to the business aspects of music; his manuscripts show evidence of careful editing, revision, and hard work (Sloboda, 1985, pp. 112–114).

Almost all famous composers engage in long periods of preparation and frequent revision. Brahms took 20 years to write his first symphony. Max Bruch's *Violin Concerto no. 1 in G Minor*, his most popular work, was rewritten almost 10 times between 1864 and 1868, including revisions after its first public performance (Schiavo, 2001). Bach's *St. Matthew Passion* was first performed in 1727, but Bach continued to revise the work over the next ten years, eventually resulting in the version that's performed today (Dennett, 1995, p. 511). Like all creativity, musical composition is 99% hard work and only 1% inspiration, and that 1% is sprinkled throughout the creative process in frequent mini-insights that are always embedded in the conscious hard work under way. Great music is rarely created in a Romantic burst of inspiration.

As we've learned in prior chapters, the Western fine arts traditions tend to be the most consistent with the Western cultural model of creativity. Like painting or poetry, classical music composition seems at first glance to be an activity that is done in private, by a solitary genius. And again, this is why creativity researchers, like other Americans, first think of these genres when they begin to study musical creativity. But if we want to develop a scientific explanation of musical creativity, we can't limit our study to European classical music. A scientific explanation must encompass all creativity, and most important, the genres of musical creativity that are most widespread and most influential in our lives. In the following sections, I'll talk about the way composition *really* happens in today's music. You'll see that it has little in common with the Hollywood image of Mozart as fictionalized in the movie *Amadeus*, writing in his sickbed in a fever of inspired creativity.

COMPOSITION IN THE RECORDING STUDIO

In the latter half of the 20th century, a significant burst of musical creativity took place in the pop arena—jazz, rock, soul, rhythm and blues, disco, and country. These songs aren't composed by solitary artists, and they're not written down. Instead, they're created as a work in progress by the entire band, working collaboratively in the studio. Phil Collins described *Genesis*'s composition process as completely improvisational; entering the studio, they would have nothing written down. Keith Strickland of the B-52s also described an improvisational rehearsal process (both quoted in Boyd, 1992). If a member of the band is credited as the writer of the song, he or she typically does no more than suggest the melodic line for the voice, the overall chord structure of the song, and the general style or genre of the piece. He or she presents that to the band, and then the individual musicians are expected to create parts for their own instruments. Their first attempts are then critically discussed by all of the band members, as musicians offer suggestions to one another.

Every musician who's experienced the tedious business of the studio knows how much hard work it is. Very few music fans are aware of the collaborative studio work that results in a popular music recording. However, a few bands have such strong cult followings that fans illegally acquire studio tapes—which contain conversation among band members, aborted first performances, warts and all—and actively trade the tapes with like-minded fans. Some widely bootlegged bands include the Grateful Dead, Bob Dylan, and the Beatles. These bootleg copies are illegal, but without being able to stop the phenomenon, record companies sometimes respond by formally releasing the most widely copied bootleg tapes on CD. In 1975, Columbia released *The Basement Tapes* with private rehearsal tapes of Bob Dylan that had been circulating for six years; in 1996 the Beatles released the six-disc *Anthology* that contained over eight hours of material, including long-circulated bootleg favorites (Kozinn, 1997).

Bootlegs provide important insights into musical creativity because we can hear how the band experimented with other versions of each song. Some of these are radically different from the version that was eventually released to the public. A pop hit becomes so embedded in a fan's brain that it seems almost a sacrilege to imagine that even a single note could have been any different. That's why bootleg recordings provide an important perspective: they make us aware of the selection processes that bands and producers go through as they decide what gets released to the public. The bootlegs make it clear that a band experiments with many different versions of a song, and may have many potentially final and releasable versions—yet they must select only one to release. The selection process is collaborative and collective, sociocultural rather than psychological.

Many finished songs are never released because there's no room left on the album or because the producer or record company decides that they won't sell enough copies to earn back the costs of production. In June 2002, the CD *A Cellar Full of Motown* was released, containing 40 fully formed singles recorded in the 1960s at the legendary Motown studio in Detroit. Although these singles were polished and ready to go, they were never released because producer Berry Gordy and the rest of the staff felt they weren't as good as the other songs that were released, and they didn't want to flood the market with too many new songs in any given year. Motown under Berry Gordy recorded many more singles than it could ever hope to successfully market. Although this might seem inefficient, it provided him with a pool of material to choose from, and he believed that this would ultimately result in more hits. When I listen to these long-lost songs today, they sound not only stylistically similar but also equal in quality to the Top 40 Motown hits that we all know so well, the ones that were released instead.

How were these 40 singles selected for the new CD from the much larger number of recordings on these basement tapes? To explain the selection, we have to look beyond the individual tastes of record company executives. For years, many of these singles had been illegally copied and widely traded among cult fans, particularly in the northern part of England, which had a network of clubs known as the "Northern Soul" scene. The Northern Soul scene was its own field, which created a new domain of 1960s soul recordings that had never been officially sold. Like much of pop culture, the initial selection was done not by the powerful gatekeepers, but by a collective grassroots emergent process. The record company made sure that these cult favorites were on the CD because they hoped that the underground scene would buy the new recordings. The selection process that picked these 40 singles was truly a distributed, social, collective process.

ELECTRONICA

Perhaps the most significant new musical genre of the 1990s was the underground genre known as "techno" or "electronica." Both are umbrella terms that uncomfortably cover a wide range of very different-sounding styles of music, and like many cultish underground scenes, insiders have created a dizzying number of terms for subgenres: house, deep house, ambient, trip hop, drum and bass. What they all share isn't so much the formal features of the music, but their method of composition.

Our mental image of a pop music composer is a pianist trying out different melodies on the keyboard, or a guitarist strumming different chords to see what sounds good. But many electronica composers don't play musical instruments and can't even read music. How can such a person create music? Electronica artists do it by digitally recording or "sampling" segments of already recorded music, building up a personal library of interesting samples on their computers' hard drives, and then using computer software to repeat the samples in loops, overlaying multiple tracks to create a polyphonic blend of sounds.

The most admired electronica songs are those that bring together the most unlikely combinations of musical genres, blending samples of 1930s field-hand chants with 1950s tiki lounge, with a sprinkling of 1960s pop orchestra swells. Electronica artist Moby, who has perhaps enjoyed the greatest popular success of any such artist, said, "I want to have the broadest possible sonic palette to draw on when I'm composing music. I wanted to hear pop records, dance records, classical records . . . On my records, I'm the composer and the musician and the engineer, but also a plagiarist and thief" (quoted in Marzorati, 2002, p. 35). Moby typically creates over 100 songs for each of his CDs, even though he knows that no more than 15 or 20 could possibly fit (Marzorati, 2002). Like Motown, he creates many more songs than the market could support, and this means that a lot of his creativity is applied at the selection stage.

The contrast with America's contemporary image of the pop musician couldn't be greater. Since the 1960s, American culture has placed a high value on a musician's authenticity. Through the 1950s, vocalists recorded songs by nameless writers that were selected by their producers. But in the 1960s this changed. Audiences began to insist that musicians write their own songs, and they wanted each song to talk about a musician's personal experience. And it went without saying that musicians would play their own instruments live, and not use any previously recorded material. Many electronica artists reject this model as obsolete. As Moby put it, "What's stranger at this point in time, given the technology and all, than a band where everybody plays one instrument, and you get one kind of music, song after song, album after album?" (quoted in Marzorati, 2002, p. 36).

Electronica composers begin by first collecting a large library of sounds—typically from other albums, but also from news reports, training films, or everyday sounds like fire alarms and cement mixers. These are all digitized and stored in a computer, and the compositional process then involves listening to and thinking about which might sound good together, and experimenting using multitrack computer sound studio software. The creative process begins to seem more like fiction writing, because writers keep notebooks and write every idea that pops into their heads—one paragraph or one character sketch at a time—and later blend and combine these bits to construct a complex story.

TRIBUTE BANDS

Popular songs act as an everyday soundtrack for each new generation of high-school and college students. But they aren't compositions in the classical music sense. The creators don't write the songs down on music paper and then hand them out to the members of the band. Instead, they're created through collaborative, performative, improvisational processes during rehearsals. Bootleg tapes or CDs, if they exist, can provide the aficionado with a window onto this collaborative compositional process. But once the master tape is finished and hundreds of thousands of CDs are manufactured and sold, the song becomes a fixed product; if anything, even more invariant than a Beethoven score.

Bands that perform the famous songs of successful bands are called cover bands or tribute bands. Their goal is to perform, live, a song that has been composed by another band, and to have their performance sound as much like the recorded composition as possible. Some bands spawn more tribute bands than others; there are probably more Grateful Dead tribute bands than for every other band combined. Other widely covered bands include Guns N' Roses and Rush.

In the past ten years, with the rapid growth of videogames, several bands have formed to perform, live, the music that accompanies the most popular videogames. As of 2010, some of the best-known of these band names included Powerglove, The Advantage, The Minibosses, and Vomitron. This is bigger business than you might think; one of my own cousins was in a band you've never heard of that made $50,000 selling CDs of videogame songs on the Internet. These bands are often invited to perform, live, at videogame conventions.

Tribute bands get little respect from serious music critics; they seem to be nothing more than wannabe rock stars, basking in reflected glory. Some may ask, "Why don't they write their own songs and perform them instead?" But they're doing the same thing as a modern symphony orchestra performing a written composition by Beethoven or Brahms. No one thinks to ask, "Why is the orchestra performing a song written by someone else? Why doesn't each city's orchestra write its own new music?" The most common answer would probably be that it's OK to replicate Beethoven's music because it is uniquely brilliant, but it's not OK to replicate late-20th-century pop music because it's not worthy. But we can't accept these subjective judgments as scientific explanations. When a band called Paradise City performs a Guns N' Roses song (Klosterman, 2002), it's a modern version of the St. Louis Symphony performing Beethoven's Ninth.

One clear difference is how the song is stored for history. Hundreds of years ago, there was no audio recording or multitrack studio technology. Composers had to create a written score using musical notation because it was the only way to preserve a song for posterity. Modern pop music instead takes advantage of recording technology and uses the sound studio itself to compose the song. You no longer need a score because the sound recording preserves the original composition more accurately than a written score ever could.

THE AUDIENCE AS COLLABORATOR

An interactive orchestral work, 3D Music, was written specifically for the Internet. It "plays" very much like a videogame (http://www.braunarts.com/3dmusic/ [accessed Aug. 26, 2011]). The work has seven "spaces" or virtual environments, and the "player/listener" chooses which spaces to enter and when. Each space has its own composed section. The player hears different music depending on where his or her on-screen character is, and which direction the player is moving to and from. You can't sit back and passively listen to this performance; you have to actively participate in its creation. Listening to 3D Music is more like playing a videogame than sitting quietly and letting the music wash over you. Listeners (or "users"?) interact with the music just like readers interact with the hypertext novels that we learned about in Chapter 17. When a composer shares control over a work's structure with the listener, our traditional notions of a composition as a fixed created product are challenged. With 3D Music, there's no authentic, authoritative version of the work. Each time it's heard, it's different, and every occasion of performance is equally authoritative.

We don't need to look at advanced computer technology to see audience influence on the compositional creative process; audiences influence musical creation indirectly all the time. For example, much of popular music is created to respond to the demands and tastes of radio listeners and major advertisers. If a radio station attracts more listeners because they like the songs that the radio station is playing, advertisers will pay more money to the station to advertise to those listeners. Country music stations, in particular, are big business. They're money-making machines, with the money coming from big advertisers. Country has been the top radio format in the United States since the late 1990s; around 20% of all radio stations play country. Yet most of country's classic artists and styles—bluegrass, country and western, western swing—are never heard on these stations. Even after the bluegrass soundtrack to the 2002 film *O Brother, Where Art Thou?* won a Grammy award, the songs on it weren't played on country stations. Why not?

Anyone paying attention to country radio's changes over the past 10 or 20 years has probably noticed that the songs are no longer about drinking and fast women—topics for men—but they're instead songs about sassy women, telling off their no-good men. The explanation for this shift starts not with the musicians, but with the major advertisers. The companies that pay for advertising time on country radio stations are the people who really control what gets played on country radio. In a sense, they're the creators of contemporary country. And "contemporary country radio is targeting young adult females," said Paul Allen, the executive director of the Country Radio Broadcasters, a trade association (quoted in Strauss, 2002, p. AR31). It's a soundtrack for suburban soccer moms, a desirable audience for consumer household goods producers such as Procter & Gamble. Young adult females influence 90% of all of the buying decisions in the household, and they haven't yet made up their minds which brands they like best. The audience research company Arbitron issued a report recently on what women want from country radio: they want family-friendly, upbeat, optimistic songs. And what radio executive won't give it to them, when their major advertisers are reading the same Arbitron report?

Unlike some other musical genres—like alternative rock or rap—country songs are still produced by an assembly-line process that has its roots in postwar Nashville (see the section later in this chapter, p. 354). Songs are written by anonymous writers; then star singers, together with their managers, search through these for a potential hit. Given this creative collaborative process—where singers are not associated with specific themes, and they're not expected to be singing about their own personal experiences—it's easy for artists to shift their songs to suit shifts in consumer taste. Country radio is a microcosm of today's entertainment industry, showing us how the mass audience collectively contributes to the creative process.

PERFORMANCE

> *There is in principle no difference between the performance of a modern orchestra or chorus and people sitting around a campfire and singing to the strumming of a guitar or a congregation singing hymns under the leadership of the organ. And there is no difference in principle between the performance of a string quartet and the improvisations at a jam session of accomplished jazz players.*
>
> —Alfred Schutz, (1964, p. 177)

To explain performance, we have to focus on the creative process rather than the created product. Composition is a creative activity that results in a created product, like a musical score or a studio recording; performance is temporary, and exists only while the band is playing. As we learned in Chapters 3 and 4, the first wave of creativity research focused on created products and creative personalities, and this led to a neglect of performance. In Chapters 5 through 7, we learned that the second wave of cognitive psychologists shifted the focus to the creative process, but they continued to focus on the process of creating products, leading to sequential stage theories that don't explain performance very well. In the 1980s and 1990s, the third wave of sociocultural researchers shifted the focus to processes of performance, and now we have a more comprehensive explanation of performance creativity.

In the European fine art tradition, performers aren't supposed to be creative; European classical music composers hate it when performers interpret their works creatively. Igor Stravinsky spoke for all composers when he stated his expectations: "Only through the performer is the listener brought in contact with the musical work. In order that the public may know what a work is like and what its value is, the public must first be assured of the merit of the person who presents the work to it and of the conformity of that presentation to the composer's will" (Stravinsky, 1947, pp. 132–133). According to Stravinsky, performers must be modest and remove their own individuality from the performance; their job is to communicate another creator's vision faithfully, not to be creative themselves. Because the Western cultural model equates creativity and novelty, it's not surprising that we don't think performers are as creative as composers.

If the ideal performer is a transparent window to the mind of the creator, then with modern recording and computer technology, who needs the performer at all? Composers can easily create their work in a computer program that will synthetically produce all of the necessary sounds, and they can record the composition on a CD on their own computer. Some contemporary composers do this, but most still write in the old-fashioned way—generating scores that will be performed later by specialists in instrumental performance. Even European classical music composers still prefer to have their music performed by real, live musicians. This suggests that Stravinsky's view is a bit extreme, that many composers believe that the variation of human performance is an important part of musical creativity.

Our prototype of the mythic composer is one of the three B's: Beethoven, Bach, or Brahms. These composers wrote scores that specified every note to be played, and added instructions for how to perform the notes—indicating which passages should be played louder, which notes should stand out, and when the tempo should speed up or slow down. From the medieval period to today, the amount of detail specified in a composer's score has changed dramatically (Grout & Palisca, 1996; Malm, 1975; Parrish, 1957). When music notation first emerged, it was meant only for experienced professionals who were likely to know the piece by heart already, and who used the notation only for occasional reminders. Then notation went through a historical process of increasing prescriptiveness, as the group of performers increased in number to include amateurs in addition to full-time professionals—as happened in musical performance in Europe over the past few centuries, with the rise of a middle class, the decreasing cost of musical instruments resulting from the Industrial Revolution, and the decreasing cost involved in printing musical scores.

Many of the most famous piano composers performed their own works during their lifetimes, and they no doubt knew their own pieces very well. Chopin was a famous virtuoso performer, and during his lifetime, it wasn't quite the same to hear another pianist play a work by Chopin. Think back to that time; imagine you're a very good amateur pianist, and you've purchased the published score of a Chopin piece. But then you attend one of his concerts and you discover that he plays it differently than it's written. Which version would you say is the right one—the one you bought two years before, or the live version performed by the composer himself? Your answer depends on whether you value performance or composition more.

Today's virtuoso performers are rarely composers; instead, they perform compositions by others. If a piano composer doesn't perform her own works, we don't think she's less creative, because we associate the creativity with the composing, not the performing. In the Western cultural model, the creation of the work is where the action is, and the performance is simply an execution of the work. But there have been many time periods and genres of music when the composer didn't specify in such detail what the performer was supposed to do. Virtuoso performers from the Renaissance through the 19th century embellished and improvised on the composer's score (Dart, 1967; Reese, 1959). In those days, the composer contributed a lesser percentage to the final performance, and more of the creativity came from the performer. Many 20th-century composers in the European tradition, including John Cage and Karlheinz Stockhausen, have reintroduced elements of improvisation into their works.

Perhaps the most important example of performance creativity is found in jazz. Miles Davis is credited as the composer of many of the songs on the seminal 1959 album *Kind of Blue*. But the song "Freddie the Freeloader," for example, is only the barest outline of a performance, and was composed to provide the performers with a framework on which to improvise. In general, the jazz community doesn't defer to the composer or to the original version when deciding how to perform a classic jazz standard. Rather, jazz performers are expected to contribute so much to the piece that the original piece may become almost unrecognizable. Needless to say, such license would constitute sacrilege in a symphony hall today—even though 200 years ago, an audience in the same hall might have rightly been outraged if the famous guest pianist didn't improvise during the performance.

IMPROVISATION

Group jazz performance is perhaps the best-known improvisational performance form in American culture. Each performance begins with a song, more or less arranged in advance, and quickly progresses to group improvisation, where each musician takes a turn improvising a solo on the initial song form. During solos, the soloist is the primary improviser; the remainder of the group is expected to direct their improvisations so that they support the soloist by reinforcing his or her creative ideas or suggesting new ideas to stimulate his or her playing.

Monson's 1996 book *Saying Something* analyzed many such examples, along with transcribed musical notation that demonstrated in wonderful detail how musicians converse in a jazz improvisation. Monson described an interview with drummer Ralph Peterson in which she played a tape of a live performance of Peterson's composition "Princess" with pianist Geri Allen and bassist Essiet Okon Essiet. During Allen's solo, Peterson's drum accompaniment was very dense, and there were several instances in which Allen and Peterson traded ideas with each other. Monson and Peterson sat together and listened closely to the tape. Monson recognized that one of the conversational exchanges seemed to be based on the distinctive, catchy pattern from Dizzy Gillespie's famous performance of "Salt Peanuts," and noted this to Peterson. He replied:

> Yeah! "Salt Peanuts" and "Looney Tunes"—kind of a combination of the two. [Drummer] Art Blakey has a thing he plays. It's like: [he sings a rhythmic phrase from the song]. And [pianist] Geri played: [he sings Allen's standard response]. So I played the second half of the Art Blakey phrase: [he sings the second part of Blakey's drum pattern]. (Monson, 1996, p. 77)

Geri Allen immediately recognized the musical quotation from her performances with Blakey, and then responded with her usual response, indicating that she recognized and appreciated Peterson's communication (musical transcripts can be found in Monson, 1996, pp. 78–79). As in this example, musical communication in jazz depends on all of the musicians knowing the jazz language extremely well—not only the notes of the songs, but even knowing how a certain performer typically plays a certain song with a specific other performer. Peterson then told Monson:

> But you see what happens is, a lot of times when you get into a musical conversation, one person in the group will state an idea or the beginning of an idea and another person will complete the idea or their interpretation of the same idea, how they hear it. So the conversation happens in fragments and comes from different parts, different voices. (Monson, 1996, p. 78)

At many points in group improvisation, rather than developing his or her own musical ideas or starting a completely new idea, each musician continues in the spirit or mood established by the prior players (Berliner, 1994, pp. 369–370). Rufus Reid told Paul Berliner how he tries to weave in the prior soloist's ideas into his own solo, but not always in an obvious way, and not always by direct quotation; he said it was more interesting to elaborate on the prior idea. In the musical conversation of jazz, as in a good everyday conversation, players borrow material from the previous phrase and then build on it.

Becker (2000) described the "etiquette" of improvisation, drawing an analogy between musical interaction and the informal and implicit rules of good social conduct. Sometimes the etiquette specifies opposed goals that are in tension. For example, jazz is democratic music, and all musicians should have the freedom to express themselves. But at the same time, players depend on one another and have to rein in their individual freedom for the good of the group.

When one performer introduces a new idea, the other performers evaluate it immediately, determining whether or not the performance will shift to incorporate the proposed new idea. The evaluation of new musical ideas is a collaborative process. Referring to a musical conversation between a trumpet and bass, bassist Richard Davis commented:

> Sometimes you might put a idea in that you think is good and nobody takes to it. . . . And then sometimes you might put an idea in that your incentive or motivation is not to influence but it does influence. (Monson, 1996, p. 88)

Composed music has a more constraining structure that the musicians must follow, but no notational system is capable of completely determining the final performance. All composed music depends on highly trained performers, capable of interpreting the notation in the proper manner. Even in composed musical performance, group creativity is necessary to an effective performance, because a score underdetermines performance.

When Peter Weeks studied chamber orchestra rehearsals, he discovered that even classical music groups have to improvisationally coordinate several aspects of the performance: the initial tempo of the piece; the rate to slow down the tempo in a *ritardando*, a passage in which the composer has indicated that the tempo should slow down; and the relative durations of the *fermata*, a mark on the score that indicates that a note should be held for an indeterminate length of time (Weeks, 1990, 1996). This is what Schutz (1964) meant when he compared an orchestra to a campfire sing-along—both of them require group interaction and collective creativity.

In smaller groups with no conductor, musicians have to coordinate their tempo so that the notes that are supposed to be played together actually end up being played together. Rasch (1988) recorded ensembles and carefully timed the onset of notes, and came up with a way to measure the degree of synchronization. He found several interesting patterns. First, the melody instruments tend to lead relative to the others, with the bass instruments second, and the middle voice in third place. (These are very small differences that are revealed only when you analyze a slowed-down recording; listening live, you'd experience them as occurring together.) Second, as the tempo of the performance got faster, the group become more synchronized. Third, as the size of the ensemble increased, the degree of synchronization declined. This is why most ensembles larger than ten musicians use a conductor. And below ten musicians, synchronization is actually better without a conductor.

Once we realize that performance creativity is like a collaborative conversation, we see that it's not created by any one of the performers. The individualist approach can partially explain what's going on, but it can't provide the complete explanation of group creativity. To explain group creativity, we also need to incorporate the sociocultural approach, bringing all approaches together in an interdisciplinary approach that analyzes collaboration, interaction, and group dynamics (also see Chapter 12).

INDIVIDUAL PERSPECTIVES

COMPOSITION

Anthony Kemp (1996) studied several hundred performers and composers in the United Kingdom and compared them to non-musicians. He found that musicians were more introverted than average, and a bit more anxious. Anxiety is one of Cattell's eight second-order factors (see Chapter 4), and it's related to increased motivation and can facilitate performance (Kemp, 1996, pp. 95–99). Music teachers, in contrast, were more extroverted than average. Kemp also found that musicians were more psychologically androgynous—that when given sex role inventories, they score high on both masculinity and femininity (Kemp, 1996, pp. 108–109), consistent with earlier studies of the creative personality reported in Chapter 4. And in studying many biographies of famous musicians, he found that very few of them showed early brilliance. They weren't prodigies; rather, they grew up practicing for hours and gradually realized their potential as adults.

Davidson and Welsh (1988) compared the composition processes of expert music students to beginning music students. They were not trained as composers; they were performance majors. But when asked to compose a piece, the experts worked with larger units—longer melodic phrases, bigger sections of the composition. This is consistent with the broader litera-ture of studies of expertise, which has demonstrated that experts group information into larger "chunks" (Ericsson et al., 2006). The experts also engaged in more reflection on their ongoing process, whereas the beginners seemed to be just trying out possibilities until one worked. Again, this is consistent with expert–novice patterns in many other domains (Ericsson et al., 2006).

Simonton (1984c) found that composers compose their best tunes between age 33 and 43, and their most famous works at the average age of 39. Their most melodically original works came after age 56. Those who became most famous had the longest careers and were the most prolific—consistent with the productivity theory of Chapter 7. The most artistically original music was composed when they were in the most difficult phases of their life (family death, financial troubles, marital troubles).

IMPROVISATION

Jeff Pressing (1988) proposed an influential model of how the mind works while improvising music. He connected musical performance with skilled performance in other domains, such as sports and typing. Many mental processes are relevant to all of these performance domains. First, because the amount of conscious attention is limited, performing at an expert level requires that the performer *automatize* substantial portions of the task so that they can be performed without conscious attention. This includes the mastery of a database of standard activity sequences that are repeatedly useful. Second, the performer must monitor the performance and correct errors if they occur. Third, the performer often anticipates possible future events so that the eventual reaction will be smoother and more natural.

With these features in mind, Pressing outlined a model of improvisation as a series of dis-tinct decision-making events. Sloboda (1985) took a similar approach, proposing that because of the time demands and the limitations of conscious attention, improvisational genres neces-sarily provide highly constraining structures that narrow the range of potential choices, thus making the decision-making task cognitively possible. Johnson-Laird (1988) likewise argued that the demands of the task will be related to the constraints. In improvisational performance, the cognitive demands are quite high; as a result, the task must be highly constrained—by song structures, genre, stock melodic phrases, and the like. In composition, in contrast, there is unlimited time, and a corresponding loosening of constraints—these tasks rely on a high degree of computational power.

Kenny and Gellrich (2002) identified eight different cognitive processes involved during improvisation: short-term anticipation, medium-term anticipation, long-term anticipation, short-term recall, medium-term recall, long-term recall, flow status, and feedback processes. Interviews revealed that the most common activities are short-term (1 to 3 seconds) and medi-um-term (3 to 12 seconds) anticipation and flow status (concentrate solely on what is being created at that moment). The other five are more likely to occur when more conscious attention is available—as, for example, in slower passages, in phrases with pauses, or when prelearned patterns are being played (pp. 124–125).

Biasutti and Frezza (2009) developed two questionnaires to study improvisation: the Improvisation Processes Questionnaire (IPQ) studies the cognitive processes involved, and the Improvisation Abilities Questionnaire (IAQ) studies the basic knowledge and skills involved.

They gave the questionnaire to 76 musicians with at least two years' experience improvising. A factor analysis of the responses resulted in five factors for IPQ and two factors for IAQ. The five factors of IPQ explained 48% of the total variance and were interpreted as follows:

- IPQ 1: Anticipation (of rhythmic development of the solo, of dynamics of the solo)
- IPQ 2: Emotive communication
- IPQ 3: Flow (nothing distracts me when I'm improvising)
- IPQ 4: Feedback (errors, or harmonic movement, affect my decisions)
- IPQ 5: Use of repertoire (I use melodic patterns or licks)

The two factors of the IAQ explained about 42% of the total variance and were interpreted as:

- IAQ 1: Musical practice
- IAQ 2: Basic skills

There were some instrumental differences. Keyboard players considered basic skills (IAQ 2) more important than brass players, guitarists, and string players. Performers who were skilled at more than one instrument received higher scores on IPQ 3, Flow.

In his 1996 book *Smooth Talkers*, Kuiper proposed an intriguing hypothesis: as the demands of the speaking situation increase, the speaker will use more and more scripted patterns, or catchphrases, during the performance. Kuiper called this *formulaic speech*, and proposed that "smooth talkers"—those with a unique fluency required in certain speech performance situations—draw on a large repertoire of formulas during their speaking. Kuiper tested his hypothesis by examining speech performance in two situations that demand high fluency: sports announcing and auctions. In each case, he examined a low-pressure context and a high-pressure one. For example, in sports announcing, he examined cricket announcing (slow, low pressure) and horse-race calling (fast, high pressure). And in auctions, he examined real-estate auctions and antique auctions at Sotheby's (low pressure), and tobacco auctions in North Carolina and wool auctions in Christchurch, New Zealand (high pressure). In auctions, for example, Kuiper's measure of "pressure" was the number of seconds it takes to make one sale. In both of the low-pressure auctions—real estate and antiques—one sale typically took well over one minute. In contrast, the high-pressure auctions took only seconds; in wool auctions, a lot is sold every 10 seconds, and in tobacco auctions, a sale is made every 5 seconds—a dramatic contrast with the slower, refined pace at Sotheby's.

Kuiper's hypothesis was supported: he found that all tobacco auctioneers used formulas; in fact, they did not use any freely created novel utterances! In the high-pressure situations, the speech was different from everyday speech because it depended on these formulaic phrases that had to be learned. High-pressure speakers drew from a stock set of standard phrases, unlike low-pressure speakers, who created sentences from scratch much like we do in everyday speech. And in high-pressure situations, the overall speech performance had a higher-level structure—with standard beginning, middle, and ends to the performance, and standard formulas for transitions between the sections.

Building on the above research, I (Sawyer, 1996) identified nine structural dimensions of performance that correlate with the degree of improvisation in the genre (Table 18.1).

Table 18.1: Nine Contrast Dimensions of Ritualized and Improvised Performance

	Ritualized	Improvisational	
1	Ossification	Revivalism	"Ossified" performances lose semantic meaning and are primarily a formal structure.
2	Low creative involvement	High creative involvement	The degree of creative involvement of the performer
3	Indexically reflexive	Indexically entailing	The degree to which a performer's actions have implications for the next actions to follow
4	Narrow genre definition	Broad genre definition	If "broad," then many different performances qualify as of that type.
5	Large ready-mades	Small ready-mades	Ready-mades are the formulaic phrases and bits that all performers memorize.
6	Low audience involvement	High audience involvement	In many improvised genres, the boundary between performer and audience is fluid.
7	Resistant to novelty	Receptive to novelty	Improvised genres undergo more rapid historical change.
8	Changes long-lasting	Changes short-lived	But those changes don't stay in place very long
9	High cultural valuation	Low valuation	More highly valued genres are more ritualized on all of the above dimensions.

I found that these dimensions covaried within performance genres, in both musical and verbal performance genres, in a wide range of cultures. I also found that verbal genres, on average, tended to be more highly ritualized than musical genres. Musical genres are almost never fully ritualized, except in those cultures that have developed a prescriptive notational system.

The degree of improvisation in a genre is a result of complex cultural and historical processes that vary quite a bit. But Table 18.1 identifies some interesting regularities that are found around the world. For example, more ritualized genres are more likely to be associated with culturally important events, such as marriage and funerals; more improvised genres are associated with more casual, everyday affairs.

FLOW

Musical performance is a complex skill that takes years of training and rehearsal to master. Talented performers seek out the flow state, a state of heightened awareness, when they're fully focused on the act of performing (Chapter 4, pp. 76–79). In the flow state, performers can lose track of time and feel themselves fully absorbed in the music. These are peak experiences, in the humanist psychology originated by Carl Rogers and Abraham Maslow (see Chapter 4, p. 77); we seek them out because they're fulfilling in their own right, not because of any external rewards that may come from engaging in the activity. Performers get into a flow state because group creativity is challenging; they have to listen to other performers while they're performing, and integrate their partners' actions into their own unfolding activity, while at the same time acting within the conventions of the genre.

Jenny Boyd (1992) interviewed 75 contemporary musicians, including famous rock and pop stars like Keith Richards, Patty Smyth, Sinéad O'Connor, and Roseanne Cash, and found that the great majority of them spoke often of a peak experience while performing, and especially while improvising. Some of them also described frequent peak experiences while working in the recording studio (including Joni Mitchell and Peter Gabriel). And all of them emphasized the importance of playing in a group with other musicians (examples include Keith Richards, David Crosby, Michael McDonald, Huey Lewis) and the role of the audience (examples include Peter Gabriel, Ringo Starr).

Group performance involves a complex interaction between the performer's conscious and unconscious minds; it can never be fully controlled by conscious awareness. Just like the writers I quoted in the last chapter, musicians skillfully balance unconscious inspiration with conscious hard work and editing. But where writers can usually separate the inspiration and the editing stages of their creative process, performers always experience both creative "stages" simultaneously; while performing they're consciously directing their actions, and also acting in a heightened state of consciousness in which the conscious mind seems removed from the process, and their action seems to come from a deeper place. This tension is perhaps most exaggerated in improvisational performance, as described by this jazz saxophonist I interviewed:

> I find what I'm playing is sometimes conscious, sometimes subconscious, sometimes it just comes out and I play it; sometimes I hear it in my head before I play it, and it's like chasing after it, like chasing after a piece of paper that's being blown across the street; I hear it in my head, and grab onto it, and follow it; but sometimes it just comes out, it falls out of my mouth. . . . When you start a solo, you're still in thinking mode; it takes a while to get yourself out of thinking mode . . . and you start giving yourself a little line to follow along, and you start following along that line, and if it's a productive thought, way of expressing yourself, you keep following it, and after a while it's like getting farther and farther into your mind, a way of burrowing in; and if you find the right thread to start with, intellectually, and keep following it, feeling it, you can turn it into something. (quoted in Sawyer, 2003c, pp. 66–67)

Improvisational performers minimize the role of the intellectual, conscious mind during performance. Yet they realize that some conscious awareness is always essential: they must create while aware of the other performers and the conventions, etiquette, and expectations of the genre: "It's all a matter of listening to the people you're playing with . . . This is a real difficulty—you have to be able to divide your senses, but still keep it coherent so you can play, so you still have that one thought running through your head of saying something, playing something, at the same time you've got to be listening to what the drummer is doing" (quoted in Sawyer, 2003c, p. 67). There's a constant tension between the performer's conscious and unconscious during performance, and each performer has to balance the tension from moment to moment. Performers say it's like riding a wave; too much of the conscious mind will slow you down and you'll slip off the back of the wave, dead in the water. But too much of the unconscious mind will make you crash over the edge.

Idealist theories can't explain performance creativity; we need an action theory, because all of the creativity occurs in the moment. The eight-stage psychological model presented in Chapters 5 through 7 has difficulty explaining performance creativity, because there don't seem to be distinct insight and evaluation stages in group creativity. Evaluation has to happen, in part, at the unconscious ideation stage; otherwise, the conscious evaluation stage would be overwhelmed, unable to properly filter the large number of musical ideas (Sawyer, 2003b). During musical improvisation new ideas come from both the conscious and the unconscious, and new ideas are also evaluated by both the conscious and the unconscious.

THE LANGUAGE OF MUSIC

Both composition and performance would be impossible if all of the musicians didn't share a common language—the language of music. We can't talk without talking in some language, and we can't create without being creative in some domain. Music is a language, too, and it couldn't exist at all without conventions. The conventions of music are so taken for granted that we don't often think about them. To begin with the most basic level, all musical notes are grouped into octaves; octaves have 12 equal tones; chords are formed in major, minor, and dominant sevenths. Over the past several centuries, a system of music notation developed in Europe to represent this 12-tone system on the page, and the widespread acceptance of the same notational conventions allows music composed anywhere to be played by musicians trained anywhere. All musicians play one of a standard set of instruments; these instruments are manufactured and can be purchased easily, teachers for the instruments can be found in almost any city, and books of technique are published for the aspiring instrumentalist.

Many psychologists have argued that the cognitive processes underlying music and language are similar in many important ways. For example, the sequential structure of a melody seems to have many parallels with the prosodic contour of a spoken verbal utterance (Lerdahl & Jackendoff, 1983). Listeners seem to listen to and process music using similar processes to the ones they use parsing a sentence (Sloboda, 1985). In a comparative analysis of brain imaging studies, Berkowitz (2010) found a high degree of overlap in brain activation between perception of speech and of melodies, between acquisition of language and music, and between spontaneous generation of speech and spontaneous generation of melodies on a keyboard. (Keeping in mind what we learned in Chapter 13 that pretty much all of the brain is active when you're engaged in music or anything else; these observations result from paired image subtraction.) These parallels are suggestive, but at present we don't know what they mean—is it syntax, or meaning, or emotion, or some general cognitive process like attention focusing, that is responsible for these parallels?

A focus on the syntax or grammar of music allows us to avoid issues of meaning—because words and sentences have meaning in a way that melodies and compositions do not. Leonard Meyer (1956) famously proposed that the referents of musical symbols were emotions, and that music was a language of emotions. Some studies have found strong correlations across listeners between specific musical structures and specific emotional responses. For example, Sloboda (1991) found that (1) tears are evoked when the harmony descends in a cycle of fifths to the tonic; (2) a new or unprepared harmony results in shivers down the spine; (3) a delay of the final cadence evoked tears. These responses occur on average, and many of the listeners reported different reactions to the same musical elements. So even though music undeniably evoked emotions in listeners, it's unlikely that music has meaning in anything like the same systematic way that language does.

I have argued (Sawyer, 1996, 2005a) that music and language are similar in an even more important way: in the ways that groups of people use them collectively, to coordinate collective action. The study of how language is used in context is called *pragmatics*. These comparisons aren't obvious at the individual level; they become visible only when one is examining a group of musicians improvising, or a group of people having a conversation—which is, at root, a form of improvised performance (Sawyer, 2001a). What these very different groups share is a focus on creating a shared experience, one that's built sequentially from each person's contributions, and one that is to some degree unpredictable—the flow of the conversation, or of the improvised music, *emerges* from the group as a whole, not from any one person's brilliance.

Like spoken language, all musical performance is based in conventions and depends on a shared language between performers and audience. We'd never say an instrumentalist isn't creative simply because he's playing an instrument that has been played before, or that a composer isn't creative because she uses a scale that many others have already used. We don't expect every aspect of a creative work to be novel. All creative works liberally draw on shared conventions, and that fact alone doesn't make us question the creativity of the work (see Chapter 11). Many of the most important conventions in a creative genre are so deeply rooted that they're second nature to creators and audiences, and aren't noticed until someone points them out.

The importance of these conventions, like many aspects of taken-for-granted culture, becomes clear only when we experience another musical culture, with a different set of musical conventions. Composer Harry Partch (1949) is legendary for creating a completely new musical culture by breaking all of these taken-for-granted conventions. Partch began by creating a new scale, with 42 equal tones instead of the 12 equal tones of the standard Western scale. Then he developed his own form of musical notation for this scale. Only then could he begin to compose in this completely novel musical language. So far so good. But choosing to discard such deeply shared conventions had major repercussions. Most important, most Western musical instruments can't play these so-called "microtones," so Partch had to invent completely new instruments, and he had to build them himself because no manufacturer was interested in making instruments that no one knew how to play.

Yet even after creating the musical language, composing the music, and building the instruments, Partch's music still couldn't be performed, because no musicians knew how to read the music or play the instruments. Partch himself had to train musicians, or else had to convince some musicians to train themselves.

Partch's compositions were performed only a few times. Before they could be performed, Partch had to spend a year in advance of the performance teaching an orchestra's worth of people how to read his notation and play his instruments. For example, at Mills College, California, Partch visited from July 1951 through February 1953, with a performance scheduled in March of 1952. In the fall, interested students volunteered, and began by building the instruments, which he'd already invented, under his direction. In the winter, he taught them his notational system and they learned to play the instruments. In the spring, they rehearsed enough compositions to fill up a two-hour performance. This entire year of effort culminated in a final performance at the end of the spring semester.

Partch's efforts no doubt qualify as radically novel. He not only created music in an existing language, but also created a new language. But this high level of novelty comes with a price: the loss of the appropriateness of the created products. There are CDs of Partch's performances available in many university music libraries (although almost never at the local music store) and most listeners find it, shall we say, an acquired taste. Partch's efforts didn't result in the creation of a new domain of music. And, even if they had, that domain would quickly take on all of the conventional properties of the 12-tone Western music that Partch rejected—standard notation, instruments, and training. It's unrealistic to expect every new generation of composers to create a completely new musical language, new instruments, and newly trained musicians, and to expect the economy to respond by building factories for a whole new set of invented instruments. Like all creativity, musical creativity depends on a shared system of creative conventions, and no one can create music without first internalizing the rules and conventions of the domain.

GENRES AND TRAJECTORIES

Lena and Peterson (2008) analyzed 60 musical genres in the United States in the 20th century and found that the 60 genres grouped naturally into four genre types, and that the genres in each genre type shared several intriguing attributes (Table 18.2). Genres of music typically begin as either Avant-garde or Scene-based and then, if successful, evolve to the Industry-based type and, potentially much later, to the Traditionalist type:

- *Avant-garde*: Very small, having no more than a dozen participants. Performing the avant-garde genre doesn't generate income and it receives very little press coverage, unless the genre is fortunate to evolve into more broadly institutionalized forms, as did thrash metal and punk.
- *Scene-based*: Performers and fans are concentrated in one local city or region; members often share similar lifestyles as well as musical taste. Examples include the early years of bluegrass, bebop, and rap.
- *Industry-based*: The primary form is the corporation. Production of such music is market-driven and targeted at specific audiences.
- *Traditionalist*: The goal is to preserve a music's heritage. Festivals and reunions are typical performance forms. Examples today include bluegrass, salsa, and Chicago blues.

There are two interesting things about this study. First is how frequently the same sets of characteristics align together, even across very different genres with no overlapping audience members. Second is how almost all genres follow the same trajectory over historical time—from left to right in Table 18.2, with the interesting exception of the IST pattern—initiated by Industry and then becoming Scene-based (an example being the Nashville sound of the 1960s). The analysis and explanation of these patterns requires a sociocultural explanation; it wouldn't be found at the individual level of analysis.

THE SOCIAL NATURE OF MUSICAL CREATIVITY

In this chapter we've learned that musical creativity is fundamentally social. Performance is more social than composition, but even composition is a lot more social than we usually realize. Cognitive psychologists who study music have examined how chords and melodies are represented in the brain, or how performers make split-second decisions during performance (Sloboda, 1988). But as we've seen in this chapter, many important aspects of musical creativity occur outside of the head of the musician: they occur in musical conversations and in interactions between musicians. This is most obvious when we consider improvisational forms of music

Table 18.2: Features of Musical Genres, as Defined by Organizational
Characteristics

	Avant-Garde	Scene-Based	Industry-Based	Traditionalist
Organizational form	Creative circle	Local scene	Corporate	Clubs, associations
Genre ideal	Create new music	Create community	Produce revenue and intellectual property	Preserve heritage
Codification of performance conventions	Low: experimental	Medium	High	Hyper: great concern about deviation
Boundary work	Against established music	Against rival musics	Market-driven	Against deviants within
Dress	Eccentric	Emblematic of genre	Mass-marketed	Stereotypic and muted

(Excerpted from Lena & Peterson, 2008, p. 702)

like American jazz. The social nature of music is a little easier to ignore if you focus only on European art music, with its detailed scores, its conducted orchestras, and its rigid division of labor between the composer and the performer.

As with the other domains of creativity examined in Part IV, we can explain our bias toward composition and European genres of music only by first understanding how our culture's conceptions of creativity influence the ways that we think about creativity. Why haven't creativity researchers, for example, studied electronica or tribute bands? Because they don't fit in with the Western cultural model of creativity. Electronica is music created by people who don't play instruments, created out of bits and pieces that were composed and performed by someone else. In the Western cultural model, this is plagiarism or theft; after all, we believe that every creator originates everything new with every creation. But if that were true, then how can we listen to a recording we've never heard before, and almost instantly know the time period in which it was recorded? How could we look at an unfamiliar painting from the last 500 years and be able to tell within 10 years or so when it was painted? And I've argued that a tribute band is, objectively speaking, not that different from a modern symphony orchestra: they both perform songs that someone else originally wrote and performed, and they try to do it exactly the same way. Yet creativity researchers have spent a lot of energy studying orchestral musicians while ignoring tribute band musicians. Orchestra musicians might be a lot more creative, but we don't know that because we haven't compared them scientifically.

It's hard to avoid the conclusion that creativity researchers have been biased toward genres of music that are culturally valued by an educated elite—the same genres that align more readily with the Western cultural model of creativity. It's the same reason that so much study has been dedicated to fine art painting, while researchers have neglected cartoons, advertisements, movies, and video games (Chapter 16). There's no longer any reason for creativity research to retain such attitudes toward the arts, attitudes that subtly reinforce cultural myths or that place special value on high-status art forms. After all, the art world itself abandoned such attitudes decades ago (see Chapter 16), and consumers have already voted with their entertainment dollars. A science of creativity must be judged on how well it explains the most widespread and most active creative domains, not on how well it explains the high-status genres of a privileged few. And ultimately, the interdisciplinary explanation of creativity that works so well to explain popular music and performance will lead to a better explanation of the fine arts, too.

KEY CONCEPTS

- Contrasts between composition and improvisation
- The influence of bootlegs on the creative process
- Contrasts between musical creativity in electronica and in instrumentally based genres
- Ritualization and improvisation

THOUGHT EXPERIMENTS

- Do you like any of the same music as your parents?
- Do your friends like the same bands that you do? If not, does this ever cause any problems?
- Do you prefer to listen to live music or recorded music? Why do you think that is?
- Do you have any friends who compose music? If so, does it sound completely original, or does it sound something like some other musician?
- Have you ever been to a symphony concert? Did you feel as if you had trouble understanding the music? What types of people were in the audience? Were they different types of persons from those you might see at a stadium concert?
- Have you ever been such a fan of a band that you listened to bootleg tapes or studio or rehearsal recordings? What did you learn about the band from those recordings?

SUGGESTED READINGS

Klosterman, C. (2002, March 17). The pretenders. *The New York Times Magazine,* 54–57.

Marzorati, G. (2002, March 17). All by himself. *The New York Times Magazine,* 32–37, 68–70.

Sawyer, R. K. (2003). *Group creativity: Music, theater, collaboration.* Mahwah, NJ: Erlbaum. [See especially Chapter 2]

Schutz, A. (1964). Making music together: A study in social relationships. In A. Brodessen (Ed.), *Collected papers, Volume 2: Studies in social theory* (pp. 159–178). The Hague, Netherlands: Martinus Nijhoff.

Weeks, P. (1990). Musical time as a practical accomplishment: A change in tempo. *Human Studies, 13,* 323–359.

THEATER

Anyone interested in processes in the natural world would be very rewarded by a study of theatre conditions. His discoveries would be far more applicable to general society than the study of bees or ants.

—Director Peter Brook, 1968, p. 99

I n 1992 and 1993, I was the pianist for one of Chicago's most popular improvisational comedy groups. Three times every weekend, Off-Off-Campus would perform to a packed house of laughing fans. Along with the eight actors and the director, I arrived at the theater an hour early for the loud and vigorous warm-up exercises. They exercised in a small circle, watching and listening closely to one another. All of the exercises were group activities, helping the group communicate instantly and think as a unit, building a group mind.

I began each show by playing an up-tempo blues on the piano, as the stage lights came on and the actors ran to the stage, pumped with adrenaline. The show always began with a game of Freeze Tag. First, one of the actors introduced the show and asked members of the audience to shout out suggestions, asking for a location or a starting line of dialog. Two performers then used this suggestion to begin an improvised scene. The actors accompanied their dialog with exaggerated gestures and broad physical movements. The audience was told to shout "Freeze!" whenever they thought the actors were in interesting physical positions. Whenever anyone shouted "Freeze!" the actors stopped talking and immediately froze in whatever body position they happened to be in. A third actor then walked up to these two and tapped one of them on the shoulder. The tapped actor left the stage. The third actor then copied that body position, and began a completely different scene with her first line of dialog, justifying their body positions but interpreting them in a new way.

Then, the actors would move on to *scene improvisation*. Table 19.1 is an improvised dialog that I videotaped during a 1993 performance by Off-Off-Campus, the first few seconds of dialog from a scene that the actors knew would last about five minutes. The audience was asked to suggest a proverb, and the suggestion given was "Don't look a gift horse in the mouth."

By turn 10, elements of the dramatic narrative are starting to emerge. We know that Dave is a storekeeper, and Ellen is a young girl. We know that Ellen is buying a present for her Dad, and

Table 19.1: Lights up. Dave is at stage right, Ellen at stage left. Dave begins
gesturing to his right, talking to himself.

1	Dave	All the little glass figurines in my menagerie, The store of my dreams. Hundreds of thousands everywhere!	Turns around to admire.
2	Ellen		Slowly walks toward Dave.
3	Dave		Turns and notices Ellen.
		Yes, can I help you?	
4	Ellen	Um, I'm looking for uh, uh, a present?	Ellen is looking down like a child, with her fingers in her mouth.
5	Dave	A gift?	
6	Ellen	Yeah.	
7	Dave	I have a little donkey?	Dave mimes the action of handing Ellen a donkey from the shelf.
8	Ellen	Ah, that's= I was looking for something a little bit bigger,	
9	Dave	Oh.	Returns item to shelf.
10	Ellen	It's for my Dad.	

(From Sawyer, 2003d)

because she is so young, probably needs help from the storekeeper. These narrative elements have emerged from the creative contributions of both actors. Although each turn's incremental contributions to the unfolding story can be identified, none of these turns fully determines the subsequent dialog, and the emergent dramatic narrative is not chosen, intended, or imposed by either of the actors.

Later in the show, the actors advanced to more experimental improvisations. They might perform a child's fairy tale chosen by the audience, in a series of different genres—ranging from science fiction to *Charlie's Angels* to opera—also shouted out by the audience. They might perform the Entrances and Exits game, where the audience chooses a word for each actor and during the scene's dialog, whenever an actor's special word is spoken, that actor must enter or leave the scene. All of these skits are fully improvised. The cast doesn't prepare anything in rehearsal; they never repeat lines, even lines that get a huge laugh. That's because the actors value pure improvisation, where no one on stage knows what will happen next. No single actor takes on a director's role and guides the performance; the dialog and the plot emerge from group collaboration.

Off-Off-Campus is based at the University of Chicago, where modern improv theater was invented in the 1950s. In 1955, a group of former students got together and formed an alternative theater group they called The Compass Players. The group's new style of improvisational theater, with its social commentary and biting satire, quickly caught on among the intellectual and artsy crowd in the university neighborhood. In 1959, many of the same actors started the Second City Theater, a legendary group that spread the improv style around the country.

In the 1980s and 1990s, improvisational theater grew dramatically in Chicago and in other cities. Now there's a wide variety of improvisation, ranging from short games like Freeze Tag that start from one or two audience suggestions, to the more experimental long-form style.

In long-form improv, the ensemble asks for an audience suggestion and then begins to improvise a one-act play that lasts 30 to 60 minutes without interruption. Long-form improv is less focused on comedy than games like Freeze Tag; it focuses instead on character and plot development. These performances often are so good that many audience members assume there's a script. But just like Off-Off-Campus, the actors work hard to avoid repeating even a single line from another night.

It's no accident that improv theater was created in the 1950s, because postwar American culture placed a high value on spontaneity in the arts—not only in theater, but also in jazz, poetry, and painting (Belgrad, 1998; Sawyer, 2000). Improv theater takes the emphasis on spontaneity to an extreme; the actors have to respond instantly, speaking the first line of dialog that comes into their heads. Pausing to analyze would cause too much delay in the performance. Only by immediately speaking the first thought can a natural-sounding dialog be sustained.

As we saw in Chapter 16, the visual arts have been heavily influenced by the creative potential of performance art, resulting in installation-specific pieces and multimedia works that integrate video images or taped sounds. *New York Times* critic Michael Kimmelman wrote in 1998, "Art today often seems to aspire to the conditions of theater and film" (p. 32). Performance may be the dominant form of creativity in contemporary U.S. society. More so than ever before, explaining creativity requires us to explain performance creativity and its place among the arts.

ORAL TRADITIONS

The current predominance of scripted theater makes it hard to imagine a time when *all* performance was improvised. But of course, this was the case at the beginning of human culture, when writing systems hadn't yet been developed. The idea that a playwright would write down a script for later performance is a relatively recent innovation in human history. Long before the invention of writing, human societies had musical and ritual performances, oral traditions that were passed from one generation to the next.

Oral traditions vary from one performance to the next. Every performance of a North Carolina tall tale or an Appalachian fiddle tune is a little different. Contemporary anthropologists, who study verbal ritual performance around the world, have documented variations in even the most sacred rituals. For example, in many performance traditions only experienced elders have acquired the skills required to speak at important rituals. But even after a lifetime of performing prayers, incantations, and sermons, they still repeat the ritual text a little differently each time. Folklorists initially viewed this as an annoying problem; their goal was to write down the "correct" version of the story or ritual, but each time they observed a performance, it was different.

In the 1970s, some anthropologists began to accept that oral traditions are not repeated verbatim, like the performances of a literate culture. These researchers began to study the improvisational creativity of the performer, and began to emphasize the ways that folklore was a living, practiced tradition. These new perspectives have changed the way we look at early European theater. They've driven home the importance of a previously neglected fact: until at least the late medieval period, many European actors remained illiterate. Some scholars, for example, believe that Shakespeare didn't write scripts, but rather taught his actors their parts orally. Scholars argue that the scripts we have today are transcriptions of actual performances, done from memory by someone in Shakespeare's group (Delbanco, 2002).

Modern theater is often traced to a popular form of entertainment called the *commedia dell'arte*, a partially improvised genre of plays originating in 16th-century Italy and thriving for the next 200 years throughout Europe. No one has ever found a script for a *commedia dell'arte* performance. Instead, what historians have found are rough outlines of plot, with brief descriptions of the characters. The actors could easily memorize these rough outlines, called *scenarios*, but all of the dialog was improvised in front of the audience. The success of a *commedia dell'arte* performance depended on the ensemble's improvisational creativity.

Literacy became more widespread in Europe during the same years that improvisation was fading out of its performance tradition. Over the 200-year period that *commedia dell'arte* was popular, literacy became much more common among actors, and the scenarios developed into more highly scripted plays. By the 19th century, this form of early improvisation had been largely replaced by scripted theater.

It wouldn't be until 1955 that improvisation returned to the theater scene. Chicago inspired an improvisation revolution in modern theater that has influenced directors, playwrights, and actor training. Chicago-style improvisation is widely considered to be America's single most important contribution to world theater. For example, British director Mike Leigh has used improvisation to develop plays since the mid-1960s. He later shifted to movie producing, and his innovative technique led to several award-winning and popular movies. His 1996 film *Secrets and Lies* won the Palme d'Or award at the Cannes Film Festival.

In 1997, the *New York Times* reported that "participatory theater"—a form of improvisation that relies heavily on audience participation—had become so popular that it had become mainstream (Marks, 1997). The granddaddy of this genre, performed since 1987 in New York, is *Tony 'n' Tina's Wedding*, a show that recreates a church wedding and reception where the audience participates in the wedding as guests. In the play *Tamara*, which played in New York City in the late 1980s, the action occurred simultaneously in several rooms, and the audience members chose a character to follow around (Caudle, 1991, p. 49). These performances are partially improvised within an overall predetermined structure. In spite of commercial success, participatory theater doesn't get much respect from the theater community. This bias grows straight out of individualist beliefs that the real creativity is in writing the script, a composed creative product generated by a single lone genius.

PERFORMING SCRIPTED PLAYS

> *[The actor] may get his ideas obviously from the author, in the same way that a painter who paints a certain object in nature is receiving his ideas and impressions from that object, but what he does is dependent intrinsically on his own creative capacity.*
> —Director Lee Strasberg, (1960, p. 83)

In scripted theater, the actors don't have to improvise the words, but the actors still have to deliver the lines so that they sound like natural human dialog. For example, when one actor stops speaking and the next one starts, the two actors have to make the transition sound natural, and this requires collaboration; the performers have to be in tune. They have to monitor the other performers' actions at the same time that they continue their own performances. As they

K: That was last <u>night</u>

J: That's what I <u>said</u> last night

    (4.0)

K: Well I—

   [

J: Getting to know you

K: ((laughs))

J: You'll ac<u>cept</u> everything but you <u>do</u> nothing

K: Wo:::::

      [

J: No: that's not true

K: Everybody's that way in certain instances (.) are they not?

J: Not <u>me</u>:, =

K: = Not <u>you</u>:, oh no

            [

J: ((laugh)) Wonderful me

                  [

K: It's your turn—It's your turn to

    get the tea

    Oh:: no (.) <u>I</u> did it six <u>months</u> ago it's

    <u>your</u> turn

          [

J: ((laughs))

             [

K: heheh

J: No

FIGURE 19.1: Transcript of conversation that was performed by a theater group exactly as it was originally spoken. The punctuation marks indicate pitch changes, volume, emphasis, and overlapping speech, which the actors were required to copy exactly. (Reprinted from *TDR/The Drama Review*, 32:3, 23–54. Bryan K. Crow "Conversational Performance and the Performance of Conversation." With permission of New York University and the Massachusetts Institute of Technology. Copyright © 1988.)

hear or see what the other performers are doing, they immediately respond by altering their own actions. They implicitly and subconsciously communicate with subtle facial expressions and gestures (Caudle, 1991, pp. 50–51).

The dialog written in a script isn't exactly like everyday conversation. To make this more obvious, theater director Brian K. Crow (1988) transcribed everyday conversation (Fig. 19.1) using the extremely detailed techniques of *conversation analysis*. Note in particular the detailed representation of pauses, overlaps, and subtle changes in pitch and volume.

Normal scripts don't have this much detail—normally, actors have to decide where to pause, and how long each pause should be; whether there should be speaker overlap at various points in the dialogue; and how to deliver each line—which words to emphasize, and with what tone of voice. When you see a transcript like Figure 19.1, you realize how much information is left out of the typical script. Everything that's put back in by the actors involves acting creativity. And although a lot of those decisions are made in rehearsal, many of them are made improvisationally every night, on stage, in front of the audience.

To teach actors how to make their dialog sound natural, a few directors and playwrights have used detailed transcripts like Figure 19.1 to generate their scripts. This style of theater is called *everyday life performance* (Hopper, 1993; Stucky, 1988, 1993). Crow used detailed transcripts of everyday dialogs to create *Conversation Pieces: An Empirical Comedy* in 1987, a production in which actors performed transcripts like Figure 19.1 exactly as written (Crow, 1988). This removes a lot of actor creativity, but it's a useful exercise for teaching actors how much creativity a normal script requires. All of the unwritten aspects of the dialog have to be improvised by the actors, and the improvisation is collaboratively managed by all actors.

THE CREATIVITY OF THE ACTOR

> *Outstanding actors like all real artists have some mysterious psychic chemistry, half conscious and yet three-quarters hidden . . . that enables them to develop their vision and their art.*
>
> —Peter Brook, (1968, p. 29)

Psychological studies of performance creativity are rare. Partly this is because acting is an ensemble art form, and it's hard to isolate the creative contribution of any one actor (Sawyer, 2003c). But it's also due to the all-too-common belief that performance is not creative, but is just execution and interpretation (Kogan, 2002). A few studies of acting creativity have identified three stages: preparation, rehearsal, and performance (Blunt, 1966; Nemiro, 1997). *Preparation* is when the actor learns the basics of acting through academic training, observing other actors in theater and in films, and observing people interacting in everyday life. The preparation stage includes some solitary activities, but for the most part actor training is social and collaborative.

The second stage, *rehearsal*, involves at least five activities:

1. Identifying something in the character that the actor can relate to
2. Using personal experiences as substitutes for the character's feelings
3. Discovering the character's objectives
4. Creating a physical persona for the character—how the character walks and moves
5. Studying the script to learn what the other characters think about the character

The rehearsal stage is mostly collaborative; although actors spend some time alone to memorize their lines, most rehearsal is done with the rest of the cast.

The third and final stage, *performance*, is the most collaborative of all. Performance involves at least five activities:

1. Focusing on the moment—what has just happened and how the character would perceive the situation at that moment, with no knowledge of how the rest of the play unfolds
2. Adjusting to other actors
3. Interacting with the audience
4. Keeping the concentration and energy level high
5. Improving the performance and keeping it fresh over repeated performances

The performance stage is what the audience sees; this is the most important to acting creativity. In improvisational performance, preparation and rehearsal don't play much of a role; almost the entire creative process occurs on stage, in front of a live audience.

PERSONALITY

The most important thing about an actor is his sincerity. If he can fake that, he's made.
—Comedian George Burns (quoted in Wilson, 1985, p. 70)

Using conventional measures of creative ability, personality psychologists long ago discovered that performing artists score higher than control groups, suggesting that performers are not simply interpreters with no creativity of their own (Lang & Ryba, 1976; Mackler & Shontz, 1965; Torrance & Khatena, 1969). In one study of actors' personality traits (Hammond & Edelmann, 1991a), the variables that distinguished the professional actors from the non-actors included:

- The actors were more privately self-conscious.
- The actors were less attentive to social comparison information.
- The actors were more honest.
- The actors were less socially anxious.
- The actors were less shy.
- The actors were more sociable.
- The actors were more sensitive to the expressive behavior of other people.

These findings are statistically significant, but as with most personality research, the effect sizes are minor and are based on group averages. As a result, these findings don't necessarily help us to explain any specific individual's creativity, in any specific production. To explain acting creativity, we need to use the sociocultural approach to analyze the collaborations of group creativity.

THE FLOW OF PERFORMANCE

Many actors believe that their performance is much better during public performance than in rehearsal (Konijn, 1991, p. 63). Social psychologists have known for decades that performance often improves in the presence of an audience; they call this *social facilitation* (Guerin, 1993). Konijn (1991) found that actors' heart rates were higher during public performance than rehearsal, indicating an elevated stress level, but the public performances were rated more highly by the actors and by expert observers, suggesting that an increased stress level improves performance. This may be why good actors welcome stage fright; it's good for performers to experience a little stress, because it increases the quality of the performance (Wilson, 1985). But there's an interesting twist: although social facilitation studies show that an audience can facilitate performance on an easy task, they also show that an audience can reduce performance on a difficult one (Geen, 1989). This paradox can be explained by Csikszentmihalyi's theory of flow, which proposes that individuals experience a flow state when the challenges of the task are perfectly matched to their own level of skill (see Chapter 4). Actors are faced with a task that would be too challenging for most of us, but they've mastered the skills necessary to perform the task. They don't experience flow in a rehearsal because that's not challenging enough: they have to seek out the additional challenge of live performance.

EXPRESSING EMOTION

A particularly important ability in performing a script is the believable communication of emotion. In 20th-century realist theater, playwrights closely focused on interpersonal relationships, and many of these involve strong emotions—dysfunctional families, alcoholism, or abusive relationships. The pioneering work of director and teacher Konstantin Stanislavsky (1863–1938) is often associated with this emotionally expressive style of acting.

It's a common belief that actors can't play emotions that they haven't experienced themselves. The idea that acting is a reliving of past emotional states is generally associated with Stanislavsky's (1936, 1962) psychological realism. Qualitative and quantitative studies have provided some evidence for this: actors who perform conventional scripted theater develop complex psychological relationships with their characters. In a series of studies in Romania, Neaçsu (Marcus & Neaçsu, 1972; Neaçsu, 1972) found that actors who had a higher capacity for reliving emotional states performed more effectively. Performing certain characters can be cathartic, allowing an actor to work out a personal dilemma through the character, or to get out certain feelings: "In a show once . . . I cried for an hour and a half on stage. Well I was never more happy-go-lucky than during the run of that show'cause I got it all out" (quoted in Nemiro, 1997, p. 235).

But this catharsis can go too far; many actors fear taking on too much of a character's identity, and worry that they'll lose themselves in the character: "To give a really brilliant performance you have to get so close to that character that you get scared. But you can't lose yourself in it" (quoted in Nemiro, 1997, p. 235). Some actors avoid roles that involve portraying emotions that would be too painful. One actor playing the part of Jesus in a play, for example, was uncomfortable because he kept comparing the goodness of Jesus to his own imperfect behavior; another actor playing in *Death of a Salesman* cried every night from genuine depression (Fisher & Fisher, 1981, p. 156). Some actors say that during the run of a play, they find it hard to keep their character out of their everyday life. In 1989, *The Guardian* reported the case of an established British actor who was removed from his role as Hamlet after he began to talk of the "demons" in the role, and began to see his father in the ghost (Hammond & Edelmann, 1991b, p. 26).

The emotional power of acting inspired the form of therapy known as *psychodrama*, originated by the Viennese theater director J. L. Moreno in the 1920s (Moreno, 1977). The rationale for psychodrama is that people may change their attitudes simply by playing a certain role. In psychodrama, the therapist works with a group of patients. At any given time, one of the patients is the center of the drama, and is encouraged to improvise his or her own character, performing critical events from childhood or from his or her current situation. The other patients in the group then improvise the other characters in the situation. Moreno's innovations have become widespread in many forms of therapy, including role playing and assertiveness training.

Yet it's too simplistic to propose that actors are carried away by their characters. As director Peter Brook reported, "The actor himself is hardly ever scarred by his efforts. Any actor in his dressing-room after playing a tremendous, horrifying role is relaxed and glowing" (Brook, 1968, p. 136). A contrary school of acting theory holds that the actor should be in complete control on stage and should not actually *feel* emotion but only *convey* emotion. This school of thought predated Stanislavsky and is often associated with French essayist Denis Diderot's famous essay *Paradox of the Comedian* (1773/1936). "Diderot's paradox" is based on the observation that emotionality could actually interfere with effective acting: "Extreme emotionality results in mediocre actors; mediocre emotionality results in most bad actors; and the absolute absence of emotionality results in sublime actors" (p. 259, my translation). After all, Diderot reasoned, if an actor had a high degree of emotionality he would be unpredictable from night to night. He might be exceptional on opening night, but by the third night his inner inspiration would have dried up. In contrast, the more intellectual, in-control actor would improve from night to night, as he reflected on each night's performance and progressively gained more insight into the character. Diderot's approach returned in the mid-20th century with Brecht's argument that the actor should play his or her character with distance (Konijn, 1991).

THE CREATIVITY OF THE ENSEMBLE

Theater is an ensemble art. Explaining theater creativity requires a sociocultural approach, because the explanation has to be based in the interpersonal dynamics among the actors. Focusing only on the inner mental states of the individual performers will miss the most fundamental aspects of performance creativity: the emergence of a unique performance from the unpredictable and always changing interactions among performers on stage.

If every group used a script like the one in Figure 19.1, there would be a lot less variability from night to night. But theater isn't about predictability. Groups attain their best performances by staying in a zone between complete predictability and being out of control. Improvisational actors have to be the most highly attuned to this zone. They can't just develop the scene in a conventional way, because that would be boring. But they also can't do something so radical that it just doesn't make sense, surprising all of the other actors and puzzling the audience. The challenge of staying in this improvisation zone leads to a flow experience, a peak mental state that performers get when they're in a particularly effective performance (Sawyer, 2001a).

But improvisation's unpredictability makes it a risky way to attain flow. It doesn't always happen, even in a group of talented, well-trained performers. Many improvising actors talk about both the high they get from a good improvisation, and the terror they feel when a performance isn't going well. The unpredictability of group creativity can be frightening because failure is public. If a painter fails, he or she can paint over the canvas; a writer can crumple up the paper and throw it away. But imagine if writers had to publish every single one of their manuscripts—that's the situation improv actors find themselves in every night. Mark Gordon, a director of and actor in The Compass Players, said, "It always felt to me like taking your pants off in front of an audience. A little terrifying" (quoted in Sweet, 1978, p. 110). Ted Flicker, director of the first St. Louis Compass and founder of the New York group The Premise, said, "Unless you've actually tasted what improvising in front of an audience feels like, you can't *imagine* the horror of it" (quoted in Sweet, 1978, p. 162). Up to a certain point, this fear can contribute to the potential for a flow experience. But once it crosses a certain threshold, the actor moves from the flow zone into the anxiety zone.

The flow state that comes from a successful performance is "something like a drug," which is also the title of a book about the improvisational Theatresports league (Foreman & Martini, 1995). Improvisers keep doing it, in spite of the lack of money and fame relative to conventional theater, television, and movies, because of the high they get from the flow experience. Comparing improvisation to conventional theater, Andrew Duncan felt that the flow experience was much greater in improvisation. After leaving Second City in 1963, he said that "I really missed that kind of company—the community, working together, respect . . . They were intense moments in your life that had meaning" (quoted in Sweet, 1978, p. 61).

Even if the individual performers are prepared and focused, a good group performance doesn't always emerge, because there are simply too many intangible factors that can't be known until the performance begins. And a group might be in group flow even when the performers don't realize it. Improvisational musicians and actors alike often describe the experience of walking off the stage at the end of the night, feeling that the performance had been really bad, and then hearing later that the audience had found it to be a stellar performance. Pete Gardner described how the improvisers always valued shows in which everything connected well, but "the audiences absolutely love the shows where there was a mass confusion." He described an experience where one friend compared a slick show with a confused show, explicitly noting that the confused and messy show was "so much better" (Sawyer, 2003c, p. 46). Inversely, most group performers can tell a story of at least one night's performance that they thought was particularly good, but later as they were discussing the performance with knowledgeable, trusted colleagues who had been in the audience, they discovered that it wasn't one of their best.

Many Chicago improvisers refer to group flow using the term *groupmind*. Group flow helps the individual actors reach their own internal flow state. Comedian Jim Belushi famously said that the high that comes from a group performance was "better than sex" (Seham, 2001, p. 64). Actor Alan Alda referred to this state, saying, "You're actually tuned into something that's inside the actor's mind and there's a kind of mental music that's played and that everybody shares" (quoted in Sweet, 1978, p. 326). Improv actors often speak of group flow as "a state of unselfconscious awareness in which every individual action seems to be the right one and the group works with apparent perfect synchronicity" (Seham, 2001, p. 64). No one actor can make this happen single-handedly; it requires a very special collaboration. The ensemble has to let it emerge from a group creative process.

INTERACTION BETWEEN ACTORS AND AUDIENCE

Peter Brook (1968) described a touring performance of *King Lear* by the Royal Shakespeare Company in the 1960s. The tour began by passing through Europe. Brook reported that "the best performances lay between Budapest and Moscow" (p. 21) and that the audience profoundly influenced the cast, even though their mastery of the English language was not great. Yet, their experience of life under communism prepared them to connect with the play's difficult themes. The actors were in peak performance and became progressively more excited as they finished the European portion of the tour and then moved to the United States. Yet after a few weeks in the United States, the spirit had gone out of the company. Brook reported that "it was the relation with the audience that had changed . . . This audience was composed largely of people who were not interested in the play; people who came for all the conventional reasons— because it was a social event, because their wives insisted, and so on" (p. 22). The actors modified their performances in an attempt to engage this different type of audience, but with limited success.

Performers feed off a good audience, and it leads the performers to rise to the best of their ability. Audiences can even affect specific moment-to-moment performance decisions. In a theater performance, an unexpected audience chuckle might lead the actors to pause a split second to let the laughter play out and die down, and they might exaggerate the next similar line by the same character, whereas on another night, an audience might not respond at that moment and the performance would be unaffected. In an improv comedy performance, a laughing audience lets the cast know they're performing well, but if there's no laughter, the cast knows they need to change something, perhaps to take the character and story development in another direction.

When one audience member reacts, whether with laughter, fear, or sadness, the others are more likely to experience that emotion or reaction as well. This group phenomenon is called *emotional contagion* (Hatfield, Cacioppo, & Rapson, 1994). This happens a lot with laughter and applause, and the larger the audience, the more extreme the effects. Examples include the extreme emotions that spread through the crowd at a sports event or a stadium concert. To understand the role of the audience, we need a sociocultural approach that explains group dynamics and communication.

THE CREATIVE PROCESS MADE VISIBLE

Most creativity research has focused on product creativity instead of performance (Sawyer, 1997a, 2003c). In scientific disciplines, creative products include theories, experimental results, and journal articles; in the arts, products include paintings, sculptures, and musical scores. In product creativity, the creative process results in a finished, fixed product. In product creativity, the creative process usually takes place in isolation, in a studio or a laboratory. It can take months or years before the final product is completed. The creator has unlimited opportunities for revision, and doesn't have to release the product until he or she is ready.

Creativity doesn't happen all in the head, as the idealist theory would have it; it happens during the hard work of execution. That's why explaining creativity requires a focus on the creative process. No creative process is ever completely predictable; there's always some improvisation. Painters constantly respond to their canvas and oils as they are painting. Each step of the painting changes the artist's conception of what he or she is doing—the first part of a painting often leads to a new insight about what to do next. Fiction writers constantly interact with the story as they write. A character or a plot line frequently emerges from the pen unexpectedly, and an experienced writer will respond and follow that new thread, in an essentially improvisational fashion. Improvisation is most important in stage performance because, unlike the painter or the writer, performers don't have an opportunity to revise their work. The improvisations of the painter can be painted over or discarded, and the writer has the power of a word processor to generate the next draft. But the improvisations that occur on stage are exposed to the audience. As a result, the audience gets to see the creative process in action, sharing not only in every unexpected inspiration but also in those disappointing attempts that fail. Fans of the popular improvisational rock band the Grateful Dead had a rule of thumb: you had to go to five concerts to be assured of getting one really inspired performance. Even the most famous artists often destroy or paint over a significant number of their canvases, and these aborted attempts are generally lost to history. But actors can never take back a bad night.

We can't explain improvisational creativity unless we focus on the collaboration and the emergence of the group. And studying improvisation can provide valuable insights into all creativity, because collaboration is important in all creative domains (see Chapter 12). In modern scientific research, these collaborations range from the group work that goes on in the laboratory to informal conversations over late-night coffee. The creative interactions of an improv theater group are much easier to study, since the analyst can hear and transcribe how this inter-action affects each actor's creative process. Performance is the creative process made visible.

Of all the world's cultures, modern European performance traditions have been the least receptive to improvisation, in both the theater and musical communities. Improvisation has often been considered to be a less refined "popular" or "folk" genre. Because most creativity researchers are also European, when they study performance they tend to focus on the perfor-mance genre that is most highly valued in European cultures: conventional, scripted theater. As psychologist Donald MacKinnon—the director of the influential Berkeley IPAR studies of cre-ativity in the 1950s—once said, creativity researchers have tended to study people too much like themselves. They're people who share the values of academic, university researchers, "the theo-retical and aesthetic" (MacKinnon, 1987, p. 121). In Csikszentmihalyi's (1996) Creativity in Later Life study, about half of the approximately 90 subjects interviewed held positions as uni-versity professors.

The Western cultural model has led us to neglect performance creativity, even though it, of all forms of creativity, provides us with the best window onto the collaboration and improvisa-tion of the creative process. We now know how the Western cultural model originated in deeply held beliefs and attitudes that are unique to individualist, European cultures. We now know that creativity is fundamentally social and collaborative; that it involves preparation, training, and hard work; and that the process is more important than the product or the personality. By explaining performance, we can ultimately better explain all creativity.

KEY CONCEPTS

- Collaborative emergence and distributed creativity
- Chicago improvisational theater
- Origins of modern theater in oral traditions
- Diderot's paradox and Stanislavsky's psychological realism
- Group flow and the group mind
- The role of the audience

THOUGHT EXPERIMENTS

- Have you and your friends ever had a special catchphrase or saying that no one outside your group understood? Do you remember how it originated? Was it one person's idea, or did it emerge collaboratively?
- Have you ever seen more than one production of the same play? How were they different?
- Have you ever seen more than one performance of the same production, with the same actors and stage set? How were they different?
- The next time you're in a religious setting, think about the performative elements of the ritual. Don't focus only on the religious officials; also examine what the audience is doing.

- The next time you're at a sports event, think about the performative elements of the event. Don't focus only on the team players; also examine the coaches, the cheerleaders, and the fans.

SUGGESTED READINGS

Crow, B. K. (1988). Conversational performance and the performance of conversation. *TDR/The Drama Review, 32*(3), 23–54.

Hammond, J., & Edelmann, R. J. (1991a). The act of being: Personality characteristics of professional actors, amateur actors and non-actors. In G. D. Wilson (Ed.), *Psychology and performing arts* (pp. 123–131). Amsterdam: Swets & Zeitlinger.

Konijn, E. A. (1991). What's on between the actor and his audience? Empirical analysis of emotion processes in the theatre. In G. D. Wilson (Ed.), *Psychology and performing arts* (pp. 59–73). Amsterdam: Swets & Zeitlinger.

Nemiro, J. (1997). Interpretive artists: A qualitative exploration of the creative process of actors. *Creativity Research Journal, 10*(2 & 3), 229–239.

Sawyer, R. K. (1998). The interdisciplinary study of creativity in performance. *Creativity Research Journal, 11*(1), 11–19.

Sawyer, R. K. (2003). *Group creativity: Music, theater, collaboration.* Mahwah, NJ: Erlbaum.

Strasberg, L. (1960). On acting. In J. D. Summerfield & L. Thatch (Eds.), *The creative mind and method: Exploring the nature of creativeness in American arts, sciences, and professions* (pp. 83–87). Austin: University of Texas Press.

SCIENCE

The greatest collective work of art of the twentieth century.

—Jacob Bronowski, 1973, p. 328, referring to physics

A re scientists really creative? After all, you might think that scientists simply discover truths by looking at the world (with the help of some very fancy equipment). The astrophysicist Subrahmanyan Chandrasekhar said that when he discovered a new fact, it appeared to him to be something "that had always been there and that I had chanced to pick up" (quoted in Farmelo, 2002a, pp. xi–xii). If a good scientific theory is just an accurate reflection of reality, then a good scientist is one whose theories directly copy reality (Barrow, 2000). And copying isn't creative.

However, this "copy theory" of science is wrong. The copy theory was famously argued by a group of mid-20th-century philosophers known as logical empiricists.[1] To an empiricist, science is a game of deduction: taking observations from experience and using them to derive statements about regularities in nature. However, when scholars began to study how scientists actually work, it turned out that empiricism and deduction weren't very good explanations. Beginning with Karl Popper just after World War II, continuing with the influential analyses of science of Thomas Kuhn, through today's studies of scientific laboratories by Bruno Latour and Karin Knorr-Cetina, we now know that scientific theories can't be derived in any simple or mechanical way from observations.

There are two main reasons why logical empiricism doesn't explain science. First, it turns out that the observed data usually fit with more than one theory. One theory might seem at first to be better at explaining certain observations, but the match is always a matter of degree, and sometimes one can't be sure. A theory that seems better at first might later turn out to have been the result of a measurement error. Because data underdetermine theory, it takes creativity to bring together all of the competing theories and all of the potentially relevant data and come up with a framework that best explains the data. Jonas Salk, the developer of the first successful vaccine against polio in 1955, described his creative process in such terms: "I recognize patterns

---

1. Also sometimes called logical positivists.

that become integrated and synthesized and I see meaning, and it's the interpretation of meaning, of what I see in these patterns." He described his moments of insight as seeing "an unfolding, as if a poem or a painting or a story or a concept begins to take form" (quoted in Csikszentmihalyi, 1996, p. 287).

Second, scientists don't always proceed by deduction; they often proceed by *induction*, starting from a theory and then designing an experiment to see if the theory is supported by reality. A classic example is Albert Einstein's general theory of relativity. Einstein had a hunch that the force of gravity warped the very structure of space and time, a very difficult concept to grasp. The general theory wasn't deduced from observation; when Einstein first proposed the theory it was just a clever speculation with no supporting data. But Einstein's theory was so appealing in its own right that scientists decided to take the time to test it.

If space really were curved by the gravity of a large planet or a big star, then faraway stars would seem to shift their position a very tiny bit when they were near a planet in the sky, because light from those stars would change direction as it passed through the warped space near that planet. With really good measuring instruments, scientists might be able to measure whether or not the observed position of a distant star really did shift when its light rays had to pass by another big object on the way to earth. But there was a complicating factor: even Newton's older theory predicted that gravity would cause light rays to bend. In 1916, Einstein used his theory to predict that the degree of light shift would be about twice that predicted by Newtonian physics. This provided a way to experimentally check the theory.

Given the measuring equipment of that time, the sun was the only body large enough to create an effect big enough that the difference between the two theories' predictions could be measured accurately. But most of the time, the sun's light made it impossible to see faraway stars behind it. The best opportunity to see these faraway stars came with the 1919 solar eclipse, when the moon would block the sun's light, allowing the stars behind it to be seen and measured. A team of British physicists led by Arthur Eddington traveled to the island of Principe, off the coast of West Africa, where they knew they'd have the best view. Eddington already believed in Einstein's theory and he was well known in Britain as an advocate of general relativity. When Eddington returned, he claimed that his observations supported Einstein's prediction, and he convinced the scientific community that general relativity was correct.

However, in the 1980s historians discovered that Eddington did not get conclusive evidence; he doctored his results. Scientists now know that there was no way Eddington could have successfully measured the light shift with the primitive equipment that he had available. In 1962 a much better-equipped British team tried to reproduce Eddington's findings. The expedition ended in failure, and the team concluded that the method was too difficult to work (Waller, 2002, pp. 48–63). Einstein's theory of general relativity turned out to be right, so this episode didn't slow the course of science. But the story shows that Einstein wasn't just copying reality when he created his theory. When scientists use induction instead of deduction, they're undeniably creative.

THE CREATIVE SCIENTIST

> *Very often the successful scientist must simultaneously display the characteristics of the traditionalist and of the iconoclast.*
>
> —Thomas S. Kuhn, (1959/1963)

Like creative personalities in general, creative scientists tend to have strong self-confidence and self-reliance, often seeming egocentric and stubborn. The famous Harvard biologist E. O. Wilson emphasized persistence and ambition, "a desire to control," and the ability "to tolerate strong rivals" (quoted in Csikszentmihalyi, 1996, p. 269). These scientists have a strong intrinsic motivation that helps them work for years on a problem. Many successful creative scientists report feeling "chosen" to be scientists in adolescence, long before they had any opportunity to prove themselves in a scientific discipline.

Catherine Cox, a student of Louis Terman at Stanford, compared the personality traits of 300 eminent scientists with nonscientists. The traits that distinguished the great scientists were a desire to excel, originality, tendency not to be changeable, determination, neatness, and accuracy of work (Cox, 1926). Summarizing the literature since Cox's 1926 study, Feist (1998, 2006b) found that on the Big Five personality traits (see Chapter 4), scientists score higher than nonscientists on Conscientiousness and Openness to Experience. Scientists have been found to be more dominant and assertive than nonscientists; they tend to be achievement driven and ambitious. And more-creative scientists score higher on these traits than less-creative scientists.

In a summary of the research on scientific expertise, Feist (2006b, pp. 106–109) found several differences between expert and novice scientists:

- Expert scientists are more willing to modify or discard hypotheses than novices.
- Experts demonstrate more cognitive complexity when they discuss their domain.
- Novices solve problems and evaluate evidence based more on commonsense representations; experts form abstract representations.
- Experts use chunking and node-linked representations of large quantities of domain knowledge.
- Experts work forward from the information given; novices work backward from a possible solution.
- Experts are more likely to discover useful analogies.

Overall, when expert scientists are compared to novice or student scientists, the experts build models that make use of analogy, metaphor, and visual imagery. They constantly test their theories against empirical evidence.

GREAT ANALOGIES IN SCIENCE

Scientific discoveries often emerge from analogies; historians have noted hundreds of analogies used by scientists (Holyoak & Thagard, 1995, p. 185). One of the most famous examples is Kekulé's discovery of the molecular structure of benzene. In the benzene molecule, the atoms combine together to form a circle of bonds. Kekulé famously reported falling half asleep and experiencing a daydream in which he imagined the atoms forming into snakelike chains, and then saw one of the snakes biting its own tail. He awoke with a start and immediately realized that benzene was a ring-shaped molecule.[2]

---

2. This story is often repeated, but there is no evidence it's true, and historians of science have uncovered a lot of evidence suggesting that it's probably false (Schaffer, 1994). Kekulé didn't report this story until

A second famous example involves magnets. By 1600 magnets had been discovered, and their properties were increasingly understood. One of the magnet experts, William Gilbert, studied the behavior of compasses—then already widely used—and also the behavior of other magnets. Gilbert then had the idea that the planet earth was a giant magnet. Analogical thinking led Gilbert to create this theory because the earth shares many properties with magnets. We now know that Gilbert was right: the earth is indeed a giant magnet.

In a third famous example, Christiaan Huygens, in his 1678 *Treatise on Light*, used an analogy between light and sound in support of his wave theory of light. Because sound traveled in waves, and light and sound shared some properties, Huygens hypothesized that light was a wave. For more than a century, this theory was shunted aside in favor of Newton's particle theory of light, but it was revived in the early 19th century by Thomas Young and Augustin Fresnel. The fact that light diffracts was suggested by observing that both sound and water waves go around corners. The wave analogy also suggested that light from two pinholes would exhibit interference, just like water waves do. Young's landmark experiments demonstrated this to be the case. Twenty-first-century quantum physics now holds to a hybrid theory in which light is both particle and wave, a "wavicle" as some physicists say.

Cognitive psychologists have learned quite a bit about how the mind thinks about analogies (see Chapter 6, pp. 119–121). They say that the phenomenon being explained is the *target*, and the metaphorical comparison is the *source* (see Chapter 6, p. 119). There are two mental steps required to have an analogical insight: first an appropriate source has to be selected, and then the source has to be matched up with the target. Psychologists have focused on answering two questions: Given a target problem or domain, how can a good source be found? And given a possible source, how can it be applied to better understand the target?

In answer to the first question, some scientists report noticing a source while they're working on a target problem. This can happen only if the scientist has already internalized a large database of potential sources—from deep experience in this domain, from work in other domains, or from life experience. Other scientists report first noticing a good source of analogy, and then noticing a target problem that they've been working on a long time.

In answer to the second question, the scientist must be able to construct representations of both the source and the target that make useful comparisons easy. This requires creative work, because the scientist has to reframe both the source and the target, emphasizing those features of each that make them most receptive to comparison. After all, the source and the target are never exactly alike. Typically, creative manipulation is required before the analogy can be made to work (Holyoak & Thagard, 1995). Kekulé's source was the snake eating its tail. He'd probably never encountered such a snake on any wooded trail, but nonetheless his mind was able to creatively construct the image.

Different analogies have different strengths and weaknesses, and it takes creativity to pick the most appropriate one for the situation. When students think of the flow of electricity in a

decades after his paper suggesting the ring structure for benzene. And Kekulé got the structure wrong: he thought the ring was composed of six hydrogen atoms, when in fact it's six carbon atoms. The correct carbon structure was discovered by Adolf Claus, although it's often retrospectively attributed to Kekulé (Schaffer, 1994). It's all an example of how a questionable story persists because it fits in well with the Western cultural model of creativity.

wire using an analogy with water flowing through pipes, they perform well on battery problems. But when they think of electricity as a crowd of people moving through a narrow corridor (with each person representing one electron), they do better on resistor problems (Gentner & Gentner, 1983).

Because many creative insights result from analogy, the psychology of analogical thinking, as reviewed in Chapter 6, can help us to explain creativity. This exciting line of research is continuing, and promises to add to our explanation of creativity.

SCIENTIFIC DISCOVERY AS PROBLEM SOLVING

Scientific discovery is a form of problem solving, and . . . the processes whereby science is carried out can be explained in the terms that have been used to explain the processes of problem solving.

—Herbert A. Simon, (1966, p. 22)

In Chapter 5, we learned that many scholars have argued that creativity is nothing more than problem solving. In science, this claim is perhaps easier to argue than in domains like painting or poetry, and many psychologists have analyzed the creative processes of scientists by using theories derived from studies of problem solving. Klahr (2000), building on the classic notion of problem solving as a search in a conceptual space (Newell & Simon, 1972; Simon, 1966; also see Chapter 5, pp. 90–91), proposed a *dual space framework*, and theorized that scientists work by simultaneously searching two distinct spaces: the *experiment space* and the *hypothesis space*. In some cases, scientists use a third space—the *data representation space*. For some complex problems, figuring out how to represent the data, and the many relationships among data, involves search-based problem solving.

These spaces require different representations, different procedures for moving in the space, and different criteria for what constitutes progress. Scientific discovery involves hypothesis space search, experiment space search, and evidence evaluation. In searching the hypothesis space, the initial state consists of some knowledge about a domain, and the goal state is a hypothesis that can account for some or all of that knowledge. This is primarily the work of theorists. In constructing experiments, scientists have to search the experiment space for a good experiment design. This is primarily the work of experimentalists. Evidence evaluation involves comparing the predictions of the hypothesis with the results obtained from the experiments. It assesses the fit between theory and evidence, and guides further search in both spaces.

As with other creative domains, scientific creativity is likely to involve a combination of well-defined and ill-defined problems. The mix varies with historical period and across research areas; when a new domain is first created, there are likely to be more ill-defined problems, and a greater need for problem-finding processes. As a domain matures, most scientists will spend the majority of their time engaged in problem-solving forms of creativity. But rarely is science only about problem solving; even in well-established domains, creative scientists need to be able to ask good questions and to formulate good problems.

MULTIPLE SIMULTANEOUS PROJECTS

In Chapter 4, we learned that creative individuals often engage in networks of enterprise, multiple overlapping simultaneous projects. Depending on the scientific field, a project can take anywhere from three months to three years or more, as it moves through preliminary pilot study, grant writing, experimental design, theoretical literature review, implementation of the experiment and gathering of data, analysis and interpretation of the results, and writing up the results for submission to a journal. Most practicing scientists schedule multiple projects so that during any given week, each of the projects will be in a different stage of development. While writing up the results of one project for a journal, another project is in the laboratory, and yet another is in the conceptual stage with theoretical speculation and library research on prior studies. A network of enterprises increases the likelihood of cross-fertilization across projects, and many of the most important insights happen when two different projects come together unexpectedly.

This kind of multitasking is supported by the modern system of apprenticeship in scientific laboratories, where each research professor is assigned several PhD students to work as research assistants. Each distinct project is parceled out to different graduate students, and they handle the day-to-day nitty-gritty details of the project. The professor acts as a project leader, managing the overall structure of each project, checking to make sure the schedule isn't excessively delayed, offering expertise to get past unexpected complications.

Successful scientists have learned how to structure their workday for maximum creativity. They shift from one project to another based on what they do most effectively at a given time of day. Original, new, and conceptual work, problem-finding work, is best done first thing in the morning. Many scientists also schedule their writing in the morning, because this involves creative conceptualization. Scientists tend to schedule the concrete, hands-on laboratory work for late morning and after lunch. Finally, many scientists report that they schedule some idle time in the late afternoon, after the concrete phase of hard work, perhaps taking a walk around campus or going for a cup of coffee. They've learned from experience that valuable insights often emerge when they get some distance from the work. Scientists then close the day by returning to writing and conceptual work, often continuing to work long after dinner.

AESTHETICS AND SCIENCE

It is more important to have beauty in one's equations than to have them fit experiment.
—Physicist Paul Dirac, winner of a Nobel Prize in Physics in 1933 (1963, p. 47)

The most creative scientists are the ones who are especially good at formulating and asking new questions. The most significant new scientific ideas, the ones that result in major revolutions, tend to be the result of a problem-finding process (Chapter 5), and it's here that science requires immense creativity.

In many scientific doctoral programs, graduate students aren't expected to come up with their own research questions. That's the responsibility of the advising professor, whose years of experience make him or her particularly good at finding problems. Even when graduate students have a pretty good idea of the kind of work they're interested in, they still need a lot of guidance on how to ask the right kind of question, and how to focus their research. In almost all graduate programs, professors' most common difficulty is teaching their doctoral students how to formulate and focus their questions appropriately (Graesser, Ozuru, & Sullins, 2010; Novak & Gowin, 1984).

How do scientists come up with good questions? Many scientists say they use aesthetic beauty rather than cold rationality. Physicists took Einstein's general theory seriously because it was beautiful. Even though there were no data to support it, its beauty made it seem likely to be true. Like a great work of art, a beautiful equation is universal and simple and has an undeniable purity and power (Farmelo, 2002a). Like great poems, equations have order; hierarchical structure; simplicity and complexity in balance, pattern, and rhythm; and symmetry (Flannery, 1991). Poems and great equations are both powerful because they pack as much meaning as possible into a small space. $E = mc2$ is enormously powerful in part because it is so simple.

Poems and great equations both act as stimuli that later can result in a wide range of unpredictable and unexpected elaborations. Each reader responds to and interprets a poem in a new way, and the poet can't control the reader's response. In a similar fashion, a great equation has repercussions through subsequent history that its discoverer could not have foreseen. Scientific equations aren't as fixed and unyielding as you might think; they're often reinterpreted in light of later discoveries and theoretical developments. Scientists have changed their interpretations of some of Einstein's and Dirac's most famous equations over the years, and Einstein's theory of relativity has developed far beyond what he imagined (Weinberg, 2002).

Of course, there are differences. Whereas poetry works only in a given language, scientific equations are universal. Whereas poets value ambiguity and intentionally leave many things unsaid, scientists intend their equations to communicate a single logical meaning. And perhaps most important, beauty in science can be misleading; the history of science is filled with discarded theories that seemed beautiful but turned out to be wrong. Einstein devoted his later career to the search for a unified field theory; because the idea was beautiful, he was convinced it was right. But no unified field theory has yet been found. Einstein rejected Heisenberg's uncertainty principle, famously saying, "God does not play dice" with the universe. But now the uncertainty principle is accepted as correct by all working physicists.

THE CREATIVITY OF SCIENCE

In the realities of today's world, scientists who are creative rarely live and work in isolation....[social] interactions are highly important and, with the evolution of science, are becoming even more so.

—Philip H. Abelson, Editor of *Science Magazine* 1962–1984 (1965, p. 603)

The logical empiricists explained science as a passive observation of the world, involving the development of logical propositions that correspond to observation. They thought of science as a body of knowledge. But research from the 1960s onward studied science as a set of practices that scientists engage in in laboratory settings. It's a subtle shift in emphasis—from knowledge itself to the ways that knowledge is generated—but it allowed us to explain scientific creativity in a new way. Scholars of scientific creativity have begun to closely examine what actually happens in laboratories, and in many cases they've been able to document the emergence of new creative insights.

Most science involves slow, methodical work, with mini-insights occurring every day. There isn't much evidence for a "burst of genius" view of creativity. Instead, scholars have discovered that scientific progress is a cooperative group effort, involving the distribution of labor and small but important contributions from each of a team of professionals.

Scientific discovery happens largely through intensive social interaction in laboratories and universities, not through isolated bursts of insight by a few great individuals. Most scientific creativity occurs in groups; the mythical image of the lone scientist working quietly into the night is a dated historical image from the 19th century. A typical scientific research team includes members with differing levels of experience—professors, postdoctoral students, and graduate students—and with different specialty backgrounds.

The historian of science Mara Beller (1999) uncovered the social processes that led to some of the key discoveries of early-20th-century quantum physics. Through a close analysis of the month-by-month interactions of the Copenhagen group, and analyses of multiple successive drafts of their most influential publications, she showed that some of the most important scientific papers of the 20th century, although formally authored by a single person, actually reveal the influence and collaboration of a circle of ten or more scientists, each working at the cutting edge of scientific knowledge, and all of them in constant communication. For example, Heisenberg's initial formulation of his famous uncertainty principle was developed in part in response to two physicists, Sentfleben and Campbell, who are now relatively unknown. It takes a very close reading of Heisenberg's papers, and a thorough knowledge of the group's collaborations, to detect these influences. Beller applied the same analysis to Bohr's legendary Como lecture, showing that the lecture juxtaposes several coexisting arguments, each addressed to a different theorist and focusing on a different issue. When we learn such facts, we realize that science is often a collaborative dialog among a close-knit community, even when only one person's name appears on the final publication.

This leads to a big problem with the Nobel prizes for science: How does one determine who deserves recognition for a given discovery or theory? No more than three scientists can receive the Nobel prize at a time. But like the Copenhagen group, most of today's scientific advances are the result of cumulative, collaborative work by many scientists. For example, the 2002 Nobel Prize in Physics was awarded to Dr. Raymond Davis Jr. and Dr. Masatoshi Koshiba for their work on solar neutrinos. Because of the three-scientist limit, the Nobel Foundation left out many other scientists who played significant roles in developing the theory of solar neutrinos: John Bahcall, Vladimir Gribov, Bruno Pontecorvo, Stanislav Mikheyev, Alexei Smirnov, Lincoln Wolfenstein, and the leaders of the Sudbury Neutrino Observatory in Canada (Johnson, 2002). The basic problem is that the Nobels assume an obsolete vision of science as resulting from solitary work, when today each great work of science is created by a collaboration, by an entire field of coauthors (also see Chapter 12, p. 232). Our 19th-century conceptions of creativity have become embedded in institutions—like the Nobel prize—that make it even harder for us to realize the sociocultural nature of creativity.

MYTHS OF GENIUS

We like to think that geniuses are often ahead of their time, but most of the stories people tell about misunderstood geniuses are inaccurate myths. For example, many biologists will tell you that an obscure Moravian monk named Gregor Mendel accidentally discovered modern genetics in 1865, and that his work was ignored for 35 years before being rediscovered in 1900 and serving as the foundation of the new science of genetics. On the 100th anniversary of the date, in April 1965, British evolutionist Sir Gavin de Beer declared: "It is not often possible to pinpoint the origin of a whole new branch of science accurately in time and place. . . . But genetics is an exception, for it owes its origins to one man, Gregor Mendel, who expounded its basic principles at Brno on 8 February and March 8, 1865" (quoted in Waller, 2002, p. 133).

But this story is false (Brannigan, 1981, pp. 89–119; Waller, 2002, pp. 132–158). An examination of what really happened shows that Mendel was working on a completely different problem—a now-discredited theory that new species result from hybridization—and he and his colleagues agreed that his work had failed to prove the theory. Although Mendel deserves credit for being one of the first to observe the ratios that helped later scientists discover genes and inheritance, many of the ideas now associated with Mendel were already widely accepted before he published his now-famous paper. Contrary to the myth, his findings were not ignored and not misunderstood; he reported them at two scientific conferences, and they were well received, although they weren't considered that radical. Mendel was not a "Mendelian" in the modern usage of the term, and he didn't realize the significance of the ratios to evolutionary theory. But today's scientists attribute ideas to his 1865 papers that Mendel didn't actually have, and that he was incapable of having given the state of science at that time.

The conventional story is false—but it survives because it fits in so well with the Western cultural model of creativity. Stories like Mendel's seem at first glance to support our individualist beliefs, but on further examination, we find that the real explanation is found at the sociocultural level of analysis.

THE CONSTRUCTION OF SCIENTIFIC GENIUS

Scientific work depends on a staff of graduate students. Otherwise, the simultaneous execution of multiple projects wouldn't be possible. And if scientists can't attract the best young graduate research assistants to their laboratories, their ideas will fade in importance. It isn't enough to simply have great ideas: you also have to be able to convince young people that they will be able to make a living and have a career by following in your footsteps.

But to maintain all of these students, a professor has to have money to pay their salaries and benefits, and to pay for the lab space and supplies to run the experiments. Successful scientists have to know how to compete for and win grants, how to budget and allocate funds, and how to manage a team of diverse individuals. Many prominent scientists say they face a difficult balancing act: the more energy they devote to these managerial tasks, the less time they have available to do real science. The size of the research team that surrounds each scientist is a result not of any individual traits of that scientist but of the nature of the scientific work in that domain, the number of graduate students choosing to enter that field, and the amount of research funding available from government and private industry.

Not all brilliant scientists become chief scientists with their own laboratories. Leading a lab requires immense administrative and leadership skills, and some good scientists are too withdrawn from social life to manage such a career. Only a scientist with the right lab, filled with the right kind of staff help, has any hope of becoming known as a genius, because the system of scientific knowledge attributes to the chief scientist the collective products of the entire lab. Mukerji's study of oceanographic lab teams (1996) showed how the collective group work of the team is ultimately attributed to the chief scientist. The chief scientist becomes "larger than life, more brilliant than any individual could be" (Mukerji, 1996, p. 274). Because the chief scientist seems to be the creator of an entire group's product, this process reinforces his or her stature and makes him or her seem ever more superhuman. However, the chief scientist only seems great because he or she is expressing the thoughts of the group.[3]

Why would members of a group prefer to have the leader get credit for their innovations rather than have the truth of collective authorship be known? Mukerji identified several social and organizational reasons. For example, sole authorship by an identified genius makes the results of the team's work more readily accepted by the scientific community, because such a creation has more authority. It fits in more readily with the Western cultural model; it's easier for our individualist culture to attribute ideas to individuals (Kasof, 1995; Markus & Kitayama, 1991). Building up the greatness of the chief scientist also gives the team's collective actions a singular identity, which is psychologically satisfying, much as the British enjoy having a king or queen to personify the national identity. The great scientist is two people in one. Of course, he or she is a brilliant scientist and is essential to the lab team. But he or she is also the social and collective face of the lab, and this second social role is the one that other scientists see in publications and conference talks. Many young researchers enter science hoping to be trained by a true genius who's doing important and significant work, and once in a lab, they naturally tend to engage in practices that reinforce the rightness of their life choice.

For all these reasons, it's in the team's collective interests to pump up the genius of the chief scientist. When one person gets credit for an entire team's work, it's not surprising that he or she seems superhuman and uniquely creative. Again, we find that it takes a sociocultural approach to look beneath the surface of first appearances, both to explain how scientific creativity really works—collectively and collaboratively—and to explain why the Western cultural model persists despite contrary evidence.

CITATION PATTERNS

Scientific fields aren't democratic. A few scientists generate the great majority of the output, and a small number of published papers receive the great majority of citations from other papers (see Chapter 15, pp. 292–293).

Output

In 1955, Wayne Dennis found that in many different scientific fields, including linguistics, geriatrics, and chemistry, the top 10% of the most prolific researchers generated half of all published work, and the 50% of the least productive researchers generated only about 15% of all published work (Dennis, 1955). Dennis's database did not include those scientists who never

---

3. Schaffer (1994) also documents several historical examples of collaborative discoveries being retrospectively attributed to solitary individuals, and suggests several reasons why scientific communities "make up discovery."

published anything at all, yet some studies suggest that about half of all PhDs from top universities never publish anything (Bloom, 1963).

It turns out that these patterns of productivity follow one of two laws known as the Price law and the Lotka law. According to the Price law, if k represents the total number of contributors to a given field, then *square root(k)* will be the predicted number of contributors who will generate half of all contributions (Price, 1963, p. 46). This results in a highly skewed distribution, one that's more skewed as the discipline grows bigger. In a discipline with 100 members, 10 individuals generate half of all output. According to the Lotka law, if n is the number of published papers, and $f(n)$ is the number of scientists publishing those papers, then $f(n)$ will be inversely proportional to $n2$, with a proportionality constant that varies with each discipline (Lotka, 1926).

A multi-agent computer simulation of a scientific discipline was developed by the sociologist of science Nigel Gilbert (1997) using a new computer technology that simulates each of the members of the group and their interactions. Gilbert programmed a small number of simple rules for how each new paper would be generated and which existing papers it would cite, then ran the simulation for 1,000 iterations. He found that the simulation reproduced the emergent macro features of Lotka's law that have been documented in real scientific disciplines (Fig. 20.1).

These findings seem odd when you consider that most personality traits are normally distributed in the population, according to the famous bell curve (Fig. 20.2). But the productivity curve in Figure 20.1 can't be explained by psychology at all; it's a sociologic phenomenon. Access to top jobs at good universities and access to large research grants is limited. Having success early on is a predictor of future success, because it increases the likelihood that future grants will be successful, and that competitive job offers will be forthcoming. At the other extreme, those who start their careers slowly tend to end up at unknown colleges, teaching large introductory courses in big lecture halls, and never have time to do the research that would gain them recognition and allow them to move to a more research-focused university (Allison, 1980).

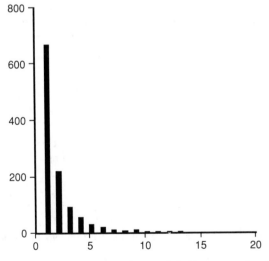

FIGURE 20.1: The number of scientific papers per author, predicted by a computer simulation, closely follows Lotka's law. (Reprinted from *Sociological Research Online*, 2(2). Gilbert 1997, with permission of *Sociological Research Online*, www.socresonline.org.uk.)

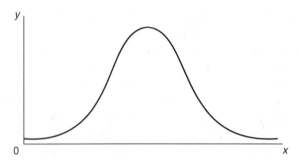

FIGURE 20.2: Normal distribution.

Citations

We've just seen that productivity varies dramatically from one scientist to another. But how do we know that the most productive scientist is the most creative? Maybe those highly productive individuals are generating a lot of worthless articles. To test this, researchers have examined citation patterns: which papers cite which other papers in their references. In some scientific disciplines, this information has been stored in computer databases for several decades, allowing for the first time in history a rigorous quantitative analysis of citation patterns across time.

It turns out that the distribution of citations is even more elitist than the distribution of productivity (Table 20.1). The graph of paper rank by citations follows an inverse power law[4] that results in a Zipf distribution: the *kth* most popular paper has *(N/k) 1/(u-1)* citations. Remarkably, the curve for all scientific disciplines is identical.[5] Such patterns aren't unique to creativity; Zipf's law does an equally good job of explaining such diverse phenomena as the size of traffic jams, the network of connections among websites, income distributions, and the population distributions of major cities (Simon, 1957). Zipf's law is found in many complex networks that have been studied by chaos and complexity theory (see Kauffman, 1993; Sawyer, 2005b).

Table 20.1: The Number of Papers Receiving Each Number of Citations

Number of Papers	Citations
1 paper	8,907 citations
64 papers	>1,000
282 papers	>500
2,103 papers	>200
633,391 papers	<10
368,110	No citations

(From Redner, 2002)

4. In an inverse power law, when both axes are transformed to a logarithmic scale, the curve declines linearly.

5. Identical if the number of citations for each paper is divided by the average number of citations for all papers in the discipline, and the paper rank is divided by the total number of papers (Redner, 2002).

Scientific domains all show skewed distributions of productivity, reputation, and success. To explain scientific creativity, we need to understand how these patterns play out in scientific domains. But an individualist approach can't explain the distribution; it's almost impossible that individual talent varies as much as the citation pattern does. The explanation for these distributions can be found only by using sociocultural approaches to examine properties of the domain and the field. Social network analysis (see Chapter 13) is a promising new methodology for studying these complex social phenomena.

COLLABORATION IN SCIENCE

Science is a very gregarious business. . . . You want to be all the time talking with people . . . it's only by interacting with other people in the building that you get anything interesting done.
     —Physicist Freeman Dyson (quoted in Csikszentmihalyi & Sawyer, 1995, p. 347)
Science is rooted in conversations.
                                    —Physicist Werner Heisenberg, 1971, p. vii

Many scientists report having key insights while engaged in discussion with colleagues—both those working the same area, and those working in radically different spheres of human inquiry. Top scientists realize that scientific creativity depends on conversations, and they do all they can to create more collaborative connections. In the days before the Internet, biologist George Klein created a worldwide network of like-minded intellectuals, held together with old-fashioned letters and stamps. After decades of such networking, Klein became a clearinghouse of ideas from physicists to poets, passing on letters to others he knew would be interested. The files of his correspondence take up dozens of cabinets near his office (Csikszentmihalyi, 1996, p. 277). Jonas Salk, the inventor of the polio vaccine, was inspired to create the Salk Institute for Biological Studies in La Jolla, California, as a forum where diverse interdisciplinary perspectives could come together in everyday hallway discussions: "I can see this done in the form of a collective mind. . . . In this kind of interaction each person helps the others see what they see" (quoted in Csikszentmihalyi, 1996, pp. 284–285).

To study these collaborative conversations, the psychologist Kevin Dunbar chose four of the top laboratories in molecular biology, and then spent a year in each of them (Dunbar, 1995, 1997). He chose 19 scientific research projects to focus on, and observed a total of 23 scientists in the four labs: four senior scientists, each in charge of one of the labs; 12 postdoctoral fellows, five graduate students, and two technicians. By videotaping weekly lab meetings, he discovered that the lab meeting is often the moment when important new ideas and concepts are generated. The lab meetings are attended by all members of the research team: the senior scientist, postdoctoral fellows, graduate students, and technicians. At the typical meeting, one of the team members presents some data from a recent study, and other members ask questions and propose new follow-up experiments. This question-and-answer session often leads the presenting scientist to reconceptualize his or her ideas; in some cases, totally new concepts are generated. The interaction in these meetings is like any other collaborative conversation; it's a spontaneous, improvisational give and take.

Watching a lab meeting allows us to see the creative process at work. Because the scientists talk out loud during the meetings, the videotape provides an external record of their creative process. Dunbar found distributed reasoning in laboratory groups. For example, different members of a group might reason about different stages of an experiment—hypothesis, methodology, and interpretation of results. Dunbar found that during lab meetings, theoretical interpretations of data, known as inductions, made by one scientist were often challenged by the others. Most people have a hard time generating alternative inductions from data, but in a group setting, each person proposes his or her own induction, creating a collaborative situation in which alternative explanations can be contrasted. The distributed reasoning of a scientific team makes the group smarter than the sum of its individual participants. Dunbar also counted the number of inductions and deductions that were *shared*—that had one premise provided by one person, and another premise provided by a different person. He found that 30% of all inductions and deductions were shared. When he interviewed members of the research team months later, they'd already forgotten where the ideas came from. If it weren't for Dunbar and his video camera, the truly social origin of these creative ideas would be lost forever. And as we've already learned, it's usually the chief scientist who gets the credit for these collaborative insights.

MULTIPLE DISCOVERY

Sociological studies of scientific creativity have long downplayed psychological factors, preferring to identify the social properties associated with creations. Sociologists argue that creativity can be analyzed as a sociological-historical process. There's empirical evidence to support this, found in the phenomenon of *multiple discovery*, when two or more independent research teams come up with the same discovery at about the same time, even though they're not in contact and are unaware of each other's work. Historians and sociologists of science have identified hundreds of such cases (Merton, 1961). Classic examples of multiple discovery include:

- The development of calculus by both Newton and Leibniz
- The prediction of the planet Neptune before it was observed, by both Adams and LeVerrier
- The formulation of the law of the conservation of energy by Mayer, Helmholtz, and Joule
- The production of oxygen by both Scheele and Priestley
- The proposal of a theory of evolution through natural selection by both Darwin and Wallace
- The invention of the telephone by both Bell and Gray

Multiple discovery is a sociological phenomenon that's found not only in science. In the recent history of book publishing, it's surprisingly common that multiple books on the same topic appear in the same year, even though each author thought it was his or her own idea, and each publisher thought it would be publishing a unique title (Rich, 2006). In 2006 alone, four books on the Boston mob, four books on climate change, and three books on the science of happiness were simultaneously published. Climate change isn't so surprising, because it's been in the news, and it's a pressing issue of our time. But there's no clear reason why the Boston mob would suddenly become a hot book topic.

Multiple discovery seems to provide evidence that an individual-level analysis can't explain creativity. Sociologists argue that with multiple discoveries, the discovery should be attributed to collective properties of the scientific discipline rather than to psychological processes in any individual scientist. Because the source of the scientific advance must lie outside any one individual and rest in the broader scientific community, we need to explain these discoveries at both an individual and a group level of analysis.

CONCLUSION

The most influential and significant scientists are immensely creative. And although their creativity can be partially explained by their internal psychology, we can explain a lot about scientific creativity by examining broader social patterns. Most scientific discoveries emerge from highly collaborative laboratory teams. Scientific disciplines are broadly cooperative systems of work. And using a sociocultural approach, we've learned that social forces conspire to reinforce the genius myth of creativity. Research teams have several incentives to falsely encourage the outside world to believe that the chief scientist had all of the key insights, even though actual research reveals that in most cases these insights collaboratively emerge from teamwork.

Two hundred years ago, when science was dominated by gentleman amateurs, it may have been possible to attribute creative advances to solitary, towering intellects. (It may have been, but don't forget that most of our well-known stories about historical scientists exaggerate the creativity myths, and distort the historical record.) But in today's era of big science, when laboratories require millions of dollars every year to pay the salaries of research teams of ten scientists or more, no scientist works alone. Today's scientists realize as well as anyone else that science is a deeply collaborative activity. When we analyze scientific work in action, we find that creative insights emerge from collaboration. Scientific creativity is both a psychological and a social process, and explaining scientific creativity requires an interdisciplinary approach.

KEY CONCEPTS

- The copy theory and logical empiricism
- Deduction versus induction
- Analogical thinking in scientific creativity
- Science as problem solving
- Citation patterns
- Multiple discovery

THOUGHT EXPERIMENTS

- You've probably heard of Albert Einstein, but you probably don't know the details of any of the theories that he's famous for. Then how do you know he's so brilliant?

- Imagine that you're in charge of government funding of scientific research. What percentage of that money would you devote to each of these areas: physics, biology, the sociology of poverty and schooling, the mental processes studied by psychology, international trade, how to design the best preschool, etc. Do you think the government's current allocation of funds is similar to what you would propose?
- How is scientific creativity different from artistic creativity? How is it the same?
- I hope I've convinced you that scientists are creative, after all. But you might still think that artists are more creative than scientists. Do you? Why or why not?

SUGGESTED READINGS

Beller, M. (1999). *Quantum dialogue: The making of a revolution.* Chicago: The University of Chicago Press.

Dunbar, K. (1997). How scientists think: On-line creativity and conceptual change in science. In T. B. Ward, S. M. Smith, & J. Vaid (Eds.), *Creative thought: An investigation of conceptual structures and processes* (pp. 461–493). Washington, DC: American Psychological Association.

Farmelo, G. (Ed.). (2002b). *It must be beautiful: Great equations of modern science.* London: Granta Books.

Holyoak, K. J., & Thagard, P. (1995). *Mental leaps: Analogy in creative thought.* Cambridge: MIT Press.

Merton, R. K. (1961). Singletons and multiples in scientific discovery: A chapter in the sociology of science. *Proceedings of the American Philosophical Society, 105*(5), 470–486.

Mukerji, C. (1996). The collective construction of scientific genius. In Y. Engeström & D. Middleton (Eds.), *Cognition and communication at work* (pp. 257–278). New York: Cambridge University Press.

Waller, J. (2002). *Einstein's luck: The truth behind some of the greatest scientific discoveries.* New York: Oxford University Press. [See especially pp. 32–63]

PART 5

EVERYDAY CREATIVITY

The Western cultural model holds that creativity is a burst of inspiration from a lone genius; that a person working alone is always more creative than a group; and that social conventions and expectations always interfere with creativity. These creativity beliefs are modern versions of the ancient idealist theory of philosophy, which states that the most important part of creativity is having an idea, and that the execution of the idea to make an actual artwork is not that important.

But in Part IV, we've learned that creativity isn't a burst of inspiration; it's mostly conscious hard work. We've learned that instead of a single moment of insight, most created products result from hard work peppered with mini-insights, and that these mini-insights don't seem that mysterious in the context of the preceding hard work. We've learned that creativity is almost never a solitary activity but that it's fundamentally social and collaborative. We've learned that the audience and the viewers play key roles in the creative process. The interdisciplinary approach gives us the ability to explain the social, collaborative hard work of creativity, and also to explain individual creative contributions.

In Part V, we'll bring all of these findings together to learn how we can increase our own creativity in everyday life. Chapter 21 focuses on creative teaching and learning, and explores what creative classrooms look like. Chapter 22 shows how to apply the research to enhance your own creativity. And Chapter 23 wraps it all up; I describe changes in global society that are changing the nature of creativity, and I make some recommendations for how creativity research might proceed.

EDUCATION AND CREATIVITY

Creative talent [is] one of our greatest national resources . . . every school and college must teach creative problem-solving both in currently established courses and in new courses specifically designed for the purpose.

Parnes & Harding, 1962, p. vii

Throughout this book, we've seen the high value placed on creativity in the world today. In the Western cultural model, "you are creative" is one of the highest compliments you can give to a person. But there's one place that seems not to welcome creativity: the classroom. Studies have shown that most teachers associate creativity with undesirable student behaviors—like being stubborn, critical, rebellious, and nonconforming (Moran, 2010, p. 336; Scott, 1999). Teachers rarely reward creativity in classrooms (Sternberg & Lubart, 1991). Teachers' least favorite students tend to be the ones who score highest on traits associated with creativity (Beghetto, 2006b; Fasko, 2000-2001; Westby & Dawson, 1995). This is even more true in some Asian countries than in Western countries (Ng & Smith, 2004). Creative children don't like school any more than teachers like them; most eminent creators say that they disliked school, many dropped out or skipped grades, and some were schooled at home by parents or tutors (Csikszentmihalyi, Rathunde, & Whalen, 1993; Goertzel & Goertzel, 1962/2004).

In the Western cultural model, schools are thought to squash creativity. This is a variant of Belief 3, that creativity is more likely when you reject convention, and Belief 4, that creative contributions tend to come from outsiders. Anyone who's worked with preschool children has seen that they display amazing creativity every day; they create dramatic fantasy worlds, or combine two different toys in a way not envisioned by the toy designers, or choose to play with the box rather than the toy inside it. Compared with the extreme creativity of children's play, schools are quite standardized and regimented; all children learn the same thing at the same time. Our image of the school is of rows of desks, all exactly the same, where teachers emphasize order and conformity (in part simply to maintain control of the classroom). In the terms used by creativity researchers, schools emphasize convergent thinking at the expense of divergent thinking.

Torrance (1965) interviewed teachers in five countries (United States, Germany, India, Greece, the Philippines) and found that teachers in all five countries disapproved of students asking questions, guessing, being independent in judgment and thinking, being intuitive, being willing to take risks, and being unwilling to accept an opinion on mere authority—and these are all behaviors associated with creativity. In contrast, all the teachers approved of uncreative behaviors including obedience, courtesy, etc. In this pioneering 1965 study, the answers varied depending on the country—teachers in the United States gave answers that were slightly less disparaging of creative behaviors, and teachers in the Philippines gave answers that were the least favorable to creativity. Forty years later, Ng and Smith (2004) compared individualist and collectivist teachers (see Chapter 14), and found that individualist teachers were more likely to promote creative behaviors in class, even if they had the potential for undesirable side effects like classroom disruption. Collectivist teachers were more likely to promote desirable behaviors, even if they were uncreative (pp. 100–101).

But I know a lot of teachers, and I don't recognize them in the above findings. The teachers I know would insist that they appreciate creative children. What's going on? One possibility is that teachers are prevented from fostering creativity by the administration, the curriculum, and other institutional constraints. One study (Andiliou & Murphy, 2010) found that teachers believe that it's possible to teach and foster creativity, but that more than half of them say that the school climate and curriculum guidelines prevent them from fostering student creativity.

A second possibility is that teachers and researchers mean different things when they refer to "creativity." Westby and Dawson (1995) asked elementary teachers to rate the top ten characteristics of creative children and the top ten of uncreative children, and they discovered that teachers have a conception of the creative child that's different from that of creativity researchers. Only 9 of the teachers' 20 characteristics of "the creative child" agreed with research; among their top ten "creativity" traits were sincere, responsible, good-natured, reliable, and logical. This suggests that to be creative and still liked by a teacher, children have to be easy to manage. Some of the teachers' bottom ten characteristics of creative children were "makes up the rules as he or she goes along," "is impulsive," and "is a noncomformist" (p. 6); yet creativity experts say these are among the top characteristics of creative children (Westby & Dawson, 1995).

Teachers associate creativity with the liberal arts and humanities, although researchers believe that creativity is manifest in all subject areas, and societies today have a great need for creativity in science, technology, engineering, and math. Some teachers associate creativity primarily with gifted students, but society would benefit from realizing the full creative potential of all students (Andiliou & Murphy, 2010). An international consensus is developing that in the 21st century, all students should graduate prepared to engage in creative thinking and acting (Benavides, Dumont, & Istance, 2008, p. 24).

I believe that schools are essential to creativity. We've learned that creativity requires a high degree of domain knowledge; for example, it takes ten years of hard work mastering a domain before one can make a creative contribution (Chapter 5, pp. 93–95). Formal schooling is quite good at delivering this domain knowledge to students. Creativity research certainly doesn't suggest that everyone would be more creative if only we got rid of all of the schools! However, schools could better foster creativity if they were transformed to better align with creativity research.

I begin the chapter by summarizing the history of research in two areas closely related to creativity: arts education, and talented and gifted education. I then shift to a discussion of contemporary research in creativity education, both in general and in specific content areas.

ARTS EDUCATION

For much of the past 50 years, creativity in education has been closely associated with the arts—music and visual arts in particular. Researchers in creativity have traditionally been closely allied with arts education researchers. The teachers who are most receptive to creativity in the classroom are arts educators, because in traditional schools, creativity is rarely found outside of arts, music, and drama classes.

There are three basic arguments in support of arts education. The first argument is that the arts are important in and of themselves, and that all educated citizens should have a solid grounding in the arts as a part of our shared cultural heritage. But the "art for art's sake" argument tends to lose in the face of tight budgets and hard choices. When financial pressures first began to affect arts programs in U.S. schools in the 1970s and increasingly in the 1980s, arts education researchers developed a second and a third argument in defense of arts education, both based on the argument that arts education provided unique cognitive benefits to the learner, and that these benefits would transfer to other content areas (including math, science, and literacy) and would result in enhanced learning across the curriculum.

The second argument is that education in the arts results in enhanced cognitive skills that then transfer to other content areas, resulting in enhanced learning of all content areas. For example, it's been hypothesized that music listening enhances spatial reasoning, that classroom drama enhances verbal achievement, and that music enhances mathematic ability. Elliot Eisner (2002b) proposed six distinctive "artistically rooted forms of intelligence": (1) experiencing qualitative relationships and making judgments; (2) working with flexible goals that emerge from the work; (3) form and content are inseparable; (4) some forms of knowledge cannot be represented propositionally; (5) thinking with a medium that has unique constraints and affordances; (6) thinking and work that results in satisfaction and flow that are inherently engaging. These new arguments emerged at the same time that the cognitive revolution spread through psychology and education research more generally (Eisner, 1982, 2002a; Gardner, 1973). Perhaps the most influential cognition and arts research was that done at Harvard's Project Zero, and the several books about arts, education, and development by Howard Gardner during the 1970s (e.g., Gardner, 1973). The primary impact of Gardner's influential 1983 book *Frames of Mind* was to provide academic support for educators who wanted to prevent schools from being narrowly focused on the "rationalist" content areas of math, science, and literacy.

It's controversial whether the arts provide unique cognitive benefits that transfer to other content areas (see Burnaford, 2007, in support, and Hetland & Winner, 2004, and Moga, Burger, Hetland, & Winner, 2000, for a critique). Yet even the strongest critics of transferable cognitive benefits nonetheless argue that arts education results in unique "habits of mind" or dispositions that may be valuable in learning other content areas (Hetland, Winner, Veenema, & Sheridan, 2007): the dispositions to observe, envision, express, reflect, stretch and explore, engage and persist, develop craft, and understand the art world.

The third argument in defense of arts education is that when the arts are integrated with instruction in another content area, such as math or science, that other content area is learned more effectively (Efland, 2002; Winslow, 1939). The claim is that when the arts are integrated with instruction in other content areas, learners achieve a deeper understanding, acquire an ability to think more flexibly using content knowledge, and develop enhanced critical thinking and creativity; the arts help teachers engage students more deeply, and reach a broader range of learning styles (Burnaford, 2007). In recent decades, arts educators use the term "interdisciplin-ary" or "arts integration" to refer to curricula that integrate the arts with other subjects (e.g. Burnaford, 2007; Cornett, 1999; Schramm, 2002; Strokrocki, 2005). Eisner (2002a) identified four possible curricular structures for arts integration: (1) in a unit focusing on a particular historical period or culture; (2) a unit that focuses on similarities and differences among art forms; (3) a unit that's centered on a major theme or idea that can be explored through the arts and other fields too; (4) a unit in which students are asked to solve a problem that has roots in both the arts and another content area.

It has proven to be exceedingly difficult to design studies that support these second and third arguments. The most exhaustive survey of research in support of transfer (argument 2) and arts integration (argument 3) is found in a 2007 report from the Arts Education Partnership (Burnaford, 2007). The most extensive critique of research in support of transfer is a meta-analysis by Lois Hetland, Ellen Winner, and colleagues (Hetland & Winner, 2004; Moga et al., 2000). The jury is still out on whether arts education enhances creativity in general. The general consensus among creativity researchers is that creativity is largely domain-specific (Chapter 3)—that the ability to be creative in any given domain, whether physics, painting, or musical performance, is based on long years of study and mastery of a domain-specific set of cognitive structures. If so, then learning how to be creative in one of the arts would not necessarily trans-fer to being creative in other content areas.

TALENTED AND GIFTED EDUCATION

Until quite recently, discussions of creativity in education were found almost exclusively within talented and gifted education.[1] Creativity assessment and instruction have long been central to gifted education programs. There's a long history of attempts to provide creative learning envi-ronments for students who are identified as gifted. Often, these are "enrichment" activities that are in addition to the regular curriculum (Subotnik & Arnold, 1994).

Through most of the 20th century, giftedness was often equated with intelligence as mea-sured by intelligence tests. But in the second half of the 20th century, there were many attempts to expand the definition of giftedness beyond IQ. In the early 1970s, the U.S. government pro-posed a six-faceted definition of giftedness, now known as the *Marland definition* (Marland, 1972). Under the Marland definition, giftedness and talent can be manifested in six areas: gen-eral intellectual ability, specific academic aptitude, creative or productive thinking, leadership ability, visual and performing arts, and psychomotor ability. This influential definition is used by almost half of all U.S. school districts (Callahan et al., 1995). Unfortunately, the second most commonly used definition of giftedness is simply an IQ cutoff score—which doesn't take creativ-ity into account at all (Hunsacker & Callahan, 1995).

---

1. The word "talented" has begun to replace "gifted" due to complex connotations of the older word. The field is sometimes called "TAG," an abbreviation for "talented and gifted." Beginning with a 1992 govern-ment report, *National Excellence: A Case for Developing America's Talent*, the word "gifted" was eliminated in favor of "outstanding talent" and "exceptional talent": "perform or show the potential for performing at remarkably high levels of accomplishment when compared with others of their age, experience, or environ-ment." The preference for "exceptional talent" has continued (see the 2010 National Academies' report).

In the 1980s and 1990s, a third phase in conceptions of giftedness began: conceptions of giftedness as being found in different domains (also see Chapter 3, pp. 58–60). These include:

- Howard Gardner's theory of multiple intelligences (Gardner, 1983; see p. 402 below)
- Robert Sternberg's triarchic theory (Sternberg, 1985a; see pp. 397–399 below)
- Joseph Renzulli's three-ring theory (Renzulli, 1978, 2005): ability, creativity, and task commitment (within the context of personality, environmental, and affective factors)
- Gagné's differentiated model of giftedness and talent (DMGT; Gagné, 1991, 1993)

Of these, Renzulli's three-ring theory has been the most influential in gifted education; it's the third most commonly used approach in gifted admissions (coming after the Marland definition and IQ scores alone). School-based programs based on this theory include Renzulli and Reis' (1985) Schoolwide Enrichment Model (also see Karnes & Bean, 2001). For Renzulli, giftedness emerges from the combination of ability, creativity, and commitment. Renzulli found that identification methods based on his theory tend to identify a larger number of minorities and girls than assessments based solely on intelligence tests (Renzulli, 1999). Sternberg (1999b) also found evidence that when creative or practical intelligence is used for selection, the resulting group is more diverse in terms of racial, ethnic, socioeconomic, and educational backgrounds than if analytic intelligence is used.

CREATIVITY TESTS IN TALENTED AND GIFTED ADMISSIONS

Most talented and gifted education programs have formal assessment procedures for admission. Almost all of these programs incorporate general intelligence, typically measured by some form of IQ test, as a primary criterion. In addition, many of these programs use one of the measures of creativity described in Chapter 3. In a study of how school districts identified gifted students, Callahan et al. (1995) found that creativity was frequently included in the district's definition of giftedness—but also found that measuring creativity was difficult. Most districts measured creativity using the Scales for Rating the Behavioral Characteristics of Superior Students (SRBCSS: Renzulli et al., 2001); a few used the TTCT-Figural or the SOI. The Callahan review also found, surprisingly, that a large number of districts use IQ and achievement tests to measure creativity (p. 32).

Many gifted programs use teacher nominations for admissions. One problem with asking teachers to nominate students for gifted programs is that teachers tend to prefer gifted children who are low in creativity to those who are highly creative (Kim, 2006; see the beginning of this chapter). This is why SRBCSS is very specific in asking the teacher to rate each student on ten characteristics:

1. Displays a great deal of curiosity about many things; is constantly asking questions about anything and everything
2. Generates a large number of ideas or solutions to problems and questions; often offers unusual ("way-out"), unique, clever responses
3. Is uninhibited in expressions of opinion; is sometimes radical and spirited in disagreement; is tenacious
4. Is a high risk taker; is adventurous and speculative

5. Displays a good deal of intellectual playfulness; fantasizes; imagines ("I wonder what would happen if. . ."); manipulates ideas (i.e., changes, elaborates upon them); is often concerned with adapting, improving, and modifying institutions, objects, and systems

6. Displays a keen sense of humor and sees humor in situations that may not appear to be humorous to others

7. Is usually aware of his impulses and more open to the irrational in himself (freer expression of feminine interest for boys, greater than usual amount of independence for girls); shows emotional sensitivity

8. Is sensitive to beauty; attends to aesthetic characteristics of things

9. Is nonconforming; accepts disorder; is not interested in details; is individualistic; does not fear being different

10. Criticizes constructively; is unwilling to accept authoritarian pronouncements without critical examination

Other instruments used to identify creative talent in students include:

- Holland (1961) Creative Activity Checklist
- Okuda, Runco, and Berger (1991) Creative Activities Checklist
- Lees-Haley (1978) Creative Behavior Inventory
- Bull and Davis (1980) Statement of Past Creative Activities
- Davis (1975) How Do You Think (HDYT) test, or its shortened version, the Group Inventory for Finding Interests II (GIFFI II; Davis & Rimm, 1982)
- Urban and Jellen (1993) Test for Creative Thinking-Drawing Production (TCT-DP)
- Smith and Carlsson (1987) Percept-Genesis test

You might expect creativity researchers to support the use of such tests in gifted program admissions. But on the contrary, most creativity researchers are nervous about placing too much weight on such tests. The typical advice you'll hear from a creativity researcher is to consider using high scores on these tests to expand the potential pool of candidates, but don't use low scores on these tests to exclude children who might otherwise qualify (Piirto, 1998, p. 99). Some colleges are taking this advice and using creativity measures as an "extra credit" possibility (J. C. Kaufman, 2009, pp. 145–147; see the discussion of the Rainbow Project on pp. 397–399). But not all school districts follow these guidelines in their creativity assessment (J. C. Kaufman, 2009, p. 144).

DOMAIN-GENERAL CREATIVITY SKILLS

Today there are thousands of students involved in extracurricular activities that emphasize creativity, including these:

- Young Authors Conventions (where children write their own books)
- Odyssey of the Mind and Destination Imagination (where groups of children invent and build mechanical devices)

- First Robotics Competition (an Olympic-style event sponsored by inventor Dean Kamen)
- Invention Conventions (where children invent things)
- Future Problem-Solving contests (where children solve pressing global problems)
- The Creative Problem Solving Program (Noller, Parnes, & Biondi, 1976)
- The Purdue Creative Thinking Program (Feldhusen et al., 1983)
- The CoRT Thinking Skills Program (de Bono, 1973)

It's been difficult to convincingly demonstrate that these programs actually increase creative ability. At first, researchers tried to prove their benefits by measuring students' divergent thinking abilities both before and after taking the creativity course. But these studies had a big weakness: because the students were told the activity would enhance their creativity, and because the students knew their divergent thinking was supposed to go up, they might have provided more answers on the post-test in a desire to conform to teacher expectations (Wallach, 1988). We'll further examine the research on creativity training effectiveness in Chapter 22.

CREATIVITY IN THE CONTENT AREAS

Instead of teaching creativity in general, a more radical approach is to teach content-area knowledge in ways that prepare students to be more creative using that knowledge. The consensus among creativity researchers is that although there are domain-general creative strategies, creativity is primarily domain-specific (see Chapter 3, pp. 58–60). Consistent with this research, many contemporary scholars have argued that creative learning should be embedded in all subject areas (e.g., Craft, Jeffrey, & Leibling, 2001; Gardner, 2007). An international consensus has developed that schools should use curricula in all subjects that result in cognitive outcomes that support creative performance (OECD, 2008).

If creativity is domain-specific, then we can't hope to produce more creative graduates simply by adding general creativity enrichment activities to the curriculum. If math and science continue to be taught in a way that doesn't foster creative thinking and problem solving, then no amount of general creativity training or arts education can help. Rather, it may be necessary to transform the ways that each subject area is taught, so that the knowledge that students acquire is of the sort that fosters creative thinking and behavior. Fortunately, an exciting new area of research, *the learning sciences*, has identified the features of this sort of knowledge (Sawyer, 2006d; Table 21.1).

In instructionism, creativity is opposed to learning, because learning is equated with mastery of what is already known. Learning is simple internalization and convergent thinking. But in the newer understanding of learning that's emerging from the learning sciences, the conceptual understanding that underlies creative behavior emerges from learning environments in which students build their own knowledge (Scardamalia & Bereiter, 2006) through exploratory talk (Mercer, 2000) and sustained argumentation (Andriessen, 2006). The constructivist view emerging from learning sciences research is that learning is always a creative process (Sawyer, 2003a).

The research shows that creativity is grounded in a deep understanding of domain knowledge (Chapter 5), and schools are essential in socializing children into creative domains. But the

Table 21.1: Contrasting Two Learning Approaches

Learning Knowledge Deeply (findings from cognitive science)	Traditional Classroom Practices (instructionism)
Deep learning requires that learners relate new ideas and concepts to previous knowledge and experience.	Learners treat course material as unrelated to what they already know.
Deep learning requires that learners integrate their knowledge into interrelated conceptual systems.	Learners treat course material as disconnected bits of knowledge.
Deep learning requires that learners look for patterns and underlying principles.	Learners memorize facts and carry out procedures without understanding how or why.
Deep learning requires that learners evaluate new ideas, and relate them to conclusions.	Learners have difficulty making sense of new ideas that are different from what they encountered in the textbook.
Deep learning requires that learners understand the process of dialog through which knowledge is created, and they examine the logic of an argument critically.	Learners treat facts and procedures as static knowledge, handed down from an all-knowing authority.
Deep learning requires that learners reflect on their own understanding and their own process of learning.	Learners memorize without reflecting on the purpose or on their own learning strategies.

(From Sawyer, 2006d)

challenge is to help students master domain knowledge so that they're prepared to be creative using that knowledge—not simply to memorize it and regurgitate it on tests.

USING CREATIVITY ASSESSMENTS IN SCHOOL

> *High but not the highest intelligence, combined with the greatest degree of persistence, will achieve greater eminence than the highest degree of intelligence with somewhat less persistence.*
>
> —Cox, (1926, p. 187)

Grades in school are only lightly correlated with adult career success (Baird, 1982, 1985; Cohen, 1984). So what other measures might be used to evaluate a person's potential for achievement—is it IQ tests, creativity tests, or some other measure? The relation between IQ and career success has been hotly debated for decades (e.g., Milgram & Hong, 1993, 1999; Ree & Earles, 1992, 1993); the outcome of this research is that IQ tests predict about 25% of the variance in school performance (Anastasi & Urbina, 1997) and 10% to 15% of the variance in job performance (Sternberg, 1999b). Ree and Earles (1992) surveyed the literature and concluded that intelligence is the best predictor of job performance.[2] High IQ predicts success in later life (Terman &

2. In a response to this article, Sternberg and Wagner (1993) noted that IQ predicts only 5% to 10% of job performance. McClelland (1993) noted that IQ predicts about 0.20; Ree and Earles (1993) in their rejoinder say it is much higher, about 0.65.

Oden, 1947, 1959), but among highly gifted children, additional IQ doesn't result in additional accomplishment (Matarazzo, 1972; Milgram & Hong, 1993, 1999).

A growing trend among admission committees is to focus not only on cognitive measures, like IQ or SAT scores, but also on emotion, motivation, and creativity (Kyllonen, Walters, & Kaufman, 2005). A survey of professors found that creativity was considered to be one of the most important abilities predicting success in graduate school (Enright & Gitomer, 1989). Creativity was one of five qualities listed in a study of potential measures to add to the GRE (Walpole, Burton, Kanyi, & Jackenthal, 2001). The Educational Testing Service (ETS) has developed two creativity measures: formulating hypotheses, and measuring constructs (Kyllonen, 2009).

There's some evidence that creativity scores predict career success and also predict adult creative accomplishments. Roberta Milgram argued that creativity is a better predictor of life success than traditional IQ tests (Milgram & Hong, 1999). Milgram and Milgram (1976) found that divergent thinking scores predicted the degree of participation and accomplishment in creative extracurricular activities, even after IQ was partialled out ($r = 0.35$ for men and 0.21 for women). There was no relation between IQ and extracurricular accomplishment, once creativity was partialled out. The bulk of the effect resulted from the relation with accomplishment in writing and in fine arts extracurricular activities, for women and men, and additionally for men, in leadership and community service. This was the entire high-school class of 60 boys and 85 girls, in a high school with high academic standards. But it's unclear that paper-and-pencil creativity tests can ever successfully predict adult creativity. Hocevar (1980) found that fluency scores were only marginally related to observed creative performance, and that the interaction of fluency and intelligence wasn't related.

The outcome variable for both the Milgram and the Hocevar studies is quantity of accomplishments, with no measure of quality (or creativity *per se*). Runco (1986) used IQ and the Wallach and Kogan (1965) tests of divergent thinking with a group of gifted fifth through eighth graders. He used a self-report of creative performance that was similar to Hocevar (1980) and Milgram and Milgram (1976). And then for quality, he asked people to describe their most creative activity, and then had those rated by two independent judges for "self-motivated and original work" (p. 1249). He found that the unique variance of fluency (apart from IQ) was related to writing and art quantity of participation (replicating Milgram & Milgram, 1976). When creativity was partialled out, IQ was related to science, performing art, and writing. But the quality of creative performance was not related to creative fluency or to IQ (p. 1252).

In sum, the research is mixed about how best to identify high-potential students. On balance, it seems that IQ tests have the strongest predictive power, although they leave the majority of the variance in adult performance unexplained—corresponding to our common-sense intuitions that the smartest people aren't always the most successful. And there's some evidence that creativity tests provide additional predictive power, both in college grades and in job performance.

THE TRIARCHIC THEORY OF HUMAN INTELLIGENCE

Psychologist Robert Sternberg has dedicated his career to the study of IQ, creativity, and performance. He hypothesized that IQ tests predict such a small percentage of job performance because they measure a person's performance in isolation, whereas in the real world, everything that we do involves working with other people, and collaborative teamwork ability isn't measured by traditional tests. Wagner and Sternberg (1986) called this practical ability *tacit knowledge*, and they developed new tests to measure it. Sternberg and Wagner (1993) found that their measures of tacit knowledge correlate 0.3 to 0.5 with job measures like rated prestige of business or institution, salary, and performance appraisals.

Sternberg (1999b) argued that instead of traditional IQ tests, we should be measuring *successful intelligence*: "the ability to achieve success in life, given one's personal standards, within one's sociocultural context" (p. 293). He argued that balanced analytic, creative, and practical abilities are necessary:

- *Analytic abilities* are used to analyze, evaluate, judge, compare, and contrast. They are typically used when the core processing components are applied to familiar problems that require abstract judgments. (These are the skills measured by traditional IQ tests and school tests like the SAT.)
- *Practical abilities* are used to implement, apply, or put into practice ideas in real-world contexts. They involve the application of the core components of intelligence to adapt to, shape, and select environments. Much of this is tacit knowledge: knowledge that is not explicitly taught and that is not verbalized, but that is nonetheless needed to work effectively.
- *Creative abilities* are used to create, invent, discover, imagine, suppose, or hypothesize. They are typically used with novel problems.

Sternberg et al. (1999) developed the *Sternberg triarchic abilities test (STAT)* to measure these three abilities. The creative measures, each with four four-item multiple-choice tests, were verbal, quantitative, and figural:

- *Verbal*: novel analogies—verbal analogies preceded by counterfactual premises like "money falls off trees"
- *Quantitative*: students had to work with novel operations, like *flix*, for which the operations differ depending on whether the first number is greater than, equal to, or different from the second
- *Figural*: students viewed a series of transformations and had to apply the rule to a new figure to complete the series

In addition, students completed three essays, one each for each of the three abilities:

- *Analytic*: Analyze the advantages and disadvantages of having police or security guards in the school building.
- *Creative*: Describe how you would reform your school system to produce an ideal one. Two additional examples of creative essay questions were: "Describe the world through the eyes of insects" and "Describe who might live and what might happen on a planet called Priumliava." The stories were scored for novelty, amount of development in the plot, and creative use of prior knowledge. Interscore reliabilities were high: 0.69, 0.75, and 0.75.
- *Practical*: State a problem in your life and state three practical solutions for resolving it.

Overall correlations among these subtests were high: for example, analytic and creative abilities correlated at 0.47. Multiple-choice items correlated more highly (0.52) and essay items more weakly (0.21). In a second study with Russian students, again the multiple-choice measures were highly correlated, and the essay items were not. Sternberg concluded that one should probably not use multiple-choice tests to measure creative or practical abilities (1999b, p. 299).

When Sternberg became Dean of the College of Arts and Sciences at Tufts University, he had a unique opportunity to apply this research to practice by introducing a new college admissions procedure. At various times, the Tufts application contained items such as (from Sternberg et al., 2006):

- **Cartoons**. Participants were given five single-frame cartoons, minus their captions, that had appeared in *The New Yorker* magazine. They had to choose three from the five, and provide a caption for each cartoon. Two trained judges rated the cartoons for cleverness, humor, and originality on a 5-point scale.
- **Written stories**. Participants were asked to write two stories, spending 15 minutes on each, choosing from the following titles: "A Fifth Chance," "2983," "Beyond the Edge," "The Octopus's Sneakers," "It's Moving Backwards," "Not Enough Time." Six judges were trained to rate the stories for originality, complexity, emotional evocativeness, and descriptiveness on 5-point scales.
- **Oral stories**. Participants were presented with five sheets of paper, each containing a set of 11 to 13 images linked by a common theme: keys, money, travel, animals playing music, humans playing music. They were told to choose two of the pages, and spend 15 minutes on each, thinking up a story, and dictating a story into a tape recorder, with no more than 5 minutes of recording time. Six judges were trained to rate the stories for originality, complexity, emotional evocativeness, and descriptiveness on 5-point scales.

Intercorrelations between pairs of these three separate measures weren't high, suggesting that there's probably not a single common factor uniting these scores (Sternberg et al., 2006, p. 334). There was a substantial correlation of 0.77 between the creativity latent variable and the SAT verbal score, but the three performance tasks were each correlated with SAT verbal at less than 0.40 (p. 335). A regression model showed that the oral stories task, the cartoon captions task, and the STAT-creative predicted college GPA beyond the SAT. As of 2010, Tufts University no longer used the multiple-choice items because they correlated so highly with SAT and across the three abilities; the essays were an optional component of the Tufts college application.

CREATIVE TEACHING

Most teacher education programs don't mention creativity at all (Mack, 1987), education textbooks don't tell teachers how to foster creativity (DeZutter, 2011), and most teachers use creative teaching techniques rarely (Schacter, Thum, & Zifkin, 2006; Torrance & Safter, 1986). But for those teachers who wish to foster student creativity, many researchers have provided lists of practices and attitudes that foster creativity (Craft, 2005, pp. 43–45; Cropley, 1997; Feldhusen & Treffinger, 1980, p. 32; Fleith, 2000; Piirto, 1998, 2004; Rejskind, 2000; Schacter, Thum, & Zifkin,

2006; Sternberg & Williams, 1996; Torrance, 1965, 1970). The following recommendations appear on many of these lists:

- Openness: Respect unusual questions and unusual ideas
- Evaluation: Have students do something without being evaluated; connect evaluation to the causes and consequences of the idea rather than to the quality of the idea; recognize and reward each child's creativity; instruct and assess creativity. Make sure that your tests include questions that require creative thinking; reward creative ideas and products. Your grading should take creativity into account; delay evaluation of student ideas until they have been fully worked out and clearly formulated.
- Surprise: Encounter the unexpected and deepen expectations.
- Trust and safety: Maintain a psychologically safe classroom environment.
- Build self-efficacy: Tell your students that they have what it takes to be creative; help students become aware of their creativity.
- Help students resist peer pressures to conform: Allow students to be odd; avoid emphasizing socialization at the expense of creative expression.
- Problem finding: Encourage questions, different responses, humor, and risk-taking. Define and redefine problems. Allow students to choose their own ways to solve problems; give them opportunities to revise and redefine.
- Model creativity: Teachers should be role models by themselves engaging in creative behaviors. Use profiles of creative people.
- Question assumptions: Encourage students to ask questions about their unstated assumptions. Take students' suggestions and questions seriously
- Encourage idea generation: Don't ask for just one response; give students time to generate multiple responses. Support and reinforce students' unusual ideas.
- Cross-fertilize ideas: Give students opportunities to think across disciplines.
- Allow time for creative thinking and incubation: Schedule ten minutes of thinking time during a class, or a longer period during the week. Allow time for students to develop and think about their creative ideas.
- Encourage sensible risks; allow mistakes; use failure as a positive.
- Encourage creative collaboration.
- Imagine other viewpoints; encourage the adoption of different perspectives.
- Motivate students to master factual knowledge; it's an important basis for creativity. Emphasize that talent is only a small part of creative production, and that discipline and practice are important. Foster the in-depth study of disciplines to enable children to go beyond their own immediate experience.
- Take an inclusive approach where students and teachers collaborate to identify problems and issues, and debate and discuss, together.

Many of these practices are found in the classrooms of good teachers everywhere, so it's not surprising that many people equate creative teaching with good teaching (Kind & Kind, 2007). But true creativity requires specific classroom designs and teacher behaviors; the teacher's role is a facilitator and fellow collaborator, joining the students in a process of knowledge building (Scardamalia & Bereiter, 2006; Sawyer, 2004). Students must be active collaborators and participants in the learning. Unfortunately, in too many classrooms, teachers are unable to engage in these creativity-fostering behaviors due to institutional pressures, including the need to cover a large amount of material (in the U.S., the curriculum is sometimes said to be "a mile wide and an inch deep") and the need to prepare students to score well on standardized tests that don't assess creativity. To transform schools to foster greater creativity in students, many things need to change:

- Student assessments should incorporate and reward creativity.
- Teacher professional development should be based in creativity research.
- Schools and districts should ensure that curricular demands don't emphasize breadth over depth.

COGNITION AND TRANSFER

Mayer (1989) defined creativity as "producing a novel method of solving a new problem" and defined creative teaching as teaching "subject matter in ways that help students to transfer what they have learned to creative problem solving" (p. 203). He defined creative learning as "when students use active learning strategies for mentally representing new material in ways that lead to problem solving transfer" (p. 203). His definition of a non-creative learner is one who's able to solve problems just like the ones presented during instruction (retention problems), but not able to solve problems that weren't explicitly taught (transfer problems). Creative learners are the students who do well on both types of problems.

Mayer summarized 16 different experiments that demonstrated that teaching with analogical models leads to improved performance on transfer problems, and thus greater creativity. On average, teaching with analogical models improved student performance on transfer problems by 64% (1989, p. 205). The implications are that to assess for creative learning, students should be tested not only on retention of specific facts, but on the ability to transfer knowledge to new problems (Mayer, 1984).

Mayer also found that when students were taught learning strategies that encouraged them to identify relational statements and to extract generalizations from texts and problem statements, they displayed greater creativity. His research suggests that schools should "teach creative learning skills within specific content domains rather than as a separate course in general learning skills" (1989, p. 204; see Chapter 22). We don't yet have a good understanding of how to teach for creativity in specific content domains; this is a promising area for future research.

In science education, there's a growing body of research on how to foster creative learning (Sawyer, 2006b). Kind and Kind (2007) presented a summary of this research; one prominent line of research focuses on introducing *inquiry-based science* into classrooms. "Inquiry-based science" has many variations, but the core of the approach is to present students with real-world problems and data, and to allow them to formulate hypotheses, design experiments, gather data, and marshal evidence in support of or against the hypotheses. These educational efforts are based on the belief that learning is more creative when learning activities mimic the real-world creative processes of scientists. The problem, according to Kind and Kind (2007), is that real inquiry almost never happens in the classroom; teachers ending up framing the children's investigative pathway, because children's naïvety as learners makes real inquiry difficult to achieve in practice. Researchers are still working to identify how to teach science in ways that foster student creativity; this too is a promising area for future research.

402   EVERYDAY CREATIVITY

THE MESHING HYPOTHESIS

Gardner (1983) criticized the claim that there's a single general factor behind human potential and performance, the *g* that IQ is purported to measure (Chapter 3). Instead, he proposed seven "intelligences": verbal, logical-mathematical, spatial-visual, bodily-kinesthetic, musical, intrapersonal, and interpersonal. (In a later work, he suggested an additional eighth intelligence of naturalist; Gardner, 1998.) Traditional intelligence tests assess only the first two or three of these intelligences: verbal, logical-mathematical, and spatial-visual. Gardner (1993) applied his theory to creative achievement, identifying one creative genius for each of his seven intelligences: T. S. Eliot, Albert Einstein, Pablo Picasso, Martha Graham, Igor Stravinsky, Sigmund Freud, and Mahatma Gandhi.

Gardner's intelligences have been widely interpreted as *learning styles*, with some people thought to learn more effectively when instruction is delivered in their preferred styles. If evidence can be found for this *Aptitude–Treatment Interaction (ATI)*, then the implications for teaching would be profound. There's at least one well-supported ATI: learners with different levels of prior knowledge need different instructional methods (Mayer, 2008; also see Pashler et al., 2008, for a review). When applied to learning styles like Gardner's intelligences, the hypothesis that there's an ATI is also known as the "meshing hypothesis" or the "matching hypothesis"—if instruction is delivered that matches the learner's preferred learning style, then more learning will occur.

Sternberg et al. (1999), in a study of his triarchic abilities model, found evidence for a matching hypothesis: students who scored highest on creative intelligence learned more when they were taught in a way that emphasized creative instruction; likewise for practical intelligence and analytic intelligence. The researchers selected 324 gifted and talented high-school students aged 14 to 18 for participation in the Yale Summer Psychology Program. They identified three groups, each strong in one of the triarchic abilities, by two criteria: (1) at least a half standard deviation above the mean for that ability; (2) at least a half standard deviation above their own scores in the other two abilities. This resulted in 112 students, about one third of all of the students, with the three groups containing 39, 38, and 35 students. An additional 40 were above the average in all three, and 47 were below the average for all three. Three different afternoon sessions were developed, one each emphasizing one of the three abilities, and then students were randomly assigned. A post-course analysis found that the matched students performed higher, for all three high-ability groups.

When Sternberg, Grigorenko, and Zhang (2008b) summarized research arguing for the importance of learning styles, their review cited only the above 1999 study as demonstrating an ATI (as pointed out by Mayer, 2008). According to Mayer, all of the other studies demonstrated that a broader method of instruction, which includes features intended for multiple learning styles, is more effective for all learners—but this isn't an ATI effect. In a response, Sternberg et al. said that they didn't advocate for matched instruction, but that all students should be taught in all three ways (Sternberg, Grigorenko, & Zhang, 2008a).

Brody (2003) closely analyzed Sternberg et al.'s 1999 study and argued that it didn't demonstrate an ATI because it dropped many participants. Brody (2003) and Gottfredson (2003) both argued that statistically, measures of *g* explain these data better; Sternberg has not addressed these criticisms (see Hunt, 2008).

Pashler et al. (2008) reviewed all of the learning styles research, and found no evidence for the meshing hypothesis that instruction should be provided in a format that meshes with the preferred learning style of the learner. The only study they found that was designed appropriately was the Sternberg et al. (1999) study, which they nonetheless criticized on several grounds: the outcome measures were of Sternberg's own design; "deviant scores" were excluded; only one third of all students were included in this study; and, the three learning styles don't correspond to any of the most popular learning styles theories and interventions.

Several other studies have found no meshing effect (e.g., Constantinidou & Baker, 2002; Massa & Mayer, 2006). Ultimately, it seems that all learners benefit when instruction is delivered in a variety of modalities and styles. All students benefit equally from creative instruction; creative teaching should not be limited to a special group of "creative students."

KEY CONCEPTS

- Teacher beliefs about creative teaching and desirable student traits
- Arts education and transfer of cognitive benefits
- The Marland definition of giftedness
- Gardner's multiple intelligence theory
- Sternberg's triarchic theory
- Renzulli's three-ring theory
- Admission to talented and gifted programs
- Creative teaching practices
- Creativity as cognitive transfer
- The meshing hypothesis and aptitude–treatment interaction (ATI)

THOUGHT EXPERIMENTS

- Can you remember a teacher who was particularly effective at fostering creativity? What did he or she do?
- Can you recall having a teacher who did not get along with the school administration? Was it because this teacher was more creative and unconventional?
- Were you ever tested for admission into a talented and gifted program? What test was used?
- Why do you think the correlation between IQ and job performance is only about 0.20? What other individual abilities do you believe could help predict job performance?
- When you applied to college, do you believe that your college application accurately represented your potential to do well in college? If not, what additional criteria should colleges be looking at?

SUGGESTED READINGS

Beghetto, R. A., & Kaufman, J. C. (2010). *Nurturing creativity in the classroom*. Cambridge, UK: Cambridge University Press.

Eisner, E. W. (2002a). *The arts and the creation of mind*. New Haven, CT: Yale University Press.

Gardner, H. (1983). *Frames of mind: The theory of multiple intelligences*. New York: Basic Books.

Hetland, L., Winner, E., Veenema, S., & Sheridan, K. M. (2007). *Studio thinking: The real benefits of visual arts education*. New York: Teachers College Press.

Sawyer, R. K. (Ed.). (2011). *The teaching paradox: Creativity in the classroom*. Cambridge, UK: Cambridge University Press.

Sternberg, R. (1985). *Beyond IQ: A triarchic theory of human intelligence*. New York: Cambridge.

HOW TO BE MORE CREATIVE

The first goal of this book is to explain creativity, drawing on the latest science provided by a broad range of scientific disciplines. But a second goal is to use the scientific research to learn how we can be more creative. While reading the chapters of this book, I hope you've already had mini-insights about how you can use these findings in your own creative activities. In this chapter, I provide specific advice for how the science of human innovation can help you be more creative in your own life.

THE TEN BELIEFS

In Chapter 1, I described the Western cultural model of creativity, and ten beliefs that are commonly found in Western countries. Before we can effectively increase our own creativity, we need to make sure that we aren't blindly adopting the Western cultural model. How does the Western cultural model stand up to the research? Throughout the chapters of this book, we've learned that some of the ten beliefs contain a grain of truth, but many of them are more myth than reality.

BELIEF 1. THE ESSENCE OF CREATIVITY IS THE MOMENT OF INSIGHT

Creative people get their great idea in a flash of insight; after that, all they have to do is execute it. They could even delegate its execution to someone else, because execution doesn't require creativity.

Grain of truth: Creative people report having insights after incubation or down time.

Reality: Our journey through the science of creativity shows that creativity rarely comes in a sudden burst of insight. Instead, scientists have discovered that creativity is mostly conscious, hard work. Insights, when they occur, tend to be rather small advances in an ongoing creative process (Chapters 5, 6, and 7). Significant creativity requires many of these small insights, over time, embedded in a lifetime of hard work, collaboration, and expertise.

Advice: To be creative, expect to work hard and have lots of small sparks, and learn how to bring them together.

BELIEF 2. CREATIVE IDEAS EMERGE MYSTERIOUSLY FROM THE UNCONSCIOUS

Creative people have radical new ideas that come out of nowhere and that can't be explained by their prior experience.

Grain of truth: Everyone has had an "Aha!" experience; it's quite ordinary to have an idea suddenly enter your conscious mind. This can even happen with something as ordinary as remembering a person's name that was on the tip of your tongue.

Reality: The Aha! experience isn't mysterious, however. Research by cognitive psychologists (Chapters 5 and 6) and cognitive neuroscientists (Chapter 10) has shown that moments of insight are generally easy to understand in terms of the previous mental trajectory of the creator. Insights are combinations of bits of domain knowledge that the creator has mastered through long years of work. And new ideas are always combinations of prior experiences and learning.

Advice: Study what has been done before. Stay on top of what everyone else is doing. Look for new ways to combine existing things.

BELIEF 3. CREATIVITY IS MORE LIKELY WHEN YOU REJECT CONVENTION

Creative people blindly ignore convention; convention is the enemy of creativity, it blocks the pure inspiration welling up from the creative spirit.

Variation: Children are more creative than adults; schools emphasize the conventions of the past, and thus squash creativity.

Like so many of our contemporary creativity beliefs, these ideas emerged only in the 19th century, along with Romanticism. In the second half of the 20th century, the idea that the artist is a person who rejects convention took an even stronger hold on the popular consciousness. Ironically, at the same time, artists were entering art schools in increasingly large numbers to be trained in the conventions of the art world. In the United States today, a greater proportion of artists have the MFA degree than at any other time in history. Yet few of us are aware of the growing influence of formal schooling in fine art.

Reality: We don't need to be worried about the influence of formal schooling on artists. It won't squash their creativity, or make them all traditionalists. Formal training and conscious deliberation are essential to creativity; as Louis Pasteur famously said, "Chance favors the prepared mind" (Dunbar, 1999; Seifert, Meyer, Davidson, Patalano, & Yaniv, 1995). Sparks of insight always follow long periods of hard work when people are immersed in convention (Chapters 5 and 11). Children often generate charming novelty, but until they master the language and conventions of a domain, they aren't capable of true creativity. Education is essential to creativity, but rote memorization isn't sufficient—creativity is based in deeper understandings that result from a focused and active form of learning (Chapters 5 and 21).

Grain of truth: Most great innovations involve breaking at least one rule. But scores of other rules stay the same; the trick is knowing all of the rules and then knowing exactly which ones to break. Knowing which rules to break requires an extremely high level of expertise that comes only after years of mastering a domain.

Grain of truth: Many schools deliver domain knowledge in a way that encourages rote memorization and doesn't foster creative thinking (Chapter 21).

Advice: Work hard to be creative. Master the conventions of the domain; pay your dues. If you're in a learning environment that doesn't foster creativity, then you may need to develop your own additional activities in which you engage in divergent thinking and problem finding, based in the domain knowledge you're learning (see Chapter 21).

BELIEF 4. CREATIVE CONTRIBUTIONS ARE MORE LIKELY TO COME FROM AN OUTSIDER THAN AN EXPERT

Sometimes the most creative people know the least about the domain. The leading people in any field are so bound up in the old way of doing things that they never have the great new ideas. It takes someone from the outside to see things in a new way; it's not important for that outsider to first learn those old ways of doing things.

Reality: Creative people are rarely outsiders. The most creative ideas come from people who are deeply familiar with a domain and immersed in it. It takes years of study and work in a domain before you can be creative.

Grain of truth: The exceptional creators who make radical contributions that advance a field have often had experience and training in a different area before they began to study that new area (see Chapter 6 on cross-fertilization).

Advice: Network; get to know everyone; seek out a senior mentor; find out who's doing what and how; put yourself in a place where you'll frequently interact with others doing the same type of work.

But don't get so specialized that you ignore everything outside of your domain. Occasionally, take some time to become familiar with the latest developments in other areas.

BELIEF 5. PEOPLE ARE MORE CREATIVE WHEN THEY'RE ALONE

People are more creative when they're alone.

Reality: Ideas often emerge in conversation, or as a result of conversations you've had before. Groups play a central role in creativity, more so today than at any other time in history (Chapter 12). Creative people are deeply connected to the field of other experts and professionals (Chapter 11).

Grain of truth: Exceptional creators spend time alone, but they also spend lots of time talking to other people. It's the alternation between social and solitary time that maximizes creativity.

Advice: To get good ideas, collaborate and talk to people.

BELIEF 6. CREATIVE IDEAS ARE OFTEN AHEAD OF THEIR TIME

Creative people are so far ahead of their time that their contemporaries don't understand them; they're recognized only after death.

We're told that Mendel's 19th-century work cross-breeding peas wasn't recognized as essential to modern genetics until 50 years later; or that the Impressionists were considered such horrible artists that their works were never displayed in the French academy.

Reality: Almost all of these examples, when examined more closely, end up failing to support the unrecognized-genius view. Mendel's work, for example, was *not* rejected as inappropriate by his peers, and it was *not* rediscovered 50 years later; the Mendel story is a historically inaccurate myth (see Chapter 20). And although the Impressionists *were* excluded from the French academy, they quickly created their own network of galleries, patrons, and like-minded colleagues; they were avidly collected by rich Americans, and many of them died with money in the bank. Research shows that creative works are almost always recognized in their own time (see Chapter 15, History).

Grain of truth: Radical, breakthrough ideas are often resisted initially, because they threaten established interests and disrupt existing institutions and relationships. It takes a confident, strong-willed individual to overcome these forms of resistance.

Advice: Build a network and make frequent use of it. Share and advertise your ideas. Your reputation and success during your lifetime are critical to creativity.

BELIEF 7. CREATIVITY IS A PERSONALITY TRAIT

Some people are born creative, and if you weren't, then you don't have much hope of being more creative.

Variation: Creativity is genetic, and some people are born with more of it.

Reality: Research has proven that creativity is *not* hereditary (Chapter 9). Despite decades of work to develop creativity tests, these tests still have a mixed record of predicting real-world creativity, suggesting that creativity isn't a stable personality trait, but rather is a situationally specific strategy (Chapters 3 and 4).

Grain of truth: There are certain dispositions that lead a person to be more likely to be original and appropriate than others. But these dispositions can be learned; they're not fixed abilities or personality traits, like IQ or extraversion.

Grain of truth: Some creativity tests can predict some portion of creativity some of the time in some situations for some people (Chapter 3).

Advice: You can be just as creative as anyone else. What makes someone creative isn't a personality trait; it's (1) mastering a creative domain; (2) the right work habits (for example, hard work interspersed with time off); (3) knowing how to select good ideas; (4) knowing how to combine and connect your ideas (Chapters 5, 6, and 7).

BELIEF 8. CREATIVITY IS BASED IN THE RIGHT BRAIN

Creativity is based in the right brain.

Reality: The most creative people use their entire brains in concert (Chapters 9 and 10). Training in a creative domain tends to increase the bilateralization of brain activity.

Grain of truth: While engaged in some cognitive tasks associated with creativity, the brain is slightly more active in the right hemisphere than the left. (However, other creative tasks are associated with increased left hemisphere activation.) A few brain imaging studies have found slightly different patterns of activation in people who score higher on creativity tests, and the majority of these seem to favor the right hemisphere (Chapter 9). But none of these tasks alone is associated with creativity. And in brain imaging studies, everyone's pattern of brain activation is more similar than different; these experiments demonstrate rather subtle statistical differences (no more than 3%).

Advice: The most creative people are more balanced than average on just about every personality trait. If your personality is extreme in some way, try to balance yourself out.

BELIEF 9. CREATIVITY AND MENTAL ILLNESS ARE CONNECTED

Creative people are more likely to be mentally ill.

Reality: There's no solid evidence that mental illness is more common among creative people than the general population (Chapter 9). There continue to be a small number of people who argue for a connection, but the consensus among creativity researchers is that those few studies that initially seemed to find a connection are methodologically flawed and don't prove that there's an association between creativity and clinical levels of mental illness.

Grain of truth: In a few creative domains—primarily fiction writing and fine art painting—there's partial evidence that more-creative people score slightly more towards the clinical end of the spectrum than less-creative people, although they don't meet diagnostic criteria for full-blown mental illness (Chapter 9).

Advice: Normal, well-balanced people are more likely to make creative contributions. However, a little bit of eccentricity doesn't hurt.

BELIEF 10. CREATIVITY IS A HEALING, LIFE-AFFIRMING ACTIVITY

This belief is supported by the research. In opposition to Belief 9, there's a preponderance of evidence that creative people are more healthy than average—beginning with the humanistic psychologists of the 1950s and the personality studies of the 1960s at Berkeley's IPAR, and continuing with contemporary studies of flow and intrinsic motivation (Chapters 4 and 9).

There are two caveats, however. First, it's not the case that people choose to engage in creative activities to heal themselves of mental disturbances. Rothenberg (1990) reported that creative people start out with the same level of psychological health as the average population, and engaging in creative activities leads them to greater health and psychological freedom than the average (pp. 46–47).

Second, it seems that this belief is more closely associated with individualist cultures rather than collectivist cultures (see Chapter 14, p. 268). Ethnographic studies have found that creative activities in collectivist cultures are less oriented towards individual self-actualization and self-expression. Thus, one might be less likely to find Belief 10 in the cultural models of creativity in collectivist cultures.

CREATIVITY TRAINING

Creativity training programs emerged in the 1960s, during the first wave of creativity research, and these programs have flourished in the decades since. Most contemporary creativity training emphasizes the same goals (Davis, 2003):

- Fostering creative attitudes
- Improving understanding of the creative process and of creative people

- Exercising creative behavior and thinking
- Teaching specific creativity techniques

If creativity can be taught, then corporate executives get very interested. After all, innovation is the holy grail of today's modern corporation. That's why many of the people offering advice about how to be more creative are highly paid management consultants. One set of creativity consultants are trained by the Lego Group AG, the Danish parent of the company that makes the world-famous children's toys. Management consultants are trained to use Lego blocks in "Serious Play" workshops with executives. It may be hard to imagine a middle-aged man with white shirt and tie playing with Legos, but the idea is becoming widespread, and some very large and serious companies have hired these consultants, including Nokia, Daimler-Chrysler, Ikea, and Alcatel. "Legos work because they let executives visualize abstract concepts like 'value chain' or 'process engineering' by actually building their interpretations of them," said Kimberly Jaussi (quoted in Gullapalli, 2002, p. B1). The Lego corporation didn't originate the idea of using Legos to teach corporations creativity; several management consulting firms had been doing it for years, including the IDEO corporation of Palo Alto, California, and the Center for Creative Leadership in Greensboro, North Carolina. As we've seen over and over again, many creations are emergent group phenomena, and the idea of using Legos for corporate creativity consulting didn't come in a moment of insight at Lego corporate headquarters. It was an emergent collective phenomenon (see Chapter 13).

These offbeat approaches to creativity training were a product of the 1990s dot-com era, when small start-ups were more receptive to unusual approaches than were large, established old-industry corporations. Consulting firms used not only Legos but also Etch A Sketches, Play-Doh, Slinkys, dramatic improvisation, painting, and singing. IDEO's training sessions had executives make hats, houses, and other objects out of wood blocks, rubber bands, and Legos (Gullapalli, 2002). The Center for Creative Leadership mixed Lego work with Tinkertoys and dominoes. The 1990s emphasis on innovation led to the casual dress of the workplace because companies believed that employees would be more creative if they were allowed to express themselves freely in their personal appearance.

HISTORY OF CREATIVITY TRAINING

Creativity training goes way back before "business casual" dress; it started with the first wave of creativity research in the 1950s and 1960s. And corporate creativity consulting didn't start in the dot-com era; creativity consulting for business has been around since at least the 1970s.

In the 1950s, Sidney Parnes and E. Paul Torrance disagreed with their colleagues: they were among the few psychologists who thought creativity could be taught (Parnes, 1993). Many personality psychologists thought that creativity was like IQ: it was fixed at birth and it couldn't be deliberately increased. The 1955 Utah Conference (see Chapter 2) focused on the "identification of creative scientific talent," not on enhancing creativity. At the third Utah Conference in 1959, Torrance and Parnes reported some results that showed that creativity training could work. As a result, the name of future conferences was changed to the "Identification *and Development* of Creative Scientific Talent" (Parnes, 1993, p. 472). By 1972, Torrance looked back at two decades of research and found 142 studies showing that training could enhance creativity (Torrance, 1972).

Creativity consulting soon followed. In Europe, Tudor Rickards held workshops for executives at the Manchester Business School in 1971, and Horst Geschka began to study corporate creativity at the Battelle Institute in Frankfurt in 1970 (Geschka, 1993). In the 1970s, these researchers moved out of the ivory tower and tried to use the psychological research of the day to develop practical, hands-on creativity training for business.

One popular training method is *morphological synthesis*. Team members list the important dimensions of an object and the range of possible attributes for each dimension, and then consider novel combinations of them. Or they divide a complex problem into its elements, and then identify possible solutions for each element and explore all the possible combinations of the different solutions. Because this method generates so many combinations, it can generate a lot of potential solutions. The biggest problem with morphological synthesis is identifying the right breakdown of the problem into its elements. This can itself take creativity, but the method can't work until you've already broken down these elements first. That's why morphological techniques are most effective for well-structured problems, and they work better for problem-solving types of creativity.

Perhaps the most popular training method is *brainstorming*, based on Alex Osborn's belief that people and groups are more creative if they begin with an idea-generating stage where everyone withholds criticism (see Chapter 12). *Synectics* is an elaboration of brainstorming that focuses on using analogies as catalysts for creativity (Gordon, 1961; see Chapter 6, pp. 119–121). The most elaborate development of Osborn's ideas is *Creative Problem Solving (CPS)*, developed by theCreative Education Foundation (CEF), a group founded by Alex F. Osborn in the 1950s in Buffalo, New York (Isaksen, Dorval, & Treffinger, 1994, 2000; Isaksen & Treffinger, 1985; Treffinger, Isaksen, & Dorval, 1994).[1] The CPS method as developed by Osborn, Parnes, and their colleagues is based on three broad recommendations (Fig. 22.1):

1. In the early stages, focus on *generating* (creative or divergent thinking). Aim for quantity of ideas rather than quality; defer judgment; and look for connections among these emerging ideas. When analyzing and choosing among ideas, shift to *focusing* (critical or convergent thinking). At this point, it's time to consider both positives and negatives, and to be more explicit about your opinions.

2. There are three components and six stages to the creative process: understanding the problem or challenge (three stages), generating ideas (one stage), and preparing for action (two stages).

3. Each of the six stages has both a generating (divergent thinking) and a focusing (convergent thinking) component. The three stages within "understanding the challenge" are constructing opportunities, exploring data, and framing problems. There's a

1. CEF was based at the University of Buffalo from 1954 to 1967, when it moved to Buffalo State. In 2002, the Buffalo State academic unit was renamed the International Center for Studies in Creativity, housed within the Creative Studies department. The Creative Education Foundation continues an independent existence as the publisher of the *Journal of Creative Behavior* and the organizer of the annual Creative Problem Solving Institute conference (CPSI); it relocated to Massachusetts in 2008.

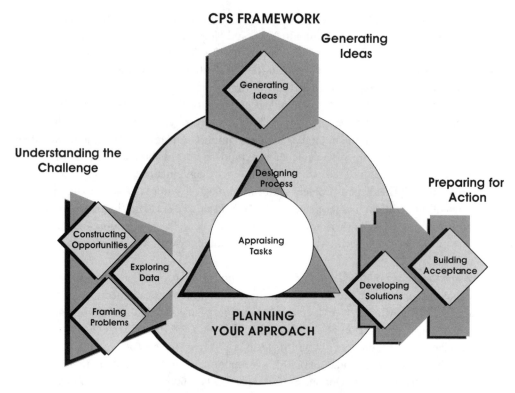

FIGURE 22.1: The six stages of creative problem solving proposed by The Creative Problem Solving Group. (Reproduced by permission. CPS Version 6.1™ is jointly owned by The Creative Problem Solving Group, Inc. and The Center for Creative Learning, Inc.: Source: Isaksen, S. G., Dorval, K. B., Treffinger, D. J. (2000). *Creative Approaches to Problem Solving: A Framework for Change*. Dubuque, Iowa: Kendall/Hunt. Figure 2.2, page 37.)

single stage for "generating ideas," the classic "brainstorming" stage. And there are two stages in "preparing for action," developing solutions and building acceptance.[2]

Many other advice books also emphasize that creativity occurs in stages, and that divergent thinking has to come first, followed by convergent thinking (e.g., Perkins, 2000). These stages are derived from the cognitive psychological approaches to creativity that we reviewed in Chapters 5, 6, and 7.

Several other creativity training programs got their start in the 1970s and 1980s, including:

- *Productive Thinking Program* (Covington et al., 1974): a self-instructional program, packaged in 15 booklets, designed for use by fifth and sixth graders. Measures of its effectiveness have produced mixed results (Nickerson, 1999).

---

2. Prior to their inclusion in Isaksen, Dorval, & Treffinger, 2000, the six stages were known as mess finding, data finding, problem finding, idea finding, solution finding, and acceptance finding.

- *CoRT or Cognitive Research Trust*, founded by Edward de Bono. The program (de Bono, 1973) is composed of six units. There was some evidence of effectiveness in a large-scale implementation with Venezuelan 10- and 11-year-olds (Nickerson, 1999).
- *The Purdue Creative Thinking Program* (Feldhusen, 1983): a set of 32 15-minute audio-taped lessons, each one focused on a famous creator from the past; worksheets, and a teacher's manual.
- *TRIZ*: The Russian acronym for "Theory of the Solution of Inventive Problems" is generally used rather than the English TSIP (Altshuller, 1988, p. 39). Altshuller (1988) proposed 40 basic methods for solving engineering problems by eliminating "technical contradictions" (p. 150; Table 22.1).

DOES CREATIVITY TRAINING WORK?

A clear, unequivocal, and incontestable answer to the question of how creativity can be enhanced is not to be found in the psychological literature.

—Nickerson, (1999, p. 407)

The most convincing test of effectiveness would be to test participants' creativity both before and after the training, and then see an increase in the assessed level of creativity. Some studies have used this method and have found that training raises scores on creativity tests. A 2004 meta-analysis (Scott, Leritz, & Mumford, 2004) of 70 prior studies found that certain creativity training programs work: those that focus on the development of cognitive skills and the heuristics involved in skill application (such as the cognitive processes reviewed in Chapters 5, 6, and 7), and those that use realistic exercises appropriate to the domain at hand (consistent with the domain specificity of creativity). The eight cognitive skills that they identified (also see Chapter 5) explained about half the variance in increased performance ($R = 0.49$). They found that a focus on more analytic methods (including critical thinking and convergent thinking) was more effective than a focus on unconstrained exploration.

Sternberg and Williams (1996) divided 86 gifted and nongifted children into two groups. All children took pretests on insightful thinking, then half of the children received instruction on insight skills. Then, all children took a posttest. Children who were taught how to solve insight problems gained more than children who were not (Davidson & Sternberg, 1984). In a related study, Ansburg and Dominowski (2000) demonstrated that very short training on verbal insight problems can improve performance on other insight problems; people who received training solved 14% to 24% more problems than a control group. Their training instructions were short (only about 400 words), and simply warned not to focus on the first or the most obvious interpretation of the problem, and emphasized the importance of looking for alternative interpretations. Cunningham and MacGregor (2008) redid this study, this time including analogous puzzle versions and realistic versions of each problem, and added in spatial problems; they found that training enhanced performance on puzzle versions, but not on real-world versions, and that training was effective with spatial puzzles but not verbal puzzles. Those who received training solved 67% of spatial puzzles; a control group solved only 27%.

Table 22.1: TRIZ: 40 Basic Methods of Eliminating Technical Contradictions, Identified by Analyzing 40,000 Patents

1	Fragmentation
2	Removal
3	Local quality
4	Asymmetry
5	Joining
6	Universality
7	Nesting
8	Counterweight
9	Preliminary counter-action
10	Preliminary action
11	Previously place cushion
12	Equipotentiality
13	Reversal
14	Spheroidality
15	Dynamism
16	Partial or satiated action
17	Moving to a new dimension
18	Use of mechanical vibrations
19	Periodic action
20	Uninterrupted useful effect
21	Rushing through
22	Turning harm to good
23	Feedback
24	Go between
25	Self-service
26	Copying
27	Cheap short life instead of expensive longevity
28	Replacement of a mechanical pattern
29	Use of pneumatic or hydraulic constructions
30	Use flexible membranes and fine membranes
31	Use porous materials
32	Using paint
33	Homogeneity
34	Discarding and regenerating parts
35	Changing the aggregate state of an object
36	The use of phase changes
37	Application of heat expansion
38	Using strong acidifiers
39	Use an inert environment
40	Use composite materials

(From Altshuller, 1988, pp. 151–168)

It's not that surprising that creativity doesn't increase much after a few hours of verbal instruction. It's more likely that long-term, sustained efforts would be more successful than short, one-shot training workshops. Cropley (1997) argued that enhancing creativity requires a long-term, multiple-intervention strategy that builds knowledge and expertise, creates exercises to build skills working with that knowledge, encourages searches for novel solutions and strategies for doing that, and evaluates progress and errors. Nickerson's summary of training studies (1999) concluded that longer-term efforts are the most successful.

CREATIVITY TRAINING IN DOMAINS

We learned in Chapter 3 that much of creativity is domain-specific. If that's true, then training that's focused on domain-general creative skills would have only limited impact, whereas training focused on a specific domain would be more successful. And research shows that creativity training *is* more effective when it focuses on a specific domain (see Chapter 3, pp. 58–60). Jay and Perkins (1997) found that training in problem finding, in a specific domain, worked. Dow and Mayer (2004) found that the most effective training was domain-specific. Baer (1998) found that training enhanced creativity, but only in the domain used in the training. He asked subjects ranging in age from 7 to 40 to create stories, poems, collages, and math word problems. Training on any one of those four areas increased the creativity of work in that area, but not in the other three areas. Dow and Mayer (2004) found that creativity training on insight problems enhanced performance only on insight problems in the same domain (verbal, mathematical, spatial, and verbal/spatial combined).

These studies are consistent with the research in Chapter 5 showing that creativity requires a person to become an extremely knowledgeable expert in his or her domain of activity. So what about those studies I reviewed in the previous section that found measurable benefits to general creativity training? One possibility (Baer, 1998) is that because all of these training programs provide a variety of domain-specific creativity training, in multiple contexts and task materials, what's actually happening is that you're learning how to be more creative in a variety of specific domains.

Creativity researchers have concluded that real-world creative performance depends both on domain-general creativity skills as well as domain-specific knowledge and skills. Although we don't yet know the exact balance, and although that balance probably varies across domains, the best advice is this: If you want to be more creative, work on general creativity skills, but also master your domain, and make sure to practice applying the general creativity skills to your chosen domain.

HUMANISTIC PSYCHOLOGY AND THE NEW AGE

> *It is ironic that our scientific objectivism about genius is mingled with a strong remnant of what looks like religious faith. The fact is that we cannot bring ourselves to renounce the dream of the superhuman . . . the post-Enlightenment guise of artistic or scientific genius.*
>
> —Marjorie Garber, (2002, p. 72)

Many advice books say that the highest level of creativity is shown in how one lives one's life. The visualization guru Shakti Gawain (1979/1982) wrote that "my life is my greatest work of art" (p. 123). Such perspectives are grounded in the 1950s humanistic psychology of Abraham Maslow and Carl Rogers, who emphasized the importance of becoming self-actualized (see Chapter 4, and the Belief 10 discussion earlier in this chapter). One's spiritual life is the ultimate creative product, and the ultimate in creativity is the process of becoming vibrant, alive, and self-actualized. Julia Cameron, author of the 1992 book *The Artist's Way*, said, "I simply wrote down the precepts of divine intervention in our lives the moment we engage our creativity and, through that, engage our Great Creator" (2002, p. 4). New Age adherents often claim that they're conduits for a deeper creativity that originates in a spiritual source. As we learned in Chapter 2, this conception of creativity goes back at least to the time of the ancient Greeks.

New Age perspectives emphasize process rather than product; creativity is a spiritual practice, not a way to generate useful products. The association of process and creativity emerged during the 1960s (in the art world) and the 1970s (in cognitive psychology). The New Age movement itself emerged during the 1970s, so it's not surprising that its assumptions about creativity reflect the general beliefs of our culture at that time.

These New Age conceptions are compatible with the Western cultural model's Belief 10, which is supported by creativity research (at least, in individualist, Western cultures). However, New Age conceptions of creativity frequently diverge from scientific research: they draw on psychoanalytic and spiritual conceptions of the unconscious, the importance of dreams, and the Jungian notions of archetypes. Many New Age writings draw from amateur anthropological studies that trot out the ethnocentric stereotypes of a century ago: that primitive peoples (or children) are more pure and are less corrupted by convention and civilization. These beliefs about creativity are hard to square with what we've learned in this book. And they're not that new, either; as we saw in Chapter 2, these conceptions of creativity originated in the 19th-century Romantic era.

In the New Age approach, people are advised "to practice art as a means of awakening" (Cushman, 1992, p. 58). The goal isn't to increase the quality and marketability of the finished product, since thinking about the final product can interfere with the spiritual effectiveness of the practice. New Age conceptions of creativity are found in many art education classes, including drawing, writing, acting, and music. Anne Cushman (1992) signed up for one of each type of class in the San Francisco area and found some common themes in all of the classes:

- Trust your intuition; honor your initial impulses.
- Stay in the present, forget about your plan, and stay attuned to the moment.
- Don't cross out or paint over, even if you change your mind.
- Create boldly, without afterthoughts or regret.
- Focus on the process, not the product.
- Create for the sheer pleasure of doing it.
- Don't analyze the result, because this isn't psychotherapy.
- Special talent is not required, and in fact technique can get in the way.
- Practice and persevere.

The question of the quality of the finished product is irrelevant; anything generated "with a profound consciousness or with total awareness is artful" (performance artist Ruth Zaporah, quoted in Cushman, 1992, p. 59).

But many of us are interested in increasing the quality of our created products. Art school students hope to generate works that will be sold and displayed in museums, and writing workshop students want to be published. Executives want their corporations to develop innovations that can be successfully marketed. But even if your eventual goal is to create a useful and marketable product, New Age instructors would argue that you should still begin your work in this process-focused, non–goal-directed way. There will be time for critical reflection and editing later. Writing instructor Natalie Goldberg told Cushman that aspiring writers shouldn't move on to this editing stage for at least two years (quoted in Cushman, 1992, p. 60).

New Age advice has some scientific support in the research on intrinsic motivation (Chapter 4). Studies have shown that people are more creative when they're internally focused and not thinking about external rewards, and New Age advice may be effective at helping people attain this "flow" state. In addition, the best of these books do a good job of dismissing some common creativity myths:

- *Only special geniuses are creative.* This myth has been proven wrong by decades of research in cognitive psychology. In Chapters 5, 6, and 7, we learned that creative processes are based in the same mental processes that every human holds.
- *Creativity is found only in the arts.* Creativity is required in all walks of life, not only in painting and poetry. And creativity is also important in everyday life—in everyday small talk, parenting, teaching, and being a good friend (Sawyer, 2001a).
- *Creativity is found only in crazy people.* The myth of the madness of creativity is incredibly resilient, despite decades of research debunking any connection (see Chapter 9).

At the same time, there is some New Age advice that perpetuates elements of the Western cultural model that aren't supported by research. "How to be an artist" (Sark, 1992) is based on the belief that children are more creative than adults. Sark gives advice like "build a perfect fort with blankets," to help us enter a childlike mindset that will make us more creative. Much of Cushman's (1992) collected advice parallels 19th-century Romantic-era beliefs that creativity originates in a pure inner nature, unconscious or divine, that exists prior to convention and society. But the research shows that creativity is based in a decade or more of training and education, that it's deeply grounded in the conventions and wisdom of existing domains, and that the best ideas emerge only after periods of hard work.

BEING AN INTELLIGENT CONSUMER OF CREATIVITY ADVICE

> Given the choice between the myth of the natural genius and the sobering reality of hard work, popular culture usually opts for the myth.
>
> —Burrell, (2004, p. 300)

When you read a creativity advice book, you need to watch out, because many of them perpetuate one or more of the Western cultural model beliefs in misleading ways. The most common advice to watch out for is as follows.

CREATIVITY IS FUN (MISLEADING VARIANT OF BELIEF 10)

The flow state of peak experience is extremely positive and self-actualizing, but it would be misleading to describe it as "fun." Creativity isn't easy or peaceful. Although creators are often in a flow state, they have to train for years and work hard to get there. And they have to constantly accept new challenges to keep themselves in the flow state; they never let themselves get too comfortable. The same activities that put a creative person in flow often seem either deathly boring or incredibly stressful to the rest of us.

CREATIVITY IS A BURST OF INSPIRATION (BELIEFS 1 AND 2)

Creativity is not a sudden burst of inspiration, a mysterious moment that you just have to wait and wish for. Rather, creativity is a long, extended process over time, in which many small, mini-insights occur throughout the work day. These mini-insights emerge directly from the hard daily work of the task, and then are immediately integrated into the ongoing work of the project. Larger insights occasionally occur, but always in the context of hard work. And most of the highly publicized stories of insight aren't true. It turns out that historians (and sometimes creators themselves) often embellish the story to make it fit better into our cultural myth of creativity, in the same way that Coleridge made up the story about how the poem "Kubla Khan" came to him suddenly in an opium-induced haze (see Chapter 17). Creative people in Western cultures also believe in the Western cultural model, and they know—at least subconsciously—that if their stories better match the Western cultural model of creativity, they'll be more likely to be judged creative.

CREATIVITY IS AN INDIVIDUAL TRAIT
(VARIANT OF BELIEFS 3, 5, AND 7)

Creativity isn't just a property of individuals, it's also a property of social groups. Modern creativity is more like an improvising jazz ensemble (Chapter 18), a collaborating group (Chapter 12), or the development of the Windows operating system (Chapter 13) than like a poet writing in solitude. But it's hard for people in individualist cultures to accept this, and creative domains in individualist countries are often structured so that the credit for an entire group's work goes to one person. Thomas Edison gets credit for all of the inventions generated by his 14-man skunk works; senior scientists get credit for the scientific advances generated by their teams of 10 or 20 scientists (see Chapter 20); movie directors get credit for a critical success even though a movie involves the creative efforts of over 100 people. For a variety of complex sociological reasons explained throughout this book, the members of a team often benefit from assigning all of the credit to the team leader, even though they have to deny their own creative role in the process.

Individual creativity is more likely to occur in collaborative groups than in solitude. That's why jazz musicians play better in groups and in front of live audiences than they do alone at home or in group rehearsal with no audience. Creators in all fields of life report their most significant insights emerging from collaborations (John-Steiner, 2000; Sawyer, 2007).

Creativity is a social phenomenon, involving variation and selection at multiple overlapping levels of analysis (Chapters 11 and 15). What movies are selected as the best in a given year?

Even before a movie is made, what about the group processes that determine which movie ideas are funded and produced? Once a movie is distributed, what group of experts decides which ones are the best, and how do they do it? How do these decisions relate to the box office, the majority vote of the ticket-buying public? And even these decisions are temporally and historically bounded; the movies that won awards 50 years ago often aren't the movies that have stood the test of time. What are the historical processes that determine which movies are judged to be the classics that deserve to be shown to each new generation?

CREATIVITY IS THE REJECTION OF CONVENTION (BELIEF 3)

For the most part, creativity accepts and builds on convention. There's a small component of novelty in most creative products, but it's always smaller than we think at the time. With 50 or 100 years' distance, almost everything being created today will sound and look the same, even though to us it seems like an incredible variety.

It wasn't freedom from social constraint that resulted in Einstein, Michelangelo, or Shakespeare. Most social systems have vested interests in the status quo, and true creative novelty is often perceived to be dangerous to those in positions of power. As a result, what creative people might really need is not the feel-good message of humanistic psychology, but rather the thick skin and big ego advocated by existentialist Salvatore Maddi (Maddi, 1975, p. 182). Recall from Chapter 3 that the 18 adjectives correlated with creativity included *confident*, *egotistical*, and *snobbish*. This kind of person doesn't sound very nice, and what Maddi advocated doesn't fit with Western cultural conceptions about creativity as the pure and good expression of the self-actualized individual.

SUMMARY

Once you're aware of how the Western cultural model influences your thinking, you're prepared to be an intelligent consumer of creativity advice. In particular, there are three things to watch out for.

First, many training programs assume that creativity is an individual process or ability, whereas we've seen that much of creativity emerges from complex social and organizational systems. And even though brainstorming is a group activity, it tends to focus on enhancing the creativity of the individuals in the group (Hennessey, 2003); it doesn't require fundamental changes to organizational structure and culture. Increasing the creativity of the employees in a company won't necessarily increase the creativity of the company; a new organizational structure or culture may be necessary, and the creativity training methods reviewed above focus instead on the individuals.

Second, high levels of creative performance require a high level of commitment and dedication, a level that's not likely to develop unless the individual finds the task intrinsically motivating. Yet very few of training programs emphasize the importance of commitment, hard work, and intrinsic motivation.

Third, many training programs emphasize the moment of creative insight as the critical feature of creativity, when most of the research suggests that insight plays a very small part in creative works. Rather, creative products result from long, complex, involved processes incorporating networks of people and long periods of hard work, during which many independent but connected mini-insights take place. Yet creativity training rarely instructs people in how to schedule and design an extended project so as to encourage and then incorporate these many sequential, incremental small insights.

In the United States and Europe, many creativity training programs are subtly influenced by the Western cultural model of creativity (Weisberg, 1986). We believe that the moment of insight is critical, so creativity consultants give us what we want: they teach us how to have more insights. But creativity researchers know that insight plays a small part, if any, in creative products. We believe that creativity is a domain-general ability or process, and creativity consultants treat it that way, too, teaching creativity as a set of domain-general processes and abilities rather than teaching individuals to become experts in their domain. We believe that the main reason we aren't creative is because of constraints and limitations in the environment, and creativity advice always associates contextual factors with limitations to creativity, rather than pointing to the large body of research showing that contextual factors are essential to creativity. We believe that creativity is a product of an individual mind, and creativity consultants focus on enhancing individual creative ability rather than changing the culture and the organization.

Creativity research shows that creativity is hard work; creativity is usually an incremental step beyond what has come before; creativity often emerges from a team, not a solitary individual; and increasing creativity often requires substantive organizational change.

INTERDISCIPLINARY ADVICE FOR CREATIVITY

The Western cultural model focuses on the individual and downplays social and cultural context. But we've learned that explaining creativity requires both individualist and sociocultural perspectives—what I've called an interdisciplinary approach. The sciences of sociology, anthropology, and history balance out the picture provided by psychology. The interdisciplinary approach presents a challenge for those of us who want to be more creative: it's hard enough to change our own cognitive processes and personality, but who has any hope of changing the whole society, or redefining cultural values and attitudes? Throughout history, from time to time, a few remarkable people have managed to change an entire society or culture. But the odds are long, and many more have tried and failed.

Fortunately, you don't have to change the world to be creative. The interdisciplinary approach emphasizes the synergy among person, domain, and field. You might not be able to change your creative domain, but you can leave your domain for another one. And when you're ready to increase your personal creativity, you can be much more effective if you've studied the domain and field that you're working in. The interdisciplinary approach recommends that you evaluate your domain and field and ask yourself: Does this domain and field, at this point in history, need someone like me?

CHOOSE A DOMAIN THAT'S RIGHT FOR YOU

Domains that are widely accessible are more likely to experience creativity. In some cultures and historical periods, elites restricted access to the domain; only a certain privileged class of people could participate. Think back to the Middle Ages, when all knowledge was written in Latin but very few Europeans spoke or read Latin. Books were rare and expensive. As a result, many creative domains were inaccessible to the great majority of the population. Now that advanced countries have near-universal literacy, and books are relatively inexpensive, creative domains are accessible to just about anyone.

Some domains are fairly advanced and most of the important problems are well known to everyone. Knowledge in the domain is well organized and well structured. If you prefer a problem-finding style of creativity, then you're likely to be frustrated in such a domain, because it needs problem solvers. Problem-finding people are better off in domains where the most important issues are unresolved, where conventions and rules are not rigidly specified, where no one even knows where to start. These tend to be relatively new areas of activity—installation art in the 1970s, or personal computer software in the 1980s, electronic music in the 1990s, sustainable technologies in the 2000s. If you prefer a problem-finding style of creativity, you'll need to keep a broad watch on the society, looking for the next new thing.

In contrast, if you prefer a problem-solving style, then you'll probably be happier in a mature domain that's been around a while. In such a domain, there are textbooks, college courses, and doctoral programs. There's probably a national association and a national conference dedicated to this one special domain. The questions are well known and the criteria for judging work are objective; everyone will know it when you come up with something new. Many people prefer the certainty of such domains; in the more ambiguous problem-finding domains, the criteria for creativity are ill defined, and there may be subjective differences of opinion in what counts as good work.

CHOOSE A FIELD THAT'S RIGHT FOR YOU

A field is more likely to experience creativity if it has formal systems of training, with teachers, mentors, and experts who can pass on the domain of known knowledge.

A field is more likely to experience creativity if it has systems in place where potentially creative young people can be identified and selected by older members of the field, and if mentor–apprentice relationships are common (Hooker, Nakamura, & Csikszentmihalyi, 2003). Newcomers to a field need experienced guidance to learn about all of the aspects of the domain that are orally transmitted, not written down in books.

A field is more likely to experience creativity if it provides opportunities for newcomers to work in the domain. Talented young people won't choose a career if there are no job opportunities, or if the field accepts only older people.

You can increase your chances of creativity by making sure you're working in a field that fits your personality and work style. Some fields are very large and require a lot of networking to stay involved and connected. That's fine if you're an extrovert, but a more introverted person might be intimidated by having to deal with 5,000 people at the annual conference. Introverts might be more comfortable in smaller fields.

In domains like math, if you have the right answer it doesn't matter whether or not people like you; the answer speaks for itself. The field becomes more important in those domains where the criteria aren't well defined, because then success requires your active involvement in the field. If you don't like dealing with people, if you don't like selling yourself, then you should be working in a domain with very explicit and objective criteria for judging works, like mathematics or theoretical physics. That way, the work will speak for itself. If you don't mind marketing and networking, then a domain that's more vague and less well defined might be fine for you.

TURN YOUR GAZE OUTWARD INSTEAD OF INWARD

Begin by becoming aware of the field that you're working in. Talk to people working in the area. Get to know the top people, who's in and who's out. Find out what cities and what universities are known as centers of creative work.

Examine the structure of the field—the gatekeepers, intermediaries, the art world—and see where you can best fit. Try to place yourself in an area where you'll be given opportunities for choice and discovery. Try to find a senior person to be your mentor.

Find out how the selection process works. Who decides what creative products are selected as useful and appropriate? What is the step-by-step procedure that they use to decide? Are decisions made without knowing the name of the work's creator, or do the gatekeepers know who they're judging? All of this information will help you to negotiate your entry into the field.

MARKET YOURSELF

Don't assume that if you build a better mousetrap, the world will beat a path to your door. The most successful creative people are very good at introducing their ideas to the field. They know who the key people are, and they know how the selection process works. They know how their new product is likely to be perceived by the field, because they've spent so much time becoming familiar with the field. They know which aspects of their idea to emphasize and which to leave unstated.

MOVE TO THE CENTER

Richard Florida (2002) noted that creativity tends to flourish in certain cities. This is a modern version of a well-known economic phenomenon known as *clustering*: the best work tends to emerge in a place where all the best people are. Simonton (1994) found that greatness is almost always found in a cultural center, rarely in a small town in the provinces. Gardner's research on the "exemplary creator" (1993) found that these exceptional individuals often grew up far from the cultural center, but before they made their most significant contributions, they moved to the center to master the domain and join the field's networks.

DON'T TRY TO BECOME CREATIVE IN GENERAL; FOCUS ON ONE DOMAIN

Try out as many domains as possible. Start with something you enjoy and then branch out from there. Choose a domain that you like and that you won't mind spending years internalizing. Take the time to build basic skills in that domain, take classes, go to graduate school, read a lot of books, listen to the experts. Expect to spend several years paying your dues before you can be truly creative; be patient yet alert to opportunity.

BE INTRINSICALLY MOTIVATED

Don't expect to be creative if your goal is to become rich and famous. Creativity almost always results from intrinsic motivation; from people who work in an area just because they love the activity itself, not because of the eventual payoff. Choose an area that you're passionate about. Creative breakthroughs take years of hard work, and you won't be able to stay the course if you love the endpoint but not the process. It's often said that even the sexiest careers involve only 10% fun stuff, with the remaining 90% being work that most people would find tedious. The most creative people are the ones who choose a career in which they actually enjoy that 90%.

DON'T GET COMFORTABLE

The flow state of peak experience tends to occur when your skills are matched by the challenges of the task. If you find that your work is becoming easier as your experience and skill level increase, then don't just sit back and get comfortable. Instead, find a way to increase the challenges facing you. Seek out new projects, move to a new company, make a lateral move, change careers.

BALANCE OUT YOUR PERSONALITY

Many creative people have what seem to be contradictory personalities; they can work at both ends of the personality spectrum. They're both masculine and feminine; they're both introverted and extroverted. They have a full range of personality styles, and they can shift to suit the situation. You can increase your odds for creativity if you broaden your personality range. For example, if you're extroverted, then work at developing the introverted side of your personality. If you're abstract and theoretical in style, then start a new project that's a little more practical and hands on.

COLLABORATE

Develop a network of close colleagues you can discuss ideas with. Share your ideas with like-minded colleagues. Schedule time for free-wheeling, unstructured discussion without a specific goal. Listen for the creative insight that emerges from the group, rather than trying to push your own ideas on everyone.

DON'T WORRY ABOUT WHO GETS CREDIT

Many of us are afraid to collaborate because we want to make sure we get the proper credit for the work that we do. We may worry that other group members won't carry their weight, or that they'll take credit for an idea that we originally had. But if you hold back during collaboration, saving your idea for later when you can present it as your own, you're hurting yourself. Ultimately, your own idea won't be as good as it would have been if it had gone through the collaborative process.

One problem is our system of copyright and patent law, which attributes each creation to a specific individual or corporation (see Sawyer, 2009a). Recent extensions of copyright far beyond the original time period envisioned by Congress are stifling our culture's creativity.[3] Fair use provisions are becoming increasingly limited, and that too is stifling creativity. These laws are based on the Western cultural model of creativity—that it's the unique possession of a single individual, and that every component of a creative product is completely novel. But most creative products are collaboratively created, and most of them are built out of existing ideas and components.

BE CONFIDENT AND TAKE RISKS

Timidity, anxiety, and fear always get in the way of creativity. Many creative people seem to others to be arrogant or to have big egos, because they have immense self-confidence that allows them to take risks. Once you have a few successes, you'll be more confident. But at first, you'll help yourself get started if you seek out an environment that's supportive of creative thinking. Don't try to start right out in a stiff, unwelcoming environment; wait until later in your career when you've had a few successes.

Being confident isn't the same thing as being naïve. Confidence will come from years of preparation in the domain, and from additional years of hard work once you've learned the domain.

TO BELIEVE OR NOT TO BELIEVE?

> *The idea of the lone hunter, or the lone voyager or explorer, who's guided by his principles and is going to get there against all odds, that self-image, as romantic and foolish as many people might consider it, is a very powerful force in making a major scientist.*
>
> —E. O. Wilson (quoted in Csikszentmihalyi, 1996, p. 269)

It's often been said that a belief doesn't have to be true to be helpful. And it might be helpful to believe in the Western cultural model even if it isn't true. I personally find myself quite attracted

---

3. See Boynton, 2004. Most scholars are opposed to the Sonny Bono Copyright Term Extension Act of 1998, which extended copyright protection an additional 20 years beyond the current term of 50 years after the author's death (in the case of corporate authors, the current term is 75 years from publication). Formal statements in opposition have been made by copyright and intellectual property law professors (http://www.public.asu.edu/~dkarjala/legmats/1998Statement.html, accessed Aug. 30, 2011) and by the American Association of University Professors (http://homepages.law.asu.edu/~dkarjala/OpposingCopyright Extension/letters/aaup-01.html, accessed Aug. 30, 2011).

to many of the New Age, spiritualist writings on creativity, even when I know they're misleading. If I'm with my friends on a Friday night, talking about my workweek, I might even use some of that language in explaining how my writing and research went. Of course, if we hope to scientifically explain creativity we can't let ourselves be sidetracked by misleading beliefs. But if our goal is to increase our own creativity, it might be helpful to believe in the Western cultural model—especially if we reside in a Western culture. Those advice books might work even if they're wrong.

Most readers of this book live in the United States, an extremely individualist culture that's very attached to the Western cultural model. But the Western cultural model emerged over several centuries; it is relatively recent (Chapter 2); and it isn't found in collectivist cultures (Chapter 14). The model thrives in the United States because it shows us as we like to imagine ourselves—the lone outsider, the rugged individualist, rejecting the stifling conventions of decaying old-world society. It almost sounds like an old cowboy movie (Shenk, 2010). It's not completely wrong; many of the beliefs are half-true—for example, creativity often starts with the individual.

The sociocultural approach is just as positive and life-affirming. It views us as social, collaborative beings. After all, the things that distinguish us from the animals are language, communication, and creativity—all fundamentally social. Together, we've created amazing things no one person could have done alone; the institutions of modern government, economy, and science are all collective, emergent phenomena. Only a sociocultural approach can explain these collective social creations. And as our society becomes progressively more advanced and complex, creativity increasingly looks more like an emergent social process than like an individual thought process.

Ultimately, the explanation of creativity requires an interdisciplinary approach, one that combines both individualist and sociocultural perspectives. You can best enhance your own creativity by working on both internal psychological factors and external contextual factors.

KEY CONCEPTS

- The grain of truth and the reality of the Western cultural model of creativity
- Effectiveness of creativity training
- Domain-general and domain-specific creativity training
- New Age conceptions of creativity
- Creativity advice based in the interdisciplinary approach to creativity

THOUGHT EXPERIMENTS

- As you've read this book, what connections have you made with your own creative experience?
- What lessons do you think are most likely to help you be creative in the future?
- Do you think you'd be more creative if you gave up the Western cultural model, or if you held onto it?

SUGGESTED READINGS

Cushman, A. (1992, March/April). Are you creative? *Utne Reader,* 52–60.

Csikszentmihalyi, M. (1996). Chapter 14 in *Creativity: Flow and the psychology of discovery and invention.* New York: HarperCollins.

Feldhusen, J. F., & Goh, B. E. (1995). Assessing and accessing creativity: An integrative review of theory, research, and development. *Creativity Research Journal, 8*(3), 231–247.

Garber, M. (2002, December). Our genius problem. *The Atlantic Monthly,* 64–72.

CHAPTER 23

CONCLUSION

The Future of Creativity

Creativity, as a term and concept, is one of the most prized commodities of capitalism, just as . . . it is one of the most cherished benefits of democracy.

—Rob Pope, 2005, p. 29

In contemporary culture, no idea is so appealing, no word put to more frequent and varied use, than creativity.

—Jacques Barzun, 1991, p. 4

To be creative is the highest achievable good. In an age in which creativity is actually a kind of moral imperative, who could imaginably be against *creativity?*

—Osborn, 2003, p. 508

In 1950, J. P. Guilford's APA address jumpstarted creativity research. And in every decade since then, creativity has become more valued and more important. In the 1950s, the United States focused on scientific creativity and the Cold War space race. In the 1960s and 1970s, U.S. culture followed the humanist psychologists of the 1950s, and many people considered artistic activity as a path to enlightened self-actualization, a private act, almost like a form of meditation. And in the first decades of the 21st century, creativity is changing once again. Creativity has moved from being a private meditative act to being essential to economic growth and competitiveness; "creativity seems today to be more or less compulsory in an increasing number of areas of life" (Osborn, 2003, p. 507).

We live in an age of mash-ups, open-source software, creative commons licensing—what legal expert Lawrence Lessig has called *free culture* (2004). The Internet has blurred the concept of creative ownership, with millions of people borrowing video clips and recorded music excerpts to generate their own combinations. Electronica music artists have for decades been creating new recordings comprising wholly existing recorded material. In 2004, the D.J. Danger Mouse brought together instrumental samples from the Beatles' *White Album* and a cappella vocals from Jay-Z's *Black Album* to create his cult hit *Grey Album*. (He was sued by EMI, copyright holder for the Beatles' *White Album*; Jay-Z, on the other hand, had released the a cappella vocals specifically with the goal of encouraging others to create mash-ups.) Despite the legal issues, *Grey Album* was reviewed in *The New Yorker* magazine (Feb. 9, 2004, issue), and was named the best album of 2004 by *Entertainment Weekly*.

On YouTube, "response videos" are some of the most widely viewed. In response videos, people parody other videos, often by changing the soundtrack. The most reused video is a speech by Hitler, from the 2004 film "Downfall," when Hitler becomes exceptionally angry and begins shouting. This clip has been excerpted and used as the basis for thousands of user-generated parody videos; if there's a new controversy or major topic of conversation, there's certain to be a version of Hitler going ballistic about it. Many of these mash-ups get millions of viewers.

At the Emmy awards in 2010, Casey Pugh's *Star Wars Uncut* won an award. This is an Internet project that invited fans to submit their own versions of their favorite 15-second scenes from the movie (www.starwarsuncut.com; accessed Aug. 30, 2011). After receiving hundreds of submissions, some made with Legos or pets, and others mash-ups with parodies from the cartoon *South Park* and other sources, Pugh edited all the clips together and then added the original musical soundtrack for continuity. This was an homage to George Lucas's original film in more ways than one; in Chapter 16 (pp. 313–314), we learned that George Lucas's *Star Wars* was itself a combination of existing visual elements.

Highly acclaimed novelist David Shields in 2010 published a book, *Reality Hunger*, built almost completely from quotations from other writers and philosophers, from Wittgenstein to DJ Spooky. Shields borrowed the quotations and taped them together to create a manifesto against boring fiction. Even though his publisher required him to include an appendix citing every source, Shields still called it "far and away the most personal book" he has ever written (Kennedy, 2010, p. 3; also see Boon, 2010, and Bartlett, 2010).

Choreographer Andrew Dinwiddie's 2008 work "The Accursed Items" is a cobbled-together sequence of dance movements borrowed from other choreographers, with their permission—they donated bits of choreography that they'd already chosen to delete from their own performances. Carla Peterson, the artistic director of Dance Theater Workshop, said, "Appropriation, sampling, referencing and dialoguing with other artists' works, notions of authorship, dissolving of genres, the rethinking of dance's relationship with movement, and with audiences, etc., are all in play" (La Rocco, 2008, p. 25). Choreographer Chase Granoff said, "You start to not always be about producing something new—you look sideways and backwards" (La Rocca, 2008, p. 25).

It was Oscar Wilde in the 19th century who said, "Good writers borrow, great writers steal." Or was it Pablo Picasso, who supposedly said, "Good artists borrow, great artists steal"? The only documentation of this quotation that I was able to find is T. S. Eliot, who in 1920 wrote "Immature poets imitate, mature poets steal" (p. 125). No one is even sure who actually said this first, or what the exact quotation is; that somehow makes the point even more strongly than the quotation itself.

Since the first edition of this book was published in 2006, a lot of Internet gurus have been preaching the message that the Internet enables a great collective genius to emerge, bringing together everyone's creative potential. Clay Shirky (2010) argued that the Internet will enable a great creative revolution by enabling our "cognitive surplus"—the hours we use unproductively, watching TV or playing video games—to be put to creative uses. Others have argued that the "wisdom of crowds" (Surowiecki, 2004) or "crowdsourcing" (Howe, 2008) will be the creative model of the future, replacing the lone artists and also replacing the graphic design and architecture firms that do most of this work today. Matt Ridley (2010) argued that all new ideas and economic advances come from interactions between people—and because the Internet is bringing people together faster and more often, living conditions for all of us will dramatically improve over the next 100 years, as the resulting creativity explosion solves all pressing social problems, and invents technologies we can only dream of today.

These recent books capture the reality of creativity today. They reject the myth of the solitary creator, and they've embraced the idea that novelty is overrated. Perhaps the United States is shifting away from the Western cultural model of creativity—away from individualist conceptions and toward collaborative, sociocultural conceptions of creativity. As the world becomes increasingly interconnected, as the economy becomes ever more globalized, as the Internet enables more democratic and distributed forms of creativity, the nature of creativity is certain to change—and conceptions of creativity will change as well, as they always have throughout history.

This is a fascinating time in the history of creativity, with the concept itself beginning to experience substantial tensions. Some commentators (e.g., Barrett, 2010; Easterly, 2010) find the futuristic optimism of Clay Shirky and Matt Ridley to be a bit off-putting. Osborn (2003) may have represented the first inkling of a backlash when he wrote of "the potentially moronic consequences of the doctrine of creativity" (p. 507) and that "we should be suspicious of the idea of creativity" (p. 522). In our public discourse, creativity is a form of individual self-realization, and also a means to economic growth. Creativity drives the profitable creative industries, like movies, television, popular music, and computer games, but it's considered essential in all industries; creativity is a required topic in many business schools. These tensions may lead to a major change in the nature of creativity. And as creativity itself changes, creativity research will have to change as well.

THE FUTURE OF CREATIVITY RESEARCH

Creativity researchers are scientists who study how new things are created by human beings. We seek to answer a basic research question: What is the best scientific explanation of how new things are created? In addition to this basic research question, creativity researchers also seek to answer an applied question: How can we use these explanations to provide advice to people, groups, and organizations about how to increase their ability to generate new and useful things?

In the past few decades, we've seen a huge growth in the scientific understanding of creativity. Creativity research attracts an increasing number of scholars, and they continue to discover new findings every year. More and more of these scientists use the interdisciplinary approach, combining individualist and sociocultural approaches. In Chapter 18 on music, for example, we examined not only the creativity of the composer, isolated at the piano, but also the group creativity of improvising jazz ensembles. In Chapter 19 on acting, we considered not only the creativity of the actor but also how the audience influences the performance. And in Chapter 17 on writing, we examined the key roles played by editors, friends, and colleagues.

When I finished writing the first edition of *Explaining Creativity* in 2003, I wrote that "creativity research is still in its infancy" (p. 315). I'm delighted to report that a lot of progress has been made since 2003. I wrote the first edition because I couldn't find an appropriate college textbook for my own creativity course. Since it was published, there have been three new creativity overviews, and three new edited volumes (see Appendix B). And I'm delighted that two new creativity journals were founded in 2006: *Thinking Skills and Creativity* and *Psychology of Aesthetics, Creativity, and the Arts*.

We now have a solid foundation for our explanation of creativity, a foundation that can guide creativity research in the future. Through these many chapters, I've identified several topics that deserve further research:

- Can we develop a creativity assessment that can be used in schools to evaluate whether a curriculum has enhanced students' creative potential? (Chapter 3)
- Research shows that play interventions result in increased scores on creativity tests (Chapter 4). What is the nature of the relationship between pretend play and creativity? What's the best way to design play interventions to enhance creativity?
- Analogical reasoning is associated with many creative breakthroughs. But it's often not a straightforward analogy; creative people often modify the source to fit the target better, or they invent a source that doesn't actually exist (Chapter 6). We don't understand these creative manipulations of analogy very well.
- New creativity assessments should be developed that measure the underlying cognitive processes identified in Chapters 5, 6, and 7; the creativity tests widely in use today originated in an earlier era of personality trait psychology.
- The process of drafting and multiple revision that's common in real-world creativity is not well understood (Chapter 7).
- Artificial creators (Chapter 8) are capable of intriguing behavior, but these programs don't simulate what we know about human mental processes. Interdisciplinary teams of psychologists and computer scientists could develop future programs in ways that are designed to evaluate different theories of the cognitive processing underlying human creative behavior.
- The potential link between ADHD and creativity warrants further examination (Chapter 9).
- There's intriguing data on productivity and age (Chapters 4 and 15), but we still don't know very much about the developmental pathways associated with creative careers. How do people choose those careers? How do they form their initial vision? When do they change careers and/or the vision?
- Regarding individualist–collectivist cultural differences, are there advantages, in some forms of group or organizational creativity, to collectivist cultural beliefs? How is group collaboration different in individualist and collectivist cultures? (Chapter 14)
- The creative process in contemporary multimedia art forms has just barely been studied: digitally animated movies; computer games; advertising and graphic design (Chapter 16).
- Neuroaesthetics, the attempt to ground aesthetic experience in the biologic brain, is a new area that warrants further study (Chapter 16).
- There has been very little study of how art is taught, and how art can be taught most effectively, at the professional levels found in art schools (Chapters 16 and 21). This topic has become increasingly important with the growth of creative and cultural industries in the major world economies.
- Contemporary collaborative genres of writing, including hypertext fiction and fan fiction, warrant further empirical study (Chapter 17). Findings that emerge from these studies

not only could provide insights into creative processes, but more generally, they could help us understand the role of information and communication technologies in group collaboration.

- The group composition processes that are common in music studios today warrant further empirical study (Chapter 18).
- Music performance has only recently attracted the attention of creativity researchers; this phenomenon warrants further scientific study, both of improvised and scored performance (Chapter 18).
- Improvisational theater has received almost no attention from creativity researchers; these genres of performance are worthy of additional study (Chapter 19).
- Studies of creativity in science, particularly of the collaborative processes in large laboratory groups and in geographically distributed teams, could result in findings that could enhance the creative productivity of future scientific collaborations (Chapter 20).
- What is the best way to design schools to foster creative learning in the content areas? What advice should we give to teachers who would like to foster creativity in their students? What sorts of curriculum design and assessments would better align with creative outcomes? These questions all remain unanswered and become increasingly relevant as creativity becomes more important to all disciplines, including science, engineering, and math (Chapters 21 and 22).

Each of my colleagues would, no doubt, generate a different list; there's no shortage of interesting questions for creativity researchers to explore. That's why I'm excited about the future of creativity research.

THE INTERDISCIPLINARY APPROACH

Only by using multiple lenses simultaneously, looking across levels, and thinking about creativity systematically, will we be able to unlock and use its secrets.
—Hennessey & Amabile, (2010, p. 590)

Most of the scientific community focuses on only one discipline at a time. Reality is organized into levels, ranging from small units—like genes and neurons—up to increasingly complex systems such as human beings, groups, societies, and cultures. Individualists study the individual's creative process; socioculturalists study the complex networks and institutions that support and evaluate individual creativity. Each discipline has its own strengths and weaknesses. Psychology is pretty good at helping us understand individual creativity, but it doesn't do such a good job of explaining why one historical period displays a burst of creative output when 100 years earlier nothing much was happening. Anthropology is good at explaining why conceptions of creativity differ in different cultures, and why individuals manifest their creativity in different ways across the globe, but it doesn't explain individual differences within cultures very well.

For a complex phenomenon like creativity, a complete understanding requires us to develop explanations at individual, organizational, and social levels. We need to understand relationships between individuals and contexts: how conventions emerge from groups of people, and how people are influenced by the conventions of a domain. Since the 1990s, scientists have increasingly focused their research on the study of complex, multileveled social phenomena (Sawyer, 2001b, 2005b). It turns out that nature is filled with examples of complex phenomena that require explanations at multiple levels of analysis, because the behavior of many systems in nature is unpredictably emergent from the interactions of the system's parts. The design of an ant colony emerges from the tiny decisions of thousands of ants; the decisions made by a human brain emerge from millions of neurons firing; a new social phenomenon emerges from the mini-insights of hundreds of people working together.

Emergence comes into play whenever scientists are trying to understand phenomena that require explanation at multiple levels of analysis. For example, scientists who study the mind and brain generally agree that although human behavior is rooted in the neurons and synapses of the brain, that brain has emergent properties that may be impossible to identify even if you know everything about neurons. Even though a creative insight is nothing more than a bunch of neurons firing, scientists agree that because of emergence, we will always need the higher-level explanations of psychology.

In the same way, even though creative groups are nothing more than the people in them, because of social emergence we often need sociocultural explanations (Sawyer, 2005b). Social emergence is the opposite of the case where one smart, creative person imposes his or her will on the group; instead, it results from the social processes of collaboration. For example, the collective creativity of an improvised jazz performance can't be explained by psychology alone. Even if we knew everything there was to know about the mental makeup of each musician, we'd still have trouble predicting the emergence of the group's improvisation, because there are so many possibilities for change at each moment. If a musician delays his or her next melodic phrase by even a second, it could have unexpected effects on the performance. As with all complex systems, small differences can balloon into large effects.

In Chapter 14, we learned that of all the world's cultures, Americans are the most individualist. And when it comes to the study of social phenomena, Americans tend to fall back on their cultural belief that the individual is primary. And individualists tend to assume that we can explain everything about creativity in terms of individual personalities and decisions. But this belief leads to a neglect of other types of creativity—the creativity of a jazz ensemble generating a brilliant group improvisation, the creativity of a scientific field as individual scientists contribute successive mini-insights, the creativity of an economy as new industries emerge through creative destruction. These are all examples of creative emergence, and a complete science of creativity should be able to explain all of them.

In this book, I've advocated an interdisciplinary approach to explain creativity at these multiple levels of analysis. Studies of science and the arts are finding that collaboration is the new norm (Sawyer, 2007). An increasingly globalized world has made us more aware that the Western cultural model isn't universal. As the Internet makes it easier for people to come together to collaborate, and as advancing scholarly knowledge makes solo publication increasingly rare and groups become the norm for creative work (Chapter 12), the explanation for creativity can't be couched only in the language of individual psychology. Explaining creativity requires both individual and sociocultural levels of explanation.

This is why creativity research in the future will be increasingly interdisciplinary, bringing together scientists who are experts in multiple levels of analysis—neurons, mental states, groups, and organizations. If creative brains generate emergent ideas that can't be explained in terms of neurons and synapses, the explanation of creativity will require mental concepts and theories.

If creative groups generate emergent phenomena that can't be fully explained in terms of individual decisions and ideas, a full explanation of creativity will require group-level concepts and theories. An interdisciplinary science of creativity has the potential to provide a more complete scientific explanation of how new things emerge from human activity. Today, we have the scientific explanation of creativity within our grasp.

APPENDICES

A NOTE ABOUT THE APPENDICES

These appendices introduce you to the *domain* and the *field* of creativity research. Appendices A through E capture the central elements of the *domain*, the collected body of knowledge that previous scholars have generated, and that have been selected by the field as valuable for future scholars to study. The complete domain is much larger, and includes all of the publications that appear in this book's reference list (and others that I didn't cite). Of all of the materials that I've read and summarized in this book, these appendices include those that are most important for a newcomer to study.

Appendices F, G, and H capture various aspects of the *field*—the social network of leading scholars (Appendix F), universities where creativity research takes place (Appendix G), and professional associations and annual conferences (Appendix H).

The domain and field are always changing; this information is current as of August 2011. For periodic updates, please visit the book website:

http://www.explainingcreativity.com

THE DOMAIN OF
CREATIVITY RESEARCH

APPENDIX A

Creativity Timeline

1913—Henri Poincaré presents his famous lecture "Mathematical Creation" at the Société de Psychologie in Paris, outlining a four-stage process of conscious hard work, unconscious incubation, illumination, and verification (available in English as Poincaré, 1913/1982).

1921—Terman begins his longitudinal study by identifying 1,000 gifted children in California schools, using IQ tests.

1926—Graham Wallas publishes *The Art of Thought*, presenting an influential stage model (derived from Poincaré, 1913/1982) of creativity as preparation, incubation, illumination, verification, and elaboration.

1931—Professor Robert P. Crawford initiates the first creative thinking course, at the University of Nebraska, based on his *attribute listing* procedure (Crawford, 1954).

1937—The first corporate creativity training program is launched at General Electric Corporation, created by A. R. Stevenson (Davis & Scott, 1971, p. ix).

1939—Alex F. Osborn conducts his first brainstorming sessions, at New York advertising agency BBDO (Osborn, 1948).

1945—Founding of the American Psychological Association's Division 10, "Psychology of Esthetics," as one of the 19 charter divisions of the APA. The name changed to "Psychology and the Arts" in 1965 (Cupchik, Arheim, & Martindale, 1996); its name recently changed once again, to "Psychology of Aesthetics, Creativity, and the Arts."

1948—Alex F. Osborn publishes *Your Creative Power*, a successful popular book that presents his brainstorming method.

1949—Founding of UC Berkeley's Institute for Personality Assessment and Research (IPAR), originally with funding from the Rockefeller Foundation, and from 1956 to 1971, with funding from the Carnegie Corporation (MacKinnon, 1978, pp. xi–xvii).

1950—J. P. Guilford's APA address, "Creativity"

1950—Founding of the U.S. National Science Foundation (NSF) and the National Science Board, established by an Act of Congress, the National Science Foundation Act, signed by President Truman. Its mission is "to promote the progress of science; to advance the national health, prosperity, and welfare; to secure the national defense" (http://www.nsf.gov/about/glance.jsp, accessed Aug. 30, 2011)

1952—Conference on Creativity hosted by the Ohio State University in Granville, Ohio, Dec. 5–8. (Two of the presentations were published in the journal *ETC* in 1954.)

1952—Industrial Research Institute holds a symposium on the nature of creative thinking (proceedings published as Olsen, 1952).

1954—Creative Education Foundation founded at the University of Buffalo by Alex F. Osborn.

1955—First Utah Conference on "The Identification of Creative Scientific Talent." Selected papers from the first three conferences were published as Taylor and Barron, 1963.

1957—Second Utah conference

1957, Oct. 4—Soviets launch Sputnik I, the first artificial satellite. On Nov. 3, Sputnik II was launched, carrying a dog named Laika. NSF funding rapidly increases, from the low tens of millions in the early 1950s to $134 million in 1959 (England, 1983).

1957–1958—A series of Interdisciplinary Symposia on Creativity are held at Michigan State University (papers published as Anderson, 1959; note that architect Alden B. Dow presented a paper; there is a creativity center named after him at Northwoods University, Michigan, with an annual conference; see Appendix H).

1958—Symposium held at the University of Colorado on "Contemporary Approaches to Creative Thinking," published as Gruber, Terrell, and Wertheimer, 1962.

1959—Third Utah Conference, published as Taylor, 1959.

1961—Fourth Utah Conference. A smaller meeting, with only six scholars: John Holland, Paul Torrance, Joseph McPherson, Hubert Brogden, Thomas Sprecher, and Calvin Taylor. The name of this, and the fifth, changed to "The Identification and Development of Creative Scientific Talent." Papers published as Taylor, 1964a.

1962—Fifth Utah Conference. Papers published as Taylor, 1964b.

1962—The journal *Hydrocarbon Processing* hosts a conference "How to develop engineering creativity" with papers published in 1962, Volume 41, Number 10.

1963—Conference on Education for Creativity in the Sciences at New York University, June 13–15, 1963. Papers published as a special issue of *Daedalus*, 1965, Volume 94, Issue 3.

1967—Founding of Harvard's Project Zero by the philosopher Nelson Goodman

1967—Founding of the *Journal of Creative Behavior* by Sidney Parnes and the Creative Education Foundation. The CEF moves from the University of Buffalo to Buffalo State.

1970—Purdue Creativity Training Program for schools begins.

1972—Publication of the Marland report on education of the gifted and talented (Marland, 1972)

1973—"Future Implications of Creativity Research" conference held at the Center for Creative Leadership (published as Taylor & Getzels, 1975, on the 25th anniversary of Guilford's 1950 speech)

1980—Dole-Bayh act becomes law, allowing universities to commercialize research.

1988—Founding of the *Creativity Research Journal* by Mark Runco at California State University, Fullerton. For its first two years, the journal was published independently by Mark Runco and the Creativity Research Center of Southern California; then it was published by Ablex for many years, and is now published by Taylor and Francis.

1999—NACCCE report: National Advisory Committee on Creative and Cultural Education, chaired by Sir Ken Robinson, presented to the UK Secretaries of Education and Employment, and of Culture, Media and Sport

1990—Founding of the *Korean Journal of Thinking and Problem Solving* (renamed in 2009 the *International Journal of Creativity & Problem Solving*)

2005—Council on Competitiveness report "Innovate America" (Council on Competitiveness, 2005), resulting from the National Innovation Initiative Summit in 2004; this report led directly to the America COMPETES Act of 2007.

2005—Business Roundtable report "Tapping America's Potential: The Education for Innovation Initiative" (Business Roundtable, 2005)

2006—UK Roberts Report "Nurturing Creativity in Young People"

2006—Founding of the *Journal of Thinking Skills and Creativity* by Rupert Wegerif (University of Exeter, UK) and Anna Craft (Open University, UK)

2006—Founding of the *Journal of Psychology of Aesthetics, Creativity, and the Arts* by co-editors Jeff Smith, Lisa Smith, and James Kaufman. (Formerly was published as the *Bulletin of Psychology and the Arts*, started by Robert Sternberg, Colin Martindale, and Sarah Benolkin.) The official journal of the American Psychological Association's Division 10, "Psychology of Aesthetics, Creativity, and the Arts."

2007—America COMPETES Act. Passed by Congress Aug, 2, 2007 (H.R. 2272), and signed into law by the President Aug, 9, 2007 (P.L. 110–69). The law authorized funds, but the funds were never appropriated.

2009—European Year of Creativity and Innovation declared by European Union

2010—National Science Board report, "Preparing the next generation of STEM innovators: Identifying and developing our nation's human capital"

APPENDIX B

Creativity Overviews

These textbooks, edited books, and review articles all present broad overviews of the scholarly research on creativity. They tend to focus on the psychology of the creative individual, and to neglect biologic, social, and cultural perspectives (exceptions include Dacey & Lennon, 1998, and Sawyer, 2006c). They are listed from older to newer within each section.

BOOKS

1983: Davis, G. A. *Creativity is forever*. Dubuque, Iowa: Kendall/Hunt. Fifth edition, 2004.

1991: Boden, M. *The creative mind: Myths and mechanisms*. New York: Basic Books. Second edition, 2004.

1992: Piirto, J. *Understanding those who create*. Dayton, OH: Ohio Psychology Press. Second edition, 1998; third edition, 2004.

1997: Runco, M. A. *Creativity research handbook, Vol. 1*. Cresskill, NJ: Hampton Press. Volumes 2 and 3 are in preparation.

1998: Dacey, J. S., & Lennon, K. H. (1998). *Understanding creativity: The interplay of biological, psychological, and social factors*. San Francisco, CA: Jossey-Bass.

1999: Sternberg, R. J. (Ed.). *Handbook of creativity*. New York: Cambridge University Press.

1999: Runco, M., & Pritzker, S. (Eds.). *Encyclopedia of creativity* (two volumes). San Diego, CA: Academic Press.

2004: Sternberg, R. J., Grigorenko, E. L., & Singer, J. L. (2004). *Creativity: From potential to realization*. Washington, DC: American Psychological Association. Sponsored by Division 10 of the APA.

2006: Sawyer, R. K. *Explaining creativity: The science of human innovation* (first edition). Oxford University Press.

2006: Weisberg, R. W. (2006). *Creativity: Understanding innovation in problem solving, science, invention, and the arts.* Hoboken, NJ: Wiley.

2007: Runco, M. A. *Creativity: Theories and themes: Research, development, and practice.* Burlington, MA: Elsevier Academic Press.

2006: Kaufman, J. C., & Sternberg, R. J. (Eds.). *The International handbook of creativity.* Cambridge University Press. Each chapter is written by scholars in different countries, providing an overview of creativity research in each country.

2009: Kaufman, J. C. *Creativity 101.* New York: Springer.

2009: Rickards, T., Runco, M. A., & Moger, S. *The Routledge companion to creativity.* London: Routledge.

2010: Kaufman, J. C., & Sternberg, R. J. (Eds.). *The Cambridge handbook of creativity.* Cambridge University Press.

REVIEW ARTICLES

Short, article-length reviews of the state of creativity research. (See Appendix E for a list of journal special issues related to creativity.)

PSYCHOLOGY OF CREATIVITY

Barron, F., & Harrington, D. M. (1981). Creativity, intelligence, and personality. *Annual Review of Psychology, 32,* 439–476.

Feldhusen, J. F., & Goh, B. E. (1995). Assessing and accessing creativity: An integrative review of theory, research, and development. *Creativity Research Journal, 8*(3), 231–247.

Piirto, J. (1999). A survey of psychological studies in creativity. In A. S. Fishkin, B. Cramond, & P. Olszewski-Kubilius (Eds.), *Investigating creativity in youth: Research and methods* (pp. 27–48). Cresskill, NJ: Hampton.

Runco, M. A. (2004). Creativity. *Annual Review of Psychology, 55,* 657–687.

Hennessey, B. A., & Amabile, T. (2010). Creativity. *Annual Review of Psychology, 61,* 569–598.

ORGANIZATIONAL CREATIVITY

Zhou, J., & Shalley, C. E. (2003). Research on employee creativity: A critical review and directions for future research. *Research in Personnel and Human Resource Management, 22,* 165–217.

Shalley, C. E., Zhou, J., & Oldham, G. R. (2004). Effects of personal and contextual characteristics on creativity: Where should we go from here? *Journal of Management, 30,* 933–958.

George, J. M. (2007). Creativity in organizations. *Academy of Management Annals, 1*(1), 439–477.

Sawyer, R. K., & Bunderson, J. S. (in press). Innovation research in organizational behavior. In A. Thakor (Ed.), *Innovation: What do we know?* Singapore: World Scientific Press.

APPENDIX C

Journals that Publish Creativity Research

All web addresses current as of August 30, 2011.

PSYCHOLOGY JOURNALS

Creativity Research Journal. Founded in 1988 by Mark A. Runco; still edited by Runco. *Little-known tidbit:* The cover graphic of an exclamation point superimposed on a head was designed by Chris Runco (see copyright page of Runco, 1994).
http://www.tandf.co.uk/journals/hcrj

Journal of Creative Behavior. The oldest journal dedicated to creativity research. Founded by the Creative Education Foundation in 1967 at Buffalo State.
http://www.creativeeducationfoundation.org/?page_id=47

Journal of Psychology, Aesthetics, and Creativity in the Arts (PACA). An official journal of the American Psychological Association (APA). Founded in 2005 by Jeff Smith, Lisa Smith, and James Kaufman, as an outgrowth of APA Division 10's *Bulletin of Psychology and the Arts*, started by Robert Sternberg, Colin Martindale, and Sarah Benolkin.
http://www.apa.org/pubs/journals/aca/index.aspx

Thinking Skills and Creativity. Founded in 2006 by Professors Anna Craft and Rupert Wegerif.
http://www.elsevier.com/wps/find/journaldescription.cws_home/706922/description

International Journal of Creativity and Problem Solving. Its original name was *The Korean Journal of Thinking and Problem Solving*, founded in 1990. The journal changed to the new name in 2009.
http://www.creativity.or.kr/about.html

TALENTED AND GIFTED JOURNALS

Roeper Review. Published since 1978 by the Roeper Institute, a non-profit corporation affiliated with the Roeper School, a private school with campuses in Bloomfield Hills and Birmingham, Michigan. Publishes "thought-provoking, informative articles that deal with research, observation, experience, theory and practice as they relate to the growth, emotions, and education of gifted and talented learners and to the cultures in which they live."
http://www.roeper.org/RoeperInstitute/RoeperReview/index.aspx

Journal for the Education of the Gifted. Published since 1999, the official publication of the Association for the Gifted. Publishes articles on gifted education, counseling, and parenting.
http://journals.prufrock.com/IJP/b/journal-for-the-education-of-the-gifted

Gifted Child Quarterly. Published since 1957 by the National Association for Gifted Children. Publishes a wide range of articles on the characteristics of gifted students, program models, curriculum, and policy.
http://gcq.sagepub.com/

ARTS AND ARTS EDUCATION JOURNALS

Journal of Aesthetics and Art Criticism. Published since 1942, the official academic journal of the American Society for Aesthetics.
http://www.wiley.com/bw/journal.asp?ref=0021-8529

Empirical Studies of the Arts. Published since 1983, the official journal of the International Association of Empirical Aesthetics. Publishes empirical studies of aesthetics, creativity, and all the arts as examined by researchers in all of the social sciences.
http://www.baywood.com/journals/PreviewJournals.asp?Id=0276-2374

Journal of Aesthetic Education. Published since 1966, an interdisciplinary journal that publishes a broad range of academic articles related to aesthetic education.
http://www.press.uillinois.edu/journals/jae.html

Research Studies in Music Education. Published since 1993, since 2008 RSME has been an official journal of the Society for Education, Music and Psychology Research (SEMPRE), which also publishes the journal *Psychology of Music.*
http://rsm.sagepub.com/

RELATED FIELDS

Digital Creativity. At the intersection of creative arts and digital technology.
http://www.tandf.co.uk/journals/NDCR

Creativity and Innovation Management. For managers and executives responsible for managing innovation.
http://www.wiley.com/bw/journal.asp?ref=0963-1690&site=1

APPENDIX D

Influential Books in Creativity Research

Under each heading, I've grouped the books chronologically, from oldest to most recent. To keep the lists focused on the domain of creativity research, I have chosen not to include books about organizational innovation, the management of technology, or entrepreneurship, and I have chosen not to include practical advice books about how to be more creative.

This is my own admittedly idiosyncratic list—my colleagues' lists might be slightly different—but I've attempted to capture our consensus, and I believe there would be a high degree of overlap among creativity researchers.

19TH CENTURY

Galton, F. (1874). *English men of science, their nature and nurture*. London: Macmillan. The first psychometric study of a large number of eminent scientists, by the man who invented both psychometrics and eugenics.

Lombroso, C. (1984/1891). *The man of genius*. New York: Garland Publishing (Originally published in Italian as *L'umo di genio*. Reprint of English language edition published by W. Scott, London, in 1891 and again in 1910). Famous for arguing that geniuses throughout history were plagued with "degeneracies," including being short, being mentally ill, and sleepwalking.

PRE-1950

Bergson, H. *Creative evolution* (1907 in French; 1911 English translation). An influential early statement of a process view of creativity rather than a product view: "Everything is obscure in the idea of creation if we think of *things* which are created and a *thing* which creates . . . There are no things, there are only actions" (p. 248).

Poincaré, H. (1913/1982). *The foundations of science*. One of the earliest descriptions of the creative process. Poincaré described four stages: conscious hard work, unconscious incubation, illumination, and verification.

Wallas, G. (1926). *The art of thought*. The classic reference for the basic four-stage model of the creative process—preparation, incubation, illumination, verification (which includes elaboration). This book is more often cited than read; and apart from Chapter IV, which describes the four stages, it is no longer cited at all.

Morgan, C. L. (1933). *The emergence of novelty*. Applies emergence theories from evolutionary biology to develop a theory of creativity that applies equally to evolution and to the human mind. This book was widely influential, particularly among the American pragmatists including G. H. Mead and John Dewey. However, today it is not well known and it is rarely read or cited.

Hadamard, J. (1945). *The psychology of invention in the mathematical field*. Princeton University Press. Inspired by Poincaré's 1913 lecture "Mathematical Creation" presenting three stages of preparation, incubation, and illumination. Highly influential; what he presents here presciently foresees much of what transpired among researchers over the next 50 years. Hadamard argues that during unconscious incubation, ideas are combining, many of them not useful but a few good combinations; the unconscious selects which ones enter consciousness. He describes what we know today as the "rest" and "selective forgetting" hypotheses of incubation (see Chapter 5, pp. 100–101), and rejects both.

Wertheimer, M. (1945). *Productive thinking*. New York: Harper & Brothers. For Gestaltists like Wertheimer, "productive thinking" goes beyond past knowledge, in contrast with "reproductive thinking," which merely applies previously acquired knowledge. This book focuses on Gestalt themes, including structural features and reorganizations, identifying gaps, inner structural relations, and structural grouping.

Terman, L. M. (1925–1959). *Genetic studies of genius*, five volumes. Each volume returned to the same group of "termites" and reported what they were doing as adults. The studies showed that high IQ in childhood predicted a successful professional life, but no creative geniuses emerged from the sample.

Osborn, A. F. (1948). *Your creative power*. New York: Charles Scribner's Sons. The first popular creativity advice book, and the book that coined the term "brainstorming."

1950s

Ghiselin, B. (1952). *The creative process: Reflections on invention in the arts and sciences*. University of California Press. An influential early collection of statements about their creative process by famous creators, including physicist Albert Einstein, surrealist painter Max Ernst, novelist D. H. Lawrence, sculptor Henry Moore, filmmaker Jean Cocteau, psychologist Carl Jung, with an influential introduction by Ghiselin.

Roe, A. (1952). *The making of a scientist*. New York: Dodd, Mead.

Kris, E. (1952). *Psychoanalytic explorations in art*. New York: International Universities Press. Outlines his theory of "regression in the service of the ego." The ego turns to the unconscious for inspiration, and then elaborates and modifies what emerges.

Osborn, A. F. (1953). *Applied imagination*. Buffalo, NY: Creative Education Foundation Press. A follow-up to his successful 1948 book.

Maslow, A. H. (1954). *Motivation and personality*. New York: Harper & Row.

Taylor, C. W. (Ed.). (1959). *The Third (1959) University of Utah Research Conference on the Identification of Creative Scientific Talent*. Salt Lake City: University of Utah Press.

1960s

Gordon, W. J. J. (1961). *Synectics: The development of creative capacity*. New York: Harper. A readable presentation of the techniques used by the Synectics consulting firm—a process that involved four types of analogy, and heavy reliance on group collaboration.

Burns, T., & Stalker, G. M. (1961). *The management of innovation*. London: Tavistock Publications. An influential critique of hierarchical bureaucracy. They contrasted strict hierarchy, which they called *mechanical*, with *organic*, flat, loosely coupled organizational forms, and argued that the latter are more innovative.

Torrance, E. P. (1962). *Guiding creative talent*. Englewood Cliffs, NJ: Prentice-Hall.

Rogers, E. M. (1962). *Diffusion of innovations*. New York: Free Press of Glencoe.

Getzels, J. W., & Jackson, P. W. (1962). *Creativity and intelligence: Explorations with gifted students*. New York: John Wiley & Sons. Analyzed a large sample of students and found that creativity measures and traditional intelligence measures like IQ were highly correlated, suggesting that creativity was not distinct from intelligence.

MacKinnon, D. W. (1962). *In search of human effectiveness*. Republished in 1978 by the Creative Education Foundation.

Taylor, C. W., & Barron, F. (Eds.). (1963). *Scientific creativity: Its recognition and development*. New York: John Wiley & Sons. Selected papers from the first three Utah Conferences.

Torrance, E. P. (1963). *Education and the creative potential*. Minneapolis, MN: University of Minnesota.

Koestler, A. (1964). *The act of creation*. New York: Macmillan. Cross-fertilization is behind all creativity; he called it *bisociation*, a mechanism that "connects previously unconnected matrices of experience" (p. 45).

Taylor, C. W. (Ed.). (1964). *Creativity: Progress and potential*. New York: McGraw-Hill Book Company. Papers from the fourth Utah Conference, held in 1961.

Taylor, C. W. (Ed.). (1964). *Widening horizons in creativity: The proceedings of the Fifth Utah Creativity Research Conference*. New York: John Wiley & Sons. The fifth Utah Conference was held in 1962.

Torrance, E. P. (1965). *Rewarding creative behavior: Experiments in classroom creativity*. Englewood Cliffs, NJ: Prentice-Hall. A collection of studies, beginning in 1959, where teachers went through various instruction in fostering creative behavior, and Torrance and his colleagues demonstrated that students who participated in "unevaluated practice" were more creative than those who were constructively evaluated.

Wallach, M. A., & Kogan, N. (1965). *Modes of thinking in young children: A study of the creativity–intelligence distinction*. New York: Holt, Rinehart & Winston. The first study that found that scores on divergent thinking tests could not be predicted from IQ scores.

Arnheim, R. (1966). *Toward a psychology of art: Collected essays*. Berkeley, CA: University of California Press.

Guilford, J. P. (1967). *The nature of human intelligence.* Presented Guilford's influential Structure of Intellect (SOI) theory.

Barron, F. (1969). *Creative persons and the creative process.* New York: Holt. Based on Barron's studies of exceptional creators at the UC Berkeley Institute for Personality Assessment Research (IPAR).

1970s

Torrance, E. P. (1970). *Encouraging creativity in the classroom.* Dubuque, IA: W. C. Brown.

Ornstein, R. E. (1972). *The psychology of consciousness.* San Francisco, CA: W. H. Freeman. This book did more than any other to popularize the left-brain/right-brain distinction, building on the research of Gazzaniga, Sperry, and others.

Wallach, M. A. (1971). *The intelligence/creativity distinction.* New York: General Learning Press. A follow-up to Wallach and Kogan (1965).

Barron, F. (1972). *Artists in the making.* New York: Seminar Press. Based on Barron's studies of exceptional creators at the UC Berkeley Institute for Personality Assessment Research (IPAR).

Marland, S. (1972). *Education of the gifted and talented (Report to the Congress of the United States by the U.S. Commissioner of Education).* Washington, DC: U.S. Government Printing Office. The famous "Marland Report," which presented a six-faceted definition of giftedness, thus expanding the definition of giftedness to include factors other than IQ.

Taylor, I. A., & Getzels, J. W. (Eds.). (1975). *Perspectives in creativity.* Chicago, IL: Aldine Publishing Company. A collection of papers presented at a conference to honor the 25th anniversary of Guilford's important 1950 APA address. The papers were originally presented at a conference at the Center for Creative Leadership in May 1973.

Getzels, J. W., & Csikszentmihalyi, M. (1976). *The creative vision.* New York: Wiley. This important book built on Csikszentmihalyi's doctoral study of MFA students at the Art Institute of Chicago by tracking them down years later to see how successful each had been, and then reporting which personality traits while in graduate school predicted career success.

Rothenberg, A. (1979). *The emerging goddess: The creative process in art, science, and other fields.* Chicago: University of Chicago Press. Defined two influential concepts: *Janusian thinking,* the "process of actively formulating simultaneous antitheses . . . actively conceiving two or more opposite or antithetical ideas, images, or concepts simultaneously" (p. 55), and *Homospatial thinking,* "actively conceiving two or more discrete entities occupying the same space, a conception leading to the articulation of new identities" (p. 69).

1980s

Perkins, D. N. (1981). *The mind's best work.* Cambridge, MA: Harvard University Press.

Winner, E. (1982). *Invented worlds: The psychology of the arts.* Cambridge: Harvard University Press.

Becker, H. (1982). *Art worlds.* Berkeley: University of California Press.

Amabile, T. (1983). *The social psychology of creativity*. New York: Springer-Verlag. Followed by the second edition: Amabile, T. (1996). *Creativity in context: Update to the social psychology of creativity*. Boulder, CO: Westview Press.

Gardner, H. (1983). *Frames of mind: The theory of multiple intelligences*. New York: Basic Books.

Kanter, R. M. (1983). *The change masters: Innovation and entrepreneurship in the American corporation*. New York: Simon & Schuster.

Simonton, D. K. (1984). *Genius, creativity, and leadership*. Cambridge, MA: Harvard University Press.

Sternberg, R. (1985). *Beyond IQ: A triarchic theory of human intelligence*. New York: Cambridge.

John-Steiner, V. (1985). *Notebooks of the mind: Explorations of thinking*. Albuquerque, NM: University of New Mexico Press.

Weisberg, R. W. (1986). *Creativity: Genius and other myths*. New York: W. H. Freeman.

Feldman, D. H. (1986). *Nature's gambit: Child prodigies and the development of human potential*. New York: Basic Books.

Isaksen, S. G. (1987). *Frontiers of creativity research: Beyond the basics*. Buffalo, NY: Bearly Limited. Contains reprints of several classic articles from the 1950s and 1960s, including Guilford's 1950 APA address, MacKinnon, Rhodes (his 1961 article that identifies the "four Ps"), and Torrance, as well as new articles commenting on the state of the field in the mid-1980s, by Guilford, Torrance, Stein, and others.

Altshuller, G. S. (1988). *Creativity as an exact science: The theory of the solution of inventive problems*. New York: Gordon and Breach Science Publishers. A comprehensive presentation of TRIZ.

Sternberg, R. J. (Ed.). (1988). *The nature of creativity*. New York: Cambridge University Press.

Simonton, D. K. (1988). *Scientific genius: A psychology of science*. New York: Cambridge University Press.

Basalla, G. (1988). *The evolution of technology*. New York: Cambridge University Press.

Wallace, D. B., & Gruber, H. E. (Eds.). (1989). *Creative people at work: Twelve cognitive case studies*. New York: Oxford University Press. Contains chapters by various scholars who use the "evolving systems approach" and focus on "networks of enterprise."

Glover, J. A., Ronning, R. R., & Reynolds, C. R. (Eds.). (1989). *Handbook of creativity*. New York: Plenum Press. The first handbook of creativity research. It's a bit unusual, because it doesn't have chapters by the best-known creativity researchers. The editors explain why in their preface: they have a "profound unhappiness with the state of research on creativity" and call it "a degenerating research program." So instead of the recognized names in the field, they chose "people of extraordinary ability" who could "step beyond the context of the literature on creativity" (p. xi). The chapters are substantial, scholarly, and worth reading to get a different perspective on the topic.

1990s

Rothenberg, A. (1990). *Creativity and madness: New findings and old stereotypes*. Baltimore, MD: Johns Hopkins Press.

Martindale, C. (1990). *The clockwork muse: The predictability of artistic change*. New York: Basic Books.

Runco, M. A., & Albert, R. S. (Eds.). (1990). *Theories of creativity*. Newbury Park, CA: Sage.

Csikszentmihalyi, M. (1990). *Flow: The psychology of optimal experience*. New York: HarperCollins.

Finke, R. (1990). *Creative imagery: Discoveries and inventions in visualization*. Hillsdale, NJ: Erlbaum. Contains most of Finke's experimental studies of visual creativity—asking participants to combine two-dimensional or three-dimensional shapes to make new inventions. A key idea is that nondirective thinking leads to a "preinventive form," an ambiguous shape or structure, which is only later interpreted. Most of this material reappears, in summary form, in Finke, Ward, and Smith, 1992.

Layton, R. (1991). *The anthropology of art* (2nd ed.). New York: Cambridge.

Boden, M. (1991). *The creative mind: Myths and mechanisms*. New York: BasicBooks. One of the best books on the topic of *artificial creators*, computer programs that simulate human creative processes.

Runco, M. A. (Ed.). (1991). *Divergent thinking*. Norwood, NJ: Ablex.

Piirto, J. (1992). *Understanding those who create*. Dayton, OH: Ohio Psychology Press. Perhaps the first textbook overview of creativity research.

Finke, R. A., Ward, T. B., & Smith, S. M. (1992). *Creative cognition: Theory, research, and applications*. Cambridge: MIT Press.

Lavie, S., Narayan, K., & Rosaldo, R. (Eds.). (1993). *Creativity/anthropology*. Ithaca: Cornell University Press.

Jamison, K. R. (1993). *Touched with fire: Manic-depressive illness and the artistic temperament*. New York: Free Press.

Weisberg, R. W. (1993). *Creativity: Beyond the myth of genius*. New York: W. H. Freeman.

Isaksen, S. G., et al. (1993). *Understanding and recognizing creativity: The emergence of a discipline*.

Gardner, H. (1993). *Creating minds*. New York: Basic Books. Applied his multiple intelligence theory to seven case studies of exceptional creators.

Subotnik, R. F., Kassan, L., Summers, E., & Wasser, A. (1993). *Genius revisited: High-IQ children grown up*. Norwood, NJ: Ablex. One last follow-up with the Terman "termites," those high-IQ teenagers who were originally identified by Louis Terman in the early 1920s.

Feldman, D. H., Csikszentmihalyi, M., & Gardner, H. (1994). *Changing the world: A framework for the study of creativity*. Westport, CT: Praeger. Reports on an important 1980s motivator of the second wave of creativity—an informal research group funded by the SSRC, and then the Andrew W. Mellon Foundation. The group included the three authors and also Howard Gruber, Jeanne Bamberger, Yadin Dudai, Helen Haste, Robert Siegler, and Robert Sternberg.

Simonton, D. K. (1994). *Greatness: Who makes history and why*. New York: Guilford.

Berliner, P. (1994). *Thinking in jazz: The infinite art of improvisation*. Chicago: University of Chicago Press.

Boden, M. A. (Ed.) (1994). *Dimensions of creativity*. Cambridge, MA: MIT Press.

Runco, M. (Ed.) (1994). *Problem finding, problem solving, and creativity*. Norwood, NJ: Ablex Publishing Corporation.

Holyoak, K. J., & Thagard, P. (1995). *Mental leaps: Analogy in creative thought*. Cambridge, MA: MIT Press.

Sternberg, R. J., & Davidson, J. E. (Eds.). (1995). *The nature of insight*. Cambridge: MIT Press.

Smith, S. M., Ward, T. B., & Finke, R. A. (Eds.). (1995). *The creative cognition approach*. Cambridge, MA: MIT Press. A collection of excellent and important papers, each summarizing cognitive research relevant to creativity conducted by the chapter's author. I cite many of these in Chapters 5, 6, and 7.

Sternberg, R. J., & Lubart, T. (1995). *Defying the crowd: Cultivating creativity in a culture of conformity*. New York: Free Press.

Csikszentmihalyi, M. (1996). *Creativity: Flow and the psychology of discovery and invention*. New York: HarperCollins.

Bennis, W., & Biederman, P. W. (1997). *Organizing genius: The secrets of creative collaboration*. Reading, MA: Addison-Wesley.

Ward, T. B., Smith, S. M., & Vaid, J. (Eds.). (1997). *Creative thought: An investigation of conceptual structures and processes*. Washington, DC: American Psychological Association.

Sawyer, R. K. (Ed.). (1997). *Creativity in performance*. Greenwich, CT: Ablex.

Runco, M. (Ed.) (1997). *Creativity research handbook: Volume 1*. Cresskill, NJ: Hampton Press. Although this is called "Volume 1," no further volumes have yet been published.

Dacey, J. S., & Lennon, K. H. (1998). *Understanding creativity: The interplay of biological, psychological, and social factors*. San Francisco, CA: Jossey-Bass. Perhaps the first overview of creativity research to include social, psychological, and biological perspectives. Still, the majority of the chapters focus on psychology; the social chapters focus on social context influences on the individual, such as family and cultural background; the two biology chapters are good, but with the rapid advances in cognitive neuroscience they are now out of date.

Belgrad, D. (1998). *The culture of spontaneity: Improvisation and the arts in postwar America*. Chicago: University of Chicago Press.

Sternberg, R. J. (Ed.). (1999). *Handbook of creativity*. New York: Cambridge University Press.

Simonton, D. K. (1999). *Origins of genius: Darwinian perspectives on creativity*. New York: Oxford University Press.

Root-Bernstein, R., & Root-Bernstein, M. (1999). *Sparks of genius: The 13 thinking tools of the world's most creative people*. Boston: Houghton-Mifflin.

2000s

John-Steiner, V. (2000). *Creative collaboration*. New York: Oxford.

Klahr, D. (2000). *Exploring science: The cognition and development of discovery processes*. Cambridge: MIT Press.

Galenson, D. W. (2001). *Painting outside the lines: Patterns of creativity in modern art*. Cambridge, MA: Harvard University Press.

Farrell, M. P. (2001). *Collaborative circles: Friendship dynamics and creative work*. Chicago: University of Chicago Press.

Cropley, A. J. (2001). *Creativity in education & learning: A guide for teachers and educators*. London: Kogan Page.

Craft, A., Jeffrey, B., & Leibling, M. (Eds.). (2001). *Creativity in education*. London: Continuum.

Kelley, T. (2001). *The art of innovation: Lessons in creativity from IDEO, America's leading design firm*. New York: Doubleday.

Florida, R. (2002). *The rise of the creative class and how it's transforming work, life, community and everyday life*. New York: Basic Books.

Candy, L., & Edmonds, E. (Eds.). (2002). *Explorations in art and technology*. Berlin: Springer.

Eisner, E. W. (2002). *The arts and the creation of mind*. New Haven, CT: Yale University Press.

Efland, A. D. (2002). *Art and cognition: Integrating the visual arts in the curriculum*. New York: Teachers College Press.

Paulus, P. B., & Nijstad, B. A. (2003). *Group creativity: Innovation through collaboration*. New York: Oxford.

Sawyer, R. K., John-Steiner, V., Moran, S., Sternberg, R., Feldman, D. H., Csikszentmihalyi, M., et al. (2003). *Creativity and development*. New York: Oxford.

Houtz, J. (Ed.). (2003). *The educational psychology of creativity*. Cresskill, NJ: Hampton Press.

Sternberg, R. J., Grigorenko, E. L., & Singer, J. L. (2004). *Creativity: From potential to realization*. Washington, DC: American Psychological Association.

von Hippel, E. (2005). *Democratizing innovation*. Cambridge, MA: MIT Press.

Pink, D. H. (2005). *A whole new mind: Why right-brainers will rule the future*. New York: Riverhead Books.

Kaufman, J. C., & Baer, J. (Eds.). (2005). *Creativity across domains: Faces of the muse*. Mahwah, NJ: Lawrence Erlbaum Associates.

Weisberg, R. W. (2006). *Creativity: Understanding innovation in problem solving, science, invention, and the arts*. Hoboken, NJ: Wiley.

Sawyer, R. K. (2007). *Group genius: The creative power of collaboration*. New York: BasicBooks.

Hetland, L., Winner, E., Veenema, S., & Sheridan, K. M. (2007). *Studio thinking: The real benefits of visual arts education*. New York: Teachers College Press.

Runco, M. A. (2007). *Creativity: Theories and themes: Research, development, and practice*. Burlington, MA: Elsevier Academic Press.

Skov, M., & Vartanian, O. (Eds.). (2009). *Neuroaesthetics*. Amityville, NY: Baywood Publishing Company.

Kaufman, J. C., & Sternberg, R. (Eds.). (2010). *The Cambridge handbook of creativity*. Cambridge, UK: Cambridge University Press.

BOOK PUBLISHERS KNOWN FOR CREATIVITY RESEARCH

Cambridge University Press. Publisher of *The international handbook of creativity*, and *The Cambridge handbook of creativity*.

Oxford University Press. Oxford has perhaps the strongest list of books related to creativity research (including, of course, this book!). Oxford titles include *Creativity and development* (2003) and *Creative collaborations* (2000), and they publish a particularly strong list in the psychology of music.

Hampton Press. For several decades, has published the book series *Perspectives on creativity*.

Routledge. Particularly strong with books by UK scholars, including *The Routledge companion to creativity*, and Rob Pope's book *Creativity: Theory, history, practice*.

I would like to acknowledge the important publishing role played by editor Barbara Bernstein in the history of creativity research, and the central editorial role played by Professor Mark A. Runco. Barbara Bernstein was an editor at Ablex Publishing Corporation (which after multiple corporate acquisitions is now part of ABC-CLIO) and responsible for creating their book series "Creativity Research Monographs," edited by Mark A. Runco. Barbara was also responsible for Ablex's decision to publish the Creativity Research Journal, *edited by Mark A. Runco (which, after multiple mergers and transitions, is now published by Taylor and Francis). When Barbara left Ablex to form Hampton Press, she continued publishing the book series with Mark Runco under the new title "Perspectives on Creativity." (Ablex continued to publish a book series using the new title "Publications in Creativity Research," with editor Robert S. Albert.)*

APPENDIX E

Journal Special Issues

These are in chronological order, starting with the oldest.

"Innovation in Science." *Scientific American*, 1958, Volume CIC, No. 3 (September 1958).

"Creativity and learning." *Daedalus*, 1965, Volume 94, Issue 3 (Summer 1965). Edited by Stephen R. Graubard, Editor of *Daedalus*. The contributors include: Jerome Weisner, Jerome Kagan, Lawrence S. Kubie, Philip H. Abelson, E. Paul Torrance, and others. Early versions of several of the papers were first presented at a Conference on Education for Creativity in the Sciences at New York University, June 13–15, 1963.

"Art, Mind, and Education. Papers on Project Zero." *Journal of Aesthetic Education*, 1988, Volume 22, Issue 1. Guest editors Howard Gardner and David Perkins.

"Discipline-Based Art Education." *Journal of Aesthetic Education*, 1988, Volume 21, Issue 2. Guest editor Marilynn J. Price.

"Creativity: Current Perspectives." *Contemporary Educational Psychology*, 1989, Volume 14, Issue 3 (July 1989). Guest editors Richard E. Ripple and Mark A. Constas.

"Play, Vygotsky, and Imagination." *Creativity Research Journal*, 1992, Volume 5, Issue 1. Editor Mark A. Runco.

"Creativity in the Moral Domain." *Creativity Research Journal*, 1993, Volume 6, Issues 1 and 2. Guest editors Howard E. Gruber and Doris B. Wallace.

"Creativity and Discovery in Biomedical Sciences." *Creativity Research Journal*, 1994, Volume 7, Issues 3 and 4. Guest editor Ken McNaughton.

"Educational Psychology of Creativity." *Educational Psychology Review*, 1995, Volume 7, Numbers 2 and 3 (separate issues).

"Can We Unravel Scientific Creativity?" *Creativity Research Journal*, 1996, Volume 9, Issues 2 and 3. Guest editor Arthur I. Miller. Papers presented at a workshop at ZIF, University of Bielefeld, Germany, July 8–11, 1994.

"Creativity from Childhood Through Adulthood." *New Directions for Child Development*, 1996, Whole issue 72. Editor Mark A. Runco.

"Art and Artists." *Creativity Research Journal*, 1997, Volume 10, Issues 2 and 3. Editor Mark A. Runco.

"Interdisciplinarity, the Psychology of Art, and Creativity." *Creativity Research Journal*, 1998, Volume 11, Issue 1. Guest editor Martin S. Lindauer.

"Creativity and Deviance." *Creativity Research Journal*, 1999, Volume 12, Issue 1. Editor Mark A. Runco.

"The Arts and Academic Achievement: What the Evidence Shows." *Journal of Aesthetic Education*, 2000, Volume 34, Issues 3 and 4. Guest editors Ellen Winner and Lois Hetland.

"Creativity and the Schizophrenia Spectrum." *Creativity Research Journal*, 2001, Volume 13, Issue 1. Guest editors Louis A. Sass and David Schuldberg.

"Creativity for the New Millennium." *American Psychologist*, 2001, Volume 56, Issue 4, Special section. Guest editors Robert J. Sternberg and Nancy K. Dess.

"Commemorating Guilford's 1950 Presidential Address." *Creativity Research Journal*, 2001, Volume 13, Issues 3 and 4. Editor Mark A. Runco.

"Festschrift for Howard E. Gruber." *Creativity Research Journal*, 2003, Volume 15, Issue 1. Editor Mark A. Runco.

"Education and Creativity." *Scandinavian Journal of Educational Research*, 2003, Volume 47, Issue 3. Guest editor Øyvind L. Martinsen.

"Creativity and Personality: Suggestions for a Theory." *Psychological Inquiry*, 2003, Volume 4, Issue 3. Responses to a lead article by Hans J. Eysenck.

"Creativity in the Workplace." *Creativity and Innovation Management*, 2004, Volume 13, Issue 3. Guest editors Todd Lubart and Petra de Weerd-Nederhof.

"A Tribute to E. Paul Torrance." *Creativity Research Journal*, 2006, Volume 18, Issue 1. Guest editors James C. Kaufman and John Baer.

"Divergent Thinking." *Creativity Research Journal*, 2006, Volume 18, Issue 3. Guest editor Mark Runco.

"Creativity and Education." *Cambridge Journal of Education*, 2006, Volume 36, Issue 3. Guest editor Pamela Burnard.

"Developing Creativity and Broad Mental Outlook in the Information Society." *Informatica*, 2006, Volume 30, Issue 4. Guest editor Vladimir Fomichov.

"In Honor of Rudolf Arnheim's Centenary (1904–)." *Psychology of Aesthetics, Creativity, and the Arts*, 2007, Volume 1, Number 1. Guest editor Gerald C. Cupchik.

"Creativity in Schools and Classrooms." *International Journal of Creativity & Problem Solving*, 2008, Volume 18, Number 2. Guest editor Ronald A. Beghetto.

"Advertising and Creativity." *Journal of Advertising*, 2008, Volume 37, Issue 4. Guest editors Sheila L. Sasser and Scott Koslow.

"Social Influence and Creativity." *Social Influence*, 2008, Volume 3, Issue 4. Guest editor Marlene Turner.

"Creativity or Conformity: Building Cultures of Creativity in Higher Education." *Innovations in Education and Teaching International*, 2008, Volume 45, Issue 3. Guest editor Annie Grove-White.

"Collaborative Creativity: Socio-cultural Perspectives." *Thinking Skills and Creativity*, 2008, Volume 3, Number 3. Guest editors Karen Littleton, Sylvia Rojas-Drummond, and Dorothy Miell.

"Creative Evaluation." *Digital Creativity*, 2009, Volume 20, Issue 3. Guest editor Stephen Boyd.

"Creativity in Dance." *Research on Dance Education: Innovations in Arts Practices*, 2009, Volume 10, Issue 3. Guest editor Edward C. Wharburton.

"Applying Thinking Skills Within Educational Settings and Beyond." *Thinking Skills and Creativity*, 2009, Volume 4, Number 3. Guest editor Robert Burden.

"New Scholars in the Field." *Psychology of Aesthetics, Creativity, and the Arts*, 2009, Volume 3, Number 1. Editors Jeffrey K. Smith, Lisa F. Smith, and James C. Kaufman.

"Personality, Psychopathology, and Original Minds." *Personality and Individual Differences*, 2009, Volume 46, Issue 8. Guest editor Gordon Claridge.

"Creativity: Simulation, Stimulation, and Studies." *Artificial Intelligence for Engineering Design, Analysis, and Manufacturing (AIEDAM)*, 2010, Volume 24, Number 2. Guest editors Mary Lou Maher, Yong Se Kim, and Nathalie Bonnardel.

"Creativity East and West." *Management and Organization Review*, 2011, Volume 6, Issue 3 (November 2011). Guest editors Michael W. Morris and Kwok Leung.

THE FIELD OF CREATIVITY RESEARCH

APPENDIX F

Important Creativity Researchers

This is my own somewhat idiosyncratic listing; I suspect most of my colleagues would agree with most of these choices, but I don't claim it represents a consensus. The boundaries of domains and fields are often fuzzy, and even more so with an interdisciplinary field like creativity research. To keep this Appendix focused and not overly long, I have intentionally focused on scientists who conduct basic research on creativity, such as psychologists and sociologists, and I have chosen not to include scholars who study business innovation and entrepreneurship, who would typically be found in schools of business or in economics departments. To the extent that creativity research represents a "field," it tends to be centered in psychology departments, with scholars from related disciplines occasionally participating.

I've grouped these people according to the decades they made their most significant contributions, although many of them made contributions outside of these periods as well.

My presentation of the creativity research domain, in Appendices A through E, is much broader and more interdisciplinary in scope than is my presentation of the field, here in Appendices F, G, and H. That's because the number of scholars who identify themselves as creativity researchers is rather small, but the number of works relevant to creativity is much larger.

Names are listed alphabetically within each time period.

PRE-1950

There wasn't a recognizable field of creativity research before the 1950s; these are scholars whose work influenced the first wave of creativity researchers in the 1950s and has continued to have an impact on research and practice today.

Genrikh S. Altshuller (1926–1988). Russian engineer who developed the TRIZ taxonomy of 40 basic types of invention by grouping 40,000 patents (see Altshuller, 1988). Following the

Gestaltists, he argued that problems are solved holistically by the identification and resolution of contradictions in the original problem state—a theory that's also consistent with the dialectical philosophy taught in the Soviet Union in Altshuller's formative years (1988, p. 32).

Alfred Binet (1857–1911). A French psychologist, developer of the first IQ test with Theodore Simon, in France, in 1905 (Binet & Simon, 1916; see A. S. Kaufman, 2009, for a more detailed history).

Karl Duncker (1903–1940). A German Gestalt psychologist. His long 1926 paper (Duncker, 1926) presented his seminal experiments with "insight problems." Many of the problems Duncker devised are still in use today, such as the candle problem and the x-ray problem.

Sigmund Freud (1856–1939). Artistic activity, neuroses, and dreams arise from the same psychodynamic processes: the repressed "primary process thought" of the unconscious emerges into consciousness.

Francis Galton (1822–1911). The founder of modern psychometrics, the science of measuring traits and abilities. Also known as the father of eugenics. He certainly believed in nature rather than nurture: "If a man is gifted with vast intellectual ability, eagerness to work, and power of working, I cannot comprehend how such a man should be repressed" (p. 79) and "social advantages are incompetent to give [eminence] to a man of moderate ability" (p. 80). Thus, he concluded that high reputation is a "fair test of high ability" (p. 87). His 1869 book *Hereditary Genius* gathered evidence to show that high ability is inherited, and is grouped by family. His argument that intelligence is inherited convinced Charles Darwin and influenced Darwin's 1871 book *Descent of Man*. An interesting piece of trivia: In 1893, he invented the method of identifying people by their fingerprints, and persuaded Scotland Yard to adopt the method.

Jacques Hadamard (1865–1963). A French mathematician, known to creativity researchers for his 1945 book (Hadamard, 1945) that presented a theory of creativity based on his interviews with exceptional creators, including Albert Einstein. His theory was similar to Poincaré's and Wallas's.

Henri Poincaré (1854–1912). A French mathematician who is known to creativity researchers for his 1913 description of his creative process as hard work, incubation, and illumination (Poincaré, 1913/1982).

B. F. Skinner (1904–1990). The public face of behaviorism in American in the middle of the 20th century. It was a common criticism of behaviorism that it could never explain creativity; it could only explain behavior that had been programmed by the environment. Skinner's response was to argue that novel behavior was largely an illusion, and that what we call creativity is based in behaviorist principles (e.g., Skinner, 1972).

Lewis M. Terman (1877–1956). A professor at Stanford who adapted Binet's test for U.S. audiences, first publishing the Stanford-Binet test in 1916 (Terman, 1916). Terman served in the U.S. military during World War I, and the test was administered to 1.7 million U.S. soldiers. Terman is famous for his important longitudinal study of over 1,500 Californian gifted children, who were identified using the Stanford-Binet IQ test and other tests; he began identifying children in 1921 and continued adding subjects through 1928 (see Terman, 1954).

Edward Thorndike (1874–1949). One of the most influential behaviorists, he is known for the *Law of Effect*—responses to a situation that are rewarded will become more likely in response to that situation. In a famous study, he observed cats as they learned to escape from puzzle boxes, and proved that they weren't using sudden insight, by showing that their learning curves showed gradual learning. He concluded that all learning is incremental, never insightful. During World War I, he developed the Alpha and Beta tests for the U.S. military.

Lev Vygotsky (1896–1934). A Soviet psychologist, widely influential among education researchers for his theory of the *zone of proximal development*, suggesting that students should be taught just a bit above their level of mastery. His first book, based on his doctoral dissertation, was *The Psychology of Art* (Vygotsky, 1922/1971).

Graham Wallas (1858–1932). Known to creativity researchers for his 1926 book (Wallas, 1926), which presented a four-stage model of the creative process: preparation, incubation, illumination, and verification/elaboration. Wallas wrote this book after he retired from his career as Professor of Political Science at the University of London.

1950–1970

Frank X. Barron (1922–2002). A founding member of the staff of the IPAR in Berkeley, California, he became a professor at the University of California, Santa Cruz in 1969 and stayed there for the rest of his career.

Alden B. Dow (1904–1983). Architect who worked with Frank Lloyd Wright. Founded the Dow Creativity Center at Northwoods University, Michigan.

Jacob Getzels (1912–2001). Professor at the University of Chicago; M. Csikszentmihalyi's doctoral advisor. Developed the concept of *problem finding* or *discovered problems* in Getzels (1964).

Harrison Gough. A member of the IPAR. Developer of the California Psychological Inventory (CPI), a personality inventory first published in 1956 and still widely used; also developed a creativity metric called the Gough Adjective Check List (ACL: Gough, 1965).

Howard E. Gruber (1922–2005). Gruber studied creativity from a Piagetian perspective. He built on Piaget's insight that the creative process was quite similar to developmental processes, in his influential analysis of Charles Darwin's notebooks. Known for his *evolving systems approach* and for his concept of *networks of enterprise*, the multiple overlapping projects that exceptional creators are involved in.

J. P. Guilford (1897–1987). Worked during World War II at the Office for Strategic Services, Assessment Center. President of the American Psychological Association in 1950, and titled his Presidential Address "Creativity," one of the most widely cited articles in creativity research (Guilford, 1950). Founded the Aptitudes Research Project at the University of Southern California in the early 1950s, funded by the Office of Naval Research. Known for his Structure of Intellect model of human ability (he abbreviated it as SI, but most people today refer to it as SOI).

Ernst Kris (1900–1957). A psychoanalytic theorist, Ernst (1952) updated Freud's view to propose that art results from a form of regression to primary process thought that was controlled by the conscious ego. He called this "regression in the service of the ego."

Donald W. MacKinnon (1903–1987). Worked during World War II at the Office for Strategic Services, Assessment Center. He was Director of Station S, a remote Maryland farmhouse that identified people who would make good spies or European resistance leaders. Founded the Institute for Personality Assessment and Research (IPAR) at the University of Berkeley in 1949. Known for an influential study of exceptionally creative architects (MacKinnon, 1962).

Abraham H. Maslow (1908–1970). Taught at Brooklyn College 1937 to 1951, then became chair of the Department of Psychology at Brandeis. One of the best-known humanist psychologists, he is famous for proposing "Maslow's hierarchy of needs," with self-actualization at the top.

Rollo May (1909–1994). An existentialist psychologist who emphasized the importance of strength and courage in creativity in his book *The Courage to Create* (May, 1975).

Sarnoff A. Mednick. Emeritus Professor at the University of Southern California. Known among creativity researchers for his 1960s proposals that creative ideas resulted from remote associations (Mednick, 1962). Developer of the Remote Associates Test (RAT). Most of his subsequent career focused on adult mental illness and schizophrenia, and their genetic bases.

Alex F. Osborn (1888–1966). A co-founder and senior executive of the New York advertising firm BBDO. Coined the term *brainstorming* and invented the technique, which was first used within BBDO. Co-developer, with Sidney Parnes, of the Creative Problem Solving (CPS) process. Author of several successful early practical books about creativity, including 1948's *Your Creative Power* and 1953's *Applied Imagination*. In 1954, founded the Creative Education Foundation in Buffalo, with a personal fortune he amassed as a successful advertising executive and from his publishing income.

Sidney J. Parnes. With Alex Osborn in the 1950s, he was co-creator of the Creative Problem Solving (CPS) process. Founder, in 1967, of the Interdisciplinary Center for Creative Studies, now known as the International Center for Studies in Creativity at Buffalo State University. For many years was director of the annual Creative Problem-Solving Institute.

Carl R. Rogers (1902–1987). A professor of psychology at the University of Wisconsin since 1957. One of the best-known humanist psychologists, he argued that creativity represented the fully actualized self. He developed *client-centered therapy*.

Morris Stein. Worked during World War II at the Office for Strategic Services, Assessment Center. Founded the Center for the Study of Creativity and Mental Health at the University of Chicago in 1952. Became director of the Research Center for Human Relations at New York University. Perhaps the first creativity researcher to emphasize the importance of social context, the "intermediaries" of the field, and interpersonal dynamics.

Calvin W. Taylor (1915–2000). Led the NSF's effort (1952–1954) to develop a test to identify the most promising future scientists for the Graduate Fellowship program. Then, as a professor at the University of Utah, organized and led the series of five Utah Conferences on "The Identification of Creative Scientific Talent" (1955, 1957, 1959, 1961, 1962). (Taylor went on to organize four additional creativity-related conferences, for a total of nine: Taylor, 1987.)

L. L. Thurstone (1887–1955). During World War I, he developed the Trade Tests for occupational classification in the U.S. Army. During World War II, he was a member of the Committee on Classification of Military Personnel of the U.S. Adjutant General's Office. A professor at the University of Chicago from 1924 to 1950, he moved to the University of North Carolina, where he was the director of the Psychometric Laboratory. Author of *The Nature of Creative Thinking* (1952).

E. Paul Torrance (1915–2003). Started his career at the University of Minnesota, where he was Director of the Bureau of Educational Research. His creativity test was originally called the Minnesota Test of Creative Thinking, later renamed the Torrance Test of Creative Thinking (TTCT; Torrance, 2002, 2008).

Michael A. Wallach. A widely published professor at Duke, best known to creativity researchers as the lead author of the 1965 Wallach and Kogan study that provided the first evidence that creativity and intelligence were not always related, contrary to earlier studies such as Getzels and Jackson (1962).

1970–1990

Robert S. Albert. Professor Emeritus of Psychology at Pitzer College. Past president of APA's Division 10, "Psychology of Aesthetics, Creativity, and the Arts"; during the 1990s, was editor of the Ablex book series "Publications in Creativity Research." Known for studies of genius, creativity, and eminence.

Teresa Amabile. After many years in the psychology department at Brandeis University, moved to Harvard School of Business in 1995. Known for her influential studies of intrinsic motivation, and of the detrimental effects of extrinsic motivation on creativity. One of the first creativity researchers to argue for a sociocultural approach, in her 1983 book *The Social Psychology of Creativity*.

Mihaly Csikszentmihalyi. Received his Ph.D. at the University of Chicago with Jacob Getzels. They worked together to follow up his 1965 dissertation study of MFA painters at the Art Institute of Chicago, and published their results in the 1976 book *The Creative Vision*. Csikszentmihalyi served as a professor at the University of Chicago for most of his career, where he published the 1990 best-seller *Flow* and 1996 *Creativity*, before moving to Claremont Graduate University.

Hans J. Eysenck (1916–1997). Personality trait psychologist and Professor at the Institute of Psychiatry in London. Widely published from the 1950s through the 1990s, he is today known for his three-trait model of personality: Neuroticism, Extraversion, and Psychoticism, measured with the Eysenck Personality Questionnaire (EPQ). Known among creativity researchers for his claim that creativity and psychoticism are correlated, below the level of manifest psychosis, due to a common predisposition towards "overinclusion."

John F. Feldhusen. Professor of Education and Psychology at Purdue for most of his career. Creator of the Purdue Creative Thinking Program. Founder of the Purdue Gifted Education Resource Institute in 1975, and its director until 1995. Served as editor of *Gifted Child Quarterly*.

David Henry Feldman. A professor of child development at Tufts University for most of his career, he is known for his studies of cognitive development, particularly his studies of childhood prodigies as published in Feldman (1986).

Howard Gardner. Co-director of Harvard's Project Zero from the early 1970s through his retirement in the 2000s. Author of over 20 books, including many based on the Project Zero studies of the cognitive foundations of artistic production and perception. Most famous for his 1983 book *Frames of Mind*, which proposed his influential theory of "multiple intelligences."

Scott Isaksen. Former Professor at Buffalo State, and a past Director of the Center for Studies in Creativity. He is one of the torchbearers for the Creative Problem Solving approach first developed by Alex Osborn and Sidney Parnes. He updated CPS to its current version in the 1980s (Isaksen & Treffinger, 1985, 1987) and is the author of several books on CPS. He is CEO and President of the Creative Problem Solving Group, based in Buffalo, NY.

Vera John-Steiner. An influential expert on Russian psychologist Lev Vygotsky. Her 1985 book *Notebooks of the Mind* was the first study of the important role of external representations in the creative process; her 2000 book *Creative Collaborations* was an influential study of collaborative pairs and teams throughout history.

Arnold M. Ludwig. M.D., Psychiatrist, Adjunct Professor of Psychiatry and Human Behavior at Brown University (2006–present). Known for his research demonstrating no link between creativity and madness.

Colin Martindale (1943–2008). President of APA Division 10, 1986–1987; President of the International Association of Empirical Aesthetics, 1994–1998; Editor of *Empirical Studies of the Arts* from 1983 to 2005. He was known for studies of the biologic foundations of creativity.

David Perkins. Co-director of Harvard's Project Zero (with Howard Gardner) for over 25 years. Author of many books on creativity and on teaching thinking.

Joseph Renzulli. An educational psychologist focused on gifted and talented education, he is known for his *three-ring model of giftedness* (Renzulli, 2005) and for his *Schoolwide Enrichment Model* (Renzulli, 1985). Developer of the summer Confratute program at the University of Connecticut, founded in 1978 for teacher professional development.

Albert Rothenberg. Professor of Psychiatry at Harvard University. Author of several influential books on creativity. Known for his concepts of "Janusian thinking," thinking of two opposed thoughts simultaneously, and "homospatial thinking," thinking of two objects occupying the same physical space.

Gudmund J. W. Smith. Retired, was Professor of Psychology at Lund University, Sweden (1960–1986). Known for his process approach to personality research. Co-author with Ingegerd Carlsson on several studies of creativity.

Donald J. Treffinger. Past Professor at Purdue; retired from Buffalo State. With Scott Isaksen, updated CPS to its current version in the 1980s (Isaksen & Treffinger, 1985, 1987). He is President of the Center for Creative Learning, Inc., in Sarasota, Florida, a firm offering consulting and training services in Creative Problem Solving (CPS).

1990—PRESENT

In preparing this list, I consulted several sources, including the editorial boards and consulting editors of all of the creativity research journals, and contributors to creativity encyclopedias and handbooks.

Prior to 1990, creativity research was dominated by scholars in the United States. In recent decades, the field has expanded dramatically to become much more international—corresponding to an increasing global awareness of the importance of creativity (Chapter 1), and that is reflected in the broader range of countries represented below. Given my location in the United States, I've no doubt neglected some important non-U.S. scholars. In particular, my awareness of creativity research in Asian countries is very low.

John M. Baer. Professor of Psychology at Rider University. Has published many studies on creativity assessment, domain specificity, and creative learning.

Mark Batey. Manchester Business School. His research focuses on creativity and personality.

Ronald A. Beghetto. Associate Professor of Educational Studies at the University of Oregon. His research focuses on creativity in schools.

Margaret A. Boden. Research Professor of Cognitive Science at the University of Sussex, UK. An influential cognitive scientist and artificial intelligence researcher, one of her areas of research is creativity in computers.

Ingegerd Carlsson. Professor of Psychology at Lund University, Sweden. With Gudmund J. W. Smith, developer of the Creative Functioning Test. Conducts brain imaging studies of the creative process.

Anna Craft. Professor of Education, University of Exeter, UK. Her research focuses on creative teaching and learning.

Bonnie Cramond. Professor of Education at the University of Georgia. Her research focuses on gifted education, and on the identification and nurturance of creativity.

Arthur Cropley. Emeritus Professor of Psychology at the University of Hamburg, Germany. His research focuses on creativity and lifelong learning.

David Cropley. Associate Professor of Engineering at the University of South Australia. His research focuses on engineering creativity, fostering creativity, and the "dark side" of creativity.

Janet E. Davidson. Associate Professor of Psychology at Lewis & Clark College, Portland, Oregon. Her doctoral advisor was Robert Sternberg at Yale. Her research focuses on giftedness, creative insight, and problem solving.

Gary A. Davis. Retired; was Professor of Educational Psychology at the University of Wisconsin, Madison (1965–1994). His research focused on gifted education; he developed the How Do You Think and the Group Inventory For Finding Interests (GIFFI) tests.

Robert Epstein. Independent scholar and journalist. Former editor-in-chief of *Psychology Today*. Known for his *generativity theory* of creativity, based in behaviorist principles that he developed studying pigeons with B. F. Skinner at Harvard.

Gregory J. Feist. Associate Professor of Psychology at San Jose State University. Founding editor of the *Journal of Psychology of Science and Technology*. Studies creativity in science, and the identification and development of scientific talent.

Cameron Ford. Associate Professor in the College of Business Administration at the University of Central Florida, where he is Founding Director of the UCF Center for Entrepreneurship and Innovation. His research focuses on creativity in the workplace, and creativity and entrepreneurship.

Elena L. Grigorenko. Associate Professor, Yale Child Study Center, and Associate Professor of Psychology at Moscow State University. A frequent co-author with Robert J. Sternberg on topics related to creativity and successful intelligence; her research focuses on learning disabilities.

Ravenna Helson. Adjunct Professor Emeritus in the Department of Psychology at the University of California, Berkeley. Her research focused on the psychology of women and creativity. Founder and Director of the Mills Longitudinal Study, which followed 120 women for 40 years.

Beth A. Hennessey. Professor of Psychology at Wellesley College. Her doctoral advisor was Teresa Amabile. Her research focuses on motivation in the creative process. Known for her development of techniques to "immunize" students from the detrimental effects of extrinsic rewards.

James C. Kaufman. Formerly of the Educational Testing Service, now a Professor of Psychology at California State University, San Bernardino. His doctoral advisor was Robert Sternberg at Yale. Has published widely on creativity and has edited many books on creativity and related topics. A founding co-editor of *Psychology of Aesthetics, Creativity, and the Arts*; editor of *The International Journal of Creativity & Problem Solving*.

Scott Barry Kaufman. Adjunct Assistant Professor of Psychology at New York University. He studies the measurement and development of talent, intelligence, and creativity.

Geir Kaufmann. Professor and Chair, Department of Organizational Psychology and Leadership, Norwegian School of Management, Norway. His research focuses on cognition, strategic imagery, and organizational innovation.

Kyung Hee Kim. Assistant Professor in the School of Education at the College of William & Mary. She studies cultural differences in creativity between Korea and America and the relationship between creativity and intelligence.

Paul Locher. Montclair State University. President of APA's Division 10, Psychology of Aesthetics, Creativity, and the Arts (2004–2005). President of the International Association of Empirical Aesthetics (2004–2006). Editor of *Empirical Studies of the Arts*. Studies empirical aesthetics, with a focus on the influence of pictorial symmetry and balance on the creation and perception of visual art.

Todd I. Lubart. Professor at Université Paris V, Université René Descartes. His doctoral advisor was Robert Sternberg at Yale. Creator, with Robert Sternberg, of the investment theory of creativity. Studies emotion and creativity and workplace creativity.

Dorothy Miell. Vice Principal and Head of College of Humanities and Social Science at the University of Edinburgh. Studies the social and communicative aspects of creativity, particularly in music making.

Roberta M. Milgram. Professor Emeritus of Education at Tel Aviv University. Her research focuses on giftedness and creativity in Israeli adolescents.

Michael Mumford. Professor of Industrial and Organizational Psychology at the University of Oklahoma. Studies the identification and measurement of creative thinking skills.

Paul B. Paulus. Professor of Psychology at the University of Texas at Arlington. Known for his experimental studies of group creativity and brainstorming.

Jane Piirto. Professor of Graduate Education at Ashland University, Ohio. Wrote the first overview of creativity research, *Understanding Those Who Create*, in 1992; it has since been republished in a second edition (1998) and a third edition (2004). Known for her "Piirto Pyramid of Talent Development," which proposes genetic, emotional, and cognitive aspects.

Jonathan A. Plucker. Professor of Educational Psychology and Cognitive Science at Indiana University. Has published on the topics of creativity and intelligence, creativity assessment, and gifted education.

Steven R. Pritzker. Professor of Psychology at Saybrook University. His research focuses on creativity in film and in writing.

Gerard J. Puccio. Department Chair at the International Center for Studies in Creativity at Buffalo State. Studies Creative Problem Solving (CPS), assessment, and leadership.

M. K. Raina. Professor and Head, Department of Educational Psychology and Foundations of Education, National Council of Educational Research and Training, New Delhi, India. His research focuses on creativity in gifted education, and cultural differences in creativity.

Ruth Richards. Professor of Psychology at Saybrook University. Studies creativity in everyday life.

Tudor Rickards. Professor of Creativity and Organizational Change at Manchester Business School, UK. His research focuses on the application of creativity-enhancing techniques. He is the developer of the "Manchester Method" of creative and applied learning.

Mark A. Runco. Director of the Torrance Center at the University of Georgia since 2009. An important leader in the field of creativity research. Founder and editor of the *Creativity Research Journal*; editor of the 1997 *Creativity Research Handbook*; co-editor of the two-volume *Encyclopedia of Creativity*; author of an undergraduate textbook, *Creativity*; author of numerous empirical journal articles; editor of many books.

Sandra W. Russ. Professor of Psychology at Case Western Reserve University. Studies the role of affect in creativity, and connections between children's play and creativity.

Keith Sawyer. Professor at Washington University in St. Louis. Author of *Explaining Creativity*. Known for studies of improvisational creativity and collaborative creativity.

Paul Silvia. Professor at the University of North Carolina at Greensboro. Has published many studies on aesthetic experience, creativity assessment, domain specificity, creativity, and intelligence.

Dean Keith Simonton. Professor at the University of California, Davis. Known for his historio-metric studies of creativity over time, using large databases containing hundreds of individuals and creative works, quantified in ways that allow broad historical patterns to be identified. His work on creativity often merges with studies of greatness and leadership.

Jeffrey K. Smith and Lisa F. Smith. Both professors at Otago University in New Zealand, and both currently co-editors of *Psychology of Aesthetics, Creativity, and the Arts*. Their research focuses on educational assessment and on the psychology of aesthetics.

Steven M. Smith. Professor of Psychology at Texas A&M University. Known for his research contributions to the creative cognition approach, with collaborators Ronald Finke and Thomas Ward.

Robert J. Sternberg. A psychologist who spent many years at Yale University as director of the PACE Center (Psychology of Abilities, Competence, and Expertise; now at Tufts). Known for his critique of intelligence testing, and his own alternative proposal for a triarchic model of human abilities, which includes creativity and practical intelligence in addition to the analytic intelligence measured by traditional IQ tests. In 2005, he moved to Tufts University as Dean of Arts and Sciences, where he modified undergraduate admissions criteria based on his research. In 2010, he became Provost at Oklahoma State University.

Ai-Girl Tan. Associate Professor of Psychological Studies at the National Institute of Education, Singapore. Her research focuses on creativity in teaching.

Oshin Vartanian. Defence Scientist at Defence R&D Canada, Toronto. Colin Martindale was his doctoral advisor, and he completed postdoctoral study in cognitive neuroscience with Dr. Vinod Goel. He studies the cognitive neuroscience of creativity, reasoning, decision making, and aesthetics.

Thomas B. Ward. Professor of psychology at the University of Alabama; Editor of the *Journal of Creative Behavior*. Studies the role of concepts in creative cognition.

Robert Weisberg. Professor at Temple University, Philadelphia, PA. A prominent advocate of the "business as usual" theory of creative cognition—that creativity is no different from other everyday mental processes. Has published several books and articles arguing that the "moment of insight" is largely mythical.

Ellen Winner. Professor of Psychology at Boston College, and Senior Research Associate at Harvard's Project Zero. Her research focuses on cognition in the arts, in typical and in gifted children.

APPENDIX G

Colleges and Universities with a Degree or Certificate in Creativity

To generate this list, I started with a similar list published in 2010 (Yudess, 2010). I then confirmed that this information was up to date as of August 2011. I removed programs that were focused on leadership, entrepreneurship, or design rather than creativity per se.

Buffalo State (also referred to as State University of New York College at Buffalo). International Center for Studies in Creativity. Undergraduate Minor in Creative Studies. Graduate Certificate in Creativity and Change Leadership. MS in Creative Studies. http://buffalostate.edu/creativity/

Drexel University. Goodwin College. Undergraduate Certificate in Creativity and Innovation. http://goodwin.drexel.edu/mep/ug_cs.php. MS in Creativity and Innovation. http://goodwin.drexel.edu/mep/ci_over.php. MS in Professional Studies: Creativity and Innovation. http://goodwin.drexel.edu/mep/g_cs.php

Saybrook University. MA in Psychology, with specialization in Creativity Studies. http://www.saybrook.edu/phs/academicprograms/psy/cs. Graduate Certificate in Creativity Studies. http://www.saybrook.edu/phs/academicprograms/certificates/creativitystudy

Texas A&M. Institute for Applied Creativity. MS and MEd in Educational Psychology: Creative Studies Specialization. PhD in Educational Psychology: Intelligence, Creativity, and Giftedness Specialization. Undergraduate Minor in Creativity Studies. http://creativity.tamu.edu/

University of California, Santa Barbara. College of Creative Studies. BS or BA degrees focusing on one of: art, biology, chemistry and biochemistry, computer science, literature, mathematics, music composition, physics. http://www.ccs.ucsb.edu/welcome/

Universidad Fernando Pessoa, Santiago de Compostela, Spain. International Masters in Creativity. International Doctorate in Creativity. Masters in Creativity and Innovation. http://www.micat.net/

University of Georgia. Torrance Center for Creativity and Talent Development. MEd, EdS, EdD, and PhD in Educational Psychology: Gifted and Creative Education Focus. http://www.coe.uga.edu/torrance/

University of Malta. Edward de Bono Institute. International MSc in Strategic Innovation and Future Creation, in partnership with University of Potsdam, Germany; Teesside University, UK; University of Turku, Finland. http://www.strategicfutures.eu/. Master in Creativity and Innovation. Secondary Area of Studies in Creativity, Innovation and Entrepreneurship. http://www.um.edu.mt/create

University of Massachusetts, Boston. Critical and Creative Thinking Graduate Program. MA in Critical and Creative Thinking. Graduate Certificate in Critical and Creative Thinking. http://www.cct.umb.edu/

CENTER WITH COURSES BUT NO DEGREE

Boise State University. College of Business and Economics. Centre for Creativity and Innovation. http://cobe.boisestate.edu/cci/

APPENDIX H

Professional Associations and Conferences

Many creativity researchers belong to one or more of these professional associations, and they present their research and socialize at one or more of these annual conferences. Other than the American Psychological Association, these associations and conferences tend to include both scholars and practitioners—creativity consultants, trainers, and educators.

All web addresses current as of August 30, 2011.

PROFESSIONAL ASSOCIATIONS

American Creativity Association. "An association of professionals from many fields whose work demands that we use deliberate creativity on a daily basis" (from the website: www.amcreativity assoc.org). Hosts an annual conference. Has affiliates in many other countries.

American Psychological Association, Division 10, Society for the Psychology of Aesthetics, Creativity, and the Arts. http://www.apa.org/divisions/div10/

China Creative Studies Institute. http://www.ccsis.org/

Creative Education Foundation. Hosts the annual CPSI conferences and publishes the *Journal of Creative Behavior*. http://www.creativeeducationfoundation.org/

Creativity European Association (CREA). An Italian affiliate of the Creative Education Foundation, equally focused on Creative Problem Solving (CPS). http://www.creaconference.com/

European Association for Creativity and Innovation. www.eaci.net. Hosts an annual conference.

Hong Kong Creative Initiatives Foundation. http://www.creative-initiatives.org/

International Forum of Creativity Organizations. Their website, http://www.ifoco.org/, lists many creativity organizations based in countries around the world, and also lists creativity conferences and events.

ANNUAL CONFERENCES

Alden B. Dow Creativity Center (founded 1978), Northwoods University, Midland, MI, has hosted an annual Creativity Conference since 1990. http://www.northwood.edu/creativitycenter/

American Creativity Association annual conference, started in 1990

Atlanta Creativity Exchange (ACE). Annual conference established in 2006 at Kennesaw State Center for Business Innovation and Creativity (near Atlanta, GA).

CREA: The Annual Conference on Creative Problem Solving Creativity & Innovation. Hosted by the Creativity European Association (CREA), and is a European partner of the U.S. CPSI conference.

Creative Problem Solving Institute (CPSI). First held at the University of Buffalo in 1949, and annually since then. http://www.cpsiconference.com/

Creativity & Cognition. The focus is on computers and creativity—both computer models of creativity, and computer systems that support creative processes and performance. First held in 1993, is now held biannually in odd-numbered years.

European Conference on Creativity and Innovation (ECCI). The first conference was held in 1987; these continue to be held in a different country in every odd-numbered year. Co-organized by EACI and a local creativity and innovation organization in the hosting country.

REFERENCES

Abbott, B. (1964). *The world of Atget*. New York: Horizon Press.

Abelson, P. H. (1965). Relation of group activity to creativity in science. *Daedalus, 94*(3), 603–614.

Abrams, M. H. (1953). *The mirror and the lamp: Romantic theory and the critical tradition*. New York: Norton.

Abrams, M. H. (1984). *The correspondent breeze: Essays on English romanticism*. New York: Norton.

Ades, D., Forge, A., & Durham, A. (1985). *Francis Bacon*. London: Thames and Hudson, Ltd.

Adorno, T. W. (2002). *Essays on music*. Berkeley, CA: University of California Press.

Aiken, M., & Hage, J. (1971). The organic organization and innovation. *Sociology, 5*, 63–82.

Alajouanine, T. (1948). Aphasia and artistic realization. *Brain, 71*, 229–241.

Albert, R. S., & Runco, M. A. (1999). A history of research on creativity. In R. J. Sternberg (Ed.), *The handbook of creativity* (pp. 16–31). New York: Cambridge.

Aldag, R. J., & Fuller, S. R. (1993). Beyond fiasco: A reappraisal of the groupthink phenomenon and a new model of group decision processes. *Psychological Bulletin, 113*, 533–552.

Allison, P. D. (1980). Inequality and scientific productivity. *Social Studies of Science, 10*, 163–179.

Alperson, P. (1984). On musical improvisation. *Journal of Aesthetics and Art Criticism, 43*, 17–29.

Alter, J. B. (1984). A factor analysis of new and standardized instruments to measure the creative potential and high-energy action preference of performing arts students: A preliminary investigation. *Personality and Individual Differences, 5*(6), 693–699.

Altshuller, G. S. (1988). *Creativity as an exact science: The theory of the solution of inventive problems*. New York: Gordon and Breach Science Publishers.

Amabile, T. (1982). Children's artistic creativity: Detrimental effects of competition in a field setting. *Personality and Social Psychology Bulletin, 8*, 573–578.

Amabile, T. (1983). *The social psychology of creativity*. New York: Springer-Verlag.

Amabile, T. (1988). A model of creativity and innovation in organizations. *Research in Organizational Behavior, 10*, 123–167.

Amabile, T. (1996). *Creativity in context: Update to the social psychology of creativity*. Boulder, CO: Westview Press. (Second edition of Amabile, 1983.)

Amabile, T., Conti, R., Coon, H., Lazenby, J., & Herron, M. (1996). Assessing the work environment for creativity. *Academy of Management Journal, 39*(5), 1154–1184.

Amabile, T. M., & Gryskiewicz, S. S. (1987). *Creativity in the R & D laboratory (Tech. Rep. #30)*. Greensboro, NC: Center for Creative Leadership.

Amit, R., Glosten, L., & Muller, E. (1993). Challenges to theory development in entrepreneurship research. *Journal of Management Studies*, 30, 815–834.

Anastasi, A., & Urbina, S. (1997). Psychological testing (7th ed.). Upper Saddle River, NJ: Prentice-Hall.

Ancona, D., & Bresman, H. (2007). *X-teams: How to build teams that lead, innovate, and succeed*. Boston, MA: Harvard Business School Press.

Ancona, D., & Caldwell, D. F. (1992). Demography and design: Predictors of new product team performance. *Organization Science, 3*, 321–341.

Anderson, F. E. (1976). Esthetic evaluations and art involvement in Australia. *Studies in Art Education, 17*, 33–43.

Anderson, H. H. (1959). *Creativity and its cultivation*. New York: Harper & Row.

Anderson, N. R., & West, M. A. (1998). Measuring climate for work group innovation: Development and validation of the team climate inventory. *Journal of Organizational Behavior, 19*, 235–158.

Andiliou, A. & Murphy, P. K. (2010). Examining variations among researchers' and teachers' conceptualizations of creativity: A review and synthesis of contemporary research. *Educational Research Review, 5*, 201–219.

Andreasen, N. C. (1987). Creativity and mental illness: Prevalence rates in writers and their first-degree relatives. *American Journal of Psychiatry, 144*(10), 1288–1292.

Andrew, J. P., Manget, J., Michael, D. C., Taylor, A., & Zablit, H. (2010). *Innovation 2010: A return to prominence, and the emergence of a new world order*. Boston, MA: Boston Consulting Group.

Andrews-Hanna, J. R., Reidler, J. S., Huang, C., & Buckner, R. L. (2010). Evidence for the default network's role in spontaneous cognition. *Journal of Neurophysiology, 104*, 322–335.

Andriessen, J. (2006). Arguing to learn. In R. K. Sawyer (Ed.), *Cambridge handbook of the learning sciences* (pp. 443–459). New York: Cambridge University Press.

Ansburg, P. I., & Dominowski, R. L. (2000). Promoting insightful problem solving. *Journal of Creative Behavior, 34*(1), 30–60.

Ansburg, P. I., & Hill, K. (2003). Creative and analytic thinkers differ in their use of attentional resources. *Personality and Individual Differences, 34*, 1141–1152.

Arenius, P., & Minniti, M. (2005). Perceptual variables and nascent entrepreneurship. *Small Business Economics, 24*, 233–247.

Arieti, S. (1976). *Creativity: The magic synthesis*. New York: Basic Books.

Arlin, P. K. (1974). *A cognitive process model of problem finding*. University of Chicago, Chicago.

Arlin, P. K. (1975). A cognitive process model of problem finding. *Educational Horizons, 54*(2), 99–106.

Arnheim, R. (1966). *Toward a psychology of art: Collected essays*. Berkeley, CA: University of California Press.

Arnheim, R. (1974). *Art and visual perception: A psychology of the creative eye*. Berkeley, CA: University of California Press. (Expanded and revised edition of the original work published in 1954).

Arnold, W. N. (1992). *Vincent van Gogh: Chemicals, crisis, and creativity*. Boston, MA: Birkhäuser.

Arnold, W. N. (2002, March 22). *Vincent van Gogh: Chemicals, crisis, and creativity*, Talk given at Washington University Department of Psychology.

Augusta, A. (1842). Sketch of the analytical engine invented by Charles Babbage, by L. F. Menabrea, with notes by the translator, Ada Augusta. http://www.fourmilab.ch/babbage/sketch.html Retrieved Sep. 1, 2011.

Azoulay, P., Zivin, J. S. G., & Wang, J. (2010). Superstar extinction. *Quarterly Journal of Economics, 125*(2), 549–589.

Bacon, F. (1868). *The works of Francis Bacon* (e. J. Spedding, R. L. Ellis & D. D. Heath, Trans. Vol. 12). London: Longman.

Baer, J. (1993). *Creativity and divergent thinking: A task-specific approach.* Hillsdale, NJ: Erlbaum.

Baer, J. (1993–1994). Why you shouldn't trust creativity tests. *Educational Leadership, 51*(4), 80–83.

Baer, J. (1998). The case for domain specificity. *Creativity Research Journal, 11*(2), 173–177.

Baer, J., & Kaufman, J. C. (2008). Gender differences in creativity. *Journal of Creative Behavior, 42*(2), 75–105.

Baer, M., Leenders, R. T. A. J., Oldham, G. R., & Vadera, A. K. (2010). Win or lose the battle for creativity: The power and perils of intergroup competition. *Academy of Management Journal, 53*(4), 827–845.

Baer, M., Oldham, G. R., Hollingshead, A. B., & Jacobsohn, G. C. (2005). Revisiting the birth order-creativity connection: The role of sibling constellation. *Creativity Research Journal, 17*(1), 67–77.

Bain, A. (1855/1977). *The senses and the intellect.* Washington, DC: University Publications of America. (Reprint of 1855 edition published by John W. Parker and Son, London.)

Baird, L. L. (1982). *The role of academic ability in high level accomplishment and general success* (College Board Report Vol. 82, No. 6). Princeton, NJ: Educational Testing Service.

Baird, L. L. (1985). Do grades and tests predict adult accomplishment? *Research in Higher Education, 23*, 3–85.

Balkundi, P., & Harrison, D. A. (2006). Ties, leaders, and time in teams: Strong inference about network structure's effects on team viability and performance. *Academy of Management Journal, 49*, 49–68.

Ball, O. E., & Torrance, E. P. (1984). *Streamlines scoring workbook: Figural A.* Bensenville, IL: Scholastic Testing Service, Inc.

Bandura, A. (1986). *Social foundations of thought and action: A social-cognitive view.* Englewood Cliffs, NJ: Prentice-Hall.

Bantel, K. A., & Jackson, S. E. (1989). Top management and innovations in banking: Does the composition of the top team make a difference? *Strategic Management Journal, 10*, 107–124.

Bargh, J. A., & Morsella, E. (2008). The unconscious mind. *Perspectives on Psychological Science, 3*, 73–79.

Barnett, H. G. (1953). *Innovation.* New York: McGraw-Hill.

Barrett, P. M. (2010, July 26–Aug. 1). The sermon on the monitor. Review of *Cognitive Surplus. Bloomberg Businessweek*, 78–79.

Barron, F. (1963a). *Creativity and psychological health: Origins of personal vitality and creative freedom.* Princeton, NJ: D. Van Nostrand Company.

Barron, F. (1963b). The disposition toward originality. In C. W. Taylor & F. Barron (Eds.), *Scientific creativity: Its recognition and development* (pp. 139–152). New York: John Wiley & Sons.

Barron, F. (1968). *Creativity and personal freedom.* Princeton, NJ: D. Van Nostrand Company, Inc.

Barron, F. (1969). *Creative persons and the creative process.* New York: Holt.

Barron, F. (1972). *Artists in the making.* New York: Seminar Press.

Barron, F., & Harrington, D. M. (1981). Creativity, intelligence, and personality. *Annual Review of Psychology, 32*, 439–476.

Barron, F., & Welsh, G. S. (1952). Artistic perception as a possible factor in personality style: Its measurement by a figure preference test. *Journal of Psychology, 33*, 199–203.

Barrow, J. D. (2000). *The universe that discovered itself.* New York: Oxford University Press.

Barthes, R. (1967). The death of the author. *Aspen Magazine, 5–6*, Section 3.

Bartlett, J. (1955). *Familiar quotations: A collection of passages, phrases, and proverbs traced to their sources in ancient and modern literature.* Boston: Little, Brown.

Bartlett, T. (2010, Oct. 22). Play it again, professor. *Chronicle of Higher Education,* A1, A10.

Barzun, J. (1991). The paradox of creativity. In H. A. Wilmer (Ed.), *Creativity: Paradoxes and reflections* (pp. 3–25). Wilmette, IL: Chiron Publications.

Basalla, G. (1988). *The evolution of technology.* New York: Cambridge University Press.

Batey, M., & Furnham, A. (2006). Creativity, intelligence, and personality: A critical review of the scattered literature. *Genetic, Social and General Psychology Monographs, 132*(4), 355–429.

Baudelaire, C. (1863/1964). *The painter of modern life, and other essays* (J. Mayne, Trans.). London: Phaidon.

Baughman, W. A., & Mumford, M. D. (1995). Process analytic models of creative capacities: Operations involved in the combination and reorganization process. *Creativity Research Journal, 8,* 37–62.

Baumeister, R. F., Schmeichel, B. J., DeWall, C. N., & Vohs, K. D. (2007). Is the conscious self a help, a hindrance, or an irrelevance to the creative process? In A. M. Columbus (Ed.), *Advances in Psychology Research* (Vol. 53, pp. 137–152). Hauppage, NY: Nova Science Publishers.

Baxandall, M. (1972). *Painting and experience in fifteenth-century Italy.* New York: Oxford University Press.

Beal, D. J., Cohen, R. R., Burke, M. J., & McLendon, C. L. (2003). Cohesion and performance in groups: A meta-analytic clarification of construct relations. *Journal of Applied Psychology, 88,* 989–1004.

Becker, G. (2000–2001). The association of creativity and psychopathology: Its cultural-historical origins. *Creativity Research Journal, 13*(1), 45–53.

Becker, H. (1982). *Art worlds.* Berkeley: University of California Press.

Becker, H. (2000). The etiquette of improvisation. *Mind, Culture, and Activity, 7*(3), 171–176.

Beeftink, F., van Eerde, W., & Rutte, C. G. (2008). The effect of interruptions and breaks on insight and impasses: Do you need a break right now? *Creativity Research Journal, 20*(4), 358–364.

Beeman, M. J., & Bowden, E. M. (2000). The right hemisphere maintains solution-related activation for yet-to-be-solved insight problems. *Memory & Cognition, 28,* 1231–1241.

Beghetto, R. A. (2006a). Creative self-efficacy: Correlates in middle and secondary students. *Creativity Research Journal, 18,* 447–457.

Beghetto, R. A. (2006b). Does creativity have a place in classroom discussions? Prospective teachers' response preferences. *Thinking Skills and Creativity, 2*(1), 1–9.

Beghetto, R. A., & Kaufman, J. C. (2010). *Nurturing creativity in the classroom.* Cambridge, UK: Cambridge University Press.

Beittel, K. R. (1972). *Mind and context in the art of drawing.* New York: Holt, Rinehart and Winston, Inc.

Beittel, K. R., & Burkhart, R. C. (1963). Strategies of spontaneous, divergent, and academic art students. *Studies in Art Education, 5*(1), 20–41.

Belgrad, D. (1998). *The culture of spontaneity: Improvisation and the arts in postwar America.* Chicago: University of Chicago Press.

Beller, M. (1999). *Quantum dialogue: The making of a revolution.* Chicago: The University of Chicago Press.

Benavides, F., Dumont, H., & Istance, D. (2008). The search for innovative learning environments. In OECD (Ed.), *Innovating to learn, learning to innovate* (pp. 21–44). Paris: OECD.

Bengtsson, S. L., Csikszentmihalyi, M., & Ullen, F. (2007). Cortical regions involved in the generation of musical structures during improvisation in pianists. *Journal of Cognitive Neuroscience, 19*(5), 830.

Bennett, W. (1980, Jan.–Feb.). Providing for posterity. *Harvard Magazine, 82,* 13–16.

Bennetts, L. (1986, Oct. 18). Alda stars in televised M*A*S*H seminar. *New York Times,* p. A11.

Bennis, W., & Biederman, P. W. (1997). *Organizing genius: The secrets of creative collaboration.* Reading, MA: Addison-Wesley.

Berge, J. T. (1999). Breakdown or breakthrough? A history of European research into drugs and creativity. *Journal of Creative Behavior, 33*(4), 257–176.

Bergson, H. (1907/1911). *Creative evolution.* New York: H. Holt. Originally published as *L'évolution créatrice* (Paris: F. Alcan, 1907).

Berkowitz, A. L. (2010). *The improvising mind: Cognition and creativity in the musical moment.* Oxford, UK: Oxford University Press.

Berkowitz, A. L., & Ansari, D. (2008). Generation of novel motor sequences: The neural correlates of musical improvisation. *Neuroimage, 41,* 535–543.

Berkowitz, A. L., & Ansari, D. (2010). Expertise-related deactivation of the right temporoparietal junction during musical improvisation. *Neuroimage, 49,* 712–719.

Berliner, P. (1994). *Thinking in jazz: The infinite art of improvisation.* Chicago: University of Chicago Press.

Berlyne, D. E. (1971). *Aesthetics and psychobiology.* New York: Appleton-Century-Crofts.

Berlyne, D. E. (Ed.). (1974). *Studies in the new experimental aesthetics: Steps toward an objective psychology of aesthetic appreciation.* Washington, DC: Hemisphere Publishing Corp.

Berman, K. B. (2003). *Transformation to transcendence: The creativity of performance through the eyes of classical musicians.* Unpublished manuscript, University of Connecticut.

Bever, T., & Chiarello, R. (1974). Cerebral dominance in musicians and nonmusicians. *Science, 185,* 137–139.

Bhattacharya, J., & Petsche, H. (2005). Drawing on mind's canvas: Differences in cortical integration patterns between artists and non-artists. *Human Brain Mapping, 26,* 1–14.

Biasutti, M., & Frezza, L. (2009). Dimensions of music improvisation. *Creativity Research Journal, 21*(2–3), 232–242.

Biebuyck, D. (1973). *The Lega: Art, initiation and moral philosophy.* Berkeley, CA: University of California Press.

Binet, A., & Simon, T. (1916/1973). *Classics in psychology: The development of intelligence in children.* New York: Arno Press. (Original work published in French in 1916.)

Bink, M. L., & Marsh, R. L. (2000). Cognitive regularities in creative activity. *Review of General Psychology, 4,* 59–78.

Birkinshaw, J., & Lingblad, M. (2001). *An evolutionary theory of intra-organisational competition.* Paper presented at the Academy of Management.

Black, D. (2000). Dreams of pure sociology. *Sociological Theory, 18*(3), 343–367.

Blair, C. S., & Mumford, M. D. (2007). Errors in idea evaluation: Preference for the unoriginal? *Journal of Creative Behavior, 41*(3), 197–222.

Blau, J. R., & Alba, R. D. (1982). Empowering nets of participation. *Administrative Science Quarterly, 27,* 363–379.

Bloom, A. (1987). *The closing of the American mind.* New York: Simon Schuster.

Bloom, B. S. (1963). Report on creativity research by the examiner's office of the University of Chicago. In C. W. Taylor & F. Barron (Eds.), *Scientific creativity* (pp. 251–264). New York: Wiley.

Bloom, B. S. (Ed.). (1985). *Developing talent in young people.* New York: Ballentine Books.

Blunt, J. (1966). *The composite art of acting.* New York: Macmillan.

Boden, M. A. (1991). *The creative mind: Myths and mechanisms.* New York: BasicBooks. (Second edition published 2004.)

Boden, M. A. (Ed.). (1994a). *Dimensions of creativity.* Boston, MA: MIT Press.

Boden, M. A. (1994b). What is creativity? In M. A. Boden (Ed.), *Dimensions of creativity* (pp. 75–117). Boston, MA: MIT Press.

Boden, M. A. (1999). Computer models of creativity. In R. J. Sternberg (Ed.), *The handbook of creativity* (pp. 351–372). New York: Cambridge.

Boden, M. A. (2004). *The creative mind: Myths and mechanisms* (revised and expanded 2d ed.). London: Routledge.

Bogen, J. E., & Bogen, G. M. (1969). The other side of the brain III: The corpus callosum and creativity. *Bulletin of the Los Angeles Neurological Societies, 34*, 191–203.

Bogen, J. E., & Bogen, G. M. (1988). Creativity and the corpus callosum. *Hemispheric Specialization, 11*(3), 293–301.

Boon, M. (2010). *In praise of copying*. Cambridge, MA: Harvard University Press.

Bouchard, T. J. (1972). A comparison of two group brainstorming procedures. *Journal of Applied Psychology, 56*, 418–421.

Bouchard, T. J., & Hare, M. (1970). Size, performance, and potential in brainstorming groups. *Journal of Applied Psychology, 54*(1), 51–55.

Bourassa, M., & Vaugeois, P. (2001). Effects of marijuana use on divergent thinking. *Creativity Research Journal, 13*, 411–416.

Bourdieu, P. (1979/1984). *Distinction: A social critique of the judgement of taste*. Cambridge, MA: Harvard University Press. (Originally published in 1979 by Les Éditions de Minuit, Paris, as *La Distinction: Critique sociale du jugement*.)

Bourdieu, P. (1993). *Fields of cultural production*. New York: Columbia University Press.

Bowden, E. M. (1997). The effect of reportable and unreportable hints on anagram solution and the Aha! experience. *Consciousness & Cognition, 6*, 545–573.

Bowden, E. M., & Beeman, M. J. (1998). Getting the right idea: Semantic activation in the right hemisphere may help solve insight problems. *Psychological Science, 9*, 435–440.

Bowden, E. M., & Jung-Beeman, M. (2003a). Aha! insight experience correlates with solution activation in the right hemisphere. *Psychonomic Bulletin and Review, 10*(3), 730–737.

Bowden, E. M., & Jung-Beeman, M. (2003b). One hundred forty-four Compound Remote Associate Problems: Short insight-like problems with one-word solutions. *Behavioral Research, Methods, Instruments, and Computers, 35*, 634–639.

Bowerman, W. G. (1947). *Studies in genius*. New York: Philosophical Library.

Bowers, K. S., Farvolden, P., & Mermigis, L. (1995). Intuitive antecedents of insight. In S. M. Smith, T. B. Ward, & R. A. Finke (Eds.), *The creative cognition approach* (pp. 27–51). Cambridge: MIT Press.

Bowers, K. S., Regehr, G., Balthazard, C., & Parker, K. (1990). Intuition in the context of discovery. *Cognitive Psychology, 22*, 72–110.

Bowles, S. (2003, June 20). Fans use their muscle to shape the movie. *USA Today*, pp. A1, A2.

Boyd, J. (1992). *Musicians in tune: Seventy-five contemporary musicians discuss the creative process*. New York: Simon & Schuster.

Boynton, A., & Fischer, B. (2005). *Virtuoso teams: Lessons from teams that changed their worlds*. Harlow, England: Pearson Education Limited.

Boynton, R. S. (2004, Jan. 25). The tyranny of copyright? *New York Times Magazine*, pp. 40–45.

Brannigan, A. (1981). *The social basis of scientific discoveries*. New York: Cambridge University Press.

Bransford, J. D., Brown, A. L., & Cocking, R. R. (Eds.). (2000). *How people learn: Brain, mind, experience, and school*. Washington, DC: National Academy Press.

Bransford, J. D., & Stein, B. S. (1984/1993). *The IDEAL problem solver* (2nd ed.). New York: W. H. Freeman and Company.

Brass, D. J. (1984). Being in the right place: A structural analysis of individual influence in an organization. *Administrative Science Quarterly, 29*, 518–539.

Brass, D. J. (1992). Power in organizations: A social network perspective. In G. Moore & J. A. Whitt (Eds.), *Research in Politics and Society* (pp. 295–323). Greenwich, CT: JAI Press.

Brody, N. (2003). Construct validation of the Sternberg Triarchic Abilities Test: Comment and reanalysis. *Intelligence, 31*, 319–330.

Bronowski, J. (1973). *The ascent of man.* Boston: Little, Brown.

Brook, P. (1968). *The empty space.* New York: Atheneum.

Brown, R. (1981). How improvised is jazz improvisation? *Jazz Research Papers, 1*, 22–32.

Brown, R. T. (1989). Creativity: What are we to measure? In J. A. Glover, R. R. Ronning, & C. R. Reynolds (Eds.), *Handbook of creativity* (pp. 3–32). New York: Plenum Press.

Brown, S., & Dissanayake, E. (2009). The arts are more than aesthetics: Neuroaesthetics as narrow aesthetics. In M. Skov & O. Vartanian (Eds.), *Neuroaesthetics* (pp. 43–57). Amityville, NY: Baywood Publishing Company.

Bruner, E. M. (1993). Epilogue: Creative persona and the problem of authenticity. In S. Lavie, K. Narayan, & R. Rosaldo (Eds.), *Creativity/anthropology* (pp. 321–334). Ithaca: Cornell University Press.

Bryan, W. L., & Harter, N. (1899). Studies on the telegraphic language: The acquisition of a hierarchy of habits. *Psychological Review, 6*(4), 345–375.

Budick, A. (2002, March 15). Creedmoor, creatively: Patients let artistic juices flow in QMA exhibit. *Newsday,* p. B3.

Bull, K. S., & Davis, G. A. (1980). Evaluating creative potential using the statement of past creative activities. *Journal of Creative Behavior, 14*, 249–257.

Burnaford, G. (2007). *Arts integration frameworks, research, & practice: A literature review.* Washington, DC: Arts Education Partnership.

Burnard, P., Craft, A., & Grainger, T. (2006). Possibility thinking. *International Journal for Early Years Education, 14*(3), 243–262.

Burns, T., & Stalker, G. M. (1961). *The management of innovation.* London: Tavistock Publications.

Burrell, B. (2004). *Postcards from the brain museum: The improbable search for meaning in the matter of famous minds.* New York: Broadway Books.

Burt, R. S. (1992). *Structural holes.* Cambridge, MA: Harvard University Press.

Burt, R. S. (2004). Structural holes and good ideas. *American Journal of Sociology, 110*(2), 349–399.

Business Roundtable. (2005). *Tapping America's potential: The education for innovation initiative.* Washington, DC: Business Roundtable.

Byrne, R. (1996). *The 2,548 best things anybody ever said.* New York: Galahad Books.

Callahan, C. M., Hunsaker, S. L., Adamas, C. M., Moore, S. D., & Bland, L. C. (1995). *Instruments used in the identification of gifted and talented students (Report No. RM-95130).* Charlottesville, VA: National Research Center on the Gifted and Talented.

Cameron, J. (1992). *The artist's way: A spiritual path to higher creativity.* Los Angeles, CA: Jeremy P. Tarcher.

Cameron, J., & Pierce, W. D. (1994). Reinforcement, reward, and intrinsic motivation: A meta-analysis. *Review of Educational Research, 64*(3), 363–423.

Campbell, D. T. (1960). Blind variation and selective retention in scientific discovery. *Psychological Review, 67*, 380–400.

Campbell, J. (2009, July 29). The real Raymond Carver. *Times Literary Supplement.*

Candy, L. (1999). *COSTART Project Artists Survey Report: Preliminary Results.* http://research.it.uts.edu.au/creative/ccrs/costart/doc/overview.rtf Retrieved Sep. 1, 2011.

Candy, L. (2002). Defining interaction. In L. Candy & E. Edmonds (Eds.), *Explorations in art and technology* (pp. 261–266). Berlin: Springer.

Candy, L., & Edmonds, E. (Eds.). (2002). *Explorations in art and technology.* Berlin: Springer.

Carey, B. (2006, Feb. 5). Searching for the person in the brain. *New York Times*, pp. WK 1, 4.

Carlsson, I., Wendt, P. E., & Risberg, J. (2000). On the neurobiology of creativity: Differences in frontal activity between high and low creative subjects. *Neuropsychologia, 38*, 873–885.

Carroll, J. (1995). *Evolution and literary theory*. Columbia, MO: University of Missouri Press.

Carroll, J. B. (1993). *Human cognitive abilities: A survey of factor-analytic studies*. New York: Cambridge University Press.

Carson, S. H., Peterson, J. B., & Higgins, D. M. (2003). Decreased latent inhibition Is associated with increased creative achievement in high-functioning individuals. *Journal of Personality and Social Psychology, 85*(3), 499–506.

Carson, S. H., Peterson, J. B., & Higgins, D. M. (2005). Reliability, validity, and factor structure of the Creative Achievement Questionnaire. *Creativity Research Journal, 17*(1), 37–50.

Cattell, R. B. (1971). *Abilities: Their structure, growth, and action*. Boston: Houghton Mifflin.

Cattell, R. B., Eber, H. W., & Tatsuoka, M. M. (1970). *Handbook for the sixteen personality factor questionnaire (16 PF)*. Champaign, IL: Institute for Personality and Ability Testing.

Caudle, F. M. (1991). An ecological view of social perception: Implications for theatrical performance. In G. D. Wilson (Ed.), *Psychology and performing arts* (pp. 45–57). Amsterdam: Swets & Zeitlinger.

Chaiken, S., & Trope, Y. (Eds.). (1999). *Dual-process theories in social psychology*. New York: Guilford.

Chapman, A. J., & Williams, A. R. (1976). Prestige effects and aesthetic experiences: Adolescents' reactions to music. *British Journal of Social and Clinical Psychology, 15*, 61–72.

Charles, R. E., & Runco, M. A. (2000–2001). Developmental trends in evaluative and divergent thinking of children. *Creativity Research Journal, 13*(3&4), 417–437.

Charlton, J. (1980). *The writer's quotation book: A literary companion*. New York: Barnes & Noble Books.

Chatterjee, A. (2003). Prospects for a cognitive neuroscience of visual aesthetics. *Bulletin of Psychology and the Arts, 4*(2), 55–60.

Chávez-Eakle, R. A. (2007). Creativity, DNA, and cerebral blood flow. In C. Martindale, P. Locher, & V. M. Petrov (Eds.), *Evolutionary and neurocognitive approaches to aesthetics, creativity, and the arts* (pp. 209–224). Amityville, NJ: Baywood Publishing.

Chell, E. (2007). Social enterprise and entrepreneurship: Towards a convergent theory of the entrepreneurial process. *International Small Business Journal, 25*, 5–23.

Chell, E. (2008). *The entrepreneurial personality: A social construction* (2nd ed.). London: Routledge.

Chen, C., Himsel, A., Kasof, J., Greenberger, E., & Dmitrieva, J. (2006). Boundless creativity: Evidence for the domain generality of individual differences in creativity. *Journal of Creative Behavior, 40*(3), 179–199.

Chidambaram, B., & Bostrom, R. P. (1996). Group development (I): An integrative review and synthesis of developmental models. *Group Decision and Negotiation, 6*, 159–187.

Child, I. L. (1968, December). The experts and the bridge of judgment that crosses every cultural gap. *Psychology Today*, 25–29.

Cho, S. H., Nijenhuis, J. T., Van Vianen, A. E. M., Kim, H.-B., & Lee, K. H. (2010). The relationship between diverse components of intelligence and creativity. *Journal of Creative Behavior, 44*(2), 125–137.

Choe, I.-S. (2006). Creativity: A sudden rising star in Korea. In J. C. Kaufman & R. J. Sternberg (Eds.), *The international handbook of creativity* (pp. 395–420). Cambridge, UK: Cambridge University Press.

Choi, J. N. (2004). Individual and contextual predictors of creative performance: The mediating role of psychological processes. *Creativity Research Journal, 16*(2 & 3), 187–199.

Christensen, P. R., Merrifield, P. R., & Guilford, J. P. (1953). *Consequences Form A-1.* Beverly Hills, CA: Sheridan Supply.

Christoff, K., Gordon, A. M., Smallwood, J., Smith, R., & Schooler, J. W. (2009). Experience sampling during fMRI reveals default network and executive systems contribution to mind wandering. *Proceedings of the National Academy of Sciences, 106*(21), 8719–8724.

Ciavarella, M. A., Buchholtz, A. K., Riordan, C. M., Gatewood, R. D., & Stokes, G. S. (2004). The big five and venture survival: Is there a linkage? *Journal of Business Venturing, 19*, 465–483.

Claridge, G. (1993). When is psychoticism psychoticism? And how does it really relate to creativity? *Psychological Inquiry, 4*(2), 184–188.

Claridge, G. (2009). Preamble. *Personality and Individual Differences, 46*, 753–754.

Clark, R. D., & Rice, G. A. (1982). Family constellations and eminence: The birth orders of Nobel Prize winners. *Journal of Psychology, 110*, 281–287.

Clark, T. (1997). *The theory of inspiration: Composition as a crisis of subjectivity in Romantic and post-Romantic writing.* Manchester, UK: Manchester University Press.

Cohen, B., & Murphy, G. L. (1984). Models of concepts. *Cognitive Science, 8*, 27–58.

Cohen, H. (1999, October 10–13). *A self-defining game for one player.* Paper presented at the Creativity & Cognition, Loughborough, UK.

Cohen, H. (2004). Public Lecture: Tate Gallery, London.

Cohen, H. (2007). Towards a diaper-free autonomy: Lecture presented at the Museum of Contemporary Art, San Diego, Aug. 4, 2007.

Cole, J. R., & Cole, S. (1972). The Ortega hypothesis. *Science, 178*, 368–375.

Collaros, P. A., & Anderson, L. R. (1969). Effect of perceived expertness upon creativity of members of brainstorming groups. *Journal of Applied Psychology, 53*, 159–163.

Collingwood, R. G. (1938). *The principles of art.* New York: Oxford University Press.

Comte, A. (1842/1854). *The positive philosophy of Auguste Comte* (H. Martineau, Trans.). New York: D. Appleton. (Originally published in French in six volumes, from 1830 to 1842.)

Constantinidou, F., & Baker, S. (2002). Stimulus modality and verbal learning performance in normal aging. *Brain and Language, 82*, 296–311.

Conti, R., Coon, H., & Amabile, T. (1996). Evidence to support the componential model of creativity: Secondary analyses of three studies. *Creativity Research Journal, 9*, 385–389.

Cooper, E. (1991). A critique of six measures for assessing creativity. *Journal of Creative Behavior, 25*(3), 194–204.

Cope, D. (2001). *Virtual music: Computer synthesis of musical style.* Cambridge, MA: MIT Press.

Copland, A. (1952). *Music and imagination.* Cambridge, MA: Harvard University Press.

Cornett, C. E. (1999). *The arts as meaning makers: Integrating literature and the arts throughout the curriculum.* Upper Saddle River, NJ: Merrill.

Cornock, S., & Edmonds, E. A. (1973). The creative process where the artist is amplified or superseded by the computer. *Leonardo, 16*, 11–16.

Coser, R. (1975). The complexity of roles as a seedbed of individual autonomy. In L. A. Coser (Ed.), *The idea of social structure: Papers in honor of Robert K. Merton* (pp. 237–263). New York: Harcourt Brace.

Costa, P. T., & McCrae, R. R. (1992). *Revised NEO personality inventory (NEO-PI-R) and NEO five-factor inventory (NEO-FFI) professional manual.* Odessa, FL: Psychological Assessment Resources.

Council on Competitiveness. (2005). *Innovate America: National innovation initiative summit and report.* Washington, DC: Council on Competitiveness.

Covington, M. V., Crutchfield, R. S., Davies, L., & Olton, R. M. (1974). *The productive thinking program: A course in learning to think.* Columbus, OH: Merrill.

Cox, C. (1926). *Genetic studies of genius, Volume 2: The early mental traits of three hundred geniuses.* Stanford, CA: Stanford University Press.

Craft, A. (2005). *Creativity in schools: Tensions and dilemmas.* New York: Routledge.

Craft, A., Jeffrey, B., & Leibling, M. (Eds.). (2001). *Creativity in education.* London: Continuum.

Crafts, H. (2002). *The bondwoman's narrative* (J. Henry Louis Gates, Trans.). New York: Warner Books.

Crain, C. (2001, October). The artistic animal. *Lingua Franca,* 28–37.

Cramond, B. (1993). The Torrance Tests of Creative Thinking: From design through establishment of predictive validity. In R. F. Subotnik & K. D. Arnold (Eds.), *Beyond Terman: Contemporary longitudinal studies of giftedness and talent* (pp. 229–254). Norwood, NJ: Ablex.

Crawford, R. P. (1954). *Techniques of creative thinking.* New York: Hawthorn Books, Inc.

Cronbach, L. J. (1968). Intelligence? Creativity? A parsimonious reinterpretation of the Wallach-Kogan data. *American Educational Research Journal, 5*(4), 491–511.

Cropley, A. J. (1997). Fostering creativity in the classroom: General principles. In M. A. Runco (Ed.), *Creativity research handbook* (Vol. 1, pp. 83–114). Cresskill, NJ: Hampton Press.

Cropley, A. J. (2001). *Creativity in education & learning: A guide for teachers and educators.* London: Kogan Page.

Cross, R., & Cummings, J. N. (2004). Tie and network correlates of individual performance in knowledge-intensive work. *Academy of Management Journal, 47*(6), 928–937.

Crow, B. K. (1988). Conversational performance and the performance of conversation. *TDR, 32*(3), 23–54.

Crozier, W. R., & Chapman, A. (1981). Aesthetic preferences: Prestige and social class. In D. O'Hare (Ed.), *Psychology and the arts* (pp. 242–278). Brighton, Sussex: Harvester Press.

Csikszentmihalyi, M. (1965). *Artistic problems and their solutions: An exploration of creativity in the arts.* Unpublished PhD thesis, University of Chicago, Chicago.

Csikszentmihalyi, M. (1975). *Beyond boredom and anxiety.* San Francisco: Jossey-Bass.

Csikszentmihalyi, M. (1988a). Motivation and creativity: Toward a synthesis of structural and energistic approaches to cognition. *New Ideas in Psychology, 6*(2), 159–176.

Csikszentmihalyi, M. (1988b). Society, culture, and person: A systems view of creativity. In R. J. Sternberg (Ed.), *The nature of creativity* (pp. 325–339). New York: Cambridge University Press.

Csikszentmihalyi, M. (1990a). The domain of creativity. In M. A. Runco & R. S. Albert (Eds.), *Theories of creativity* (pp. 190–212). Newbury Park, CA: Sage.

Csikszentmihalyi, M. (1990b). *Flow: The psychology of optimal experience.* New York: HarperCollins.

Csikszentmihalyi, M. (1993). Does overinclusiveness equal creativity? *Psychological Inquiry, 4*(2), 188–189.

Csikszentmihalyi, M. (1994). The domain of creativity. In D. H. Feldman, M. Csikszentmihalyi, & H. Gardner (Eds.), *Changing the world: A framework for the study of creativity* (pp. 135–158). Westport, CT: Praeger Publishers.

Csikszentmihalyi, M. (1996). *Creativity: Flow and the psychology of discovery and invention.* New York: HarperCollins.

Csikszentmihalyi, M. (1999). Implications of a systems perspective for the study of creativity. In R. J. Sternberg (Ed.), *The handbook of creativity* (pp. 313–335). New York: Cambridge.

Csikszentmihalyi, M., & Getzels, J. W. (1988). Creativity and problem finding in art. In F. H. Farley & R. W. Neperud (Eds.), *The foundations of aesthetics, art & art education* (pp. 91–116). New York: Praeger.

Csikszentmihalyi, M., Rathunde, K., & Whalen, S. (1993). *Talented teenagers: The roots of success and failure.* New York: Cambridge University Press.

Csikszentmihalyi, M., & Sawyer, R. K. (1995). Creative insight: The social dimension of a solitary moment. In R. J. Sternberg & J. E. Davidson (Eds.), *The nature of insight* (pp. 329–363). Cambridge: MIT Press.

Cummings, J. (2004). Work groups, structural diversity, and knowledge sharing in a global organization. *Management Science, 50*, 352–364.

Cunningham, J. B., & MacGregor, J. N. (2008). Training insightful problem solving: Effects of realistic and puzzle-like contexts. *Creativity Research Journal, 20*(3), 291–296.

Cunningham, J. B., MacGregor, J. N., Gibb, J., & Haar, J. (2009). Categories of insight and their correlates: An exploration of relationships among classic-type insight problems, rebus puzzles, remote associates and esoteric analogies. *Journal of Creative Behavior, 43*(4), 262–280.

Cupchik, G. C., Arnheim, R., & Martindale, C. (1996). A history of Division 10 (Psychology and the Arts): Through the eyes of past presidents. In D. A. Dewsbury (Ed.), *Unification through division: Histories of the divisions of the American Psychological Association* (Vol. 4, pp. 9–34). Washington, DC: American Psychological Association.

Cushman, A. (1992, March/April). Are you creative? *Utne Reader*, 52–60.

Dacey, J. S., & Lennon, K. H. (1998). *Understanding creativity: The interplay of biological, psychological, and social factors*. San Francisco, CA: Jossey-Bass.

Dailey, L., & Mumford, M. D. (2006). Evaluative aspects of creative thought: Errors in appraising the implications of new ideas. *Creativity Research Journal, 18*(3), 367–384.

Damasio, A. R. (2001). Some notes on brain, imagination, and creativity. In K. H. Pfenninger & V. R. Shubik (Eds.), *The origins of creativity* (pp. 59–68). New York: Oxford University Press.

Dansky, J. L. (1980). Make-believe: A mediator of the relationship between play and associative fluency. *Child Development, 51*, 576–579.

Dansky, J. L., & Silverman, I. W. (1973). The effects of play on associative fluency in preschool-aged children. *Developmental Psychology, 9*, 38–43.

Dansky, J. L., & Silverman, I. W. (1975). Play: A general facilitator of associative fluency. *Developmental Psychology, 11*, 104.

Dart, T. (1967). *The interpretation of music* (4th ed.). London: Hutchinson.

Dasgupta, S. (1994). *Creativity in invention and design: Computational and cognitive explorations of technological originality*. Cambridge, UK: Cambridge University Press.

Davidson, J. E. (1995). The suddenness of insight. In R. J. Sternberg & J. E. Davidson (Eds.), *The nature of insight* (pp. 125–156). Cambridge, MA: MIT Press.

Davidson, J. E., & Sternberg, R. J. (1984). The role of insight in intellectual giftedness. *Gifted Child Quarterly, 28*, 58–64.

Davidson, L., & Welsh, P. (1988). From collections to structure: The developmental path of tonal thinking. In J. A. Sloboda (Ed.), *Generative processes in music: The psychology of performance, improvisation, and composition* (pp. 260–285). New York: Oxford.

Davis, G. A. (1975). In frumious pursuit of the creative person. *Journal of Creative Behavior, 9*, 75–87.

Davis, G. A. (1983). *Creativity is forever*. Dubuque, IA: Kendall-Hunt Publishers. (Fifth edition, 2004.)

Davis, G. A. (2003). Identifying creative students, teaching for creative growth. In N. Colangelo & G. A. Davis (Eds.), *Handbook of gifted education* (3rd ed., pp. 312–324). Boston, MA: Pearson Education.

Davis, G. A., & Rimm, S. (1982). Group inventory for finding interests (GIFFI) I and II: Instruments for identifying creative potential in the junior and senior high school. *Journal of Creative Behavior, 16*, 50–57.

Davis, G. A., & Scott, J. A. (1971). *Training creative thinking*. New York: Holt, Rinehart and Winston, Inc.

Day, R. S. (1988). Alternative representations. In G. H. Bower (Ed.), *The psychology of learning and motivation* (Vol. 22, pp. 261–305). New York: Academic Press.

de Bono, E. (1973). *CoRT thinking.* Blanford, England: Direct Educational Services.

de Manzano, Ö., Cervenka, S., Karabanov, A., Farde, L., & Ullén, F. (2010). Thinking outside a less intact box: Thalamic dopamine D2 receptor densities are negatively related to psychometric creativity in healthy individuals. *PLos One, 5*(5), e10670.

Deci, E. L. (1975). *Intrinsic motivation.* New York: Plenum Press.

Deci, E. L., & Ryan, R. M. (1985). *Intrinsic motivation and self-determination.* New York: Plenum Press.

Decuyper, S., Dochy, F., & Van den Bossche, P. (2010). Grasping the dynamic complexity of team learning: An integrative model for effective team learning in organisations. *Educational Research Review, 5*(2), 111–133.

Delbanco, N. (2002, July). In praise of imitation. *Harper's Magazine,* 57–63.

Dennett, D. (1995). *Darwin's Dangerous Idea: Evolution and the meanings of life.* New York: Simon & Schuster.

Dennis, A. R., & Valacich, J. S. (1993). Computer brainstorms: More heads are better than one. *Journal of Applied Psychology, 78*(4), 531–537.

Dennis, W. (1955). Variations in productivity among creative workers. *Scientific Monthly, 79,* 180–183.

Dennis, W. (1958). The age decrement in outstanding scientific contributions: Fact or artifact? *American Psychologist, 13,* 457–460.

Dennis, W. (1966). Creative productivity between the ages of 20 and 80 years. *Journal of Gerontology, 21,* 1–8.

Denoyelle, F. (2002, June, July, August). Photographie: Les voies de la reconnaissance. *Sciences Humaines, 37,* 41–43.

DePalma, A. (1992, June 17). Hard sell for top universities: Finding new chiefs. *New York Times,* p. B11.

Deppman, J., Ferrer, D., & Groden, M. (Eds.). (2004). *Genetic criticism: Texts and avant-textes.* Philadelphia: University of Pennsylvania Press.

Devereux, G. (1961). Art and mythology. In B. Kaplan (Ed.), *Studying personality cross-culturally* (pp. 361–386). Evanston, IL: Row, Peterson.

Dewey, J. (1934). *Art as experience.* New York: Perigree Books.

DeYoung, C. G., Flanders, J. L., & Peterson, J. B. (2008). Cognitive abilities involved in insight problem solving: An individual differences model. *Creativity Research Journal, 20*(3), 278–290.

DeZutter, S. (2011). Professional improvisation and teacher education: Opening the conversation. In R. K. Sawyer (Ed.), *Structure and improvisation in creative teaching* (pp. 27–50). New York: Cambridge University Press.

Diamond, M. C., Scheibel, A. B., Murphy, G. M., & Harvey, T. (1985). On the brain of a scientist: Albert Einstein. *Experimental Neurology, 88,* 198–204.

Diderot, D. (1936). Paradoxe sur le Comédien. In F. C. Green (Ed.), *Diderot's writings on the theatre* (pp. 249–317). New York: Cambridge. (Original work published in 1773.)

Diehl, M., & Stroebe, W. (1987). Productivity loss in brainstorming groups: Toward the solution of a riddle. *Journal of Personality and Social Psychology, 53*(3), 497–509.

Diehl, M., & Stroebe, W. (1991). Productivity loss in idea-generating groups: Tracking down the blocking effect. *Journal of Personality and Social Psychology, 61,* 392–403.

Dietrich, A. (2004). The cognitive neuroscience of creativity. *Psychonomic Bulletin and Review, 11*(6), 1011–1026.

Dijksterhuis, A., & Nordgren, L. F. (2006). A theory of unconscious thought. *Perspectives on Psychological Science, 1*(2), 95–109.

Dimaggio, O., & Useem, M. (1978). Social class and arts consumption: The origins and consequences of class differences in exposure to the arts in America. *Theory and Society, 5,* 141–161.

Dirac, P. (1963). The evolution of the physicist's picture of nature. *Scientific American, 208*(5), 45–53.

Dissanayake, E. (1988). *What is art for?* Seattle, WA: University of Washington.

Domino, G. (1970). Identification of potentially creative persons using the Adjective Check List. *Journal of Consulting and Clinical Psychology, 35,* 48–51.

Dominowksi, R. L., & Dallob, P. (1995). Insight and problem solving. In R. J. Sternberg & J. E. Davidson (Eds.), *The nature of insight* (pp. 33–62). Cambridge: MIT Press.

Donnat, O. (2002, June, July, August). Entre passade et passion: Les amateurs. *Sciences Humaines, 37,* 70–73.

Dow, G. T., & Mayer, R. E. (2004). Teaching students to solve insight problems: Evidence for domain specificity in creativity training. *Creativity Research Journal, 16*(4), 389–402.

Dudek, S. Z. (1993). Creativity and psychoticism: An *overinclusive* model. *Psychological Inquiry, 4*(2), 190–192.

Dunbar, K. (1995). How scientists really reason: Scientific reasoning in real-world laboratories. In R. J. Sternberg & J. E. Davidson (Eds.), *The nature of insight* (pp. 365–395). Cambridge: MIT Press.

Dunbar, K. (1997). How scientists think: On-line creativity and conceptual change in science. In T. B. Ward, S. M. Smith & J. Vaid (Eds.), *Creative thought: An investigation of conceptual structures and processes* (pp. 461–493). Washington, DC: American Psychological Association.

Dunbar, K. (1999). How scientists build models: In vivo science as a window on the scientific mind. In L. Magnani, N. J. Nersessian & P. Thagard (Eds.), *Model-based reasoning in scientific discovery* (pp. 85–99). New York: Kluwer Academic/Plenum Press.

Duncker, K. (1926). A qualitative (experimental and theoretical) study of productive thinking (solving of comprehensive problems). *The Pedagogical Seminary and Journal of Genetic Psychology, 33,* 642–708.

Dutton, D. (2001). What is genius? *Philosophy and Literature, 25,* 181–196.

Eagleton, T. (2003). *After theory.* London: Allen Lane.

Easterly, W. (2010, June 13). A high-five for the invisible hand. Review of *The Rational Optimist. New York Times,* p. BR 20.

Ebert, R. (1997, October 22). Film, the snubbed art. *New York Times,* p. A23.

Eckblad, M., & Chapman, L. J. (1986). Development and validation of a scale for hypomanic personality. *Journal of Abnormal Psychology, 95,* 214–222.

Edwards, B. (1979). *Drawing on the right side of the brain: A course in enhancing creativity and artistic confidence.* Los Angeles: J. P. Tarcher.

Efland, A. D. (2002). *Art and cognition: Integrating the visual arts in the curriculum.* New York: Teachers College Press.

Einstein, A., & Infeld, L. (1938). *The evolution of physics.* New York: Simon and Schuster.

Eisenberg, E. M. (1990). Jamming: Transcendence through organizing. *Communication Research, 17*(2), 139–164.

Eisenberg, J., & Thompson, W. F. (2003). A matter of taste: Evaluating improvised music. *Creativity Research Journal, 15,* 287–296.

Eisenberger, R., & Cameron, J. (1996). Detrimental effects of reward: Reality or myth? *American Psychologist, 51*(11), 1153–1166.

Eisenberger, R., & Rhoades, L. (2001). Incremental effects of rewards on creativity. *Journal of Personality and Social Psychology, 81,* 728–741.

Eisenberger, R., & Selbst, M. (1994). Does reward increase or decrease creativity? *Journal of Personality and Social Psychology, 66,* 1116–1127.

Eisenstadt, J. M. (1978). Parental loss and genius. *American Psychologist, 33,* 211–223.

Eisner, E. W. (1982). *Cognition and curriculum: A basis for deciding what to teach.* New York: Longman.

Eisner, E. W. (2002a). *The arts and the creation of mind.* New Haven, CT: Yale University Press.

Eisner, E. W. (2002b). What can education learn from the arts about the practice of education? In *The encyclopedia of informal education (available online at http://www.infed.org/biblio/eisner_arts_and_ the_practice_or_education.htm).*

Ekvall, G. (1996). Organizational climate for creativity and innovation. *European Journal of Work and Organizational Psychology, 5*(1), 105–123.

Eliot, T. S. (1920/1950). *The sacred wood: Essays on poetry and criticism.* London: Methuen & Co., Ltd. (Seventh edition 1950.)

Eliot, T. S. (1971). *The waste land: A facsimile and transcript of the original drafts including the annotations of Ezra Pound.* New York: Harcourt Brace Jovanovich.

Elkins, J. (2001). *Why art cannot be taught: A handbook for art students.* Urbana, IL: University of Illinois Press.

Ellis, H. (1904). *A study in British genius.* London: Hurst and Blackett.

Ellwood, S., Pallier, G., Snyder, A., & Gallate, J. (2009). The incubation effect: Hatching a solution? *Creativity Research Journal, 21*(1), 6–14.

Elman, J. L., Bates, E. A., Johnson, M. H., Karmiloff-Smith, A., Parisi, D., & Plunkett, K. (1996). *Rethinking innateness: A connectionist perspective on development.* Cambridge, MA: MIT Press.

Engell, J. (1981). *The creative imagination: Enlightenment to romanticism.* Cambridge, MA: Harvard.

England, J. M. (1983). *A patron for pure science: The National Science Foundation's formative years, 1945–1957.* Washington, DC: National Science Foundation.

Enright, M. K., & Gitomer, D. H. (1989). *Toward a description of successful graduate students (GRE Board Professional Rep. No. 89–09, GRE Board Research Rep. 85–17R).* Princeton, NJ: Educational Testing Service.

Envick, B. R., & Langford, M. (2000). The five-factor model of personality: Assessing entrepreneurs and managers. *Academy of Entrepreneurship Journal, 6,* 6–17.

Epstein, J. S. (Ed.). (1994). *Adolescents and their music: If it's too loud, you're too old.* New York: Garland Publishing.

Epstein, R. (1990). Generativity theory and creativity. In M. A. Runco & R. S. Albert (Eds.), *Theories of creativity* (pp. 116–140). Newbury Park, CA: Sage.

Epstein, R. (1999). Generativity theory. In M. A. Runco & S. R. Pritzker (Eds.), *Encyclopedia of creativity* (Vol. 1, pp. 759–766). San Diego, CA: Academic Press.

Ericsson, K. A., Charness, N., Feltovich, P. J., & Hoffman, R. R. (Eds.). (2006). *The Cambridge handbook of expertise and expert performance.* New York: Cambridge University Press.

Ericsson, K. A., Krampe, R. T., & Tesch-Römer, C. (1993). The role of deliberate practice in the acquisition of expert performance. *Psychological Review, 100*(3), 273–305.

Estrada, C. A., Isen, A. M., & Young, M. J. (1994). Positive affect influence creative problem solving and reported source of practice satisfaction in physicians. *Motivation and Emotion, 18,* 285–299.

European Union. (2009). *Manifesto.* Brussels, Belgium: European Ambassadors for Creativity and Innovation.

Evans, K. B., & Sims-Jr., H. P. (1997). Mining for innovation: The conceptual underpinnings, history and diffusion of self-directed work teams. In C. L. Cooper & S. E. Jackson (Eds.), *Creating tomorrow's organizations: A handbook for future research in organizational behavior* (pp. 269–291). New York: Wiley.

Eysenck, H. J. (1947/1961). *Dimensions of personality.* London: Routledge & Kegan Paul.

Eysenck, H. J. (1993). Creativity and personality: Suggestions for a theory. *Psychological Inquiry, 4*(3), 147–178.

Eysenck, H. J. (1995). *Genius: The natural history of creativity*. New York: Cambridge.

Eysenck, H. J., & Eysenck, S. B. G. (1975). *Manual of the Eysenck Personality Questionnaire*. San Diego, CA: EDITS.

Eysenck, H. J., & Eysenck, S. B. G. (1976). *Psychoticism as a dimension of personality*. London: Hodder & Stoughton.

Eysenck, M. W. (1990). Creativity. In M. W. Eysenck (Ed.), *The Blackwell dictionary of cognitive psychology* (pp. 86–87). Oxford, UK: Basil Blackwell.

Farmelo, G. (2002a). Foreword: It must be beautiful. In G. Farmelo (Ed.), *It must be beautiful: Great equations of modern science* (pp. ix–xvi). London: Granta Books.

Farmelo, G. (Ed.). (2002b). *It must be beautiful: Great equations of modern science*. London: Granta Books.

Farnsworth, P. R. (1969). *The social psychology of music* (2nd ed.). Ames, IA: Iowa State University Press.

Farrell, M. P. (2001). *Collaborative circles: Friendship dynamics and creative work*. Chicago: University of Chicago Press.

Fasko, D. (2000–2001). Education and creativity. *Creativity Research Journal, 13*(3/4), 317–327.

Feinstein, J. S. (2006). *The nature of creative development*. Stanford, CA: Stanford Business Books.

Feist, G. J. (1998). A meta-analysis of personality in scientific and artistic creativity. *Personality and Social Psychology Review, 2*(4), 290–309.

Feist, G. J. (2006a). The development of scientific talent in Westinghouse Finalists and members of the National Academy of Sciences. *Journal of Adult Development, 13*, 23–35.

Feist, G. J. (2006b). *The psychology of science and the origins of the scientific mind*. New Haven, CT: Yale University Press.

Feist, G. J. (2010). The function of personality in creativity: The nature and nurture of the creative personality. In J. C. Kaufman & R. J. Sternberg (Eds.), *The Cambridge handbook of creativity* (pp. 113–130). Cambridge, UK: Cambridge University Press.

Feist, G. J., & Runco, M. A. (1993). Trends in the creativity literature: An analysis of research in the *Journal of Creative Behavior* (1967–1989). *Creativity Research Journal, 6*(3), 271–286.

Feldhusen, J. F. (1983). The Purdue creative thinking program. In I. S. Sato (Ed.), *Creativity research and educational planning* (pp. 41–46). Los Angeles, CA: Leadership Training Institute for the Gifted and Talented.

Feldhusen, J. F., & Goh, B. E. (1995). Assessing and accessing creativity: An integrative review of theory, research, and development. *Creativity Research Journal, 8*(3), 231–247.

Feldhusen, J. F., & Treffinger, D. J. (1980). *Creative thinking and problem solving in gifted education*. Dubuque, IA: Kendall/Hunt.

Feldman, D. H. (1974). Universal to unique. In S. Rosner & L. E. Abt (Eds.), *Essays in creativity* (pp. 45–85). Croton-on-Hudson, NY: North River Press.

Feldman, D. H. (1980). *Beyond universals in cognitive development*. Norwood, NJ: Ablex.

Feldman, D. H. (1986). *Nature's gambit: Child prodigies and the development of human potential*. New York: Basic Books.

Feldman, D. H. (2003). The creation of multiple intelligences theory: A study in high-level thinking. In R. K. Sawyer et al., *Creativity and development* (pp. 139–185). New York: Oxford.

Feldman, D. H., Csikszentmihalyi, M., & Gardner, H. (1994). *Changing the world: A framework for the study of creativity*. Westport, CT: Praeger.

Fine, G. A. (2004). *Everyday genius: Self-taught art and the culture of authenticity*. Chicago, IL: University of Chicago Press.

Fineberg, J. D. (1997). *The innocent eye: Children's art and the modern artist*. Princeton, NJ: Princeton University Press.

Fineberg, J. D. (Ed.). (1998). *Discovering child art: Essays on childhood, primitivism and modernism*. Princeton, NJ: Princeton University Press.

Fink, A., Benedek, M., Grabner, R. H., Staudt, B., & Neubauer, A. C. (2007). Creativity meets neuroscience: Experimental tasks for the neuroscientific study of creative thinking. *Methods, 42*, 68–76.

Fink, A., Grabner, R. H., Benedek, M., Reishofer, G., Hauswirth, V., Fally, M., et al. (2009). The creative brain: Investigation of brain activity during creative problem solving by means of EEG and fMRI. *Human Brain Mapping, 30*, 734–748.

Finke, R. (1990). *Creative imagery: Discoveries and inventions in visualization*. Hillsdale, NJ: Erlbaum.

Finke, R. A., & Slayton, K. (1988). Explorations of creative visual synthesis in mental imagery. *Memory & Cognition, 16*(3), 252–257.

Finke, R. A., Ward, T. B., & Smith, S. M. (1992). *Creative cognition: Theory, research, and applications*. Cambridge, MA: MIT Press.

Fiore, S. M., & Schooler, J. W. (1998). Right hemisphere contributions to creative problem solving: Converging evidence for divergent thinking. In M. Beeman & C. Chiarello (Eds.), *Right hemisphere language comprehension: Perspectives from cognitive neuroscience* (pp. 349–371). Mahwah, NJ: Erlbaum.

Fish, S. (1980). *Is there a text in this class? The authority of interpretive communities*. Cambridge: Harvard.

Fisher, S., & Fisher, R. L. (1981). *Pretend the world is funny and forever: A psychological analysis of comedians, clowns, and actors*. Hillsdale, NJ: Lawrence Erlbaum Associates.

Fiske, A. P., Kitayama, S., Markus, H. R., & Nisbett, R. E. (1998). The cultural matrix of social psychology. In D. T. Gilbert, S. T. Fiske, & G. Lindzey (Eds.), *The handbook of social psychology* (pp. 915–981). New York: McGraw-Hill.

Fitzsimons, G. M., Chartrand, T. L., & Fitzsimons, G. J. (2008). Automatic effects of brand exposure on motivated behavior: How Apple makes you "think different." *Journal of Consumer Research, 35*(1), 21–35.

Flanagan, D. P., Ortiz, S. O., & Alfonso, V. C. (2007). *Essentials of Cross-Battery Assessment with C/D ROM* (2nd ed.). New York: Wiley.

Flannery, M. C. (1991). Science and aesthetics: A partnership for science education. *Science Education, 75*(5), 577–593.

Flavell, J. H., & Draguns, J. (1957). A microgenetic approach to perception and thought. *Psychological Bulletin, 54*(3), 197–217.

Fleith, D. d. S. (2000). Teacher and student perceptions of creativity in the classroom environment. *Roeper Review, 22*(3), 148–157.

Fleming, L., & Marx, M. (2006). Managing creativity in small worlds. *California Management Review, 48*(4), 6–26.

Florida, R. (2002). *The rise of the creative class and how it's transforming work, life, community and everyday life*. New York: Basic Books.

Foreman, K., & Martini, C. (1995). *Something like a drug: An unauthorized oral history of Theatresports*. Alberta, Canada: Red Deer College Press.

Forge, A. (1967). The Abelam artist. In M. Freedman (Ed.), *Social organization: Essays presented to Raymond Firth* (pp. 65–84). London: Frank Cass and Co. Ltd.

Frasier, M. M. (1990). *Torrance verbal and figural tests: Measuring general creative thinking processes*. Paper presented at the Annual Meeting of the American Educational Research Association.

Freud, S. (1907/1989). Creative writers and day-dreaming. In P. Gay (Ed.), *The Freud reader* (pp. 436–443). New York: Norton. (Paper originally presented Dec. 6, 1907).

Freud, S. (1917/1966). *Introductory lectures on psycho-analysis* (J. Strachey, Trans.). New York: Norton.

Friedman, R. A. (2002, Tuesday, June 4). Connecting depression and artistry. *New York Times*, p. D6.

Friend, T. (1998, Sept. 14). Copy cats. *New Yorker*, 51–57.

Frith, S. (1978). *The sociology of rock*. London: Constable.

Fry, E. F. (Ed.). (1970). *On the future of art*. New York: Viking Press.

Fuchs-Beauchamp, K. D., Karnes, M. B., & Johnson, L. J. (1993). Creativity and intelligence in preschoolers. *Gifted Child Quarterly, 37*, 113–117.

Furnham, A. (2008). *Personality and intelligence at work*. London: Routledge.

Furnham, A., Crump, J., Batey, M., & Chamorro-Premuzic, T. (2009). Personality and ability predictors of the "consequences" test of divergent thinking in a large non-student sample. *Personality and Individual Differences, 46*, 536–540.

Gagné, F. (1991). Toward a differentiated model of giftedness and talent. In N. Colangelo & G. A. Davis (Eds.), *Handbook of gifted education* (pp. 65–80). Boston: Allyn and Bacon.

Gagné, F. (1993). Constructs and models pertaining to exceptional human abilities. In K. A. Heller, F. J. Monks, & A. H. Passow (Eds.), *International handbook of research and development of giftedness and talent* (pp. 63–85). Oxford: Pergamon Press.

Galenson, D. W. (2001). *Painting outside the lines: Patterns of creativity in modern art*. Cambridge, MA: Harvard University Press.

Galinsky, A., & Kray, L. J. (2004). From thinking about what might have been to sharing what we know: The role of counterfactual mind-sets on information sharing in groups. *Journal of Experimental Social Psychology, 40*, 606–618.

Gallupe, R. B., Bastianutti, L. M., & Cooper, W. H. (1991). Unblocking brainstorms. *Journal of Applied Psychology, 76*, 137–142.

Gallupe, R. B., & Cooper, W. H. (1990). Average time to speak vs. keyboard ideas [Unpublished raw data]. Queen's University School of Business, Kingston, Ontario, Canada.

Galton, F. (1869/1962). *Hereditary genius: An inquiry into its laws and consequences*. Cleveland, OH: Meridian Books. (Original work published 1869.)

Galton, F. (1874). *English men of science, their nature and nurture*. London: Macmillan.

Galton, F. (1875). The history of twins, as a criterion of the relative powers of nature and nurture. *Frasier's Magazine, 12*, 566–576.

Gantchev, D. (2007). *Assessing the economic contribution of creative industries: WIPO's experience*. Paper presented at the WIPO International Conference on Intellectual Property and the Creative Industries.

Garaigordobil, M. (2006). Intervention in creativity with children aged 10 and 11 years: Impact of a play program on verbal and graphic-figural creativity. *Creativity Research Journal, 18*(3), 329–345.

Garber, M. (2002, December). Our genius problem. *Atlantic Monthly*, 64–72.

Gardner, H. (1973). *The arts and human development: A psychological study of the artistic process*. New York: Wiley.

Gardner, H. (1975). *The shattered mind*. New York: Knopf.

Gardner, H. (1982). *Art, mind, and brain: A cognitive approach to creativity*. New York: Basic Books.

Gardner, H. (1983). *Frames of mind: The theory of multiple intelligences*. New York: Basic Books.

Gardner, H. (1988). Creativity: An interdisciplinary perspective. *Creativity Research Journal, 1*(1), 8–26.

Gardner, H. (1993). *Creating minds*. New York: Basic Books.

Gardner, H. (1999). *Intelligence reframed: Multiple intelligences for the twenty-first century*. New York: Basic Books.

Gardner, H. (2007). *Five minds for the future*. Boston, MA: Harvard Business School Press.

Gargiulo, M., & Benassi, M. (2000). Trapped in your own net? Network cohesion, structural holes, and the adaptation of social capital. *Organization Science, 11*, 183–196.

Gartner, J. (2005). *The hypomanic edge: The link between (a little) craziness and (a lot of) success in America*. New York: Simon & Schuster.

Gates, H. L. (2002, Feb. 18). The fugitive. *New Yorker*, 104.

Gawain, S. (1979/1982). *Creative visualization*. New York: Bantam Books. (Original work published by Whatever Publishing, March 1979.)

Gazzaniga, M. (1970). *The bisected brain*. New York: Appleton-Century-Crofts.

Gazzaniga, M. (1995). Principles of human brain organization derived from split-brain studies. *Neuron, 14*, 217–228.

Gazzaniga, M. (2000). Cerebral specialization and interhemispheric communication: Does the corpus callosum enable the human condition? *Brain, 123*(7), 1293–1326.

Gazzaniga, M., Ivry, R. B., & Mangun, G. R. (2002). *Cognitive neuroscience: The biology of the mind* (2nd ed.). New York: Norton.

Gedo, J. E. (1996). *The artist & the emotional world: Creativity and personality*. New York: Columbia University Press.

Geen, R. G. (1989). Alternative conceptions of social facilitation. In P. B. Paulus (Ed.), *Psychology of group influence* (2nd ed., pp. 15–51). Hillsdale, NJ: Erlbaum.

Geertz, C. (1966/1973). *The interpretation of cultures*. New York: Basic Books. (Original work published 1966.)

Gelman, R., & Brenneman, K. (1994). First principles can support both universal and culture-specific learning about number and music. In L. A. Hirschfeld & S. A. Gelman (Eds.), *Mapping the mind: Domain specificity in cognition and culture* (pp. 369–390). New York: Cambridge University Press.

Gentner, D. (1989). The mechanisms of analogical learning. In S. Vosniadou & A. Ortony (Eds.), *Similarity and analogical reasoning* (pp. 199–241). Cambridge, UK: Cambridge University Press.

Gentner, D., & Gentner, D. R. (1983). Flowing waters or teeming crowds: Mental models of electricity. In D. Gentner & A. L. Stevens (Eds.), *Mental models* (pp. 99–129). Mahwah, NJ: Erlbaum.

George, J. M. (2007). Creativity in organizations. *Academy of Management Annals, 1*(1), 439–477.

Geraghty, M. (1997, Jan. 31). Art schools change admissions policies to place more emphasis on academics. *Chronicle of Higher Education*, A27–A28.

Gerard, A. (1774/1966). *An essay on genius*. Munich, Germany: Fink Verlag.

Gerbrands, A. A. (1967). *Wow-Ipits: Eight Asmat carvers of New Guinea*. The Hague: Mouton.

Geschka, H. (1993). The development and assessment of creative thinking techniques: A German perspective. In S. G. Isaksen, M. C. Murdock, R. L. Firestien, & D. J. Treffinger (Eds.), *Nurturing and developing creativity: The emergence of a discipline* (pp. 215–236). Norwood, NJ: Ablex.

Getzels, J. W. (1964). Creative thinking, problem-solving, and instruction. In E. R. Hilgard (Ed.), *Theories of learning and instruction* (pp. 240–267). Chicago: University of Chicago Press.

Getzels, J. W. (1987). Creativity, intelligence, and problem finding: Retrospect and prospect. In S. G. Isaksen (Ed.), *Frontiers of creativity research* (pp. 88–102). Buffalo, NY: Bearly Limited.

Getzels, J. W., & Csikszentmihalyi, M. (1976). *The creative vision*. New York: Wiley.

Getzels, J. W., & Jackson, P. W. (1962). *Creativity and intelligence: Explorations with gifted students*. New York: John Wiley & Sons.

Ghiselin, B. (1952). *The creative process: Reflections on invention in the arts and sciences*. Berkeley, CA: University of California Press.

Gick, M. L., & Holyoak, K. J. (1980). Analogical problem solving. *Cognitive Psychology, 12*, 306–355.

Gick, M. L., & Lockhart, R. S. (1995). Cognitive and affective components of insight. In R. J. Sternberg & J. E. Davidson (Eds.), *The nature of insight* (pp. 197–228). Cambridge: MIT Press.

Gilbert, N. (1997). A simulation of the structure of academic science. *Sociological Research Online, 2*(2), http://www.socresonline.org.uk/2/2/3.html.

Gingras, L. M., Arenberg, D., Zonderman, A. B., Kawas, C., & Costa, P. T. (2008). The effects of aging on researchers' publication and citation patterns. *PLoS One, 3*, e4048.

Gist, M. E., & Mitchell, T. R. (1992). Self-efficacy: A theoretical analysis of its determinants and malleability. *Academy of Management Review, 17*(2), 183–211.

Gladwell, M. (2002, July 22). The talent myth. *New Yorker*, 28–33.

Glazer, E. (2009). Rephrasing the madness and creativity debate: What is the nature of the creativity construct? *Personality and Individual Differences, 46*, 755–764.

Glover, J. A., Ronning, R. R., & Reynolds, C. R. (Eds.). (1989). *Handbook of creativity*. New York: Plenum Press.

Glucksberg, S. (1962). The influence of strength of drive on functional fixedness and perceptual recognition. *Journal of Experimental Psychology, 63*, 36–41.

Goel, V., & Vartanian, O. (2005). Disassociating the roles of right ventral lateral and dorsal lateral prefrontal cortex in generation and maintenance of hypotheses in set-shift problems. *Cerebral Cortex, 15*, 1170–1177.

Goertzel, M. G., Goertzel, V., & Goertzel, T. G. (1978). *Three hundred eminent personalities*. San Francisco, CA: Jossey-Bass.

Goertzel, V., & Goertzel, M. G. (1962/2004). *Cradles of eminence* (2nd ed.). Scottsdale, AZ: Great Potential Press.

Goldberg, E., Podell, K., & Lovell, M. (1994). Lateralization of frontal lobe functions and cognitive novelty. *Journal of Neuropsychiatry and Clinical Neurosciences, 6*, 371–378.

Goldberg, N. (1986). *Writing down the bones: Freeing the writer within*. Boston, MA: Shambala.

Goldstein, K. (1944). The mental changes due to frontal lobe damage. *Journal of Psychology, 17*, 187–208.

Goldstein, T. R., & Winner, E. (2009). Living in alternative and inner worlds: Early signs of acting talent. *Creativity Research Journal, 21*(1), 117–124.

Goldwater, R. (1938/1967). *Primitivism in modern art*. Cambridge, MA: Harvard University Press. (Original work published 1938.)

Golomb, C. (2002). *Child art in context: A cultural and comparative perspective*. Washington, DC: APA Press.

Gordon, W. J. J. (1961). *Synectics: The development of creative capacity*. New York: Harper & Row, Publishers.

Gottfredson, L. S. (2003). Dissecting practical intelligence: Its claims and evidence. *Intelligence, 31*, 343–398.

Gough, H. G. (1976). Studying creativity by means of word association tests. *Journal of Applied Psychology, 61*, 348–353.

Gough, H. G. (1979). A creative personality scale for the Adjective Check List. *Journal of Personality and Social Psychology, 37*(8), 1398–1405.

Gough, H. G., & Heilbrun, A. B. (1965). *The Adjective Checklist manual*. Palo Alto, CA: Consulting Psychologists Press.

Graburn, N. H. H. (Ed.). (1976). *Ethnic and tourist arts*. Berkeley, CA: University of California Press.

Graesser, A., Ozuru, Y., & Sullins, J. (2010). What is a good question? In M. G. McKeown & L. Kucan (Eds.), *Bringing reading research to life*. New York: Guilford.

Granovetter, M. (1973). The strength of weak ties. *American Journal of Sociology, 6*, 1360–1380.

Granovetter, M. (1982). The strength of weak ties: A network theory revisited. In P. V. Marsden & N. Lin (Eds.), *Social structure and network analysis* (pp. 105–130). Beverly Hills, CA: Sage.

Green, G. S. (1981). A test of the Ortega hypothesis in criminology. *Criminology, 19,* 45–52.

Greenberg, C. (1961/1996, April 14). The Jackson Pollock market soars. *New York Times Magazine,* 115–116. (Originally published in the April 16, 1961 issue.)

Greeno, J. G. (2006). Learning in activity. In R. K. Sawyer (Ed.), *Cambridge handbook of the learning sciences* (pp. 79–96). New York: Cambridge.

Griffin, M., & McDermott, M. R. (1998). Exploring a tripartite relationship between rebelliousness, openness to experience and creativity. *Social Behavior and Personality, 26*(4), 347–356.

Griskevicius, V., Cialdini, R. B., & Kenrick, D. T. (2006). Peacocks, Picasso, and parental investment: The effects of romantic motives on creativity. *Journal of Personality and Social Psychology, 91*(1), 63–76.

Grønhaug, K., & Kaufmann, G. (Eds.). (1988). *Innovation: A cross-disciplinary perspective.* Oslo, Norway: Norwegian University Press.

Grout, D. J., & Palisca, C. V. (1996). *A history of Western music* (5th ed.). New York: Norton.

Gruber, H. E. (1974). *Darwin on man: A psychological study of scientific creativity.* Chicago: University of Chicago.

Gruber, H. E. (1988). The evolving systems approach to creative work. *Creativity Research Journal, 1,* 27–51.

Gruber, H. E., & Davis, S. N. (1988). Inching our way up Mount Olympus: The evolving-systems approach to creative thinking. In R. J. Sternberg (Ed.), *The nature of creativity* (pp. 243–270). New York: Cambridge University Press.

Gruber, H. E., Terrell, G., & Wertheimer, M. (1962). *Contemporary approaches to creative thinking.* New York: Atherton Press.

Guerin, B. (1993). *Social facilitation.* New York: Cambridge University Press.

Guerrilla Girls. (1998). *The Guerrilla Girls' bedside companion to the history of Western art.* New York: Penguin Books.

Guilford, J. P. (1950). Creativity. *American Psychologist, 5*(9), 444–454.

Guilford, J. P. (1959). *Personality.* New York: McGraw-Hill.

Guilford, J. P. (1967). *The nature of human intelligence.* New York: McGraw-Hill.

Guilford, J. P. (1970). Creativity: Retrospect and prospect. *Journal of Creative Behavior, 4*(3), 149–168.

Guilford, J. P. (1971). Some misconceptions regarding measurement of creative talents. *Journal of Creative Behavior, 5,* 77–87.

Guilford, J. P., & Hoepfner, R. (1971). *The analysis of intelligence.* New York: McGraw-Hill.

Guilford, J. P., Merrifield, P. R., & Wilson, R. C. (1958). *Unusual Uses Test.* Orange, CA: Sheridan Psychological Services.

Gullapalli, D. (2002, Aug. 16). To do: Schedule meeting, play with Legos. *Wall Street Journal,* p. B1.

Haacke, H. (1975). *Framing and being framed: 7 works 1970–75.* Halifax, NS: The Press of the Nova Scotia College of Art and Design.

Hadamard, J. (1945). *The psychology of invention in the mathematical field.* Princeton, NJ: Princeton University Press.

Hall, W. B. (1972). A technique for assessing aesthetic predispositions: Mosaic Construction Test. *Journal of Creative Behavior, 6*(4), 225–235.

Halpern, D. (1989). *Thought and knowledge: An introduction to critical thinking* (2nd ed.). Hillsdale, NJ: Erlbaum.

Hambrick, D. C., Cho, T., & Chen, M. (1996). The influence of top management team heterogeneity on firms' competitive moves. *Administrative Science Quarterly, 41,* 659–684.

Hammond, J., & Edelmann, R. J. (1991a). The act of being: Personality characteristics of professional actors, amateur actors and non-actors. In G. D. Wilson (Ed.), *Psychology and performing arts* (pp. 123–131). Amsterdam: Swets & Zeitlinger.

Hammond, J., & Edelmann, R. J. (1991b). Double identity: The effect of the acting process on the self-perception of professional actors—two case illustrations. In G. D. Wilson (Ed.), *Psychology and performing arts* (pp. 24–44). Amsterdam: Swets & Zeitlinger.

Hampton, J. A. (1987). Inheritance of attributes in natural concept conjunctions. *Memory & Cognition, 15*(1), 55–71.

Hansen, M. T. (1999). The search-transfer problem: The role of weak ties in sharing knowledge across organizational subunits. *Administrative Science Quarterly, 37*, 422–447.

Hargadon, A. B. (2003). *How breakthroughs happen: The surprising truth about how companies innovate.* Boston, MA: Harvard Business School Press.

Hargadon, A. B., & Bechky, B. A. (2006). When collections of creatives become creative collections: A field study of problem solving at work. *Organization Science, 17*, 484–500.

Harlow, H. F., Harlow, M. K., & Meyer, D. R. (1950). Learning motivated by a manipulation drive. *Journal of Experimental Psychology, 40*, 228–234.

Harrington, D. M., Block, J., & Block, J. H. (1983). Predicting creativity in preadolescence from divergent thinking in early childhood. *Journal of Personality and Social Psychology, 45*, 609–623.

Harris, N. (1966). *The artist in American society: The formative years 1790–1869.* New York: Simon and Schuster.

Hatfield, E., Cacioppo, J. T., & Rapson, R. L. (1994). *Emotional contagion.* New York: Cambridge.

Hayes, J. R. (1989). *The complete problem solver* (2nd ed.). Hillsdale, NJ: Erlbaum.

Heausler, H. L., & Thompson, B. (1988). Structure of the Torrance Tests of Creative Thinking. *Educational and Psychological Measurement, 48*, 463–468.

Hébert, T. P., Cramond, B., Spiers-Neumeister, K. L., Millar, G., & Silvian, A. F. (2002). *E. Paul Torrance: His life, accomplishments, and legacy.* Storrs, CT: University of Connecticut, National Research Center on the Gifted and Talented.

Heinich, N. (1993). *Du peintre a l'artiste.* Paris: Minuit.

Heisenberg, W. (1971). *Physics and beyond.* New York: Harper and Row.

Helson, R. (1990). Creativity in women: Inner and outer views over time. In M. A. Runco & R. S. Albert (Eds.), *Theories of creativity* (pp. 46–58). Newbury Park, CA: Sage.

Helstrup, T., & Anderson, R. E. (1991). Imagery in mental construction and decomposition tasks. In R. H. Logie & M. Denis (Eds.), *Mental images in human cognition* (pp. 229–240). Amsterdam: North Holland.

Hemphill, J. (2003). Interpreting the magnitudes of correlation coefficients. *American Psychologist, 58*, 78–80.

Henderson, M. (2003, Feb. 17). "Genetic changes" triggered man's artistic abilities. *London Times.*

Hennessey, B. A. (2003). Is the social psychology of creativity really social? Moving beyond a focus on the individual. In P. B. Paulus & B. A. Nijstad (Eds.), *Group creativity: Innovation through collaboration* (pp. 181–201). New York: Oxford.

Hennessey, B. A., & Amabile, T. (2010). Creativity. *Annual Review of Psychology, 61*, 569–598.

Hennessey, B. A., & Zbikowski, S. (1993). Immunizing children against the negative effects of reward: A further examination of intrinsic motivation training techniques. *Creativity Research Journal, 6*, 297–308.

Henshilwood, C. S., d'Errico, F., Yates, R., Jacobs, Z., Tribolo, C., Duller, G. A. T., et al. (2002). Emergence of modern human behavior: Middle stone age engravings from South Africa. *Science, 295*(5558), 1278–1280.

Herrnstein, R. J., & Murray, C. (1994). *The bell curve: Intelligence and class structure in American life.* New York: Free Press.

Hetland, L., & Winner, E. (2004). Cognitive transfer from arts education to non-arts outcomes: Research evidence and policy implications. In E. W. Eisner & M. D. Day (Eds.), *Handbook of research and policy in art education* (pp. 135–162). Mahwah, NJ: Erlbaum.

Hetland, L., Winner, E., Veenema, S., & Sheridan, K. M. (2007). *Studio thinking: The real benefits of visual arts education.* New York: Teachers College Press.

Hill, K. G., & Amabile, T. M. (1993). A social psychological perspective on creativity: Intrinsic motivation and creativity in the classroom and workplace. In S. G. Isaksen, M. C. Murdock, R. L. Firestien, & D. J. Treffinger (Eds.), *Understanding and recognizing creativity: The emergence of a discipline* (pp. 400–432). Norwood, NJ: Ablex.

Hill, R. (1978, July). Dozens of uses for versatile Velcro fasteners. *Popular Science,* 110–112.

Hirschfeld, L. A., & Gelman, S. A. (Eds.). (1994). *Mapping the mind: Domain specificity in cognition and culture.* New York: Cambridge University Press.

Hocevar, D. (1980). Intelligence, divergent thinking, and creativity. *Intelligence, 4,* 25–40.

Hocevar, D., & Bachelor, P. (1989). A taxonomy and critique of measurements used in the study of creativity. In J. A. Glover, R. R. Ronning, & C. R. Reynolds (Eds.), *Handbook of creativity* (pp. 53–75). New York: Plenum Press.

Holland, D., & Quinn, N. (1987). *Cultural models in language and thought.* Cambridge, UK: Cambridge University Press.

Holland, J. L. (1961). Creative and academic performance among talented adolescents. *Journal of Educational Psychology, 52,* 136–147.

Holland, J. L. (1997). *Making vocational choices: A theory of vocational personalities and work environments* (3rd ed.). Odessa, FL: Psychological Assessment Resources.

Hollanders, H. (2009). Measuring innovation: The European Innovation Scoreboard. In E. Villalba (Ed.), *Measuring creativity* (pp. 27–40). Luxembourg: European Union.

Hollenberg, D. (1978). Performance review: Ran Blake/Ray Bryant trio. *Downbeat, 45*(10), 40–42.

Holt, J. (1964). *How children fail.* New York: Pitman Publishing Corporation.

Holyoak, K. J., & Thagard, P. (1995). *Mental leaps: Analogy in creative thought.* Cambridge, MA: MIT Press.

Homma, M., Tajima, K., & Hayashi, M. (1995). The effects of misperception of performance in brainstorming groups. *Japanese Journal of Experimental Social Psychology, 34,* 221–231.

Honour, H., & Fleming, J. (1999). *World history of art* (5th ed.). London: Lawrence King.

Hooker, C., Nakamura, J., & Csikszentmihalyi, M. (2003). The group as mentor: Social capital and the systems model of creativity. In P. B. Paulus & B. A. Nijstad (Eds.), *Group creativity: Innovation through collaboration* (pp. 225–244). New York: Oxford.

Hoppe, K. D. (1988). Hemispheric specialization and creativity. *Psychiatric Clinics of North America, 11*(3), 303–315.

Hoppe, K. D., & Kyle, N. L. (1990). Dual brain, creativity, and health. *Creativity Research Journal, 3,* 150–157.

Hopper, R. (1993). Conversational dramatism and everyday life performance. *Text and Performance Quarterly, 13,* 181–183.

Horn, J. L., & Cattell, R. B. (1966). Refinement and test of the theory of fluid and crystallized intelligence. *Journal of Educational Psychology, 57,* 253–270.

Horn, J. L., & Noll, J. (1997). Human cognitive capacities: Gf-Gc theory. In D. P. Flanagan, J. L. Genshaft & P. L. Harrison (Eds.), *Life-span developmental psychology: Research and theory* (pp. 423–466). New York: Academic Press.

Horng, J., & Lin, L. (2009). The development of a scale for evaluating creative culinary products. *Creativity Research Journal, 21,* 54–63.

Hotz, R. L. (2009a, Friday, May 22). Heady theories on the contours of Einstein's genius. *Wall Street Journal,* p. A9.

Hotz, R. L. (2009b, Friday, June 19). A wandering mind heads straight toward insight. *Wall Street Journal,* p. A11.

Houtz, J. (Ed.). (2003). *The educational psychology of creativity.* Cresskill, NJ: Hampton Press.

Howard-Jones, P. A., Blakemore, S.-J., Samuel, E. A., Summers, I. R., & Claxton, G. (2005). Semantic divergence and creative story generation: An fMRI investigation. *Cognitive Brain Research, 25,* 240–250.

Howe, J. (2008). *Crowdsourcing: Why the power of the crowd is driving the future of business.* New York: Crown Business.

Huang, G. T. (2003, May). Machining melodies. *Technology Review,* p. 26.

Huber, J. C. (1998). Invention and inventivity as a special kind of creativity, with implications for general creativity. *Journal of Creative Behavior, 32*(1), 58–72.

Huettel, S. A., Song, A. W., & McCarthy, G. (2009). *Functional magnetic resonance imaging* (2nd ed.). Sunderland, MA: Sinauer Associates.

Hughes, R. (1984). The rise of Andy Warhol. In B. Wallis (Ed.), *Art after modernism: Rethinking representation* (pp. 45–58). New York: New Museum of Contemporary Art/David Godine.

Hughes-Freeland, F. (2007). "Tradition and the individual talent": T. S. Eliot for anthropologists. In E. Hallam & T. Ingold (Eds.), *Creativity and cultural improvisation* (pp. 207–222). Oxford, UK: Berg.

Hulbert, A. (2003). *Raising America: Experts, parents, and a century of advice about children.* New York: Alfred A. Knopf.

Hunsaker, S. L., & Callahan, C. M. (1995). Creativity and giftedness: Published instrument uses and abuses. *Gifted Child Quarterly, 39,* 110–114.

Hunt, E. (2008). Applying the theory of successful intelligence to education—The good, the bad, and the ogre: Commentary on Sternberg et al. (2008). *Perspectives on Psychological Science, 3,* 509–515.

Hutchins, E. (1995). *Cognition in the wild.* Cambridge: MIT Press.

Hutt, C., & Bhavnani, R. (1976). Predictions from play. In J. S. Bruner, A. Jolly & K. Sylva (Eds.), *Play: Its role in development and evolution* (pp. 216–219). New York: Penguin.

Hyams, N. B., & Graham, W. K. (1984). Effects of goal setting and initiative on individual brainstorming. *Journal of Social Psychology, 123,* 283–284.

Ibarra, H. (1992). Homophily and differential returns: Sex differences in network structure and access in an advertising firm. *Administrative Science Quarterly, 37,* 277–303.

Isaksen, S. G. (1987). *Frontiers of creativity research: Beyond the basics.* Buffalo, NY: Bearly Limited.

Isaksen, S. G., Dorval, K. B., & Treffinger, D. J. (1994). *Creative approaches to problem solving: A framework for change.* Buffalo, NY: Creative Problem Solving Group.

Isaksen, S. G., Dorval, K. B., & Treffinger, D. J. (2000). *Creative approaches to problem solving: A framework for change* (2nd ed.). Buffalo, NY: Creative Problem Solving Group.

Isaksen, S. G., & Gaulin, J. P. (2005). A reexamination of brainstorming research: Implications for research and practice. *Gifted Child Quarterly, 49*(4), 315–329.

Isaksen, S. G., Murdock, M. C., Firestien, R. L., & Treffinger, D. J. (Eds.). (1993). *Understanding and recognizing creativity: The emergence of a discipline.* Norwood, NJ: Ablex.

Isaksen, S. G., & Puccio, G. J. (1988). Adaptation-innovation and the Torrance Tests of Creative Thinking: The level-style issue revisited. *Psychological Reports, 63,* 659–670.

Isaksen, S. G., & Treffinger, D. J. (1985). *Creative problem solving: The basic course.* Buffalo, NY: Bearly Ltd.

Isen, A. M., Daubman, K. A., & Nowicki, G. P. (1987). Positive affect facilitates creative problem solving. *Journal of Personality and Social Psychology, 52*(6), 1122–1131.

Isen, A. M., Labroo, A. A., & Durlach, P. (2004). An influence of product and brand name on positive affect: Implicit and explicit measures. *Motivation and Emotion, 28*(1), 43–63.

Iser, W. (1978). *The act of reading: A theory of aesthetic response.* Baltimore: Johns Hopkins University Press.

Jacobson, T., Schubotz, R. I., Höfel, L., & Craman, D. Y. (2006). Brain correlates of aesthetic judgment of beauty. *Neuroimage, 29*, 276–285.

James, W. (1880). Great men, great thoughts, and the environment. *Atlantic Monthly, 46*(276), 441–459.

Jamison, K. R. (1989). Mood disorders and patterns of creativity in British writers and artists. *Psychiatry, 52*, 125–134.

Jamison, K. R. (1993). *Touched with fire: Manic-depressive illness and the artistic temperament.* New York: Free Press.

Jamison, K. R. (1995, February). Manic-depressive illness and creativity. *Scientific American*, 62–67.

Janis, I. L. (1972). *Victims of groupthink: A psychological study of foreign-policy decisions and fiascos.* Boston: Houghton Mifflin Company.

Jaussi, K. S., Randel, A. E., & Dionne, S. D. (2007). I am, I think I can, and I do: The role of personal identity, self-efficacy, and cross-application of experiences in creativity at work. *Creativity Research Journal, 19*, 247–258.

Jay, E. S., & Perkins, D. N. (1997). Problem finding: The search for mechanism. In M. A. Runco (Ed.), *Creativity research handbook* (Vol. 1, pp. 257–293). Cresskill, NJ: Hampton Press.

Jehn, K. A., Northcraft, G. B., & Neale, M. A. (1999). Why differences make a difference: A field study of diversity, conflict, and performance in work groups. *Administrative Science Quarterly, 44*, 741–763.

Jellen, H. G., & Urban, K. K. (1989). Assessing creative potential worldwide: The first cross-cultural application of the test for creative thinking-drawing production (TCT-DP). *Gifted Education, 6*, 78–86.

Johnson, G. (1997, Nov. 11). Undiscovered Bach? No, a computer wrote it. *New York Times*, pp. B9, B10.

Johnson, G. (2002, Oct. 13). Oil and water: Why prizes and science don't mix. *New York Times*, pp. Section 4 (Week in Review), Page 3.

Johnson, J. E. (1976). Relations of divergent thinking and intelligence test scores with social and nonsocial make-believe play of preschool children. *Child Development, 47*, 1200–1203.

Johnson-Laird, P. N. (1987). Reasoning, imagining, and creating. *Bulletin of the British Psychological Society, 40*, 121–129.

Johnson-Laird, P. N. (1988). Freedom and constraint in creativity. In R. J. Sternberg (Ed.), *The nature of creativity* (pp. 202–219). New York: Cambridge.

John-Steiner, V. (1985). *Notebooks of the mind: Explorations of thinking.* Albuquerque, NM: University of New Mexico Press.

John-Steiner, V. (2000). *Creative collaboration.* New York: Oxford.

Joncich, G. (1964). A culture-bound concept of creativity: A social historian's critique, centering on a recent American research report. *Educational Theory, 14*(3), 133–143.

Jones, B. F. (2010). Age and great invention. *Journal of Economics and Statistics, 92*(1), 1–14.

Joy, S. (2006). What should I be doing, and where are they doing it? Scholarly productivity of academic psychologists. *Psychological Science, 1*, 346–364.

Juda, A. (1949). The relationship between highest mental capacity and psychic abnormalities. *American Journal of Psychiatry, 106*, 296–307.

Jung-Beeman, M. (2005). Bilateral brain processes for comprehending natural language. *Trends in Cognitive Science, 9,* 512–518.

Jung-Beeman, M., Bowden, E. M., & Haberman, J. (2002). *The Aha! experience and semantic activation in the cerebral hemispheres.* Paper presented at the 9th Annual Meeting of the Cognitive Neuroscience Society.

Jung-Beeman, M., Bowden, E. M., Haberman, J., Frymaire, J. L., Arambel-Lui, S., Greenblatt, R., et al. (2004). Neural activity when people solve verbal problems with insight. *PLoS Biology, 2*(4), 0500–0510.

Jurgensen, J. (2006, Saturday/Sunday, Sept. 16–17). Rewriting the rules of fiction. *Wall Street Journal,* pp. P1, P4.

Kaeppler, A. L. (1987). Spontaneous choreography: Improvisation in Polynesian dance. *Yearbook for Traditional Music, 19,* 13–22.

Kakutani, M. (1997, Sept. 28). Never-ending saga. *New York Times Magazine,* 40–41.

Kane, M. J., Brown, L. H., McVay, J. C., Silvia, P. J., Myin-Germeys, I., & Kwapil, T. R. (2007). For whom the mind wanders, and when. *Psychological Science, 18*(7), 614–621.

Kant, I. (1781/1900). *Critique of pure reason* (J. M. D. Meiklejohn, Trans.). New York: The Colonial Press. (Original work published 1781.)

Kanter, R. M. (1983). *The change masters: Innovation and entrepreneurship in the American corporation.* New York: Simon & Schuster.

Kao, J. (1996). *Jamming: The art and discipline of business creativity.* New York: HarperCollins.

Kaplan, C. A., & Simon, H. A. (1990). In search of insight. *Cognitive Psychology, 22,* 374–419.

Kaplan, R., & Kaplan, S. (1989). *The experience of nature: A psychological perspective.* New York: Cambridge University Press.

Kapur, R. L., Subramanyam, S., & Shah, A. (1997). Creativity in Indian science. *Psychology & Developing Societies, 9,* 161–187.

Karmiloff-Smith, A. (1992). *Beyond modularity: A developmental perspective on cognitive science.* Cambridge, MA: MIT Press.

Karnes, F. A., & Bean, S. M. (Eds.). (2001). *Methods and materials for teaching the gifted.* Waco, TX: Prufrock Press.

Kasof, J. (1995). Explaining creativity: The attributional perspective. *Creativity Research Journal, 8*(4), 311–366.

Kauffman, S. A. (1993). *The origins of order: Self-organization and selection in evolution.* New York: Oxford.

Kaufman, A. B., Kornilov, S. A., Bristol, A. S., Tan, M., & Grigorenko, E. L. (2010). The neurobiological foundation of creative cognition. In J. C. Kaufman & R. J. Sternberg (Eds.), *The Cambridge handbook of creativity* (pp. 216–232). Cambridge, UK: Cambridge University Press.

Kaufman, A. S. (2009). *IQ testing 101.* New York: Springer.

Kaufman, A. S., & Kaufman, N. L. (2004). *Kaufman Assessment Battery for Children—Second Edition (KABC-II) administration and scoring manual.* Circle Pines, MN: American Guidance Service.

Kaufman, G. (2003). What to measure? A new look at the concept of creativity. *Scandinavian Journal of Educational Research, 47*(3), 235–251.

Kaufman, J. C. (2005). The door that leads into madness: Eastern European poets and mental illness. *Creativity Research Journal, 17*(1), 99–103.

Kaufman, J. C. (2009). *Creativity 101.* New York: Springer.

Kaufman, J. C., & Baer, J. (2004). Sure, I'm creative—but not in math! Self-reported creativity in diverse domains. *Empirical Studies of the Arts, 22,* 143–155.

Kaufman, J. C., & Baer, J. (Eds.). (2005). *Creativity across domains: Faces of the muse.* Mahwah, NJ: Lawrence Erlbaum Associates.

Kaufman, J. C., Baer, J., & Cole, J. C. (2009). Expertise, domains, and the consensual assessment technique. *Journal of Creative Behavior, 43*(4), 223–233.

Kaufman, J. C., Baer, J., Cole, J. C., & Sexton, J. D. (2008). A comparison of expert and nonexpert raters using the consensual assessment technique. *Creativity Research Journal, 20*(2), 171–178.

Kaufman, J. C., & Beghetto, R. A. (2009). Beyond big and little: The four C model of creativity. *Review of General Psychology, 13*(1), 1–12.

Kaufman, J. C., Cole, J. C., & Baer, J. (2009). The construct of creativity: Structural model for self-reported creativity ratings. *Journal of Creative Behavior, 43*(2), 119–132.

Kaufman, J. C., Lee, J., Baer, J., & Lee, S. (2007). Captions, consistency, creativity, and the consensual assessment technique: New evidence of reliability. *Thinking Skills and Creativity, 2*, 96–106.

Kaufman, J. C., Plucker, J. A., & Baer, J. (2008). *Essentials of creativity assessment.* New York: Wiley.

Kaufman, J. C., & Sternberg, R. J. (Eds.). (2006). *The international handbook of creativity.* Cambridge, UK: Cambridge University Press.

Kaufman, J. C., & Sternberg, R. J. (Eds.). (2010). *The Cambridge handbook of creativity.* Cambridge, UK: Cambridge University Press.

Kaufman, S. B. (2007). Review of *Explaining Creativity: The Science of Human Innovation. Psychology of Aesthetics, Creativity, and the Arts, 1*(1), 47–51.

Kaufmann, G. (1988). Problem solving and creativity. In K. Grønhaug & G. Kaufmann (Eds.), *Innovation: A cross-disciplinary perspective* (pp. 87–137). Oslo, Norway: Norwegian University Press.

Kavolis, V. (1968). *Artistic expression: A sociological analysis.* New York: Cornell University Press.

Keck, S. L. (1997). Top management team structure: Differential effects by environmental context. *Organization Science, 8*(2), 143–156.

Kelley, T. (2001). *The art of innovation: Lessons in creativity from IDEO, America's leading design firm.* New York: Doubleday.

Kelly, G., Crawford, T., & Green, J. (2001). Common task and uncommon knowledge: Dissenting voices in the discursive construction of physics across small laboratory groups. *Linguistics & Education, 12*(2), 135–174.

Kemp, A. E. (1996). *The musical temperament.* Oxford, UK: Oxford University Press.

Kennedy, R. (2010, Sunday, Feb. 28). The free-appropriation writer. *New York Times,* p. WK 3.

Kenny, B. J., & Gellrich, M. (2002). Improvisation. In R. Parncutt & G. E. McPherson (Eds.), *The science and psychology of music performance: Creative strategies for teaching and learning* (pp. 117–134). New York: Oxford.

Kenrick, D. T., Griskevicius, V., Neuberg, S. L., & Schaller, M. (2010). Renovating the pyramid of needs: Contemporary extensions built upon ancient foundations. *Perspectives on Psychological Science, 5*(3), 292–314.

Keri, S. (2009). Genes for psychosis and creativity: A promotor polymorphism of the *neuregulin 1* gene is related to creativity in people with high intellectual achievement. *Psychological Science, 20*(9), 1070–1073.

Kerr, H. L., & Bruun, S. E. (1983). The dispensability of member effort and group motivation losses: Free rider effects. *Journal of Personality and Social Psychology, 44*, 78–94.

Kessler, R. C., McGonagle, K. A., Zhao, S., Nelson, C. B., Hughes, M., Eshlemann, S., et al. (1994). Lifetime and twelve-month prevalence of DSM-III-R psychiatric disorders in the United States: Results from the National Comorbidity Survey. *Archives of General Psychiatry, 51*, 8–19.

Kiersey, D., & Bates, M. (1978). *Please understand me: Character and temperament types.* Del Mar, CA: Promethean Nemesis.

Kim, K. H. (2005). Can only intelligent people be creative? *Journal of Secondary Gifted Education, 16*, 57–66.

Kim, K. H. (2006). Can we trust creativity tests? A review of the Torrance Tests of Creative Thinking (TTCT). *Creativity Research Journal, 18*(1), 3–4.

Kim, K. H. (2008). Meta-analyses of the relationship of creative achievement to both IQ and divergent thinking test scores. *Journal of Creative Behavior, 42*(2), 106–130.

Kimmelman, M. (1998, Sunday, Aug. 9). Installation art moves in, moves on. *New York Times*, Section 2, p. 1 and 32.

Kind, P. M., & Kind, V. (2007). Creativity in science education: Perspectives and challenges for developing school science. *Studies in Science Education, 43*, 1–37.

King, L. A., Walker, L. M., & Broyles, S. J. (1996). Creativity and the five-factor model. *Journal of Research in Personality, 30*, 189–203.

King, N., & Anderson, N. (1995). *Innovation and change in organizations*. London: Routledge.

Kinney, D. K., & Richards, R. L. (2007). Artistic creativity and mood disorders: Are they connected? In C. Martindale, P. Locher & V. M. Petrov (Eds.), *Evolutionary and neurocognitive approaches to aesthetics, creativity, and the arts* (pp. 225–237). Amityville, NJ: Baywood Publishing.

Kirton, M. J. (1976). Adaptors and innovators: A description and measure. *Journal of Applied Psychology, 61*, 622–629.

Kirton, M. J. (1978). Have adaptors and innovators equal levels of creativity? *Psychological Reports, 42*, 695–698.

Kirton, M. J. (1988). Adaptors and innovators: Problem solvers in organizations. In K. Grønhaug & G. Kaufmann (Eds.), *Innovation: A cross-disciplinary perspective* (pp. 65–85). Oslo, Norway: Norwegian University Press.

Klahr, D. (2000). *Exploring science: The cognition and development of discovery processes*. Cambridge: MIT Press.

Klahr, D., & Simon, H. A. (1999). Studies of scientific discovery: Complementary approaches and convergent findings. *Psychological Bulletin, 125*(5), 524–543.

Klein, R. G., & Edgar, B. (2002). *The dawn of human culture*. New York: John Wiley.

Klinger, E. (2009). Daydreaming and fantasizing: Thought flow and motivation. In K. D. Markman, W. M. P. Klein, & J. A. Suhr (Eds.), *Handbook of imagination and mental simulation* (pp. 225–239). New York: Psychology Press.

Klosterman, C. (2002, March 17). The pretenders. *New York Times Magazine*, 54–57.

Knight, D., Pearce, C. L., Smith, K. G., Olian, J. D., Sims, H. P., Smith, K. A., et al. (1999). Top management team diversity, group process, and strategic consensus. *Strategic Management Journal, 20*, 445–465.

Köhler, W. (1925). *The mentality of apes*. London: Routledge & Kegan Paul.

Koestler, A. (1964). *The act of creation*. New York: Macmillan.

Kogan, N. (1974). Creativity and sex differences. *Journal of Creative Behavior, 8*(1), 1–14.

Kogan, N. (2002). Careers in the performing arts: A psychological perspective. *Creativity Research Journal, 14*(1), 1–16.

Kogan, N., & Pankove, E. (1974). Long-term predictive validity of divergent-thinking tests: Some negative evidence. *Journal of Educational Psychology, 66*, 802–810.

Kohn, N., & Smith, S. M. (2009). Partly versus completely out of your mind: Effects of incubation and distraction on resolving fixation. *Journal of Creative Behavior, 43*(2), 102–118.

Kolb, B., & Whishaw, I. Q. (2003). *Fundamentals of human neuropsychology (5th edition)*. New York: Worth Publishers.

Konijn, E. A. (1991). What's on between the actor and his audience? Empirical analysis of emotion processes in the theatre. In G. D. Wilson (Ed.), *Psychology and performing arts* (pp. 59–73). Amsterdam: Swets & Zeitlinger.

Kotovsky, K. (2003). Problem solving: Large/small, hard/easy, conscious/nonconscious, problem-space/problem-solver. In J. E. Davidson & R. J. Sternberg (Eds.), *The psychology of problem solving* (pp. 373–383). New York: Cambridge.

Kounios, J., Fleck, J., Green, D. L., Payne, L., Stevenson, J. L., Bowden, E. M., et al. (2008). The origins of insight in resting-state brain activity. *Neuropsychologia, 46*, 281–291.

Kounios, J., Frymaire, J. L., Bowden, E. M., Fleck, J., Subramaniam, K., Parrish, T. B., et al. (2006). The prepared mind: Neural activity prior to problem presentation predicts subsequent solution by sudden insight. *Psychological Science, 17*(10), 882–290.

Kozinn, A. (1997, Oct. 8). Bootlegging as a public service: No, this isn't a joke. *New York Times*, p. B2.

Kris, E. (1952). *Psychoanalytic explorations in art*. New York: International Universities Press.

Kristeller, P. O. (1983). "Creativity" and "tradition." *Journal of the History of Ideas, 44*(1), 105–113.

Kubie, L. S. (1958). *The neurotic distortion of the creative process*. Lawrence, KS: University of Kansas Press.

Kuhn, A. (1925). *Lovis Corinth*. Berlin: Im Propyläen-Verlag.

Kuhn, T. S. (1959/1963). The essential tension: Tradition and innovation in scientific research. In C. W. Taylor & F. Barron (Eds.), *Scientific creativity: Its recognition and development* (pp. 341–354). New York: John Wiley & Sons. (From a paper presented at the third Utah Conference on Creativity in 1959).

Kuiper, K. (1996). *Smooth talkers: The linguistic performance of auctioneers and sportscasters*. Mahwah, NJ: Lawrence Erlbaum Associates.

Kuper, A. (1988). *The invention of primitive society*. London: Routledge.

Kurtzberg, T. R. (2005). Feeling creative, being creative: An empirical study of diversity and creativity in teams. *Creativity Research Journal, 17*(1), 51–65.

Kyllonen, P. C. (2009). *The tried, the true, and the transpiring in creativity assessment*. Paper presented at the "Can creativity be measured?" conference held in Brussels, Belgium, May 28–29, 2009.

Kyllonen, P. C., Walters, A. M., & Kaufman, J. C. (2005). Noncognitive constructs and their assessment in graduate education. *Educational Assessment, 10*(3), 153–184.

Kyvik, S., & Olsen, T. B. (2008). Does the aging of tenured academic staff affect the research performance of universities? *Scientometrics, 76*, 439–455.

La Rocco, C. (2008, Sunday, Aug. 24). Say, just whose choreography is this? *New York Times*, p. AR 25.

Lamott, A. (1994). *Bird by bird: Some instructions on writing and life*. New York: Pantheon Books.

Lang, R. J., & Ryba, K. A. (1976). The identification of some creative thinking parameters common to the artistic and musical personality. *British Journal of Educational Psychology, 46*, 267–279.

Lange-Eichbaum, W. (1930/1932). *The problem of genius*. New York: Macmillan. (Original work published 1930.)

Langley, P., & Jones, R. (1988). A computational model of scientific insight. In R. J. Sternberg (Ed.), *The nature of creativity* (pp. 177–201). New York: Cambridge University Press.

Lant, T. K., Milliken, F. J., & Batra, B. (1992). The role of managerial learning and interpretation in strategic persistence and reorientation: An empirical exploration. *Strategic Management Journal, 13*, 585–608.

Larey, T. S. (1994). *Convergent and divergent thinking, group composition, and creativity in brainstorming groups*. Unpublished doctoral dissertation, University of Texas, Arlington.

Larey, T. S., & Paulus, P. B. (1999). Group preference and convergent tendencies in small groups: A content analysis of group brainstorming performance. *Creativity Research Journal, 12*(3), 175–184.

Larkin, J. H., & Simon, H. A. (1987). Why a diagram is (sometimes) worth ten thousand words. *Cognitive Science, 11*, 65–99.

Larson, J. R., Christiansen, C., Abbott, A. S., & Franz, T. M. (1996). Diagnosing groups: Charting the flow of information in medical decision-making teams. *Journal of Personality and Social Psychology, 71*, 315–330.

Lau, S., & Cheung, P. C. (2010). Developmental trends of creativity: What twists of turn do boys and girls take at different grades? *Creativity Research Journal, 22*(3), 329–336.

Lau, S., Hui, A. N. N., & Ng, G. Y. C. (Eds.). (2004). *Creativity: When East meets West*. Singapore: World Scientific Publishing Co. Pte. Ltd.

Laughlin, P. R., Hatch, E. C., Silver, J. S., & Boh, L. (2006). Groups perform better than the best individuals on letters-to-numbers problems: Effects of group size. *Journal of Personality and Social Psychology, 90*(4), 644–651.

Lavie, S., Narayan, K., & Rosaldo, R. (Eds.). (1993). *Creativity/anthropology*. Ithaca: Cornell University Press.

Layton, R. (1991). *The anthropology of art* (2nd ed.). New York: Cambridge.

Lazear, E. P. (2005). Entrepreneurship. *Journal of Labor Economics, 23*(4), 649–680.

Leary, W. E. (2002, Oct. 22). The inquiring minds behind 200 years of inventions. *New York Times*, p. F4.

Lees-Haley, P. R. (1978). *Creative behavior inventory*. Huntsville, AL: Basic Research, Inc.

Lehman, H. C. (1953). *Age and achievement*. Princeton, NJ: Princeton University Press.

Lena, J. C., & Peterson, R. A. (2008). Classification as culture: Types and trajectories of music genres. *American Sociological Review, 73*, 697–718.

Lenat, D. B. (1977). The ubiquity of discovery. *Artificial Intelligence, 9*, 257–286.

Lenat, D. B. (1983). The role of heuristics in learning by discovery: Three case studies. In R. S. Michalski, J. G. Carbonell, & T. M. Mitchell (Eds.), *Machine learning: An artificial intelligence approach* (pp. 243–306). Palo Alto, CA: Tioga.

Lencioni, P. (2002). *The five dysfunctions of a team: A leadership fable*. San Francisco, CA: Jossey-Bass.

Lerdahl, F., & Jackendoff, R. (1983). *A generative theory of tonal music*. Cambridge, MA: MIT Press.

Lessig, L. (2004). *Free culture: The nature and future of creativity*. New York: Penguin.

Leung, K., Au, A., & Leung, B. W. C. (2004). Creativity and innovation: East-West comparisons with an emphasis on Chinese societies. In S. Lau, A. N. N. Hui, & G. Y. C. Ng (Eds.), *Creativity: When east meets west* (pp. 113–135). Singapore: World Scientific Publishing Co.

Lezak, M. D. (1995). *Neuropsychological assessment* (3rd ed.). New York: Oxford University Press.

Li, A. K. (1978). Effects of play on novel responses in kindergarten children. *Alberta Journal of Educational Research, 24*(1), 31–36.

Li, A. K. (1985). Correlates and effects of training in make-believe play on preschool children. *Alberta Journal of Educational Research, 31*, 70–79.

Lieberman, A. F. (1977). Preschoolers' competence with a peer: Relations with attachment and peer experience. *Child Development, 48*, 1277–1287.

Lieberman, M. D., Gaunt, R., Gilbert, D. T., & Trope, Y. (2002). Reflection and reflexion: A social cognitive neuroscience approach to attributional inference. *Advances in Experimental Social Psychology, 34*, 199–249.

Lim, W., & Plucker, J. A. (2001). Creativity through a lens of social responsibility: Implicit theories of creativity with Korean samples. *Journal of Creative Behavior, 35*(2), 115–130.

Limb, C. J., & Braun, A. R. (2008). Neural substrates of spontaneous musical performance: An fMRI study of jazz improvisation. *PLos One, 3*(2), e1679.

Lincoln, J. R., & Miller, J. (1979). Work and friendship ties in organizations: A comparative analysis of relational networks. *Administrative Science Quarterly, 24*, 181–199.

Litchfield, R. C. (2008). Brainstorming reconsidered: A goal-based view. *Academy of Management Review, 33*, 649–668.

Lockhart, R. S., Lamon, M., & Gick, M. L. (1988). Conceptual transfer in simple insight problems. *Memory & Cognition, 16*(1), 36–44.

Logothetis, N. K. (2008). What we can do and what we cannot do with fMRI. *Nature, 453*, 869–878.

Lombroso, C. (1984/1891). *The man of genius.* New York: Garland Publishing. (Originally published in Italian as *L'umo di genio*. Reprint of English language edition published by W. Scott, London, in 1891 and again in 1910.)

Lonergan, D. C., Scott, G. M., & Mumford, M. D. (2004). Evaluative aspects of creative thought: Effects of appraisal and revision standards. *Creativity Research Journal, 16*, 231–246.

Lorblanchet, M. (2002, June, July, August). L'art des premiers hommes: Entretien avec Michal Lorblanchet. *Sciences Humaines, 37*, 8–11.

Lord, A. B. (1960). *The singer of tales.* New York: Cambridge University Press.

Lotka, A. J. (1926). The frequency distribution of scientific productivity. *Journal of the Washington Academy of Sciences, 16*, 317–323.

Lubart, T. (2010). Cross-cultural perspectives on creativity. In J. C. Kaufman & R. J. Sternberg (Eds.), *The Cambridge handbook of creativity* (pp. 265–278). Cambridge, UK: Cambridge University Press.

Lubart, T., & Sternberg, R. J. (1995). An investment approach to creativity: Theory and data. In S. M. Smith, T. B. Ward, & R. A. Finke (Eds.), *The creative cognition approach* (pp. 269–302). Cambridge, MA: MIT Press.

Ludwig, A. M. (1992). Creative achievement and psychopathology: Comparison among professions. *American Journal of Psychotherapy, 46*(3), 330–356.

Ludwig, A. M. (1995). *The price of greatness: Resolving the creativity and madness controversy.* New York: The Guilford Press.

Lung, C., & Dominowksi, R. L. (1985). Effects of strategy instructions and practice on nine-dot problem solving. *Journal of Experimental Psychology: Learning, Memory, and Cognition, 11*(4), 804–811.

Luo, J., & Knoblich, G. (2007). Studying insight problem solving with neuroscientific methods. *Methods, 42*, 77–86.

Machiavelli, N. (1992). *The prince: a revised translation, backgrounds, interpretations, marginalia* (R. M. Adams, Trans.). New York: Norton.

Mack, R. W. (1987). Are methods of enhancing creativity being taught in teacher education programs as perceived by teacher educators and student teachers? *Journal of Creative Behavior, 21*, 22–33.

MacKinnon, D. W. (1962). The nature and nurture of creative talent. *American Psychologist, 17*(7), 484–495.

MacKinnon, D. W. (1962/1978). What makes a person creative? In D. W. MacKinnon (Ed.), *In search of human effectiveness* (pp. 178–186). New York: Universe Books. (Originally published in Saturday Review, Feb. 10, 1962, pp. 15–17, 69).

MacKinnon, D. W. (1978). *In search of human effectiveness.* Buffalo, NY: Creative Education Foundation.

MacKinnon, D. W. (1987). Some critical issues for future research in creativity. In S. G. Isaksen (Ed.), *Frontiers of creativity research* (pp. 119–130). Buffalo, NY: Bearly.

Mackler, B., & Shontz, F. C. (1965). Life style and creativity: An empirical investigation. *Perceptual and Motor Skills, 20*, 873–896.

Mackworth, N. H. (1965). Originality. *American Psychologist, 20*, 51–66.

Maddi, S. R. (1975). The strenuousness of the creative life. In I. A. Taylor & J. W. Getzels (Eds.), *Perspectives in creativity* (pp. 173–190). Chicago: Aldine Publishing Company.

Maduro, R. (1976). *Artistic creativity in a Brahmin painter community*. Berkeley, CA: Center for South and Southeast Asian Studies.

Maginn, B. K., & Harris, R. J. (1980). Effects of anticipated evaluation on individual brainstorming performance. *Journal of Applied Psychology, 65*, 219–225.

Malevich, K. S. (1919/1968). On new systems in art. In T. Anderson (Ed.), *Essays on art 1915–1933* (pp. 83–117). London: Rapp and Whiting.

Mall, A. S. (2007). Structure, innovation and agency in pattern construction: The *Kolam* of Southern India. In E. Hallam & T. Ingold (Eds.), *Creativity and cultural improvisation* (pp. 55–78). Oxford, UK: Berg.

Malm, W. P. (1975). Shoden: A study in Tokyo festival music. When is variation an improvisation? *Yearbook of the International Folk Music Council, 7*, 44–66.

Mann, P. H. (1969). *The romantic novel: A survey of reading habits*. London: Mills & Boon Limited.

Marcus, S., & Neaçsu, G. (1972). La structure psychologique du talent dramatique. *Revue Roumaine des Sciences Sociales, Série de Psychologie, 16*(2), 133–149.

Marcuse, H. (1970). Art as a form of reality. In E. F. Fry (Ed.), *On the future of art* (pp. 123–134). New York: The Viking Press.

Markman, A. B., Yamauchi, T., & Makin, V. S. (1997). The creation of new concepts: A multifaceted approach to category learning. In T. B. Ward, S. M. Smith & J. Vaid (Eds.), *Creative thought: An investigation of conceptual structures and processes* (pp. 179–208). Washington, DC: American Psychological Association.

Marks, P. (1997, Tuesday, April 22). When the audience joins the cast. *New York Times*, pp. B1, B7.

Markus, H. R., & Kitayama, S. (1991). Culture and the self: Implications for cognition, emotion, and motivation. *Psychological Review, 98*(2), 224–253.

Marland, S. P. (1972). *Education of the gifted and talented (Report to the Congress of the United States by the U.S. Commissioner of Education)*. Washington, DC: U.S. Government Printing Office.

Marsden, P. V., & Campbell, K. E. (1984). Measuring tie strength. *Social Forces, 63*, 482–501.

Martin, T. (2009, Oct. 30). Beginners by Raymond Carver: review. *Telegraph*.

Martindale, A. (1972). *The rise of the artist in the middle ages and early renaissance*. London: Thames and Hudson.

Martindale, C. (1990). *The clockwork muse: The predictability of artistic change*. New York: Basic Books.

Martindale, C., & Hines, D. (1975). Creativity and cortical activation during creative, intellectual, and EEG feedback tasks. *Biological Psychology, 3*, 71–80.

Marzorati, G. (2002, March 17). All by himself. *New York Times Magazine*, pp. 32–37, 68–70.

Maslow, A. H. (1954). *Motivation and personality*. New York: Harper & Row.

Maslow, A. H. (1959). Creativity in self-actualizing people. In H. H. Anderson (Ed.), *Creativity and its cultivation* (pp. 83–95). New York: Harper & Row.

Mason, M. F., Norton, M. I., Van Horn, J. D., Wegner, D. M., Grafton, S. T., & Macrae, N. (2007). Wandering minds: The default network and stimulus-independent thought. *Science, 315*, 393–395.

Massa, L. J., & Mayer, R. E. (2006). Testing the ATI hypothesis: Should multimedia instruction accommodate verbalizer-visualizer cognitive style? *Learning and Individual Differences, 16*, 321–336.

Matarazzo, J. D. (1972). *Wechsler's measure and appraisal of adult intelligence* (5th ed.). New York: Oxford University Press.

Mathisen, G. E., & Einarsen, S. (2004). A review of instruments assessing creative and innovative environments within organizations. *Creativity Research Journal, 16*(1), 119–140.

Max, D. T. (1998, Aug. 9). The Carver chronicles. *New York Times Magazine*, pp. 34–40, 51, 56–57.

May, R. (1959). The nature of creativity. In H. H. Anderson (Ed.), *Creativity and its cultivation* (pp. 55–68). New York: Harper & Row.

May, R. (1969). *The courage to create*. New York: Norton.

Mayer, R. E. (1984). Aids to prose comprehension. *Educational Psychologist, 20*, 30–42.

Mayer, R. E. (1989). Cognitive views of creativity: Creative teaching for creative learning. *Contemporary Educational Psychology, 14*, 203–211.

Mayer, R. E. (2008). Incorporating individual differences into the science of learning: Commentary on Sternberg et al. (2008). *Perspectives on Psychological Science, 3*, 507–508.

McClelland, D. C. (1993). Intelligence is not the best predictor of job performance. *Current Directions in Psychological Science, 2*(1), 5–6.

McCorduck, P. (1991). *Aaron's code: Meta-art, artificial intelligence, and the work of Harold Cohen*. New York: W. H. Freeman.

McCrae, R. R. (1987). Creativity, divergent thinking, and openness to experience. *Journal of Personality and Social Psychology, 52*(6), 1258–1265.

McCrae, R. R., Arenberg, D., & Costa, P. T. (1987). Declines in divergent thinking with age: Cross-sectional, longitudinal, and cross-sequential analyses. *Psychology and Aging, 2*, 130–137.

McCrae, R. R., & Costa, P. T. (1997). Personality trait structure as a human universal. *American Psychologist, 52*, 509–516.

McGrew, K. S. (2005). The Cattell-Horn-Carroll theory of cognitive abilities. In D. P. Flanagan & P. L. Harrison (Eds.), *Contemporary intellectual assessment: Theories, tests and issues* (2nd ed., pp. 136–181). New York: Guilford.

McGrew, K. S. (2009). CHC theory and the human cognitive abilities project: Standing on the shoulders of the giants of psychometric intelligence research. *Intelligence, 37*, 1–10.

McKinsey & Company. (2009). *"And the winner is . . .": Capturing the promise of philanthropic prizes*. San Francisco, CA: McKinsey & Company.

McLurkin, J. (2002). The swarm orchestra: Temporal synchronization and spatial division of labor for large swarms of autonomous robots. http://groups.csail.mit.edu/mac/projects/amorphous/6.978/final-papers/jamesm-final.pdf Retrieved Sep. 1, 2011.

McNeill, D. (1992). *Hand and mind: What gestures reveal about thought*. Chicago: University of Chicago.

McNemar, Q. (1964). Lost: Our intelligence? Why? *American Psychologist, 19*, 871–882.

McPherson, M., Smith-Lovin, L., & Cook, J. M. (2001). Birds of a feather: Homophily in social networks. *Annual Review of Sociology, 27*, 415–444.

Medin, D. L., & Shoben, E. J. (1988). Context and structure in conceptual combination. *Cognitive Psychology, 20*, 158–190.

Mednick, S. A. (1962). The associative basis of the creative process. *Psychological Review, 69*(3), 220–232.

Mednick, S. A., & Mednick, M. T. (1967). *Remote associates test examiner's manual*. Boston: Houghton Mifflin.

Meehan, J. (1976). *The metanovel: Writing stories by computer*. Unpublished doctoral dissertation, Yale University, New Haven, CT.

Meehan, J. (1981). TALE-SPIN. In R. C. Schank & C. J. Riesbeck (Eds.), *Inside computer understanding: Five programs plus miniatures* (pp. 197–226). Mahwah, NJ: Erlbaum.

Mehra, A., Kilduff, M., & Brass, D. J. (2001). The social networks of high and low self-monitors: Implications for workplace performance. *Administrative Science Quarterly, 46*, 121–146.

Menand, L. (1998, Feb. 9). What is "art"? *New Yorker*, 39–41.

Mercer, N. (2000). *Words and minds: How we use language to think together*. London: Routledge.

Merges, R. P. (1995). The economic impact of intellectual property rights: An overview and guide. *Journal of Cultural Economics, 19*, 103–117.

Merton, R. K. (1949/1968). *Social theory and social structure.* New York: Free Press.

Merton, R. K. (1961). Singletons and multiples in scientific discovery: A chapter in the sociology of science. *Proceedings of the American Philosophical Society, 105*(5), 470–486.

Metcalfe, J. (1986). Feeling of knowing in memory and problem solving. *Journal of Experimental Psychology: Learning, Memory, and Cognition, 12*(2), 288–294.

Metcalfe, J. (1986). Premonitions of insight predict impending error. *Journal of Experimental Psychology: Learning, Memory, and Cognition, 12,* 623–634.

Metcalfe, J., & Wiebe, D. (1987). Intuition in insight and noninsight problem solving. *Memory & Cognition, 15*(3), 238–246.

Meyer, L. (1956). *Emotion and meaning in music.* Chicago: University of Chicago Press.

Meyer, R. E. (1989). Systematic thinking fostered by illustration in scientific text. *Journal of Educational Psychology, 81,* 240–246.

Meyer, T. D. (2002). The hypomanic personality scale, the big five, and their relationship to depression and mania. *Personality and Individual Differences, 32,* 649–660.

Michael, W. B., Rosenthal, B. G., & DeCamp, M. A. (1949). An experimental investigation of prestige-suggestion for two types of literary material. *Journal of Psychology, 28,* 303–323.

Middleton, D., & Edwards, D. (1990). Collective remembering. In D. Middleton & D. Edwards (Eds.), *Collective remembering* (pp. 23–45). Newbury Park, CA: Sage.

Milgram, R. M., & Hong, E. (1993). Creative thinking and creative performance in adolescents as predictors of creative attainments in adults: A follow-up study after 18 years. *Roeper Review, 15,* 135–139.

Milgram, R. M., & Hong, E. (1999). Creative out-of-school activities in intellectually gifted adolescents as predictors of their life accomplishment in young adults: A longitudinal study. *Creativity Research Journal, 12,* 77–87.

Milgram, R. M., & Milgram, N. (1976). Creative thinking and creative performance in Israeli children. *Journal of Educational Psychology, 68,* 255–259.

Miller, G. F. (2000). *The mating mind: How sexual choice shaped the evolution of human nature.* New York: Doubleday.

Miller, G. F. (2001). Aesthetic fitness: How sexual selection shaped artistic virtuosity as a fitness indicator and aesthetic preferences as mate choice criteria. *Bulletin of Psychology of the Arts, 2*(1), 20–25.

Miner, A. S., Bassoff, P., & Moorman, C. (2001). Organizational improvisation and learning: A field study. *Administrative Science Quarterly, 46,* 304–337.

Miner, J. B. (1997). The expanded horizon for achieving entrepreneurial success. *Organizational Dynamics, Winter,* 54–67.

Mintzberg, H. (1983). *Structure in fives: Designing effective organizations.* Englewood Cliffs, NJ: Prentice-Hall.

Mittler, C. A. (1976). An instructional strategy designed to overcome the adverse effects of established student attitudes toward works of art. *Studies in Art Education, 17,* 13–31.

Mobley, M. I., Doares, L., & Mumford, M. D. (1992). Process analytic models of creative capacities: Evidence for the combination and reorganization process. *Creativity Research Journal, 5,* 125–156.

Moga, E., Burger, K., Hetland, L., & Winner, E. (2000). Does studying the arts engender creative thinking? Evidence for near but not far transfer. *Journal of Aesthetic Education, 34*(3/4), 91–104.

Monson, I. (1996). *Saying something: Jazz improvisation and interaction.* Chicago: University of Chicago Press.

Moore, H. (1952/1985). Notes on sculpture. In B. Ghiselin (Ed.), *The creative process: A symposium* (pp. 68–73). Berkeley, CA: University of California Press. (Original work published 1952.)

Moore, M. (1985). The relationship between the originality of essays and variables in the problem-discovery process: A study of creative and non-creative middle school students. *Research in the Teaching of English, 19*(1), 84–95.

Moore, M. T. (1990). Problem finding and teacher experience. *Journal of Creative Behavior, 24*, 39–58.

Moore, M. T. (1993). Implications of problem finding on teaching and learning. In S. G. Isaksen, M. C. Murdock, R. L. Firestien & D. J. Treffinger (Eds.), *Nurturing and developing creativity: The emergence of a discipline* (pp. 51–69). Norwood, NJ: Ablex.

Moran, S. (2010). Creativity in school. In K. Littleton, C. Wood, & J. K. Staarman (Eds.), *International handbook of psychology in education* (pp. 319–359). Bingley, UK: Emerald Group Publishing Ltd.

Morelli, G. A., Rogoff, B., Oppenheim, D., & Goldsmith, D. (1992). Cultural variation in infants' sleeping arrangements: Questions of independence. *Developmental Psychology, 28*(4), 604–613.

Morelock, M. J., & Feldman, D. H. (1999). Prodigies. In M. A. Runco & S. R. Pritzker (Eds.), *Encyclopedia of creativity* (Vol. 2, pp. 449–456). San Diego, CA: Academic Press.

Moreno, J. L. (1977). *Psychodrama* (3 vols.). Beacon, NY: Beacon House.

Morgan, C. L. (1933). *The emergence of novelty.* London: Williams & Norgate Ltd.

Mukerji, C. (1996). The collective construction of scientific genius. In Y. Engeström & D. Middleton (Eds.), *Cognition and communication at work* (pp. 257–278). New York: Cambridge University Press.

Mullen, B., Johnson, C., & Salas, E. (1991). Productivity loss in brainstorming groups: A meta-analytic integration. *Basic and Applied Social Psychology, 12*(1), 3–23.

Mullineaux, P. Y., & Dilalla, L. F. (2009). Preschool pretend play behaviors and early adolescent creativity. *Journal of Creative Behavior, 43*(1), 41–57.

Mumford, M. D. (1995). Situational influences on creative achievement: Attributions or interactions? *Creativity Research Journal, 8*(4), 405–412.

Mumford, M. D. (2003). Where have we been, where are we going? Taking stock in creativity research. *Creativity Research Journal, 15*(2 & 3), 107–120.

Mumford, M. D., Baughman, W. A., Maher, M. A., Constanza, D. P., & Supinski, E. P. (1997). Process-based measures of creative problem-solving skill: IV. Category combination. *Creativity Research Journal, 10*(1), 59–71.

Mumford, M. D., Baughman, W. A., & Sager, C. E. (2003). Picking the right material: Cognitive processing skills and their role in creative thought. In M. A. Runco (Ed.), *Critical creative processes* (pp. 19–68). Cresskill, NJ: Hampton Press.

Mumford, M. D., Baughman, W. A., Supinski, E. P., & Maher, M. A. (1996a). Process-based measures of creative problem-solving skills: II. Information encoding. *Creativity Research Journal, 9*(1), 77–88.

Mumford, M. D., Baughman, W. A., Threlfall, K. V., Supinski, E. P., & Constanza, D. P. (1996b). Process-based measures of creative problem-solving skills: I. Problem construction. *Creativity Research Journal, 9*(1), 63–76.

Mumford, M. D., Supinski, E. P., Threlfall, K. V., & Baughman, W. A. (1996c). Process-based measures of creative problem-solving skills: III. Category selection. *Creativity Research Journal, 9*(4), 395–406.

Mumford, M. D., & Gustafson, S. B. (1988). Creativity syndrome: Integration, application, and innovation. *Psychological Bulletin, 103*(1), 27–43.

Nagel, E. (1961). *The structure of science: Problems in the logic of scientific explanation.* New York: Harcourt, Brace & World.

Nakamura, F. (2007). Creating or performing worlds? Observations on contemporary Japanese calligraphy. In E. Hallam & T. Ingold (Eds.), *Creativity and cultural improvisation* (pp. 79–98). Oxford, UK: Berg.

Nakamura, J., & Csikszentmihalyi, M. (2003). Creativity in later life. In R. K. Sawyer et al., *Creativity and development* (pp. 186–216). New York: Oxford.

Nakamura, J., Shernoff, D., & Hooker, C. (2009). *Good mentoring.* San Francisco, CA: Jossey-Bass.

Neaçsu, G. (1972). L'Unité de la transposition et de l'expressivité: Indice fondamental du talent scénique. *Revue Roumaine des Sciences Sociales, Série de Psychologie, 16*(1), 3–15.

Negroponte, N. (2003, February). Creating a culture of ideas. *Technology Review,* 34–35.

Negus, K., & Pickering, M. (2004). *Creativity, communication and cultural value.* London: Sage Publications.

Nemeth, C. (1986). Differential contributions of majority and minority influence. *Psychological Review, 93*(1), 23–32.

Nemeth, C. J., & Goncalo, J. A. (2005). Collaborations from afar: The benefits of independent authors. *Creativity Research Journal, 17*(1), 1–8.

Nemiro, J. (1997). Interpretive artists: A qualitative exploration of the creative process of actors. *Creativity Research Journal, 10*(2 & 3), 229–239.

Newell, A., Shaw, J. C., & Simon, H. A. (1962). The processes of creative thinking. In H. E. Gruber, G. Terrell, & M. Wertheimer (Eds.), *Contemporary approaches to creative thinking* (pp. 63–119). New York: Atherton Press.

Newell, A., & Simon, H. A. (1972). *Human problem solving.* Englewood Cliffs, NJ: Prentice-Hall.

Newhall, B. (1964). *The history of photography.* New York: Museum of Modern Art.

Ng, A. K. (2001). *Why Asians are less creative than Westerners.* Englewood Cliffs, NJ: Prentice Hall.

Ng, A. K., & Smith, I. (2004). Why is there a paradox in promoting creativity in the Asian classroom? In S. Lau, A. N. N. Hui, & G. Y. C. Ng (Eds.), *Creativity: When East meets West* (pp. 87–112). Singapore: World Scientific Publishing Co. Pte. Ltd.

Nicholls, J. G. (1972). Creativity in the person who will never produce anything original and useful: The concept of creativity as a normally distributed trait. *American Psychologist, 27,* 717–727.

Nichols, R. C. (1978). Twin studies of ability, personality and interest. *Homo, 29*(3), 158–173.

Nickerson, R. S. (1999). Enhancing creativity. In R. J. Sternberg (Ed.), *The handbook of creativity* (pp. 392–430). New York: Cambridge.

Nicolson, A. (2006, Sept. 30 – Oct. 1). God's work via committee. *The Wall Street Journal,* p. P14.

Nicolson, H. (1947). The health of authors. *Lancet,* 709–714.

Niu, W. (2006). Development of creativity research in Chinese societies: A comparison of mainland China, Taiwan, Hong Kong, and Singapore. In J. C. Kaufman & R. J. Sternberg (Eds.), *The international handbook of creativity* (pp. 374–394). Cambridge, UK: Cambridge University Press.

Niu, W., & Sternberg, R. J. (2002). Contemporary studies on the concept of creativity: The East and West. *Journal of Creative Behavior, 36*(4), 269–284.

Noller, R. B., Parnes, S. J., & Biondi, A. M. (1976). *Creative Actionbook.* New York: Scribner.

Norlander, T. (1999). Inebriation and inspiration? A review of the research on alcohol and creativity. *Journal of Creative Behavior, 33*(1), 22–44.

Norlander, T., Erixon, A., & Archer, T. (2000). Psychological androgyny and creativity: Dynamics of gender role and personality trait. *Social Behavior and Personality, 28,* 423–436.

Norlander, T., & Gustafson, R. (1996). Effects of alcohol on scientific thought during the incubation phase of the creative process. *Journal of Creative Behavior, 30,* 231–248.

Norlander, T., & Gustafson, R. (1997). Effects of alcohol on picture drawing during the verification phase of the creative process. *Creativity Research Journal, 10,* 355–362.

Norlander, T., & Gustafson, R. (1998). Effects of alcohol on a divergent figural fluency test during the illumination phase of the creative process. *Creativity Research Journal, 11,* 265–274.

Novak, J. D., & Gowin, D. B. (1984). *Learning how to learn.* New York: Cambridge University Press.

Nunamaker, J. F., Applegate, L. M., & Konsynski, B. R. (1987). Facilitating group creativity: Experience with a group decision support system. *Journal of Management Information Systems, 3,* 5–19.

Obstfeld, D. (2005). Social networks, the *Tertius Iungens* orientation, and involvement in innovation. *Administrative Science Quarterly, 50*, 100–130.

OECD. (2008). *Innovating to learn, learning to innovate.* Paris, France: OECD.

Offner, A. K., Kramer, T. J., & Winter, J. P. (1996). The effects of facilitation, recording, and pauses on group brainstorming. *Small Group Research, 27*(2), 283–298.

Ohlsson, S. (1992). Information-processing explanations of insight and related phenomena. In M. T. Keane & K. J. Gilhooly (Eds.), *Advances in the psychology of thinking* (Vol. 1, pp. 1–44). London: Harvester Wheatsheaf.

Okuda, S. M., Runco, M. A., & Berger, D. E. (1991). Creativity and the finding and solving of real-world problems. *Journal of Psychoeducational Assessment, 9*, 45–53.

Olsen, F. (Ed.). (1952). *The nature of creative thinking: A monograph.* New York: Industrial Research Institute. Report of a symposium presented at the May 5–7, 1952, meeting of the Industrial Research Institute, Skytop Club, Skytop, Pennsylvania.

Ornstein, R. E. (1972). *The psychology of consciousness.* San Francisco, CA: W. H. Freeman.

Ornstein, R. E. (1997). *The right mind: Making sense of the hemispheres.* New York: Harcourt Brace.

Oromaner, M. (1985). The Ortega hypothesis and influential articles in American sociology. *Scientometrics, 7*, 3–10.

Orr, A. H. (1996, Summer). Dennett's strange idea (Review of *Darwin's Dangerous Idea* by Daniel C. Dennett). Boston Review, Available online at http://bostonreview.net/BR21.3/Orr.html, accessed Sep. 1, 2011.

Ortega y Gasset, J. (1932). *The revolt of the masses* (A. Kerrigan, Trans.). New York: Norton.

Ortony, A. (1979). Beyond literal similarity. *Psychological Review, 86*, 161–180.

Osborn, A. F. (1948). *Your creative power.* New York: Charles Scribner's Sons.

Osborn, A. F. (1953). *Applied imagination.* Buffalo, NY: Creative Education Foundation Press.

Osborn, T. (2003). Against "creativity": A philistine rant. *Economy and Society, 32*(4), 507–525.

Over, R. (1982). The durability of scientific reputation. *Journal of the History of the Behavioral Sciences, 18*, 53–61.

Owen, S. V., & Baum, S. M. (1985). The validity of the measurement of originality. *Educational and Psychological Measurement, 45*, 939–944.

Ox, J. (2002). The color organ and collaboration. In L. Candy & E. Edmonds (Eds.), *Explorations in art and technology* (pp. 211–218). Berlin: Springer.

Oxley, N. L., Dzindolet, M. T., & Paulus, P. B. (1996). The effects of facilitators on the performance of brainstorming groups. *Journal of Social Behavior and Personality, 11*(4), 633–646.

Park, D. C., & Huang, C.-M. (2010). Culture wires the brain: A cognitive neuroscience perspective. *Perspectives on Psychological Science, 5*(4), 391–400.

Parks, T. (2002, Oct. 24). Tales told by the computer. *New York Review of Books*, 49–51.

Parnes, S. J. (1993). A glance backward and forward. In S. G. Isaksen, M. C. Murdock, R. L. Firestien, & D. J. Treffinger (Eds.), *Understanding and recognizing creativity: The emergence of a discipline* (pp. 471–474). Norwood, NJ: Ablex.

Parnes, S. J., & Harding, H. F. (1962). Preface. In S. J. Parnes & H. F. Harding (Eds.), *A source book for creative thinking* (pp. v–viii). New York: Charles Scribner's Sons.

Parrish, C. (1957). *The notation of medieval music.* New York: Pendragon Press.

Partch, H. (1949). *Genesis of a music.* Madison, WI: University of Wisconsin Press.

Pashler, H., McDaniel, M., Rohrer, D., & Bjork, R. (2008). Learning styles: Concepts and evidence. *Psychological Science in the Public Interest, 9*(3), 105–119.

Pater, W. (1873/1986). *The Renaissance: Studies in art and poetry* (E. Adam Phillips, Trans.). New York: Oxford University Press.

Patrick, A. S. (1986). The role of ability in creative "incubation." *Personality and Individual Differences, 7*(2), 169–174.

Paulus, P. B., & Dzindolet, M. T. (1993). Social influence processes in group brainstorming. *Journal of Personality and Social Psychology, 64,* 575–586.

Paulus, P. B., Larey, T. S., & Dzindolet, M. T. (2001). Creativity in groups and teams. In M. Turner (Ed.), *Groups at work: Theory and research* (pp. 319–338). Mahwah, NJ: Erlbaum.

Paulus, P. B., Larey, T. S., & Ortega, A. H. (1995). Performance and perceptions of brainstormers in an organizational setting. *Basic and Applied Social Psychology, 17,* 249–265.

Paulus, P. B., & Nijstad, B. A. (2003). *Group creativity: Innovation through collaboration.* New York: Oxford.

Peck, J. (2005). Struggling with the creative class. *International Journal of Urban and Regional Research, 29*(4), 740–770.

Peele, S., & DeGrandpre, R. (1995, July 1). My genes made me do it. *Psychology Today,* online at http://www.psychologytoday.com/node/25675, accessed Sep. 1, 2011.

Peiry, L. (2001). *Art brut: The origins of outsider art.* Paris: Flammarion.

Pelled, L. H., Eisenhardt, K. M., & Xin, K. R. (1999). Exploring the black box: An analysis of work group diversity, conflict, and performance. *Administrative Science Quarterly, 44,* 1–28.

Pellegrini, A. D. (1992). Rough-and-tumble play and social problem solving flexibility. *Creativity Research Journal, 5,* 13–26.

Perkins, D. N. (1994). Creativity: Beyond the Darwinian paradigm. In M. A. Boden (Ed.), *Dimensions of creativity* (pp. 119–142). Cambridge, MA: MIT Press.

Perkins, D. (2000). *The Eureka effect: The art and logic of breakthrough thinking.* New York: W. W. Norton.

Perkins, D. N. (1981). *The mind's best work.* Cambridge, MA: Harvard University Press.

Perkins, D. N. (1983). Novel remote analogies seldom contribute to discovery. *Journal of Creative Behavior, 17,* 223–239.

Perry-Smith, J. E. (2006). Social yet creative: The role of social relationships in facilitating individual creativity. *Academy of Management Journal, 49,* 85–101.

Perry-Smith, J. E., & Shalley, C. E. (2003). The social side of creativity: A static and dynamic social network perspective. *Academy of Management Review, 28,* 89–106.

Perry-Smith, J. E., & Shalley, C. E. (2006). *Team creativity: The role of informal interactions.* Paper presented at the Academy of Management Annual Meeting.

Pfeiffer, J. E. (1982). *The creative explosion: An inquiry into the origins of art and religion.* New York: Harper & Row Publishers.

Pfenninger, K. H., & Shubik, V. R. (2001). Insights into the foundations of creativity: A synthesis. In K. H. Pfenninger & V. R. Shubik (Eds.), *The origins of creativity* (pp. 213–236). New York: Oxford University Press.

Piirto, J. (1991). Why are there so few? (Creative women: Visual artists, mathematicians, musicians). *Roeper Review, 13,* 142–147.

Piirto, J. (1992). *Understanding those who create.* Dayton, OH: Ohio Psychology Press.

Piirto, J. (1998). *Understanding those who create* (2nd ed.). Dayton, OH: Ohio Psychology Press.

Piirto, J. (1999). A survey of psychological studies in creativity. In A. S. Fishkin, B. Cramond, & P. Olszewski-Kubilius (Eds.), *Investigating creativity in youth: Research and methods* (pp. 27–48). Cresskill, NJ: Hampton.

Piirto, J. (2004). *Understanding creativity* (Revised edition of *Understanding those who create*, 2nd ed., 1998). Scottsdale, AZ: Great Potential Press.

Piirto, J. (2009). The personalities of creative writers. In S. B. Kaufman & J. C. Kaufman (Eds.), *The psychology of creative writing* (pp. 3–22). Cambridge, UK: Cambridge University Press.

Pink, D. H. (2005). *A whole new mind: Why right-brainers will rule the future*. New York: Riverhead Books.

Planck, M. (1949). *Scientific autobiography and other papers* (F. Gaynor, Trans.). New York: Philosophical Library.

Plucker, J. A. (1999). Is the proof in the pudding? Reanalyses of Torrance's (1958 to present) longitudinal studies data. *Creativity Research Journal, 12*, 103–114.

Plucker, J. A., Beghetto, R. A., & Dow, G. T. (2004). Why isn't creativity more important to educational psychologists? Potentials, pitfalls, and future directions in creativity research. *Educational Psychologist, 39*(2), 83–96.

Plucker, J. A., & Dana, R. Q. (1998). Alcohol, tobacco, and marijuana use: Relationships to undergraduate students' creative achievement. *Journal of College Student Development, 39*(5), 472–483.

Plucker, J. A., & Makel, M. C. (2010). Assessment of creativity. In J. C. Kaufman & R. J. Sternberg (Eds.), *The Cambridge handbook of creativity* (pp. 48–73). Cambridge, UK: Cambridge University Press.

Poe, E. A. (1846). The philosophy of composition. *Graham's Magazine, 28*, 163–167.

Poincaré, H. (1913/1982). *The foundations of science*. Washington, DC: University Press of America.

Policastro, E., & Gardner, H. (1999). From case studies to robust generalizations: An approach to the study of creativity. In R. J. Sternberg (Ed.), *Handbook of creativity* (pp. 213–225). Cambridge, UK: Cambridge University Press.

Pope, R. (2005). *Creativity: Theory, history, practice*. London: Routledge.

Posner, M. I., & Raichle, M. E. (1994). *Images of mind*. New York: Scientific American Library.

Post, F. (1994). Creativity and psychopathology: A study of 291 world-famous men. *British Journal of Psychiatry, 165*, 22–34.

Postmes, T., Spears, R., & Cihangir, S. (2001). Quality of decision making and group norms. *Journal of Personality and Social Psychology, 80*, 918–930.

Pound, E. (1954). A retrospect. In T. S. Eliot (Ed.), *Literary essays of Ezra Pound* (pp. 3–14). London: Faber and Faber Ltd.

Poze, T. (1983). Analogical connections: The essence of creativity. *Journal of Creative Behavior, 17*(4), 240–258.

Preckel, F., Holling, H., & Weise, M. (2006). Relationship of intelligence and creativity in gifted and non-gifted students: An investigation of threshold theory. *Personality and Individual Differences, 40*, 159–170.

Pressing, J. (1988). Improvisation: Methods and models. In J. A. Sloboda (Ed.), *Generative processes in music: The psychology of performance, improvisation, and composition* (pp. 129–178). New York: Oxford.

Price, D. (1963). *Little science, big science*. New York: Columbia University Press.

Price, D. (1965). Networks of scientific papers. *Science, 149*, 510–515.

Prince, G. M. (1970). *The practice of creativity: A manual for dynamic group problem solving*. New York: Harper & Row, Publishers.

Prinzhorn, H. (1922/1972). *Artistry of the mentally ill*. New York: Springer-Verlag. (Original work published in 1922 as *Bildnerei der Geisteskranken*, Berlin: Verlag Julias Springer.)

Pritzker, S., & Runco, M. A. (1997). The creative decision-making process in group situation comedy writing. In R. K. Sawyer (Ed.), *Creativity in performance* (pp. 115–141). Norwood, NJ: Ablex.

Qualifications and Curriculum Authority (QCA). (2005). *Creativity: Find it, promote, promoting pupils' creative thinking and behaviour across the curriculum at key stages 1 and 2, practical materials for schools*. London: Qualifications and Curriculum Authority.

Quetelet, A. (1835/1969). *A treatise on man and the development of his faculties*. Gainesville, FL: Scholars' facsimiles and reprints. (A facsimile reproduction of the English translation of 1842 of the 1835 French original.)

Quinn, J. B. (1985, May–June). Managing innovation: Controlled chaos. *Harvard Business Review, 63,* 73–80.

Radway, J. A. (1991). *Reading the romance: Women, patriarchy, and popular literature* (2nd ed.). Chapel Hill: University of North Carolina Press. (First edition published 1984.)

Raichle, M. E. (2009). A paradigm shift in functional brain imaging. *Journal of Neuroscience, 29*(41), 12729–12734.

Raina, M. K. (1993). Ethnocentric confines in creativity research. In S. G. Isaksen, M. C. Murdock, R. L. Firestien, & D. J. Treffinger (Eds.), *Understanding and recognizing creativity: The emergence of a discipline* (pp. 435–453). Norwood, NJ: Ablex.

Raina, M. K. (1999). Cross-cultural differences. In M. A. Runco & S. R. Pritzker (Eds.), *Encyclopedia of creativity* (Vol. 1, pp. 453–464). San Diego, CA: Academic Press.

Ramachandran, V. S. (2004). *A brief tour of human consciousness: From impostor poodles to purple numbers.* New York: Pi Press.

Rasch, R. A. (1988). Timing and synchronization in ensemble performance. In J. A. Sloboda (Ed.), *Generative processes in music: The psychology of performance, improvisation, and composition* (pp. 70–90). Oxford, UK: Clarendon Press.

Raskin, E. (1936). Comparison of scientific and literary ability: A biographical study of eminent scientists and men of letters of the nineteenth century. *Journal of Abnormal and Social Psychology, 31*(1), 20–35.

Ray, D. J., & Blaker, A. A. (1967). *Eskimo masks: Art and ceremony.* Seattle, WA: University of Washington Press.

Reason, J. T., & Lucas, D. (1984). Using cognitive diaries to investigate naturally occurring memory blocks. In J. E. Harris & P. E. Morris (Eds.), *Everyday memory, actions and absentmindedness* (pp. 53–69). London: Academic Press.

Redner, S. (2002, Nov. 13). *The statistical mechanics of popularity.* Paper presented at the Department of Physics colloquium, Washington University.

Ree, M. J., & Earles, J. A. (1992). Intelligence is the best predictor of job performance. *Current Directions in Psychological Science, 1*(3), 86–89.

Ree, M. J., & Earles, J. A. (1993). *g* is to psychology what carbon is to chemistry: A reply to Sternberg and Wagner, McClelland, and Calfee. *Current Directions in Psychological Science, 2*(1), 11–12.

Reese, G. (1959). *Music in the Renaissance* (rev. ed.). New York: W. W. Norton.

Reichardt, J. (1971). *The computer in art.* London: Studio Vista.

Reiterer, S., Pereda, E., & Bhattacharya, J. (2009). Measuring second language proficiency with EEG synchronization: How functional cortical networks and hemispheric involvement differ as a function of proficiency in second language speakers. *Second Language Researcher, 25*(1), 77–106.

Rejskind, G. (2000). TAG teachers: Only the creative need apply. *Roeper Review, 22*(3), 153–157.

Renzulli, J. S. (1978). What makes giftedness? Reexamining a definition. *Phi Delta Kappan, 60,* 180–184, 261.

Renzulli, J. S. (1999). Reflections, perceptions, and future directions. *Journal for the Education of the Gifted, 23,* 125–146.

Renzulli, J. S. (2005). The three-ring definition of giftedness: A developmental model for promoting creative productivity. In R. J. Sternberg & J. E. Davidson (Eds.), *Conceptions of giftedness* (2nd ed., pp. 246–280). New York: Cambridge University Press.

Renzulli, J. S., & Reis, S. M. (1985). *The schoolwide enrichment model: A comprehensive plan for educational excellence.* Mansfield Center, CT: Creative Learning Press.

Renzulli, J. S., Smith, L., White, A., Callahan, C., & Hartman, R. (2001). *Scales for rating the behavioral characteristics of superior students* (rev. ed.): *Manual and nine rating scales.* Mansfield Center, CT: Creative Learning Press.

Restak, R. (1993). The creative brain. In J. Brockman (Ed.), *Creativity: The reality club 4* (pp. 164–175). New York: Simon & Schuster.

Reuter, M., Panksepp, J., Schnabel, N., Kellerhoff, N., Kempel, P., & Hennig, J. (2005). Personality and biological markers of creativity. *European Journal of Personality, 19*, 83–95.

Reznikoff, M., Domino, G., Bridges, C., & Honeyman, M. (1973). Creative abilities in identical and fraternal twins. *Behavior Genetics, 3*(4), 365–377.

Rhodes, C. (2000). *Outsider art: Spontaneous alternatives*. London: Thames & Hudson Ltd.

Rhodes, M. (1961). An analysis of creativity. *Phi Delta Kappan, 42*(7), 305–310.

Rich, M. (2006, April 11). Boston mob, party of 4: Authors publish in packs. *New York Times*, pp. B1, B7.

Rich, M. (2007, Oct. 17). The real Carver: Expansive or minimal? *New York Times*, p. B1.

Richards, R., Kinney, D. K., Benet, M., & Merzel, A. P. C. (1988a). Assessing everyday creativity: Characteristics of the lifetime creativity scales and validation with three large samples. *Journal of Personality and Social Psychology, 54*, 476–485.

Richards, R., Kinney, D. K., Lunde, I., Benet, M., & Merzel, A. P. C. (1988b). Creativity in manic-depressives, cyclothymes, their normal relatives, and control subjects. *Journal of Abnormal Psychology, 97*(3), 281–288.

Richards, R. L. (1981). Relationships between creativity and psychopathology: An evaluation and interpretation of the evidence. *Genetic Psychology Monographs, 103*(Second Half), 261–324.

Ridley, M. (2010). *The rational optimist: How prosperity evolves*. New York: Harper.

Robins, L. N., & Regier, D. A. (Eds.). (1991). *Psychiatric disorders in America: The Epidemiological Catchment Area Study*. New York: The Free Press.

Rockefeller Brothers Fund. (1958). *The pursuit of excellence: Education and the future of America; panel report V of the Special Studies Project*. Garden City, NY: Doubleday.

Rodan, S., & Galunic, D. C. (2004). More than network structure: How knowledge heterogeneity influences managerial performance and innovativeness. *Strategic Management Journal, 25*, 541–562.

Roe, A. (1952a). *The making of a scientist*. New York: Dodd, Mead.

Roe, A. (1952b). The psychologist examines 64 eminent scientists. *Scientific American, 187*(5), 21–25.

Roediger, H. L., & Neely, J. H. (1982). Retrieval blocks in episodic and semantic memory. *Canadian Journal of Psychology, 36*(2), 213–242.

Rogers, C. R. (1954). Toward a theory of creativity. *ETC: A Review of General Semantics, 11*(4), 249–260.

Rogers, C. R. (1961). *On becoming a person: A therapist's view of psychotherapy*. Boston, MA: Houghton-Mifflin.

Rogers, E. M. (1962). *Diffusion of innovations*. New York: Free Press of Glencoe.

Rogoff, B. (1998). Cognition as a collaborative process. In D. Kuhn & R. S. Siegler (Eds.), *Handbook of child psychology* (5th ed., Vol. 2): *Cognition, perception, and language* (pp. 679–744). New York: Wiley.

Roid, G. H. (2003). *Stanford-Binet intelligence scales* (5th ed.). Itasca, IL: Riverside.

Root-Bernstein, R., & Root-Bernstein, M. (1999). *Sparks of genius: The 13 thinking tools of the world's most creative people*. Boston: Houghton-Mifflin.

Root-Bernstein, R. S., Bernstein, M., & Garnier, H. (1993). Identification of scientists making long-term, high-impact contributions, with notes on their methods of working. *Creativity Research Journal, 6*, 329–343.

Root-Bernstein, M., & Root-Bernstein, R. (2006). Imaginary worldplay in childhood and maturity and its impact on adult creativity. *Creativity Research Journal, 18*(4), 405–425.

Rosaldo, R., Lavie, S., & Narayan, K. (1993). Introduction: Creativity in anthropology. In S. Lavie, K. Narayan, & R. Rosaldo (Eds.), *Creativity/anthropology* (pp. 1–8). Ithaca: Cornell University Press.

Rose, A. M. (1969). Four interviews. *Arts Magazine, 43.*

Rosengren, K. E. (1985). Time and literary fame. *Poetics, 14,* 157–172.

Rosenthal, S. (2011). Tao Te Ching. Retrieved Sep. 1, 2011, from http://www.vl-site.org/taoism/ttcstan1.html

Rosner, S., & Abt, L. E. (1974). Conclusions. In S. Rosner & L. E. Abt (Eds.), *Essays in creativity* (pp. 191–200). Croton-on-Hudson, NY: North River Press.

Ross, B. M. (1976). Preferences for nonrepresentational drawings by Navaho and other children. *Journal of Cross-Cultural Psychology, 7,* 145–156.

Rothenberg, A. (1979). *The emerging goddess: The creative process in art, science, and other fields.* Chicago: University of Chicago Press.

Rothenberg, A. (1990). *Creativity and madness: New findings and old stereotypes.* Baltimore, MD: Johns Hopkins Press.

Rothenberg, A. (2001). Bipolar illness, creativity, and treatment. *Psychiatric Quarterly, 72*(2), 131–147.

Rothstein, E. (1997, Oct. 26). Where a democracy and its money have no place. *New York Times,* pp. AR1, 39.

Rowatt, W. C., Nesselroade, K. P., Beggan, J. K., & Allison, S. T. (1997). Perceptions of brainstorming in groups: The quality over quantity hypothesis. *Journal of Creative Behavior, 31*(2), 131–150.

Rowe, J., & Partridge, D. (1993). Creativity: A survey of AI approaches. *Artificial Intelligence Review, 7,* 43–70.

Rubin, D. C. (1995). *Memory in oral traditions: The cognitive psychology of epic, ballads, and counting-out rhymes.* New York: Oxford University Press.

Rudowicz, E. (2004). Creativity: Developmental and cross-cultural issues. In S. Lau, A. N. N. Hui, & G. Y. C. Ng (Eds.), *Creativity: When East meets West* (pp. 55–86). Singapore: World Scientific Publishing Co.

Runco, M. A. (1984). Teachers' judgments of creativity and social validation of divergent thinking tests. *Perceptual and Motor Skills, 59,* 711–717.

Runco, M. A. (1986). Predicting children's creative performance. *Psychological Reports, 59,* 1247–1254.

Runco, M. A. (1989). The creativity of children's art. *Child Study Journal, 19*(3), 177–189.

Runco, M. A. (Ed.). (1991a). *Divergent thinking.* Norwood, NJ: Ablex.

Runco, M. A. (1991b). The evaluative, valuative, and divergent thinking of children. *Journal of Creative Behavior, 25,* 311–319.

Runco, M. A. (1993, May). *Critical creative thought.* Paper presented at the Wallace Symposium, University of Kansas.

Runco, M. A. (Ed.). (1994). *Problem finding, problem solving, and creativity.* Norwood, NJ: Ablex Publishing Corporation.

Runco, M. A. (1997). *Creativity research handbook, Volume one.* Cresskill, NJ: Hampton Press.

Runco, M. A. (2003). Idea evaluation, divergent thinking, and creativity. In M. A. Runco (Ed.), *Critical creative processes* (pp. 69–94). Cresskill, NJ: Hampton Press.

Runco, M. A. (2004). Creativity. *Annual Review of Psychology, 55,* 657–687.

Runco, M. A. (2007). *Creativity: Theories and themes: Research, development, and practice.* Burlington, MA: Elsevier Academic Press.

Runco, M. A., & Albert, R. S. (1986). The threshold theory regarding creativity and intelligence: An empirical test with gifted and nongifted children. *Creative Child and Adult Quarterly, II*(4), 213–218.

Runco, M. A., & Albert, R. S. (Eds.). (1990). *Theories of creativity.* Newbury Park, CA: Sage.

Runco, M. A., & Bahleda, M. D. (1987). Implicit theories of artistic, scientific, and everyday creativity. *Journal of Creative Behavior, 20*, 93–98.

Runco, M. A., & Chand, I. (1994). Problem finding, evaluative thinking, and creativity. In M. A. Runco (Ed.), *Problem finding, problem solving, and creativity* (pp. 40–76). Norwood, NJ: Ablex.

Runco, M. A., & Dow, G. T. (2004). Assessing the accuracy of judgments of originality on three divergent thinking tests. *Korean Journal of Thinking and Problem Solving, 14*(2), 5–14.

Runco, M. A., & Johnson, D. (1993). Parents' and teachers' implicit theories of children's creativity. *Child Study Journal, 23*(2), 91–113.

Runco, M. A., & Okuda, S. M. (1988). Problem discovery, divergent thinking, and the creative process. *Journal of Youth and Adolescence, 17*(3), 211–220.

Runco, M. A., Plucker, J. A., & Lim, W. (2000–2001). Development and psychometric integrity of a measure of ideational behavior. *Creativity Research Journal, 13*, 393–400.

Runco, M. A., & Pritzker, S. (Eds.). (1999). *Encyclopedia of creativity*. New York: Academic Press.

Runco, M. A., & Richards, R. (1997). *Eminent creativity, everyday creativity, and health*. Norwood, NJ: Ablex.

Runco, M. A., & Smith, W. R. (1992). Interpersonal and intrapersonal evaluations of creative ideas. *Personality and Individual Differences, 13*, 295–302.

Runco, M. A., & Vega, L. (1990). Evaluating the creativity of children's ideas. *Journal of Social Behavior and Personality, 5*, 439–452.

Rushton, J. P. (1990). Creativity, intelligence, and psychoticism. *Personality and Individual Differences, 11*, 1291–1298.

Russ, S. W. (1996). Development of creative processes in children. In M. A. Runco (Ed.), *Creativity from childhood through adulthood: The developmental issues* (pp. 31–42). San Francisco, CA: Jossey-Bass.

Russ, S. W., Robins, A. L., & Christiano, B. A. (1999). Pretend play: Longitudinal prediction of creativity and affect in fantasy in children. *Creativity Research Journal, 12*(2), 129–139.

Sacks, O. (1970). *The man who mistook his wife for a hat*. New York: Harper Collins.

Saltelli, A., & Villalba, E. (2009). How about composite indicators? In E. Villalba (Ed.), *Measuring creativity* (pp. 17–24). Luxembourg: European Union.

Sandkühler, S., & Bhattacharya, J. (2008). Deconstructing insight: EEG correlates of insightful problem solving. *PLoS One, 3*(1), e1459.

Sante, L. (1998, Jan. 4). They know what we like. *New York Times Book Review*, p. 8.

Sarton, M. (1980). *Writings on writing*. Orono, ME: Puckerbrush Press.

SARK. (1992). *Inspiration sandwich: Stories to inspire our creative freedom*. Berkeley, CA: Celestial Arts/ Ten Speed Press.

Sass, L. (1992). *Madness and modernism: Insanity in the light of modern art, literature, and thought*. New York: Basic Books.

Sass, L. A. (2000–2001). Schizophrenia, modernism, and the "creative imagination": On creativity and psychopathology. *Creativity Research Journal, 13*(1), 55–74.

Sass, L. A., & Schuldberg, D. (2000–2001). Introduction to special section on creativity and the schizophrenia spectrum. *Creativity Research Journal, 13*(1), 1–4.

Sawyer, R. K. (1993). He blinded me with science: Review of Colin Martindale, *The clockwork muse: The predictability of artistic change*. *Creativity Research Journal, 6*, 461–464.

Sawyer, R. K. (1996). The semiotics of improvisation: The pragmatics of musical and verbal performance. *Semiotica, 108*(3/4), 269–306.

Sawyer, R. K. (Ed.). (1997a). *Creativity in performance*. Greenwich, CT: Ablex.

Sawyer, R. K. (1997b). *Pretend play as improvisation: Conversation in the preschool classroom.* Mahwah, NJ: Lawrence Erlbaum Associates.

Sawyer, R. K. (2000). Improvisation and the creative process: Dewey, Collingwood, and the aesthetics of spontaneity. *Journal of Aesthetics and Art Criticism, 58*(2), 149–161.

Sawyer, R. K. (2001a). *Creating conversations: Improvisation in everyday discourse.* Cresskill, NJ: Hampton Press.

Sawyer, R. K. (2001b). Emergence in sociology: Contemporary philosophy of mind and some implications for sociological theory. *American Journal of Sociology, 107*(3), 551–585.

Sawyer, R. K. (2003a). Emergence in creativity and development. In R. K. Sawyer, V. John-Steiner, S. Moran, R. Sternberg, D. H. Feldman, M. Csikszentmihalyi, & J. Nakamura (Eds.), *Creativity and development* (pp. 12–60). New York: Oxford.

Sawyer, R. K. (2003b). Evaluative processes during group improvisational performance. In M. A. Runco (Ed.), *Critical creative processes* (pp. 303–327). Cresskill, NJ: Hampton Press.

Sawyer, R. K. (2003c). *Group creativity: Music, theater, collaboration.* Mahwah, NJ: Erlbaum.

Sawyer, R. K. (2003d). *Improvised dialogues: Emergence and creativity in conversation.* Westport, CT: Greenwood.

Sawyer, R. K. (2004). Creative teaching: Collaborative discussion as disciplined improvisation. *Educational Researcher, 33*(2), 12–20.

Sawyer, R. K. (2005a). Music and conversation. In D. E. Miell, R. MacDonald & D. Hargreaves (Eds.), *Musical communication* (pp. 45–60). Oxford, UK: Oxford University Press.

Sawyer, R. K. (2005b). *Social emergence: Societies as complex systems.* New York: Cambridge.

Sawyer, R. K. (2006a). Analyzing collaborative discourse. In R. K. Sawyer (Ed.), *Cambridge handbook of the learning sciences* (pp. 187–204). New York: Cambridge.

Sawyer, R. K. (Ed.). (2006b). *Cambridge handbook of the learning sciences.* New York: Cambridge University Press.

Sawyer, R. K. (2006c). *Explaining creativity: The science of human innovation.* New York: Oxford.

Sawyer, R. K. (2006d). The new science of learning. In R. K. Sawyer (Ed.), *Cambridge handbook of the learning sciences* (pp. 1–16). New York: Cambridge.

Sawyer, R. K. (2006e). The schools of the future. In R. K. Sawyer (Ed.), *Cambridge handbook of the learning sciences* (pp. 567–580). New York: Cambridge.

Sawyer, R. K. (2007). *Group genius: The creative power of collaboration.* New York: BasicBooks.

Sawyer, R. K. (2008). Creativity, innovation, and obviousness. *Lewis & Clark Law Review, 2*(12), 461–487.

Sawyer, R. K. (2009a). The collaborative nature of innovation. *Journal of Law and Policy, 30,* 293–324.

Sawyer, R. K. (2009b). Writing as a collaborative act. In S. B. Kaufman & J. C. Kaufman (Eds.), *The psychology of creative writing* (pp. 166–179). New York: Cambridge University Press.

Sawyer, R. K. (Ed.). (2011). *Structure and improvisation in creative teaching.* New York: Cambridge University Press.

Sawyer, R. K., & Bunderson, J. S. (in press). Innovation research in organizational behavior. In A. Thakor (Ed.), *Innovation: What do we know?* Singapore: World Scientific Press.

Sawyer, R. K., & DeZutter, S. (2009). Distributed creativity: How collective creations emerge from collaboration. *Psychology of Aesthetics, Creativity, and the Arts, 3*(2), 81–92.

Sawyer, R. K., John-Steiner, V., Moran, S., Sternberg, R., Feldman, D. H., Csikszentmihalyi, M., et al. (2003). *Creativity and development.* New York: Oxford.

Scardamalia, M., & Bereiter, C. (2006). Knowledge building. In R. K. Sawyer (Ed.), *Cambridge handbook of the learning sciences* (pp. 97–115). New York: Cambridge University Press.

Schacter, J., Thum, Y. M., & Zifkin, D. (2006). How much does creative teaching enhance elementary students' achievement? *Journal of Creative Behavior, 40*(1), 47–72.

Schaffer, S. (1994). Making up discovery. In M. A. Boden (Ed.), *Dimensions of creativity* (pp. 13–51). Cambridge: MIT Press.

Schank, R. C. (1988). Creativity as a mechanical process. In R. J. Sternberg (Ed.), *The nature of creativity* (pp. 220–238). New York: Cambridge University Press.

Schiavo, P. (2001, Fall). Comments: Wolfgang Amadeus Mozart. *St. Louis Symphony Orchestra Stagebill,* 24b–24c.

Schlaug, G. (2006). The brain of musicians: A model for functional and structural adaptation. *Annals of the New York Academy of Sciences, 930,* 281–299.

Schlesinger, J. (2009). Creative misconceptions: A closer look at the evidence for the "mad genius" hypothesis. *Psychology of Aesthetics, Creativity, and the Arts, 3*(2), 62–72.

Schneider, E. (1953). *Coleridge, opium, and Kubla Khan.* Chicago: University of Chicago Press.

Schooler, C. (1972). Birth order effects: Not here, not now! *Psychological Bulletin, 78,* 161–175.

Schooler, J. W., Fallshore, M., & Fiore, S. M. (1995). Insight and problem solving. In R. J. Sternberg & J. E. Davidson (Eds.), *The nature of insight* (pp. 559–587). Cambridge: MIT Press.

Schooler, J. W., & Melcher, J. (1995). The ineffability of insight. In S. M. Smith, T. B. Ward, & R. A. Finke (Eds.), *The creative cognition approach* (pp. 97–133). Cambridge: MIT Press.

Schooler, J. W., Ohlsson, S., & Brooks, K. (1993). Thoughts beyond words: When language overshadows insight. *Journal of Experimental Psychology: General, 122*(2), 166–183.

Schramm, S. L. (2002). *Transforming the curriculum: Thinking outside the box.* Lanham, MD: Scarecrow Education.

Schuldberg, D. (2000–2001). Six subclinical "spectrum" traits in "normal creativity." *Creativity Research Journal, 13*(1), 5–16.

Schumpeter, J. (1942/1975). *Capitalism, socialism, and democracy.* New York: Harper.

Schutz, A. (1964). Making music together: A study in social relationships. In A. Brodessen (Ed.), *Collected papers* (Vol. 2): *Studies in social theory* (pp. 159–178). The Hague: Martinus Nijhoff.

Schwartz, B. (1982). Reinforcement-induced behavioral stereotypy: How not to teach people to discover rules. *Journal of Experimental Psychology: General, 111,* 23–59.

Schwartz, D. L. (1995). The emergence of abstract representations in dyad problem solving. *Journal of the Learning Sciences, 4*(3), 321–354.

Scott, C. L. (1999). Teachers' biases towards creative children. *Creativity Research Journal, 12*(4), 321–328.

Scott, G., Leritz, L. E., & Mumford, M. D. (2004). The effectiveness of creativity training: A quantitative review. *Creativity Research Journal, 16*(4), 361–388.

Seabrook, J. (1997, Jan. 6). Why is the force still with us? *New Yorker,* 40–53.

Seger, C. A., Desmond, J. E., Glover, G. H., & Gabrieli, J. D. (2000). Functional magnetic resonance imaging evidence for right-hemisphere involvement in unusual semantic relationships. *Neuropsychology, 14,* 361–369.

Seham, A. E. (2001). *Whose improv is it anyway? Beyond Second City.* Jackson, MS: University Press of Mississippi.

Seifert, C. M., Meyer, D. E., Davidson, N., Patalano, A. L., & Yaniv, I. (1995). Demystification of cognitive insight: Opportunistic assimilation and the prepared-mind perspective. In R. J. Sternberg & J. E. Davidson (Eds.), *The nature of insight* (pp. 65–124). Cambridge: MIT Press.

Selfe, L. (1977). *Nadia: A case of extraordinary drawing ability in an autistic child.* New York: Academic Press.

Sethi, R., Smith, D. C., & Park, C. W. (2001). Cross-functional product development teams, creativity, and the innovativeness of consumer products. *Journal of Marketing Research, 38,* 73–85.

Seyba, M. E. (1984). *Imaging: A different way of thinking.* Hawthorne, NJ: Educational Impressions.

Sfard, A. (2002). The interplay of intimations and implementations: Generating new discourse with new symbolic tools. *Journal of the Learning Sciences, 11*(2–3), 319–357.

Shalley, C. E., & Perry-Smith, J. E. (2001). Effects of social-psychological factors on creative performance: The role of informational and controlling expected evaluation and modeling experience. *Organizational Behavior and Human Decision Processes, 84,* 1–22.

Shalley, C. E., Zhou, J., & Oldham, G. R. (2004). Effects of personal and contextual characteristics on creativity: Where should we go from here? *Journal of Management, 30,* 933–958.

Shane, S. (1992). Why do some societies invent more than others? *Journal of Business Venturing, 7*(1), 29–47.

Shane, S. (1993). Cultural influences on national rates of innovation. *Journal of Business Venturing, 8*(1), 59–73.

Shelley, P. B. (1901). *The complete poetical works of Shelley* (G. E. Woodberry, Trans.). Boston, MA: Houghton Mifflin.

Shelley, P. B. (1965). *A defence of poetry.* Indianapolis, IN: Bobbs-Merrill.

Shenk, J. W. (2010, Sept. 14). Two is the magic number: A new science of creativity. *Slate,* id 2267004.

Shepard, R. N. (1978). Externalization of mental images and the act of creation. In B. S. Randhawa & W. E. Coffman (Eds.), *Visual learning, thinking, and communication* (pp. 133–189). New York: Academic Press.

Sheth, B. R., Sandkühler, S., & Bhattacharya, J. (2008). Posterior beta and anterior gamma oscillations predict cognitive insight. *Journal of Cognitive Neuroscience, 21*(7), 1269–1279.

Shields, D. (2010). *Reality hunger: A manifesto.* New York: Knopf.

Shirky, C. (2010). *Cognitive surplus: Creativity and generosity in a connected age.* New York: Penguin Press.

Shostak, M. (1993). The creative individual in the world of the !Kung San. In S. Lavie, K. Narayan, & R. Rosaldo (Eds.), *Creativity/anthropology* (pp. 54–69). Ithaca: Cornell University Press.

Shulman, S. (2002). *Unlocking the sky: Glenn Hammond Curtiss and the race to invent the airplane.* New York: HarperCollins.

Silver, H. R. (1981). Calculating risks: The socio-economic foundations of aesthetic innovations in an Ashanti carving community. *Ethnology, 20,* 101–114.

Silvia, P. J. (2007). Review of the book *Group Genius: The Creative Power of Collaboration. Psychology of Aesthetics, Creativity, and the Arts, 1,* 254–255.

Silvia, P. J. (2008a). Creativity and intelligence revisited: A latent variable analysis of Wallach and Kogan (1965). *Creativity Research Journal, 20*(1), 34–39.

Silvia, P. J. (2008b). Discernment and creativity: How well can people identify their most creative ideas? *Psychology of Aesthetics, Creativity, and the Arts, 2*(3), 139–146.

Silvia, P. J., & Kaufman, J. C. (2010). Creativity and mental illness. In J. C. Kaufman & R. J. Sternberg (Eds.), *The Cambridge handbook of creativity* (pp. 381–394). Cambridge, UK: Cambridge University Press.

Silvia, P. J., Martin, C., & Nusbaum, E. C. (2009). A snapshot of creativity: Evaluating a quick and simple method for assessing divergent thinking. *Thinking Skills and Creativity, 4,* 79–85.

Silvia, P. J., Winterstein, B. P., & Willse, J. T. (2008a). Rejoinder: The madness to our method: Some thoughts on divergent thinking. *Psychology of Aesthetics, Creativity, and the Arts, 2*(2), 109–114.

Silvia, P. J., Winterstein, B. P., Willse, J. T., Barona, C. M., Cram, J. T., Hess, K. I., et al. (2008b). Assessing creativity with divergent thinking tasks: Exploring the reliability and validity of new subjective scoring methods. *Psychology of Aesthetics, Creativity, and the Arts, 2*(2), 68–85.

Simon, H. A. (1957). *Models of man, social and rational.* New York: Wiley.

Simon, H. A. (1966). Scientific discovery and the psychology of problem solving. In R. G. Colodny (Ed.), *Mind and cosmos: Essays in contemporary science and philosophy* (pp. 22–40). Pittsburgh, PA: University of Pittsburgh Press.

Simon, H. A. (1977). *Boston studies in the philosophy of science: Vol. 54. Models of discovery.* Boston: Reidel.

Simon, H. A., & Chase, W. (1973). Skill in chess. *American Scientist, 61*, 364–403.

Simon, R. J. (1974). The work habits of eminent scientists. *Sociology of Work and Occupations, 1*, 327–335.

Simonton, D. K. (1976). Biographical determinants of achieved eminence: A multivariate approach to the Cox data. *Journal of Personality and Social Psychology, 33*, 218–226.

Simonton, D. K. (1983). Formal education, eminence, and dogmatism. *Journal of Creative Behavior, 17*, 149–162.

Simonton, D. K. (1984a). Artistic creativity and interpersonal relationships across and within generations. *Journal of Personality and Social Psychology, 46*, 1273–1286.

Simonton, D. K. (1984b). Creative productivity and age: A mathematical model based on a two-step cognitive process. *Developmental Review, 4*(1), 77–111.

Simonton, D. K. (1984c). *Genius, Creativity, and leadership.* Cambridge, MA: Harvard University Press.

Simonton, D. K. (1988a). Creativity, leadership, and chance. In R. J. Sternberg (Ed.), *The nature of creativity* (pp. 386–426). New York: Cambridge University Press.

Simonton, D. K. (1988b). *Scientific genius: A psychology of science.* New York: Cambridge University Press.

Simonton, D. K. (1994). *Greatness: Who makes history and why.* New York: Guilford.

Simonton, D. K. (1997a). Creative productivity: A predictive and explanatory model of career trajectories and landmarks. *Psychological Review, 104*(1), 66–89.

Simonton, D. K. (1997b). Creativity in personality, developmental, and social psychology: Any links with cognitive psychology? In T. B. Ward, S. M. Smith & J. Vaid (Eds.), *Creative thought: An investigation of conceptual structures and processes* (pp. 309–324). Washington, DC: American Psychological Association.

Simonton, D. K. (1999a). Creativity from a historiometric perspective. In R. J. Sternberg (Ed.), *The handbook of creativity* (pp. 116–133). New York: Cambridge.

Simonton, D. K. (1999b). *Origins of genius: Darwinian perspectives on creativity.* New York: Oxford University Press.

Simonton, D. K. (2007). Review of Creativity: Theories and Themes. *Psychology of Aesthetics, Creativity, and the Arts, 1*, 251–252.

Simonton, D. K. (2011). *Great flicks: Scientific studies of cinematic creativity and aesthetics.* New York: Oxford University Press.

Singapore Ministry of Education. (2002). Masterplan 2. Available online at http://ictconnection.edu-mall.sg/. Accessed Sep. 1, 2011.

Singer, J. L., & Antrobus, J. S. (1963). A factor-analytic study of daydreaming and conceptually-related cognitive and personality variables. *Perceptual and Motor Skills, 17*, 187–209.

Sio, U. N., & Rudowicz, E. (2007). The role of an incubation period in creative problem solving. *Creativity Research Journal, 19*(2–3), 307–318.

Skinner, B. F. (1968). *The technology of teaching.* New York: Appleton-Century-Crofts.

Skinner, B. F. (1972). A lecture on "having" a poem. In B. F. Skinner (Ed.), *Cumulative record: A selection of papers* (pp. 345–355). New York: Appleton-Century-Crofts.

Skov, M., & Vartanian, O. (Eds.). (2009). *Neuroaesthetics*. Amityville, NY: Baywood Publishing Company.

Sligh, A. C., Connors, F. A., & Roskos-Ewoldsen, B. (2005). Relation of creativity to fluid and crystallized intelligence. *Journal of Creative Behavior, 39,* 123–136.

Slivka, R. (1971, October). Laugh-in in clay. *Craft Horizons, 31,* 39–47, 63.

Sloboda, J. (Ed.). (1988). *Generative processes in music*. New York: Oxford.

Sloboda, J. A. (1985). *The musical mind: The cognitive psychology of music*. New York: Oxford.

Sloboda, J. A. (1991). Music structure and emotional response: Some empirical findings. *Psychology of Music, 19,* 110–120.

Smallwood, J., & Schooler, J. W. (2006). The restless mind. *Psychological Bulletin, 132*(6), 946–958.

Smith, E. E., & Osherson, D. N. (1984). Conceptual combination with prototype concepts. *Cognitive Science, 8*(4), 337–361.

Smith, G. J. W., & Carlsson, I. (1987). A new creativity test. *Journal of Creative Behavior, 21*(1), 7–14.

Smith, G. J. W., & Carlsson, I. (1990). *The CFT: A test of the creative function*. Stockholm: Psykologiforlaget.

Smith, L. P. (1961). Four words: Romantic, originality, creative, genius. In *S. P. E. Tracts, I–XX* (Vol. I, pp. 521–566). London: Oxford University Press.

Smith, P. K., & Whitney, S. (1987). Play and associative fluency: Experimenter effects may be responsible for previous positive findings. *Developmental Psychology, 23,* 49–53.

Smith, S. M. (1995). Fixation, incubation, and insight in memory and creative thinking. In S. M. Smith, T. B. Ward, & R. A. Finke (Eds.), *The creative cognition approach* (pp. 135–156). Cambridge: MIT Press.

Smith, S. M., & Blankenship, S. E. (1989). Incubation effects. *Bulletin of the Psychonomic Society, 27*(4), 311–314.

Smith, S. M., & Dodds, R. (1999). Incubation. In M. A. Runco & S. Pritzker (Eds.), *Encyclopedia of creativity*. San Diego, CA: Academic Press, pp. 39–44.

Sparrowe, R. T., Liden, R. C., Wayne, S. J., & Kraimer, M. L. (2001). Social networks and the performance of individuals and groups. *Academy of Management Journal, 44*(2), 316–325.

Spearman, C. (1923). *The nature of intelligence and the principles of cognition*. London: Macmillan.

Sperry, R. W., Gazzaniga, M. S., & Bogen, J. E. (1969). Interhemispheric relationships: The neocortical commissures; syndromes of hemispheric disconnection. In P. J. Vinken & G. W. Bruyn (Eds.), *Disorders of speech, perception, and symbolic behaviour* (pp. 273–290). New York: Wiley Interscience.

Springer, S. P., & Deutsch, G. (1993). *Left brain, right brain*. San Francisco, CA: W. H. Freeman & Company. (First edition published 1981.)

Spurzheim, J. K. (1826). *The anatomy of the brain, with a general view of the nervous system*. London, UK: S. Highley.

Srinivasan, N. (2007). Cognitive neuroscience of creativity: EEG based approaches. *Methods, 42,* 109–116.

Standage, T. (1998). *The Victorian Internet: The remarkable story of the telegraph and the nineteenth century's on-line pioneers*. New York: Walker and Company.

Stanislavsky, K. (1936). *An actor prepares*. New York: Theatre Arts.

Stanislavsky, K. (1962). *Building a character*. New York: Theatre Arts Books.

Starko, A. J. (1999). Problem finding: A key to creative productivity. In A. S. Fishkin, B. Cramond, & P. Olszewski-Kubilius (Eds.), *Investigating creativity in youth: Research and methods* (pp. 75–96). Cresskill, NJ: Hampton.

Stasser, G., Taylor, L. A., & Hanna, C. (1989). Information sampling in structured and unstructured discussions of three- and six-person groups. *Journal of Personality and Social Psychology, 57*, 67–78.

Stasser, G., & Titus, W. (1985). Pooling of unshared information in group decision making: Biased information sampling during discussion. *Journal of Personality and Social Psychology, 48*, 1467–1478.

Stasser, G., & Titus, W. (2003). Hidden profiles: A brief history. *Psychological Inquiry, 14*(3&4), 304–313.

Stein, M. I. (1958). Toward developing more imaginative creativity in students. In R. M. Cooper (Ed.), *The two ends of the log* (pp. 69–75). Minneapolis, MN: University of Minnesota Press.

Stein, M. I. (1961/1963). Creativity in a free society. *Educational Horizons, 41*, 115–130. (Reprinted with minor changes from the October 1961 issue of *Graduate Comment* at Wayne State University, Detroit, MI.)

Stein, M. I. (1967). Creativity and culture. In R. L. Mooney & T. A. Razik (Eds.), *Explorations in creativity* (pp. 109–119). New York: Harper & Row.

Stein, M. I. (1974). *Stimulating creativity* (Vol. 1): *Individual procedures.* San Francisco, CA: Academic Press.

Stein, M. I. (1987). Creativity research at the crossroads: A 1985 perspective. In S. G. Isaksen (Ed.), *Frontiers of creativity research: Beyond the basics* (pp. 417–427). Buffalo, NY: Beary Limited.

Steinberg, L. (1972). *Other criteria: Confrontations with twentieth-century art.* New York: Oxford.

Steiner, I. D. (1972). *Group processes and productivity.* New York: Academic Press.

Steiner, W. (1996, March 10). In love with the myth of the "outsider." *New York Times,* pp. H45, H48.

Sternberg, R. (1985a). *Beyond IQ: A triarchic theory of human intelligence.* New York: Cambridge.

Sternberg, R. J. (1985b). Implicit theories of intelligence, creativity, and wisdom. *Journal of Personality and Social Psychology, 49*(3), 607–627.

Sternberg, R. J. (Ed.). (1988). *The nature of creativity.* New York: Cambridge University Press.

Sternberg, R. J. (1996). *Successful intelligence.* New York: Simon & Schuster.

Sternberg, R. J. (Ed.). (1999a). *Handbook of creativity.* New York: Cambridge University Press.

Sternberg, R. J. (1999b). The theory of successful intelligence. *Review of General Psychology, 3*(4), 292–316.

Sternberg, R. J. (2003). The development of creativity as a decision-making process. In R. K. Sawyer (Ed.), *Creativity and development* (pp. 91–138). New York: Oxford.

Sternberg, R. J. (2006). Stalking the elusive creativity quark: Toward a comprehensive theory of creativity. In P. Locher, C. Martindale, & L. Dorfman (Eds.), *New directions in aesthetics, creativity, and the arts* (pp. 79–104). Amityville, NY: Baywood Publishing Company.

Sternberg, R. J., & Collaborators, T. R. P. (2006). The Rainbow Project: Enhancing the SAT through assessments of analytic, practical, and creative skills. *Intelligence, 34*, 321–350.

Sternberg, R. J., Conway, B. E., Ketron, J. L., & Bernstein, M. (1981). People's conceptions of intelligence. *Journal of Personality and Social Psychology, 41*, 37–55.

Sternberg, R. J., & Davidson, J. E. (Eds.). (1995). *The nature of insight.* Cambridge: MIT Press.

Sternberg, R. J., & Dess, N. K. (2001). Creativity for the new millennium. *American Psychologist, 56*(4), 332.

Sternberg, R. J., Grigorenko, E. L., Ferrari, M., & Clinkenbeard, P. (1999). A triarchic analysis of an aptitude-treatment interaction. *European Journal of Psychological Assessment, 15*(1), 3–13.

Sternberg, R. J., Grigorenko, E. L., & Singer, J. L. (2004). *Creativity: From potential to realization.* Washington, DC: American Psychological Association.

Sternberg, R. J., Grigorenko, E. L., & Zhang, L. (2008a). A reply to two stylish critiques: Response to Hunt (2008) and Mayer (2008). *Perspectives on Psychological Science, 3*(6), 516–517.

Sternberg, R. J., Grigorenko, E. L., & Zhang, L. (2008b). Styles of learning and thinking matter in instruction and assessment. *Perspectives on Psychological Science, 3*, 486–506.

Sternberg, R. J., & Lubart, T. (1991). An investment theory of creativity and its development. *Human Development, 34*, 1–31.

Sternberg, R. J., & Lubart, T. (1995). *Defying the crowd: Cultivating creativity in a culture of conformity.* New York: Free Press.

Sternberg, R. J., & Lubart, T. (1996). Investing in creativity. *American Psychologist, 51*, 677–688.

Sternberg, R. J., & Lubart, T. (1999). The concept of creativity: Prospects and paradigms. In R. J. Sternberg (Ed.), *The handbook of creativity* (pp. 3–15). New York: Cambridge.

Sternberg, R. J., & Wagner, R. K. (1993). The g-ocentric view of intelligence and job performance is wrong. *Current Directions in Psychological Science, 2*(1), 1–5.

Sternberg, R. J., & Williams, W. M. (1996). *How to develop student creativity.* Alexandria, VA: Association for Supervision and Curriculum Development.

Stevenson, H. H., & Sahlman, W. A. (1989). The entrepreneurial process. In P. Burns & J. Dewhurst (Eds.), *Small business and entrepreneurship* (pp. 94–157). Houndsmills: Macmillan Education.

Storr, A. (1972). *The dynamics of creation.* New York: Atheneum.

Strack, F., & Deutsch, R. (2004). Reflective and impulsive determinants of social behavior. *Personality and Social Psychology Review, 8*, 220–247.

Strasberg, L. (1960). On acting. In J. D. Summerfield & L. Thatch (Eds.), *The creative mind and method: Exploring the nature of creativeness in American arts, sciences, and professions* (pp. 83–87). Austin, TX: University of Texas Press.

Strauss, N. (2002, March 24). The country music country radio ignores. *New York Times*, pp. AR1, AR31.

Stravinsky, I. (1947). *The poetics of music.* Cambridge, MA: Harvard University Press.

Stroebe, W. (2010). The graying of academia: Will it reduce scientific productivity? *American Psychologist, 65*(7), 660–673.

Stroebe, W., & Diehl, M. (1994). Why groups are less effective than their members: On productivity losses in idea-generating groups. *European Review of Social Psychology, 5*, 271–303.

Stroebe, W., & Frey, B. S. (1982). Self-interest and collective action: The economics and psychology of public goods. *British Journal of Social Psychology, 21*, 121–137.

Strokrocki, M. (Ed.). (2005). *Interdisciplinary art education: Building bridges to connect disciplines and cultures.* Reston, VA: National Art Education Association.

Stucky, N. (1988). Unnatural acts: Performing natural conversation. *Literature in Performance, 8*(2), 28–39.

Stucky, N. (1993). Toward an aesthetics of natural performance. *Text and Performance Quarterly, 13*, 168–180.

Subotnik, R. F., & Arnold, K. D. (1994). Longitudinal study of giftedness and talent. In R. F. Subotnik & K. D. Arnold (Eds.), *Beyond Terman: Contemporary longitudinal studies of giftedness and talent* (pp. 1–23). Norwood, NJ: Ablex.

Subotnik, R. F., Karp, D. E., & Morgan, E. R. (1989). High IQ children at mid-life: An investigation into the generalizability of Terman's genetic studies of genius. *Roeper Review, 11*(3), 139–144.

Subotnik, R. F., Kassan, L., Summers, E., & Wasser, A. (1993). *Genius revisited: High-IQ children grown up.* Norwood, NJ: Ablex.

Subramaniam, K., Kounios, J., Parrish, T. B., & Jung-Beeman, M. (2009). A brain mechanism for facilitation of insight by positive affect. *Journal of Cognitive Neuroscience, 21*(3), 415–432.

Sulloway, F. (1996). *Born to rebel: Birth order, family dynamics, and creative lives.* New York: Pantheon Books.

Surowiecki, J. (2004). *The wisdom of crowds: Why the many are smarter than the few and how collective wisdom shapes business, economies, societies, and nations*. New York: Doubleday.

Sutton, R. I., & Hargadon, A. B. (1996). Brainstorming groups in context: Effectiveness in a product design firm. *Administrative Science Quarterly, 41*, 685–718.

Sweet, J. (1978). *Something wonderful right away: An oral history of the Second City & the Compass Players*. New York: Avon Books.

Taggar, S. (2002). Individual creativity and group ability to utilize individual creative resources: A multilevel model. *Academy of Management Journal, 45*(2), 315–330.

Talbot, R. J. (1993). Creativity in the organizational context: Implications for training. In S. G. Isaksen, M. C. Murdock, R. L. Firestien, & D. J. Treffinger (Eds.), *Nurturing and developing creativity: The emergence of a discipline* (pp. 177–215). Norwood, NJ: Ablex.

Tardif, T. Z., & Sternberg, R. J. (1988). What do we know about creativity? In R. J. Sternberg (Ed.), *The nature of creativity* (pp. 429–440). New York: Cambridge University Press.

Taylor, C. (1989). *Sources of the self: The making of the modern identity*. Cambridge, UK: Cambridge University Press.

Taylor, C. W. (1959). Some concerns about certain factors in the creativity movement: Spontaneous discussion of total group. In C. W. Taylor (Ed.), *Research Conference on the Identification of Creative Scientific Talent* (pp. 282–286). Salt Lake City, UT: University of Utah Press.

Taylor, C. W. (Ed.). (1959). *The Third (1959) University of Utah Research Conference on the Identification of Creative Scientific Talent*. Salt Lake City, UT: University of Utah Press.

Taylor, C. W. (1962). A tentative description of the creative individual. In S. J. Parnes & H. F. Harding (Eds.), *A source book for creative thinking* (pp. 169–184). New York: Charles Scribner's Sons.

Taylor, C. W. (Ed.). (1964a). *Creativity: Progress and potential*. New York: McGraw-Hill Book Company.

Taylor, C. W. (Ed.). (1964b). *Widening horizons in creativity: The proceedings of the Fifth Utah Creativity ReCearch conference*. New York: John Wiley & Sons.

Taylor, C. W., & Barron, F. (Eds.). (1963). *Scientific creativity: Its recognition and development*. New York: John Wiley & Sons.

Taylor, D. W., Berry, P. C., & Block, C. H. (1958). Does group participation when using brainstorming facilitate or inhibit creative thinking? *Administrative Science Quarterly, 3*(1), 23–47.

Taylor, I. A., & Getzels, J. W. (Eds.). (1975). *Perspectives in creativity*. Chicago, IL: Aldine Publishing Company.

Taylor, M. C., & Saarinen, E. (1994). *Imagologies: Media philosophy*. London: Routledge.

Terman, L. M. (1916). *The measurement of intelligence*. Boston, MA: Houghton-Mifflin.

Terman, L. M. (1922). A new approach to the study of genius. *Psychological Review, 29*(4), 310–318.

Terman, L. M. (Ed.). (1925). *Genetic studies of genius* (Vol. 1): *Mental and physical traits of a thousand gifted children*. Stanford, CA: Stanford University Press.

Terman, L. M., & Oden, M. H. (1947). *Genetic studies of genius* (Vol. 4): *The gifted child grows up*. Stanford, CA: Stanford University Press.

Terman, L. M., & Oden, M. H. (1959). *Genetic studies of genius* (Vol. 5): *The gifted group at mid-life*. Stanford, CA: Stanford University Press.

Tierney, J. (2010, June 29). Discovering the virtues of a wandering mind. *New York Times*, p. D1.

Tierney, P. A., & Farmer, S. M. (2002). Creative self-efficacy: Its potential antecedents and relationship to creative performance. *Academy of Management Journal, 45*(6), 1137–1148.

Tierney, P. A., & Farmer, S. M. (2004). The Pygmalion process and employee creativity. *Journal of Management, 30*(3), 413–432.

Tomkins, C. (2002, Aug. 5). Man of steel. *New Yorker*, 52–63.

Tonelli, G. (1973). Genius from the renaissance to 1770. In P. P. Wiener (Ed.), *Dictionary of the history of ideas* (pp. 293–298). New York: Scribner's.

Torrance, E. P. (1962). *Guiding creative talent.* Englewood Cliffs, NJ: Prentice-Hall.

Torrance, E. P. (1963). *Education and the creative potential.* Minneapolis, MN: University of Minnesota.

Torrance, E. P. (1965). *Rewarding creative behavior: Experiments in classroom creativity.* Englewood Cliffs, NJ: Prentice-Hall.

Torrance, E. P. (1968). A longitudinal examination of the fourth-grade slump in creativity. *Gifted Child Quarterly, 12*, 195–199.

Torrance, E. P. (1970). *Encouraging creativity in the classroom.* Dubuque, IA: W. C. Brown.

Torrance, E. P. (1972). Can we teach children to think creatively? *Journal of Creative Behavior, 6*, 114–143.

Torrance, E. P. (1974). *Torrance Tests of Creative Thinking: Norms-technical manual.* Princeton, NJ: Personnel Press/Ginn.

Torrance, E. P. (1981). Predicting the creativity of elementary school children (1958–1980)—and the teacher who "made a difference." *Gifted Child Quarterly, 25*, 55–62.

Torrance, E. P. (1983). Role of mentors in creative achievement. *Creative Child and Adult Quarterly, 8*, 8–15.

Torrance, E. P. (2008). *The Torrance Tests of Creative Thinking: Norms-technical manual.* Bensenville, IL: Scholastic Testing Service.

Torrance, E. P., & Khatena, J. (1969). Originality of imagery in identifying creative talent in music. *Gifted Child Quarterly, 13*, 3–8.

Torrance, E. P., & Safter, H. T. (1986). Are children becoming more creative? *Journal of Creative Behavior, 20*, 1–13.

Torrance, E. P., & Safter, H. T. (1989). The long-range predictive validity of the Just Suppose Test. *Journal of Creative Behavior, 23*, 219–223.

Treffinger, D. J. (1986). Research on creativity. *Gifted Child Quarterly, 30*(1), 15–19.

Treffinger, D. J., Isaksen, S. G., & Dorval, K. B. (1994). *Creative problem solving: An introduction* (rev. ed.). Sarasota, FL: Center for Creative Learning.

Triandis, H. C. (1994). *Culture and social behavior.* New York: McGraw-Hill.

Triandis, H. C. (1995). *Individualism & collectivism.* Boulder, CO: Westview Press.

Trollope, A. (1883/1989). *Anthony Trollope: An illustrated autobiography.* Wolfeboro, NH: Alan Sutton Publishing.

Tuckman, B. W. (1965). Developmental sequence in small groups. *Psychological Bulletin, 63*, 384–389.

Tuckman, B. W., & Jensen, M. A. (1977). Stages in small group development revisited. *Group and Organizational Studies, 2*, 419–427.

Tuomi, I. (2002). *Networks of innovation: Change and meaning in the age of the Internet.* New York: Oxford.

Turner, S. R. (1994). *The creative process: A computer model of storytelling and creativity.* Mahwah, NJ: Erlbaum.

Turner, V. (1969). *The ritual process.* Harmondsworth, England: Penguin Books.

Tusa, J. (2003). *On creativity: Interviews exploring the process.* London: Methuen.

Tushman, M. L. (1977). Special boundary roles in the innovation process. *Administrative Science Quarterly, 22*, 587–605.

Tylor, E. B. (1889). *Primitive culture: Researches into the development of mythology, philosophy, religion, language, art, and custom.* New York: Holt. (Original work published 1871.)

Urban, K. K., & Jellen, H. G. (1993). *Manual for the test for creative thinking: Drawing production.* Hanover, Germany: University of Hanover.

US Department of Education. (1993). *National excellence: A case for developing America's talent.* Washington, DC: U.S. Department of Education, Office of Educational Research and Improvement.

Uzzi, B., & Spiro, J. (2005). Collaboration and creativity: The small world problem. *American Journal of Sociology, 111*(2), 447–504.

Van der Vegt, G. S., & Bunderson, J. S. (2005). Learning and performance in multidisciplinary teams: The importance of collective team identification. *Academy of Management Journal, 48*(3), 532–547.

Vandenberg, S. G. (Ed.). (1968). *Progress in human behavior genetics.* Baltimore, MD: Johns Hopkins Press.

Varnedoe, K., & Gopnik, A. (1990). *High & low: Modern art, popular culture.* New York: Museum of Modern Art.

Vartanian, O. (2009). Conscious experience of pleasure in art. In M. Skov & O. Vartanian (Eds.), *Neuroaesthetics* (pp. 261–273). Amityville, NY: Baywood Publishing Company.

Vartanian, O., & Goel, V. (2007). Neural correlates of creative cognition. In C. Martindale, P. Locher, & V. M. Petrov (Eds.), *Evolutionary and neurocognitive approaches to aesthetics, creativity, and the arts* (pp. 195–207). Amityville, NJ: Baywood Publishing.

Veblen, T. (1919). The intellectual preeminence of Jews in modern Europe. *Political Science Quarterly, 34,* 33–42.

Verstijnen, I. M. (1997). *Sketches of creative discovery: A psychological inquiry into the role of imagery and sketching in creative discovery.* Technische Universiteit, Delft, The Netherlands.

Verstijnen, I. M., van Leeuwen, C., Goldschmidt, G., Hamel, R., & Hennessey, J. M. (1998). Creative discovery in imagery and perception: Combining is relatively easy, restructuring takes a sketch. *Acta Psychologica, 99,* 177–200.

Vinacke, W. E. (1952). *The psychology of thinking.* New York: McGraw-Hill.

von Hippel, E. (2005). *Democratizing innovation.* Cambridge, MA: MIT Press.

Vygotsky, L. S. (1971). *The psychology of art.* Cambridge: MIT Press. (Originally published in Russian in 1922.)

Waddell, C. (1998). Creativity and mental illness: Is there a link? *Canadian Journal of Psychiatry, 43,* 166–172.

Wageman, R. (1995). Interdependence and group effectiveness. *Administrative Science Quarterly, 40,* 145–180.

Wagner, R. K., & Sternberg, R. J. (1986). Tacit knowledge and intelligence in the everyday world. In R. J. Sternberg & R. K. Wagner (Eds.), *Practical intelligence: Nature and origins of competence in the everyday world* (pp. 51–83). New York: Cambridge University Press.

Wakefield, J. F. (1985). Towards creativity: Problem finding in a divergent-thinking exercise. *Child Study Journal, 15,* 265–270.

Wakefield, J. F. (1991). The outlook for creativity tests. *Journal of Creative Behavior, 25*(3), 184–193.

Wallace, D. B., & Gruber, H. E. (Eds.). (1989). *Creative people at work: Twelve cognitive case studies.* New York: Oxford University Press.

Wallach, A. (1997, Oct. 12). Is it art? Is it good? And who says so? *New York Times,* p. AR36.

Wallach, M. A. (1971). *The intelligence/creativity distinction.* New York: General Learning Press.

Wallach, M. A. (1986). Creativity testing and giftedness. In D. Horowitz & M. O'Brien (Eds.), *The gifted and talented: Developmental perspectives* (pp. 99–123). Washington, DC: American Psychological Association.

Wallach, M. A. (1988). Creativity and talent. In K. Grønhaug & G. Kaufmann (Eds.), *Innovation: A cross-disciplinary perspective* (pp. 13–27). Oslo: Norwegian University Press.

Wallach, M. A., & Kogan, N. (1965). *Modes of thinking in young children: A study of the creativity-intelligence distinction*. New York: Holt, Rinehart & Winston.

Wallach, M. A., & Wing Jr, C. W. (1969). *The talented student: A validation of the creativity-intelligence distinction*. New York: Holt, Rinehart and Winston.

Wallas, G. (1926). *The art of thought*. New York: Harcourt, Brace and Company.

Waller, J. (2002). *Einstein's luck: The truth behind some of the greatest scientific discoveries*. New York: Oxford University Press.

Waller, N. G., Bouchard Jr., T. J., Lykken, D. T., Tellegen, A., & Blacker, D. M. (2003). Creativity, heritability, familiality: Which word does not belong? *Psychological Inquiry, 4*(3), 235–237.

Walpole, M. B., Burton, N. W., Kanyi, K., & Jackenthal, A. (2001). *Selecting successful graduate students: In-depth interviews with GRE users (GRE Board Research Report No. 99–11R, ETS Research Report 02–8)*. Princeton, NJ: Educational Testing Service.

Ward, J. (2006). *The student's guide to cognitive neuroscience*. Hove, UK: Psychology Press.

Ward, T. B. (1994). Structured imagination: The role of category structure in exemplar generation. *Cognitive Psychology, 27*, 1–40.

Ward, T. B. (2001). Creative cognition, conceptual combination, and the creative writing of Stephen R. Donaldson. *American Psychologist, 56*(4), 350–354.

Ward, T. B., Smith, S. M., & Finke, R. A. (1999). Creative cognition. In R. J. Sternberg (Ed.), *Handbook of creativity* (pp. 189–212). Cambridge: Cambridge University Press.

Ward, T. B., Smith, S. M., & Vaid, J. (1997a). Conceptual structures and processes in creative thought. In T. B. Ward, S. M. Smith & J. Vaid (Eds.), *Creative thought: An investigation of conceptual structures and processes* (pp. 1–27). Washington, DC: American Psychological Association.

Ward, T. B., Smith, S. M., & Vaid, J. (Eds.). (1997b). *Creative thought: An investigation of conceptual structures and processes*. Washington, DC: American Psychological Association.

Warrington, E. K., James, M., & Kinsbourne, M. (1966). Drawing disability in relation to laterality of cerebral lesion. *Brain, 89*, 53–82.

Weeks, P. (1990). Musical time as a practical accomplishment: A change in tempo. *Human Studies, 13*, 323–359.

Weeks, P. (1996). Synchrony lost, synchrony regained: The achievement of musical coordination. *Human Studies, 19*, 199–228.

Wegener, B. (1991). Job mobility and social ties: Social resources, prior job, and status attainment. *American Sociological Review, 56*, 60–71.

Wegner, D. M. (1986). Transactive memory: A contemporary analysis of the group mind. In B. Mullen & G. Goethals (Eds.), *Theories of group behavior* (pp. 185–208). New York: Springer-Verlag.

Wehner, L., Csikszentmihalyi, M., & Magyari-Beck, I. (1991). Current approaches used in studying creativity: An exploratory investigation. *Creativity Research Journal, 4*(3), 261–271.

Weick, K. E. (1969). *The social psychology of organizing*. Reading, MA: Addison-Wesley.

Weick, K. E. (2001). *Making sense of the organization*. London: Blackwell.

Weinberg, S. (2002). Afterword: How great equations survive. In G. Farmelo (Ed.), *It must be beautiful: Great equations of modern science* (pp. 253–257). London: Granta Books.

Weiner, R. P. (2000). *Creativity & beyond: Cultures, values, and change*. Albany, NY: State University of New York Press.

Weisberg, R. W. (1986). *Creativity: Genius and other myths*. New York: W. H. Freeman.

Weisberg, R. W. (1988). Problem solving and creativity. In R. J. Sternberg (Ed.), *The nature of creativity* (pp. 148–176). New York: Cambridge University Press.

Weisberg, R. W. (1993). *Creativity: Beyond the myth of genius.* New York: W. H. Freeman.

Weisberg, R. W. (1995). Prolegomena to theories of insight in problem solving: A taxonomy of problems. In R. J. Sternberg & J. E. Davidson (Eds.), *The nature of insight* (pp. 157–196). Cambridge, MA: MIT Press.

Weisberg, R. W. (2006). *Creativity: Understanding innovation in problem solving, science, invention, and the arts.* Hoboken, NJ: Wiley.

Weisberg, R. W., & Alba, J. W. (1981). An examination of the alleged role of "fixation" in the solution of several "insight" problems. *Journal of Experimental Psychology: General, 110*(2), 169–192.

Wells, D. H. (1996). Forced incubation. *Creativity Research Journal, 9*(4), 407–409.

Welsh, G. S. (1969). *Gifted adolescents: A handbook of test results.* Greensboro, NC: Prediction Press.

Welsh, G. S. (1975). *Creativity and intelligence: A personality approach.* Chapel Hill, NC: Institute for Research in Social Science.

Wenzel, M. (1972). *House decoration in Nubia.* London: Duckworth.

Wertheimer, M. (1945). *Productive thinking.* New York: Harper & Brothers.

West, M. A. (2002). Sparkling fountains or stagnant ponds: An integrative model of creativity and innovation implementation in work groups. *Applied Psychology: An International Review, 51*(3), 355–424.

West, M. A. (2003). Innovation implementation in work teams. In P. B. Paulus & B. A. Nijstad (Eds.), *Group creativity: Innovation through collaboration* (pp. 245–276). New York: Oxford.

West, M. A., & Farr, J. L. (Eds.). (1990). *Innovation and creativity at work: Psychological and organizational strategies.* New York: Wiley.

Westby, E. L., & Dawson, V. L. (1995). Creativity: Asset or burden in the classroom? *Creativity Research Journal, 8*(1), 1–10.

White, E. W. (1966). *Stravinsky: The composer and his works.* Berkeley, CA: University of California Press.

White, H. A., & Shah, P. (2006). Uninhibited imaginations: Creativity in adults with attention-deficit/hyperactivity disorder. *Personality and Individual Differences, 40,* 1121–1131.

Whitman, R. D., Holcomb, E., & Zanes, J. (2010). Hemispheric collaboration in creative subjects: Cross-hemisphere priming in a lexical decision task. *Creativity Research Journal, 22*(2), 109–118.

Whyte, W. H. (1956). *The organization man.* New York: Simon and Schuster.

Wicklund, R. A. (1989). The appropriation of ideas. In P. B. Paulus (Ed.), *Psychology of group influence* (2nd ed., pp. 393–423). Hillsdale, NJ: Erlbaum.

Wiersema, M. F., & Bantel, K. A. (1992). Top management team demography and corporate strategy change. *Academy of Management Journal, 35,* 91–121.

Wilford, J. N. (2002, Tuesday, Feb. 26). When humans became human. *New York Times,* pp. D1, D5.

Wilkenfeld, M. J. (1995). *Conceptual combinations: Does similarity predict emergence?* Unpublished master's thesis, Texas A&M University, College Station, TX.

Wilkinson, A. (2002, May 27). Moody toons: The king of the cartoon network. *New Yorker,* 76–81.

Williams, F. E. (1991). *Creativity assessment packet: Test manual.* Austin, TX: PRO-ED.

Williams, W. M., & Sternberg, R. J. (1988). Group intelligence: Why some groups are better than others. *Intelligence, 12,* 351–377.

Willis, P. (1990). *Common culture: Symbolic work at play in the everyday cultures of the young.* Boulder, CO: Westview Press.

Wilson, G. (1985). *The psychology of the performing arts.* London: Croom Helm.

Winner, E. (1982). *Invented worlds: The psychology of the arts.* Cambridge: Harvard University Press.

Winslow, L. (1939). *The integrated school art program.* New York: McGraw-Hill.

Winterson, J. (2009, Oct. 17–18). In praise of the crack-up. *Wall Street Journal*, p. W3.

Wisniewski, E. J. (1997). Conceptual combination: Possibilities and esthetics. In T. B. Ward, S. M. Smith, & J. Vaid (Eds.), *Creative thought: An investigation of conceptual structures and processes* (pp. 51–81). Washington, DC: American Psychological Association.

Wisniewski, E. J., & Gentner, D. (1991). On the combinatorial semantics of noun pairs: Minor and major adjustments to meaning. In G. B. Simpson (Ed.), *Understanding word and sentence* (pp. 241–284). New York: Elsevier.

Witelson, S. F., Kigar, D. L., & Harvey, T. (1999). The exceptional brain of Albert Einstein. *Lancet, 353*, 2149–2153.

Wittkower, R., & Wittkower, M. (1963). *Born under Saturn*. London: Shenval.

Wolf, J. (1998, August 23). The blockbuster script factory. *New York Times Magazine*, pp. 32–35.

Woodcock, R. W., McGrew, K. S., & Mather, N. (2001). *Woodcock-Johnson III Tests of Cognitive Abilities*. Itasca, IL: Riverside.

Woody, E., & Claridge, G. (1977). Psychoticism and thinking. *British Journal of Social and Clinical Psychology, 16*, 241–248.

Wordsworth, W. (1800/1957). *Wordsworth's preface to lyrical ballads* (W. J. B. Owen, Trans.). Copenhagen: Rosenkilde and Bagger. (Original work published 1800.)

Wuchty, S., Jones, B. F., & Uzzi, B. (2007). The increasing dominance of teams in the production of knowledge. *Science, 316*, 1036–1039.

Wypijewski, J. (Ed.). (1997). *Painting by numbers: Komar and Melamid's scientific guide to art*. New York: Farrar, Straus and Giroux.

Yaniv, I., & Meyer, D. E. (1987). Activation and metacognition of inaccessible stored information: Potential bases for incubation effects in problem solving. *Journal of Experimental Psychology: Learning, Memory, and Cognition, 13*, 187–205.

Yuasa, M. (1974). The shifting center of scientific activity in the west: From the 16th to the 20th century. In N. Shigeru, D. L. Swain & Y. Eri (Eds.), *Science and society in modern Japan* (pp. 81–103). Tokyo: Tokyo University Press.

Yudess, J. (2010). Colleges and Universities with Degree or Certificate Bearing Programs in Creativity. *Journal of Creative Behavior, 44*(2), 139–142.

Zaidel, D. W. (2005). *Neuropsychology of art: Neurological, cognitive, and evolutionary perspectives*. Hove, UK: Psychology Press.

Zaidel, D. W. (2009). Brain and art: Neuro-clues from intersection of disciplines. In M. Skov & O. Vartanian (Eds.), *Neuroaesthetics* (pp. 153–170). Amityville, NY: Baywood Publishing Company.

Zaimov, K., Kitov, D., & Kolev, N. (1969). Aphasie chez un peintre. *Encephale, 68*, 377–417.

Zha, P., Walczyk, J. J., Griffith-Ross, D. A., Tobacyk, J. J., & Walczyk, D. F. (2006). The impact of culture and individualism-collectivism on the creative potential and achievement of American and Chinese adults. *Creativity Research Journal, 18*(3), 355–366.

Zhao, H., & Jiang, G. (1986). Life-span and precocity of scientists. *Scientometrics, 9*, 27–36.

Zhou, J. (2003). When the presence of creative coworkers is related to creativity: Role of supervisor close monitoring, developmental feedback, and creative personality. *Journal of Applied Psychology, 88*, 413–422.

Zhou, J., & Shalley, C. E. (2003). Research on employee creativity: A critical review and directions for future research. *Research in personnel and human resource management, 22*, 165–217.

Ziman, J. M. (Ed.). (2000). *Technological innovation as an evolutionary process*. New York: Cambridge University Press.

Zuckerman, H. (1974). The scientific elite: Nobel laureates' mutual influence. In R. S. Albert (Ed.), *Genius and eminence* (pp. 171–186). New York: Pergamon Press.

INDEX

Note: Page numbers followed by "*f*", "*t*", or "n" refer to figures, tables, or notes, respectively.